Handbook of Parenting

Volume 1
Children and Parenting

Handbook of Parenting

Volume 1
Children and Parenting

Edited by
Marc H. Bornstein
National Institute of Child Health and Human Development

LEA LAWRENCE ERLBAUM ASSOCIATES, PUBLISHERS
1995 Mahwah, New Jersey   Hove, UK

Lawrence Erlbaum Associates, Inc., Publishers
10 Industrial Avenue
Mahwah, New Jersey 07430

Library of Congress Cataloging-in-Publication Data

Handbook of parenting / edited by Marc H. Bornstein.
        p. cm.
     Includes bibliographical references and indexes.
     Contents: v. 1. Children and parenting — v. 2. Biology and ecology of
parenting — v. 3. Status and social conditions of parenting — v. 4. Applied and
practical parenting.
     ISBN 0-8058-1085-4 (cloth : set : alk. paper). — ISBN 0-8058-1892-8 (cloth
: v. 1 : alk. paper). — ISBN 0-8058-1893-6 (cloth : v. 2 : alk. paper). — ISBN
0-8058-1894-4 (cloth : v. 3 : alk. paper). — ISBN 0-8058-1895-2 (cloth: v. 4 :
alk. paper).
     1. Parenting. 2. Parents. I. Bornstein, Marc H.
HQ755.8.H357 1995
649'.1--dc20
                                                                95-30114
                                                                CIP

Books published by Lawrence Erlbaum Associates are printed on acid-free paper,
and their bindings are chosen for strength and durability.

Printed in the United States of America
10 9 8 7 6 5 4 3 2

For *Marian* and *Harold Sackrowitz*

Contents of Volume 1:
Children and Parenting

Foreword

Edward Zigler
Yale University

Parenting has been described as the most challenging and complex of all the tasks of adulthood. It can also be argued that there is no undertaking that is more important to the life of the human community. Yet that community rarely offers adequate guidance, support, or preparation for parenthood; with today's mobile life style and changing family structure, even the cross-generational passing down of parental wisdom that once occurred is no longer common. Our understanding of what it means to be a parent has undergone considerable revision and has taken on many new dimensions.

Today's parents face what may be unprecedented levels of social and economic stress. The growing incidence of such major social problems as poverty, homelessness, violence, crime, and substance abuse makes it difficult for parents to create a decent life for themselves, much less protect their offspring from harm and plan for their children's future. Such stress is most deeply felt by economically disadvantaged and single parents, most of whom are women. In many cases the double disadvantage of poverty and single parenting is combined with extreme youth: The number of teen births continues to rise, making the future precarious for both the child and her young mother.

Among two-parent families in the U.S., both parents typically work outside the home to make ends meet. Although about 44 percent of single mothers with children under 3 work outside the home, an even larger number (57 percent) of under-3s in two-parent families have mothers in the labor force. Thus, there is a special stress even among parents fortunate enough to have employment: the stress of having too little time to spend with one's child. The typical child spent about 30 hours per week with a parent in 1965; by the 1980s, this interaction time had declined to about 17 hours.

These are truly hard times for parents. And to make matters worse, a large number of adults in the so-called "sandwich" generation are called on to assume care of their own elderly parents, even as they struggle to nurture their young children. What's more, parents living in the United States must tackle all of these challenges largely without the considerable social supports offered by other industrialized nations. Such supports include paid parental leaves, government-subsidized child care, health care, parent education, and other services for families. Although there has been an increased interest in supportive programming and some improvement in meeting family needs, such as the passage of an unpaid parental leave in the form of the Family and

Medical Leave Act, parents in most communities, and the practitioners who serve them, are themselves in need of both nurturance and guidance.

The *Handbook of Parenting* should prove invaluable in meeting this need for expert guidance, and the knowledge imparted by the four volumes of the *Handbook* may also help to meet the critical need for increased family supports by enlightening policymakers. At minimum, the stellar contributors assembled for the *Handbook of Parenting* succeed admirably in their attempt to capture and describe the myriad aspects of parenting today.

This is not a handbook in the sense of a manual, although the chapters describing what it is like, for example, to parent a child born prematurely or how to foster sound moral development in one's offspring offer valuable insights that will guide parents. Rather, the volumes that make up the *Handbook* offer a comprehensive account of the state of our scientific and social knowledge regarding virtually every facet of parenting, from a social history of the topic to its psychological, educational, medical, legal, and even its public policy aspects.

These volumes have an extraordinary scope in that the authors share with us an impressive breadth, as well as depth, of experience and learning. The writers are acknowledged experts in their individual fields, and they represent a remarkable diversity of perspective. But this comprehensive approach is essential to reveal the social ecology of parenthood. Just as we have learned that the child does not develop in isolation from the environments of the family, home, school, and child-care setting, parenting also does not take place in a social vacuum.

All of the forces that make up the larger sociopolitical world create the context in which parents must nurture, educate, and struggle to understand their children, and themselves as parents. The *Handbook of Parenting* offers us a detailed roadmap to that context and it tells us a good deal about the needs, beliefs, troubles, wishes, and triumphs of the parents who inhabit our increasingly complex society. The contributors to this excellent compendium have provided a great resource for parents and for the clinicians, educators, and other professionals who attempt to assist parents in carrying on their important work as guardians of the next generation.

Foreword

Robert A. Hinde
St. John's College, Cambridge

It is easy to forget how rapidly ideas about parenting have changed. I was brought up as a Truby King baby. Influenced by this New Zealand pediatrician, my father, also a physician, believed that babies should be fed on a strict 6-hour schedule. Whenever we visited my father after our first child was born, at 6 p.m. he would start to fidget in his chair and say, "Isn't it time he was nursed?" But by then I was much influenced by Niko Tinbergen, the Nobel Prize winning ethologist and my mentor, who used to say "When the baby cries, it is a sign stimulus to the mother requiring attention, and she in turn is predisposed to respond with caregiving behavior." The parenting books that I remember from that time were mostly concerned with caring for the physical needs of the baby, but there was the early Spock, letting the child express himself or herself, and all that. With John Bowlby, psychological issues came right to the fore, with emphasis on the importance of the parent–child relationship and the nature of the child's attachment to the parent.

Now that we recognize that parenting depends on the baby as well as the parent, now that we see the importance of sensitive parenting, of gentle control and setting limits, of scaffolding and the furthering of exploration, we feel we have gotten it right. Have we? An historical eye should tell us there is no reason to think that the changes we have seen will just stop here. Quite apart from the possibility of new insights, the world is changing, and parenting practice is inevitably influenced by the world outside. That is clearly shown by the dilemma that Bowlby bequeathed—babies need a sensitive caregiver, but post-World War II cultural norms led mothers to want something outside the home— a frustrated mother is not a happy mother, and a mother who is not happy is unlikely to be a sensitive caregiver. So we must beware of thinking we have final solutions.

We may not have a final solution, we may not be right on all counts, but at least we know now that we cannot rely on ubiquitously applicable firm dicta about "what parents should do." Parenting practices must fit the child, the parents, and the culture. And if we are to move toward that goal we must have, not generalizations and precepts, but knowledge of process, of the dynamics of parent–child interaction and its consequences for the child and for the parent.

That is why these volumes will without doubt be a pediatric landmark. They synthesize what we now know about parenting practices, about the dynamics of parent–child relationships, about the family context in which parenting occurs, and about the role of cultural norms. And they do so not by making broad generalizations but by bringing together different views, different aspects, and different problems that arise. For example, most of the research on parenting has been done in Europe and North America, and it is easy to slip into assuming that a generalization about parenting in the United States is a generalization about parenting. One of the most refreshing things about these volumes is that so many of the authors recognize the limits of their generalizations, and point to the need for more cross-cultural data. They leave no room for thinking that the dynamics of the mother–daughter relationship, for example, is just the same in Burundi and Boston, or even in Cambridge, England and Cambridge, Massachusetts. The way the volumes are organized shows not only that mothers in general are different from fathers (which is not to say that the one cannot take on the other's role), but that parents are not the only ones who parent, and that children of different ages and with different problems need different sorts of treatment. It implies that parenting has multiple determinants—hormonal, psychological, social, sociological, cultural, historical, and eco-logical.

The diversity of approaches in these volumes will elicit different responses, but I would emphasize three issues. First, parenting practices must fit the child. Parent–child interaction differs with gender of parent and gender of child, and perhaps should so differ. The issues for infants differ from those of middle and later childhood and adolescence; and they differ for healthy children and children with handicaps. Second, it is the parent–child *relationship* that matters. And, as many of the authors emphasize, this is not something that is imposed by the parent, but something that is co-constructed by parent and child. They are in it together, for better or worse. That means that in real life, one is always dealing with a particular parent and a particular child co-constructing a particular relationship: Parental sensitivity means sensitivity to this child and not necessarily to that one.

Third, because parenting has multiple determinants, there are multiple ways in which parents can be helped. Parents' attitudes and beliefs are important, and most parents are eager for advice. But beyond that, in many parts of the world, there is much that can be done to smooth their way, to increase the chances that they will be able to provide a secure base for their children to lead full and happy lives. And that raises another issue, of how parents' lives are changed materially, socially, and psychologically by what they have become. However, this book is about parenting and not about parents.

I'm sure this book will be a landmark, and I am sure that many will be profoundly grateful to Marc Bornstein and all who have taken part in this challenging and timely enterprise.

Preface

Does parenting come naturally, or must we learn how to parent? What does it mean to be the parent of a preterm baby, of twins, or of a child with a disability? To be an older parent, or one who is divorced, disabled, or abusing drugs? How do personality, knowledge, and world view affect parenting skills? What roles do history, social class, and culture play in shaping parenthood? How should parents relate to schools, daycare, pediatricians, and other everyday nonfamilial influences on their children? These are just a few of the many questions addressed in the *Handbook of Parenting*. This is not a book on how to parent, but rather one on *what being a parent is all about*.

Put succinctly, parents create people. It is the particular and continuing task of parents to prepare the next generation for the physical, economic, and psychosocial situations in which it is to survive and thrive. Whatever other influences on child development there may be, parents are the "final common pathway" to childhood oversight and caregiving, development and stature. Human social inquiry—at least since the Athenians expressed interest in Spartan childrearing practices—has almost always, as a matter of course, included reports of parenting.

Despite the fact that most people become parents and everyone who ever lived has had parents, parenting remains a mystifying subject about which almost everyone has opinions, but about which few people agree. Freud once listed bringing up children as one of the three "impossible professions"—the other two being governing nations and psychoanalysis. One would probably encounter as many views as the number of people one cares to ask about the relative merits of being an at-home or working mother, about whether daycare, family care, or parent care is best for a child, about whether parenting depends on intuition or technique. Moreover, we are witnessing the emergence of striking permutations on the theme of parenting: single parenthood, blended families, lesbian and gay parents, teen versus 50s first-time moms and dads.

The *Handbook of Parenting* is concerned with different types of parents—mothers and fathers, single, adolescent, and adoptive parents—with basic characteristics of parenting—behaviors, knowledge, beliefs, and expectations about parenting—with forces that shape parenting—how employment, social class, culture, and environment contribute to parenthood—with problems faced by parents—the special circumstances of handicap, unhappy marriage, or drug addiction—and with practical concerns of parenting—how to talk to pediatricians, promote children's health, foster social adjustment and cognitive competence, interact with schools, and mediate with children's peers. Contributors to the *Handbook of Parenting* have worked in different ways toward understanding all these diverse aspects of parenting, and all look to the most recent research and thinking in the field to shed light on many topics every parent has wondered about at one time or another.

The *Handbook of Parenting* is divided into four volumes, each with two parts:

Volume 1 concerns children and parenting. Human development is too subtle, dynamic, and intricate to admit that parental caregiving alone determines the course and outcome of ontogeny. Volume 1 of the *Handbook of Parenting* begins intentionally with essays concerned with how children influence parenting. The chapters in Part I, "Parenting Children and the Elderly," discuss the special demands and unique rewards of parenting infants, toddlers, youngsters in middle childhood, and adolescents as well as the modern notion of parenting the elderly. The chapters in Part II, "Parenting Various Kinds of Children," discuss such common matters as parenting siblings and girls versus boys as well as more unique situations of parenting twins, children born preterm, and those with special needs, such as Down syndrome, aggressive and withdrawn disorders, and notable talent.

Volume 2 concerns the biology and ecology of parenting. To be understood as a whole, the psychophysiological and sociological determinants of parenting need to be brought into the picture. Volume 2 relates parenting to its biological roots and sets parenting in its ecological framework. The chapters in Part I, "Biology of Parenting," examine hormonal and psychobiological determinants of parenting in nonhumans and in human beings, parenting in other species, and biological universals in human parenting. The chapters in Part II, "Ecology of Parenting," examine maternal and dual-earner employment status and parenting, socioeconomic, ethnic, cultural, environmental, and historical issues associated with parenting, and also provide a developmental contextual perspective on parenting.

Volume 3 concerns the status and social conditions of parenting. Someone must parent children, and the different someones who do each have their own habits. Volume 3 distinguishes among the cast of characters responsible for parenting and is revealing of the psychological make-ups and social interests of those individuals. Chapters in Part I, "Who Is the Parent," consider successively mothering, fathers and families, single parenthood, grandparenthood, adolescent parenthood, nonparental caregiving, sibling caregivers, parenting adopted children, parenting in divorced and remarried families, and lesbian and gay parenthood. The chapters in Part II, "Social Conditions of Parenting," consider determinants of the transition to parenting, parents' knowledge, expectations, beliefs, and attitudes toward childrearing, as well as parenting in relation to social networks, public policy, and the law.

Volume 4 concerns applied and practical parenting. Parenting is not easy, nor does it go well all of the time. Volume 4 describes problems of parenting and how they are (sometimes) overcome as well as the promotion of positive parenting practices. The chapters in Part I, "Applied Issues in Parenting," explore maternal deprivation, marital interaction and parenting, parenting with a sensory or physical disability, psychologically depressed and substance abusing parents, and parental dysfunction in child maltreatment. The chapters in Part II, "Practical Considerations in Parenting," explore parents and their children's doctors, health promotion, and discipline and child compliance, parenting vis-à-vis children's moral development and cognitive competence, everyday stresses and parenting, the roles which child temperament, television, and play have in parenting, and parents and their children's associations with peers, childcare, and schools.

Each chapter in the *Handbook of Parenting* addresses a different but central topic in parenting; each is rooted in current thinking and theory as well as classical and modern research in that topic; each has been written to be read and absorbed in a single sitting. Each chapter follows (more or less) closely a standard organization, including an introduction to the chapter as a whole, followed by historical considerations of the topic, a discussion of central issues and theory, a review of classical and modern research, forecasts of future directions of theory and research, and a conclusion section. Of course, each chapter considers contributors' own convictions and research, but contributors to the *Handbook of Parenting* present all major points of view and central lines of inquiry and interpret them broadly. The *Handbook of Parenting* is intended to be comprehensive and state-of-the-art. To state that parenting is complex is to understate the obvious. As the scope of the *Handbook of Parenting* shows, parenting is naturally and closely allied with many other fields.

The *Handbook of Parenting* is concerned less with child outcomes of parenting, and more with the nature and dimensions of variations in parenting per se. Beyond an impressive range of information, readers will find passim typologies of parenting (e.g., authoritarian–autocratic, indulgent–permissive, indifferent–uninvolved, authoritative–reciprocal), theories of parenting (e.g., psychoanalytic, etho-logical, behavioral, sociobiological), conditions of parenting (e.g., mother vs. father, cross-cultural, situation-by-age-by-style), recurrent themes in parenting studies (e.g., attachment, transaction, eco-logical systems), and even aphorisms (e.g., "A child should have strict discipline in order to develop a fine, strong character," "The child is father to the man"). Patterns of parenting may converge, reflecting inherent truisms, or the historical intersection of styles, or the increasing prevalence of a single pattern through migration or dissemination via mass media. In the end, parents wish to promote general competencies in their offspring, and some do so in manifestly similar ways. Others do so in different ways, and of course specific patterns of parenting are adapted to specific settings and needs. Therefore, variation in parenting philosophies, values, beliefs, ideas, and practices are widespread.

In the course of editing this *Handbook,* I wrote extensive notes abstracting central messages and critical points of view expressed in each chapter fully intending to construct a comprehensive introduction to these volumes. In the end, I took away two significant impressions from my own efforts and the texts of my collaborators in this work. First, my notes cumulated to a near-monograph on parenting ... clearly inappropriate for an introduction. Second, when all was written and done, I found the chorus of contributors to the *Handbook* more eloquent and compelling than my own lone voice could ever be. Each chapter in the *Handbook* begins with an introduction that lays out, in a clarity, expressiveness, and force I could only envy, the meanings and implications of that contribution and that perspective to the parenting whole. In lieu of one introduction, readers are urged to browse the many introductions that lead the way into the *Handbook of Parenting.*

The *Handbook of Parenting* appears at an altogether critical time in the history of parenting. The family generally, and parenting specifically, are today in a greater state of flux and re-definition than perhaps at any other time. One cannot but be impressed on the biological front that artificial insemination now renders postmenopausal women capable of childbearing and with the possibility of designing babies. Similarly on the sociological front, single parenthood is a modern day fact of life, adult child dependency is on the rise, and parents are ever less certain of their roles, even in the face of rising environmental and institutional demands that they take increasing responsibility for their charges, as well as the future.

Once upon a time, parenting was a seemingly simple thing: Mothers mothered. Fathers fathered. Today, parenting has many motives, many meanings, and many manifestations. Parenting is now viewed as immensely time consuming and effortful. The perfect mother or father or family is now firmly a figment of the imagination. Society recognizes "subdivisions" of the call: genetic mother, gestational mother, biological mother, birth mother, social mother. For some, altruistic individual sacrifices that mark parenting are actually directed at offspring for the sole and selfish purpose of passing ones's genes onto succeeding generations. Is this the motive a mother has for planning a second child when her adolescent first, stricken with leukemia, desperately needs matching bone marrow for transplant? Others still wonder aghast at how a mother could stand before a sympathetic nation when she knows full well that she has condemned her two babies to a fearful passing. A multitude of factors influence the unrelenting onrush of decisions that surround parenting—biopsychological, dyadic, contextual. Recognizing this complexity is important to informing people's thinking about parenting, especially information-hungry parents themselves. The *Handbook of Parenting* embraces, expresses, and explores the myriad motives, meanings, and manifestations of parenting.

Parenting has never come with a handbook ... until now.

ACKNOWLEDGMENTS

I would like to express my deep gratitude to the staff at Lawrence Erlbaum Associates who made the *Handbook of Parenting* more than I ever could: Judith Amsel, Lawrence Erlbaum, Sharon Levy, Arthur M. Lizza, Anne Patricia Monaghan, Joseph Petrowski, and Robin Marks Weisberg.

—Marc H. Bornstein

Contents of Volume 2: Biology and Ecology of Parenting

Contents of Volume 3:
Status and Social Conditions of Parenting

Contents of Volume 4:
Applied and Practical Parenting

Introduction to
Handbook of Parenting
Volume 1
Children and Parenting

The first volume of the *Handbook of Parenting* concerns itself with parenting children at different stages of development and children with special interests. Chapters in Part I, "Parenting Children and the Elderly," first review distinctive developmental issues and achievements of each age period, as they constitute the special array of characteristics parents must expect and cope with at that stage. Specific developmental characteristics can be expected to influence specifics of parenting. Thus, Marc Bornstein on parenting infants, Carolyn Edwards on parenting toddlers, Andrew Collins, Michael Harris, and Amy Susman on parenting during middle childhood, and Grayson Holmbeck, Roberta Paikoff, and Jeanne Brooks-Gunn on parenting adolescents all evaluate developmental issues and achievements particular to each stage and then discuss the salient features of parenting children at that stage. These chapters present the reader with common themes of parenting but at the same time address special interests pertinent to each point in development. In the last chapter in Part I, Steven Zarit and David Eggebeen attend to parent–child relationships in adulthood and old age, exploring the two-way street between care of the elderly by adult children and contributions the elderly make to their adult children's parenting.

Chapters in Part II of Volume 1, "Parenting Various Kinds of Children," address parenting issues surrounding common and special groups of children. On the everyday side, Wyndol Furman deals with parenting siblings and Beverly Fagot with parenting boys and girls. Less common, Hugh Lytton and Jagjit Singh report on parenting twins, and Susan Goldberg and Barbara DiVitto on parenting children born preterm. Robert Hodapp takes up the challenge of parenting children with Down syndrome and other types of mental retardation, and Kenneth Rubin, Shannon Stewart, and Xinyin Chen parents of aggressive and withdrawn children. Finally, David Henry Feldman and Jane Piirto examine parenting talented children. Features and models of parenting in these familiar and rare circumstances reveal fascinating resemblances and particularities.

Chapters in Volume 1 of the *Handbook of Parenting* on children and parenting are complemented by those in Volumes 2, 3, and 4. Volume 2 concerns the biology and ecology of parenting: To be understood as a whole, the psychophysiological and sociological determinants of parenting need to be brought into the picture, and Volume 2 relates parenting to its biopsychological roots and sets parenting in its ecological context. Volume 3 concerns the status and social conditions of parenting: Someone must parent children, and the different someones who do each have their own practices: Volume 3 distinguishes among the cast of characters responsible for parenting and reveals more about their psychological make-ups and social interests. Volume 4 concerns applied and practical parenting: Parenting is not easy, nor does it go well all of the time, and Volume 4 describes problems of parenting and how they are (sometimes) overcome as well as steps toward the promotion of positive parenting practices.

PART I

PARENTING CHILDREN AND THE ELDERLY

1

Parenting Infants

Marc H. Bornstein
National Institute of Child Health and Human Development

INTRODUCTION

New parents around the world are called by similar sounding familial kin terms, like /ma/, /pa/, and /da/. Why? The linguistic theorist Jakobson (1971) once proposed the romantic view that parents adopt as names for themselves the sounds that infants first produce. Jakobson (1969) claimed that, when they first begin to speak, infants' articulations are limited to a set of sounds that follow a universal pattern of development based on the anatomical structure of the oral cavity and vocal tract and on ease of motor control (Kent, 1984). In this view, certain sound combinations—consonants articulated at the lips (/m/ and /p/) or teeth (/d/), and vowels articulated at the back of the oral cavity (/a/)—have primacy because their production maximizes contrasts. Thus, infants' earliest sound combinations consist of front consonants with back vowels. Significantly, of several logically possible combinations, the front-consonant–back-vowel pairs /pa/, /da/, and /ma/ are used as parental kin terms in nearly 60 percent of more than 1,000 of the world's languages, many more than would be expected by chance (Murdock, 1959). It seems that parents of infants have adopted as generic labels for themselves their infants' earliest vocal productions.

Nothing rivets the attention or stirs the emotions of adults more than the birth of a child. By their very coming into existence, infants forever alter the sleeping, eating, and working habits of their parents; they change who parents are and how parents define themselves. Infants keep parents up late into the night or cause them to abandon late nights to accommodate early waking; they require parents to give up a rewarding career to care for them or take a second job to support them; they lead parents to make new circles of friends with others in similar situations and sometimes cause parents to lose or abandon old friends who are not parents. Yes, parents even seem to take for themselves the names that infants bestow. Parenting an infant is a 168-hour-a-week job, whether by the parents themselves or by a surrogate who is on call, because the human infant is totally dependent on parents for survival. Unlike the newborn colt, which is on its feet within minutes of birth, or the newborn chick, which forages on its own more or less immediately, the human infant cannot walk, talk, or even ingest food without the aid of a competent caregiver. In a given year, approximately 4 million new babies are born in the

3

United States, and worldwide each day more than three quarters of a million adults experience the joys and heartaches, challenges and rewards of becoming new parents (National Center for Health Statistics, 1994; Population Reference Bureau, 1993). The wonder is that every day, 11,000 babies are born in the United States—a number equivalent to the population of a small town—and yet everyone is unique and special.

Infancy encompasses only a small fraction of the average person's life expectancy, but it is a period highly attended to and invested in by parents all over the world. Parenting responsibilities are greatest during infancy, when the child is most dependent on caregiving and the ability to cope alone is minimal. Not by chance, infants' physiognomic structure is especially attractive to adults; infants engender responsibility, and they make undeniable demands; infants are also fun to observe, to talk to, and to play with; infants do not know how to be agonistic, deceiving, or malicious. Further, infancy is a period of rapid development in practically all spheres of human expression, and people are perennially fascinated by the dramatic ways in which the helpless and disorganized newborn human transforms into the competent and curious, frustrating and frustrated child.

Reciprocally, infants may profit most from parental care. Infancy is the phase of the life cycle when adult caregiving is thought to exert extremely salient influences. Not only does caregiving occur at its most intense levels then, but infants are thought to be particularly susceptible and responsive to external events. The sheer amount of interaction between parent and child is greatest in infancy; parents spend more than twice as much time with their infants as they do with their children in middle childhood (Hill & Stafford, 1980). In effect, adult (or other more mature) caregivers are responsible

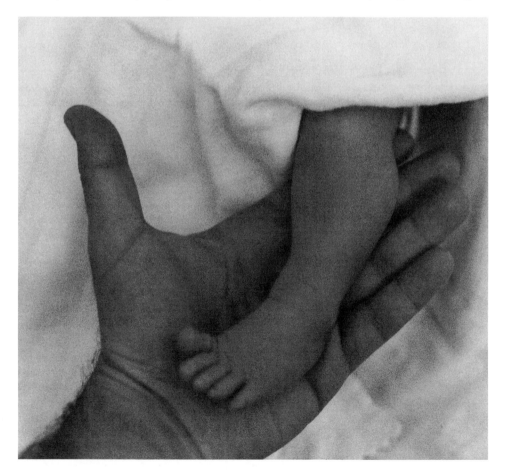

for determining most, if not all, of infants' earliest experiences. It is the particular and continuing task of parents to enculturate children, that is, to prepare them for the physical, economic, and psychosocial situations characteristic of the context and culture in which they are to survive and thrive (Benedict, 1938; Bornstein, 1991; LeVine, 1988). Parents everywhere appear highly motivated to carry out this task, and infants are likewise invested in their parents. At a very early age, they appear to recognize and prefer the sights, sounds, and smells of these caregivers, and over the course of the first year develop deep and lifelong attachments to them.

At their best, parent and infant activities are characterized by intricate patterns of synchronous interactions and sensitive mutual understandings (Bornstein, 1989a; Bornstein & Tamis-LeMonda, 1990; Kaye, 1982; Stern, 1985). In one study, 2- to 4-month-olds were observed while interacting with their mothers (Murray & Trevarthen, 1985). Infants first viewed real-time images of their mothers interacting with them via closed-circuit television, and during this period infants were seen to react with normal interest and pleasure. Immediately afterward, infants watched a videotaped recording of those same images; this time, however, the infants exhibited signs of distress. The negative reactions observed were considered to arise out of the lack of synchrony that these babies experienced. Even months-old infants express sensitivity to the presence or absence of appropriate parenting interactions.

In this chapter, salient features of parenting infants are presented. First, a brief history of interest in parenting infants is reviewed, followed by a discussion of the theoretical significance attached to parenting infants. Next, characteristics of infants and infant development that are especially meaningful for parenting are described, including developmental changes in state, stature, and physical abilities, perceiving, thinking, acquiring language, expressing emotions, and interacting socially. Then, the main part of the chapter reviews principles of parenting infants, including direct and indirect effects, parenting behaviors and beliefs, stylistic differences between mothers and fathers, and the mechanisms of action of principles of parenting. Afterward, forces that shape parenting during infancy are outlined, including biology, personality, infant effects, and various social, socioeconomic, and cultural determinants. Finally, nonparental (i.e., sibling, familial, and nonfamilial) infant caregiving is described.

A BRIEF HISTORY OF PARENTING INFANTS

Infancy is an easily definable stage of life, based on biological and mental data as well as social convention. Infants creep and crawl, whereas the young and the old walk and run; infants do not speak, whereas the young and old do. Infancy defines the period of life between birth and the emergence of language approximately $1\frac{1}{2}$ to 2 years into childhood. Our generic terms "infant" and "baby" both have their origins in language-related concepts. The word *infant* derives from the Latin *in* + *fans*, translated literally as "nonspeaker," and the word *baby* shares a Middle English root with "babble" (another front-consonant–back-vowel combination). Harkness and Super (1983, p. 223) suggested that "a primary function of culture in shaping human experience is the division of the continuum of human development into meaningful segments, or 'stages.'... All cultures ... recognize infancy as a stage of human development." Our *newborn* and *infant* are for the Chagga of Tanganyika *mnangu* (the "incomplete one") and *mkoku* ("one who fills lap"). For us, a child is an infant until she talks, and becomes a toddler when he walks; for the Alor of the Lesser Sundra Islands, the first stage of infancy lasts from birth to the first smile, and the second stage from the smile to the time when the child can sit alone or begins to crawl (Mead & Newton, 1967, in Fogel, 1984). Infancy achieved recognition as an independent and significant stage in the life cycle in pre-Classical times, and the Romans depicted infancy as a period in the career of a typical man on "biographical" sarcophagi. Indeed, artists everywhere and throughout the ages have represented infancy as typically a first age or stage in the life span (Bornstein, in preparation). Iconographically, infants symbolize origins and beginnings.

Informal interest and concerns for parenting infants have been driven in large measure by perennial questions about the relative roles of heredity and experience on the course of child development. Speculation on the subject dates back centuries to ancient Egypt, the code of Hammurabi, and the pre-Socratic philosophers (French, in this *Handbook*). Plato (1970) theorized about the significance of infancy in this respect; Henri IV of France had the physician Jean Héroard (1868) document experiences of the dauphin Louis from his birth in 1601; and no less modern scientific and cultural figures than Charles Darwin and Sigmund Freud initiated scientific observations of infants and theoretical speculations about the role of infancy in development.

The formal study of parenting infants had its beginnings in attempts by philosopher, educator, or scientist parents to do systematically what parents around the world do naturally everyday—simply observe their babies. The first-ever studies of children were diary descriptions of infants in their natural settings written by their own parents, or "baby biographies" (Darwin, 1877; Hall, 1891; Preyer, 1882; Rousseau, 1762; Taine, 1877; Tiedemann, 1787; also see Jaeger, 1985, and Wallace, Franklin, & Keegan, 1994). Darwin, who founded evolutionary theory with the *Origin of Species* (1859), published observations he had made in the early 1840s on his firstborn son William Erasmus, nicknamed "Doddy." Darwin's (1877) "Biographical Sketch of an Infant" gave great impetus to infancy studies (Dixon & Lerner, 1992). In succeeding years, baby biographies grew in popularity around the world—whether they were scientific documents, parents' private personal records, or illustrations of educational practices—and they still appear today (e.g., Brazelton, 1969; Church, 1966; Mendelson, 1990; Stern, 1990). Perhaps the most influential of the modern baby biographers was Piaget (e.g., 1952), whose writings and theorizing refer chiefly to observations of his own young children.

Reciprocally, these systematic observations of infancy heightened awareness in parents and provoked formal studies of how to guide infant development, that is, of *parenting*. Historians and sociologists of family life have documented evolving patterns of primary concern in infant care. They contend that, on account of high rates of infant mortality (e.g., Beales, 1985), parents in early times may have cared for but resisted emotional investment in the very young (Dye & Smith, 1986; Slater, 1977–1978), a point of view that persists where especially dire childrearing circumstances reign (Scheper-Hughes, 1989). One historian theorized that parents have generally improved in their orientation to and treatment of the very young because parents have, through successive generations, improved in their ability to identify and empathize with the special qualities of early childhood (deMause, 1975). Today, advice on parenting infants can be found in professional compendia such as *Effective Care in Pregnancy and Childbirth* (Chalmers, Enkin, & Keirse, 1989), which provides a comprehensive treatment of virtually all aspects of prenatal and perinatal development; in classic "how to" books, such as *Dr. Spock's Baby and Child Care* (Spock & Rothenberg, 1992) and *Babyhood* and *Your Baby and Child* (Leach, 1983, 1989); as well as in numerous popular periodicals that overflow local drugstore magazine racks.

THE THEORETICAL SIGNIFICANCE ATTACHED
TO PARENTING DURING INFANCY

From the perspective of the formal study of parenting, infancy attracts attention in part because a provocative debate rages concerning the significance of events occurring in infancy for later development. Two extreme points of view vie. Proponents of one viewpoint contend that infancy is not particularly influential because experiences and habits of infancy have little (if any) long-term predictive significance in the life course. Others argue contrariwise that experiences and habits developed in infancy are of crucial significance; that is, the social orientations, personality styles, and intellectual predilections established at the start fix enduring patterns. Either the invisible foundation and frame of the edifice are always and forever critical to the structure, or once erected what really matters is upkeep and renovation. Whichever, theoreticians and researchers have been surprisingly hard pressed to confirm or to refute the significance of the child's earliest experiences to the course and eventual outcome of development.

Prominently, psychoanalysis propunded the importance of early experience. Thus, Freud (1949) focused attention on infancy, suggesting that the ways babies are treated establish lifelong personality traits. He theorized that child development is characterized by critical phases during which certain experiences take on unusual significance. Infancy defines the oral phase during which experiences and activities centered on the mouth, notably feeding, are particularly salient. Freud asserted that, if the baby's needs for oral gratification were overindulged or underindulged in the oral stage, the baby would grow into an adult who continually seeks oral gratification. Overlapping the end of infancy, according to Freud, the oral phase is succeeded by the anal phase. During this period, parent–infant interactions center on toilet training; long-term personality consequences associated with this phase likely involve stubbornness and obsessiveness. Erikson (1950) portrayed infant experiences provided by parents differently, but also asserted that experiences in infancy can exert telling influences on later development. Erikson described eight developmental stages, each marked by an emotional crisis. From oral sensory experiences, Erikson suggested, infants develop basic trust or mistrust in others. He also theorized that whether infants develop basic trust has implications for the way they negotiate the next muscular anal stage of development, in which the key issue is establishing autonomy or shame. With respect to toilet training, Erikson emphasized not the anal organs, but the status of toilet training as a battleground of wills as the child tries to exert initial control. Modern proponents of the psychodynamic school continue to see infancy as critical for the basic differentiation of self (e.g., S. Greenspan & N. T. Greenspan, 1985; Mahler, Pine, & Bergman, 1975; Stern, 1985).

Like the psychoanalysts, behaviorists and learning theorists also stressed the significance of infant experiences in the lifecourse (e.g., Dollard & Miller, 1950; Watson, 1924/1970). Behaviorists eschew the idea that infancy should be set apart; but for them as well an organism's early experiences are crucial because they are first, have no competing propensities to replace, and thus yield easy and rapid learning. Moreover, in the learning view, early behavior patterns lay the foundation for more complex ones. Students of the constructivist school of development, beginning with Piaget (1952), have likewise theorized that capacities of later life build on simple developments that emerge early in life.

The exceptional role of infant experiences has also been emphasized by other theorists, including embryologists and ethologists (e.g., Lorenz, 1935; Tinbergen, 1951, 1963). In the view of those who study developmental physiology and animal behavior, the immature nervous system is in its most plastic state, and predetermined "sensitive periods" mark the early maturation of organisms. During these periods, various structural developments and behavioral tendencies are maximally susceptible to influence by specific types of experience (see Bornstein, 1989c). The sensitive period concept assigns great weight to infant experiences because it holds that experiences that occur in that period are likely to be of long-lasting influence and that, once that period has passed, those specific experiences no longer exert the same formative influence on the developing organism. Demonstrations of sensitive periods in lower animals (such as imprinting) accord biological and scientific credibility to the potency of early experience, and this notion has been integrated into many portraits of human infant growth and development. Indeed, the neoteny of human infancy (the prolongation of this period, especially in human beings) is thought to have special adaptive significance.

Not all developmental theoreticians espouse the view that experiences of infancy are formative. Some have, with equally compelling arguments, suggested that experiences in infancy are peripheral or ephemeral, in the sense that they exert little or no enduring effect on the balance of development. These individuals attribute the engine and controls of development instead to biology and maturation and to influences of later experience. The embryologist Waddington (1962) contended, based on principles of growth such as canalization, that early experiences, if influential, are not determinative (see, too, Erikson, 1950; Kagan, 1971; McCall, 1981; Scarr & Kidd, 1983). Infancy may be a period of plasticity and adaptability to transient conditions, but those effects may not persist or they may be altered by subsequent conditions. "There is no more reason to assume that irritability during the first six months will leave persistent structural residues than that a child who has perspired a lot during her first three months, because she was born in North Carolina in the middle of July, will take with her into late childhood psychological remnants of these bouts of excessive perspiration" (Kagan,

1984, p. 105). In the normal range of experience, many things have a predetermined course; alternatively, varied kinds of experience can correct or reverse the effects of early experience. The infant may not predict the adult.

Infancy is the first phase of extrauterine life, and the characteristics we develop and acquire then may be formative and fundamental in the sense that they endure or (at least) constitute features that later developments or experiences build on or modify. Infancy is only one phase in the life span, however, and so development will also be shaped by experiences after infancy. Parenting the infant does not fix the course or outcome of development, but it makes sense that effects have causes and the start exerts an impact on the end. Parenting is central to infancy, to development, and to long-term investment in children (Trivers, 1986). So, we are motivated to know about the meaning and importance of infancy as much for itself, and out of the desire to improve the lives of infants, as for what infancy may herald about later life. Indeed, social anthropological inquiry has almost always included reports of infant life and adults' first efforts at parenting (Bornstein, 1991; French, in this *Handbook*). Parents are fundamentally invested in infants: their survival, their socialization, and their education.

IMPLICATIONS FOR PARENTING
OF CHARACTERISTICS PECULIAR TO INFANCY
AND INFANT DEVELOPMENT

For parents and professionals alike, the pervasiveness, rapidity, and clarity of changes in infancy engender both fascination and action. The most remarkable of these domains of change involve the growing complexity of the nervous system; alterations in the shape and capacity of the body and its muscles; the sharpening of sensory and perceptual capacity; increases in the ability to make sense of, understand, and master objects in the world; the advent of communication; the formation of specific social bonds; and the emergence of characteristic personal and social styles. Each of these domains of infant development fundamentally influences parenting. Parenting is also thoroughgoingly affected by the context in which these developmental changes occur.

Developing Domains in Infancy

During infancy, children are transformed from immature beings unable to move their limbs in a coordinated manner to individuals who control complicated sequences of muscle contractions and flections in order to walk, reach, or grasp, and from beings who can only cry or babble to those who make their needs and desires abundantly clear. During infancy, children learn how to make sense of and understand objects in the world, form their first social relationships, and learn to express and read basic human emotions. Infants develop individual personalities and social styles. Nonetheless, parents escort their children through these dramatic "firsts." Not surprisingly, all of these developmental dynamics are closely tracked by parents, all shape parenting, and all are, in turn, shaped by parents.

State.   Infants vary in how soon they establish a predictable schedule of behavioral states (Parmelee & Sigman, 1983), and their regularity or lack thereof has critical implications for infant care and development as well as for parental well-being. State determines how infants present themselves; much of what infants learn about people, their own abilities, and the object world is acquired during periods of quiet alertness and attentiveness. Infant state likewise influences adult behavior; adults rather soothe distressed babies than try to play with them. Infants who are temperamentally fretful elicit different patterns of care than do infants who cry only infrequently (Sanson & Rothbart, in this *Handbook*). The amount of time infants spend in different states even determines whether they are alone or with their parents: Babies are usually with their mothers when awake, and alone when asleep. At the same time, infant state is modifiable: Cole (1992) documented cultural variation in even so basic a biological function as newborn entrainment to the day–night cycle. Among the Kipsigis, a tribe of the Kenyan desert, infants sleep with their mothers at night and are permitted to nurse on demand. During the day, they are strapped to their mothers' backs, accompanying them on daily rounds of farming, household chores, and social activities. These babies often nap while their mothers go about their work, and so they do not begin to sleep through the night until many months later than do, for example, U.S. American infants. State organization and getting "on schedule" are subject to parent-mediated experiential influences.

Physical stature and psychomotor abilities.   Infancy is the stage of greatest physical and nervous system development. Growth through the first two postnatal years is manifest even on casual observation because of its magnitude and scope. On average, the newborn measures about 20 inches (51 cm) and weighs about 7½ pounds (3.2 kg). In the year after birth, a baby's length grows by half, and a baby's weight approximately triples.

These physical changes are paralleled by numerous advances in motor skills. Consider the eagerness with which parents await their child's first step. This achievement signifies an important stage in infant independence, permitting new means of exploring the surroundings and of determining when and how much time infants spend near their parents. By walking, the baby asserts individuality, maturity, and self-mindedness. These changes, in turn, affect the ways in which parents treat the child: How parents organize the baby's physical environment and even how they speak to the walking, as opposed to the crawling, baby differ substantially.

Again, psychomotor growth reflects the influence of parenting practices: W. Dennis and M. G. Dennis (1940) suggested that relative locomotor delay in Hopi Native Americans reflected Hopi babies' traditional early constriction on the cradleboard; Mead and MacGregor (1951) proposed that the manner in which Balinese mothers habitually carry their infants promoted unique motor patterns; and Ainsworth (1967) attributed advanced Ganda infant motor abilities to a nurturing climate of physical freedom. Super (1976) found highly developed sitting, standing, and walking among Kipsigis babies, but retarded head lifting, crawling, and turning over. Kipsigis mothers deliberately "teach" their infants to sit, stand, and walk, and mothers teaching their babies to crawl relates systematically to the average age of infant crawling. Antecedent to parental behaviors, expectations also play an influential role. For example, Jamaican mothers expect their infants to sit and to walk relatively early, whereas Indian mothers living in the same city in England expect their infants to crawl relatively late. In each case, infants develop in accordance with their mothers' expectations (Hopkins & Westra, 1990).

Perceiving and thinking.   During infancy, the capacities to take in information through the major sensory channels, to make sense of the environment, and to attribute meaning to information improve dramatically. Although it is not always apparent, there is no question that infants have an active mental life. Thirty years under the watchful eyes of researchers (catching up with parents) have documented that infants are constantly learning and developing new ideas, and that they do so in many different ways (see Bornstein & Lamb, 1992). Infants actively scan the environment; pick up, encode, and process information; and they aggregate over their experiences (Bornstein, 1992). Newborns are equipped to hear, to orient to, and to distinguish sounds, and babies seem especially primed to perceive and to appreciate sound in the dynamic form and range of adult speech (Trehub & Hsing-Wu, 1977). Newborns also identify particular speakers—notably mother—right after birth (DeCasper & Spence, 1986), apparently on the basis of prenatal exposure to her voice. By their preference reactions, newborns also give good evidence that they possess a developed sense of smell (Steiner, 1979), and babies soon suck presumptively at the smell of their mothers; reciprocally, mothers recognize the scent of their babies with only 1 or 2 days experience (Porter, Bologh, & Makin, 1988). By middle infancy, babies attend closely to faces, discriminate among facial expressions associated with different emotions (Nelson, 1987), and even distinguish variations in the intensity of some emotional expressions (Kuchuk, Vibbert, & Bornstein, 1986). At this point, how parents appear will meaningfully supplement what they have to say. Looking is not solely a source of information acquisition, of course; gaze is also a basic means to social exchange. Eye-to-eye contact between infant and caregiver is rewarding to both and sets in motion routines and rhythms of social interaction and play.

As a consequence of infants' information-processing skills (Bornstein, 1989d), parents' displays for imitation during infancy provide a particularly efficient mechanism for infants acquiring information of all sorts—just by listening and watching. When infants imitate and what they imitate are disputed research issues (Anisfeld, 1991), but the significance of observational learning from infancy is not.

Infancy culminates with the development of representational thinking and language. In the first year, for example, play with objects is predominantly characterized by sensorimotor manipulation, and mouthing and fingering, whose goal appears to be extraction of information about objects. In the second year, children's object play takes on an increasingly symbolic quality as they enact activities performed by self, others, and objects in simple pretense scenarios, for example, by pretending to drink from empty teacups or to talk on toy telephones (Bornstein & O'Reilly, 1993; K. H. Rubin, Fein, & Vandenberg, 1983). Maternal play influences infant play (Bornstein, Haynes, O'Reilly, & Painter, 1994; Užgiris & Raeff, in this *Handbook*), and cross-cultural comparisons confirm that, in cultures where parents emphasize particular types of play, very young children tend to engage in those types of play (Farver, 1993; Tamis-LeMonda, Bornstein, et al., 1990).

Speaking and understanding.   Early in life, infants communicate by means of emotional expressions like crying. However, babies quickly display the capacity to organize speech sounds, as indicated by babbling. In remarkably short order, the infant's repertoire of communicative tokens expands to include gestures and a growing range of social signals that eventuate in spoken language. The comprehension of speech combined with the generation of unique utterances rank among the major cognitive achievements of the infancy period, but the motivation to acquire language is social and is born in interaction, usually with parents. That is, the acquisition of first language reflects the child's early and rich exposure to the parent-provided target language environment as much as it reflects competencies that are part of the child.

In short, language learning is active, but always embedded in the larger context of adult–infant social communication. Thus, components of the young infant's very earliest babbles are influenced by local auditory input, and infants born into different language settings rapidly speak the language of their local community. Experienced phoneticians and lay French monolingual adult judges listened to pure samples of babbling from 6-, 8-, and 10-month-old French, Arabic, and Chinese babies from Paris, Tunis or Algiers, and Hong-Kong, respectively; as languages, French, Arabic, and Cantonese differ from one another in voice quality, stress, and proportion of consonantal versus vocalic sounds (Boysson-Bardies, Sagart, & Durand, 1984). The judges were asked to identify which babbling samples came from French babies. The phoneticians correctly classified the country of origin in 6-month-olds; both the trained and lay groups correctly distinguished the patrimony of 8- and 10-month-olds. Because the language the infant hears is the only conceivable cause of such an effect, it is highly likely that the "speech" of infants as young as 6 months of age is influenced by the language they hear. Parent-provided experiences swiftly and surely channel early speech development toward the adult target language. In the space of about 2 years, infants master language without explicit instruction and without noticeable effort, but they always speak in the language to which they have been exposed.

Emotional expressivity and temperament.   Emotional expressions give evidence about how babies respond to events, and new parents pay special attention to infants' emotions in their efforts to manage and modify them (Kaye, 1982). The advent of emotional reactions—whether the first elicited smiles or the earliest indications of stranger wariness—cue meaningful transitions for caregivers. Parents consider them to indicate emerging individuality—as cues not only to what the child's behavioral style is like now, but what it may be like in future years. Reciprocally, by the second half of the first year, parents' emotional expressions are meaningful to infants (Klinnert, Campos, Sorce, Ende, & Svejda, 1983; Nelson, 1987). Infants respond emotionally to the affective expressions they observe in other people as when, for example, their caregivers are depressed (Field, in this

Handbook), to different vocal correlates of emotional expression, and to coordinated vocal and facial features of emotional expressions (A. J. Caron, R. F. Caron, & MacLean, 1988). Infants as young as 1 year understand specific object or event referents of a communication (Churcher & Scaife, 1982), and they respond to emotional messages, showing signs of distress when witnessing angry interactions between family members (Cummings, Zahn-Waxler, & Radke-Yarrow, 1981).

Beyond emotional exchange, infants influence parenting by their individuality of temperament. Variation in activity level, mood, soothability, and emotional intensity define dimensions of temperament individuality by which parents typically characterize their infants. Just as parents and caregivers try to interpret, respond to, and manage infants' emotional states, they also devote considerable energy to identifying, adapting to, and channeling the temperament of their infants (Bornstein & Lamb, 1992; Sanson & Rothbart, in this *Handbook*). Infants come into the world with simple yet influential behavioral proclivities. Babies who are congenitally distractible, for example, are likely to learn slowly about objects they see or hear because they do not attend to or concentrate on them for sufficient periods. Temperament has consequences for interaction and development.

Just as in other spheres of infant life, cultural differences in ideology influence context and help to determine the interaction between emotional expression or temperament and parenting. No doubt some temperament proclivities of the infant transcend culture: Some smiles are more equal than others, and an infant's smile is first among equals. "Difficult" babies are characterized by frequent and intense expressions of negative emotion, and they demand and (perhaps) receive more attention than do "easy" babies (Pettit & J. Bates, 1984), regardless of culture. But adults from different cultural backgrounds surely socialize the emotional displays of their infants by responding in accordance with culture-specific requirements or interpretations of infants' expressions and emotions (Harkness & Super, 1985; Super & Harkness, 1986). For example, infants universally respond to separation from parents in characteristic ways (Ainsworth, Blehar, Waters, & Wall, 1978; LeVine & Miller, 1990), but mothers may perceive and interpret their reactions differently according to cultural values. Anglo-American and Puerto Rican mothers both prefer infants who display a balance of autonomy and dependence. However, Anglo-American mothers attend to and place more emphasis on the presence or absence of individualism, whereas Puerto Rican mothers focus more on characteristics associated with a sociocentric orientation, that is, the child's ability to maintain proper conduct in a public place (Harwood, 1992). Thus, the meaning of infant behavior for parents is a complex function of act and context. Although in some circumstances difficultness may be associated with long-term negative consequences, among Ethiopian infants otherwise dying of starvation, difficult temperament, which elicited adult attention and feeding, proved vitally adaptive (DeVries & Sameroff, 1984).

Social life.   Infancy encompasses the gradual dawning of social awareness and is characterized by babies taking increasing responsibility for maintaining sequences of social interaction. The development of emotional relationships with other people—mainly parents—constitutes one of the most important aspects of social development in infancy. By the middle of the first year, the social infant bears little resemblance to the asocial neonate: 7-month-olds clearly understand and (can) respect rules of reciprocity in interactions. Between 6 and 12 months of age, infants increasingly initiate interaction using directed social behaviors like gaze, whereas mothers more frequently initiate games, terminate or redirect infants' activities, and issue verbal requests (Green, Gustafson, & West, 1980).

Once infants develop the capacity to recognize specific people, they begin to interact preferentially with, and gradually form attachments to these adults who have been consistently and reliably accessible during their first months of life. A major step in socioemotional development is defined by the formation of these enduring relationships. Attachment formation is a product of the convergence of built-in tendencies on the part of infants and propensities of adults to respond in certain ways to infants' cues and needs (Ainsworth et al., 1978; Bowlby, 1969). As discussed later, the ways in which individual adults respond to babies vary depending on a variety of factors, including their gender, their personalities, their current social, emotional, and economic circumstances, their infants' characteristics, their own life histories, as well as their ideology and culture.

The nature of parent–infant interactions provides a medium within which the chrysalis of the child's future life germinates and grows. Continuities in interaction across diverse contexts in the infant's social ecology ensure that characteristics of interactions with parents carry over to interactions infants have with other classes of social partners, like caregivers and peers (Clarke-Stewart, Allhusen, & Clements, in this *Handbook*; Ladd & Le Sieur, in this *Handbook*). The quality of parent–infant relationships could shape infants' relationships with others by affecting their willingness and ability to engage in interactions with others, as well as influencing the likelihood that they will benefit from those interactions.

The developmental changes that take place in individuals during the 2½ years after their conception—the prenatal and infancy periods—are more dramatic and thoroughgoing than any others in the life span. The body, the mind, and the ability to operate meaningfully in and on the world all develop with intensity. That dynamism, in turn, engages the world, for infants do not grow and change in a vacuum. Every facet of the world they touch as they grow and change acts on them in return. These reciprocal relations ultimately cast parenting in a featured role.

Developmental Change in Infancy

The nature of the game in infancy is change, and children change at their own rate. Yesterday, Jonathan may have stayed in the spot where he was placed, today he is creeping, and next week he will be crawling faster than his mother can catch him. Another same-age child may not begin to locomote for two more months. Coping with dynamic change in the context of individual variation presents a major challenge to all new parents.

Infancy is dynamic change.   Infant development involves parallel and rapid biological, psychological, and sociological events, and infancy is synonymous with structural change. Parents must track and anticipate or respond to developments on these many fronts. Crying in 6-month-olds and behavioral inhibition in 18-month-olds may look different, but the underlying source construct of fear may be the same. Moreover, normal development in some spheres of infancy may be nonlinear in nature, stalling sometimes, or even regressing temporarily (Bever, 1982; Harris, 1983; Strauss & Stavy, 1981). Parents need to know about and learn to recognize these complications and subtleties.

Infant growth well exemplifies a "systems" perspective on development, in the sense that the organization of the whole changes as the infant matures and is exposed to new experiences, and transformations take place at many levels at once (e.g., Thelen, 1989, 1990). The advent of one behavioral subsystem brings with it a host of new experiences that influence and are influenced by changes in related component processes. Bertenthal and Campos (1990) provided an extended discussion of this systems approach using self-produced locomotion as an illustration. The emergence of this activity involves not only an advance in motor skills, it also affects a diverse number of structures and functions, such as visual-vestibular adaptation, visual attention to changes in the environment, social referencing, and emotions. For example, babies who have begun to crawl are better able to locate hidden objects and may have a new appreciation (and hence fear) of heights. Pulling up to a standing position and walking (which occurs sometime between 11 and 15 months) also have major implications for both social and cognitive development. A dramatic change in perspective has occurred: A whole new array of objects can be approached, explored, manipulated, and mastered—or broken. Although the infant is totally dependent on adults for stimulation, the toddler rapidly acquires the ability to explore and to self-stimulate. In the social domain, the ability to stand signals significant changes in the infant's role vis-à-vis parenting figures. In the second year, toddlers initiate activities with parents more than 85 percent of the time (B. L. White, Kaban, Shapiro, & Attanucci, 1977). Standing infants seem more grown up to adults, who in turn treat them so. With each advance, parents' behaviors toward infants change. Parents must now be vigilant about a range of new, and possibly dangerous, circumstances. Much more than before, parents must communicate that infants need to regulate their own behavior.

Infancy is individual variation.   The number of notable developmental achievements occurring during infancy is amazing (especially when infancy is viewed as a proportion of the entire life span), but normal variability in the timing of these achievements is equally compelling. Every infant is original. Interest in the origins and expression of this variability occupies a central position in thinking about infant development and parenting. The age at which individual infants achieve a given developmental milestone typically varies enormously (some children say their first word at 9 months, others at 29 months), just as infants of a given age vary dramatically among themselves on nearly every index of development (at 1 year, some toddlers comprehend 10 words, others 75; and some produce zero words, others nearly 30). Of course, when and how their toddlers talk or walk or whatever exercises a psychological impact on parents, even if the long-term significance of a given child's performance is meaningful only for extreme cases.

Individual variation in infant emotion and temperament is equally fascinating and has significant implications for each child's development (J. E. Bates, 1987; Sanson & Rothbart, in this *Handbook*). For example, some infants inherit or develop enduring dispositions that elicit negative perceptions from caregivers. Difficult babies have hunger cries that are higher-pitched, and adults perceive them as more aversive and demanding (Lounsbury & J. E. Bates, 1982). Further, maternal perceptions of difficultness in the first 6 months of life predict their perceptions of aggressiveness and anxiety in children when they are 3 to 5 years old (J. E. Bates, Maslin, & Frankel, 1985).

Developing Infants

Parenting an infant is akin to trying to hit a moving target, with each everchanging infant developing in fits and starts at different paces. Across this spectrum of developmental issues and matters that parents must confront, infants themselves are mute but potent. The very young neither understand their parents' speech nor respond to them verbally. At the same time, infants are also notoriously uncooperative and seem unmotivated to perform or conform. Still other pervasive infant characteristics vex parents or give pause—depending on a parent's perspective or the moment: Infants possess limited attention spans and, in addition to lacking speech, have limited response repertoires; they are also, especially in the earlier months, motorically incompetent or inept. Yet infants are consistent and voracious in their demands. Parents need to interpret aspects of infant function unambiguously, and must accomplish this in spite of changes and fluctuations in infant state. Perhaps the major problem faced by parents of infants is that, at base, they are constantly trying to divine what is "inside the baby's head"—what infants want, what they know, how they feel, what they will do next about the people and things around them, and whether they understand and are affected by those same people and things. Thus, parents of infants seem constantly in search of patterns, often even on the basis of single transient instances. New parents have the job of disambiguating novel, complex, and rapidly emerging uncertain information and, at the same time, are called to parent appropriately and effectively. Most face the formidable challenges of infancy with psychological naiveté. But parents do not meet these tests totally unprepared. Beyond blind biodeterminism, culture generally equips parents for understanding and interpreting the developing domains of infancy as well as it's vicissitudes.

PRINCIPLES OF PARENTING INFANTS

Infants do not and cannot grow up as solitary individuals; parenting constitutes an initial and all-encompassing ecology of infant development. Mothers and fathers guide the development of their infants via many direct and indirect means. Biological parents contribute to the genetic makeup of their infants. All parents shape their infants' experiences. Parents also influence their infants by virtue of each partner's influence on the other. Parents influence infant development both by their behaviors and by their beliefs. In this respect, similarities as well as differences in mothers' and fathers' actions and attitudes affect the nature and course of infant development, and they do so according to different mechanisms and following different models.

Direct and Indirect Effects

Most mothers and fathers contribute directly to the nature and development of their infants by passing on biological characteristics. Modern behavior genetics argues that characteristics of offspring in a host of different realms—including height and weight, intelligence, and temperament—reflect inheritance in substantial degree (e.g., Bouchard, Lykken, McGue, Segal, & Tellegen, 1990; Plomin, 1989).

Although parental genes certainly contribute to infant proclivities and abilities in different domains, all prominent theories of development put experience in the world as either the principal source of individual growth or as a major contributing component (Dixon & Lerner, 1992; Kuhn, 1992). Studies of children with genetic backgrounds that differ from those of their nurturing families provide a powerful means of evaluating the impacts of heredity and experience on infant development (e.g., Ho, 1987; Plomin, 1989; Plomin & DeFries, 1985). In (ideal) natural experiments of adoption, the child shares genes but little if any of the same environment with biological parents, and the child shares an environment but few if any genes with adoptive parents. Studies of 1-year-olds, their biological parents, and their adoptive parents show, for example, that the rate of development of communicative competence and cognitive abilities relates to the general intelligence of the baby's biological mother (IQ) and also to the behavior of the adoptive mother (imitating and responding contingently to infant vocalization). These results point to direct roles for *both* heredity and experience in parenting infants (Hardy-Brown, 1983; Hardy-Brown & Plomin, 1985). Thus, evidence for heritability effects neither negates nor diminishes equally compelling evidence for the direct effects of caregiving functions of parents. To cite even the most obvious example, genes must contribute to making siblings very much alike, but (as we all know) siblings are normally very different, and siblings' different experiences contribute to making them distinctive individuals (Dunn & Plomin, 1991). Even within the same family and home setting, parents (and other factors) create distinctive effective environments for different children.

Empirical research attests to the short- and long-term influences of parent-provided experiences in infant development. Maternal attentiveness and mood during feeding in the first months predict 3-year child language comprehension (Bee et al., 1982). Mothers' affectionate touching, rocking, holding, and smiling at their 6-month-olds predicts cognitive/language competence at 2 years (Olson, J. E. Bates, & Bayles, 1984). Analyses of the influences of maternal interactions on the growth of vocabulary and verbal intelligence in young children show that mothers who speak more, prompt more, and respond more during the first year have 6-month-olds to 4-year-olds who score higher in standardized evaluations (e.g., Bornstein, 1985; Bornstein & Tamis-LeMonda, 1989, 1990; Tamis-LeMonda & Bornstein, 1989, 1990; Vibbert & Bornstein, 1989). Even features of the parent-outfitted physical environment appear to influence infant development directly (Wachs & Chan, 1986): Parents who provide their toddlers with new toys and change their room decorations are also likely to name objects more, but the physical parameters of the environment exert an influence on child language acquisition in and of themselves, and not simply as a function of parental naming.

Indirect effects are more subtle and less noticeable than direct effects, but perhaps no less meaningful. Primary among this type of effect is marital support and communication. Conflicts and disagreements between couples increase with the birth of a first baby, and marital satisfaction decreases from pregnancy to early childhood (Belsky, Lang, & Rovine, 1985; C. P. Cowan et al., 1985; Grossman, Eichler, & Winikoff, 1980). Parents' attitudes about themselves and their marriages during this transition influence the quality of their interactions with their children and in turn their children's development (C. P. Cowan & P. A. Cowan, 1992). Parents who feel negative about themselves and their marriage are more authoritarian with their children (i.e., their interactions tend to be cold and unresponsive), and they are less able to set limits than parents who have more positive feelings. Mothers who report supportive relationships with "secondary parents" (husbands, lovers, or grandparents) are more competent and sensitively responsive to their infants than are women who lack such relationships (Feiring, 1976; Ladd & Le Sieur, in this *Handbook*; Parke, in this *Handbook*).

In the extreme, conflict between spouses may reduce the availability of an important source of support in early childrearing, namely one's partner. Short of that, parents embroiled in marital conflict may have difficulty attending to the sometimes subtle signals infants use to communicate their needs. Infants in these homes may learn that caregivers are unreliable sources of information or assistance in stressful situations. For example, uncertain 1-year-olds are less likely to look to their maritally dissatisfied fathers for information or clarification than are infants of more satisfied fathers (Dickstein & Parke, 1988). In one study, the influence of the husband–wife relationship on mother–infant interaction in a feeding context was assessed (Pedersen, 1975). Ratings were made of the quality of mother–infant interaction during home observations when the infants were 4 weeks of age. Feeding competence referred to the appropriateness of the mother in managing and pacing feeding without disrupting the baby and to her showing sensitivity to the baby's needs for either stimulation of feeding or brief rest periods during the course of feeding. In addition, the husband–wife relationship was assessed via interview. Neonatal assessments (Brazelton, 1973) were also available. When fathers were more supportive of mothers, evaluating maternal skills more positively, mothers were more competent in feeding babies. (Of course, competent mothers could elicit more positive evaluations from their husbands.) The reverse held for marital discord: High tension and conflict in the marriage were associated with more inept feeding on the part of the mother. The marital relationship also predicted the status and well-being of the infant assessed by Brazelton scores. With an alert baby, the father evaluated the mother more positively; with a motorically mature baby, there appeared to be less tension and conflict in the marriage.

Research shows both direct and indirect effects of parenting on infants. In addition, both parents' behaviors and beliefs matter.

Parenting Behaviors

Perhaps most salient in the phenomenology of the infant are actual experiences provided by mother and father. Before children are old enough to enter informal or formal social learning situations, like play groups and school, much of their worldly experience stems directly from interactions they have within the family. In that context (at least in Western cultures), two adult caregiving figures are responsible for determining most, if not all, of infants' experiences. A small number of domains of parenting interactions have been identified as a common "core" of parental care. They have been studied for their variation, stability, continuity, and covariation, as well as for their correspondence with and prediction of infant development.

Domains of parenting infants. In infrahuman primates, the majority of maternal behaviors consist simply in biologically requisite feeding, grooming, protecting, and the like (Bard, in this *Handbook*). The content of parent–infant interactions is more dynamic, varied, and arbitrary in human beings. Moreover, there is initially asymmetry in parent and child contributions to interactions and control: Postinfancy, children play more active and anticipatory roles in interaction, whereas initial responsibility for adaptation in child development lies unambiguously with the parent.

Four superordinate categories of human parental caregiving (and reciprocally for the infant, experiences) can be identified: They are nurturant, material, social, and didactic. These categories apply to the infancy period and to normal caregiving. Not all forms of parenting, or parenting domains appropriate for older children (e.g., punishment), are incorporated or accounted for in this taxonomy. Although these modes of caregiving are conceptually and operationally distinct, in practice caregiver–infant interaction is intricate and multidimensional, and infant caregivers regularly engage in combinations of them. Together, these modes are the most prominent of caregivers' activities with babies, and they are perhaps universal, even if their instantiation or emphases in terms of frequency or duration vary across cultures. For their part, human infants are reared in, influenced by, and adapt to a physical and social ecology commonly characterized by the elements in this taxonomy.

1. *Nurturant caregiving* meets the physical requirements of the infant. Infant mortality is a perennial concern (UNICEF, 1993), and parents are responsible for promoting infants' wellness and preventing their illness from the moment of conception—and even earlier. Parents in virtually all higher species nurture the very young, providing sustenance, protection, supervision, grooming, and the like. Parents shield infants from many risks and stressors. Nurturance is prerequisite for infants' survival and well-being.

2. *Material caregiving* encompasses those ways in which parents provision and organize the infant's physical world. Adults are responsible for the number and variety of inanimate objects (toys, books, tools) available to the infant, the level of ambient stimulation, the limits on physical freedom, and the overall physical dimensions of babies' experiences.

3. *Social caregiving* includes the variety of visual, verbal, affective, and physical behaviors parents use in engaging infants in interpersonal exchanges. Rocking, kissing, tactile comforting, smiling, vocalizing, and playful face-to-face contact are illustrative of interpersonal social interactions. Parental displays of warmth toward children peak in infancy and decline thereafter, an effect likely explained by the fact that displays of warmth early on can involve physical expressions of affection that they do not as children get older. Social caregiving includes the regulation of affect as well as the management of infant social relations with others, including relatives, nonfamilial caregivers, and peers.

4. *Didactic caregiving* consists of the variety of strategies parents use in stimulating infants to engage and understand the environment outside the dyad. Didactics include focusing the baby's attention on properties, objects, or events in the surroundings; introducing, mediating, and interpreting the external world; describing and demonstrating; as well as provoking or providing opportunities to observe, to imitate, and to learn. Normally, didactics increase toward the end of infancy and after.

Four significant developmental characteristics distinguish these domains of parenting. The first has to do with variation among individual parents. Adults differ considerably among themselves in terms of their caregiving behaviors, even when they come from the same culture and from socioeconomically homogeneous groups. For example, the language that parents address to infants varies enormously. One study reported that, even when relatively homogeneous in terms of education and socioeconomic status, some mothers talk to their 4-month-olds during as little as 3 percent and some during as much as 97 percent of a naturalistic home observation (Bornstein & Ruddy, 1984). Thus, the range in amount of language that washes over babies is virtually as large as it can be. This is not to say that there are not also systematic group differences by SES or culture (there are; discussed later).

The second feature of parenting has to do with stability of individual variation over time, and the third with continuity over time. These perspectives on caregiving add meaning to infants' experiences. Stability gives evidence of consistency in the relative ranks of individuals in a group over time, and continuity gives evidence of consistency in the absolute level of group performance; the two are independent. One study examined activities of mothers toward their firstborn infants between the time babies were 2 and 5 months of age (Bornstein & Tamis-LeMonda, 1990). This study recorded two kinds of mothers' encouraging attention, two kinds of speech, and maternal bids to social play in relation to infants' own exploration and vocalization. Table 1.1 provides a conceptual summary of some findings, distinguishing activities that are stable and unstable (in terms of rank order of individual differences), as well as those that are continuous and discontinuous (in terms of change in absolute level). Notable is the fact that every cell in the table is represented with a significant maternal activity. Some parenting activities are stable and continuous as infants age. Total maternal speech to baby is an example. Other activities are stable and discontinuous, showing either a general developmental increase (e.g., didactic stimulation) or a decrease (e.g., the sing-song tones of "infant-directed" speech). Some activities are unstable and continuous (e.g., social play), whereas others are unstable and discontinuous, showing either a general developmental increase (e.g., the normal conversational tones of "adult-directed" speech) or a decrease (e.g., social stimulation). Other studies have examined consistency of maternal behavior toward first- and secondborns when each child was 1 and 2 years old (Dunn, Plomin, & Daniels, 1986; Dunn, Plomin, & Nettles, 1985); at both times, moderate to high levels of stability emerged in maternal affectionate verbal responsiveness and controlling behavior. Summarizing across a wide variety of samples, time intervals, and types of home assessments, Gottfried (1984) determined that parent-provided experiences in the United States tend to be stable during the early years (see, too, Belsky, Taylor, & Rovine, 1984). Klein (1988) also found that Israeli mothers are stable in the amounts of learning experiences they provide in different situations of caregiving between middle infancy and the time their toddlers reach 2 years of age.

Individual parents do not vary much in their activities from day to day, but parenting activities change over longer periods, and in response to children's development. The ratio of positive to negative phrases mothers make in reference to their infants increases across the first postpartum year, and there is a corresponding reduction in time devoted to caregiving activities (Fleming, Ruble, Flett, & Van Wagner, 1990). Sensitive parents also tailor their behaviors to match their infants' developmental progress (Adamson & Bakeman, 1984; Carew, 1980), for example, by providing more didactic experiences as infants age (Klein, 1988). Indeed, parents express sensitivity both to infant age and, more especially, to infant capacity or performance (Bellinger, 1980): The mean length of mothers' utterances tends to match the mean length of those of their 1½- to 3½-year-olds (McLaughlin, D. White, McDevitt, & Raskin, 1983).

The fourth characteristic of these different categories of parenting has to do with their relative independence from one another. Classical authorities, including notably psychoanalysts and ethologists, once conceptualized maternal behavior as a more or less unitary construct—often denoted "good," "sensitive," "warm," or "adequate"—despite the wide range of activities mothers naturally engage in with infants (e.g., Ainsworth et al., 1978; Mahler et al., 1975; Rohner, 1985; Winnicott, 1957). In other words, the thinking was that parents behave in consistent ways across domains of interaction, time, and context. The four domains described here constitute coherent, but mutually distinctive constructs. Mothers who engage in more face-to-face play are not necessarily or automatically those who engage in didactics more, and vice versa. This is true in U.S. American as well as in English, French, and Japanese mothers (Bornstein, Azuma, Tamis-LeMonda, & Ogino, 1990; Bornstein & Tamis-LeMonda, 1990; Bornstein, Tamis-LeMonda, Pêcheux, & Rahn, 1991; Bornstein, Toda, Azuma, Tamis-LeMonda, & Ogino, 1990; Dunn, 1977). In other words, individual mothers appear to emphasize particular kinds of activities with their infants.

Mutual responsiveness. Infant caregiving is further differentiated by responsibility and lead. In Western industrialized cultures, parents are generally acknowledged to take principal responsibility for structuring exchanges: They engage infants in early game play (e.g., Hodapp, Goldfield, &

TABLE 1.1
Developmental Stability and Continuity in Maternal Activities in Early Infancy

Developmental Stability	Developmental Continuity		
	Yes	*No*	
		Increase	*Decrease*
Stable	Speech[a]	Didactic stimulation	Infant-directed speech
Unstable	Social play	Adult-directed speech	Social stimulation

[a]For example, across early infancy, mothers speak to their infants approximately the same amount in total (*continuity*), and those mothers who speak more when their infants are younger speak more when their infants are older, just as those mothers who speak less when their infants are younger speak less when their infants are older (*stability*).

Boyatzis, 1984) as well as in turn-taking in verbal interchange (e.g., Vandell & Wilson, 1987). Frequently, then, thinking about parent–infant relationships highlights parents as agents of infant socialization with infants conceived of as passive recipients. To a considerable degree, however, parenting infants is a two-way street. Surely, infants cry to be fed and changed, and when they wake they are ready to play. Sometimes, parents' initiatives are proactive; often, however, they are reactive and interactive.

Responsiveness is a major issue to be considered in parenting infants (Ainsworth et al., 1978; Bornstein, 1989e). Although responsiveness may take many guises, studies show that parents who respond promptly, reliably, and appropriately to their babies' signals give babies a good message from the start. They tell their children that they can trust their parents to be there for them. They give their children a sense of control and of self. Babies cry and the mother comes; babies already feel they have an effect on the world. A baby whose parent has been unresponsive is frequently angry because the parent's inaccessibility may be painful and frustrating; further, because of uncertainty about the parent's responsiveness, the infant may be apprehensive and readily upset by stressful situations (Rubin, Stewart, & Chen, in this *Handbook*).

Infants deliberately search for and use others' (parents') emotional (facial, vocal, gestural) expressions to help clarify uncertain and evaluate novel events, a phenomenon called social referencing (Campos & Stenberg, 1981; Feinman, 1982; Feinman & Lewis, 1983). At 9 to 12 months of age, infants look to mothers and fathers for emotional cues and are influenced by both positive and negative adult expressions (Dickstein & Parke, 1988; Hirshberg & Svejda, 1990). Indeed, they may position themselves so they can keep mother's face in view (Sorce & Emde, 1981). That negative qualities of caregivers' emotional expressions—distress, disgust, fear, anger—influence infant behavior seems sensible given that the important message in a parent's emotional expressions is that the event is (or is not) dangerous or threatening to the baby. Infants play less with unusual toys when their mothers show disgust compared with pleasure, and when the same toys are presented a few minutes later, they show the same responses, even though mothers may no longer pose distinct emotional expressions but are instead silent and neutral (Hornik, Risenhoover, & Gunnar, 1987). Infants of depressed mothers show inferior social referencing skills, perhaps because their mothers provide less frequent or certain facial and vocal cues and fewer modeling responses (Field, in this *Handbook*).

Responsiveness has been observed as a typical parenting characteristic of mothers in different parts of the world (Bornstein et al., 1992). Certainly, some types of responsiveness in mothers are similar and some types vary relative to divergent cultural goals of parenting. Mothers in different cultures do not vary substantially in responding to infant vocal distress or nondistress. Responsiveness to distress, for example, is thought to have evolved an adaptive significance for eliciting and maintaining proximity and care. However, mothers respond variuosly in more discretionary interactions, as in determining which infant attentional behaviors to respond to and how to respond to them. For example, following cultural expectations, Japanese mothers emphasize emotional exchange within the dyad in responsive interactions with their babies, whereas U.S. American mothers promote language and emphasize the world outside the dyad (Bornstein et al., 1992).

Parenting infants gone awry.   Before leaving a consideration of how parents behave toward infants, some reality testing is in order. In everyday life, parenting infants does not always go well and right. Infanticide was practiced historically (French, in this *Handbook*), but it is very rare (although not unknown) today (Eisenberg, 1990). Nonetheless, the local 10 o'clock news too often begins with horrific telecasts of some diabolical instance of infant maltreatment. Short of such outright pathology, numerous other risks alter postnatal parenting and compromise the innocent infant (Carnegie Corporation of New York, 1994): More than one-quarter of births in the United States are to unmarried mothers. More than one-quarter of children under 3 live below the federal poverty level. One in three victims of physical abuse is a baby. In the inner city, nearly one-half of women giving birth test positive for cocaine use at the time of delivery. Less than one-half of American 2-year-olds are fully immunized. If they are kissed as the ultimate gesture of political caring, infants have always and in every society still suffered physical and psychological neglect and abuse: from parents who are distressed and so supervise their children less closely and understand their children less well (Wahler & Dumas, 1989), to those who have abused drugs and simply fail to attend to their parenting responsibilities (Bernstein, Jeremy, Hans, & Marcus, 1984; K. Burns, Chethik, W. J. Burns, & Clark, 1991).

Parenting Beliefs

When their infants are only 1 month of age, 99 percent of mothers believe that babies can express interest, 95 percent joy, 84 percent anger, 75 percent surprise, 58 percent fear, and 34 percent sadness (W. Johnson, Emde, Pennbrook, Stenberg, & Davis, 1982). These judgments may reflect infants' expressive capacities or contextual cues, or mothers' subjective inferences. In response to specific questions, mothers describe infants' vocal and facial expressions, along with their gestures and arm movements, as the bases of these judgments (W. Johnson et al., 1982; Klinnert, Sorce, Emde, Stenberg, & Gaensbauer, 1984). Because mothers commonly respond differently to distinct emotional messages they perceive in their infants, they have frequent opportunities to have their inferences corrected or fine-tuned depending on how their babies respond. Thus, there is good reason for investing confidence in many maternal beliefs about infants.

Parents' beliefs—whether more specifically, their ideas, knowledge, understanding, on attitudes—hold a consistently popular place in the study of parent–infant relationships (Goodnow & Collins, 1990; Holden, in this *Handbook*). Parental beliefs are conceived to serve many functions; they may generate and shape parental behaviors, mediate the effectiveness of parenting, or help to organize parenting because they affect parents' sense of self and competence (Darling & Steinberg, 1993; Maccoby & Martin, 1983; McGillicuddy-De Lisi & Sigel, in this *Handbook*; Murphey, 1992; K. H. Rubin & Mills, 1992). In observing and understanding childrearing beliefs, one may come to determine how and why parents behave in the ways they do.

Consider the role of parents' own theories of development. Goodnow (1986) proposed that most parents harbor implicit assumptions regarding relations between developing behavior and age, for example, and that parents continually assess their children's level of development when formulating how best and most productively to interact with them. Parents' beliefs fluctuate to some degree, as they actively acquire new information about children through observations, experimentation, feedback, and so forth.

A determinative role of parental beliefs is found in reports about infants. Based on their long-term, intimate experience with them, parents surely know their own infants better than anyone else does. For that reason, parents (or other close caregivers) can provide valid and insightful reports about them (Thomas, Chess, Birch, Hertzig, & Korn, 1963). However, parental report invites problems of bias owing, for example, to parents' subjective viewpoint, personality disposition, unique experiences, and other factors. One study compared maternal and observer ratings of infant activity (operationalized in terms of reaching, kicking, and other explicit motor behaviors) when infants were by themselves, with mother, and with observer, on two separate occasions, each time in the different situations (Bornstein, Gaughran, & Seguí, 1991). Mother–observer assessments agreed, but only moderately. Historically, evaluations of convergence between maternal reports and assessments of infants by (significant) others (father, caregiver, or observer) have yielded only moderate levels of agreement (e.g., J. E. Bates, 1987; Hagekull, Bohlin, & Lindhagen, 1984). Apparently, different observers have different amounts of information about baby, and they carry with them unique perspectives that have been shaped by different prior experiences; these perspectives influence their judgments of infants (Sameroff, Seifer, & Elias, 1982; Vaughn, Taraldson, Crichton, & Egeland, 1981).

Nonetheless, parents' perceptions are still valuable in their own right, that is, as contributors to understanding parenting forces at work in the development of infants (J. E. Bates, 1987; Bornstein et al., 1991; St. James-Roberts & Wolke, 1984). Their beliefs play a role in infant development.

Mothers who see their infants as being difficult, for example, are less likely to pay attention or respond to their children's positive overtures. In this way, parental perceptions per se may foster a temperamentally difficult attribute because they lead adults to treat children more negatively.

Significantly, parents of infants in different cultures appear to cling to different ideas about the meaning and significance of their own parenting behaviors as well as of the behaviors of their infants (e.g., Bornstein et al., in press; Goodnow & Collins, 1990; Palacios, 1990). Parents act on culturally defined beliefs as much or more than on what their senses tell them. Parents in Samoa think of young children as having an angry and willful character, and, independent of what children might actually say, universally acknowledge that the child's first word is "tae"— Samoan for "shit" (Ochs, 1988). Parents who believe that they can or cannot affect their infants' temperament, intelligence, or what have you, modify their parenting accordingly. Parents in Mexico promote play in very young children as a forum of interpersonal sensitivity experience, whereas parents in the United States are prone to attach a greater cognitive value to play (Farver, 1993). The ways in which parents (choose to) interact with their infants appear to relate to culturally prevailing belief systems.

Descriptions of the characteristics of parenting beg the question: How do parental behaviors and beliefs develop? After a brief interlude that compares maternal and paternal parenting and discusses mechanisms of parenting effects on infants, we return to explore forces that shape parenting infants.

Mothers and Fathers

Most people would agree that mothers normally play the central role in their children's development, especially in infancy (Barnard & Martell, in this *Handbook*), even if historically fathers' social and legal claims and responsibilities on children were preeminent (French, in this *Handbook*). Cross-cultural surveys attest to the primacy of biological mothers in caregiving (e.g., Leiderman, Tulkin, & Rosenfeld, 1977), and theorists, researchers, and clinicians have been concerned with mothering, rather than parenting, in recognition of this fact. Western industrialized nations have witnessed increases in the amount of time fathers spend with their children; in reality, however, fathers typically assume little responsibility for infant care and rearing, and fathers are primarily helpers (Young, 1991). On average, mothers spend between 65 and 80 percent more time than fathers do in direct one-to-one interaction with their infants (Parke, in this *Handbook*). Mothers spend more time with babies than do fathers whether in the United States (Kotelchuck, 1976; Pedersen & Robson, 1969), the U.K. (Jackson, 1987), Australia (Russell, 1983), or France or Belgium (Szalai, 1972). Mothers also interact with and take care of babies and toddlers more than fathers (Belsky, Gilstrap, & Rovine, 1984; Collins & G. Russell, 1991; Greenbaum & Landau, 1982; Montemayor, 1982; G. Russell & A. Russell, 1987). Fathers may withdraw from their infants when they are unhappily married; mothers typically do not.

Fathers are neither inept nor uninterested in interacting with their infants, however. When feeding infants, for example, both fathers and mothers respond to infants' cues, either with social bids or by adjusting the pace of their feeding (Parke & Sawin, 1980). Mothers and fathers alike touch and look more closely at an infant after the infant has vocalized (Parke & Sawin, 1975), and both equally increase their rates of speech to baby following baby vocalization.

Although fathers are capable of performing sensitively, they tend to yield responsibility for child care to their wives when not asked to demonstrate their competence (Parke, in this *Handbook*). Mothers and fathers also interact with and care for their infants in complementary ways; that is, they tend to share the labor of caregiving and engage infants emphasizing different types of interactions (Bornstein, Maital, & Tal, 1994). When in face-to-face play with their 2-week-old to 6-month-old babies, for example, mothers tend to be rhythmic and containing, whereas fathers provide staccato bursts of both physical and social stimulation (Yogman, 1982). Mothers are more likely to hold their infants in the course of caregiving, whereas fathers are more likely to do so when playing with babies or in response to infants' requests to be held. With older infants, mothers tend to engage in less physically stimulating, unpredictable, and arousing play than fathers do (Parke, in this *Handbook*). When mother–infant and father–infant play were contrasted in a developmental analysis (Power,

1985), both mothers and fathers followed interactional rules of sharing attentional focus on a toy with baby; however, mothers tended to follow the baby's focus of interest, whereas fathers tended to establish the attentional focus themselves. In research involving both traditional American families (Belsky et al., 1984) and traditional and nontraditional Swedish families, where father was primary caregiver (Lamb, A. M. Frodi, M. Frodi, & Hwang, 1982), parental gender was found to exert a greater influence in these respects than, say, parental role or employment status: Mothers are more likely to kiss, hug, talk to, smile at, tend, and hold their infants than fathers, regardless of degree of involvement in caregiving. In general, mothers are associated with infant caregiving, whereas fathers are identified with playful interactions (Clarke-Stewart, 1980).

Mothers and fathers alike are sensitive to infant language status, but here too they appear to play complementary roles with regard to the quality and quantity of speech they direct to infants (Rondal, 1980). On the one hand, maternal and paternal speech to infants displays many of the same simplification processes. On the other hand, mothers are more "in tune" with their infants' linguistic abilities: Mother utterance length relates to child utterance length, whereas father utterance length does not. Father speech is lexically more diverse than mother speech. It is shorter, and fathers correct children's speech less often and place more verbal demands on the child; it thereby "pulls" for higher levels of performance (McLaughlin et al., 1983; Rondal, 1980). Despite the low quantity of interaction and variant style, however, infants become attached to their fathers as they do to their mothers.

Mechanisms of Parenting Effects on Infants

Parents' behaviors and beliefs influence infants and infant development via different paths. A common assumption in parenting is that the overall level of parental involvement or stimulation affects the infant's overall level of development (see Maccoby & Martin, 1983). An illustration of the simplest model suggests that the development of language in infants is determined (at least to some degree) by the language infants hear. Mothers' single-word utterances are just those that appear earliest in their children's vocabularies (Chapman, 1981), and specific characteristics of maternal speech appear to play a big part in children's specific styles of speech as well (E. Bates, Bretherton, & Snyder, 1988).

The nature of interactions. Increasing evidence suggests, however, that sophisticated mechanisms function in explaining parenting effects. First, specific (rather than general) parental activities appear to relate concurrently and predictively to specific (rather than general) aspects of infant competence or performance and, second, parent and infant mutually influence one another through time.

The *specificity principle* states that specific experiences at specific times exert specific effects over specific aspects of infant growth in specific ways (e.g., Bornstein, 1989a; Bradley, Caldwell, & Rock, 1988; Tamis-LeMonda & Bornstein, 1994). Several such associations were observed in one example longitudinal study of relations between mothers and their 2- to 5-month-olds (Bornstein & Tamis-LeMonda, 1990). For instance, mothers who encouraged their infants to attend to the mothers themselves had babies who later looked more at their mothers and less at the environment, whereas mothers who encouraged attention to the environment had babies who explored external properties, objects, and events more and their mothers less.

The *transactional principle* of development recognizes that the characteristics of individuals shape their experiences and reciprocally, that experiences shape the characteristics of individuals through time (Sameroff, 1983). Biological endowment and experience mutually influence development from birth onward, and one life force affects the other as development proceeds throughout the life span (Lerner & Busch-Rossnagel, 1981). By virtue of their unique characteristics and propensities—state of arousal, perceptual awareness, cognitive status, emotional expressiveness, and individuality of temperament—infants actively contribute, through their interactions with their parents, toward producing their own development. Infants influence which experiences they will be exposed to as well as how they interpret those experiences and how those experiences might affect them (Scarr & McCartney, 1983). Infant and parent bring distinctive characteristics to, and each is believed to be changed as a result of, every interaction; both then enter the next round of interaction as "different" individuals. Vygotsky (1978) contended that, as a central feature of this transactional perspective, the more advanced or expert partner (the mother) will raise the level of performance and of competence of the less advanced or expert partner (the infant), and the "dynamic systems" perspective posits that reciprocity between mother and infant specifically facilitates higher level forms of interaction (Fogel & Thelen, 1987). Thus, Lea, who is alert and responsive, invites her mother's stimulation; Lea's enthusiastic response is rewarding to her parents who stimulate her more, which in turn further enriches her life.

The specificity and transactional principles together propel development from infancy onward. Normally, parent and infant behaviors dovetail. The working model of parenting infants and infant development is that specific experiences at specific times affect specific aspects of the child's growth in specific ways *and* that specific infant abilities and proclivities affect specific experiences and specific aspects of development.

Models of interaction effects.   Parenting behaviors or beliefs appear to affect development in infancy via different pathways. A parent-provided experience may influence the infant at a particular time point, and the consequence for the infant endures, independent of earlier or later parenting (and, perhaps, independent of any contribution of the infant). This model is consonant with a sensitive period interpretation of parenting effects (e.g., Bornstein, 1989c). An alternative possible pathway is that parent-provided experiences influence infant development cumulatively; that is, a parent-provided experience at any one time does not necessarily exceed an effective threshold in affecting the infant, but meaningful longitudinal relations are structured by similar parenting interactions continually repeating and aggregating through time (e.g., Olson et al., 1984). Of course, there is nothing to prevent both sensitive period and cumulative impact models of parenting influence from operating simultaneously in different spheres of infant development. It would be shortsighted to assume that different kinds of parenting exert independent and linear effects over infant development. Such a position fails to consider significant complex and conditional effects of caregiving. Parenting of specific sorts might affect development monistically, but often different behaviors also often combine in conditional ways; parenting affects development over short or over long periods; it's effects may be immediate, or they may need to aggregate; and some may be direct, others indirect.

Summary

Parents influence their infants directly via their genes, behaviors, and beliefs as well as indirectly via their influence on one another. Despite the dynamic range and complexity of individual activities that are naturally a part of parenting infants, major domains of parent–infant interaction have been operationally distinguished; they include nurturing, provisioning the environment, interacting socially, and stimulating cognitively. These domains are conceptually separable, and each is developmentally significant. The attitudes parents hold about their infants can be as meaningful for development as their activities with their babies. Mothers typically take more responsibility for and engage in infant caregiving more than fathers, but fathers play complementary and important roles. Parent-provided experiences affect infants via different mechanisms of action, but tend to follow signal principles of specificity and transaction.

FORCES THAT SHAPE PARENTING INFANTS

A key step toward fully understanding parenting is to evaluate the forces that first shape it. The origins of individual variation in maternal and paternal caregiving—whether behaviors or beliefs—are extremely complex, but certain factors seem to be of paramount importance: biological determinants;

personality characteristics; actual or perceived characteristics of infants; and contextual influences, including social situational factors, socioeconomic status, and culture.

Biological Determinants of Parenting

Basic physiology is mobilized to support parenting (Corter & Fleming, in this *Handbook*; Rosenblatt, in this *Handbook*), and parenting normally first arises out of biological processes associated with pregnancy and parturition. Prenatal biological events—parental age, diet, and stress, as well as other factors such as contraction of disease, exposure to environmental toxins, and even anesthetics—also affect postnatal parenting.

H. Papoušek and M. Papoušek (in this *Handbook*) have developed the notion that some infant caregiving practices are biologically "wired" into human beings. Intuitive parenting, as it is called, involves responses that are developmentally suited to the age and abilities of the child, and they often have the goal of enhancing adaptation and development. Parents regularly enact intuitive parenting programs in an unconscious fashion—that is, such programs do not require the time and effort typical of conscious decision making, and, being more rapid and efficient, they utilize less attentional reserve.

An example of intuitive parenting is the use of infant-directed speech. Parents (as well as others) habitually and unconsciously modulate myriad aspects of their communication with infants to match infants' presumed or evaluated competencies. Special characteristics of such infant-directed speech include prosodic features (higher pitch, greater range of frequencies, more varied and exaggerated intonation), simplicity features (shorter utterances, slower tempo, longer pauses between phrases, fewer embedded clauses, fewer auxiliaries), redundancy features (more repetition over shorter amounts of time, more immediate repetition), lexical features (special forms like "mama"), and content features (restriction of topics to the child's world) (Fernald, 1989; M. Papoušek, H. Papoušek, & Bornstein, 1985). Cross-cultural developmental study attests that infant-directed speech is (essentially) universal (Jacobson, Boersma, Fields, & Olson, 1983; H. Papoušek & M. Papoušek, in this *Handbook*; Snow, 1977; but see Ratner & Pye, 1984). Indeed, parents find it difficult to resist or modify such intuitive behaviors, even when asked to do so (Trevarthen, 1979). Additional support for the premise that these interactions with infants are intuitive comes from observations that nonparents (males and females) who have little prior experience with infants modify their speech as parents do, when an infant is actually present or even when asked to imagine speaking to one (Jacobson et al., 1983). Further, 2- to 3-year-old children engage in such systematic language adjustments when speaking to their year-old siblings as opposed to their mothers (Dunn & Kendrick, 1982). When communicating with their infants, deaf vocally incompetent mothers modify their sign language the way hearing mothers use infant-directed speech (Erting, Prezioso, & Hynes, 1990).

Parental Personality

Parenting also reflects enduring personality traits (Belsky, 1984; Lamb & Easterbrooks, 1981). Features of personality favorable to good parenting might include empathic awareness, predictability, nonintrusiveness, and emotional availability (Martin, 1989). Perceived effectance is also likely to affect parenting because parents who feel effective are reinforced and thus motivated to engage in further interaction with their infants, which in turn provides them with additional opportunities to read their infants' signals fully, interpret them correctly, and respond appropriately; the more rewarding the interaction, the more motivated are parents to seek "quality" interactions again.

Within the normal range, characteristics such as self-centeredness and adaptability will be especially pertinent to infant caregiving. Adult adaptability may be vital in the first few months when infants' activities appear unpredictable and disorganized, their cues less distinct and well-differentiated, and infants themselves generally less "readable." Self-centeredness can lead to difficulties when adults fail to put infants' needs before their own (Dix, 1991). Middle-class married women who are more preoccupied with themselves, as measured by physical and sexual concerns, show less effective parenting patterns in the postpartum year (Grossman et al., 1980). Directed inward, these mothers may not show appropriate sensitivity to their children's needs (C. P. Cowan & P. A. Cowan, 1992), a situation that also seems to prevail among teen mothers.

Negative characteristics of personality, whether transient or permanent, are likely to affect parenting infants adversely. For example, depression might reflect an enduring psychological characteristic, or it may be fleeting, as in response to economic circumstances, or even follow the birth the baby (Field, in this *Handbook*). Depressed mothers fail to experience—and convey to their infants—much happiness with life. Such feelings no doubt diminish responsiveness or discoordinate interactions (Tronick & Gianino, 1986), and so depressed parenting may have short- as well as long-term consequences for infants (Lyons-Ruth, Zoll, Conell, & Grunebaum, 1986). Field (1984) observed that, in face-to-face interactions, infants of depressed mothers show less positive and more negative facial affect, vocalize less, protest more, and seem to make less effort to change or improve their lot than do infants of nondepressed mothers.

Thus, aspects of adult personality help to shape parenting. Further, through intergenerational transmission, purposefully or unintentionally, one generation may psychologically influence the parenting behaviors and beliefs of the next (Van IJzendoorn, 1992). (Intergenerational transmission may follow genetic or experiential pathways.) So, for example, a mother's experiences with her own mother may have far-reaching effects on her personality and parenting. Mothers who report having had secure and realistic perceptions of their attachments to their own mothers are themselves more likely to have securely attached infants.

A dynamic view of personality influences leads to the conclusion that a parent's personality is also molded by diverse formative experiences that are contemporaneous with infant parenting. Thus, infants themselves as well as contextual settings condition parental behaviors and beliefs.

Infant Effects

Manifest as well as subtle characteristics of infants can be expected to influence parenting (and, in turn, infant development). So-called infant effects may be of different kinds. Some are universal and common to all infants; others include effects unique to a parent's particular infant or situation.

Some physical features of infancy probably affect parents everywhere in similar ways. By the conclusion of the first trimester, fetuses are felt to move in utero ("quickening"), and soon after (with support) fetuses may survive outside the womb ("viability"). These are significant markers in the life of the child *and* in the lives and psyches of the child's parents. After birth, the infant's nature as well as certain actions are likely to influence parenting. The newborn has a large head dominated by a disproportionately large forehead, widely spaced sizeable eyes, a small and snub nose, an exaggeratedly round face, and a small chin. The ethologist Lorenz (1943) argued that these physiognomic features of "babyishness" provoke adults to express reflexively nurturant and solicitous reactions toward babies—even across different species (Alley, 1981, 1983). Under ordinary conditions, specific infant behaviors predictably elicit caregiving or other specific responses from parents (Bell & Harper, 1977; Bornstein et al., 1992). From the time of birth, babies exercise several effective signals that are at their disposal: Crying will motivate adults to approach and soothe, and smiling will encourage adults to stay near.

Other structural characteristics of infants manifestly affect parenting and the quality of parent–infant interaction; infant health status, gender, and age are three significant factors. Preterm infants, for example, are more passive and reactive than are term infants of comparable age, and their mothers are more active and directive (Goldberg & DiVitto, in this *Handbook*). Such differences actually attest to heightened sensitivity on the part of mothers of preterms. Parental patterns of interaction with infant girls and boys are a second more complicated infant effect. On the one hand, there is evidence that parenting infant girls and boys is surprisingly similar (Fagot, in this *Handbook*; Lytton & Romney, 1991; Maccoby & Jacklin, 1974). On the other hand, newborn nurseries provide color-coded blankets, diapers, and so forth; gifts, beginning with the baby shower, are carefully selected by sex; and infants are uniformly dressed in sex-typed clothing (M. Shakin, D. Shakin, & Sternglanz, 1985). Infant gender, as is well known, fundamentally organizes parents' initial descriptions, impressions, and expectations (J. Condry & S. Condry, 1976; J. Rubin, Provenzano, & Luria, 1974). Finally, infant development per se, a third structural infant effect, exerts pervasive control over parental behavior. For example, over the second half of the first year of life, as infants begin to achieve verbal and other competencies, mothers appear to expect that their infants need and can process more information about themselves and their surroundings. Cross-cultural data on maternal language in this period show clearly that mothers of younger infants favor affect-laden speech but that, as infants achieve more sophisticated levels of motor exploration and cognitive comprehension, mothers everywhere increasingly orient, comment, and prepare their babies for the world outside the dyad using more information-laden speech (Bornstein et al., 1992).

Still other characteristics of infants may be idiosyncratic, but they are no less stimulating to parents. Goldberg (1977), for example, taxonomized some salient infant characteristics that affect parents in broad ways: They include responsiveness, readability, and predictability. Responsiveness refers to the extent and quality of infant reactivity to stimulation. Readability refers to the definitiveness of infant behavioral signals: An "easily read" infant is one who produces unambiguous cues that allow caregivers to recognize state quickly, interpret signals promptly, and thus respond contingently. Predictability refers to the degree to which infant behaviors can be anticipated reliably. Babies possess unique profiles of these three characteristics.

Infant temperament also influences adults and the effectiveness of adult ministrations. Having a temperamentally easy baby (one who is relatively happy, predictable, soothable, and sociable) may enhance a mother's feelings that she is efficacious, good, and competent. Even perceptions are critical. Mothers who perceive their babies as temperamentally easy consider themselves to be better mothers than mothers who see their babies as difficult (Deutch, Ruble, Fleming, Brooks-Gunn, & Stangor, 1988). Further, the same behavioral intervention may rapidly soothe one infant yet seem totally ineffective for another, leading parents of different infants to reach very different conclusions about their competence as parents, despite similarities in their parenting per se (Sanson & Rothbart, in this *Handbook*).

Contexts of Parenting

Biology, personality, and perceptions of role responsibilities constitute factors that influence parenting from the start. But societal factors channel behaviors and beliefs of infants' parents as well. Social support, social class, and culture encourage divergent patterns of parenting perceptions and practices. In some places, infants are reared in extended families in which care is provided by many relatives; in others, mothers and babies are isolated from almost all social contexts. In some groups, fathers are treated as irrelevant social objects; in others, fathers are assigned complex responsibilities for children.

Family social situation.   Infant parenting is influenced by family configuration, level of parental stress, and status of parents, among other social-situational factors. For example, about one half of babies born in a given year are firstborns, and firstborns receive more attention and better care as infants and toddlers than laterborns (Furman, in this *Handbook*). Mothers of firstborns engage, respond to, stimulate, talk to, and express positive affection to their babies more often than mothers of laterborns, even when first and laterborn babies show no difference in their behavior, indicating that these maternal behaviors do not reflect mothers' responding to differences in infants (Belsky et al., 1984). However, mothers are more prone to rate their firstborns as difficult (J. E. Bates, 1987), which may derive from the fact that firstborns actually are more difficult babies or, alternatively, because first-time mothers are less at ease with their infants and thus tend to perceive them as more demanding. Multiparas report higher self-efficacy than primiparas (Fish & Stifter, 1993). One of the more dramatic changes in family dynamics is the one that takes place when a second baby is born (Belsky, Rovine, & Fish, 1991; Mendelson, 1990; Stewart, 1990), thus the social and physical ecologies of the first- and laterborn are thoroughgoingly different (Dunn & Plomin, 1991). The births of later children alter the roles of each family member and forever affect the ways in which each interacts with all others. Parents of a secondborn infant are in many ways, therefore, not the same as parents of a firstborn in terms of behaviors or beliefs, and the mere presence of older siblings puts its own stamp on parent–infant interactions.

Even though the absolute frequency of "daily hassles" reported by parents of infants is about the same as for children of other ages, new parents do not rate the intensity and salience of those hassles as high (Crnic & Booth, 1991). Infancy may well represent a "honeymoon period" in which parents recognize the difficultness of parenting chores and choose not to make as stressful attributions about them. In contrast, as children become more autonomous, parents attempt to assert their own control over events and are more likely to feel stressed. Parents also begin to attribute greater willfulness to children's behavior once they make the transition out of infancy.

Certain choices new mothers make and situations they find themselves in exert enormous influences over parenting. About one-half of new mothers in the United States have not finished high school, are not married, or are teenagers themselves when their baby is born (Center for the Study of Social Policy, 1993; Honig, in this *Handbook*). Having a baby is a major transition in a person's life, marked by dramatic changes in information seeking, self-definition, and role responsibility (Belsky, 1984; C. P. Cowan & P. A. Cowan, 1992; Deutsch et al., 1988). Teenage mothers are thought to have lower levels of ego strength, to be less mature emotionally and socially, and to lack a well-formed maternal self-definition, perhaps because they themselves are negotiating their own developmental issues and are unskilled on account of a lack of life experience (Brooks-Gunn & Chase-Lansdale, in this *Handbook*). Overall, perhaps one-half of babies start life disadvantaged in some way because of their parents.

Financial and social stresses adversely affect general well-being and health in parents and demand attention and emotional energy from them. This, in turn, may reduce their attentiveness, patience, and tolerance toward children (Crnic & Acevedo, in this *Handbook*). Emotional integration or isolation from potential support networks mitigate or exacerbate these effects in new parents (Cochran & Niego, in this *Handbook*; Rogosch, Cicchetti, Shields, & Toth, in this *Handbook*). Well-supported mothers are less restrictive and punitive with their infants than are less well-supported mothers, and frequency of contacts with significant others improves the quality of parent–child relationships (Crnic, Greenberg, Ragozin, Robinson, & Basham, 1983; Powell, 1980) as well as parents' sense of their own effectance and competence (Abernathy, 1973). Mothers report that community and friendship support are beneficial, but intimate support from husbands (those indirect effects mentioned earlier) has the most general positive consequences for maternal competence (Crnic et al., 1983).

SES.   Socioeconomic status exerts differential effects on parental behavior with infants. Mothers in different SES groups behave similarly in certain ways, however SES orders the home environment and other behaviors of parents toward infants (Bornstein, Haynes, Suwalsky, & Galperin, 1994; Field & Pawlby, 1980; Hoff-Ginsberg, 1991; Ninio, 1980). Middle- compared to lower-SES parents typically provide more opportunities for variety in daily stimulation, more appropriate play materials, and more total stimulation, for example (Gottfried, 1984).

Significantly, middle-class mothers converse with their infants more, and in systematically more sophisticated ways, than do lower class mothers, even though young infants (presumably) understand little direct speech (Tulkin, 1977). Functionally, they acknowledge their infants' actions or attempt to engage them in conversation as opposed to limiting their utterances to directions and corrections. Lexically and syntactically, they expose their infants to a richer vocabulary, longer sentences, and greater numbers of word roots (Hoff-Ginsberg, 1991). Such social class differences in maternal speech to infants are pervasive across cultures. In Israel, for example, upper class mothers talk, label, and ask "what" questions more often than do lower middle-class mothers (Ninio, 1980). Thus, in a variety of ways, higher-SES mothers encourage their infants and toddlers in language and expand their communicative abilities. Such encouragement undoubtedly facilitates self-expression; higher SES babies produce more sounds in the first months of life than do lower SES babies (Papoušek et al., 1985). Whether parental SES (in the normal range) is associated with infant biocognitive functioning (Mayes & Bornstein, in press), it is consistently associated with cognitive development and achievement in childhood (Hoff-Ginsberg & Tardif, in this *Handbook*; McCall, 1977).

The lower class mother is likely to have been a poorer student, making it unlikely she will turn to books readily as sources of information about pregnancy and parenthood; among middle-class women, reading material is primary (Furstenberg, Brooks-Gunn, & Chase-Lansdale, 1989; Hofferth & Hayes, 1987; Young, 1991). Middle-class, more than lower class, parents also seek out and absorb expert advice about child development (Lightfoot & Valsiner, 1992). Indeed, social class and culture pervasively influence the complexity and resourcefulness with which mothers view infant development (Palacios, 1990; Sameroff & Feil, 1985).

Culture. Cultural variation in behavior is always impressive, whether observed among different ethnic groups in one society or among groups in different parts of the world. As illustrations throughout this chapter attest, cross-cultural comparisons show that virtually all aspects of parenting infants—whether behaviors or beliefs—are informed by cultural practices. For example, an investigation of developmental timetables in new mothers from Australia versus Lebanon found that cultural differences influenced expectations of children much more than other factors, such as experiences observing their own children, comparing them to other children, and receiving advice from friends and experts (Goodnow, Cashmore, Cotton, & Knight, 1984).

Culture influences parenting patterns and child development from very early in infancy through such factors as when and how parents care for infants, the extent to which parents permit infants freedom to explore, how nurturant or restrictive parents are, which behaviors parents emphasize, and so forth (Benedict, 1938; Bornstein, 1991; Erikson, 1950; Whiting, 1981). Japan and the United States represent a provocative case study for cultural comparison of infant caregiving, as these two countries maintain reasonably similar levels of modernity and living standards, and both are child centered. At the same time, the two differ dramatically in terms of history, culture, beliefs, and childrearing goals (e.g., Azuma, 1986; Bornstein, 1989b; Caudill, 1973). Japanese mothers expect early mastery of emotional maturity, self-control, and social courtesy in their young, whereas American mothers expect early mastery of verbal competence and individual action in theirs (Hess, Kashiwagi, Azuma, Price, & Dickson, 1980). American mothers promote autonomy and organize social interactions with infants so as to foster physical and verbal assertiveness and independence, and they promote interest in the external environment. Japanese mothers organize social interactions so as to consolidate and strengthen closeness and dependency within the dyad (e.g., Befu, 1986; Doi, 1973; Kojima, 1986) and to indulge infants (Levine & M. I. White, 1986; White, 1986). Thus, Japanese mothers are responsive to infants' social orientation, whereas American mothers respond more to infants' orienting to the environment. When responding to their infants' social overtures, Japanese mothers tend to direct their infants' attention to themselves, whereas American mothers tend to direct their infants' attention away from themselves and to the environment. Japanese mothers organize infant pretense in ways that encourage incorporation of a partner in play; by contrast, American mothers encourage investigation at exploratory and functional play levels. For Americans, parents' play with infants and the toys used during play are more frequently the set and topic of communication; for Japanese, the play setting serves to mediate dyadic exchange and interaction (see Bornstein, Azuma, et al., 1990; Bornstein, Tal, & Tamis-LeMonda, 1991; Bornstein, Toda, et al., 1991; Tamis-LeMonda, Bornstein, et al., 1992).

Parents in different cultures show some striking similarities in interacting with their infants as well. Whether converging patterns in mothers reflect an inherent truism of caregiving across certain societies, the historical convergence of parenting styles, or the increasing prevalence of a single childrearing pattern through migration or dissemination via mass media is difficult, if not impossible, to determine. In the end, different peoples (presumably) wish to promote similar general competencies in their young. Some do so in manifestly similar ways. Others appear to do so in different ways, and of course, culture-specific patterns of childrearing are adapted to each specific society's settings and needs (Lerner, 1989; Valsiner, 1987).

Summary

Parenting is the confluence of many complex tributaries of influence; some arise within the individual, whereas others have external sources. Some reactions felt toward babies may be reflexive and universal; others are idiosyncratic and vary with personality. By virtue of their temperament and the quality and contingency of their own responsiveness, infants have a major impact on how parents behave and how parents perceive their own effectiveness. Family social situation, class, and culture play major roles in shaping parenting and the ecology of infancy. The childrearing practices of one's own context may seem "natural," but may actually be rather unusual when compared with those of other groups. Few nations in the world are characterized by cultural homogeneity; class differences within Western industrialized countries color infantrearing practices just as surely as larger cross-cultural differences do. Cultural ideology also makes for subtle, but potentially meaningful, differences in patterns of parent behaviors and beliefs toward infants.

NONPARENTAL CAREGIVERS AND INFANTS

Historically and contemporaneously, direct infant care by a biological parent is more the exception than the rule. Siblings or other young children often care for infants, and in different cultures now and in the past infants have usually been tended by nonparental care providers—aunts and grandmothers, nurses and slaves, day-care providers and metaplot—whether in family day care at home, day-care facilities, village centers, or fields. Many individuals—other than mother and father— "parent" infants.

Siblings

In many cultures around the world, especially in non-Western nonindustrialized countries, infants may be found in the care of an older sister or brother (Weisner, 1982; Zukow, in this *Handbook*). In such situations, siblings typically spend most of their child-tending time involved in unskilled nurturant caregiving, thereby freeing adults for more rewarding economic activities (Werner, 1984). In Western and industrialized societies, by contrast, siblings are seldom entrusted with much responsibility for parenting infants per se and are themselves engaged in activities preparatory for maturity.

Sibling relationships display features of both adult–infant and peer–infant systems (Pepler, Corter, & Abramovitch, 1982). On the one hand, sibling–infant dyads share common interests and have more similar behavioral repertoires than do adult–infant dyads. On the other hand, sibling pairs resemble adult–infant pairs to the extent that they differ in experience and levels of both cognitive and social ability (Abramovitch, Corter, & Lando, 1979; Lamb, 1978). Older siblings tend to "lead" interactions and engage in more dominant, assertive, and directing behaviors. Reciprocally, infants often take special note of what their older siblings do; they follow, imitate, and explore the toys recently abandoned by older children. Of course, this strategy maximizes infant learning about the environment from the older child. Older siblings spend at least some time teaching object-related and social skills to their younger siblings (including infants), and the amount of teaching increases with the age of the older child (Minnett, Vandell, & Santrock, 1983; Pepler, 1981; Stewart, 1983). Older preschool-age firstborns create more "intellectual" (e.g., language mastery) and "social" (e.g., game) experiences for their infant siblings than do younger preschool-age firstborns (Teti, Bond, & Gibbs, 1986) and so may influence cognitive and social skills of infants through teaching and modeling (Zajonc, 1983). Older sisters and brothers also learn about themselves and about others as a result of parenting their younger siblings (Mendelson, 1990).

Related and Nonrelated Adult Caregivers

Infants commonly encounter a social world that extends beyond the immediate family. In some societies, multiple caregiving is natural (e.g., Bornstein et al., 1994; Morelli & Tronick, 1991). Today, the majority of infants in the United States are cared for on a regular basis by someone other than a parent (Phillips, 1991). Families of all kinds have need for supplementary care for their infants.

A common form of nonparental familial care involves relatives such as grandparents (Smith, in this *Handbook*). Parents with infants are very likely to receive support from their own parents (Eggebeen, 1992; Eggebeen & Hogan, 1990; Spitze & Logan, 1992). The maternal grandmother is acknowledged to play an especially critical role in the life of infants of teen and ethnic minority mothers (Brooks-Gunn & Chase-Lansdale, in this *Handbook;* Garcia Coll, Meyer, & Brillon, in this *Handbook*).

Nonrelated family day-care providers constitute another common form of infant caregiving. Usually these are women who provide care in their own homes; other infants are cared for by nonrelatives in the baby's own home; the balance attend day-care centers (Clarke-Stewart, Allhusen, & Clements, in this *Handbook*).

It was once believed that only full-time mothers could provide infants with the care they needed in order to thrive: These beliefs were fostered by literatures on the adverse effects of maternal deprivation (Bowlby, 1951; Rutter, in this *Handbook*). Theory maintained that infants become attached to those persons who have been associated over time with consistent, predictable, and appropriate responses to their signals as well as to their needs, and that attachment was critical to the development of a healthy and normal personality. Since the 1960s, however, some social critics have argued that high-quality nonparental infant day care is possible and that the normalcy of infants' emotional attachments to parents appears to depend, not on the quantity of time that parents spend with their infants, but on the quality of parents' interactions with them (Lamb, Ketterlinus, & Fracasso, 1992).

Siblings, grandparents, and various nonparents play salient roles in infant care, offering degrees of nurturing, stimulation, and entertainment that vary depending on a variety of factors—including age, gender, age gap, quality of attachment, personality, and so forth. Often infant caregivers behave in a complementary fashion to one another, dividing the full labor of infant caregiving among themselves by individually emphasizing parenting responsibilities and activities (Bornstein et al., 1994). Still unclear are the implications of these diverse patterns of early "parenting" relationships for infants' development.

CONCLUSIONS

Because of the unique nature of the infant as well as the range, magnitude, and implications of developmental change that occurs early in life, infancy is intensely fascinating and undeniably appealing, but challenging and formidable in the extreme for parents. The popular belief that parent-provided experiences during infancy exert powerful influences on later behavior or personality has been fostered from many quarters. Nevertheless, human behavior is quite malleable, and plasticity remains a feature of adaptation long after infancy. Although not all infant experiences are critical for later development, and single events are rarely formative, some infant experiences doubtlessly have long-lasting effects. Certainly, little and big consistencies of parenting aggregate over infancy to construct the person.

Parents intend much in their interactions with their infants: They promote their infants' mental development through the structures they create and the meanings they place on those structures, and they foster emotional understanding and development of self through the models they portray and the values they display. The complex of parent behaviors with infants is divisible into domains, and parents tend to show consistency over time in certain of those domains. Some aspects of parenting are frequent or significant from the get-go, and decrease after; others wax over the course of infancy. The types of interactions that infants have with their parents also vary. Mothers assume primary responsibility for child care within the family (as they typically do), and mother–infant interactions are characterized by nurturant and verbal activities; father–infant interactions are dominated by play. As a result, infants' relationships with their two parents are distinctive from a very early age. The interactive and intersubjective aspects of parent and infant activities have telling consequences for the after-infancy development of the child. Researchers and theoreticians today do not ask *whether* parenting affects infant development, but *which* parent-provided experiences affect *what* aspects of development *when* and *how*. They are interested also to learn the ways in which individual children are so affected, as well as the ways individual children affect their own development.

A full understanding of what it means to parent infants depends on the ecologies in which that parenting takes place. Within-family experiences appear to have a major impact during the first years of life. The nuclear family triad—mother, father, infant—constitutes the primary context within which infants grow and develop. Family constitution, social class, and cultural variation affect patterns of childrearing and exert salient influences on the ways in which infants are reared and what is expected of them as they grow. Infants also form relationships with siblings and grandparents as well as other nonfamilial caregivers. Large numbers of infants have significant experiences outside the family—often through enrollment in alternative care settings—and the effects of out-of-home care vary depending on its type and quality, as well as on characteristics of infants and their families. These early relationships with mothers, fathers, siblings, and others all ensure that the parenting that the young infant experiences is rich and multifaceted.

Biology, personality, beliefs and intuitions, aspects of economic, social, and cultural circumstances, and quality of intimate relationships all play important roles in determining the nature of infant parenting. Of course, infants bring individual social styles and an active mental life to everyday interactions with adults that shape their caregiving experiences too. Infants alter the environment as they interact with it, and they interpret the environment in their own ways. The transactional view asserts that parent and infant convey distinctive characteristics to every interaction, and both are changed as a result. In other words, parent and infant actively co-construct one another through time.

Infancy is a distinctive period, a major transition, and a formative phase in human development. Infants assume few responsibilities and are not at all self-reliant. Rather, parents have central roles to play in infants' survival, social growth, emotional maturity, and cognitive maturation. With the birth of a baby, a parent's life is forever changed. The pattern that those changes assume, in turn, shapes the experiences of infants and, with time, the people they become. Parent and infant chart that course together. Infancy is a starting point of life for both infant and parent.

ACKNOWLEDGMENTS

I thank H. Bornstein, J. Genevro, J. Suwalsky, and B. Wright for comments and assistance.

REFERENCES

Abernathy, V. (1973). Social network and response to the maternal role. *International Journal of Sociology of the Family, 3*, 86–96.

Abramovitch, R., Corter, C., & Lando, B. (1979). Sibling interaction in the home. *Child Development, 50*, 997–1003.

Adamson, L. B., & Bakeman, R. (1984). Mothers' communicative acts: Changes during infancy. *Infant Behavior and Development, 7*, 467–478.

Ainsworth, M. (1967). *Infancy in Uganda*. Baltimore, MD: Johns Hopkins University Press.

Ainsworth, M. D. S., Blehar, M. D., Waters, E., & Wall, S. (1978). *Patterns of attachment: A psychological study of the strange situation*. Hillsdale, NJ: Lawrence Erlbaum Associates.

Alley, T. R. (1981). Head shape and the perception of cuteness. *Developmental Psychology, 17*, 650–654.

Alley, T. R. (1983). Infantile head shape as an elicitor of adult protection. *Merrill-Palmer Quarterly, 29*, 411–427.

Anisfeld, M. (1991). Neonatal imitation. *Developmental Review, 11*, 60–97.

Azuma, H. (1986). Why study child development in Japan? In H. Stevenson, H. Azuma, & K. Hakuta (Eds.), *Child development and education in Japan* (pp. 3–12). New York: Freeman.

Bates, E., Bretherton, I., & Snyder, L. (1988). *From first words to grammar*. New York: Cambridge University Press.

Bates, J. E. (1987). Temperament in infancy. In J. D. Osofsky (Ed.), *Handbook of infant development* (pp. 1101–1149). New York: Wiley.

Bates, J. E., Maslin, C. A., & Frankel, K. A. (1985). Attachment security, mother–child interaction, and temperament as predictors of behavior problem ratings at age three years. In I. Bretherton & E. Waters (Eds.), Growing points of attachment theory and research. *Monographs of the Society for Research in Child Development, 50* (Serial No. 209).

Beales, R. W. (1985). The child in seventeenth-century America. In J. M. Hawes & N. R. Hiner (Eds.), *American childhood* (pp. 3–56). Westport, CT: Greenwood Press.

Bee, H. L., Barnard, K. E., Eyres, S. J., Gray, C. A., Hammand, M. A., Spietz, A. L., Snyder, C., & Clark, B. (1982). Prediction of IQ and language skill from perinatal status, child performance, family characteristics, and mother–infant interaction. *Child Development, 53*, 1134–1156.

Befu, H. (1986). Social and cultural background for child development in Japan and the United States. In H. W. Stevenson, H. Azuma, & K. Hakuta (Eds.), *Child development and education in Japan* (pp. 13–27). San Francisco: Freeman.

Bell, R. Q., & Harper, L. (1977). *Child effects on adults*. Hillsdale, NJ: Lawrence Erlbaum Associates.

Bellinger, D. (1980). Consistency in the pattern of change in mother's speech: Some discriminant analyses. *Journal of Child Language, 7*, 469–487.

Belsky, J. (1984). The determinants of parenting: A process model. *Child Development, 55*, 83–96.

Belsky, J., Gilstrap, B., & Rovine, M. (1984). The Pennsylvania Infant and Family Development Project I: Stability and change in mother–infant and father–infant interaction in a family setting—1- to 3- to 9-months. *Child Development, 55*, 692–705.

Belsky, J., Lang, M. E., & Rovine, M. (1985). Stability and change in marriage across the transition to parenthood: A second study. *Journal of Marriage and the Family, 47*, 855–865.

Belsky, J. Rovine, M., & Fish, M. (1991). The developing family system. In M. Gunnar (Ed.), *Minnesota symposia on child psychology: Vol. 22. Systems and development* (pp. 119–166). Hillsdale, NJ: Lawrence Erlbaum Associates.

Belsky, J., Taylor, D., & Rovine, M. (1984). The Pennsylvania Infant and Family Development Project, II: The development of reciprocal interaction in the mother–infant dyad. *Child Development, 55*, 706–717.

Benedict, R. (1938). Continuities and discontinuities in cultural conditioning. *Psychiatry, 1*, 161–167.

Bernstein, V., Jeremy, R. J., Hans, S., & Marcus, J. (1984). A longitudinal study of offspring born to methadone-maintained women: II. Dyadic interaction and infant behavior at four months. *American Journal of Drug and Alcohol Abuse, 10*, 161–193.

Bertenthal, B. I., & Campos, J.J. (1990). A systems approach to the organizing effects of self-produced locomotion during infancy. In C. Rovee-Collier (Ed.), *Advances in infancy research* (Vol. 6, pp. 1–60). Norwood, NJ: Ablex.

Bever, T. G. (1982). *Regressions in mental development*. Hillsdale, NJ: Lawrence Erlbaum Associates.

Bornstein, M. H. (1985). How infant and mother jointly contribute to developing cognitive competence in the child. *Proceedings of the National Academy of Sciences (U.S.A.), 82*, 7470–7473.

Bornstein, M. H. (1989a). Between caretakers and their young: Two modes of interaction and their consequences for cognitive growth. In M. H. Bornstein & J. S. Bruner (Eds.), *Interaction in human development* (pp. 197–214). Hillsdale, NJ: Lawrence Erlbaum Associates.

Bornstein, M. H. (1989b). Cross-cultural developmental comparisons: The case of Japanese-American infant and mother activities and interactions. What we know, what we need to know, and why we need to know. *Developmental Review, 9*, 171–204.

Bornstein, M. H. (1989c). Sensitive periods in development: Structural characteristics and causal interpretations. *Psychological Bulletin, 105*, 179–204.

Bornstein, M. H. (1989d). Stability in early mental development: From attention and information processing in infancy to language and cognition in childhood. In M. H. Bornstein & N. A. Krasnegor (Eds.), *Stability and continuity in mental development: Behavioral and biological perspectives* (pp. 147–170). Hillsdale, NJ: Lawrence Erlbaum Associates.

Bornstein, M. H. (Ed.). (1989e). *Maternal responsiveness: Characteristics and consequences*. San Francisco: Jossey-Bass.

Bornstein, M. H. (1991). Approaches to parenting in culture. In M. H. Bornstein (Ed.), *Cultural approaches to parenting* (pp. 3–19). Hillsdale, NJ: Lawrence Erlbaum Associates.

Bornstein, M. H. (1992). Perception across the life cycle. In M. H. Bornstein & M. E. Lamb (Eds.), *Developmental psychology: An advanced textbook* (3rd ed., pp. 155–209). Hillsdale, NJ: Lawrence Erlbaum Associates.

Bornstein, M. H. (in preparation). *Infancy as a stage of life*. Unpublished manuscript, National Institute of Child Health and Human Development, Bethesda, MD.

Bornstein, M. H., Azuma, H., Tamis-LeMonda, C. S., & Ogino, M. (1990). Mother and infant activity and interaction in Japan and in the United States: I. A comparative macroanalysis of naturalistic exchanges. *International Journal of Behavioral Development, 13*, 267–287.

Bornstein, M. H., Gaughran, J. M., & Seguí, I. (1991). Multimethod assessment of infant temperament: Mother questionnaire and mother and observer reports evaluated and compared at 5 months using the Infant Temperament Measure. *International Journal of Behavioral Development, 14*, 131–151.

Bornstein, M. H., Haynes, O. M., O'Reilly, A. W., & Painter, K. (1994). *Solitary and collaborative pretense play in early childhood: Sources of individual variation in the development of representational competence.* Unpublished manuscript, National Institute of Child Health and Human Development, Bethesda, MD.

Bornstein, M. H., Haynes, O.M.H., Suwalsky, J.T.D., & Galperin, C. (1994, April). *Family socioeconomic status and mother–infant relations: The United States and Argentina.* Paper presented to the International Conference on Infant Studies, Paris, France.

Bornstein, M. H., & Lamb, M. E. (1992). *Development in infancy: An introduction* (3rd ed.). New York: McGraw-Hill.

Bornstein, M. H., Maital, S., & Tal, J. (1994). *The (further) division of labor in parenting.* Unpublished manuscript, National Institute of Child Health and Human Development, Bethesda, MD.

Bornstein, M. H., & O'Reilly, A. W. (Eds.). (1993). *The role of play in the development of thought.* San Francisco: Jossey-Bass.

Bornstein, M. H., & Ruddy, M. (1984). Infant attention maternal stimulation: Prediction of cognitive linguistic development in singletons and twins. In H. Bouma & D. Bouwhuis (Eds.), *Attention and performance* (Vol. X, pp. 433–445). London: Lawrence Erlbaum Associates.

Bornstein, M. H., Tal, J., Rahn, C., Galperín, C. Z., Pêcheux, M.-G., Lamour, M., Azuma, H., Toda, S., Ogino, M., & Tamis-LeMonda, C. S. (1992). Functional analysis of the contents of maternal speech to infants of 5 and 13 months in four cultures: Argentina, France, Japan, and the United States. *Developmental Psychology, 28*, 593–603.

Bornstein, M. H., Tal, J., & Tamis-LeMonda, C. S. (1991). Parenting in cross-cultural perspective: The United States, France, and Japan. In M. H. Bornstein (Ed.), *Cultural approaches to parenting* (pp. 69–90). Hillsdale, NJ: Lawrence Erlbaum Associates.

Bornstein, M. H., & Tamis-LeMonda, C. S. (1989). Maternal responsiveness and cognitive development in children. In M. H. Bornstein (Ed.), *Maternal responsiveness: Characteristics and consequences* (pp. 49–61). San Francisco: Jossey-Bass.

Bornstein, M. H., & Tamis-LeMonda, C. S. (1990). Activities and interactions of mothers and their firstborn infants in the first six months of life: Covariation, stability, continuity, correspondence, and prediction. *Child Development, 61*, 1206–1217.

Bornstein, M. H., Tamis-LeMonda, C. S., Pascual, L., Haynes, O. M., Painter, K., Galperín, C., & Pêcheux, M.-G. (in press). Ideas about parenting in Argentina, France, and the United States. *International Journal of Behavioral Development.*

Bornstein, M. H., Tamis-LeMonda, C. S., Pêcheux, M.G., & Rahn, C. W. (1991). Mother and infant activity and interaction in France and in the United States: A comparative study. *International Journal of Behavioral Development, 14*, 21–43.

Bornstein, M. H., Tamis-LeMonda, C. S., Tal, J., Ludemann, P., Toda, S., Rahn, C. W., Pêcheux, M.-G., Azuma, H., & Vardi, D. (1992). Maternal responsiveness to infants in three societies: The United States, France, and Japan. *Child Development, 63*, 808–821.

Bornstein, M. H., Toda, S., Azuma, H., Tamis-LeMonda, C. S., & Ogino, M. (1990). Mother and infant activity and interaction in Japan and in the United States: II. A comparative microanalysis of naturalistic exchanges focused on the organization of infant attention. *International Journal of Behavioral Development, 13*, 289–308.

Bouchard, T. J., Lykken, D. T., McGue, M., Segal, N. L., & Tellegen, A. (1990). Sources of human psychological differences: The Minnesota study of twins reared apart. *Science, 250*, 223–228.

Bowlby, J. (1951). *Maternal care and mental health.* Geneva: World Health Organization.

Bowlby, J. (1969). *Attachment and loss.* New York: Basic Books.

Boysson-Bardies, B. de, Sagart, L., & Durand, C. (1984). Discernible differences in the babbling of infants according to target language. *Journal of Child Language, 11*, 1–15.

Bradley, R. H., Caldwell, B. M., & Rock, S. L. (1988). Home environment and school performance: A ten-year follow-up and examination of three models of environmental action. *Child Development, 59*, 852–867.

Brazelton, T. B. (1969). *Infants and mothers: Differences in development.* New York: Dell.

Brazelton, T. B. (1973). *Neonatal behavioral assessment scale.* (Clinics in Developmental Medicine, No. 50). Philadelphia: Lippincott.

Burns, K., Chethik, L., Burns, W. J., & Clark, R. (1991). Dyadic disturbances in cocaine-abusing mothers and their infants. *Journal of Clinical Psychology, 47*, 316–319.

Campos, J. J., & Stenberg, C. R. (1981). Perception, appraisal and emotion: The onset of social referencing. In M. E. Lamb & L. R. Sherrod (Eds.), *Infant social cognition: Empirical and theoretical considerations* (pp. 273–314). Hillsdale, NJ: Lawrence Erlbaum Associates.

Carew, J. V. (1980). Experience and the development of intelligence in young children at home and in day care. *Monographs of the Society for Research in Child Development, 45* (Serial No. 187).

Carnegie Corporation of New York (1994). *Starting points: Meeting the needs of our youngest children.* New York: Author.

Caron, A. J., Caron, R. F., & MacLean, D. J. (1988). Infant discrimination of naturalistic emotional expressions: The role of face and voice. *Child Development, 59,* 604–616.

Caudill, W. (1973). The influence of social structure and culture on human behavior in modern Japan. *Journal of Nervous and Mental Disease, 157,* 240–257.

Center for the Study of Social Policy. (1993). *Kids count data book: State profiles of child well-being.* Washington, DC: Annie E. Casey Foundation.

Chalmers, I, Enkin, M., & Keirse, M. J.N.C. (Eds.). (1989). *Effective care in pregnancy and childbirth.* New York: Oxford University Press.

Chapman, R. S. (1981). Cognitive development and language comprehension in 10- to 21-month-olds. In R. E. Stark (Ed.), *Language behavior in infancy and early childhood* (pp. 359–394). New York: Elsevier/North Holland.

Church, J. (Ed.). (1966). *Three babies: Biographies of cognitive development.* New York: Vintage Books.

Churcher, J., & Scaife, M. (1982). How infants see the point. In G. Butterworth & P. Light (Eds.), *Social cognition* (pp. 110–136). Brighton, Sussex: Harvester.

Clarke-Stewart, K. A. (1980) The father's contribution to children's cognitive and social development in early childhood. In F. A. Pedersen (Ed.), *The father–infant relationship: Observational studies in the family setting* (pp. 111–146). New York: Praeger.

Cole, M. (1992). Culture in development. In M. H. Bornstein & M. E. Lamb (Eds.), *Developmental psychology: An advanced textbook* (3rd ed., pp. 731–789). Hillsdale, NJ: Lawrence Erlbaum Associates.

Collins, W. A., & Russell, G. (1991). Mother–child and father–child relationships in middle childhood and adolescence: A developmental analysis. *Developmental Review, 11,* 1–38.

Condry, J., & Condry, S. (1976). Sex differences: A study of the eye of the beholder. *Child Development, 47,* 812–819.

Cowan, C. P. & Cowan, P. A. (1992). *When partners become parents.* New York: Basic Books.

Cowan, C. P., Cowan, P. A., Heming, G., Garrett, E., Coysh, W. S., Curtis-Boles, H., & Boles, A. J. (1985). Transitions to parenthood: His, hers, and theirs. *Journal of Family Issues, 6,* 451–481.

Crnic, K. A., & Booth, C. L. (1991). Mothers' and fathers' perceptions of daily hassles of parenting across early childhood. *Journal of Marriage and the Family, 53,* 1042–1050.

Crnic, K. A., Greenberg, M. T., Ragozin, A. S., Robinson, N. M., & Basham, R. B. (1983). Effects of stress and social support on mothers and premature and fullterm infants. *Child Development, 54,* 209–217.

Cummings, M. E., Zahn-Waxler, C., & Radke-Yarrow, M. (1981). Young children's responses to expressions of anger and affection by others in the family. *Child Development, 52,* 1274–1282.

Darling, N., & Steinberg, L. (1993). Parenting style as context: An integrative model. *Psychological Bulletin, 113,* 487–496.

Darwin, C. R. (1859). *Origin of species.* London: John Murray.

Darwin, C. (1877). Biographical sketch of an infant. *Mind, 2,* 285–294.

DeCasper, A. J., & Spence, M. J. (1986). Prenatal maternal speech influences newborns' perception of speech sounds. *Infant Behavior and Development, 9,* 133–150.

deMause, L. (1975). The evolution of childhood. In L. deMause (Ed.), *The history of childhood* (pp. 1–73). New York: Harper.

Dennis, W., & Dennis, M. G. (1940). The effect of cradling practices upon the onset of walking in Hopi children. *Journal of Genetic Psychology, 56,* 77–86.

Deutsch, F. M., Ruble, D. N., Fleming, A., Brooks-Gunn, J., & Stangor, C. (1988). Information-seeking and self-definition during the transition to motherhood. *Journal of Personality and Social Psychology, 55,* 420–431.

DeVries, M. W., & Sameroff, A. J. (1984). Culture and temperament: Influences on infant temperament in three East African societies. *American Journal of Orthopsychiatry, 54,* 83–96.

Dickstein, S., & Parke, R. D. (1988). Social referencing in infancy: A glance at fathers and marriage. *Child Development, 59,* 506–511.

Dix, T. (1991). The affective organization of parenting: Adaptive and maladaptive processes. *Psychological Bulletin, 110,* 3–25.

Dixon, R. A., & Lerner, R. M. (1992). A history of systems in developmental psychology. In M. H. Bornstein & M. E. Lamb (Eds.), *Developmental psychology: An advanced textbook* (3rd ed., pp. 3–58). Hillsdale, NJ: Lawrence Erlbaum Associates.

Doi, T. (1973). *The anatomy of dependence* (J. Bester, Trans.). Tokyo: Kodansha International.

Dollard, J., & Miller, N. (1950). *Personality and psychotherapy.* New York: McGraw-Hill.

Dunn, J. B. (1977). Patterns of early interaction: Continuities and consequences. In H. R. Schaffer (Ed.), *Studies in mother–infant interaction* (pp. 438–456). London: Academic Press.

Dunn, J., & Kendrick, C. (1982). *Siblings: Love, envy, and understanding.* Cambridge, MA: Harvard University Press.

Dunn, J., & Plomin, R. (1991). *Separate lives: Why siblings are so different.* New York: Basic Books.

Dunn, J. F., Plomin, R., & Daniels, D. (1986). Consistency and change in mothers' behavior toward young siblings. *Child Development, 57,* 348–356.

Dunn, J. F., Plomin, R., & Nettles, M. (1985). Consistency of mother's behaviour toward infant siblings. *Developmental Psychology, 21,* 1188–1195.

Dye, N. S., & Smith, D. B. (1986). Mother love and infant death, 1750–1920. *Journal of American History, 73,* 329–353.

Eggebeen, D. J. (1992). Family structure and intergenerational exchanges. *Research on Aging, 14,* 427–447.

Eggebeen, D. J., & Hogan, D. P. (1990). Giving between generations in American families. *Human Nature, 1*, 211–232.

Eisenberg, L. (1990). The biosocial context of parenting in human families. In N. A. Krasnegor & R. S. Bridges (Eds.), *Mammalian parenting: Biochemical, neurobiological, and behavioral determinants* (pp. 9–24). New York: Oxford University Press.

Erikson, E. (1950). *Childhood and society*. New York: Norton.

Erting, C. J., Prezioso, C., & Hynes, M. O. (1990). The interactional context of deaf mother–infant communication. In V. Volterra & C. Erting (Eds.), *From gesture to language in hearing and deaf children* (pp. 97–106). Berlin: Springer-Verlag.

Farver, J. M. (1993). Cultural differences in scaffolding pretend play: A comparison of American and Mexican mother–child and sibling–child pairs. In K. MacDonald (Ed.), *Parent–child play: Descriptions and implications* (pp. 349–366). Albany, NY: State University of New York Press.

Feinman, S. (1982). Social referencing in infancy. *Merrill-Palmer Quarterly, 28*, 445–470.

Feinman, S., & Lewis, M. (1983). Social referencing and second order effects in ten-month-old infants. *Child Development, 54*, 878–887.

Feiring, C. (1976, March). *The preliminary development of a social systems model of early infant–mother attachment*. Paper presented to the Eastern Psychological Association, New York.

Fernald, A. (1989). Intonation and communicative intent in mothers' speech to infants: Is the melody the message? *Child Development, 60*, 1497–1510.

Field, T. M. (1984). Early interactions between infants and their postpartum depressed mothers. *Infant Behavior and Development, 7*, 517–522.

Field, T. M., & Pawlby, S. (1980). Early face-to-face interactions of British and American working- and middle-class mother–infant dyads. *Child Development, 51*, 250–253.

Fish, M., & Stifter, C. A. (1993). Mother parity as a main and moderating influence on early mother–infant interaction. *Journal of Applied Developmental Psychology, 14*, 557–572.

Fleming, A. S., Ruble, D. N., Flett, G. L., & Van Wagner, V. (1990). Postpartum adjustment in first-time mothers: Changes in mood and mood content during the early postpartum months. *Developmental Psychology, 26*, 137–143.

Fogel, A. (1984). *Infancy: Infant, family, and society*. St. Paul, MN: West Publishing.

Fogel, A., & Thelen, E. (1987). Development of early expressive and communicative action: Reinterpreting the evidence from a dynamic systems perspective. *Developmental Psychology, 23*, 747–761.

Freud, S. (1949). *An outline of psycho-analysis*. New York: Norton.

Furstenberg, F. F., Jr., Brooks-Gunn, J., Chase-Lansdale, L. (1989). Teenaged pregnancy and child bearing. *American Psychologist, 44*, 313–320.

Goldberg, S. (1977). Infant development and mother–infant interaction in urban Zambia. In P. H. Leiderman, S. R. Tulkin, & A. Rosenfeld (Eds.), *Culture and infancy: Variations in the human experience* (pp. 211–245). New York: Academic Press.

Goodnow, J. (1986). Adult social cognition: Implications of parents' ideas for approaches to development. In M. Perlmutter (Ed.), *Cognitive perspectives on children's social and behavioral development: The Minnesota Symposia on Child Psychology* (Vol. 18, pp. 287–324). Hillsdale, NJ: Lawrence Erlbaum Associates.

Goodnow, J. J., Cashmore, J., Cotton, S., & Knight, R. (1984). Mothers' developmental timetables in two cultural groups. *International Journal of Psychology, 19*, 193–205.

Goodnow, J. J., & Collins, W. A. (1990). *Development according to parents: The nature, sources, and consequences of parents' ideas*. Hillsdale, NJ: Lawrence Erlbaum Associates.

Gottfried, A. W. (Ed.). (1984). *Home environment and early cognitive development*. Orlando, FL: Academic Press.

Green, J. A., Gustafson, G. E., & West, M. J. (1980). Effects of infant development on mother–infant interactions. *Child Development, 51*, 199–207.

Greenbaum, C. W., & Landau, R. (1982). The infants exposure to talk by familiar people: Mothers, fathers and siblings in different environments. In M. Lewis & L. Rosenblum (Eds.), *The social network of the developing infant* (pp. 229–247). New York: Plenum.

Greenspan, S., & Greenspan, N. T. (1985). *First feelings*. New York: Viking.

Grossman, F. K., Eichler, L. W., & Winikoff, S. A. (1980). *Pregnancy, birth and parenthood*. San Francisco: Jossey-Bass.

Hagekull, B., Bohlin, G., & Lindhagen, K. (1984). Validity of parental reports. *Infant Behavior and Development, 7*, 77–92.

Hall, G. S. (1891). Notes on the study of infants. *Pedagogical Seminary, 1*, 127–138.

Hardy-Brown, K. (1983). Universals in individual differences: Disentangling two approaches to the study of language acquisition. *Developmental Psychology, 19*, 610–624.

Hardy-Brown, K., & Plomin, R. (1985). Infant communicative development: Evidence from adoptive and biological families for genetic and environmental influences on rate differences. *Developmental Psychology, 21*, 378–385.

Harkness, S., & Super, C. M. (1983). The cultural construction of child development: A framework for the socialization of affect. *Ethos, 11*, 221–231.

Harkness, S., & Super, C. M. (1985). Child–environment interactions in the socialization of affect. In M. Lewis & C. Saarni (Eds.), *The socialization of emotions* (pp. 21–36). New York: Plenum.

Harris, P. L. (1983). Infant cognition. In M. M. Haith & J. J. Campos (Vol. Eds.) & P. H. Mussen (Series Ed.), *Handbook of child psychology: Vol. 2. Infancy and developmental psychobiology* (pp. 689–782). New York: Wiley.

Harwood, R. L. (1992). The influence of culturally derived values on Anglo and Puerto Rican mothers' perceptions of attachment behavior. *Child Development, 63,* 822–839.

Héroard, J. (1868). *Journal de Jean Héroard sur l'enfance et la jeunesse de Louis XIII (1601–1628).* [*Jean Héroard's journal of the childhood and youth of Louis XIII (1601–1628)*]. Paris: Eud. Soulie et Ed. de Barthelemy.

Hess, R. D., Kashiwagi, K., Azuma, H., Price, G. C., & Dickson, W. P. (1980). Maternal expectations for mastery of developmental tasks in Japan and the United States. *International Journal of Psychology, 15,* 259–271.

Hill, C. R., & Stafford, F. P. (1980). Parental care of children: Time diary estimate of quantity, predictability and variety. *Journal of Human Resources, 15,* 219–239.

Hirshberg, L. M., & Svejda, M. (1990). When infants look to their parents: I. Infants' social referencing of mothers compared to fathers. *Child Development, 61,* 1175–1186.

Ho, H. Z. (1987). Interaction of early caregiving environment and infant developmental status in predicting subsequent cognitive performance. *British Journal of Developmental Psychology, 5,* 183–191.

Hodapp, R. M., Goldfield, E. C., & Boyatzis, C. J. (1984). The use and effectiveness of maternal scaffolding in mother–infant games. *Child Development, 55,* 772–781.

Hofferth, S. L., & Hayes, C. D. (Eds.). (1987). *Risking the future: Adolescent sexuality, pregnancy, and childbearing* (Vol. 2). Washington, DC: National Academy of Sciences Press.

Hoff-Ginsberg, E. (1991). Mother–child conversation in different social classes and communicative settings. *Child Development, 62,* 782–796.

Hopkins, B., & Westra, T. (1990). Motor development, maternal expectation, and the role of handling. *Infant Behavior and Development, 13,* 117–122.

Hornik, R., Risenhoover, N., & Gunnar, M. (1987). The effects of maternal positive, neutral, and negative affective communications on infant responses to new toys. *Child Development, 58,* 937–944.

Jackson, S. (1987). Great Britain. In M. E. Lamb (Ed.), *The father's role: Cross-cultural perspectives* (pp. 29–57). Hillsdale, NJ: Lawrence Erlbaum Associates.

Jacobson, J. L., Boersma, D. C., Fields, R. B., & Olson, K. L. (1983). Paralinguistic features of adult speech to infants and small children. *Child Development, 54,* 436–442.

Jaeger, S. (1985). The origin of the diary method in developmental psychology. In G. Eckhardt, W. G. Bringmann, & L. Sprung (Eds.), *Contributions to a history of developmental psychology* (pp. 63–74). Berlin: Mouton.

Jakobson, R. (1969). *Child language, aphasia and phonological universals.* New York: Humanities Press. (Original work published 1941)

Jakobson, R. (1971). Why "Mama" and "Papa"? In A. Bar-Adon & W. F. Leopold (Eds.), *Child language* (pp. 212–217). Englewood Cliffs, NJ: Prentice-Hall.

Johnson, W., Emde, R. N., Pennbrook, B., Stenberg, C., & Davis, M. (1982). Maternal perception of infant emotion from birth through 18 months. *Infant Behavior and Development, 5,* 313–322.

Kagan, J. (1971). *Change and continuity in infancy.* New York: Wiley.

Kagan, J. (1984). *The nature of the child.* New York: Basic Books.

Kaye, K. (1982). *The mental and social life of babies.* Chicago: University of Chicago Press.

Kent, R. D. (1984). The psychobiology of speech development: Co-emergence of language and a movement system. *American Journal of Physiology, 246,* R888–R894.

Klein, P. S. (1988). Stability and change in interaction of Israeli mothers and infants. *Infant Behavior and Development, 11,* 55–70.

Klinnert, M., Campos, J. J., Sorce, J., Emde, R. N., & Svejda, M. (1983). Emotions as behavior regulators: Social referencing in infancy. In R. Plutchik & H. Kellerman (Eds.), *Emotions in early development* (Vol. 2, pp. 57–86). New York: Academic Press.

Klinnert, M., Sorce, J., Emde, R. N., Stenberg, C., & Gaensbauer, T. (1984). Continuities and change in early affective life: Maternal perceptions of surprise, fear, and anger. In R. N. Emde & R. J. Harmon (Eds.), *Continuities and discontinuities in development* (pp. 339–354). New York: Plenum.

Kojima, H. (1986). Japanese concepts of child development from the mid-17th to mid-19th century. *International Journal of Behavioral Development, 9,* 315–329.

Kotelchuck, M. (1976). The infants' relationship to the father: Experimental evidence. In M. E. Lamb (Ed.), *The role of the father in child development* (pp. 329–344). New York: Wiley.

Kuchuk, A., Vibbert, M., & Bornstein, M. H. (1986). The perception of smiling and its experiential correlates in 3-month-old infants. *Child Development, 57,* 1054–1061.

Kuhn, D. (1992). Cognitive development. In M. H. Bornstein & M. E. Lamb (Eds.), *Developmental psychology: An advanced textbook* (3rd ed., pp. 211–272). Hillsdale, NJ: Lawrence Erlbaum Associates.

Lamb, M. E. (1978). The development of sibling relationships in infancy: A short-term longitudinal study. *Child Development, 49,* 1189–1196.

Lamb, M. E., & Easterbrooks, M. A. (1981). Individual differences in parental sensitivity: Origins, components, and consequences. In M. E. Lamb & L. R. Sherrod (Eds.), *Infant social cognition: Empirical and theoretical considerations* (pp. 127–153). Hillsdale, NJ: Lawrence Erlbaum Associates.

Lamb, M. E., Frodi, A. M., Frodi, M., & Hwang, C.-P., (1982). Characteristics of maternal and paternal behavior in traditional and nontraditional Swedish families. *International Journal of Behavioral Development, 5*, 131–141.

Lamb, M. E, Ketterlinus, R, & Fracasso, M. (1992). Parent–child relations. In M. H. Bornstein & M. E. Lamb (Eds.), *Developmental psychology: An advanced textbook* (3rd ed., pp. 465–518). Hillsdale, NJ: Lawrence Erlbaum Associates.

Leach, P. (1983). *Babyhood*. New York: Alfred A. Knopf.

Leach, P. (1989). *Your baby & child*. New York: Alfred A. Knopf.

Leiderman, P. H., Tulkin, S. R., & Rosenfeld, A. (Eds.). (1977). *Culture and infancy: Variations in the human experience*. New York: Academic Press.

Lerner, R. M. (1989). Developmental contextualism and the life span view of person-context interaction. In M. H. Bornstein & J. S. Bruner (Eds.), *Interaction in human development* (pp. 217–239). Hillsdale, NJ: Lawrence Erlbaum Associates.

Lerner, R. M., & Busch-Rossnagel, N. A. (1981). *Individuals as producers of their development: A lifespan perspective*. New York: Academic Press.

LeVine, R. A. (1988). Human parental care: Universal goals, cultural strategies, individual behavior. In R. A. LeVine, P. M. Miller, & M. M. West (Eds.), *Parental behavior in diverse societies* (pp. 3–12). San Francisco: Jossey-Bass.

LeVine, R. A., & Miller, P. M. (Eds.). (1990). Cross-cultural validity of attachment theory [Special issue]. *Human Development, 33*, 2–80.

LeVine, R. A., & White, M. I. (1986). *Human conditions: The cultural basis of educational development*. London: Routledge & Kegan Paul.

Lightfoot, C., & Valsiner, J. (1992). Parental belief systems under the influence: Social guidance of the construction of personal cultures. In I. E. Sigel, A. V. McGillicuddy-De Lisi, & J. J. Goodnow (Eds.), *Parental belief systems: The psychological consequences for children* (2nd ed., pp. 393–414). Hillsdale, NJ: Lawrence Erlbaum Associates.

Lorenz, K. (1935). Der Kumpan in der Umwelt des Vogels. *Journal für Ornithologie, 83,* 137–213, 289–413.

Lorenz, K. (1943). Die angeborenen formen moglicher arfahrund. *Zeitschrift für Tierpsychologie, 5*, 233–409.

Lounsbury, M. L., & Bates, J. E. (1982). The cries of infants and different levels of perceived temperamental difficultness: Acoustic properties and effects on listeners. *Child Development, 53*, 677–686.

Lyons-Ruth, K., Zoll, D., Conell, D., & Grunebaum, H. U. (1986). The depressed mother and her one-year-old infant: Environment, interaction, attachment and infant development. In E. Tronick & T. Field (Eds.) *Maternal depression and infant disturbance* (pp. 61–83). New York: Jossey-Bass.

Lytton, H., & Romney, D. M. (1991). Parents' differential socialization of boys and girls: A meta-analysis. *Psychological Bulletin, 109*, 267–296.

Maccoby, E. E., & Jacklin, C. N. (1974). *The psychology of sex differences*. Stanford, CA: Stanford University Press.

Maccoby, E. E., & Martin, J. A. (1983). Socialization in the context of the family: Parent–child interaction. In E. M. Hetherington (Vol. Ed.) & P. H. Mussen (Series Ed.), *Handbook of child psychology: Vol. 4. Socialization, personality, and social development* (pp. 1–101). New York: Wiley.

Mahler, M., Pine, A., & Bergman, F. (1975). *The psychological birth of the human infant*. New York: Basic.

Martin, J. A. (1989). Personal and interpersonal components of responsiveness. In M. H. Bornstein (Ed.), *Maternal responsiveness: Characteristics and consequences* (pp. 5–14). San Francisco: Jossey-Bass.

Mayes, L. C., & Bornstein, M. H. (in press). Infant information-processing performance and maternal education. *Early Development and Parenting*.

McCall, R. B. (1977). Childhood IQ's as predictors of adult educational and occupational status. *Science, 197*, 482–483.

McCall, R. B. (1981). Nature-nurture and the two realms of development: A proposed integration with respect to mental development. *Child Development, 52*, 1–12.

McLaughlin, B., White, D., McDevitt, T., & Raskin, R. (1983). Mothers' and fathers' speech to their young children: Similar of different? *Journal of Child Language, 10*, 245–252.

Mead, M., & MacGregor, F. C. (1951). *Growth and culture*. New York: Putnam's Sons.

Mendelson, M. J. (1990). *Becoming a brother: A child learns about life, family, and self*. Cambridge, MA: MIT Press.

Minnett, A. M., Vandell, D. L., & Santrock, J. W. (1983). The effects of sibling status on sibling interaction: Influence of birth order, age spacing, sex of child, and sex of sibling. *Child Development, 54*, 1064–1072.

Montemayor, R. (1982). The relationship between parent–adolescent conflict and the amount of time adolescents spend alone with parents and peers. *Child Development, 53*, 1512–1519.

Morelli, G. A., & Tronick, E. Z. (1991). Parenting and child development in the Efe foragers and Lese farmers of Zaire. In M. H. Bornstein (Ed.), *Cultural approaches to parenting* (pp. 91–113). Hillsdale, NJ: Lawrence Erlbaum Associates.

Murdock, G. P. (1959). Cross-language parallels in parental kin terms. *Anthropological Linguistics, 1*, 1–5.

Murphey, D. A. (1992). Constructing the child: Relations between parents' beliefs and child outcomes. *Developmental Review, 12*, 199–232.

Murray, L., & Trevarthen, C. (1985). Emotional regulation of interactions between two-month-olds and their mothers. In T. M. Field & N. A. Fox (Eds.), *Social perception in infants* (pp. 177–197). Norwood, NJ: Ablex.

National Center for Health Statistics. (1994). *Births, marriages, divorces, and deaths for 1993* (Monthly Vital Statistics Rep. Vol. 42, No. 12). Hyattsville, MD: Public Health Service.

Nelson, C. A. (1987). The recognition of facial expressions in the first two years of life: Mechanisms of development. *Child Development, 58,* 889–909.

Ninio, A. (1980). Picture-book reading in mother–infant dyads belonging to two subgroups in Israel. *Child Development, 51,* 587–590.

Ochs, E. (1988). *Culture and language development: Language acquisition and language socialization in a Samoan village.* New York: Cambridge University Press.

Olson, S. L., Bates, J. E., & Bayles, K. (1984). Mother–infant interaction and the development of individual differences in children's cognitive competence. *Developmental Psychology, 20,* 166–179.

Palacios, J. (1990). Parents' ideas about the development and education of their children. Answers to some questions. *International Journal of Behavioral Development, 13,* 137–155.

Papoušek, M., Papoušek, H., & Bornstein, M. H. (1985). The naturalistic vocal environment of young infants: On the significance of homogeneity and variability in parental speech. In T. M. Field & N. Fox (Eds.), *Social perception in infants* (pp. 269–297). Norwood, NJ: Ablex.

Parke, R. D., & Sawin, D. B. (1975, April). *Infant characteristics and behavior as elicitors of maternal and paternal responsibility in the newborn period.* Paper presented at the biennial meeting of the Society for Research in Child Development, Denver.

Parke, R. D., & Sawin, D. B. (1980). The family in early infancy: Social interactional and attitudinal analyses. In F. A. Pedersen (Ed.), *The father–infant relationship: Observational studies in the family setting* (pp. 44–70). New York: Praeger.

Parmelee, A. H., & Sigman, M. D. (1983). Perinatal brain development and behavior. In M. M. Haith & J. J. Campos (Vol. Eds.) & P. H. Mussen (Series Ed.), *Handbook of child psychology: Vol. 2. Infancy and developmental psychobiology* (pp. 95–155). New York: Wiley.

Pedersen, F. A. (1975, September). *Mother, father and infant as an interactive system.* Paper presented at the annual convention of the American Psychological Association, Chicago.

Pedersen, F. A., & Robson, K. S. (1969). Father participation in infancy. *American Journal of Orthopsychiatry, 39,* 466–472.

Pepler, D. (1981, April). *Naturalistic observations of teaching and modeling between siblings.* Paper presented at the biennial meeting of the Society for Research in Child Development, Boston.

Pepler, D., Corter, C., & Abramovitch, R. (1982). Social relations among children: Comparison of sibling and peer interaction. In K. H. Rubin & H. S. Ross (Eds.), *Peer relationships and social skills in childhood* (pp. 209–227). New York: Springer-Verlag.

Pettit, G. S., & Bates, J. (1984). Continuity of individual differences in the mother–infant relationship from 6 to 13 months. *Child Development, 55,* 729–739.

Piaget, J. (1952). *The origins of intelligence in children.* New York: Norton.

Phillips, D. (1991). Day care for young children in the United States. In E. C. Melhuish & P. Moss (Eds.), *Day care for young children* (pp. 161–184). London: Routledge.

Plato. (1970). *The laws* (T. J. Saunders, Trans.). Middlesex, England: Penguin.

Plomin, R. (1989). Environment and genes: Determinants of behavior. *American Psychologist, 44,* 105–111.

Plomin, R., & DeFries, J. C. (1985). *The origins of individual differences in infancy: The Colorado Adoption Project.* New York: Academic Press.

Population Reference Bureau. (1993). *1993 World population data sheet.* Washington, DC: Author.

Porter, R. H., Bologh, R. D., & Makin, J. W. (1988). Olfactory influences on mother–infant interactions. In C. Rovee-Collier & L. P. Lipsitt (Eds.), *Advances in infancy research* (Vol. 5, pp. 39–69). Norwood, NJ: Ablex.

Powell, D. R. (1980). Personal social networks as a focus for primary prevention of child maltreatment. *Infant Mental Health Journal, 1,* 232–239.

Power, T. G. (1985). Mother and father–infant play: A developmental analysis. *Child Development, 56,* 1514–1524.

Preyer, W. (1882/1888–1889). *Die seele des kindes.* Leipsig: Grieben. Published in English in 1888–1889 as *The mind of the Child, Parts 1 & 2* (H. W. Brown, Trans.). New York: Appleton. Reprint edition 1973 by Arno Press, New York.

Ratner, N. B., & Pye, C. (1984). Higher pitch in BT is not universal: Acoustic evidence from Quiche Mayan. *Journal of Child Language, 11,* 512–522.

Rohner, R. (1985). *The warmth dimension.* Beverly Hills, CA: Sage.

Rondal, J. A. (1980). Fathers' and mothers' speech in early language development. *Journal of Child Language, 7,* 353–369.

Rousseau, J. J. (1762). *Emile.* New York: Barron's Educational Series.

Rubin, K. H., Fein, G. G., & Vandenberg, B. (1983). Play. In E. M. Hetherington (Vol. Ed.) & P. H. Mussen (Series Ed.), *Handbook of child psychology: Vol. 4. Socialization, personality, and social development* (pp. 693–774). New York: Wiley.

Rubin, K. H., & Mills, R. S. L. (1992). Parents' thoughts about children's socially adaptive and maladaptive behaviors: Stability, change, and individual differences. In I. Sigel, J. Goodnow, & A. McGillicuddy-De Lisi (Eds.), *Parental belief systems* (pp. 41–68). Hillsdale, NJ: Lawrence Erlbaum Associates.

Rubin, J., Provenzano, F., & Luria, Z. (1974). The eye of the beholder: Parents' view of sex of newborns. *American Journal of Orthopsychiatry, 43,* 720–731.

Russell, G. (1983). *The changing role of fathers?* St. Lucia, Queensland: University of Queensland Press.

Russell, G., & Russell, A. (1987). Mother–child and father–child relationships in middle childhood. *Child Development, 58,* 1573–1585.

Sameroff, A. J. (1983). Developmental systems: Contexts and evolution. In W. Kessen (Vol. Ed.) & P. H. Mussen (Series Ed.), *Handbook of child psychology: Vol. 1. History, theory, and methods* (pp. 237–294). New York: Wiley.

Sameroff, A. J., & Feil, L. A. (1985). Parental concepts of development. In I. E. Sigel (Ed.), *Parental belief systems: The psychological consequences for children* (pp. 83–100). Hillsdale, NJ: Lawrence Erlbaum Associates.

Sameroff, A., Seifer, R., & Elias, P. (1982). Sociocultural variability in infant temperament ratings. *Child Development, 53,* 164–173.

Scarr, S., & Kidd, K. K. (1983). Developmental behavior genetics. In M. M. Haith & J. J. Campos (Vol. Eds.) & P. H. Mussen (Series Ed.), *Handbook of child psychology: Vol. 2. Infancy and developmental psychobiology* (pp. 345–433). New York: Wiley.

Scarr, S., & McCartney, K. (1983). How people make their own environments: A theory of genotype-environment effects. *Child Development, 54,* 424–435.

Scheper-Hughes, N. (1989). Death without weeping. *Natural History, 98*(10), 8–16.

Shakin, M., Shakin, D., & Sternglanz, S. H. (1985). Infant clothing: Sex labeling for strangers. *Sex Roles, 12,* 955–963.

Slater, P. G. (1977–1978). From the cradle to the coffin: Parental bereavement and the shadow of infant damnation in Puritan society. *Psychohistory Review, 6,* 4–24.

Snow, C. E. (1977). Mothers' speech research: From input to interactions. In C. E. Snow & C. A. Ferguson (Eds.), *Talking to children: Language input and acquisition* (pp. 31–49). Cambridge: Cambridge University Press.

Sorce, J. F., & Emde, R. N. (1981). Mother's presence is not enough: Effect of emotional availability on infant exploration. *Developmental Psychology, 17,* 737–745.

Spitze, G., & Logan, J. (1992). Helping as a component of parent–adult-child relations. *Research on Aging, 14,* 291–312.

Spock, B., & Rothenberg, M. B. (1992). *Dr. Spock's baby and child care.* New York: Pocket Books.

St. James-Roberts, I., & Wolke, P. (1984, April). *Towards a systems theory of infant temperament.* Paper presented at the fourth biennial International Conference on Infant Studies, New York.

Steiner, J. E. (1979). Human facial expressions in response to taste and smell stimulation. In H. Reese & L. Lipsitt (Eds.), *Advances in child development and behavior* (Vol. 13, pp. 257–295). New York: Academic Press.

Stern, D. (1985). *The interpersonal world of the infant.* New York: Basic Books.

Stern, D. (1990). *Diary of a child.* New York: Basic Books.

Stewart, R. B. (1983). Sibling interaction: The role of the older child as teacher for the younger. *Merrill-Palmer Quarterly, 29,* 47–68.

Stewart, R. B. (1990). *The second child: Family transition and adjustment.* Newbury Park, CA: Sage.

Strauss, S., & Stavey, R. (1981). U-shaped behavioral growth: Implications for theories of development. In W. W. Hartup (Ed.), *Review of child development research* (Vol. 6, pp. 547–599). Chicago: University of Chicago Press.

Super, C. M. (1976). Environmental effects on motor development: The case of "African infant precocity." *Developmental Medicine and Child Neurology, 18,* 561–567.

Super, C. M., & Harkness, S. (1986). Temperament, development, and culture. In R. Plomin & J. Dunn (Eds.), *The study of temperament: Changes, continuities, and challenges* (pp. 131–149). Hillsdale, NJ: Lawrence Erlbaum Associates.

Szalai, A. (Ed.). (1972). *The use of time: Daily activities of urban and suburban populations in twelve countries.* The Hague: Mouton.

Taine, H. A. (1877). Taine on the acquisition of language by children. *Mind, 2,* 252–259.

Tamis-LeMonda, C. S., & Bornstein, M. H. (1989). Habituation and maternal encouragement of attention in infancy as predictors of toddler language, play, and representational competence. *Child Development, 60,* 738–751,

Tamis-LeMonda, C. S., & Bornstein, M. H. (1990). Language, play and attention at one year. *Infant Behavior and Development, 13,* 85–98.

Tamis-LeMonda, C. S., & Bornstein, M. H. (1994). Specificity in mother–toddler language-play relations across the second year. *Developmental Psychology, 30,* 283–292.

Tamis-LeMonda, C. S., Bornstein, M. H., Cyphers, L., Toda, S., & Ogino, M. (1992). Language and play at one year: A comparison of toddlers and mothers in the United States and Japan. *International Journal of Behavioral Development, 15,* 19–42.

Teti, D. M., Bond, L. A., & Gibbs, E. D. (1986). Sibling-created experiences: Relationships to birth-spacing and infant cognitive development. *Infant Behavior and Development, 9,* 27–42.

Thelen, E. (1989). Self-organization in developmental processes: Can systems approaches work? In M. Gunnar & E. Thelen (Eds.), *Systems and development: The Minnesota Symposium on Child Psychology* (Vol. 22, pp. 77–117). Hillsdale, NJ: Lawrence Erlbaum Associates.

Thelen, E. (1990). Dynamical systems and the generation of individual differences. In J. Colombo & J. Fagen (Eds.), *Individual differences in infancy: Reliability, stability, prediction* (pp. 19–44). Hillsdale, NJ: Lawrence Erlbaum Associates.

Thomas, A., Chess, S., Birch, H., Hertzig, M., & Korn, S. (1963). *Behavioral individuality in childhood*. New York: New York University Press.

Tiedemann, D. (1787). Beobachtungen über die Entwicklung der Seelenfähigkeiten bei Kindern. *Hessische Beiträge zur Gelehrsamkeit und Kunst, 2*, 313–315 *3*, 486–488. (Trans. as: Observations on the development of the mental faculties of children. *Pedagogical Seminary*, 1927, *34*, 205–230).

Tinbergen, N. (1951). *The study of instinct*. Oxford: Oxford University Press.

Tinbergen, N. (1963). On aims and methods of ethology. *Zeitschrif für Tierpsychologie, 20*, 410–433.

Trehub, S. E., & Hsing-wu, C. (1977). Speech as reinforcing stimulation for infants. *Developmental Psychology, 13*, 121–124.

Trevarthen, C. (1979). Communication and cooperation in early infancy: A description of primary intersubjectivity. In M. Bullowa (Ed.), *Before speech: The beginning of interpersonal communication* (pp. 321–347). Cambridge: Cambridge University Press.

Trivers, R. (1986). *Social evolution*. Menlo Park, CA: Benjamin Cummings.

Tronick, E. Z., & Gianino, A. F. (1986). The transmission of maternal disturbance to the infant. In E. Z. Tronick & T. Field (Eds.), *Maternal depression and infant disturbance* (pp. 5–11). New York: Wiley.

Tulkin, S. R. (1977). Dimensions of multicultural research in infancy and early childhood. In P. H. Leiderman, S. R. Tulkin, & A. Rosenfeld (Eds.), *Culture and infancy: Variations in the human experience* (pp. 567–586). New York: Academic Press.

UNICEF. (1993). *Facts for life*. New York: Author.

Valsiner, J. (Ed.). (1987). *Cultural context and child development*. Norwood, NJ: Ablex.

Vandell, D.L., & Wilson, K.S. (1987). Infants' interactions with mother, sibling, and peer: Contrasts and relations between interaction systems. *Child Development, 58*, 176–186.

Van IJzendoorn, M. H. (1992). Intergenerational transmission of parenting: A review of studies in nonclinical populations. *Developmental Review, 12*, 76–99.

Vaughn, B., Taraldson, B., Crichton, L., & Egeland, B. (1981). The assessment of infant temperament: A critique of the Carey Infant Temperament Questionnaire. *Infant Behavior and Development, 4*, 1–17.

Vibbert, M., & Bornstein, M. H. (1989). Specific associations between domains of mother–child interaction and toddler referential language and pretense play. *Infant Behavior and Development, 12*, 163–184.

Vygotsky, L. (1978). *Mind in society*. Cambridge, MA: Harvard University Press.

Wachs, T. D., & Chan, A. (1986). Specificity of environmental action, as seen in environmental correlates of infants' communication performance. *Child Development, 57*, 1464–1474.

Waddington, C. H. (1962). *New patterns in genetics and development*. New York: Columbia University Press.

Wahler, R. G., & Dumas, J. E. (1989). Attentional problems in dysfunctional mother–child interactions. *Psychological Bulletin, 105*, 116–130.

Wallace, D. B., Franklin, M. B., & Keegan, R. T. (1994). The observing eye: A century of baby diaries. *Human Development, 37*, 1–29.

Watson, J. B. (1924/1970). *Behaviorism*. New York: Norton.

Weisner, T. (1982). Sibling interdependence and child caretaking: A cross-cultural view. In M. E. Lamb & B. Sutton-Smith (Eds.), *Sibling relationships* (pp. 305–327). Hillsdale, NJ: Lawrence Erlbaum Associates.

Werner, E. E. (1984). *Kith, kin, and hired hands*. Baltimore, MD: University Park Press.

White, B. L., Kaban, B., Shapiro, B., & Attanucci, J. (1977). Competence and experience. In I. C. U giris & F. Weizmann (Eds.), *The structuring of experience* (pp. 115–152). New York: Plenum.

White, M. (1986). *The Japanese educational challenge: A commitment to children*. New York: Free Press.

Whiting, J. M. W. (1981). Environmental constraints on infant care practices. In R. H. Munroe, R. L. Munroe, & B. B. Whiting (Eds.), *Handbook of cross-cultural human development* (pp. 155–179). New York: Garland STPM Press.

Winnicott, D. W. (1957). *Mother and child: A primer of first relations*. New York: Basic Books.

Yogman, M. W. (1982). Development of the father–infant relationship. In H. E. Fitzgerald, B. M. Lester, & M. W. Yogman (Eds.), *Theory and research in behavioral pediatrics* (pp. 221–280). New York: Plenum.

Young, K. T. (1991). What parents and experts think about infants. In F. S. Kessel, M. H. Bornstein, & A. J. Sameroff (Eds.), *Contemporary constructions of the child* (pp. 79–90). Hillsdale, NJ: Lawrence Erlbaum Associates.

Zajonc, R. B. (1983). Validating the confluence model. *Psychological Bulletin, 93*, 457–480.

2

Parenting Toddlers

Carolyn Pope Edwards
University of Kentucky

INTRODUCTION

The age period bridging between infancy and early childhood (the 1½- or 2-year period between about 12 and 36 months of age) is often referred to as *toddlerhood*. Although toddlerhood is unquestionably a time of rapid growth and change, there is no consensus as to whether it is a distinct developmental phase, or stage, of childhood (i.e., a period of development bounded by fundamental reorganizations in cognitive and socioemotional capacities and with a unique pattern of developmental issues, tasks, and achievements). If toddlerhood is not a genuine phase or stage, then it must be a prominent subphase at the cusp of infancy and childhood, and it may be asked whether toddlers are more properly classified with infants or young children with regard to the capabilities and limitations—the delights and puzzlements—they present to caregiving adults.

This uncertainty about whether or not toddlerhood is a distinct stage of childhood can be illuminated by looking at the professional literature. For example, many older developmental and early childhood education texts (especially those less influenced by the psychoanalytic perspective) do not include a major section on the toddler period. For example, child development texts, such as those by Gardner (1978) and Seifert and Hoffnung (1987), simply divide childhood into three periods (infancy; early childhood, or preschool years; and middle childhood, or school years). In contrast, some newer texts and editions follow the lead of Stone and Church (1973) and separate out toddlerhood as a distinct stage of child development (Black, Puckett, & Bell, 1992); others explicitly address toddler developments as the second half of infancy (e.g., Papalia & Olds, 1987; J. A. Schickedanz, D. I. Schickedanz, Hansen, & Forsyth, 1993) or the phase of infancy transitional to childhood (e.g., M. Cole & S. R. Cole, 1989; Mussen, Conger, Kagan, & Huston, 1990). In a parallel way, experts writing for parents of young children have tended increasingly to recognize the uniqueness of toddler concerns by devoting to this age group either an entire book (e.g., Brazelton, 1974; Rubin, Fisher, & Doering, 1980) or a major section of a book (e.g., Leach, 1977). These patterns are mirrored in the field of early childhood education, where there is a burgeoning literature on toddler education and care; most state regulations for licensing child-care programs require higher staff–child ratios for the 15- to 33-month age group than for 3- to 4-year-old children, yet not so high as what is required for children under 15 months.

Thus, recent years have witnessed a sharpening interest and awareness in the special capacities and requirements of toddlers, as research on the second and third years of life has exploded and more young children have come under the supervision of professional educators and caregivers. Clearly there is a consensus of practical opinion and applied professional belief in contemporary America that the tasks of nurturing and guiding children just past the threshold of mobility and language present significantly different challenges from parenting or teaching either younger infants or preschool and kindergarten children.

Indeed, these practical opinions track and correspond rather closely to the portrait of toddlers painted by the American research literature. This chapter reviews several of the classic and emerging theoretical perspectives on development during the toddler years. Then it discusses some of the most important issues addressed by current research on the parenting of children during their second and third years of life. It closes with a brief analysis of how new theories and findings about toddler development have been translated into practical advice for parents. Theorists from many perspectives—psychoanalytic, cognitive-structuralist, information-processing, attachment theory—have made attempts to define the central psychosocial and/or cognitive tasks of the toddler period, and their efforts have been subjected to the theoretical scrutiny of critics versed in childrearing customs in non-Western societies. Empirical researchers, meanwhile, have attempted to operationalize the themes of the toddler period in behavioral terms and establish the underlying processes of developmental change, including the processes of socialization that most affect toddler growth and development. Finally, writers seeking to offer the benefits of new thinking and new knowledge to parents have offered their opinions—often based as much on personal experience and observation as on empirical evidence—to successive generations of anxious mothers and fathers. After briefly reviewing the theoretical perspectives, this chapter surveys the empirical findings concerning toddler development and socialization and then briefly appraises several advice books to parents, which have been most popular as well as esteemed by both professionals and the general public. Thus, three portraits of the parenting of toddlers are put forward for comparison.

THEORETICAL PERSPECTIVES ON TODDLER DEVELOPMENT

It is clear at the outset that much current child development literature features a common vocabulary and presents overlapping images of the defining developmental tasks confronting the toddler. From the parental point of view, of course, the hallmarks of the toddler period are weaning, walking, and talking—in academic language: separation-individuation, motility, and communicative competence. The scientific perspective incorporates this commonsense parental perspective and then goes beyond it by hypothesizing underlying structural changes that are most fundamental to healthy growth and development for the child. Developmental tasks are those major, pressing issues on the mind or agenda of the developing child and that occupy much of the child's emotional and interactional energy. Cultural communities may differ in the order and timing of developmental tasks, and the significance they place on each task for describing the maturity of the child, but the tasks can be predicted to be universal. Although different theorists cast these tasks in slightly different ways, the following tasks, or developmental themes, are most frequently named in the current literature:

1. *autonomy and independence*, or the emergence of capacities to function at one remove (physical and psychological) from the adult and to begin to master simple skills of daily living, such as feeding and dressing, toileting and personal hygiene, sleeping apart from the mother, and playing without adult facilitation;

2. *categorical self-concept and beginning self-reflection*, or the capacity for self-recognition in the mirror, awareness of the self as a source of actions, ideas, words, and feelings, and beginning reflective self-evaluation;

3. *impulse- or self-control*, or the emergence of capacities related to affective and behavioral regulation and compliance with adult expectations, including abilities to wait, resist temptation, defer gratification, and follow rules and directions even when not immediately monitored;

4. *empathy, morality, and standards*, or the emergence of abilities related to becoming prosocial and taking into account others' perspective and needs, learning moral and cultural rules and standards, and feeling anxiety or distress when standards are violated;

5. *gender identity and sex-role identification*, or the emergence of capacities to label and identify the gender of self and others, know some of the appropriate behaviors and attributes of males and females of various ages, understand the stability of gender over the life course, and prefer to imitate and affiliate with others of one's gender;

6. *becoming a member of society*, or establishing one's own place as a member of a larger family or kinship grouping, including functioning in a childhood play group and learning how to engage appropriately in social interaction across a variety of domains, such as teaching and learning, dominance and responsibility, nurturance and dependency, play and sociability.

Psychoanalytic and Neo-Psychoanalytic Theories

The aforementioned six themes have grown out of the classic and emerging theoretical literature on toddler development. Psychoanalytic theorists were perhaps the first to define developmental tasks for the second and third year of life, and strongly shaped our thinking in regard to the developmental tasks of autonomy and impulse-control. The classic psychoanalytic account of the period of childhood just past infancy focuses on issues surrounding control of aggression and bodily functions. Sigmund Freud portrayed young children as assertive and willful beings whose strivings for independence and sexual gratification bring them into inevitable conflict with socializing, restraining adults. In the first edition of *Three Essays on the Theory of Sexuality,* Freud (1901–1905; collected, 1953) defined latency as all of childhood up to puberty and claimed there were but two interruptions of latency prior to puberty: infantile orality and preschool genitality (see Mueller & Cohen, 1986). In later writings, however, Freud (1920, 1949) argued that the sexual impulse increases progressively all through the early years, expressed in three overlapping waves: the *oral* phase of the first year; the *sadistic-anal* phase peaking in Year 2 or 3, where satisfaction is sought in aggression and in excretion; and the *phallic* phase of Years 4 and 5. Freud (1920) discussed how during the sadistic-anal phase the outer world is first seen by children as a hostile force opposed to their pursuit of pleasure. Battles over when and how to express aggression and to pass their excretions are children's first hint of external and internal conflict (Freud, 1920, p. 324). Thus, an important legacy of Freud's theory is the centrality of issues of conflict to our understanding of toddler experience.

Several other psychoanalysts since Freud considered infant development and elaborated his ideas regarding developments during the second and third year of life, always making conflict a central point of interest. Erikson (1950), for example, accepted Freud's proposal that transformations in aggressive and sexual drives form the core of the emerging personality, but he reconceived the psychosexual stages as *psychosocial* and saw the oral, anal, and genital zones as modalities for encounters between children and parents—encounters strongly shaped by the cultural environment. Erikson, who was influenced by anthropological research, described how in many traditional rural cultural communities parents are casual about elimination and leave it to older children to gradually lead children out to the bush, whereas in Western middle-class societies, pressures for clean, orderly, and punctual behavior sometimes lead to early and harsh emphasis on toilet training. Erikson highlighted the conflict issue by claiming that the necessary alternation of first retaining, then expelling, the products of the bowels gives the anal modality its special potential for creating both internal and external tension. In laying out *eight psychosocial stages of man*, he elaborated on this duality through the metaphor of *autonomy versus shame and doubt* as representing the pivotal issue of the second and third year. Parents, Erikson argued, support their children through this crisis by letting their toddlers make choices in ways that do not harm themselves or others, by helping them to play and assert themselves safely and independently, and by rewarding and sharing in their accomplishments. Ever since Erikson, the focus on the battle for autonomy has dominated American understanding of toddler development, with at least preliminary awareness of the role of the family and culture in intensifying or attenuating toddlers' struggles for maturity.

The themes of autonomy and conflict have been taken up by neo-psychoanalytic theorists such as Spitz (1965) and Mahler, whose theories encompass the first 3 years but differentiate more substages than Freud and Erikson. Thus, the toddler period becomes subdivided into two or three phases. For example, Mahler, Pine, and Bergman (1975) conceptualized the process of ego development during infancy as involving two parallel but intertwined strands they called *separation* and *individuation*. The toddler period involves the three stages of *practicing* (a drive toward separateness from the mother based on the exhilarating discovery of walking), *rapprochement* (an ambivalent, contested re-engagement with the mother, involving both demanding dependency and insistent self-reliance), and *individuation* (the establishment of a lasting sense of separateness from mother with a balanced sense of personal powers and dependencies). As with autonomy, the child is helped toward psychological separateness and individuation by a mother who tolerates ambivalence and negativism and responds flexibly to conflicting demands.

Cognitive-Structuralist Theories

Jean Piaget's cognitive-structural theory of the growth of intelligence during childhood has been the second major influence shaping the contemporary understanding of the developmental tasks of toddlerhood. According to this theory, the sensorimotor stage of infancy concludes at about 18–24 months of age with the attainment of representational thought, or *symbolization*—an event ushering in the long preoperational stage that does not culminate until the achievement of concrete operational intelligence. Thus, the toddler period, in Piaget's theory, is not differentiated as a separate phase; younger toddlers (under about 18 months) are cognitively still infants, and older toddlers (18–36 months) more resemble preschool children. The cognitivist revolution has led, in the United States, to an urgent sense that parents of toddlers *should* facilitate and support the development of representational competencies—language and symbolic play—by providing such things as the following: a cognitively rich and stimulating environment (that invites children to ask and answer their own questions; Duckworth, 1972); partnership and intersubjectivity in object play and exploration (e.g., Hubley & Trevarthen, 1979); dialogue that promotes concept-formation and abstraction ("cognitive distance" between the subjective and objective, self and others, objects and their properties, ideas and actions; Sigel, 1986); and a social environment generally supportive of curiosity, self-directed play and investigation, and competence motivation.

Contemporary cognitivists (e.g., Damon, 1977; Fischer, 1980; Kagan, 1971; Kaye, 1982; McCall, Eichorn, & Hogarty, 1977) have found much to agree with Piaget's (1952) substantive descriptions of sensorimotor and preoperational development and, more generally, with the hypothesis that there are several major phases in young children's capacities to construct knowledge out of sensory perceptions and motoric actions and use that knowledge for remembering, problem solving, coordinating with others, and constructing concepts of the self and others. In attempting to correct or refine Piaget's theory and descriptions, some theorists formulated alternative frameworks based on their own empirical research (see Fogel, 1984, pp. 297–305). These theories contain points of overlap with one another but do not exactly match in number of discrete stages or in times of transition between stages; they do agree in presenting a more domain-specific and highly age-graded account of toddlerhood than did Freud, Erikson, and Piaget. Furthermore, they highlight and extend Piaget's hypotheses about the construction of a categorical self-concept (understanding of the self as a distinct entity and agent; Theme 2) and elaborate how the child constructs identities for self and others.

Theorists coming from an information-processing perspective sought to specify the ways in which the mind handles and manipulates the information presented to it by the environment. McCall et al. (1977), for example, set forth five stages of early mental development informed by Piaget's formulations. During the stage called *objectification of environmental entities*, young toddlers (about 13–21 months) search for new means and understand the existence of objects independent of their actions. For example, when blocked in reaching for a ball that has rolled under the couch, the child persists in crying for it and tries alternate ways of getting it, such as going around to the back. The older toddler (beyond 21 months), at *symbolic relations*, conceptualizes and symbolizes relations between objects, solves problems involving mental combinations and insight, and has the capacity for two- or three-word sentences. Such a child can secure the ball that has rolled under the couch by looking for a stick to use as a tool.

Fischer's (1980) theory integrates Piagetian and information-processing approaches into a system of 10 hierarchical cognitive *skill levels*, organized into three tiers: sensorimotor, representational, and abstract. During the sensorimotor period, the infant or younger toddler controls first one, then two, then three or more, sensorimotor schemas (skills) at a time. The older toddler, in contrast, has typically advanced to the representational tier; at Skill Level 4, this child can cognitively control one symbolic representation (concept, label, category) at a time, for example, using the word "girl" to label a peer. At Skill Level 5, the child (usually of preschool age) can cognitively control and coordinate two representations at once, for example, thinking about how someone must be either a girl or a boy. Finally, at Skill Level 6, the child (usually of early school age) can control and coordinate many symbolic representations simultaneously, for example, constructing a system relating the male–female dimension to masculine–feminine differences in clothing, toys, adult jobs, and so forth. Fischer's system is useful in conceptualizing how the thinking of the 2- to 3-year-old toddler differs from that of both the sensorimotor infant and the 4- to 5-year-old child, and how these cognitive transitions lead to pervasive changes during the early childhood years in causal reasoning, role understanding, identity formation, and other aspects of social-cognitive understanding (Fischer, Hand, Watson, Van Parys, & Tucker, 1984).

Other theorists emphasized the transformative power of emerging symbolization on affect and self-regulation. Sroufe (1979) reinterpreted the development of affect and attachment through a perspective informed by both psychoanalytic and cognitivist modes of thinking: he distinguished a *practicing* stage seen in the young toddler (12–18 months) from the *emergence of self-concept* seen in the older toddler (18–36 months) in terms of the new emotions experienced. Elation, anxiety, and petulance are prominent during practicing; positive self-evaluation, shame, and defiance come with the emergence of self-concept. Kopp (1982) outlined discontinuous phases of *coping and self-regulation* from a social skills perspective, synthesizing the findings on early childhood cognitive advances documented by many investigators. From about age 12 to 18 months, the young toddler achieves *control*, or abilities to initiate, maintain, and terminate physical acts based on elementary awareness of the social demands of a situation: initial self-monitoring, self-inhibition of previously prohibited behavior, and compliance appear. For example, in the presence of something dangerous that the toddler has been taught not to touch, the child will look toward his mother and back away from the object. From about 24 to 36 months, older toddlers achieve *self-control*, that is, the ability to comply with requests, to delay specific activities due either to self-instruction or another's demand, and to monitor their behavior according to caregiver expectations in the absense of the caregiver. Such a child will shake his head, "no," and refrain from touching the dangerous object even when the mother is out of the room. The achievement of self-control involves major growth in self-awareness, knowledge of social standards, recall memory, and ability to delay or inhibit responding.

Attachment Theories

A third loosely connected group of theories clarified another central issue for the toddler period: children's *entry into larger social systems beyond the mother–infant dyad* (Theme 6 earlier), involving relationships with immediate and extended family members, as well as with peers, secondary caregivers, neighbors, and others outside the family. Attachment theory, first proposed by Bowlby (1969), proved a useful corrective to the prevailing behavioristic view that the child's orientation toward caregivers was based on "dependency motives" conditioned through satisfaction of the child's primary and secondary needs (Gewirtz, 1972). Attachment theory lays out developmental phases of the child's progressive entry into widening social networks. Infancy, it can be summarized, is the preeminent time for the mother–child dyad (Barnard & Martell, in this *Handbook*; Bornstein, in this *Handbook*) infants show passing interest and pleasure in people other than their primary caregivers but they do not function well or for long out of visual and auditory range of an attachment figure. They may enjoy interacting with persons other than an attachment figure, but they do not require such playmates for optimal development. During the toddler period, in contrast, when children have accomplished the developmental work involved in establishing mature mother–infant reciprocity and partnership (Sander, 1962) on the basis of shared rhythms, intentions, and memory (Kaye, 1982), they now begin to display appetite for establishing strong and lasting relationships—attachments and friendships—with other persons. Mueller and Cohen (1986) referred to "peer hunger" as first seen during the toddler period, but perhaps it is "people hunger," a desire for long-term partners with whom to establish reciprocal relationships and gain social experience, skill, knowledge, and confidence. Mothers play a key role, not yet fully understood, in mediating toddlers' entry into these wider social relationships and influencing the affective responses, communicative styles, and social repertories their children bring to the task of forming meaningful and sustainable relationships and associations (Barnard & Martell, in this *Handbook*; Ladd, Profilet, & Hart, 1992). They may also help by providing their child with opportunities for making friends or by supervising their child's play and coaching them in sharing, entering a group, or solving a dispute as necessary (Parke, Cassidy, Burks, Carson, & Boyum, 1992).

Attachment theory, however, provided more than another discourse to discuss the outlines of toddler development. It also provided hypotheses about the importance of developmental transitions themselves as opportunities for early intervention to correct disturbances in parent–child interaction. Brazelton's (1992) framework interpreted, or re-framed, the stressful periods of the parent–child relationship that predictably occur at transition points as the most positive and productive moments (*touchpoints*) for professionals to help parents gain insight into their children and support their development of competence and individuality. Touchpoints are the culturally universal and predictable times that occur just before major spurts of motor, cognitive, or emotional growth; they are characterized by behavioral disintegration and regression in the child and by stress on the parent–child system. With regard to the toddler period, these points normatively occur at age 12 months, 15 months, 18 months, 2 years, and 3 years. Thus, for Brazelton, both infancy and toddlerhood represented particularly rich times for outside intervention precisely because both age periods contain many transitions and moments of disorganization and reorganization.

Critiques from a Cross-Cultural Perspective

Each of these theoretical perspectives has received criticism from different quarters, and each has continually evolved on the basis of new research and dialogue within the scientific community. As Maccoby (1992) noted, socialization theories have shown striking continuities but also sweeping changes over this century. They have generally evolved from grand and inclusive to modest and domain specific. They have changed from unidirectional (parent behaviors as causes, child behaviors as effects) to bidirectional and transactional. Their explanations of the underlying causes and processes of development have evolved from simple to complex.

Socialization theories have also evolved in response to critiques of cultural limitation, that is, that they are too heavily based on a narrow empirical base of research and philosophical and psychological assumptions of advanced Western societies. Three such lines of criticism focus substantively on toddler development and parent–toddler relationships.

One line of criticism addresses the classic account of the toddler's drive for autonomy and separateness (Theme 1), which, it is claimed, appears incorrect as a thematic description of toddler development in many non-Western cultural communities (Edwards, 1989). For example, in Zinacantan, Mexico, a Mayan community in the Chiapas Highlands, the transition from infancy to early childhood is not typified by resistant toddlers demanding and asserting control over toileting and other self-help skills (the familiar "No! *I* can do it!"), but instead by watchful, imitative children who acquire toilet training and other elements of self-care with a minimum of fuss. Clothing is simple; dirt floors and yards can be easily swept; the emotions of pride or shame and guilt do not seem to be at issue. Indeed, Zinacanteco toddlers appear not to assert separateness and to push away from encircling mothers, but rather the opposite: to struggle to cope with an unsought physical distancing initiated by mothers, who until then had kept them calm, quiet, and peaceful by carrying them under a shawl on the back and nursing them frequently. Previously all-giving mothers now reserve their privileges for a new baby. The displaced toddlers, often appearing listless and dejected, frequently hover in their mothers' vicinity and seem equally disturbed by the weaning process and the lost pleasures of being carried and sleeping next to the mother's body at night. After an extended period of adjustment, however, these children seem to accept their change in status and to rebound as active members of the children's multiage courtyard play group. Mothers in Zinacantan, as in other similar cultures, do not see themselves as playmates or conversational partners for their infants and young children; rather, they delegate these roles to siblings and other family members (Edwards, 1993; Edwards & Whiting, 1993). Greenfield, Brazelton, and Childs (1989), describing Zinacanteco infancy, hypothesized that the infant care practices lay the groundwork for the development of toddlers who watch closely, imitate elders, and respond to others, rather than taking the initiative to make others respond to them:

> An all pervasive concept in Zinacanteco culture is the contrast between *bankilal* and *itz'inal*, older and younger brother [senior and junior rank]. … Applied to social relations and interaction in the family, the basic rule is that older people have authority over and command respect from younger people. … Under this analysis, Zinacanteco practices organized around nursing could form the roots of socialization into a society that values intact transmission of culture from the older generation to the younger. … emphasizing the *responsiveness* rather than the *initiative* of the younger member of a dyad in social interactions in early infancy continued into childhood, when "good" children were assessed by their obedience to their parents. (Greenfield et al., 1989, p. 189)

These descriptions of Zinacanteco toddlerhood correspond in rough outline to many other descriptions of toddler behavior in rural, non-Western communities (Edwards, 1993; Farver, 1983; Whiting & Edwards, 1988). Albino and Thompson (1956) made intensive clinical observations of how Zulu toddlers reacted to the customary practice of sudden weaning and noticed the following disturbances: clinging, refusals to respond, aggression toward mother, sucking of objects, repetitive behavior (such as rocking), messing and naughtiness (such as playing with fire, spilling food, throwing dirt), fretfulness or crying, disturbed sleep and bed wetting, subdued apathy. Following the period of disturbance, however, the Zulu children quite suddenly developed behaviors normally expected of older children, such as helping with household tasks, increased facility in speech, and a greater independence of adult support.

After weaning, it seems that in many non-Western communities, toddlers begin to function without constant maternal attention and to play well and get most of their needs met within the multiage playgroup of siblings and courtyard cousins. This is illustrated in the following description of Embu children living in Kenya:

> The influence of siblings and peers appears to be quite important for the Embu [Kenyan] toddlers' development. Older sisters were frequently the caregivers who listened to and talked to their younger sibling. Furthermore, those toddlers most involved in sustained social interaction developed the most rapidly, and social interactions almost always involved other children rather than adults. (Sigman et al., 1988, p. 1259)

These descriptions do not fit well with the portrait of a self-initiated drive for autonomy and separateness—what Brazelton (1974) called the "Declaration of Independence" of the 1-year-old—widely accepted in American child development and parenting literature as the normative pattern.

In place of the psychoanalytic account, Weisner (1989a, 1989b, 1993) suggested that the language of increasing "interdependence" (or "shared social support") rather than "independence" best describes the developmental goal of parents in many cultures around the world. Whiting and Edwards (1988; Edwards, 1992, 1993; Whiting, 1980, 1983) proposed examining without theoretical presumption the cross-cultural universals and variations in behavior that young children demonstrate to and elicit from social partners, using as a point of reference the four major age grades defined by Margaret Mead: the *lap child* (infant), *knee child* (toddler), *yard child* (preschooler), and *community child* (school child). They then theorized about age-specific *developmental agendas*, such as seeking responsiveness from others (lap child), discovering the limits of the physical and social environments (knee child), establishing a position in the childhood pecking order (yard child), and seeking symbolic knowledge and to compete with same-sex peers (community child).

Findings from comparative studies of parental developmental expectations make clear that parents from different cultures do not agree on the expected age that children should acquire various competancies, nor on how crucial these various competencies are for maturity (Goodnow, in this *Handbook*). For example, Americans regard social skills with peers and verbal articulateness and assertiveness to be very important for young children and push for early achievement of these skills, whereas Italians regard sensitivity to the needs of others and graciousness in entering and exiting from social situations to be signs of maturity (Edwards, 1992; Edwards, Gandini, & Forman, 1993; Edwards, Gandini, & Giovannini, in press). Super and Harkness (1986; Harkness & Super, 1983) likewise argued that developmental stages are influenced by cultural experiences and demarcated differently around the world:

> The definition of developmental stages is in part a culturally shared response to the observable aspects of human development, and thus it seems reasonable to expect universal elements in stages as defined by all cultures. ... Cultures vary, however, in their choice of different aspects of development as the critical ones for defining growth. ... The result, we hypothesize, is that cultures will vary not only in the timing of roughly comparable developmental stages, but also in the developmental issues which are seen as primary to each stage. (Harkness & Super, 1983, p. 223)

The bottom line of these arguments is that before concluding what is *the* central or defining developmental task of the toddler period, we need more complete information on toddler development and behavior in a wide variety of cultural settings. Thus, even the list of six themes proposed earlier—autonomy, self-awareness, impulse control, emergence of standards, gender identity, and becoming a member of society—should be considered tentative and subject to cross-cultural validation.

Rogoff, Mistry, Goncu, and Mosier (1991, 1993) developed a second line of criticism of the standard theoretical accounts, focusing on issues of cognitive development. Drawing on Vygotsky's (1962, 1978) theory of cognitive development, Rogoff argued that cognitive as well as social development occur in cultural contexts, through interaction of children with more competent partners in situations of *guided participation*. The Piagetian account, Rogoff claimed, leads researchers to attend chiefly to situations in which a parent and a young child interact with each other around a toy or engage in face-to-face talk or play. In reality, at least for many children around the world, most learning and development take place not in situations where adults and children are focused on each other but rather jointly participating in a task or social activity engaging their shared interest, such as cooking, weaving, visiting, or celebrating. In studies of toddlers in four cultures (Rogoff et al., 1993), adults are seen to *scaffold* their children's ("apprentices") learning, first through choosing and structuring their activities, then through various forms of tacit communication and explicit verbal guidance. The kinds of behaviors that adults can do to extend toddlers' cognitive competence include recruiting the child's interest in a task, simplifying the task, motivating the child to maintain effort, calling attention to important discrepancies between what the child has accomplished and the ideal solution, controlling frustration and risk, and demonstrating the ideal solution (Wood, Bruner, & Ross, 1976). However, the preferred way in which the adult scaffolds the toddler's learning is strongly affected by culture (Rogoff et al., 1993). In some contexts, for example, among Mayan families in the Highlands of Guatemala, caregivers and toddlers *jointly* and *mutually* contribute to the direction of activity in everyday moments of problem solving. The caregivers orient their toddlers to an activity, monitor what unfolds, and offer help and suggestions when needed, but meanwhile they also *simultaneously* attend to other persons present or activities taking place (such as with older children). Mayan toddlers, for their part, watch closely the progress of events taking place around them and sensitively share the leadership for problem solving. In contrast, in other contexts, such as among middle-class Turkish and European-American families, caregivers and toddlers prefer to take turns and *alternate*, rather than share, the task of directing activity, and both mother and child focus *exclusively* on one activity and one social partner at a time. Such findings are proving fruitful in opening up new lines of research on the ways in which children appropriate their culture through processes of participation and negotiation with more competent experts (Farver, 1993).

A third vein of criticism draws from the work of developmental sociolinguists. Ochs and Schieffelin (1984) called for a new conceptualization of childhood socialization based on merging this domain with the study of language acquisition. The forms, functions, and message content of children's early language in natural settings, they argued, should be documented and examined for "the ways in which they *organize* and *are organized by* culture" (p. 276). Using Ochs's transcripts of Samoan adult–child speech, Schieffelin's transcripts of the Kaluli of Papua New Guinea, and a synthesis of American child language studies, they created three very different portraits of early parent–child communication patterns. They saw not one choreography of normal parent–toddler speech, but rather many (within and across societies) shaped by the interaction of biological predispositions with cultural role- and rule-systems. Sociolinguistic research is yielding a growing corpus of ethnographic studies that detail the socialization of early communication in cultural context (Schieffelin & Ochs, 1986).

Summary

The classic and more recent theoretical descriptions of the toddler period together yield a fairly integrated picture of developmental tasks faced during the second and third years. Such tasks, which occupy much of the emotional and interactional energy of the developing child, include: (1) learning to function autonomously, that is, at one remove from the caregiver, and beginning to help in an appropriate way as defined by family and culture with the ordinary routines of self-care and daily living; (2) categorical self-concept and beginning self-reflection; (3) impulse and self-control, the precursors of self-regulation in the absense of the caregiver; (4) the beginnings of moral conscience, including sensitivity to the violation of standards and organized emotional themes of hurt feelings, empathy toward the plight of others, fear of punishment, guilt, shame, and desire to repair; (5) gender identity, beginning knowledge of sex roles, and beginning preference for acting like and affiliating with others of one's gender; and (6) becoming a member of society in the sense of taking a place in the larger family and kinship network and in a childhood play group.

Critiques of this literature by anthropologists, cross-cultural psychologists, and sociolinguists made the point that toddler development cannot be adequately described without introducing further theoretical perspectives based on Vygotsky's (1962, 1978) writings and using naturalistic observations that clarify the meaning systems and communication processes involved in socialization. Furthermore, whereas certain developmental tasks may be universal, cultural groups may nevertheless differ in what age and order they impose these tasks on the child, and in how significant or insignificant they claim each task to be in evaluating a child's maturity. Moreover, cultures differ in whether their ultimate goal is "interdependence" or "independence" and to whom (mother versus child) they assign the leading role in the push for separateness. Americans and Western Europeans tend to see the drive for separateness as coming from the child, who is considered to want to push away from the mother, whereas peoples in rural village communities in sub-Saharan Africa, South and Central America, and other parts of the world place the mother in charge of creating psychological separation and distance—against the toddler's expected resistance (Edwards, 1989).

CLASSICAL AND MODERN RESEARCH ON TODDLER DEVELOPMENT

In addition to the strides made in theorizing about the developmental tasks of the toddler period, recent years have also witnessed an outpouring of empirical research focusing on toddler behavioral development and parent–child interaction during the second and third years of life. The research findings provide further insight on how children move through the developmental tasks already discussed. However, in current developmental texts, the discussions of findings are not usually organized by developmental tasks or themes, but rather by behavioral domains that can readily be operationalized and observed. In the remainder of this chapter, research findings relevant to the parenting of toddlers shall be reviewed, using the subheadings commonly found in the child development literature: (1) self-concept and self-reflection; (2) compliance and noncompliance; (3) empathy and the emergence of standards; (4) gender identity and sex-role identification; and (5) cognitive and communicative competence. Of course, the topics of self-concept, emergence of standards, and gender identity (one, three, and four) obviously correspond to earlier themes. The topic of compliance and noncompliance corresponds to the developmental task or theme of impulse and self-control. The topic of cognitive and communicative competence relates not to any one single theme; the issues here are broader than psychosocial tasks and underlie all of them simultaneously. Yet another well-studied topic that could be reviewed, attachment (related to the themes of autonomy and becoming a member of society), is addressed elsewhere in this *Handbook*.

Self-Concept and Self-Reflection

Extensive studies of children's self-recognition by Lewis and his colleagues (Lewis & Brooks-Gunn, 1979; Lewis, Sullivan, Stranger, & Weiss, 1989) established that toddlers between about 15 and 18 months of age begin to recognize themselves in the mirror. At the same age they typically also begin to label themselves by names and use personal pronouns, such as "I" and "me" (Baldwin, 1897; Kagan, 1981). These behaviors are taken as evidence that the child has formed a "categorical self-concept," or the awareness that the self is a separate, physical entity and a source of actions, words, ideas, and feelings.

This new concept of the self as entity and agent, in turn, serves as the basis for a second major achievement, the beginning of reflective self-evaluation, that is, the ability to reflect on whether or not one can meet an achievement standard or accomplish a task, such as fulfill a parent's request. Stipek, Recchia, and McClintic (1992) found that as children approached age 2, they showed pridelike responses when succeeding with a toy (such as pushing shapes into a sorting box or hammering pegs into a pounding bench), and they sought recognition by calling their mothers' attention to their accomplishments. Mothers who tended to praise their toddlers more frequently had children who spontaneously showed more pride (even when not being praised). On the other hand, competitive standards of success ("winning" and "losing" against someone else) seemed to have little meaning to toddlers before age 3. In speculating about the implications of their findings for parenting, Stipek, Recchia, and McClintic commented that the capacity for reflective self-evaluation opens the child up to learning about parental and cultural values: Parents' approval and disapproval teaches the child, first, that some things they do can please other people as well as themselves, and second, about desirable outcomes and standards. The children "should become at least somewhat dependent on adults to identify socially valued outcomes" (Stipek et al., 1992, p. 19) and they should begin to internalize the forms in which praise and blame are expressed to them, for example, the words, postures, and emotions commonly used with them should become their working models for proper emotional expression in evaluating self and others (Kitayama & Markus, 1994).

Compliance and Noncompliance

During the second year of life, children become capable of learning their family's and community's standards for proper and desirable behavior. Indeed, socialization pressures begin in earnest during the second or third year of life in most cultural communities around the world (Kopp, 1982; Maccoby & Martin, 1983; Whiting, 1983; Whiting & Edwards, 1988). Some demands for mature behavior are elicited by the 2-year-olds' budding interest in the world around them, desire to participate in adult work (Reingold, 1982), and new abilities to imitate complex adult and peer routines evidencing competence (Kuczynski, Zahn-Waxler, & Radke-Yarrow, 1987). Other socialization pressures arise in response to the management problems presented by toddlers' emerging mobility and exploratory behaviors. Toddlers elicit many commands from both adults and older children that serve to protect them from physical dangers ("Stay away from the fire," "The sun is hot"), infection ("Don't drink that water," "Stop eating dirt"), and wandering too far ("Don't cross the road"). Toddlers also receive frequent admonishments concerning cleanliness and hygiene ("Go wash yourself"), basic etiquette ("Greet your grandmother"), care of clothing and household property ("That will break"), and other simple rules and standards. If what they are doing is perceived as annoying or intrusive, they receive commands to go away, to desist, or not to interrupt. In some cultural communities, 3-year-olds may even begin to receive commands related to meaningful household and subsistence tasks; in such places, assigning the toddler a chore or errand is seen as nurturant and complimentary—a way to flatter children as grownups and include them in the family group (Edwards & Whiting, 1993; Weisner, 1989a). Thus, the study of the growth of compliance, the ability and willingness to modulate behavior in accordance with caregiver commands and expectations, has been one of the most active areas of toddler research. One limitation, however, is that most of the research relates to North American families, the types most likely to believe in continuing high levels of parent–child interaction during the toddler period. The findings, therefore, would not seem to apply to the kinds of rural subsistence communities, previously mentioned, that use the toddler period as a time to wean the child from mother's bed, back, and breast, and re-direct much of the child's dependency out toward the family as a whole. Compliance issues are certainly present in the latter, too, but the close analyses of mother–child communication and interaction surrounding growth of self-regulation have yet to be conducted in such non-Western settings.

Developmental studies of resistance and negativism are not new in the United States; they were prevalent in the 1920s and 1930s (Kopp, 1992). This work, along with Gessell's (1940) findings, firmly established the stereotype of "the terrible twos." Taken together, earlier studies do reveal a peak of resistant and negativistic behaviors at about 2 years, with a steady decline by age 4 (E. R. Dubin & R. Dubin, 1963; Spitz, 1957; Wenar, 1982).

In response to maternal requests for cooperation, child compliance increases from toddler to preschool to school years (Whiting & Edwards, 1988). In a nonthreatening play situation, even children under 2 comply when they understand a command and do not comply when they do not understand (Kaler & Kopp, 1990). Such commands activate not simply cooperation but actual joyful enthusiasm from children age 18 to 24 months, when the commands are accompanied by clarity, sensitivity in interrupting the child's ongoing behavior, and an attentive and appreciative response to the children's performance (Reingold, Cook, & Kolowitz, 1987). The pleasure taken in achievement and in fitting one's actions to the words of the adults seems to account for toddlers' readiness to do what parents ask.

However, when the situation is nonplayful, or when the adult forcefully insists on breaking contact or interaction with the child, toddler behavior is not always so cooperative (Power & Chapieski, 1986). Schneider-Rosen and Wenz-Gross (1990) studied age changes in toddler compliance to both mothers and fathers in a variety of tasks typical of situations with which children are often confronted: told to play independently and not interrupt a busy parent; told to stop playing in order to read a book with the parent; told to clean up toys and put them away; told to sit quietly and not touch a toy; and told to work on a difficult problem alone. The different tasks elicited different patterns of responses and age trends, suggesting different underlying task demands. Neither fathers nor mothers elicited more cooperation overall. Age relations were complex, and the authors interpreted the findings as pointing to a transition and behavioral reorganization at about 24 months. Prior to this age, behavior is under the control of external monitors (adults), and children are very motivated to comply. Following age 2, behavior may be influenced more by the child's sense of autonomy and internal control systems involving language, memory, and the ability to inhibit responding.

Many studies have documented developmental changes in the ways that young children express their noncompliance. Passive noncompliance and direct defiance are the strategies typical of younger toddlers, whereas bargaining, negotiation, and direct refusal are the more mature strategies typical of older toddlers and preschool children (Kopp, 1992; Kuczynski & Kochanska, 1990; Kuczynski, Kochanska, Radke-Yarrow, & Girnius-Brown, 1987). These changes in noncompliant behavior are accompanied by changes in the control strategies used by mothers. Simple distraction and physical guidance (e.g., showing, leading by the hand) are used more by mothers of young toddlers, whereas verbal suggestion, reasoning, and counternegotiation are used more by the mothers of older, more verbal children (Kuczynski et al., 1987). Thus, both mothers and children show evolving "techniques of persuasion" they employ with each other.

Crying and tantruming are other forms of resistant noncompliance often seen in toddlers. Brazelton (1992) argued that temper tantrums in the second year reflect the child's inner turmoil, the struggle between dependence and independence, and are best handled by parents who stand back and allow their child to regain control. By moving beyond crying and tantruming, the child demonstrates emotional regulation, which is an important component of self-regulation. Matheny (reported in Kopp, 1992) observed children in laboratory settings for the Louisville Twin Study and found negative emotional tone to increase sharply between 12 and 18 months, to decline somewhat by 24 months, and to shift strongly back toward more positive tone by 30 months. Similarly, Kopp (1992), in home and laboratory observations, found a peak for crying (both short bouts and longer tantrums) at 18 to 21 months of age, with a clear drop by 36 months.

Besides providing a window into the development of self-regulation, the study of compliance and noncompliance offers a way to examine the development of reciprocity in parent–child relations (Parpal & Maccoby, 1985). Affective reciprocity has been amply documented; for example, highly negative London 2- to 4-year-olds were found to have more negative mothers (Downdey & Pickles, 1991), but the cause-and-effect relations within the cycle of reciprocity are complex. Maccoby and Martin (1983) made a useful distinction between "situational" compliance (immediate obedience, often based on factors such as threat of punishment or promise of reward) and "receptive" compliance (a long-term, reciprocity-based, readiness to cooperate with expectations). Power assertive techniques, such as yelling and punishment, they argued, may well be effective in the short run because they generate some degree of fear and submission to authority, yet less effective in the long run because they must be resorted to more and more frequently as time goes on and they do not create a general cooperative attitude on the part of the child—what Maccoby and Martin (1983) called a "readiness to be socialized." In support of this hypothesis, both Power and Chapieski (1986) and Crockenberg and Litman (1990) found better 2-year compliance to be associated with mothers' use of guidance and nonassertive methods of control, whereas defiance was associated with power-assertive techniques and physical punishment. Lytton's (1979) study of 21-year-old boys based on parents' "compliance diaries" found consistent enforcement of rules and frequency of joint play and cooperative activities to be related to high levels of compliance, and love-withdrawal and other forms of psychological punishment related to low compliance. "Responsiveness," however, is a quality that parents as well as children help create in a relationship. Some extremely difficult toddlers, who are aggressive, unyielding, and unruly in the face of their parents' attempts at guidance, help create the devastating "cycles of coercion" analyzed by Patterson (1982; Chamberlain & Patterson, in this *Handbook*).

The key to enlisting the toddler's willing compliance, suggested Westerman (1990), may be more than simple reciprocity but instead interaction behaviors that are *well coordinated* with the child's, in the sense that parent behaviors scaffold the child's effort, fit with what the child is doing, add to it, and set the stage for what the child might do next. Mothers of 3- to 4-year-olds, who were identified as having compliance problems, were compared with other mothers at the same preschools, and the former were judged less successful in coordinating with their children on a block task (Westerman, 1990). Parpal and Maccoby (1985) trained mothers in responsive play that scaffolded their children's play with toys, and found that these children subsequently increased in compliance. The point, then, may not be simply that parents should apply firm, responsive control (following Baumrind's, 1972, well-known paradigm for authoritative parenting), but that they work toward a certain type of control, within a context of generally positive emotion and sense of well-being, that leads the toddler toward learning and success.

Empathy and the Emergence of Standards

During the second year, an early moral sense, including sensitivity to flawed objects and distress when a standard is violated or cannot be met, clearly emerges (Kagan, 1981). This moral sense parallels their new capacities for self-reflective evaluation, described earlier. Children show anxiety("something is wrong") when they see someone hurt, an object is broken, or an important rule is violated. At first children exhibit a strong, unspecific arousal and may not be sure whether to react with positive or negative emotion (Zahn-Waxler, Radke-Yarrow, Wagner, & Chapman, 1992), but at around age 2 their reactions become more differentiated. By age 3, a number of organized socioemotional themes have emerged to serve as the basis of childhood morality and conscience: shame, guilt, reparation, empathy, pride, hurt feelings (Eisenberg & Murphy, in this *Handbook*; Emde, Biringen, Clyman, & Oppenheim, 1991).

Research has determined the effects of different parental behaviors in influencing children's responses and in helping them modulate and organize their emotional responses into constructive actions, such as apologizing, offering sympathy or comfort, seeking to assist or repair, going for help, and inhibiting future transgression. Maternal modeling is important: Maternal sensitivity and reasoning have been found to relate positively to empathic, prosocial responses during the second year of life. For example, when mothers show concern and talk about who was hurt, and why, their toddlers show more empathy and attempts to help someone in pain (Zahn-Waxler, Radke-Yarrow, & King, 1979). Conversely, parents who subject their toddlers to abuse at home, have children who do not show concern in response to the distress of a day-care classmate, but instead react with disturbing and unusual sorts of behavior (not seen in comparable nonabused children), such as with physical attacks, fear, and anger at the victim (Main & George, 1985; Rogosch, Cicchetti, Shields, & Toth, in this *Handbook*).

Girls and boys do not respond identically to the distress of others, however, even during the toddler period. Although boys are as prosocially active as girls (often offering instrumental help or seeking to repair), girls show more empathic concern and tend to mirror or copy the affective experience of the other more (Zahn-Waxler et al., 1992, p. 134): "Typically, these are seen as indicators of joining in the emotional experience of others, and there is a long history of discussion regarding why females are sometimes more prone than males to participate in others' affective states."

Temperament may be another factor besides gender that affects how a child feels when a standard is violated and that may predict how parents can most effectively get the child to comply. Kochanska (1993) proposed that individuals vary in intensity of *affective discomfort* (arousal, fear, shame, anxiety, guilt, remorse) occasioned by transgression (committed or anticipated). Evidence from several laboratories suggests that there are stable individual differences in susceptibility to fearful arousal and anxiety, corresponding to consistent physiological patterns (Deinstbier, 1984; Feinman,

1982; Goldsmith & Campos, 1986; Kochanska, 1991). The question as to whether anxiety or fearfulness is a continuous dimension (e.g., more or less anxious) or better conceptualized as discrete types (e.g., shy versus not shy) remains unresolved (Kagan, 1992). But different temperaments may call for different parenting styles to ensure optimal development of a moral self. Subtle methods may work best with a highly anxious child, whereas parents of imperturbable children may need to shift to alternatives that do not rely on the child's anxiety, shame, or guilt to be effective—perhaps emphasizing positive emotions such as pride, competence motivation, and desire to please. Otherwise, parents of less perturbable children may find themselves resorting to higher and higher levels of anger and punishment to control their child, and the stage will be set for a negative cycle of coercion and formation of an aggressive, uncontrollable child (Patterson, 1982).

Gender Identity and Sex-Role Identification

During the second and third years of life, children take several important steps along the road to constructing a *gender identity* (the knowledge that one is and always will be a male or female) and *sex-role identification* (consisting of sex-role knowledge and preferences). Parents of children this age may be becoming more mindful of their child's masculinity or femininity; as toddlers' language development accelerates, parents may correct children's use of gender labels and pronouns, and they may find that the clothes and toys available or that their children prefer are more obviously sex linked. Issues of gender, nevertheless, are not yet as central and exciting to the toddler as they will be during preschool and adolescent eras. Instead, age groups (baby, child, adult) stand out as the most salient and interesting social categories to toddlers because they point to what toddlers feel are the most noteworthy distinctions in people's size, competence, and activities (for instance, who gets fed a bottle, sleeps in a crib, wears a diaper, rides a bike, drives a car, and so on; see Edwards, 1986).

By 2½ or 3 years, most children have become fairly accurate in labeling photographs of themselves and others by gender (C. Etaugh, Grinnell, & A. Etaugh, 1989). Children typically master gender nouns ("boy," "girl," "man," "woman,") before pronouns ("he," "she," and so forth) and correctly apply labels to others before consistently labeling themselves. Not before age 4, however, have children correctly constructed the idea that gender category is stable over time, as in this vignette (from Edwards, 1986, p. 58):

> Teacher: "Lisa, are you a girl or a boy?"
> Lisa (age 3): "I'm a girl, but when I'm 4, I'll be a boy."

By age 3 or 4, children are certain about their own gender; they have formed one of the most stable self-categorizations they will make in their lifetimes (Kohlberg, 1966).

During the same period, from watching television, reading books, and observing the world around them, children are also beginning to construct sex-role knowledge and stereotypes. By age 3, children have been found to be aware of sex-role differences for adult possessions, adult tasks, and children's toys (Weinraub, Clemens, Sockloff, Ethridge, Gracely, & Myers, 1984).

Sex-typed preferences also emerge early. Around age 2 for girls and age 3 for boys, children begin to direct more of their social approaches to same-sex play partners; without yet seeking to exclude or avoid opposite-sex children, they yet show a beginning attraction or preference for others of their own gender, especially when in group situations (Maccoby, 1988; Whiting & Edwards, 1988).

What causes these differences? The role of parental socialization in sex-role development has been closely studied and debated for many years (Fagot, in this *Handbook*). Current evidence strongly indicates that both gender identification and preference for same-sex partners are driven by cognitive processes rather than social reinforcement (Maccoby, 1988). The drawing apart of boys and girls in social play is seen universally across cultures whenever children are present in sufficient numbers for choice to be a factor; gender segregation is always strongest in same-age rather than mixed-age groups, and hence is a more dominant feature of play at school than within the home or nearby yard (Whiting & Edwards, 1988). Rather than being created by adult reinforcement, gender segregation seems lessened when an adult is present (e.g., when several children of both sexes gather around a teacher to hear a story at nursery school; Maccoby, 1988).

The role of reinforcement in helping produce sex-typed behavior is not discounted, but it does need to be understood in new and more complex ways. First, already by age 2, reinforcements for sex-typed behavior are most effective when processed in terms of gender (Fagot, 1985, p. 1102; in this *Handbook*): "Girls' peer groups gave the message, play with those like you; but they do not limit [sanction] play behaviors by category in the same way that boys do. We see that the male peer group starts defining [sanctioning] what is *not male* very early, and that the behaviors defined as not male drop out of the boy's repertoire." Second, although parental socialization is no longer believed to account for sex differences in dominance and aggressive behaviors (now understood to be hormonally mediated), nevertheless parents surely play a role in children's development of some sex-typed behavior. Current research examines parents as co-participants with children in a system of preferences and meanings; they sometimes "steer" toddlers toward sex-typed behavior (e.g., Weitzman, Birns, & Friend, 1985), but more often "join" with the children in influential ways. For example, Caldera, Huston, and O'Brien (1989) found parents of toddlers (observed in the laboratory) to follow their children in play with either same-sex or cross-sex toys, but they became more involved and excited with same-sex toys. The sex-stereotyped toys, moreover, themselves elicited sex-typed play: Trucks evoked different, noisier, more active play than did play with feminine toys, no matter the sex of parent or sex of child. These findings are reminiscent of Whiting and Edwards' (1988) claim that, from a cross-cultural perspective, parents exert their strongest sex-role socialization through the settings and activities to which they assign boys versus girls, rather than through praise or reprimands that are intended to modulate behavior. Moreover, parents are not the only adults influential in young children's sex-role development, and many studies (e.g., Fagot, Hagan, Leinbach, & Kronsberg, 1985) have found that adults act in more sex-stereotyped ways when they do not know a child well and hence are in a more ambiguous situation. Relatives, neighbors, and new acquaintances may play heightened roles in creating worlds of gendered meaning for very young children.

Cognitive and Communicative Competence

Throughout the 1960s and early 1970s, the vulnerability of infants and young children to environmental deprivation was a rallying cry for researchers, educators, and policymakers. Hunt (1961), Fowler (1962), and others, resonating to the social idealism of the times, galvanized a wave of early intervention programs and evaluation research aimed at understanding and eradicating educational disadvantages ascribed to socioeconomic background. In the 1980s, however, the earlier optimism was not so much vanquished as tempered and transformed into more cautious and narrowly defined efforts aimed at specific target populations, for example, early intervention efforts for infants and toddlers with disabilities or identified risks, child abuse prevention and treatment, and early treatment of speech and communication disorders. Knowledge about form and process in developmental change during the first 3 years of life exploded, but it has brought with it a certain wisdom and prudence associated with increased awareness of, first, the complexities of the questions and the limits of what we know, second, the contribution the child makes to situations and interactions, and third, the huge range in normal childrearing environments, goals, and expectations found throughout history and around the world.

Thus, current reports of correlational connections between early experience and later competence are tempered by the proviso that genetic influences may be intervening in some of the complex ways summarized by Scarr (1992), who noted that biological parents provide their children with both genes and environments, that different children do not evoke the same responses from others, and that children make selective choices about what parts of the physical and social environment to which they will devote time and attention. Recognizing these facts, recent research studies have often taken advantage of longitudinal designs or other methodological safeguards to make it more possible to argue direction of causality.

It seems hard to discount all causal relations between early experience and later mental competence, however. For example, Bradley and associates (1989) reported on an extensive 3-year longitudinal study involving six sites and three ethnic groups in North America. Correlations between the HOME Inventory (Caldwell & Bradley, 1978; a measure of the quality of the physical and social environment) and mental test scores increased during the second year of life and then stabilized during the third. Parental responsivity and availability of stimulating play materials were more strongly related to subsequent mental test scores than were the socioeconomic status variables. Cross-lag correlations supported the interpretation of bidirectional influences, but with more evidence of the environment shaping the child than of the child shaping the environment.

Many experts on infancy, such as Fogel (1984) and Kagan (1971), however, stopped believing that early experiences are inherently more important than experiences at any other time in life; instead, self-righting forces in the individual and in the environment are operative throughout the life span. Others (e.g., Fowler, 1986) claimed that early experiences are important and formative, but that the hard problem is to identify phenomena of a magnitude sufficient to make a long-term impact—sufficient to override the continuing accumulation of multiple, competing experiences. Fowler (1986) argued that research must be more focused and ask more complex, multivariate questions, looking at specific experiences, and also their exact timing and duration, in relation to particular outcomes.

McCall (1981) proposed a model that attributes causal power to dimensions of the environment but in different ways prior to versus after the second year of life. The model portrays early development as looking like a shovel or scoop (narrow at the top, then rapidly widening out). McCall argued that during the first 18 months of life, development proceeds along a fairly narrow, fixed, species-typical path, at least as long as species-typical, appropriate environments prevail. After the first 2 years, however, environmental influences and organismic factors (such as temperament or learning style) are more likely to have a formative impact, and children's development fans out into a greater variety of normal types of outcomes. Thus, the toddler period, 18 months to 3 years, represents the time when the scoop first "fans out," and cultural, socioeconomic, familial, and organismic differences are more and more implicated in the scenario of children's development.

Whichever model of the influence of early experiences turns out to be correct, evidence is accumulating for the relation of specific experiences to specific outcomes in cognitive and language development. For example, Wachs (1982) found that exploratory play skills in the second and third year are best enhanced by caregivers' providing responsive objects (such as rattles and balls), as well as an overall variety of objects, during the first year. The development of spatial relations and perspective-taking are best predicted by the avoidance of noise, confusion, and environmental overcrowding during the first 2 years. Wachs (1982; Wachs & Gruen, 1982) developed a concept of *environmental specificity*, and argued that some forms of stimulation should be introduced at specific ages, and others should be dropped; for example, from 12 to 24 months, toddlers should be provided with an environment with more temporal/spatial regularity, avoidance of restriction and coercion, and opportunities for exploration and social interaction; but after 36 months, floor freedom and responsive objects can be eliminated. Early experiences require later reinforcement to remain influential: "The vast majority of early experiences, *taken in isolation*, will not have lasting effects unless later experiences occur which stabilize the effects of the initial experiences" (Wachs & Gruen, 1982, p. 220).

There is also evidence for specificity in the social environment-organism interaction, although these relations are not always confirmed as predicted (e.g., Bornstein, Vibbert, Tal, & O'Donnell, 1992). For instance, in a longitudinal, experimental design, Slade (1987) found that mothers' availability for interactive play and conversation contributed to toddlers' symbolic (pretend) play, across the age period from 20 to 28 months. *Semantic contingency*, an immediate matching of adult speech to the topic or content of the child's utterance (e.g., "You like that truck across the street? It's a big dump truck!") has been replicated as effective in promoting more rapid language development in toddlerhood (Bohannon & Stanowicz, 1988; Cross, 1978; Rice, 1989; Smolak & Weinraub, 1983). The adult may repeat the child's utterance, expand on it, use the child's word in a question, repeat a child's phrase with grammatical correction, or request clarificaton. Vocabulary development during toddlerhood has been related to overall amount of parent speech (Huttenlocher, Haight, Bryk, Seltzer, & Lyons, 1991) and to adults' tendencies to describe aspects of the environment that are at that moment occupying the child's attention (e.g., "Yes, that bird [you're looking at] is big and blue") (P. Dunham & F. Dunham, 1992; Valdez-Menchaca & Whitehurst, 1988). Social interactive routines, such as book reading, are strongly supportive of vocabulary development and emergent print literacy (Bus & van IJzendoorn, 1988). As Fogel (1984, p. 287) concluded, "Maternal vocalization, contingent responsiveness, and involvement become important between six and twenty-four months, after which a lack of restrictiveness and providing opportunities to interact with other people are the best predictors of cognitive and language development."

Summary

Several content areas of toddler development have received intensive psychological study and much knowledge and understanding of underlying processes has been gained for the issues of self-concept, compliance/noncompliance, moral development, gender identity, and cognitive and language development. Moreover, theoretical analyses of these content areas showed strong and encouraging signs of a maturing field of knowledge: There has been a synthesis of findings and joining of vocabularies across formerly separate research traditions. For example, in work on the growth of self-regulation (e.g., Kopp, 1982, 1992), analyses of the cognitive underpinnings were drawn together from the Genevan tradition, Vygotskian and Russian psychology, and the American functionalist point of view.

Antecedent–consequent relations, however, still remained difficult to nail down. The standards for what is considered convincing evidence of parental causation were increased, and bidirectional, multicausational models became the goal. Both research investigators and textbook writers became increasingly cautious in generalizing about socialization effects, lasting influences of early experience, and the like.

TRANSLATION OF THEORY AND RESEARCH
INTO PRACTICAL INFORMATION

During recent years, many of the major findings on toddler development became available to parents in summary and simplified form through the medium of advisory literature. Parents who wanted expert advice on care and guidance of their toddlers had many books from which to choose. Women's and parenting magazines often featured articles addressing toddler developments.

Many works focused on emotional development. Fraiberg's (1959) *The Magic Years* was a psychoanalytic account of the age period of 18 months to 3 years, when parents need to assist children in acquiring selfhood, conscience, and self-control. Her organizing metaphor for the toddler, "the magician," referred to the primitive belief that the whole world (including thoughts, wishes, and words) were under one's own omnipotent control. S. Greenspan and N. T. Greenspan's (1985) *First Feelings,* another psychoanalytic account, described six emotional milestones during the first 4 years. The early toddler period (9–18 months) involves the emergence of an organized sense of self, whereas the later period (18–36 months) focuses on "creating emotional ideas." This book was intended to help parents understand such problems as supporting a rich emotional life for their child, setting limits, and coping with their own and their child's fears. Brazelton's (1974) *Toddlers and Parents* integrated an Eriksonian perspective (autonomy versus shame and doubt) into a framework that explored temperamental differences among withdrawn, demanding, and hyperactive children; also, the book addressed contemporary childrearing issues such as maternal employment and single parenthood (see, too, Brazelton's *Touchpoints,* 1992). Brazelton's volumes re-framed childhood problems into strengths, and stressful transitions into moments of openness and opportunity for change on the part of both parents and children.

Lickona's (1983) *Raising Good Children,* one of the few parenting books to start from a cognitive-structuralist theoretical base, used Kohlberg's (1969) six-stage developmental model of moral judgment. This work was intended to assist parents to understand typical childhood reasoning, achieve fairness in conflict resolution, reason and communicate with children, and use books and television to aid moral education. Lickona summarized the toddler years as laying the foundation for moral development, including respect for authority and accomodation to reasonable rules and requests. One-year-olds are said to need from their parents opportunities for safe exploration, limits, alternatives, distraction, reinforcement for desirable behavior, and logical consequences for misbehavior; by contrast, 2½-year-olds also require thought-provoking questions, stories with a moral lesson, time-outs, rhyming rules, and physical punishment only as a last resort.

Books that described toddler development for parents in a comprehensive way included Leach's (1977) *Your Baby and Child,* F. Caplan and T. Caplans' (1977) *The Second Twelve Months of Life,* and Rubin et al.'s (1980) *Your Toddler.* These books presented child development norms and medical information, with the Caplan book offering a detailed month-by-month organization. Motor development and common toddler behaviors such as "testing limits," biting, and difficulties with sharing received much more attention than they did in the child development literature. Advice to parents was not organized around emotional themes, as in the psychoanalytic accounts, but rather around daily routines and common problems, such as feeding and weaning; putting the child to sleep (and nighttime waking); dressing, changing, and toilet training; limit setting and discipline; coping with family changes; responding to accidents and common illnesses; and providing toys, games, and opportunities for play with peers. Many legacies of psychoanalytic theory remained, however, such as sensitivity to the place of conflict and ambivalence to the toddler period, along with issues more properly attributed to the influence of other theories, such as highlighting symbolic thinking, language development, and the importance of active exploration and pretend play.

All of this expert advice to parents, then, provided another kind of synthesis of what has been learned in the last few decades of theorizing and research on toddler development. Moreover, though presented without much evidentiary basis, the advisory literature also integrated what the professionals believed about how parents can best deal with ordinary toddler problems, the sticking points of the daily routine, and the emotional upheavals commonly experienced.

CONCLUSIONS

The last 30 years have witnessed an explosion of new knowledge about the second and third years of life, accompanied by growing awareness of the special issues of this age period and the effects of differing parenting strategies. Toddlerhood is more and more recognized as a separate phase or stage of child development, bounded by "infancy" on the one side and "early childhood" on the other; some authorities even subdivide toddlerhood into discrete subphases, although there is no consensus on whether there are two or three subphases and what is the normative age of transition between subphases.

There is substantial agreement, however, on the developmental tasks faced during the second and third years, which include the following:

(1) learning to function independently or interdependently (at one remove from the caregiver) and beginning to help in an appropriate way as defined by family and culture with the ordinary routines of self-care and daily living.

(2) self-concept and beginning self-reflection.

(3) impulse- and self-control, the precursors to self-regulation in the absense of the caregiver.

(4) the beginnings of moral conscience, including sensitivity to the violation of standards and organized emotional themes of hurt feelings, empathy toward the plight of others, fear of punishment, guilt, shame, and desire to repair.

(5) gender identity, beginning knowledge of sex roles, and beginning preference for acting like and affiliating with others of one's gender.

(6) becoming a member of society in the sense of taking a place in the larger family grouping and in a childhood play group.

Cultures appear to differ in the age they expect mastery of these competencies by the child, their order, and how significant each is considered in defining the child's maturity. Moreover, cultures differ in whether the ultimate goal of socialization is autonomy or interdependence and whether they put upon the parent or the child the responsibility for leading the way toward the child's more self-reliant functioning.

The content areas of toddler development that have been most studied by developmental psychologists include compliance/noncompliance, moral development, gender identity, language development, and cognitive development. A great deal is now known about the descriptive details of development, for both typically and nontypically developing toddlers. Moreover, theoretical writings about the underlying processes and antecedent-consequences relations show increasing synthesis of findings across formerly separate theoretical traditions and a joining of vocabularies, as in the work on the growth of self-control and self-regulation.

Although socialization processes in the field of toddler development are by no means fully understood, standards are nevertheless higher for what is considered convincing evidence, and bidirectional, multicausational, and transactional models have become the goal. Parents are no longer made the whipping boys for all childhood disabilities and disturbed outcomes. Researchers and textbook writers have become more conservative in speculating about how socialization takes place and the lasting impacts of early experience. As a result, in advisory books and articles for parents, socialization is increasingly talked of as a two-way street, and parents' expectations for what they can (or should) accomplish through their childrearing efforts are more moderate than they were for the previous generation. Moreover, greater knowledge about many details of toddler development has translated into a greater quantity and quality of popular literature about this age period. More information has become available to parents to assist them in negotiating everyday problems, understanding their individual child's temperament, growth, and development, and reframing their child's vulnerabilities and stressful periods into "stengths" and "opportunities."

It still remains the case, however, that in spite of greater knowledge of cultural differences in childrearing and the existence of subcultural diversity within American society, the definition of good parenting assumed in the expert literature remains fairly unitary and traditional. The assumed definition complements widely shared American ideals and goals for healthy child development; the literature helps parents facilitate their child's early and continued school success, friendships with peers, self-confidence, increasing independence from one's family of origin, individuality and emotional autonomy, capacity for intimacy, pleasure in work and play, and achievement motivation. As yet there is little attention or consideration given toward what kind of toddler parenting might lead toward alternative values that may be required in future generations, such as moderated appetite for individual choices and consumer goods, lifelong interdependency with extended family, and a more calm and unhurried lifestyle with more continuity of meaningful relationships and fewer transitions and stresses on children. Perhaps these alternative questions represent areas of future inquiry: In the study of socialization, history indicates that greater knowledge inevitably creates new concerns and a questioning of assumptions that limit the validity of that knowledge.

REFERENCES

Albino, R. C., & Thompson, V. J. (1956). The effects of sudden weaning on Zulu children. *British Journal of Medical Psychology, 29*(3–4), 177–210.

Baldwin, J. M. (1897). *Social and ethical interpretations in mental development.* New York: Macmillan.

Baumrind, D. (1972). Socialization and instrumental competence in young children. In W. W. Hartup (Ed.), *The young child: Reviews of research* (Vol. 2, pp. 202–274). Washington, DC: National Association for the Education of Young Children.

Black, J. K., Puckett, M. B., & Bell, M. J. (1992). *The young child: Development from prebirth through age eight.* New York: Merrill.

Bowlby, J. (1969). *Attachment.* New York: Basic Books.

Bohannon, J. N. III, & Stanowicz, L. (1988). The issue of negative evidence: Adult responses to children's language errors. *Developmental Psychology, 24,* 684–689.

Bornstein, M. H., Vibbert, M., Tal, J. & O'Donnell, K. (1992). Toddler language and play in the second year: Stability, covariation, and influences of parenting. *First Language, 12,* 323–338.

Bradley, R. H., Caldwell, B. M., Rock, S. L., Barnard, K. E., Gray, C., Hammond, M. A., Mitchell, S., Siegel, L., Ramey, C. R., Gottfried, A. W., & Johnson, D. L. (1989). Home environment and cognitive development in the first 3 years of life: A collaborative study involving six sites and three ethnic groups in North America. *Developmental Psychology, 25,* 217–235.

Brazelton, T. B. (1974). *Toddlers and parents: A declaration of independence.* New York: Dell.

Brazelton, T. B. (1992). *Touchpoints.* Reading, MA: Addison-Wesley.

Bus, A. G., & van IJzendoorn, M. H. (1988). Mother–child interactions, attachment, and emergent literacy: A cross-sectional study. *Child Development, 59,* 1262–1272.

Caldera, Y. M., Huston, A. C., & O'Brien, M. (1989). Social interactions and play preferences of parents and toddlers with feminine, masculine, and neutral toys. *Child Development, 60,* 70–76.

Caldwell, B., & Bradley, R. (1978). *Home Observation for Measurement of the Environment: Administration Manual.* Little Rock, AR: University of Arkansas.

Caplan, F., & Caplan, T. (1977). *The second twelve months of life: A kaleidoscope of growth.* New York: Grosset & Dunlap.

Cole, M., & Cole, S. R. (1989). *The development of children.* New York: Freeman.

Crockenberg, S. C., & Litman, C. (1990). Autonomy as competence in 2-year-olds: Maternal correlates of child defiance, compliance, and self-assertion. *Developmental Psychology, 26,* 961–971.

Cross, T. G. (1978). Mothers' speech and its association with rate of language acquisition in young children. In N. Waterson & C. Snow (eds.), *The development of communication* (pp.199–216). London: Wiley.

Damon, W. (1977). *The social world of the child.* San Francisco: Jossey-Bass.

Deinstbier, R. A. (1984). The role of emotion in moral socialization. In C. Izard, J. Kagan, & R. B. Zajonc (Eds.), *Emotions, cognitions, and behaviors* (pp. 484–513). New York: Cambridge University Press.

Dowdney, L., & Pickles, A. R. (1991). Expression of negative affect within disciplinary encounters: Is there dyadic reciprocity? *Developmental Psychology, 27,* 606–617.

Duckworth, E. (1972). The having of wonderful ideas. *Harvard Education Review, 42,* 217–231.

Dubin, E. R., & Dubin, R. (1963). The authority inception period in socialization. *Child Development, 34,* 885–898.

Dunham, P., & Dunham, F. (1992). Lexical development during middle infancy: A mutually driven infant–caregiver process. *Developmental Psychology, 28,* 414–420.

Edwards, C. P.(1986). *Promoting social and moral development in young children: Creative approaches for the classroom.* New York: Teacher's College.

Edwards, C. P. (1989). The transition from infancy to early childhood: A difficult transition, and a difficult theory. In V.R. Bricker & G.H. Gossen (Eds.), *Ethnographic encounters in Southern Mesoamerica: Essays in honor of Evon Z. Vogt, Jr.* (pp. 167–175). Austin, TX: University of Texas.

Edwards, C. P. (1992). Cross-cultural perspectives on family–peer relations. In R. D. Parke & G. W. Ladd (Eds.), *Family-peer relationships: Modes of linkage* (pp.285–316). Hillsdale, NJ: Lawrence Erlbaum Associates.

Edwards, C. P. (1993). Behavioral sex differences in children of diverse cultures: The case of nurturance to infants. In M. Pereira & L. Fairbanks (Eds.), *Juveniles—Comparative socioecology* (pp. 327–338). New York: Oxford University.

Edwards, C. P., Gandini, L., & Giovannini, D. (in press). The contrasting developmental timetables of parents and preschool teachers in two cultural communities. In S. Harkness & C. Super (Eds.), *Parental cultural belief systems.* New York: Guilford.

Edwards, C. P., Gandini, L. & Forman, G. (Eds.). (1993). *The hundred languages of children: The Reggio Emilia approach to early childhood education.* Norwood, NJ: Ablex.

Edwards, C. P., & Whiting, B. B. (1993). "Mother, older sibling, and me": The overlapping roles of caregivers and companions in the social world of two- to three-year-olds in Ngeca, Kenya. In K. MacDonald (Ed.), *Parent–child play: Descriptions and implications* (pp. 305–329). Albany: State University of New York.

Emde, R.N., Biringen, Z., Clyman, R.B., & Oppenheim, D. (1991). The moral self of infancy: Affective core and procedural knowledge. *Developmental Review, 11,* 251–270.

Erikson, E. (1950). *Childhood and society.* New York: Norton.

Etaugh, C., Grinnell, K., & Etaugh, A. (1989). Development of gender labeling: Effect of age of pictured children. *Sex Roles, 21*, 769–773.

Fagot, B. I. (1985). Beyond the reinforcement principle: Another step toward understanding sex role development. *Developmental Psychology, 21*, 1097–1104.

Fagot, B. I., Hagan, R., Leinbach, M. D., & Kronsberg, S. (1985). Differential reactions to assertive and communicative acts of toddler boys and girls. *Child Development, 56*, 1499–1505.

Farver, J. M. (1993). Cultural differences in scaffolding pretend play: A comparison of American and Mexican mother–child and sibling–child pairs. In K. MacDonald (Ed.), *Parent–child play: Descriptions and implications* (pp. 349–366). Albany: State University of New York Press.

Feinman, S. (1982). Social referencing in infancy. *Merrill-Palmer Quarterly, 28*, 445–470.

Fogel, A. (1984). *Infancy: Infant, family, and society.* St. Paul: West.

Fischer, K. W. (1980). A theory of cognitive development: The control and construction of hierarchies of skills. *Psychological Review, 87*, 477–531.

Fischer, K. W., Hand, H. H., Watson, M. W., Van Parys, M. M., & Tucker, J. L. (1984). Putting the child into socialization. In L. Katz (Ed.), *Current topics in early childhood education* (Vol. 5, pp. 27–72). Norwood, NJ: Ablex.

Fowler, W. (1962). Cognitive learning in infancy and early childhood. *Psychological Bulletin, 59*, 116–152.

Fowler, W. (Ed.). (1986). *Early experience and the development of competence.* San Francisco: Jossey-Bass.

Fraiberg, S. H. (1959). *The magic years: Understanding and handling the problems of early childhood.* New York: Scribner's.

Freud, S. (1953). *Three essays on the theory of sexuality.* In J. Strachey (Ed. and Trans.), *The standard edition of the complete psychological works of Sigmund Freud* (Vol. 7, pp.125–230). London: Hogarth. (Original work published 1901–1905)

Freud, S. (1920). *A general introduction to psychoanalysis* (J. Riviere, Trans.). New York: Washington Square Press.

Freud, S. (1949). *An outline of psycho-analysis* (J. Strachey, Trans.) New York: Norton.

Gardner, H. (1978). *Developmental psychology.* Boston: Little, Brown.

Gesell, A. (1940). *The first five years of life: A guide to the study of the preschool child.* New York: Harper & Brothers.

Gewirtz, J. L. (Ed.). (1972). *Attachment and dependency.* Washington, DC: Winston.

Goldsmith, H. H., & Campos, J. J. (1986). Fundamental issues in the study of early temperament: The Denver Twin Temperament Study. In M. E. Lamb, A. L. Brown, & B. Rogoff (Eds.), *Advances in developmental psychology* (Vol. 4, pp. 231–283). Hillsdale, NJ: Lawrence Erlbaum Associates.

Greenfield, P. M., Brazelton, T. B., & Childs, C. P. (1989). From birth to maturity in Zinacantan: Ontogenesis in cultural context. In V. R. Bricker & G. H. Gossen (Eds.), *Ethnographic encounters in Southern Mesoamerica: Essays in honor of Evon Z. Vogt, Jr.* (pp. 177–216). Austin, TX: University of Texas.

Greenspan, S., & Greenspan, N. T. (1985). *First feelings.* New York: Viking.

Harkness, S., & Super, C. M. (1983). The cultural construction of child development: A framework for the socialization of affect. *Ethos, 11*, 221–231.

Hubley, P., & Trevarthen, C. (1979). Sharing a task in infancy. In I. E. Ugiris (Ed.), *Social interaction and communication during infancy* (pp. 57–80). San Francisco: Jossey-Bass.

Hunt, J. M. (1961). *Intelligence and experience.* New York: Ronald Press.

Huttenlocher, J., Haight, W., Bryk, A., Seltzer, M., & Lyons, T. (1991). Early vocabulary growth: Relation to language input and gender. *Developmental Psychology, 27*, 236–248.

Kagan, J. (1971). *Change and continuity in infancy.* New York: Wiley.

Kagan, J. (1981). *The second year: The emergence of self-awareness.* Cambridge, MA: Harvard University Press.

Kagan, J. (1992). Yesterday's premises, tomorrow's promises. *Developmental Psychology, 28*, 990–997.

Kaler, S. R., & Kopp, C. (1990). Compliance and comprehension in very young toddlers. *Child Development, 61*, 1997–2003.

Kaye, K. (1982). *The mental and social life of babies.* Chicago: University of Chicago.

Kitayama, S., & Markus, H. R. (1994). *Emotion and culture.* Washington, DC: American Psychological Association.

Kochanska, G. (1991). Socialization and temperament in the development of guilt and conscience. *Child Development, 62*, 250–263.

Kochanska, G. (1993). Toward a synthesis of parental socialization and child temperament in early development of conscience. *Child Development, 64*, 325–347.

Kohlberg, L. (1966). A cognitive-developmental analysis of children's sex-role concepts and attitudes. In E. E. Maccoby (Ed.), *The development of sex differences* (pp. 82–173). Stanford, CA: Stanford University Press.

Kohlberg, L. (1969). Stage and sequence: The cognitive developmental approach to socialization. In D. A. Goslin (Ed.), *Handbook of socialization theory and research* (pp. 347–480). Chicago: Rand McNally.

Kopp, C. B. (1982). The antecedents of self-regulation: A developmental perspective. *Developmental Psychology, 18*, 199–214.

Kopp, C. B. (1992). Emotional distress and control in young children. In N. Eisenberg & R. A. Fabes (Eds.), *Emotion and its regulation in early development* (pp. 41–56). San Francisco: Jossey-Bass.

Kuczynski, L., & Kochanska, G. (1990). Development of children's noncompliance strategies from toddlerhood to age 5. *Developmental Psychology, 26*, 398–408.

Kuczynski, L., Kochanska, G., Radke-Yarrow, M., & Girnius-Brown, O. (1987). A developmental interpretation of young children's noncompliance. *Developmental Psychology, 23*, 799–806.

Kuczynski, L., Zahn-Waxler, C., & Radke-Yarrow, M. (1987). Development and content of imitation in the second and third years of life: A socialization perspective. *Developmental Psychology, 23,* 276–282.

Ladd, G. W., Profilet, S. M., & Hart, C. H. (1992). Parents' management of children's peer relations. In R. D. Parke & G. W. Ladd (Eds.), *Family-peer relationships: Modes of linkage* (pp. 215–281). Hillsdale, NJ: Lawrence Erlbaum Associates.

Leach, P. (1977). *Your baby & child: From birth to age five.* New York: Knopf.

Lewis, M., & Brooks-Gunn, J. (1979). *Social cognition and the acquisition of self.* New York: Plenum.

Lewis, M., Sullivan, M., Stranger, C., & Weiss, M. (1989). Self development and self-conscious emotions. *Child Development, 60,* 146–156.

Lickona, T. (1983). *Raising good children.* New York: Bantam.

Lytton, H. (1979). Disciplinary encounters between young boys and their mothers: Is there a contingency system? *Developmental Psychology, 15,* 256–268.

Maccoby, E. E. (1988). Gender as a social category. *Developmental Psychology, 24,* 755–765.

Maccoby, E. E. (1992). The role of parents in the socialization of children: An historical overview. *Developmental Psychology, 28,* 1006–1017.

Maccoby, E. E., & Martin, J. A. (1983). Socialization in the context of the family: Parent–child interaction. In P. H. Mussen (Series Ed.) & E. M. Hetherington (Vol. Ed.), *Handbook of child psychology: Vol. 4. Socialization, personality, and social development* (pp. 1–101). New York: Wiley.

Mahler, M., Pine, F., & Bergman, A. (1975). *The psychological birth of the human infant.* New York: Basic Books.

Main, M., & George, C. (1985). Responses of abused and disadvantaged toddlers to distress in agemates: A study in the day care setting. *Developmental Psychology, 21,* 407–412.

McCall, R. B. (1981). Nature–nurture and two realms of development: A proposed integration with respect to mental development. *Child Development, 52,* 1–12.

McCall, R. B., Eichorn, D. H., & Hogarty, P. S. (1977). Transitions in early mental development. *Monographs of the Society for Research in Child Development, 42* (Serial No. 150).

Mueller, E. C., & Cohen, D. (1986). Peer therapies and the little latency: A clinical perspective. In E. C. Mueller & C. R. Cooper (Eds.), *Process and outcome in peer relations* (pp. 161–183). New York: Academic Press.

Mussen, P. H., Conger, J. J., Kagan, J. & Huston, A. C. (1990). *Child development and personality* (7th ed.). New York: Harper & Row.

Ochs, E., & Schieffelin, B. B. (1984). Language acquisition and socialization. In R. A. Shweder & R. A. LeVine (Eds.), *Culture theory: Essays on mind, self, and emotion* (pp. 276–320). New York: Cambridge University Press.

Papalia, D. E., & Olds, S. W. (1987). *A child's world: Infancy through adolescence.* New York: McGraw-Hill.

Parpal, M., & Maccoby, E. E. (1985). Maternal responsiveness and subsequent child compliance. *Child Development, 56,* 1326–1334.

Parke, R. D., Cassidy, J., Burks, V. M., Carson, J. L., & Boyum, L. (1992). Familial contributions to peer competence among young children: The role of interactive and affective processes. In R.D. Parke & G. W. Ladd (Eds.), *Family–peer relationships: Modes of linkage* (pp. 107–134). Hillsdale, NJ: Lawrence Erlbaum Associates.

Patterson, G.R. (1982). *Coercive family process.* Eugene, OR: Castalia Press.

Piaget, J. (1952). *The origins of intelligence in children.* New York: International Universities Press.

Power, T. G., & Chapieski, M. L. (1986). Childrearing and impulse control in toddlers: A naturalistic investigation. *Developmental Psychology, 22,* 271–275.

Reingold, H. (1982). Little children's participation in the work of adults: A nascent prosocial behavior. *Child Development, 53,* 114–125.

Reingold, H., Cook, K., & Kolowitz, V. (1987). Commands activate the behavior and pleasure of 2-year-old children. *Developmental Psychology, 23,* 146–151.

Rice, M. L. (1989). Children's language acquisition. *American Psychologist, 44,* 149–156.

Rogoff, B., Mistry, J., Goncu, A., & Mosier, C. (1991). Cultural variation in the role relations of toddlers and their families. In M. H. Bornstein (Ed.), *Cultural approaches to parenting* (pp. 173–183). Hillsdale, NJ: Lawrence Erlbaum Associates.

Rogoff, B., Mistry, J., Goncu, A., & Mosier, C. (1993). Guided participation in cultural activity by toddlers and caregivers. *Monographs of the Society for Research in Child Development, 58*(8, Serial No. 236).

Rubin, R. R., Fisher, J. J. III, & Doering, S. G. (1980). *Your toddler: Ages 1 and 2.* New York: Macmillan.

Sander, L. W. (1962). Issues in early mother–child interaction. *Journal of the American Academy of Child Psychiatry, 1,* 141–166.

Scarr, S. (1992). Developmental theories for the 1990s: Development and individual differences. *Child Development, 63,* 1–19.

Schickedanz, J. A., Schickedanz, D. I., Hansen, K., & Forsyth, P. D. (1993). *Understanding children* (2nd ed.). Mountain View, CA: Mayfield.

Schieffelin, B. B., & Ochs, E. (1986). *Language socialization across cultures.* Cambridge: Cambridge University Press.

Schneider-Rosen, K., & Wenz-Gross, M. (1990). Patterns of compliance from eighteen to thirty months of age. *Child Development, 61,* 104–112.

Seifert, K. L., & Hoffnung, R. J. (1989). *Child and adolescent development.* Boston: Houghton Mifflin.

Sigel, I. E. (1986). Early social experience and the development of representational competence. In W. Fowler (Ed.), *Early experience and the development of competence* (pp. 49–65). San Francisco: Jossey-Bass.

Sigman, M., Neumann, C., Carter, E., Cattle, D. J., D'Souza, S. D., & Bwibo, N. (1988). Home interactions and the development of Embu toddlers in Kenya. *Child Development, 59*, 1251–1261.

Slade, A. (1987). A longitudinal study of maternal involvement and symbolic play during the toddler period. *Child Development, 58*, 367–375.

Smolak, L., & Weinraub, M. (1983). Maternal speech: Strategy or response? *Journal of Child Language, 10*, 369–380.

Spitz, R. A. (1957). *No and yes: On the genesis of human communication*. New York: International Universities Press.

Spitz, R. (1965). *The first year of life*. New York: International Universities Press.

Sroufe, L.A. (1979). Socioemotional development. In J. Osofsky (Ed.), *Handbook of infant development* (pp. 462–516). New York: Wiley.

Stipek, D., Recchia, S., & McClintic, S. (1992). Self-evaluation in young children. *Monographs of the Society for Research in Child Development, 57*(1, Serial No. 226).

Stone, L. J., & Church, J. (1973). *Childhood and adolescence: A psychology of the growing person* (3rd ed.). New York: Random House.

Super, C. M., & Harkness, S. (1986). The developmental niche: A conceptualization at the interface of child and culture. *International Journal of Behavioral Development, 9*, 545–569.

Valdez-Menchaca, M.C., & Whitehurst, G.J. (1988). The effects of incidental teaching on vocabulary acquisition by young children. *Child Development, 59*, 1451–1459.

Vygotsky, L. S. (1962). *Thought and language*. Cambridge, MA: MIT Press.

Vygotsky, L. S. (1978). *Mind in society: The development of higher psychological processes*. Cambridge, MA: Harvard University Press.

Wachs, T. D. (1982). Early experience and early cognitive development: The search for specificity. In I. U giris & J. Hunt (Eds.), *Research with scales of psychological development in infancy* . Champaign, IL: University of Illinois Press.

Wachs, T. D., & Gruen, G. E. (1982). *Early experience and human development*. New York: Plenum.

Weinraub, M., Clemens, L. P., Sockloff, A., Ethridge, T., Gracely, E., & Myers, B. (1984). The development of sex role stereotypes in the third year: Relationships to gender labeling, gender identity, sex-typed toy preference, and family characteristics. *Child Development, 55*, 1493–1503.

Weisner, T. (1989a). Cultural and universal aspects of social support for children: Evidence from the Abaluyia of Kenya. In D. Belle (Ed.), *Children's social networks and social supports* (pp. 70–90). New York: Wiley.

Weisner, T. (1989b). Comparing sibling relationships across cultures. In P. G. Zukow (Ed.), *Sibling interaction across cultures* (pp. 11–22). New York: Springer-Verlag.

Weisner, T. (1993). Overview: Sibling similarity and difference in different cultures. In C. W. Nuckolls (Ed.), *Siblings in South Asia* (pp. 1–18). New York: Guilford.

Weitzman, N., Birns, B., & Friend, R. (1985). Traditional and nontraditional mothers' communication with their daughters and sons. *Child Development, 56*, 894–898.

Wenar, C. (1982). On negativism. *Human Development, 25*, 1–23.

Westerman, M. A. (1990). Coordination of maternal directives with preschoolers' behavior in compliance-problem and healthy dyads. *Developmental Psychology, 26*, 621–630.

Whiting, B. B. (1980). Culture and social behavior: A model for the development of social behavior. *Ethos, 8*, 95–116.

Whiting, B. B. (1983). The genesis of prosocial behavior. In D. L. Bridgeman (Ed.), *The nature of prosocial development: Interdisciplinary theories and strategies* (pp. 221–242). New York: Academic.

Whiting, B. B., & Edwards, C. P. (1988) *Children of different worlds: The formation of social behavior.* Cambridge, MA: Harvard University.

Wood, D., Bruner, J., & Ross, G. (1976). The role of tutoring in problem-solving. *Journal of Child Psychology and Psychiatry, 17*, 89–100.

Zahn-Waxler, C., Radke-Yarrow, M., & King, R. A. (1979). Child-rearing and children's prosocial initiations toward victims in distress. *Child Development, 50*, 319–330.

Zahn-Waxler, C., Radke-Yarrow, M., Wagner, E., & Chapman, M. (1992). Development of concern for others. *Developmental Psychology, 28*, 126–136.

3

Parenting During Middle Childhood

W. Andrew Collins
Michael L. Harris
Amy Susman
Institute of Child Development, University of Minnesota

INTRODUCTION

Parents of children between the ages of 6 and 12—the period commonly referred to as middle childhood—face challenges arising from both maturational changes in the children themselves and from socially imposed constraints, opportunities, and demands impinging on them. Children in diverse societies enter a wider social world at about age 6 and begin to determine their own experiences, including their contacts with particular others, to a greater degree than previously. In the years before adolescence, transitions occur in physical maturity, cognitive abilities and learning, the diversity and impact of relationships with others, and access to new settings, opportunities, and demands. These changes inevitably alter the amount, kind, content, and impact of interactions between parents and children. This chapter addresses the question of how the distinctive challenges and achievements of middle childhood affect parent–child relationships and the processes of socialization that occur within families.

The chapter includes five main sections. The first section provides a brief overview of historical considerations in the study of parenting of 6- to 12-year-olds. The second section outlines key normative changes in children that affect parenting during middle childhood. The third section reviews changes in parent–child relationships in which parenting issues are embedded. The fourth section distills findings from research on the question of what issues of parenting and of parent–child relationships are especially linked to the distinctive changes of the period. These include adapting processes of control, fostering self-management and responsibility, facilitating positive relationships outside of the family, and maintaining contacts with schools and other out-of-home settings. The concluding section underscores the key themes from research and notes persistent questions about the distinctiveness of parenting during middle childhood.

HISTORICAL CONSIDERATIONS

In diverse cultures, early middle childhood historically marked a major shift in children's relationships with adults. The age of 6 or 7 was the time at which children were absorbed into the world of adults, helping to shoulder family responsibilities and working alongside their elders. Well into the eighteenth century in Western nations, many children left home by the age of 6 or 7 to work as servants in other households (Aries, 1962). Thus, if children remained at home, their parents became more like supervisors or overseers; if children entered service, adults other than their parents assumed these primary roles. The assumption that children were capable of tasks now largely reserved for adults was consistent with a general attitude toward forcing infants and young children toward behavioral rectitude and submissiveness to authority (see French, in this *Handbook*).

In recent times, changing concepts of the family and the advent of formal schooling removed children of this age from wide participation in adult society. In industrialized nations today, 6- to 12-year-old children have continued to be set apart from younger ages because they correspond to the first segment of the compulsory school years. Schooling provides a distinctive social definition of children and social structures that constrain and channel development during this period. This secular change has meant that rather than taking on adult responsibilities, as was the case in earlier periods, middle childhood primarily is concerned with preparation for eventual responsibility. Children's preparation for adulthood is conducted not only by parents, but also by institutions and persons outside of the family. Thus, the central contemporary issue of parenting during middle childhood is how parents most effectively adjust their interactions, cognitions, and affectional behavior to the changing characteristics of children, in order to maintain appropriate influence and guidance during age-graded transitions toward greater autonomy (Collins, 1992). The next section outlines these normative changes and some implications for parent–child relationships.

NORMATIVE CHANGES IN CHILDREN DURING MIDDLE CHILDHOOD

To most parents in industrialized societies, middle childhood is less distinctive as a period of development than infancy, toddlerhood, or adolescence. The age period of 6 to 12 is nevertheless universally set apart by major transition points in human development. This section briefly reviews changes in children that set the stage for changes in parenting during middle childhood.

Changes in Children

Normative changes during middle childhood result both from maturation and socially prescribed transitions. These changes include cognitive competence and the growth of knowledge, transitions in social contexts and relationships, increased vulnerability to stress, altered functions of the self, and self-regulation and social responsibility.

Cognitive competence and the growth of knowledge. Cognitive changes greatly expand capacities for solving problems and gaining necessary information to become increasingly competent and resourceful. For parents, changes in cognitive competence necessitate alterations ranging from the content of conversations, strategies for control and influence over children's behavior, and expectations regarding competence and self-regulation.

Three characteristic changes of middle childhood are noteworthy. One is a growing ability to reason in terms of abstract representations of objects and events. For children younger than 5 to 7 years, cognition characteristically involves limitations on the number of objects that can be thought about at one time, and systematic or abstract reasoning is relatively rare (Edwards, in this *Handbook*). Most children gain capacities between ages 6 and 9 that enable them to reason effectively about increasingly complex problems and circumstances; and, by 10 to 12 years, children begin to show increased abilities for generalizing across concrete instances and for systematic problem solving and reasoning (Fischer & Bullock, 1984). Second, children begin to organize tasks more maturely and independently than in early childhood (Brown, Bransford, Ferrara, & Campione, 1983; Siegler, 1989). This more systematic behavior entails adopting goals for activities, subordinating knowledge and actions in the service of a superordinate plan, and monitoring one's own activities and mental processes. Third, increases occur in both the opportunity and the capacity for acquiring information and for using new knowledge in reasoning, thinking, problem solving, and action (Carey, 1985; Chi, Glaser, & Rees, 1982). Compared to younger children, 6- to 12-year-olds thus can solve more difficult, abstract intellectual problems in school and can master increased, more complex responsibilities at home and in other common settings.

These cognitive expansions are accompanied by increased challenges to integrate knowledge and abilities for understanding self and others, relationships, communities, and societies. A primary achievement of middle childhood is the ability to adopt the perspectives of others, which facilitates recognition of possible reasons for others' actions and reactions (Dunn & Slomkowski, 1992; Selman, 1980). This ability underlies increasingly greater social competence during middle childhood, including skills for describing and explanations of conditions and events that can be comprehended by others (e.g., Whitehurst & Sonnenschein, 1981), for deception and for detecting deception in others (e.g., DePaulo, Jordan, Irvine, & Laser, 1982), and for more differentiated predictions about the behavior of other children (e.g., Droege & Stipek, 1993). In addition, knowledge and understanding of social roles expand. Gender-role concepts increase in complexity (Serbin, Powlishta, & Gulko, 1993), and concepts of parent–child relationships move toward notions of mutual caring and responsibility, rather than focusing on children's dependency and parents' gratification of children's needs (Selman, 1980). A further implication is that 6- to 12- year-olds attain greater understanding of such fundamental life experiences as conception, illness, and death (Bibace & Walsh, 1981; Campbell, 1975; Lazar & Torney-Purta, 1991).

These achievements underlie distinctive patterns of behavior and responsiveness during middle childhood and, consequently, alter the demands on parents. As an example, parents typically must provide more elaborate and compelling explanations and justifications in order to have the same degree of impact that, in earlier years, could be achieved by distracting or admonishing a child.

Social contexts and relationships.   Six- to 12-year-olds experience a rapidly widening social world. Social *networks* expand significantly during middle childhood, incorporating extrafamilial adults and peers. In particular, middle-childhood experiences exert considerable pressure to develop capacities for creating and maintaining connections with peers (Hartup, 1984, 1989; Higgins & Parsons, 1983; Ladd & Le Sieur, in this *Handbook*). Entry into school especially increases the number and kinds of developmental tasks and influences that children encounter. For parents, these experiences outside of the family often create additional burdens and responsibilities for monitoring children's activities and choices of companions at a distance and for facilitating positive behavior and development.

Whereas families are the primary contexts for children's exchanges with others during infancy and early childhood, 6- to 12-year-olds spend less time in the company of adults and family members, relative to peers and other adults outside of the family. The shifts are most pronounced between the ages of 6 and 9. (Not until early adolescence, however, do contacts with peers, rather than those with adults, dominate social networks; Feiring & Lewis, 1991a, 1991b; Holmbeck, Paikoff, & Brooks-Gunn, in this *Handbook*).

The need for *social support* from a variety of others, moreover, is more apparent in middle childhood than in earlier years. Contrary to stereotypes, perceptions of parents as sources of both emotional support and instrumental help typically remain stable across age groups during middle childhood (Hunter & Youniss, 1982). At the same time, 6- to 12-year-olds identify distinctive social needs served by different persons in their networks (Furman & Buhrmester, 1992; Reid, Landesman, Treder, & Jaccard, 1989; Zarbatany, Hartmann, & Rankin, 1990). To maintain these extended networks, children must learn to cooperate on more complex tasks and to work in groups over which adults exercise less oversight (Berndt, 1981; Brady, Newcomb, & Hartup, 1983). By ages 10 to 12, children become notably more skilled in using goal-directed planful strategies to initiate, maintain, and cooperate within peer relationships. One implication of these skills is greater ability to manage conflicts with peers (Parker & Gottman, 1989; Selman & Schultz, 1989). Consequently, parents may spend less time in direct management of peer relations. Children who do not gain these skills are at a disadvantage for optimal social development and at risk for a variety of later problems (Parker & Asher, 1987).

Peer relationships play an increasingly complementary role to that of parents during middle childhood (Hartup, 1984). Perceptions of peers as sources of intimacy increase with age. Although parental and peer influences work in the same direction for most children, peers often provide experience in areas in which families can have limited impact, especially in situations requiring an understanding of give-and-take with others of equal power and status (e.g., collaborative tasks). For the most part, parental and peer influences are reciprocal: The family system provides children with basic skills for smooth, successful peer relationships; and children may bring to their families from their peer groups knowledge, expectations, and behavioral tactics that foster parents' adaptations to the characteristics of a rapidly maturing child (Hartup, 1979; Youniss, 1980).

Schools typically provide increasing opportunities and challenges for peer relations and self-management. Classrooms, playgrounds, and school buses are primary settings for peer interactions and greater opportunities for more diverse contacts than children would otherwise encounter (Hartup, 1984). At the same time, structural changes in school environments may complicate tasks of forming and maintaining stable relationships with peers (Eccles et al., 1993; Epstein, 1989). For example, the social field for children initially is the classroom, and most interactions are only with one teacher; whereas in the later grades, the entire school is the social field, with multiple teachers, classrooms, and common spaces (Minuchin & Shapiro, 1983). For parents, monitoring of school experiences may become more difficult as the number of teachers and settings increases. In addition, many parents must arrange for and interact with out-of-home child-care personnel and with adults who provide instruction and supervision in out-of-school learning and recreational settings (Collins, 1984; Honig, in this *Handbook*). Clearly, the transitions of middle childhood generate new tasks for parents, as well as developmental challenges for children.

Vulnerability to stress.   Parenting during middle childhood is exacerbated by an increase in risks and stressors for children during middle childhood, relative to early childhood. Although children between ages 6 and 12 are generally the healthiest segment of the population in industrialized countries (Shonkoff, 1984), for many the physical transitions of middle childhood and the secular trend toward earlier puberty hasten exposure to some of the health risks of adulthood. Accidents, the major cause of death during childhood, increase at this time. During the past decade, tobacco, alcohol, and other drug use have become more common for children in the middle-childhood age group (Shonkoff, 1984).

The risk of exposure to violence during middle childhood is increasing as well (Lorion & Saltzman, 1993; Osofsky, Wewers, Hann, & Fick, 1993; Richters & Martinez, 1993). Children's perceptions of violence in their communities are correlated positively with their reports of fearfulness, distress, and depression at home and at school (Bell & Jenkins, 1993; Martinez & Richters, 1993; Osofsky et al., 1993). Furthermore, exposure to violence and victimization at home is associated with a variety of emotional and behavior problems and diminished school performance (Emery, 1989). Recent studies show the risk of exposure to violence to be as great for 6- to 8-year-olds as for 10- to 12-year-olds. The ready availability of weapons to individuals of all ages increases the likelihood of being a victim or perpetrator of violence during the middle childhood years.

Six- to 12-year-olds generally may be vulnerable to different stressors than children of other ages (Compas, 1987; Garmezy, 1983; Maccoby, 1983, 1984). For example, these children generally are less distressed by short-term separations from parents than are younger children, but grieve more intensely and over a longer period of time over the death of a parent (Rutter, 1983). Certain resources for coping with stress, moreover, may be more readily available to 6- to 12-year-olds than to younger children. Among these are greater knowledge of strategies for coping with uncontrollable stress, which may modulate the degree of children's vulnerability (Altshuler & Ruble, 1989; Compas, 1987; Maccoby, 1983), and availability of social support (Dubow & Tisak, 1989; Dubow, Tisak, Causey, Hryshko, & Reid, 1991).

Parents may play a role by monitoring the degree of risk associated with school and neighborhood settings and imposing appropriate safety measures, including training children to respond to high-risk situations. Furthermore, parents are critical sources of social support to children in coping with risky, threatening conditions. Children's perceptions that persons are available with whom they can talk, discuss problems, and so forth have been found to help children cope with the stress of multiple personal and social changes during middle childhood and the transition to adolescence (Dubow & Tisak, 1989; Dubow et al., 1991; Hirsch & Rapkin, 1987).

Development of self-concept, self-regulation, and social responsibility. Children's descriptions of themselves become more stable and more comprehensive in middle childhood (Damon & Hart, 1988). This shift partly reflects the growth of cognitive concepts and awareness of cultural norms and expectations for performance. In addition, self-evaluation intensifies as exposure to more varied persons and social contexts stimulates comparisons between self and others and provides evaluative feedback about characteristics, skills, and abilities (Higgins & Parsons, 1983; Markus & Nurius, 1984). The role of parents in these processes is discussed further later.

Linked to changing concepts of self are greater capacities for self-control and self-regulation. For most children, impulsive behavior declines steadily from early childhood into middle childhood (Maccoby, 1984). To attain mature self-regulatory capacities, however, also requires knowledge of the self, emotions, and cognitive capacities to redirect attention and focus on long-term goals and to take account of others' views and needs (Markus & Nurius, 1984). Parents contribute to the development of capacities for self-regulation by exposing children to standards of conduct and models of socially valued behaviors and by providing rewards and punishments in accord with those standards (Brody & Shaffer, 1982). Furthermore, parents can stimulate cognitive components of self-regulation through discussion and reasoning that invoke principles for discerning right from wrong and that emphasize the consequences of transgressions (Chapman & McBride, 1992; Dunn & Slomkowski, 1992; Eisenberg & Murphy, in this *Handbook*; Walker & Taylor, 1991).

Increasing self-regulation potentially affects many aspects of parenting during middle childhood. Parents ordinarily expect more autonomy and independence in tasks at school and at home, including peer-group activities (Hartup, 1984). Parents gradually allow children to assume more responsibility for interacting with health care personnel and for mastering and acting on information and instructions about medication, specific health practices, and evolving lifestyle issues with implications for physical and mental well-being (Shonkoff, 1984). These transitions lay the groundwork for greater autonomy in adolescence and young adulthood.

NORMATIVE CHANGES IN PARENT–CHILD RELATIONSHIPS

Concurrent with these individual changes of middle childhood are characteristic patterns of parent–child interactions and relationships that distinguish this period from earlier and later years of life.

Interactions and Affective Expression

Interactions between parents and children become less frequent in middle childhood. Parents are with children less than half as much as before the beginning of school (Hill & Stafford, 1980). This decline in time together is relatively greater for parents with lower levels of education.

Overt *affection* by parents (Baldwin, 1946; Roberts, J. H. Block, & J. Block, 1984) and by children (J. Newson & E. Newson, 1968, 1976) also decreases during middle childhood. Children report that parents are less accepting toward them during the later years of middle childhood (Armentrout & Burger, 1972). Although this finding is sometimes attributed to decreased warmth toward children in middle childhood than in early childhood (e.g., Baldwin, 1946), a more likely explanation is that displays of warmth less often involve physical expressions of affection as children mature. For example, longitudinal data (Roberts et al., 1984) show that, despite a decrease between ages 3 and 12 in displays of physical affection, parents report little change in their enjoyment of parenting, having positive regard for their child, or having respect for the child's opinions and preferences.

Parents and children alike are less likely to display and experience negative emotions in these interactions. Emotional outbursts, such as temper tantrums, and coercive behaviors of children toward other family members ordinarily begin to decline in early childhood (Goodenough, 1931; J. Newson & E. Newson, 1968, 1976; Patterson, 1982). This trend continues during middle childhood, and the frequency of disciplinary encounters also decreases steadily between the ages of 3 and 9 (Clifford, 1959). Nevertheless, several emotional characteristics of interactions with 6- to 12-year-olds may complicate parents' management of their relationships with children. Compared to preschool children, 6- to 12-year-olds are more likely to sulk, become depressed, avoid parents, or engage in passive noncooperation with their parents (Clifford, 1959). Furthermore, children become increasingly likely to attribute conflicts with parents to the inadequacy of parental helping behaviors, disappointment in the frequency of parent–child interactions, and, in preadolescence, to perceive failures to fulfill parent-role expectations and a lack of consensus on familial and societal values (Fisher & Johnson, 1990).

Mother–child and father–child relationships. Some aspects of relationships are differentiated by gender. In general, mothers and children spend more time together than do fathers and children (Parke, in this *Handbook*; G. Russell & A. Russell, 1987). When both parents and child are together, however, mothers and fathers initiate interaction with children with equal frequency (Noller, 1980; G. Russell & A. Russell, 1987); and children's initiations toward each parent are similar (G. Russell & A. Russell, 1987). As in early life, fathers are relatively more involved in physical/outdoor play interactions, whereas mothers report more frequent interactions involving caregiving and household tasks. In observational studies with both parents present, though, fathers and mothers engaged in caregiving to a similar degree.

Both positive and negative emotional expressions and conflictual interactions are more likely in mother–child than in father–child interactions (Bronstein, 1984; G. Russell & A. Russell, 1987). This may reflect the greater amount of time and greater diversity of shared activities involving mothers. There is some indication that interactions with sons are more affectively marked than those with daughters, although whether these emotions are relatively more positive or negative is inconsistent across studies (Bronstein, 1984; Margolin & Patterson, 1975; Noller, 1980; G. Russell & A. Russell, 1987; Salt, 1991).

Several differences commonly expected for interactions with mothers and with fathers have not been supported by research results. In Roberts et al.'s (1984) longitudinal study, for example, both mothers and fathers reported increased attention to school achievement and homework during middle childhood. Furthermore, studies of parental reinforcements for instances of behaviors such as competitiveness, autonomous achievement, or competence in cognitive or play activities generally show negligible differences between mothers and fathers (Bronstein, 1984; G. Russell & A. Russell, 1987). Collins and G. Russell (1991) argued that few parental differences emerge in middle childhood. Furthermore, alterations in complementarity between mother–child and father–child relationships are more likely to be occur during adolescence than during middle childhood (see Holmbeck, Paikoff, & Brooks-Gunn, in this *Handbook*).

Mutual cognition. Parents' and children's cognitions about each other and about issues of mutual relevance also change during middle childhood, especially the latter part of the period. Most studies indicate relative congruity in the perceptions of 10- to 11-year-olds and their parents concerning matters in which parents' authority is legitimate (Smetana, 1989), whereas incongruity becomes more likely during adolescence. Even in late middle childhood (roughly, 10–12 years of age), however, significant cognitive disparities occur. Alessandri and Wozniak (1987) found that 10- to 11-year-olds perceive their parents' beliefs about them less accurately than do 15- to 16-year-olds. In a 2-year follow-up study (Alessandri & Wozniak, 1989), the congruency of perceptions between parents and children in the younger group (now age 12–13) had increased, whereas the perceptions of members of the older age group (age 17–18) and their parents had not become more congruent. Perhaps characteristics of children during middle childhood stimulate a process of changing expectancies about children's behavior that continues into the adolescent years.

The degree to which parents and children maintain mutual patterns of cognitions may influence the course of their relationship during the middle childhood years. Maccoby (1984; Maccoby & Martin, 1983) speculated that mutual cognitions are more significant determinants of relationship qualities in middle childhood than in earlier periods. By the time a child reaches middle childhood, shared experiences have created extensive expectancies about the probable reactions of both parents and children. These expectancies then guide each person's behavior in interactions with the other.

To summarize, changes in parent–child relationships create new paradigms for interaction that affect when and how parents will respond to the behavior of children during middle childhood. Although partly resulting from adaptations to developmental changes that have already occurred, these relational patterns also affect responses to further changes during and beyond middle childhood. The next section examines findings from research on parenting of 6- to 12-year-olds.

RESEARCH ON PARENTING DURING MIDDLE CHILDHOOD

Developmental changes in children and parallel alterations in relationships between parents and children raise the question of whether middle childhood is a distinctive period of parenting. This section addresses two related questions: What distinctive tasks devolve parents during the middle childhood years, and what characteristics of effective parenting have emerged in studies of 6- to 12-year-olds?

Research findings on four central issues of parenting entailed by the developmental changes of middle childhood are examined: adapting control processes, fostering self-management and a sense of responsibility, facilitating positive relationships with others, and managing experiences in extrafamilial settings.

Adapting Control Processes

Changes in interactions between parents and children, together with age-graded activities and experiences, necessitate different strategies for exerting influence over children's behavior (Maccoby, 1984). These strategies may involve different disciplinary practices than in early childhood, more extensive use of shared regulation of children's behavior, and altered patterns for effective control.

Disciplinary practices. Parenting young children typically involves distraction and physically assertive strategies for preventing harm and gaining compliance. In middle childhood, however, parents report less frequent physical punishment and increasing use of techniques such as deprivation of privileges, appeals to children's self-esteem or sense of humor, arousal of children's sense of guilt, and reminders that children are responsible for what happens to them (Clifford, 1959; J. Newson & E. Newson, 1976; Roberts et al., 1984). These techniques may reflect changes in parents' attributions about the degree to which children should be expected to have control over their behavior and also a greater tendency to regard misbehavior as deliberate intent and, thus, as warranting both parental anger and punishment (Dix, Ruble, Grusec, & Nixon, 1986).

Maccoby (1984) speculated that children's responses to parents' control attempts during middle childhood are affected by changes in children's concepts of the basis for parental authority. Whereas preschoolers view parental authority as resting on the power to punish or reward, children in early middle childhood increasingly believe parental authority derives from all the things that parents do for them. After about age 8, parents' expert knowledge and skill also are seen as reasons to submit to their authority (Braine, Pomerantz, Lorber, & Krantz, 1991; Damon, 1977). Consequently, Maccoby (1984) speculated that parental appeals based on fairness, the return of favors, or reminders of the parents' greater knowledge and experience may increase in effectiveness during middle childhood, with parents less often feeling compelled to resort to promises of reward or threats of punishment. This line of reasoning implies that, during middle childhood, parents may find it easier to follow the disciplinary practices that have been found most effective in fostering patterns of self-regulated, socially responsible behavior, namely, an emphasis on the implications of children's actions for others (*induction*), rather than on use of parents' superior power to coerce compliance (Hoffman, 1970; Saltzstein, 1976).

Co-regulation.   Decreasing face-to-face interactions during middle childhood put additional pressures on parents' strategies for exerting control over children's behavior. Different methods are appropriate because of the age and capabilities of children and also because children must be trained to regulate their own behavior for longer periods of time. At the same time, children's increased capabilities for planfulness and goal-directedness and for more effective communication of plans and wishes to parents permit greater collaboration on mutually acceptable plans and more effective monitoring through conversations about children's activities (Ainsworth, 1989; Maccoby, 1984). Maccoby (1984) specified the responsibilities of both parents and children in their cooperative process:

> First, [parents] must monitor, guide, and support their children at a distance—that is, when the children are out of their presence; second, they must effectively use the times when direct contact does occur; and third, they must strengthen in their children the abilities that will allow them to monitor their own behavior, to adopt acceptable standards of good and bad behavior, to avoid undue risks, and to know when they need parental support or guidance. Children must be willing to inform parents of their whereabouts, activities, and problems so that parents can mediate and guide when necessary; parents must keep informed about events occurring outside their presence and must coordinate agendas that link the daily activities of parents and child. (pp. 191–192)

Effective control in middle childhood.   Maccoby's formulation implies that effective parental control processes are tantamount to training of skills for self-regulation. A key component of effective control is parental *monitoring*, which requires careful attention to children's behavior and associated contingencies. Monitoring is integral to *child-centered* control techniques, in which parents exert influence by sensitively fitting their behavior to behavioral cues from children, rather than allowing the parents' own needs to drive parent–child interactions (Maccoby & Martin, 1983). Ineffective parental monitoring repeatedly has been linked to antisocial behavior in middle childhood and adolescence (Patterson, 1982, 1986; Pulkinnen, 1982; Tolan & Loeber, 1993).

The effectiveness of monitoring, however, depends on the parents' general style of control. The outcomes for children appear to be most positive when parents practice child-centered patterns of discipline, accompanied by clearly communicated demands, parental monitoring, and an atmosphere of acceptance toward the child (authoritative parenting; Baumrind, 1989; Maccoby, 1984; Maccoby & Martin, 1983). For example, attentive, responsive care appears to be positively linked to the development of self-esteem, competence, and social responsibility. The meager evidence now available from other cultures indicates that optimal childrearing practices frequently include somewhat more restrictiveness than is usually implied by North American findings with middle-class families (e.g., Chao, in press; Kelley, Power, & Wimbush, 1992; R. P. Rohner & Pettingill, 1985; R. P. Rohner & E. C. Rohner, 1981). In every society, however, responsiveness to children's needs and support for their development appears to foster competent, responsible behaviors. Darling and Steinberg (1993) argued that a context of responsive, supportive, child-centered parental style affects the impact of specific parental practices, such as monitoring of children's behavior.

A component of common models of effective parenting, firmness of control, appears to be a fairly stable characteristic of parents across the years from 6 to 12. Emmerich (1962) found that parents of 6- to 10-year-olds described their childrearing along two dimensions: nurturance-restrictiveness (running from positive, facilitating reactions to negative, interfering reactions) and power (amount of active control exerted by the parent, including both rewards and punishments). In a comparison across age groups, Emmerich found no consistent increase or decrease in either dimension. Similarly, Armentrout and Burger (1972) found that children's perceptions of firmness of control showed little variation across groups from age 9 to 13 years. Most experts now believe that firmness alone is an inadequate indicator of effective control. Lewis (1981) argued that correlations with firm control actually may be attributable to children's willingness to be socialized. She proposed that, in many families, firmness of control co-exists with responsive, child-centered parenting, which in turn enhances children's motivation to respond positively to their parents' socialization practices.

To summarize, middle childhood does not induce changes in parents' typical styles of childrearing. As in other periods, effective childrearing entails both attentiveness and responsiveness to children's needs and expectations of age-appropriate behavior. Nevertheless, during middle childhood, patterns from earlier life are altered in ways that fundamentally affect the exchanges between parents and children and the implications of those exchanges for further development. These changes involve a gradual transition toward greater responsibility for children in regulating their own behavior and interactions with others.

Fostering Self-Management and Social Responsibility

Alterations in parents' management and control activities partly result from children's own developing self-management skills. Although parents do not abruptly relinquish control any more than children abruptly become autonomous, children's enhanced self-management skills probably contribute to a gradual transition from parental regulation of children's behavior to self-regulation by the child (Maccoby, 1984).

This implicit transfer of regulatory responsibility has long been considered a hallmark of adolescent development (Holmbeck et al., in this *Handbook*). Maccoby (1984) argued, however, that the transfer process begins earlier and lasts longer than has commonly been assumed. She contends that the transfer of power from parents to children involves a three-phase developmental process: parental regulation, co-regulation, and, finally, self-regulation. In the intermediate period of co-regulation, parents retain general supervisory control but expect children to exercise gradually more extensive responsibilities for moment-to-moment self-regulation. This co-regulatory experience in turn lays the groundwork for greater autonomy in adolescence and young adulthood.

In several recent formulations (Grusec & Goodnow, 1994; Kuczynski, 1991; Youniss, 1983), co-regulation, rather than autonomous self-regulation, is treated as the norm for both parent–child and other relationships. In this view, interdependence is essential to social relationships at every age, and socialization entails more mature and complex forms of interdependence with age. Maccoby (1992, p. 1013) characterized the effective goal of authoritative parenting as "inducting the child into a system of reciprocity." Training for autonomy is seen, not as preparing children for freedom from the regulatory influences of others, but as enhancing capabilities for responsible exercise of autonomy, while recognizing one's interdependence with others (Hill & Holmbeck, 1986; Youniss, 1983). Thus, parenting in middle childhood is less a matter of gradually yielding control than of transforming patterns of responsibility in response to new characteristics and challenges.

Variations in parents' behavior toward children are correlated with several distinctive aspects of self-management and responsibility: incidence of prosocial and undercontrolled, often antisocial, behavior; internalization of moral values; and increasing responsibility for self-care and for collective well-being. These links are discussed in the following sections.

Incidence of prosocial and antisocial behavior.   Behaviors that either benefit or harm others are increasingly inversely related, beginning in early childhood (for reviews, see Parke & Slaby, 1983; Radke-Yarrow, Zahn-Waxler, & Chapman, 1983). During middle childhood, normative changes in the tendency to behave impulsively, increases in planfulness and other executive processes, greater capacity for understanding the impact of one's actions on others, and knowledge of what is required for helpfulness (Barnett, Darcie, Holland, & Kobasigawa, 1982) imply that prosocial behavior would become more likely and undercontrolled, antisocial behavior less likely. Differentiation of appropriate settings for displaying anger and aggression also increases during middle childhood (Underwood, Coie, & Herbsman, 1992). Parents contribute to the development of prosocial norms. Parents' use of explanations that emphasize the implications of children's behavior for others is associated with helpful, emotionally supportive behavior toward others (Brody & Shaffer, 1982; Hoffman, 1970). Furthermore, parents generally are perceived as sources of social support (Furman & Buhrmester, 1992). Children's perceptions that persons who are available with whom they can talk, discuss problems, and so forth are correlated positively with prosocial behaviors and attitudes, such as empathy, tolerance of differences, and understanding of others (Bryant, 1985).

An aspect of self-regulation of particular significance during middle childhood is the control of hostile aggressive actions. Although the overall likelihood of aggressive behavior is reduced relative to early childhood, 6- to 12-year-olds' aggression is more often hostile and person oriented than in early childhood (Hartup, 1974; Shantz & Voydanoff, 1973). Parental behaviors and family environments have repeatedly been associated with the likelihood of antisocially aggressive behavior (Tolan & Loeber, 1993). A key linking the two appears to be biased processing of interpersonal cues (Dodge, Bates, & Pettit, 1990). Children generally regard acts that are unintended, unforseeable, and unavoidable as less blameworthy and less deserving of retaliation than other actions (Shantz & Voydanoff, 1973). Habitually aggressive children frequently show biases toward attributing hostile intent to others in ambiguous situations (Dodge, 1980), and these biases are related to a history of harsh parental discipline in early childhood (Weiss, Dodge, Bates, & Pettit, 1992). Furthermore, parents' indifferent, unresponsive behavior toward children is associated with tendencies toward antisocial behavior (Patterson, 1982; Pulkinnen, 1982). Antisocial tendencies place children at risk for peer rejection and school failure during middle childhood and for involvement in antisocial behavior in adolescents and young adulthood (Patterson, DeBaryshe, & Ramsey, 1989). Thus, antisocial behavior is the nexus of a longitudinal process linking ineffective parenting and personal and social dysfunction.

Internalization of moral values.   Parents enhance social understanding by appealing to concerns for others and stimulating more cognitively complex reasoning about moral issues (Bearison & Cassell, 1975; Hoffman, 1970; Walker & Taylor, 1991). During middle childhood, these parental techniques may become more effective because of increasing abilities for understanding others' experiences and feelings (Shantz, 1983). The implications for behavior come from the well-established correlation between parental disciplinary approaches based on warmth, other-oriented induction, and infrequent use of coercive discipline without explanations and signs of "conscience"—confessing misdeeds, offering reparations, feeling guilty (Eisenberg & Murphy, in this *Handbook*; Rest, 1983).

Responsibility for self and collective well-being.   The term *responsibility* encompasses broad behavioral expectations, including "(a) following through on specific interpersonal agreements and commitments, (b) fulfilling one's social role obligations, and (c) conforming to widely held social and moral rules of conduct" (Ford, Wentzel, Wood, Stevens, & Siesfeld, 1989, p. 405). Parental practices associated with the development of prosocial behavior and acquisition of moral values during middle childhood can be regarded as factors in the development of responsibility generally (Eisenberg & Murphy, in this *Handbook*).

More specific strategies, however, involve parental expectations regarding household tasks and other activities considered relevant to the welfare of the family as a whole. Parents generally believe that expecting children to carry out household tasks not only provides valuable work experience, but also teaches about expected relationships with others (Goodnow, in this *Handbook*; Goodnow & Collins, 1990). Goodnow (1988) viewed division of responsibility for household tasks as an instance of distributive justice, referring not only to the distribution of labor for efficiency's sake, but also distribution in the sense of relational goals such as obligation, justice, and reciprocity.

Assigning household tasks may mean somewhat different things at different ages. Warton and Goodnow (1991) found developmental progressions from middle childhood into adolescence in the understanding of distributional principles, such as direct-cause responsibility ("people should take care of the areas that they mess up"). This progression involves moving from a direct assertion of responsibility (e.g., "It's Mom's job") or an emphasis on some concrete details of the situation, to the understanding of the principle ("John should clean up the playroom because he and his friends were playing down there, and I wasn't involved"), followed by a move toward a modified, rather than rigid use of the principle (e.g., "John made this mess, but he has to do his paper route on time; he'll help me out some other time"). Although parents of 6- to 12-year-olds are most likely to be dealing with the first two phases of this progression, discussions emphasizing the third view of equality may have impact on the growth of concepts of responsibility during middle childhood. Amato (1989) reported that, for 8- to 9-year-olds, rearing environments characterized by high levels of parental control and parental support, along with high allocation of household responsibility, are associated with broad competence at tasks.

To summarize, fostering self-management and responsibility probably involves a more gradual process than is implied by the common image of parents' transferring control to their children. Co-regulatory processes, in which parents allocate responsibilities for gradually broader self-management to children, while retaining oversight, probably influence children through two key processes: training for effective self-management and enhancing capacities for interdependence, both with persons more powerful than they and with persons of equal power (Baumrind, 1989; Youniss, 1983).

Facilitating Positive Relationships

Capacities for interdependence are fundamentally important to well-being and development throughout life. The development of supportive relationships during middle childhood is influenced by relationships with parents in earlier periods, as well as during middle childhood, and their impact enhances competence in and beyond the middle-childhood years.

Sibling relationships. Sibling relationships become increasingly positive, egalitarian, and companionable during middle childhood (Dunn, 1992; Dunn & McGuire, 1992; Vandell, Minnett, & Santrock, 1987). The degree to which this occurs, however, is related to parental interactions with both siblings. Bryant and Crockenberg (1980) studied the sibling relationships of 10- to 11-year-old girls with their sisters, who were 2 to 3 years younger. The daughters whose mothers fell above the group average in responsiveness to their daughters' needs showed more prosocial behavior and less hostility toward their siblings than the daughters of mothers who were below average in responsiveness. Rates of positive, negative, and controlling behaviors directed by mothers toward each child are positively correlated with the rates of such behaviors directed by siblings toward each other (Stocker, Dunn, & Plomin, 1989).

Parents' treating siblings differently has also been linked to negative relationships between the siblings. In the Bryant and Crockenberg study discussed earlier, mothers who showed favoritism to one child over the other in the degree of parental responsiveness had children who were more likely to behave with hostility toward one another. Brody, Stoneman, and McCoy (1992) found evidence that both parents' direct behavior toward each child and their differences in their behavior toward their children are linked to sibling relationships. In this research, rates of fathers' and mothers' positive behavior directed to each child were associated with siblings' positive behavior toward each other; and both negative parental behavior generally and differences in behavior toward the children were associated with negative sibling interactions. It is not possible to say whether parents' treating children differently during middle childhood affects sibling relationships more than differential behavior in other life periods. Children who perceive that they are treated less positively than their sibling, however, are somewhat more likely than their sibling to show negative personality adjustment in adolescence (Daniels, Dunn, Furstenberg, & Plomin, 1985).

Parent–peer interrelations.   Parents facilitate their children's positive peer relationships indirectly and directly throughout childhood (Hartup, 1992; Parke, MacDonald, Beitel, & Bhavnagri, 1988). Indirect or *stage-setting* effects subsume the advantages of positive, accepting, secure parent–child relationships on children's capacities for forming and maintaining smooth, prosocial relationships with others (e.g., Dishion, 1990; Sroufe & Fleeson, 1986). Direct or *intervention* effects refer to parents' management of their children's relations with other children and the transmission of specific social skills for effective interactions with peers (Parke & Bhavnagri, 1989).

In general, the parental correlates of positive relations with peers in middle childhood parallel the more extensive findings from studies of preschool children (Hartup, 1984). In middle childhood, mothers and fathers of well-liked children are emotionally supportive, infrequently frustrating and punitive, and discouraging of antisocial behavior in their children (Dekovic & Janssens, 1992; Winder & Rau, 1962). The families of these children are generally low in tension and are marked by affection toward, and parental satisfaction with, their children (Elkins, 1958). Furthermore, social skills that are significant to successful peer relations (e.g., self-confidence, assertiveness, and effectiveness with other same-gender children) are correlated with a history of affection from both parents and dominance from the same-gender parent (Hoffman, 1961). In recent research with 8- and 9-year-old children and their parents, popularity with peers was positively correlated with children's perceptions of positive relationships with parents and observational measures of fathers' receptivity to children's proposed solutions on a teaching task (Henggeler, Edwards, Cohen, & Summerville, 1991).

These findings imply both direct and indirect links between parent and peer relationships, but leave open the question of how such links come about. Relevant evidence on one possible process comes from a study of 5- and 6-year-old White, middle-class children and their parents (Cassidy, Parke, Butkovsky, & Braungart, 1992). The children in this study were more effective with peers if their parents were emotionally expressive. The relation was most pronounced for children who showed understanding of emotions, including emotional expressions, experiences, conditions, and effective action and feeling responses. Thus, the impact of the emotional tenor of parent–child relationships may be especially great for those children who are capable of inferring positive principles of interpersonal behavior from experiences with parents and siblings.

Parent–child interaction patterns have also been linked to less positive behavior in middle childhood (Dishion, 1990; Patterson, 1982, 1986; Patterson & Bank, 1989; Vuchinich, Bank, & Patterson, 1992). In two cohorts of boys, age 9 to 10 years, Dishion (1990) found that erratic monitoring and ineffective disciplinary practices marked the families of rejected boys, as did higher levels of family stress, lower socioeconomic status, and evidence of more behavioral and academic problems for the boys themselves. Parents' ineffective disciplinary practices increased the likelihood of peer rejection by enhancing the likelihood of antisocial behavior and academic failure. Later analysis of these data, along with data from a 2-year follow-up (Vuchinich et al., 1992), showed a reciprocal relation between parental ineffectiveness and child behavior: Parental discipline in these families was ineffective partly because the children behaved antisocially, but the ineffective discipline also helped to maintain these antisocial tendencies. These isolated pieces of evidence indicate that parent–child and peer relationships are linked through complex, multiple processes.

Timing of effects.   Considerable uncertainty exists about whether links between parent–child relationships and interpersonal competence during middle childhood reflect concurrent relationships or the longer history of interactions between parent and child. Current longitudinal research indicates impressive stabilities between parent–child relationships in infancy and early childhood and extrafamilial relationships in middle childhood (e.g., Elicker, Englund, & Sroufe, 1992; Sroufe, Carlson,

& Shulman, in press). These findings come from research on *attachment*, or individuals' feeling of confidence in the responsiveness of one person in particular (see Bornstein, in this *Handbook*).

In these studies, security of attachment to caregivers at 12 and 18 months was associated with a variety of indicators of competence with peers at 10 to 12 years of age (Elicker et al., 1992; Hiester, Carlson, & Sroufe, 1993; Sroufe et al., in press; Urban, Carlson, Egeland, & Sroufe, 1991). The securely attached children were more likely to be rated highly by adults on broad-based social and personal competence and were less dependent on adults. These children also spent more time with peers, were more likely to form friendships, and were more likely to have friendships characterized by openness, trust, coordination, and complexity of activity. They also spent more time in, and functioned more effectively in, groups and were more likely to follow implicit rules of peer interactions than children with histories of insecure attachment. An example comes from research on same-gender versus cross-gender peer interactions. During middle childhood, frequency of cross-gender interactions is negatively correlated with social skills and popularity. Insecurely attached children more frequently engaged in cross-gender interactions than securely attached children did (Sroufe, Bennett, Englund, Urban, & Shulman, 1993). In general, the links between security of attachment and social competence with peers in middle childhood were similar to links found in preschool (Sroufe et al., in press). That is, at age 6 to 12, children show similar patterns of orientation to peers and teachers as they did in early childhood; and both the early- and middle-childhood patterns are correlated with attachment measures taken during the first 2 years of life.

These correlations may mean that relationships with parents have similar characteristics across time. Parents who provided responsive, child-centered care in infancy may be more likely to adapt those patterns of care to the support and guidance needed by children in later years, thus providing continuity of care. The researchers suggest two other possibilities. First, the patterns of behavior formed in early relationships may persist, eliciting characteristically different patterns of reactions from others in later life. That is, positive relationships with peers may result from skillful interpersonal behavior by the securely attached child. Or, perhaps children carry forward from early relationships an internal working model of interpersonal relations (Bowlby, 1973). Internal working models are inferred cognitive representations or prototypes of one's key relationships that incorporate behaviors, feelings, and expectancies of reactions from others.

These possibilities are not mutually exclusive, and all three may contribute to the complex linkages between familial and peer relationships. Some recent longitudinal analyses imply that early relationships are probably linked to middle-childhood peer competence via internal working models (Fury, 1993; McCrone, Carlson, & Loewen, 1991; Ramirez, Carlson, Gest, & Egeland, 1991). Children's internal working models of relationships were assessed at ages 4, 8, and 12 years. There were clear contrasts among groups varying in early attachment scores in early- and middle-childhood measures of internal working models. Together, infant attachment scores and later measures of internal working models accounted for 44 percent of the variance in ratings of social competence at age 12; early attachment alone, however, was not reliably related to later social competence. Important questions remain, such as whether and how representations themselves are affected by variations in relationships after infancy, but findings to date imply that parenting in middle childhood partly is rooted in relational patterns established in earlier periods of life.

Beyond middle childhood. It should be noted that temporal linkages between familial and extrafamilial relationships run forward, as well as backward, in time. Rejection by peers, which consistently has been linked to relationships with parents and siblings in childhood, is a compelling marker of long-term developmental disadvantage (Parker & Asher, 1987). Individuals with unsatisfactory peer relations in childhood have been shown to be at greater risk for behavioral problems, school failure, and emotional maladjustment in childhood and adolescence and for mental health problems and criminality in adulthood. Parent–child relationships appear to affect these developmental outcomes via their impact on antisocial behavior and academic failure in middle childhood (Patterson, DeBaryshe, & Ramsey, 1989).

More positive linkages to parent–child relationships have also been documented. Franz, McClelland, and Weinberger (1991) reported longitudinal follow-ups of individuals who were first studied at age 5, together with their mothers (Sears, Maccoby, & Levin, 1957). The participants were measured at age 41 on a indicator of "conventional social accomplishment," defined as having a long happy marriage, children, and relationships with close friends at midlife (Vaillant, 1977). Franz and her colleagues found that having a warm and affectionate father and mother at age 5 was correlated with affiliative behaviors and reports of good relationships with significant others 36 years later. These characteristics of parents also were associated with higher levels of generativity, work accomplishment, psychological well-being, lower level of strain, and less use of emotion-focused coping styles in adulthood. In a separate analysis with this same sample, parents' characteristics at age 5 were associated with empathic concern at age 31 (Koestner, Franz, & Weinberger, 1990). As in the shorter term longitudinal findings described earlier, a variety of possible processes may account for this link between middle-childhood familial relationships and these varied adult characteristics.

Parent–peer cross-pressures.   One widely invoked possible linkage between parent–child and peer relationships in middle childhood is an inverse one: Namely, increasing involvement with peers may be associated with decreasing engagement with and influence of parents. This linkage, though, has only limited and narrow support in the literature. A more common finding is that attitudes toward both parents and peers are more favorable than unfavorable throughout middle childhood and adolescence (Harris & Tseng, 1957). Within this general stability, however, some change does occur. For example, the number of children reporting positive attitudes toward parents declines moderately during middle childhood, although attitudes toward peers generally do not become more favorable during this period.

With respect to endorsement of attitudes held by parents versus peers, the inverse relation occurs only for antisocial behavior and, furthermore, is not especially intense prior to puberty (Hartup, 1984). In a cross-sectional study of 9-, 12-, 15-, and 17- year-old children, Berndt (1979) charted age-related patterns of conformity to parents and peers regarding prosocial, neutral, and antisocial behaviors. Antisocial behavior, in this instance, refers to such activities as cheating, stealing, trespassing, and minor destruction of property. Children and adolescents alike conformed to both parents and friends regarding prosocial behavior; there was some decline across ages in conformity to parents, but not peers, on neutral behaviors; and conformity to peers regarding antisocial behaviors increased between ages 8 and 15 (Grades 3–9), but not beyond. Thus, there is relatively little evidence that pronounced parent–peer cross-pressures are characteristic of middle childhood.

More disruptive shifts may occur in families in which parents fail to maintain age-appropriate, child-centered control patterns. Several studies indicate that conformity to peers may be more likely in families in which relationships with parents are perceived as unsatisfactory. Fuligni and Eccles (1993) collected self-report questionnaires on this topic from 1,771 12- and 13-year-olds. They found that children who believed their parents continued the same patterns of power assertion and restrictiveness they had used in earlier years were higher in an extreme form of peer orientation. Furthermore, those who perceived few opportunities to be involved in decision making, as well as no increase in these opportunities, were higher in both extreme peer orientation and peer advice seeking. Studies of school-age children and early adolescents in self-care also show greater susceptibility to peer influence cross-pressures when parent–child relationships are less warm and involve less regular parental monitoring (Galambos & Maggs, 1991; Steinberg, 1986).

Social support for parents.   Parents' perceptions of a supportive network beyond the family also influence their behavior and children's development (Cochran & Niego, in this *Handbook*). For example, perceived social support has been found to facilitate effectiveness of interventions in troubled families (Wahler, 1980). In contrast, isolation from community support systems is often characteristic of abusive families (e.g., Emery, 1989; Garbarino, 1977; Rogosh, Cicchetti, Shields, & Toth, in this *Handbook*).

To summarize, qualities of relationships with parents have significant implications for development in and beyond middle childhood. Furthermore, linkages to other periods indicate that middle-childhood experiences are inextricable from developmental influences and processes across the life span. A variety of possible processes may link middle-childhood family relationships to both earlier and later functioning, but to date these have been given only piecemeal consideration.

Managing Extrafamilial Experiences

As children move into settings beyond the family, parents increasingly must monitor extrafamilial settings and negotiate with nonfamilial adults on behalf of children. Of these, the most prominent is school (Connors & Epstein, in this *Handbook*). In addition, many parents must arrange for afterschool care by others or must establish and monitor arrangements for self-care by children.

School.   U.S. children typically spend more than 15,000 hours in school from the time they enter school at around age 6, until they graduate from high school at about age 18. This is almost as much time as they spend at home. Schools advance both academic knowledge and knowledge of cultural norms and values and provide essential supports for learning literacy skills, which greatly extend the cognitive capacities in many different areas (Fischer & Bullock, 1984; Good & Weinstein, 1986; Linney & Seidman, 1989). Experiences in school also affect children's views of their own abilities to learn and their actual achievement and adjustment (Harter, 1983; Minuchin & Shapiro, 1983).

Family experiences are linked to children's successful adaptation to the sometimes difficult demands of schooling (Connors & Epstein, in this *Handbook*). A history of shared work and play activities with parents is positively linked to a smooth entry into school, whereas early interactions characterized by a controlling parent and a resisting child, or by a directing child, are correlated with poor adjustment (Barth & Parke, 1993; Moorehouse, 1991).

Children express more satisfaction with school when the authority structure of classrooms is similar to the authority practices they encounter at home (Epstein, 1983; Hess & Holloway, 1984). Furthermore, parenting styles consistently have been linked to school success. Authoritative styles that emphasize encouragement, support for child-initiated efforts, clear communication, and a child-centered teaching orientation in parent–child interactions are associated with higher achievement than are strategies characterized by punishment for failure, use of a directive teaching style, and discouragement of child-initiated interactions (Baumrind, 1973; Hess, Holloway, Dickson, & Price, 1984; Hess & McDevitt, 1984; Hess, Shipman, Brophy, & Bear, 1969; Norman-Jackson, 1982). These correlations have been found in studies with both Euro-American and African-American families. Similar patterns have been documented in studies with adolescents from a variety of ethnic and subcultural groups within North America (Steinberg, Elmen, & Mounts, 1989). These latter findings show that authoritative parenting has been found to be associated with higher school grades and lower incidence of behavior problems in school, compared to authoritarian or permissive parenting styles. In addition to parental control strategies, school achievement during middle childhood has also been associated, negatively, with family environments characterized by interparent and parent–child hostility (Feldman & Wentzel, 1990).

Parents' expectations regarding children's achievement also are implicated in school success (Stevenson & Newman, 1986). For example, perceptions of children's ability are more closely related to children's achievement than their actual ability as measured by standardized tests (Parsons, Adler, & Kaczala, 1982). Furthermore, expectations have an impact from the beginning of schooling. Entwisle and Hayduk (1982) examined U.S. parents' expectations for their children's school performance each year between the age of 6 and 9. For both middle- and working-class children, parents' expectations were strong influences on children's first marks. After age 6, the influence of working-class parents appeared to be considerably less than that of their middle-class counterparts (Connors & Epstein, in this *Handbook*; Hoff-Ginsberg & Tardiff, in this *Handbook*). Similar findings are reported by Alexander and Entwisle (1988).

In European-American middle-class families, correlations are found between achievement and parental expectations into the preadolescent years (Hess et al., 1984; Parsons et al., 1982; Stevenson & Newman, 1986). Changes in expectations often occur during the early school years, however, and these changes are difficult to explain. Children's performance in school may affect these expectations, of course. Alexander and Entwisle (1988) found significant impact of first-grade (age 6) achievement on parents' subsequent expectations for children's school performance. In other instances, contrasting expectations emerge for children who are equivalent in classroom grades and in test scores. For example, although parents' expectations for math performance do not differ by gender at the beginning of school, males are expected to do better than females by the beginning of second grade (Entwisle & Baker, 1983).

High parental expectations also appear to be a key factor in cross-national differences in school achievement during middle childhood. Stevenson and Lee (1990) examined parental correlates of substantially lower levels of academic achievement by U.S. children, as compared to those in China and Japan. They found that U.S. parents have lower expectations for and assign less importance to school achievement alone than Asian parents do; furthermore, U.S. mothers are more likely to regard achievement primarily as a reflection of innate ability, whereas Asian mothers emphasize the importance of hard work in attaining academic excellence. Compared to parents in China and Japan, as well as immigrant parents in the United States, parents born in the United States are more likely to believe that general cognitive development, motivation, and social skills are more important than academic skills (Okagaki & Sternberg, 1993; Stevenson & Lee, 1990). Thus, not only expectations about children's achievement, but the importance assigned to mastery of school tasks per se, affect the impact of parents on their children's school experiences.

Parental expectations may affect children's achievement through effects on their self-esteem. Children with high self-esteem generally perform better in school and other tasks than children with less positive views of themselves (Harter, 1983). This linkage has led some educators to hope that, by intervening to improve self-esteem generally, children's school performance could be improved. In general, however, efforts to improve self-esteem alone as a means of improving academic performance have been unsuccessful. Apparently, children's sense of themselves as competent in academic endeavors needs to be tied to specific successes in learning (Dweck, 1986; Harter, 1983; Minuchin & Shapiro, 1983). A single intervention is unlikely to improve self-esteem if the child is dealing with multiple areas of difficulty (Harter, 1983).

Family difficulties, such as divorce, are also linked to children's school learning and to their emerging self-concepts (Hetherington & Stanley-Hagan, in this *Handbook*). In the first year or two after a divorce, children from one-parent families have been found to be absent from school more often, to study less effectively, and to be more disruptive in the classroom (Hetherington, M. Cox, & R. Cox, 1982). Furthermore, these children's relationships with classmates are disrupted, and teachers observe difficulties in their general social behavior. Girls were seen to be more dependent, and boys were perceived as more aggressive and less able to maintain attention and effort at assigned tasks—and in general as less academically competent (Hetherington et al., 1982). On the other hand, one important context may compensate for difficulties in the other, as when family members provide support for school difficulties, or teachers and classmates help to buffer children's distress over family problems (Wallerstein & Kelly, 1980).

Parents' involvement with schools and with children's school-related tasks is also positively correlated with children's school performance. Parental involvement is variously defined as expectations of school performance, verbal encouragement, direct reinforcement of school-relevant behaviors, general academic guidance or support, and children's perceptions of parents' influence on school progress (Fehrmann, Keith, & Reimers, 1987). Regardless of definition, research findings show generally positive effects of parental involvement on measures of achievement (e.g., achievement test scores, grades) in the elementary grades. Correlations are less impressive in the secondary grades, perhaps because common forms of parental involvement are perceived as intrusions on autonomy.

Several factors mediate the effects of parental involvement, however. Darling and Steinberg (1993) contended that the impact of parental involvement in schooling may depend on general parental style of childrearing. Among authoritative parents (those who characteristically showed responsive, child-centered behavior and clear expectations for child behavior), involvement was highly correlated with academic achievement, in comparison to involvement of authoritarian (restrictive, parent-centered, controlling) parents. It seems likely that authoritative parents' involvement is interpreted as reflecting interest in and support for children's school-related activities, whereas authoritarian parents' involvement may be perceived as intrusive, controlling, and implying disrespect and lack of trust for the child.

The most studied area of parental involvement in schooling is homework. Leone and Richards (1989) found that 11- and 12-year-old students in the top one third of their classes spent significantly more time working on homework, including time spent working with a parent on school assignments. Other studies have shown negative correlations, perhaps because parents are more likely to become involved in homework when children have not been doing well on their own (Miller & Kelley, 1991). Under these conditions, however, parental involvement was generally effective in improving test scores in mathematics. This is most likely when parents have been exposed to training in how best to help their children complete homework assignments. Parental attitudes toward the importance of homework, like attitudes toward the importance of school achievement generally, vary cross-nationally (Chen & Stevenson, 1989).

Afterschool care.   Large numbers of 6- to 12-year-olds are alone without immediate adult supervision for significant amounts of time. Estimates place the total amount of time alone at 21 percent of children's waking hours, although parents' themselves typically give much lower estimates. Often, these times alone are irregularly scheduled (e.g., while parents run errands) and may involve siblings being left alone together. Many 6- to 12-year-olds, however, regularly spend time alone while parents are at work (Rodman, Pratto, & Nelson, 1985).

Few general differences in academic performance or psychosocial status are apparent when children in adult care arrangements are compared to those in self-care arrangements. Vandell and Corasaniti (1988) reported that 8- and 9-year-olds in center care showed lower academic achievement and lower acceptance by peers than children in other care arrangements, including mother care. Surprisingly, "latchkey" children—children who are at home alone after school— were not generally disadvantaged relative to mother care children. The reasons for the deficits observed in children cared for in centers are not clear.

Negative effects are most likely when children on their own are not monitored regularly and when they are free to spend time away from home with peers (Galambos & Maggs, 1991; Steinberg, 1986). These arrangements are more common in the preadolescent years than the early elementary years. Older children are more susceptible to peer influences and more likely to engage in problem behaviors than children who stay at home and those who are in regular telephone contact with parents. The negative effects from being allowed to roam may result partly from generally less positive parent–child relationships. For girls particularly, permissive self-care arrangements are associated with lowered perceptions of parental acceptance and higher levels of parent–child conflicts (Galambos & Maggs, 1991). Among these preadolescents and younger children alike, regular arrangements for parental monitoring and clear expectations for letting parents know where the child is seem to overcome the potential negative effects of self-care (Galambos & Maggs, 1991; Steinberg, 1986; Vandell & Corasaniti, 1988).

In summary, parents' involvement in children's lives away from home entails many of the same principles and processes that determine their effectiveness in more direct exchanges. Appropriate monitoring, in the context of warm, accepting relationships, is associated with positive school adjustment and academic achievement and with benign impact of self-care arrangements. Although these areas of children's lives require different forms of parental involvement, the general style of parents' relationships with children is a key factor in the impact of out-of-home experiences on development during middle childhood.

CONCLUSIONS

Parenting during middle childhood encompasses adaptation to distinctive transformations in human development that affect not only the current well-being of children, but carry significant implications for later life. The age of 5 to 7 years is universally regarded as "the age of reason" (Rogoff, Pirrotta, Fox, & White, 1975). In non-Western cultures, children are assumed to develop new capabilities at this age and are often assigned expanded roles and responsibilities in their families and communities. Although the transition to adultlike responsibilities is less pronounced in Western industrialized societies, 6- to 12-year-olds are expected to show greater autonomy and responsibility in some arenas.

The unique experiences of individual children in middle childhood partly reflect changes experienced by virtually all children of this age and also the interpersonal relationships and the characteristics of particular communities and social institutions. Such factors as urban versus rural residence, family and domestic group status, parental and nonparental child-care arrangements, tasks typically assigned to children, and the role of women in the society have all been demonstrated to affect important dimensions of childhood socialization in both industrialized and developing countries (Weisner, 1984).

Common changes in children and in relationships have raised two key questions that underlie the framework outlined in this chapter. One is the question of whether parenting during middle childhood is distinctively different from parenting in other age periods. Although the particular forms of parental behavior and parent-child interaction vary considerably, certain issues arise in virtually all families of 6- to 12-year-olds in industrialized societies: exercising regulatory influence while facilitating increasing self-regulation, maintaining positive bonds while fostering a distinctive sense of self, providing groundwork for effective relationships and experiences outside of the family (Collins, 1984). These issues are integral to parent–child relationships from birth, although often in less obtrusive or more rudimentary forms than in middle childhood and remain central in the adolescent years and, to a lesser degree, in early adulthood (White, Speisman, & Costos, 1983).

The distinctiveness of parenting 6- to 12-year-olds largely arises from the relative novelty and salience of the issues. Middle childhood is a period of intensifying transitions, many of which require parents to extend their activities on behalf of the child to interactions with others, including teachers, peers, and other families. In addition, behaviors of children toward parents change, as the result of cognitive, emotional, and social transitions. Consequently, both the scope of the issues and the interpersonal modes available for addressing them are altered in middle childhood.

Current models of socialization imply that the most effective parental responses to changes in children's behavior is a combination of child-centered flexibility and adherence to core values and expectancies for approved behavior (Baumrind, 1989; Darling & Steinberg, 1993; Dix, 1991; Grusec & Goodnow, 1994; Hoffman, 1994; Maccoby, 1992). The evidence to date suggests that this combination may be more complex in middle childhood than in other periods. Furthermore, the balance between assuring continuity and adapting to child-driven change may be more difficult to maintain in and after middle childhood than in early childhood. It seems likely, however, that the capacity for age-appropriate adaptation is not exclusive to effective parenting in this period, but is inherent in the characteristics of effective parenting at every age.

An implied, but less directly addressed, question in this chapter concerns the linkages between parenting and individual development during middle childhood and in later periods. These associations are more often implicit than explicit. Nevertheless, research findings have documented some key connections. The most extensively replicated finding is that parenting styles marked by authoritativeness toward children, but clearly child-centered attitudes and concerns, is correlated with a variety of positive outcomes that attain salience in middle childhood and that are predictive of successful adaptation in later life. These include peer acceptance, school success, competence in self-care, and competence and responsibility in a broad array of tasks. Equally well established is the finding that parenting behavior and attitudes dominated by parental concerns, rather than child characteristics and needs, are associated with less positive outcomes on all of these variables. The latter must be regarded as middle-childhood risk factors for long-term dysfunction.

A caveat is that the evidence on middle-childhood correlates of later dysfunction does not distinguish cases in which negative conditions were experienced for the first time in middle childhood and those in which there is a longer history of parenting problems. Nevertheless, manifestations of these negative conditions in middle childhood must be regarded as compelling indications of the signficance of parental contributions to development during and after middle childhood.

REFERENCES

Ainsworth, M. D. S. (1989). Attachments beyond infancy. *American Psychologist, 44*, 709–716.

Alessandri, S. M., & Wozniak, R. H. (1987). The child's awareness of parental beliefs concerning the child: A developmental study. *Child Development, 58*, 316–323.

Alessandri, S. M., & Wozniak, R. H. (1989). Continuity and change in intrafamilial agreement in beliefs concerning the adolescent: A follow-up study. *Child Development, 60*, 335–339.

Alexander, K. L., & Entwisle, D. R. (1988). Achievement in the first 2 years of school: Patterns and processes. *Monographs of the Society for Research in Child Development, 53*(2, Serial No. 218).

Altshuler, J. L., & Ruble, J. L. (1989). Developmental changes in children's awareness of strategies for coping with uncontrollable stress. *Child Development, 60*, 1337–1349.

Amato, P. R. (1989). Family processes and the competence of adolescents and primary school children. *Journal of Youth and Adolescence, 18*, 39–53.

Aries, P. (1962). *Centuries of childhood.* New York: Knopf.

Armentrout, V. A., & Burger, G. K. (1972). Children's reports of parental child-rearing behaviors at five grade levels. *Developmental Psychology, 7*, 44–48.

Baldwin, A. L. (1946). Differences in parent behavior toward three- and nine- year-old children. *Journal of Personality, 15*, 143–165.

Barnett, K., Darcie, G., Holland, C., & Kobasigawa, A. (1982). Children's cognitions about effective helping. *Developmental Psychology, 18*, 267–277.

Barth, J. M., & Parke, R. D. (1993). Parent–child relationship influences on children's transition to school. *Merrill-Palmer Quarterly, 39*, 173–195.

Baumrind, D. (1973). The development of instrumental competence through socialization. In A. D. Pick (Ed.), *Minnesota symposia on child psychology* (Vol. 7, pp. 3–46). Minneapolis: University of Minnesota Press.

Baumrind, D. (1989). Rearing competent children. In W. Damon (Ed.), *Child development today and tomorrow* (pp. 349–378). San Francisco: Jossey-Bass.

Bearison, D. J., & Cassell, T. Z. (1975). Cognitive decentration and social codes: Communication effectiveness in young children from differing family contexts. *Developmental Psychology, 11*, 29–36.

Bell, C. C., & Jenkins, E. J. (1993). Community violence and children on Chicago's Southside. *Psychiatry, 56*, 46–54.

Berndt, T. J. (1979). Developmental changes in conformity to peers and parents. *Developmental Psychology, 15*, 608–616.

Berndt, T. J. (1981). Age changes and changes over time in prosocial intentions and behavior between friends. *Developmental Psychology, 17*, 408–416.

Bibace, R., & Walsh, M. (1981). Children's conceptions of illness. In R. Bibace & M. Walsh (Eds.), *Children's conceptions of health, illness, bodily functions: New directions for child development* (No. 14). San Francisco: Jossey-Bass.

Bowlby, J. (1973). *Attachment and loss: Vol. 2. Separation.* New York: Basic Books.

Brady, J. E., Newcomb, A. F., & Hartup, W. W. (1983). Context and companion as determinants of cooperation and competition in middle childhood. *Journal of Experimental Child Psychology, 36*, 396–412.

Braine, L. G., Pomerantz, E., Lorber, D., & Krantz, D. H. (1991). Conflicts with authority: Children's feelings, actions, and justifications. *Developmental Psychology, 27*, 829–840.

Brody, G. H., & Shaffer, D. R. (1982). Contributions of parents and peers to children's moral socialization. *Developmental Review, 2*, 31–75.

Brody, G. H., Stoneman, Z., & McCoy, J. K. (1992). Associations of maternal and paternal direct and differential behavior with sibling relationships: Contemporaneous and longitudinal analyses. *Child Development, 63*, 82–92.

Bronstein, P. (1984). Differences in mothers' and fathers' behaviors toward children: A cross-cultural comparison. *Developmental Psychology, 20*, 995–1003.

Brown, A., Bransford, J., Ferrara, R., & Campione, J. (1983). Learning, remembering, and understanding. In P. H. Mussen (Ed.), *Handbook of child psychology* (Vol. 3, pp. 77–166). New York: Wiley.

Bryant, B., & Crockenberg, S. (1980). Correlates and dimensions of prosocial behavior: A study of female siblings with their mothers. *Child Development, 51,* 529–544.

Bryant, B. (1985). The neighborhood walk: Source of support in middle childhood. *Monographs of the Society for Research in Child Development, 50* (3, Serial No. 210).

Campbell, J. (1975). Illness is a point of view: The development of children's concepts of illness. *Child Development, 46,* 92–100.

Carey, S. (1985). *Conceptual change in childhood.* Cambridge, MA: MIT Press.

Cassidy, J., Parke, R. D., Butkovsky, L., & Braungart, J. M. (1992). Family–peer connections: The roles of emotional expressiveness within the family and children's understanding of emotions. *Child Development, 63,* 603–618.

Chao, R. (1994). Beyond parental control and authoritarian parenting style: Understanding Chinese parenting through the cultural notion of training. *Child Development, 65,* 1111–1119.

Chapman, M., & McBride, M. L. (1992). The education of reason: Cognitive conflict and its role in intellectual development. In C. U. Shantz & W. W. Hartup (Eds.), *Conflict in child and adolescent development* (pp. 36–69). New York: Cambridge University Press.

Chen, C., & Stevenson, H. W. (1989). Homework: A cross-cultural examination. *Child Development, 60,* 551–561.

Chi, M. T., Glaser, R., & Rees, E. (1982). Expertise in problem solving. In R. Sternberg (Eds.), *Advances in the psychology of human intelligence* (Vol 1., pp. 7–76). Hillsdale, NJ: Lawrence Erlbaum Associates.

Clifford, E. (1959). Discipline in the home: A controlled observational study of parental practices. *Journal of Genetic Psychology, 95,* 45–82.

Collins, W. A. (Ed.). (1984). *Development during middle childhood: The years from six to twelve.* Washington, DC: National Academy of Sciences Press.

Collins, W. A. (1992). Parents' cognitions and developmental changes in relationships during adolescence. In I. E. Sigel, A. V. McGillicuddy-DeLisi, & J. J. Goodnow (Eds.), *Parental belief systems: The psychological consequences for children* (2nd ed., pp. 175–198). Hillsdale, NJ: Lawrence Erlbaum Associates.

Collins, W. A., & Russell, G. (1991). Mother–child and father–child relation-ships in middle childhood and adolescence. *Developmental Review, 11,* 99–136.

Compas, B. D. (1987). Coping with stress during childhood and adolescence. *Psychological Bulletin, 101*(3), 393–403.

Damon, W. (1977). *The social world of the child.* San Francisco: Jossey-Bass.

Damon, W. &. Hart, D. (1988). *Self-understanding in childhood and adolescence.* New York: Cambridge University Press.

Daniels, D., Dunn, J., Furstenberg, F. F., Jr., & Plomin, R. (1985). Environmental differences within the family and adjustment differences within pairs of adolescent siblings. *Child Development, 56,* 764–774.

Darling, N., & Steinberg, L. (1993). Parenting style as context: An integrative model. *Psychological Bulletin, 113,* 487–496.

Dekovic, M., & Janssens, J.M.A.M. (1992). Parents' child-raring style and child's sociometric status. *Developmental Psychology, 28*(5), 925–932.

DePaulo, B., Jordan, A., Irvine, A., & Laser, P. (1982). Age changes in the detection of deception. *Child Development, 53,* 701–709.

Dishion, T. J. (1990). The family ecology of boys' peer relations in middle childhood. *Child Development, 61,* 874–892.

Dix, T. (1991). The affective organization of parenting: Adaptive and maladaptive process. *Psychological Bulletin, 110,* 3–25.

Dix, T., Ruble, D., Grusec, J., & Nixon, S. (1986). Social cognition in parents: Inferential and affective reactions to children of three age levels. *Child Development, 57,* 879–894.

Dodge, K. A. (1980). Social cognition and children's aggressive behavior. *Child Development, 51,* 162–170.

Dodge, K. A., Bates, J. E., & Pettit, G. S. (1990). Mechanisms in the the cycle of violence. *Science, 250,* 1678–1683.

Droege, K. L., & Stipek, D. J. (1993). Children's use of dispositions to predict classmates' behavior. *Developmental Psychology, 29*(4), 646–654.

Dubow, E. F., & Tisak, J. (1989). The relation between stressful life events and adjustment in elementary school children: The role of social support and social problem-solving skills. *Child Development, 60,* 1412–1423.

Dubow, E. F., Tisak, J., Causey, D., Hryshko, A., & Reid, G. (1991). A two-year longitudinal study of stressful life events, social support, and social problem-solving skills: Contributions to children's behavioral and academic adjustment. *Child Development, 62,* 583–599.

Dunn, J. (1992). Sisters and brothers: Current issues in developmental research. In F. Boer & J. Dunn (Eds.), *Children's sibling relationships: Developmental and clinical issues* (pp. 1–17). Hillsdale, NJ: Lawrence Erlbaum Associates.

Dunn, J., & McGuire, S. (1992). Sibling and peer relationships in childhood. *Journal of Child Psychology and Psychiatry, 33,* 67–105.

Dunn, J., & Slomkowski, C. (1992). Conflict and the development of social understanding. In C. U. Shantz & W. W. Hartup (Eds.), *Conflict in child and adolescent development* (pp. 70–92). New York: Cambridge University Press.

Dweck, C. (1986). Motivational processes affecting learning. *American Psychologist, 41,* 1040–1048.

Eccles, J. S., Midgley, C., Wigfield, A., Buchanan, C. M., Reuman, D., Flanagan, C., & MacIver, D. G (1993). Development during adolescence: The impact of stage-environment fit on young adolescents' experiences in schools and in families. *American Psychologist, 48*, 90–101.

Elicker, J., Englund, M., & Sroufe, L. A. (1992). Predicting peer competence and peer relationships in childhood from early parent–child relationships. In R. D. Parke & G. W. Ladd (Eds.), *Family–peer relationships: Modes of linkage* (pp. 77–106). Hillsdale, NJ: Lawrence Erlbaum Associates.

Elkins, D. (1958). Some factors related to the choice status of ninety eighth-grade children in a school society. *Genetic Psychology Monographs, 58*, 2076–2272.

Emery, R. (1989). Family violence. *American Psychologist, 44*, 321–328.

Emmerich, W. (1962). Variations in the parent roles as a function of parents' sex and the child's sex and age. *Merrill-Palmer Quarterly, 8*, 1–11.

Entwisle, D., & Baker, D. P. (1983). Gender and young children's expectations for performance in arithmetic. *Developmental Psychology, 29*, 200–209.

Entwisle, D., & Hayduk, L. (1982). *Early schooling.* Baltimore: Johns Hopkins University Press.

Epstein, J. L. (1983). Longitudinal effects of family–school–person interactions on student outcomes. In A. Kerckhoff (Ed.), *Research in sociology of education and socialization* (Vol. 4, pp. 90–130). Greenwich, CT: JAI Press.

Epstein, J. L. (1989). The selection of friends: Changes across the grades and in different school environments. In T. J. Berndt & G. W. Ladd (Eds.), *Peer relationships in child development* (pp. 158–187). New York: Wiley.

Fehrmann, P. G., Keith, T. Z., & Reimers, T. M. (1987). Home influence on school learning: Direct and indirect effects of parental involvement on high-school grades. *Journal of Educational Research, 80*, 330–337.

Feiring, C., & Lewis, M. (1991a). The development of social networks from early to middle childhood: Gender differences and the relation to school competence. *Sex Roles, 25*, 237–253.

Feiring, C., & Lewis, M. (1991b). The transition from middle childhood to early adolescence: Sex differences in the social network and perceived self-competence. *Sex Roles, 24*, 489–509.

Feldman, S. S., & Wentzel, K. R. (1990). Relations among family interaction patterns, classroom self-restraint, and academic achievement in preadolescent boys. *Journal of Educational Psychology, 82*, 813–819.

Fischer, K. W., & Bullock, D. (1984). Cognitive development in school-age children: Conclusions and new directions. In W. A. Collins (Ed.), *Development during middle childhood: The years from six to twelve* (pp. 70–146). Washington, DC: National Academy of Sciences Press.

Fisher, C. B., & Johnson, B. L. (1990). Getting mad at mom and dad: Children's changing views of family conflict. *International Journal of Behavioral Development, 13*, 31–48.

Ford, M. E., Wentzel, K. R., Wood, D., Stevens, E., & Siesfeld, G. A. (1989). Processes associated with integrative social competence: Emotional and contextual influences on adolescent social responsibility. *Journal of Adolescent Research, 4*, 405–425.

Franz, C. E., McClelland, D. C., & Weinberger, J. (1991). Childhood antecedents of conventional social accomplishment in midlife adults: A 36-year prospective study. *Journal of Personality and Social Psychology, 60*(4), 586–595.

Fuligni, A. J., & Eccles, J. S. (1993). Perceived parent–child relationships and early adolescents' orientation toward peers. *Developmental Psychology, 29*(4), 622–632.

Furman, W., & Buhrmester, D. (1992). Age and sex differences in perceptions of networks of personal relationships. *Child Development, 63*, 103–115.

Fury, G. (1993, March). *The relations between infant attachment history and representations of relationships in school-age family drawings.* Paper presented at the biennial meeting of the Society for Research in Child Development, New Orleans, LA.

Galambos, N. L., & Maggs, J. L. (1991). Out-of-school care of young adolescents and self-reported behavior. *Developmental Psychology, 27*, 644–655.

Garbarino, J. (1977). The human ecology of child maltreatment: A conceptual model for research. *Journal of Marriage and the Family, 39*, 721–736.

Garmezy, N. (1983). Stressors of childhood. In N. Garmezy & M. Rutter (Eds.), *Stress, coping, and development in children* (pp. 43–84). New York: McGraw-Hill.

Good, T. L., & Weinstein, R. S. (1986). Schools make a differences: Evidence, criticisms, and new directions. *American Psychologist, 41*, 1090–1097.

Goodenough, F. L. (1931). *Anger in young children.* Minneapolis: University of Minnesota Press.

Goodnow, J. J. (1988). Children's household work: Its nature and functions. *Psychological Bulletin, 103*, 5–26.

Goodnow, J. J., & Collins, W. A. (1990). *Development according to parents: The nature, sources, and consequences of parents' ideas.* London, England: Lawrence Erlbaum Associates.

Grusec, J., & Goodnow, J. J. (1994). The impact of parental discipline methods on the child's internalization of values: A reconceptualization of current points of view. *Developmental Psychology, 30*, 4–19.

Harris, D. B., & Tseng, S. (1957). Children's attitudes towards peers and parents as revealed by sentence completions. *Child Development, 28*, 401–411.

Harter, S. (1983). Developmental perspectives on the self system. In P. H. Mussen (Ed.), *Handbook of child psychology* (Vol. 4, pp. 275–385). New York: Wiley.

Hartup, W. W. (1974). Aggression in childhood: Developmental perspectives. *American Psychologist, 29,* 226–341.

Hartup, W. W. (1979). Two social worlds of childhood. *American Psychologist, 34,* 944–950.

Hartup, W. W. (1984). The peer context in middle childhood. In W. A. Collins (Ed.), *Development during middle childhood: The years from six to twelve* (pp. 240–282). Washington, DC: National Academy Press.

Hartup, W. W. (1989). Social relationships and their developmental significance. *American Psychologist, 44,* 120–126.

Hartup, W. W. (1992). Friendships and their developmental significance. In H. McGurk (Ed.), *Childhood social development: Contemporary perspectives* (pp. 175–205). London: Routledge.

Henggeler, S. W., Edwards, J. J., Cohen, R., & Summerville, M. B. (1991). Predicting changes in children's popularity: The role of family relations. *Journal of Applied Developmental Psychology, 12,* 205–218.

Hess, R. D., & Holloway, S. D. (1984). Family and school as educational institutions. In R. D. Parke (Ed.), *Review of child development research: The family* (Vol. 7, pp. 179–222). Chicago: University of Chicago Press.

Hess, R. D., Holloway, S. D., Dickson, W. P., & Price, G. G. (1984). Maternal variables as predictors of children's school readiness and later achievement in vocabulary and mathematics in sixth grade. *Child Development, 55,* 1902–1912.

Hess, R. D., & McDevitt, T. M. (1984). Some cognitive consequences of maternal intervention techniques: A longitudinal study. *Child Development, 55,* 2017–2030.

Hess, R. D., Shipman, V. C., Brophy, J. E., & Bear, R. M. (1969). *The cognitive environments of urban preschool children: Follow-up phase.* Unpublished manuscript, Graduate School of Education, University of Chicago.

Hetherington, E. M., Cox, M., & Cox, R. (1982). Effects of divorce on parents and children. In M. Lamb (Ed.), *Non-traditional families: Parenting and child development* (pp. 233–288). Hillsdale, NJ: Lawrence Erlbaum Associates.

Hiester, M., Carlson, E., & Sroufe, L. A. (1993, March). *The evolution of friendships in preschool, middle childhood, and adolescence: Origins in attachment history.* Paper presented at the biennial meeting of the Society for Research in Child Development, New Orleans, LA.

Higgins, E. T., & Parsons, J. E. (1983). Social cognition and the social life of the child: Stages as subcultures. In E. T. Higgins, D. N. Ruble, & W. W. Hartup (Eds.), *Social cognition and social development: A sociocultural perspective* (pp. 15–62). New York: Cambridge University Press.

Hill, C. R., & Stafford, F. P. (1980). Parental care of children: Time diary estimate of quantity, predictability and variety. *Journal of Human Resources, 15,* 219–239.

Hill, J., & Holmbeck, G. (1986). Attachment and autonomy during adolescence. In G. J. Whitehurst (Ed.), *Annals of child development* (Vol. 3, pp. 145–189). Greenwich, CT: JAI Press.

Hirsch, B. J., & Rapkin, B. D. (1987). The transition to junior high school: A longitudinal study of self-esteem, psychological symptomatology, school life, and social support. *Child Development, 58,* 1235–1243.

Hoffman, M. L. (1970). Moral development. In P. H. Mussen (Ed.), *Carmichael's manual of child psychology* (Vol. 2, pp. 261–359). New York: Wiley.

Hoffman, M. L. (1994). Discipline and internalization. *Developmental Psychology, 30,* 26–28.

Hunter, F. T., & Youniss, J. (1982). Changes in functions of three relations during adolescence. *Developmental Psychology, 18,* 806–811.

Kelley, M. L., Power, T. G., & Wimbush, D. D. (1992). Determinants of disciplinary practices in low-income black mothers. *Child Development, 63,* 573–582.

Koestner, R., Franz, C., & Weinberger, J. (1990). The family origins of empathic concern: A 26-year longitudinal study. *Journal of Personality and Social Psychology, 58,* 709–717.

Kuczynski, L. (1991, April). Emerging conceptions of children's responses to parental control. In D. Jacobvitz (Chair), *New perspectives on child compliance, noncompliance, and parental control.* Symposium conducted at the meeting of the Society for Research in Child Development, Seattle.

Lazar, A., & Torney-Purta, J. (1991). The development of the subconcepts of death in young children: A short-term longitudinal study. *Child Development, 62,* 1321–1333.

Leone, C. M., & Richards, M. H. (1989). Classwork and homework in early adolescence: The ecology of achievement. *Journal of Youth and Adolescence, 18,* 531–548.

Lewis, C. C. (1981). The effects of parental firm control: A reinterpretation of findings. *Psychological Bulletin, 90,* 547–564.

Linney, J. A., & Seidman, E. (1989). The future of schooling. *American Psychologist, 44,* 336–340.

Lorion, R. P., & Saltzman, W. (1993). Children's exposure to community violence: Following a path from concern to research to action. *Psychiatry, 56,* 55–65.

Maccoby, E. E. (1983). Social-emotional development and response to stressors. In N. Garmezy & M. Rutter (Eds.), *Stress, coping, and development in children* (pp. 217–234). New York: McGraw-Hill.

Maccoby, E. E. (1984). Middle childhood in the context of the family. In W. A. Collins (Ed.), *Development during middle childhood: The years from six to twelve* (pp. 184–239). Washington, DC: National Academy of Sciences Press.

Maccoby, E. E. (1992). The role of parents in the socialization of children: An historical overview. *Developmental Psychology, 28,* 1006–1017.

Maccoby, E. E., & Martin, J. A. (1983). Socialization in the context of the family: Parent–child interaction. In P. H. Mussen (Ed.), *Handbook of child psychology* (Vol. 4, pp. 1–101). New York: Wiley.

Margolin, G., & Patterson, G. (1975). Differential consequences provide by mothers and fathers for their sons and daughters. *Developmental Psychology, 11*, 537–538.

Markus, H., & Nurius, P. (1984). Self-understanding and self-regulation in middle childhood. In W. A. Collins (Ed.), *Development during middle childhood: The years from six to twelve* (pp. 147–183). Washington, DC: National Academy of Sciences Press.

Martinez, P. & Richters, J. E. (1993). The NIMH Community Violence Project II: Children's distress symptoms associated with violence exposure. *Psychiatry, 56*, 22–35.

McCrone, E., Carlson, E., & Loewen, G. (1991, April). *Thematic analysis of friendship motivation related to attachment history: Constructive replication of McAdams and Losoff (1984).* Poster presented at the biennial meeting of the Society for Research in Child Development, Seattle.

Miller, D. L., & Kelley, M. L. (1991). Interventions for improving homework performance: A critical review. *School Psychology Quarterly, 6*, 174–185.

Minuchin, P., & Shapiro, E. (1983). The school as a context for social development. In P. H. Mussen (Ed.), *Handbook of child psychology* (Vol. 4, pp. 197–274). New York: Wiley.

Moorehouse, M. J. (1991). Linking maternal employment patterns to mother–child activities and children's school competence. *Developmental Psychology, 27*, 295–303.

Newson, J., & Newson, E. (1968). *Four years old in an urban community.* Chicago: Aldine.

Newson, J., & Newson, E. (1976). *Seven years old in the home environment.* New York: Wiley.

Noller, P. (1980). Cross-gender effects in two-child families. *Developmental Psychology, 16*, 159–160.

Norman-Jackson, J. (1982). Family interactions, language development, and primary reading achievement of black children in families of low income. *Child Development, 53*, 349–358.

Okagaki, L., & Sternberg, R. J. (1993). Parental beliefs and children's school performance. *Child Development, 64*, 36–56.

Osofsky, J. D., Wewers, S., Hann, D. M., & Fick, A. C. (1993). Chronic community violence: What is happening to our children? *Psychiatry, 56*, 36–45.

Parke, R. D., & Bhavnagri, N. P. (1989). Parents as managers of children's peer relationships. In D. Belle (Ed.), *Children's social networks and social supports* (pp. 241–259). New York: Wiley.

Parke, R. D., MacDonald, K. B., Beitel, A., & Bhavnagri, N. (1988). The role of the family in the development of peer relationships. In R. Peters & R. J. McMahon (Eds.), *Social learning systems approaches to marriage and the family* (pp. 17–44). New York: Brunner/Mazel.

Parke, R. D., & Slaby, R. G. (1983). The development of aggression. In P. H. Mussen (Ed.), *Handbook of child psychology* (Vol. 4, pp. 547–642). New York: Wiley.

Parker, J. G., & Asher, S. R. (1987). Peer relations and later personal adjustment: Are low-accepted children "at risk?" *Psychological Bulletin, 102*, 357–389.

Parker, J. G., Gottman, J. M. (1989). Social and emotional development in a relational context: Friendship interactions from early childhood to adolescence. In T. J. Berndt & G. W. Ladd (Eds.), *Peer relationships in child development* (pp. 95–131). New York: Wiley.

Parsons, J. E., Adler, T. F., & Kaczala, C. M. (1982). Socialization of achievement attitudes and beliefs: Parental influences. *Child Development, 53*, 310–321.

Patterson, G. R. (1982). *Coercive family processes.* Eugene, OR: Castalia Press.

Patterson, G. R. (1986). Performance models for antisocial boys. *American Psychologist, 41*, 432–444.

Patterson, G. R., & Bank, L. (1989). Some amplifier and dampening mechanisms for pathologic processes in families. In M. R. Gunnar & E. Thelen (Ed.), *Systems and development: Vol. 22, The Minnesota symposia on child psychology* (pp. 167–210). Hillsdale, NJ: Lawrence Erlbaum Associates.

Patterson, G. R., DeBaryshe, B. D., & Ramsey, E. (1989). A developmental perspective on antisocial behavior. *American Psychologist, 44*, 329–335.

Pulkinnen, L. (1982). Self-control and continuity from childhood to adolescence. In P. B. Baltes & O. G. Brim (Eds.), *Life-span development and behavior* (Vol. 4, pp. 64–105). New York: Academic Press.

Radke-Yarrow, M., Zahn-Waxler, C., & Chapman, M. (1983). Children's prosocial dispositions and behavior. In P. H. Mussen (Ed.), *Handbook of child psychology* (Vol. 4, pp. 469–546). New York:Wiley.

Ramirez, M., Carlson, E., Gest, S., & Egeland, B. (1991, July). *The relationship between children's behavior at school and internal representations of their relationships as measured by the sentence completion method.* Paper presented at the biennial meeting of the International Society for the Study of Behavioral Development, Minneapolis, MN.

Reid, M., Landesman, S., Treder, R., & Jaccard, J. (1989). "My family and friends": Six- to twelve-year old children's perceptions of social support. *Child Development, 60*, 896–910.

Rest, J. R. (1983). Morality. In P. H. Mussen (Ed.), *Handbook of child psychology* (Vol. 3, pp. 556–629). New York: Wiley.

Richters, J. E., & Martinez, P. (1993). The NIMH Community Violence Project: I. Children as victims and witnesses to violence. *Psychiatry, 56*, 7–21.

Roberts, G. C., Block, J. H., & Block, J. (1984). Continuity and change in parents' child-rearing. *Child Development, 55*, 586–597.

Rodman, H., Pratto, D. J., & Nelson, R. S. (1985). Child care arrangements and children's functioning: A comparison of self-care and adult-care children. *Developmental Psychology, 21*, 413–418.

Rogoff, B. S., M., Pirrotta, S., Fox, N., & White, S. (1975). Age of assignment of roles and responsibilities in children: A cross-cultural survey. *Human Development, 18*, 353–369.

Rohner, R. P., & Pettengill, S. M. (1985). Perceived parental acceptance-rejection and parental control among Korean adolescents. *Child Development, 56*, 524–528.

Rohner, R. P., & Rohner, E. C. (1981). Parental acceptance-rejection and parental control: Cross-cultural codes. *Ethnology, 20*, 245–260.

Russell, G., & Russell, A. (1987). Mother–child and father–child relationships in middle childhood. *Child Development, 58*, 1573–1585.

Rutter, M. L. (1983). Stress, coping, and development: Some issues and some questions. In N. Garmezy & M. Rutter (Eds.), *Stress, coping, and development in children* (pp. 1–41). New York: McGraw-Hill.

Salt, R. E. (1991). Affectionate touch between fathers and preadolescent sons. *Journal of Marriage and the Family, 53*, 545–554.

Saltzstein, H. D. (1976). Social influence and moral development: A perspective on the role of parents and peers. In T. Lickona (Ed.), *Moral development and behavior: Theory, research, and social issues* (pp. 253–265). New York: Holt, Rinehart & Winston.

Sears, R. R., Maccoby, E. E., & Levin, H. (1957). *Patterns of child rearing*. Evanston, IL: Row, Peterson.

Selman, R. (1980). *The growth of interpersonal understanding: Developmental and clinical applications*. New York: Academic Press.

Selman, R., & Schultz, L. H. (1989). Children's strategies for interpersonal negotiation with peers: An interpretive/empirical approach to the study of social development. In T. J. Berndt & G. W. Ladd (Eds.), *Peer relationships in child development* (pp. 371–406). New York: Wiley.

Serbin, L. A., Powlishta, K. K., & Gulko, J. (1993). The development of sex-typing in middle childhood. *Monographs of the Society for Research in Child Development, 58*(2, Serial No. 232).

Shantz, C. U. (1983). Social cognition. In P. H. Mussen (Ed.), *Handbook of child psychology* (Vol. 3, pp. 495–555). New York: Wiley.

Shantz, C. U., & Voydanoff, D. A. (1973). Situational effects on retaliatory aggression at three age levels. *Child Development, 44*, 149–153.

Siegler, R. (1989). Five principles of cognitive development. *Annual Review of Psychology, 40*, 353–379.

Shonkoff, J. P. (1984). The biological substrate and physical health in middle childhood. In W. A. Collins (Ed.), *Development during middle childhood: The years from six to twelve* (pp. 24–69). Washington, DC: National Academy of Sciences Press.

Smetana, J. G. (1989). Adolescents' and parents' reasoning about actual family conflict. *Child Development, 60*, 1052–1067.

Sroufe, L. A., Bennett, C., Englund, M., Urban, J., & Shulman, S. (1993). The significance of gender boundaries in preadolescence: Contemporary correlates and antecedents of boundary violation and maintenance. *Child Development, 64*, 455–466.

Sroufe, L. A., & Fleeson, J. (1986). Attachment and the construction of relationships. In W. Hartup & Z. Rubin (Eds.), *Relationships and development* (pp. 51–71). New York: Cambridge University Press.

Sroufe, L. A., Carlson, E., & Shulman, S. (in press). The development of individuals in relationships: From infancy through adolescence. In D. C. Funder, R. D. Parke, C. Tomlinson-Keasey, & K. Widaman (Eds.), *Studying lives through time: Approaches to personality and development* (pp. 315–342). Washington, DC: American Psychological Association.

Steinberg, L. (1986). Latchkey children and susceptibility to peer pressure: An ecological analysis. *Developmental Psychology, 22*, 433–439.

Steinberg, L., Elmen, J. D., & Mounts, N. S. (1989). Authoritative parenting, psychosocial maturity, and academic success among adolescents. *Child Development, 60*, 1424–1436.

Stevenson, H. W., & Lee, S. Y. (1990). Contexts of achievement. *Monographs of the Society for Research in Child Development, 55*(1–2, Serial No. 221).

Stevenson, H. W., & Newman, R. S. (1986). Long-term prediction of achievement and attitudes in mathematics and reading. *Child Development, 57*, 646–659.

Stocker, C., Dunn, J., & Plomin, R. (1989). Sibling relationships: Links with child temperament, maternal behavior, and family structure. *Child Development, 60*, 715–727.

Tolan, P. H., & Loeber, R. (1993). Antisocial behavior. In P. H. Tolan & B. Cohler (Eds.), *Handbook of clinical research and practice with adolescents* (pp. 307–331). New York: Wiley.

Underwood, M. K., Coie, J. D., & Herbsman, C. R. (1992). Display rules for anger and aggression in school-age children. *Child Development, 63*, 366–380.

Urban, J., Carlson, E., Egeland, B., & Sroufe, L. A. (1991). Patterns of individual adaptation across childhood. *Development and Psychopathology, 3*, 445–460.

Vaillant, G. E. (1977). *Adaptation to life*. Boston: Little, Brown.

Vandell, D. L., & Corasaniti, M. A. (1988). The relation between third graders' after-school care and social, academic, and emotional functioning. *Child Development, 59,* 868.875.

Vandell, D. L., Minnett, A. M., Santrock, J. W. (1987). Age differences in sibling relationships during middle childhood. *Journal of Applied Developmental Psychology, 8,* 247–257.

Vuchinich, S., Bank, L., & Patterson, G. R. (1992). Parenting, peers, and the stability of antisocial behavior in preadolescent boys. *Developmental Psychology, 28*(3), 510–521.

Wahler, R. G. (1980). Parent insularity as a determinant of generalization success in family treatment. In S. Salzinger, J. Antrobus, & J. Glick (Eds.), *The ecosystem of the sick child* (pp. 187–200). New York: Academic Press.

Walker, L. J., & Taylor, J. H. (1991). Family interactions and the development of moral reasoning. *Child Development, 62,* 264–283.

Wallerstein, J. S., & Kelly, J. B. (1980). *Surviving the break-Up: How children and parents cope with divorce.* New York: Basic Books.

Warton, P. M., & Goodnow, J. J. (1991). The nature of responsibility: Children's understanding of "your job." *Child Development, 62,* 156–165.

Weisner, T. S. (1984). Ecocultural niches of middle childhood: A cross-cultural perspective. In W. A. Collins (Ed.), *Development during middle childhood: The years from six to twelve* (pp. 335–369). Washington, DC: National Academy of Sciences Press.

Weiss, B., Dodge, K. A., Bates, J. E., & Pettit, G. S. (1992). Some consequences of early harsh discipline: Child aggression and a maladaptive social information processing style. *Child Development, 63,* 1321–1335.

White, K. M., Speisman, J. C., & Costos, D. (1983). Young adults and their parents. In H. D. Grotevant & C. R. Cooper (Eds.), *Adolescent development in the family: New directions in child development* (No. 22, pp. 61–76). San Francisco: Jossey-Bass.

Whitehurst, G. J., & Sonnenschein, S. (1981). The development of informative messages in referential communication: Knowing when versus knowing how. In W. P. Dickson (Eds.), *Children's oral communication skills* (pp. 127–142). New York: Academic Press.

Winder, C. L., & Rau, L. (1962). Parental attitudes associated with social deviance in preadolescent boys. *Journal of Abnormal and Social Psychology, 64,* 418–424.

Youniss, J. (1980). *Parents and peers in social development: A Sullivan-Piaget perspective.* Chicago: University of Chicago Press.

Youniss, J. (1983). Social construction of adolescence by adolescents and parents. In H. D. Grotevant & C. R. Cooper (Eds.), *Adolescent development in the family: New directions for child development* (No. 22, pp. 93–109). San Francisco: Jossey–Bass.

Zarbatany, L., Hartmann, D. P., & Rankin, D. B. (1990). The psychological functions of preadolescent peer activities. *Child Development, 61,* 1067–1080.

4

Parenting Adolescents

Grayson N. Holmbeck
Loyola University Chicago
Roberta L. Paikoff
University of Illinois, Chicago
Jeanne Brooks-Gunn
Teachers College, Columbia University

INTRODUCTION

It is only recently that parenting has become a discrete and much researched topic in the literature on adolescent development, distinguishable from work on parenting children of other ages. Indeed, as recently as 1980, there was so little research on the topic of family relationships during adolescence that one author was unable to complete a handbook-length review on the topic (Adelson, 1980, 1985). In sharp contrast, the time since has witnessed the emergence of considerable interest in parent–child relationships during the adolescent period (Petersen, 1988). Vast improvements in both the quality and quantity of research on adolescents and their families have led to several recent reviews focusing on the integration of this research literature (Collins, 1990; Hill, 1987; Paikoff & Brooks-Gunn, 1991; Steinberg, 1990).

Despite the appearance of these reviews, there has been no serious attempt to review the literature on parent–adolescent relationships from a "parenting" perspective. Thus, this chapter focuses specifically on the task of parenting adolescent children (Kidwell, Fischer, Dunham, & Baranowski, 1983). The chapter is divided into five sections. The first section reviews the pattern of developmental and contextual changes that occur in the child during adolescence and speculates on the implications that each has for parenting. More specifically, it briefly reviews the biological, cognitive, social-cognitive, emotional, self-definitional, and contextual changes that impact on the task of parenting. Developmental change requires the parenting task to change in several respects, but particularly with regard to issues of flexibility, responsivity, supervisory responsibilities, and the like. The second section reviews developmental concerns that parents experience as their children make the transition to adolescence, again speculating on how such concerns alter the parenting task. There may be links between developmental concerns of adolescents and developmental concerns of parents; stressors that confront parents during this stage of the family life cycle may have a significant effect on the parenting task. The third section examines adolescent outcomes of parenting, with a particular focus on findings relevant to adolescent competence and adjustment difficulties. Research relevant to the following dimensions of parenting is reviewed: parenting style, parenting practices, changes in parenting practices during the transition to adolescence, discrepancies between parent and adolescent viewpoints regarding important family issues, and parent–adolescent conflict. In past research, certain parenting styles and practices have been linked with favorable adolescent outcomes. Moreover, adolescents appear to benefit when parents demonstrate sensitivity to the developmental needs of their children, when discrepancies between the perceptions of parents and adolescents are acknowledged, and when parents respond adaptively to parent–adolescent conflict. In the fourth section, we examine effects of both parent and child gender on parenting practices. Differences between mother–adolescent and father–adolescent relationships are highlighted, as are more specific dyadic differences. Finally, our conclusions are summarized at the end of the chapter and several directions for future work in this area are reviewed.

DEVELOPMENTAL AND CONTEXTUAL CHANGES IN THE CHILD: IMPLICATIONS FOR PARENTING

Whereas children in the United States and other Western cultures are presumed to need intensive and extensive monitoring and supervision, the goal of parenting during the adolescent period is in some sense to produce independent and autonomous offspring, albeit in a context of caring and connected family relationships (Hill & Holmbeck, 1986). Thus, in the ideal, parenting during this period becomes less dominated by parental authority and power. Changes in the goals and challenges of parenting are likely due to developmental changes that occur in the child during the transition to adolescence. At a more complex level, developmental changes in the child also may interact with parents' own life situation and developmental concerns to influence the task of parenting. This section reviews the relevant literature on the developmental and contextual changes in the child that occur during the adolescent period. Development during the transition to adolescence involves biological, cognitive, emotional, self-definitional, and contextual changes in the child (Hill, 1980b), all of which may necessitate changes in the parenting task. Each type of change is reviewed in turn, with particular attention to the implications of each change for parenting.

Biological Changes

Pubertal changes that define the entry into the adolescent life phase are the most comprehensive biological changes since those of the first year of life (Brooks-Gunn & Reiter, 1990; Paikoff & Brooks-Gunn, 1991). The onset of pubertal change is often considered the beginning of *early adolescence* (roughly age 11–14 years; Steinberg, 1993), a developmental period that can be distinguished from *middle adolescence* (roughly age 15–18 years) and *late adolescence* (roughly age 18–21 years). During early adolescence, changes occur in the levels of hormones, as regulated by the hypothalamus, pituitary gland, and the gonads (Petersen & Taylor, 1980). These changes result in the visible physical changes of puberty (e.g., breast growth in girls; facial hair in boys, changes in body muscle and body fat in both genders) as well as those that are not visible (e.g., menarche in girls; testicular growth in boys; pubic hair development in both). Although adolescents progress through the events of puberty in largely the same sequence (within gender), the rate of progression through puberty, as well as the timing of particular pubertal events, vary widely (Brooks-Gunn & Reiter, 1990; Evelyth & Tanner, 1976).

    The physiological and physical events of puberty have been examined with regard to their effects on the psychological and social functioning of the adolescent (Paikoff & Brooks-Gunn, 1990). For example, menarche is not the traumatic experience that much psychoanalytic literature has portrayed.

Rather, girls experience many different feelings, ranging from positive to negative (Brooks-Gunn, 1984; Greif & Ulman, 1982). Discussions with mothers (fathers are almost never informed by daughters about their menarche) tend to center around logistics and physical symptoms, and rarely focus on feelings (Brooks-Gunn & Ruble, 1982; Ruble & Brooks-Gunn, 1982). Limited work with boys suggests that initial ejaculation (or "spermarche") is a relatively pleasant experience, but also seldom discussed with parents (Gaddis & Brooks-Gunn, 1985).

The changes of puberty may result in intraindividual changes that impact on the adolescent's relationship with parents (Brooks-Gunn & Zahaykevich, 1989; Buchanan, Eccles, & Becker, 1992). For example, hormonal changes could directly impact on parent–child relationships due to enhanced irritability and negative emotionality on the part of the adolescent (Buchanan et al., 1992). Visible pubertal changes may result in comments from parents and others. For example, in a study of girls' responses to puberty, parents were mentioned as the most frequent teasers regarding breast growth; anger was the primary affective response reported by girls (Brooks-Gunn, 1984; Brooks-Gunn & Warren, 1988). Pubertal changes that are not visible and known only to the adolescent may not be discussed in the relationship, creating altered patterns of communication. Any or all of these changes may lead to increases in conflict and emotional distance in parent–child relationships during the pubertal period (e.g., Hill, Holmbeck, Marlow, Green, & Lynch, 1985a, 1985b; Holmbeck & Hill, 1991; Papini, Datan, & McCluskey-Fawcett, 1988; Steinberg, 1987a; although, see Laursen & Collins, 1994, for a different interpretation of these data). This association between conflict and pubertal change may also be bidirectional (Belsky, Steinberg, & Draper, 1991; Brooks-Gunn, Graber, & Paikoff, 1994; Graber, Brooks-Gunn, & Warren, in press; Moffitt, Caspi, Belsky, & Silva, 1992; Steinberg, 1988).

The biological changes of early adolescence result in a reproductively mature individual, and are linked to changes in the expectations of parents and other adults regarding child behavior (Collins, 1990; Eccles et al., 1993; Freedman-Doan, Arbreton, Harold, & Eccles, 1993; Paikoff & Brooks-Gunn, 1991). As children mature physically, parents may begin to feel they can expect more mature behavior, simultaneously wishing to monitor their child's interactions with the other sex more intensely (especially for daughters; see Hill & Lynch, 1983). Parents of adolescents are also more likely to infer intentionality in the behavior of their offspring than are parents of preadolescents (Dix, Ruble, Grusec, & Nixon, 1986; Goodnow & Collins, 1990). It is likely that expectations on the part of parents about what it "means" to have an adolescent in the home may have an impact on their parenting behaviors (Collins, 1990). For example, if parents endorse "storm and stress" beliefs about adolescence (Buchanan et al., 1990; Holmbeck & Hill, 1988), they may be more likely to "put the brakes on" when their child becomes pubertal, due to anticipatory fears of rebelliousness and conflict. Pubertal changes may also change the affective nature of the parent–child relationship (e.g., Holmbeck & Hill, 1991), particularly for fathers and daughters, as both parties may feel less comfortable expressing physical affection than previously (Hill, 1988; also see Brooks-Gunn & Zahaykevich, 1989, for anecdotal evidence). At adolescence, the parent's task is to incorporate these biological changes into their own image of the child, as well as to confront the meaning of the child's increasingly adultlike appearance.

Cognitive and Social-Cognitive Changes

Considerable controversy exists regarding whether *qualitative* shifts occur in the thinking of children during the adolescent years (see Keating, 1990; Lapsley, 1990). Most investigators agree, however, that problem-solving abilities improve incrementally, particularly with regard to the spontaneous generation of alternatives as well as the complexity of the process by which alternatives are evaluated. Such abilities are fostered in school environments, where assignments and discussion may increasingly involve debate and critical evaluation. The cognitive changes of adolescence also may enable the child to incorporate multiple viewpoints, or to think systematically about persons or relationships (Damon & Hart, 1982; Selman, 1980).

Within the larger area of cognitive change, the subset of studies examining social cognition, or changes in abilities to consider and reflect on social relationships, are perhaps most relevant to consideration of parenting and parent–adolescent relationships (also see Brooks-Gunn & Paikoff, 1992). This literature has focused both on content (adolescents' descriptive statements about themselves, friends, or family) and structure (complexity, sophistication, and integration of adolescents' descriptions). With regard to content, there appears to be a shift from an emphasis on physical and material aspects to more psychological descriptions of self and relationships (Berndt, 1986; Harter, 1983; Livesley & Bromley, 1973; Montemayor & Eisen, 1977). Structural approaches to adolescent social cognition have, for the most part, adapted Piagetian stages to the description of social reasoning in a variety of domains. As with more general work on cognitive development, these approaches have been plagued by the inability to define particular shifts in the quality of social reasoning, finding instead relatively large and nonspecific stages that overlap, without being able to specify behavioral links. The most comprehensive have been provided by Selman (1980) and by Youniss and colleagues (Youniss, 1980; Youniss & Smollar, 1985). Both find overall support for changes in adolescent thinking about parent–child relationships that incorporate greater integration and sophistication, as well as improved abilities to appreciate the importance of social reciprocity and mutuality in the parent–child relationship, and (in the case of Selman) enhanced capacities for coordinating multiple perspectives on social relationships.

It has been hypothesized that these cognitive changes, many of which are fostered in the school environment, may result in more confrontative interactions with parents, as adolescents increasingly begin to question and debate parental rules and expectations (Collins, 1990; Smetana, 1988b). Smetana (1988a, 1988b, 1989) suggested that differences arise between parents and children at adolescence regarding their beliefs about the legitimacy of parental jurisdiction over particular issues, due to children's increased questioning of the appropriateness of parental control. Although contentious debates and interchanges between parents and children most surely occur prior to adolescence, increases in sophistication and complexity of thought allow adolescents to manifest more adultlike reasoning, making such interchanges potentially more prolonged and more challenging for parents. Thus, as parents and children negotiate the transition toward adulthood, the parenting task begins to require more sophisticated reasoning in limit setting coupled with flexibility and a willingness to allow for change in rules and rule regulation (Kidwell et al., 1983).

The ability to think more complexly about people and relationships allows adolescents to integrate positive as well as negative perceptions of parents, potentially facilitating the process of parental de-idealization (Blos, 1979; Fuhrman & Holmbeck, in press; Lamborn & Steinberg, 1993; Ryan & Lynch, 1989; Steinberg & Silverberg, 1986). Hence, another possible precipitating factor in changes in the parent–child relationship at adolescence involves the child's realization that the parent is not perfect and the child's potential willingness to discuss this issue with the parent.

Emotional and Self-Definitional Changes

Pubertal and cognitive changes of adolescence are often linked to changes in perceptions of the self and others. Changes in emotionality or affective expression are linked to the *meaning* assigned to these new perceptions of self and other (e.g., positive or negative feelings regarding the worth or the agency of the self and others). The valence of these emotions in turn may have implications for the parent–child relationship and for the parenting task at adolescence.

The majority of work on adolescent affective expression has focused on depression or negative emotionality (Brooks-Gunn & Paikoff, 1992; Brooks-Gunn & Petersen, 1991; Petersen et al., 1993). Increases in negative affective expression occur from preadolescence to middle adolescence; evidence suggests that slight increases occur population-wide, although individual variation in factors such as timing of pubertal development and cumulative number of life changes (see later) have been associated with increased depressive affect as well (Brooks-Gunn, 1991; Brooks-Gunn & Paikoff, 1992; Petersen, Sarigiani & Kennedy, 1991).

Despite overall increases in depressive affect, it is also clear that the majority of adolescents have relatively stable self-feelings (Brooks-Gunn, 1991; Kandel & Davies, 1986; Savin-Williams & Demo, 1984) and do not become extremely depressed or require clinical services. Approximately 20 percent of adolescents experience intense difficulties (Hauser & Bowlds, 1990; Offer, 1987), and it is probably the case that many of these adolescents were already having adjustment difficulties as children (Loeber, 1989; Robins, 1978). The presence of emotional difficulties may impact on an adolescent's willingness to participate in the parent–child relationship, and the degree of communication or closeness between parent and adolescent. Such difficulties may also influence the degree to which a parent feels engaged in interaction with the adolescent or competent to assist in the adolescent's continued passage toward maturity. Indeed, poor familial relationships have been consistently linked to adolescent depressive affect, although the direction of the association remains unclear (Carlton-Ford, Paikoff, & Brooks-Gunn, 1991b; Petersen et al., 1993).

Controversy surrounds the role of child temperament and personality in contributing to variation in parenting behavior (Belsky, 1984; Sroufe, 1985; Thomas & Chess, 1977). Of particular note is the relatively consistent finding that parent or child psychiatric symptomatology is linked to more extreme disturbances in the parent–child relationship at adolescence (Hauser & Bowlds, 1990; Hibbs, Hamburger, Kruesi, & Rapoport, 1992). In particular, maternal depression has often been considered as predictive of problematic parent–child relationships (Dodge, 1990; Field, in this *Handbook*; Hammen, Burge, & Stansbury, 1990); these difficulties may be exacerbated by either a "match" or "mismatch" in depression between parent and child. In less extreme circumstances, it is likely that relatively small increases in depressive affect at adolescence will go largely unrecognized by parents—a relatively consistent body of methodological evidence suggests that one of the areas of disagreement between parents and children is in their rating of the child's internalizing behavior problems; parents are likely to underrate child depression and anxiety (Achenbach, McConaughy, & Howell, 1987). It is thus an additional parenting task to attempt to keep lines of communication open so that parents are aware of adolescents' negative affect, as well as to be flexible in seeking help for their adolescent children when negative emotional states become particularly problematic.

Contextual Changes

A host of contextual changes characterizes the transition from childhood to adolescence as well as the adolescent period. We focus on changes in peer relationships, changes in the school context, and the problems that result from the accumulation of changes and major life events during adolescence.

Changes in peer relationships. At the same time that physical and cognitive changes are occurring, changes in friendship and peer relationships occur as well. Peer relationships fill important emotional needs beginning relatively early in childhood, because they allow children to interact in "horizontal" ways amongst relative equals, in contrast to their more "vertical" relationships with adults (Hartup, 1983, 1989). At adolescence, however, relationships with peers assume more central importance, and are likely to become more intimate and be based on the sharing of thoughts, ideas, and opinions, as well as activities (Berndt & Perry, 1990; Savin-Williams & Berndt, 1990). Both girls and boys may be more likely to share initial experiences of pubertal maturation with friends rather than with parents (Brooks-Gunn, Samelson, Warren, & Fox, 1986; Gaddis & Brooks-Gunn, 1985); this "selective sharing" may in turn lead to increases in emotional distance between parents and children during the pubertal period (although this premise has not been tested empirically).

It has frequently been suggested in the popular media that during adolescence children begin to rely more heavily on the influence of peers (and, more particularly, their friends) than parents. In fact, little empirical evidence supports this premise (Brown, 1990). Although the influence of peer groups and friendships increases across adolescence, parents retain primary influence over major decision making regarding life values, goals, and future decisions (Berndt, 1979, 1982; Brown, 1990). From the parents' perspective, however, the changes in influence that do occur, coupled with popular media images of the adolescent and the parent–adolescent relationship, may invoke concerns over loss of influence.

Parents may wish to supervise closely their children's peer relationships (particularly in mixed-sex groupings or dating relationships), but they also are likely to recognize the importance of these adolescent relationships to emotional well-being. Adolescents are likely to choose friendships based on their own relationship history; thus, their friends are likely to be relatively similar to their parents on dimensions of values and attitudes (Block, Haan, & Smith, 1969; Brown, 1990). Even slight differences between parental and friendship values, however, may be disconcerting to parents. The task of parenting adolescents requires parents simultaneously to encourage the formation of friendship and dating relationships with same- and opposite-sex peers as well as to monitor the activities of the friendship group. Adolescents are far more likely than younger children to spend unsupervised time with peers. It is in such situations that important peer socialization occurs; however, it is also the case that these time periods involve heightened possibilities for risk-taking or problem behaviors.

Changes in school context.   As adolescents' relationships within the peer context change, so do the social contexts in which adolescents spend both structured and free time. In the United States, children frequently move from elementary to junior high or middle school during the young adolescent years. Eccles and her collaborators (Eccles et al., 1993; Eccles & Midgley, 1990) suggested that the structure and organization of many middle or junior high schools is at odds with the developmental needs of the early adolescent period and thus may increase the stressfulness of the adolescent transition. These organizational changes often involve more fragmented days (e.g., moving from classroom to classroom and from teacher to teacher rather than staying in one room the majority of the day), and a transition from smaller, more personal elementary schools to larger middle or junior high schools (Eccles & Midgley, 1990; Simmons & Blyth, 1987). Such changes are undertaken with the goal of promoting increased autonomy and maturity among young adolescents; the timing of these changes, however, appears to have important emotional and social consequences for individual adolescents (Simmons & Blyth, 1987) and may occur too early for optimal benefit of most (Eccles & Midgley, 1990).

Organizational changes in the school context require parents to assist the child in negotiating the new system and the increased responsibilities and challenges of this life transition. Unfortunately, the manner in which parents provide such assistance has not received intensive study. Collins (1990) hypothesized that the encouragement of more questioning and more critical thought in the school setting may be incorporated into parent–child dialogues, and thus result in exacerbated conflicts between parents and children. Parents may need to respond to changes in the child, which first manifest themselves in the school context. Work with children of earlier ages has unearthed important links between early parent–child behavior and individual differences in resource seeking and utilization in preschool (Sroufe, 1983) and in the elementary school years (Sroufe, Egeland, & Kreutzer, 1990); the extent to which school behavior influences later parent–child relationships is not known.

Accumulation of changes.   The rise in mental health problems (and, in particular, depressive affect) at adolescence may be linked to the sheer frequency and cumulative effect of multiple life events and major social and contextual transitions (Petersen et al., 1991; Simmons, Burgeson, & Reef, 1988; Smolak, Levine, & Gralen, 1993). Self-esteem and depressive affect have been associated with the cumulative number of life events, such that larger numbers of life events are linked to more negative affect (e.g., higher depression, lower self-esteem; see Baydar et al., 1992; Simmons et al., 1988). Petersen et al. (1991) reported that the gender differences found in depressive affect at adolescence are explained by the greater propensity of girls to experience multiple challenges (in particular, pubertal change coupled with school transition) than boys; however, the linear finding discussed earlier (e.g., more life events leading to overall higher levels of depressive affect) holds for both boys and girls (Simmons et al., 1988).

In response to the multiple changes and challenges of the young adolescent period, parents must be able to take perspective on the adolescent's life and the multiple events and challenges experienced by the child, and to anticipate and help prepare the child for resultant stress. Similar to the changes of infancy, toddlerhood, and middle childhood, adolescence is a time when changes and challenges occur in multiple systems. Unlike those periods, however, parents must now cope with multiple changes in an organism capable of reflecting and constructing meaning from these changes. Continued flexibility and fluidity in the parenting task is necessary to assist with these changes.

Summary

Developmental and contextual changes in the child during the transition from childhood to adolescence require the parenting task to change in terms of greater flexibility and responsivity. Generally speaking, however, little empirical work has been done on associations between developmental changes in the child and the task of parenting. Parents are often challenged to change the way they manage their relationship with their child. For instance, some of the most difficult parenting challenges during the adolescent years are likely to involve negotiating a relationship with a reproductively mature child; revising and modifying household discussions and debate, as well as rules and regulations; negotiating the level of supervision and monitoring, while facilitating the child's peer socialization; and the need for a heightened degree of perspective taking on the part of the parent. It is likely that challenges such as these will necessitate changes in one's parenting style and practices and also may result in increases in parent–adolescent conflict. The next section reviews the developmental concerns of parents and the implications that such concerns have for the task of parenting.

DEVELOPMENTAL ISSUES OF PARENTS: IMPLICATIONS FOR PARENTING

Not only do adolescents experience a host of intraindividual changes during the transition to adolescence, but parents may as well. Available evidence suggests there may be more marital dissatisfaction and physical and identity concerns on the part of parents of adolescents, as compared to parents of younger children (Preto & Travis, 1985; Silverberg & Steinberg, 1987, 1990; Steinberg & Silverberg, 1987; Wilson & Gottman, in this *Handbook*). Whether these indices of discomfort and dissatisfaction reflect midlife issues of the parent, the stresses of parenting an adolescent, or a combination of the two is not known. Some scholars have posited a connection between the changes of the younger and older generations (Kidwell et al., 1983). That is, parents' tendency to reevaluate their goals, values, and beliefs may be, in part, a reaction to the development of their own offspring (Preto & Travis, 1985). The adolescent is developing physically, cognitively, and sexually at a time when parents are questioning their status in each of these very same areas. Both adolescents and parents may be simultaneously confronted with struggles related to personal goals, relationship concerns, and issues of autonomy (Farrell & Rosenberg, 1981; Preto & Travis, 1985).

Research has supported some of these speculations. As adolescents gradually distance themselves emotionally from their same-sex parents (as opposed to their opposite-sex parents), mothers and fathers are more likely to report midlife concerns, reappraisal, and less marital satisfaction (Silverberg & Steinberg, 1987; Steinberg & Silverberg, 1987). Parents also report higher levels of personal stress during periods when their offspring are making demands for increased levels of autonomy and when there are more conflicts over such autonomy demands than during periods when there are fewer autonomy demands and conflicts (Small, Eastman, & Cornelius, 1988). Finally, there is some evidence to suggest that, in families where mothers are in the process of completing their own reproductive years at the same time that their daughters are beginning to mature physically, both mothers and daughters appear to experience more difficulties, particularly in the area of eating concerns (Paikoff, Brooks-Gunn, & Carlton-Ford, 1991). Thus, there may be predictable associations between adolescents' and parents' developmental changes and concerns and these associations may be causally linked (Silverberg & Steinberg, 1990). Given that the adolescent phase of the family life cycle appears to be stressful for parents, it is likely that such an increase in stress will impact on the tasks of parenting.

Level of marital conflict (Amato & Keith, 1991; Fauber, Forehand, Thomas, & Wierson, 1990; Grych & Fincham, 1990; Hetherington & Anderson, 1988; Hetherington & Clingempeel, 1992), maternal and paternal psychopathology (Dodge, 1990; Hauser & Bowlds, 1990; Rutter, 1990), as well as other major and minor life events and stressors have been found to impact the quality of parenting and adolescent adjustment and could be expected to impact parents' and adolescents' responses to developmental change. Highly stressed family systems may be less responsive or less adaptively responsive to developmental changes in the offspring.

THE TASKS OF PARENTING: IMPLICATIONS FOR ADOLESCENT ADJUSTMENT

What is known about the task of parenting during the adolescent period? We divide this section into five parts: parenting style, parenting practices, changes in parenting during the transition to adolescence, discrepancies between adolescents' and parents' views of family issues, and parent–adolescent conflict. In drawing a distinction between parenting practices and parenting style, we were influenced by the reviews by Maccoby and J. Martin (1983) and by Darling and Steinberg (1993). Maccoby and Martin (1983) reviewed child outcomes of parenting styles (e.g., authoritarian-autocratic, indulgent-permissive) separately from outcomes of specific practices (e.g., induction). Darling and Steinberg (1993) also argued that the distinction between parenting style and parenting practices is critical, insofar as parents who do not differ in their style of parenting may differ greatly in the practices they employ to achieve their socialization goals. Parenting practices are hypothesized by Darling and Steinberg (1993) to have a direct effect on adolescent outcomes. Parenting style, on the other hand, is hypothesized to have an indirect effect on outcome via its influence on the *relationship* between parenting practices and outcome. That is, parenting style is a context that influences the relative effectiveness of parenting practices.

Parenting Style

Based primarily on factor analyses of interview and questionnaire data, early work on parenting style during childhood and adolescence (Becker, 1964; Schaefer, 1959; see Darling & Steinberg, 1993; Maccoby & J. Martin, 1983; B. Martin, 1975, for reviews) suggested that parenting may be described globally along two dimensions: warmth–hostility and permissiveness–restrictiveness (Becker, 1964). Later, Baumrind (1968) developed a tripartite classification system whereby parents could be categorized as authoritarian, authoritative, or permissive. Although narrowly conceived of as a typology of parental control, Baumrind's classification system proved to be more broadly useful in differentiating parents across other dimensions of parenting as well (e.g., warmth, communication style). Baumrind (1980, 1991) used the terms *responsiveness* and *demandingness* as labels for parenting dimensions that are not unlike those that emerged in the early studies (e.g., Becker, 1964).

Using the same terms, Maccoby and J. Martin (1983) devised a fourfold scheme where parents could be classified as authoritarian–autocratic, indulgent–permissive, authoritative–reciprocal, or indifferent–uninvolved. Placement into a category is based on a parents' distribution of scores (representing high and low levels of responsiveness and demandingness) from questionnaire, interview, and/or observational methods. Children and adolescents coming from *authoritarian–autocratic* homes (i.e., high demandingness, low responsiveness) experience a style of parenting characterized by power assertion, where obedience to rules is expected and where children are often not permitted to make demands on parents. In such a parenting environment, there is little warmth and verbal give-and-take between parents and their children, and physical punishment is more likely in such homes. Children and adolescents from *indulgent–permissive* homes (i.e., low demandingness, high responsiveness) have parents who are reasonably responsive but avoid regulating the behavior of their offspring. Such parents impose few rules on their children, make relatively few demands for mature behavior, avoid the use of punishment, and tend to be tolerant of a wide range of behavior (Maccoby & J. Martin, 1983). *Indifferent–uninvolved* parents (i.e., low demandingness, low responsiveness) tend to limit the amount of time they devote to the parenting task, thus limiting the degree to which they are exposed to the inconveniences of parenting (Maccoby & J. Martin, 1983). Many important parenting functions are often absent from these homes (e.g., a long-term commitment to rule-enforcement). Finally, parents who evidence an *authoritative–reciprocal* (i.e., high demandingness, high responsiveness) parenting style are responsive to the demands of their offspring but, at the same time, expect their children to be responsive to their demands (Baumrind, 1968; Darling & Steinberg, 1993; Maccoby & J. Martin, 1983). Such parents encourage verbal give and take (hence the label "reciprocal"), enforce rules when necessary, have clear expectations for mature behavior, and encourage independence. They foster psychological autonomy by encouraging their children to express their own opinions (Steinberg, 1990). Such parents also make a point of explaining their assertions and providing rationales for rules and regulations.

Parenting style and adjustment outcomes. Over the past 25 years, dozens of studies have been conducted to examine the child and adolescent outcomes of varying levels of parental demandingness and responsiveness. Across most outcome measures and across most questionnaire and observational measures of parenting, research with young children suggests that those who are exposed to authoritative rearing are rated as more competent and as having higher levels of self-esteem, moral development, impulse control, and subjective feelings of independence than are children from other types of parenting environments. Empirical findings for parents of adolescents are very similar to those that have emerged for younger children. Steinberg and his colleagues conducted several self-report questionnaire studies based on Maccoby and J. Martin's (1983) fourfold typology (e.g., Lamborn, Mounts, Steinberg, & Dornbusch, 1991; Steinberg, 1990). They used the following labels for different parenting style subtypes: *authoritative, authoritarian, indulgent,* and *neglectful.* As with children, and virtually regardless of the outcome assessed, authoritative parenting yields the most favorable outcomes for adolescents (Lamborn et al., 1991).

More specifically, Steinberg found that when one or more components of authoritative parenting are missing, adverse outcomes typically occur. Adolescents from authoritarian homes score high on measures of obedience but low on measures of self-competence. Adolescents from a permissive parenting background are self-confident but evidence higher levels of substance use and school difficulties. Finally, adolescents from neglectful homes evidence the lowest scores on competence and the highest scores on behavior problems, as compared with the other three forms of parenting. Given these findings, it appears that responsiveness and demandingness are each related to their own set of adolescent outcomes. Whereas responsiveness appears to facilitate the development of self-esteem and social skills, demandingness appears to foster impulse-control and social responsibility (Steinberg, 1990).

Parent–adolescent and peer–adolescent relationships have also been studied within the same design; results from this line of research suggest that parenting style is associated with peer-group membership (e.g., Durbin, Darling, Steinberg, & Brown, 1993). For example, authoritatively reared adolescents are more likely to be in peer groups that endorse *both* parent and peer values. Employing longitudinal data, Steinberg, Lamborn, Dornbusch, and Darling (1992) found that parents from authoritative homes are also more likely to be involved in their child's schooling. Such parental involvement in the school was found, in turn, to promote school success.

Contextual variations in the effects of parenting style.   Although the benefits of authoritative parenting appear to cut across different ethnic groups and level of socioeconomic status (e.g., Steinberg, Mounts, Lamborn, & Dornbusch, 1991), there may be exceptions to this general conclusion. Steinberg and his colleagues examined links between academic performance and adolescents' reports of parenting (Darling & Steinberg, 1993; Dornbusch, Ritter, Leiderman, Roberts, & Fraleigh, 1987; Steinberg, Dornbusch, & Brown, 1992; Steinberg, Elmen, & Mounts, 1989; Steinberg, Mounts, Lamborn, & Dornbusch, 1991). In this research, authoritatively reared Asian-American and African-American adolescents are no more likely to exhibit superior school performance than are their nonauthoritatively reared counterparts (Steinberg et al., 1991). On the other hand, adolescents from European-American or Hispanic-American households who report authoritative parenting are advantaged with respect to academic performance as compared to those coming from nonauthoritative households. These findings may be due to a variety of factors. The goals toward which parents socialize their children may differ across ethnic groups. Or, the goals of parenting may be the same, but the actual parenting behaviors may differ across different cultures (Darling & Steinberg, 1993). Even if parents' goals and behaviors are similar, parenting behaviors may have different meanings for adolescents from varying cultural or ethnic backgrounds (Spencer & Dornbusch, 1990). Another set of explanations focuses more on poverty, because ethnicity and poverty are so highly related (Duncan, Brooks-Gunn, & Klebanov, in press; McLoyd, 1990; Spencer & Dornbusch, 1990). Clearly, much work is needed on ethnic and social class variations in parenting style and the outcomes of parenting (Spencer & Dornbusch, 1990).

Parenting Practices

A conceptualization of the parenting task that relies solely on parenting styles, and especially parenting typologies, may miss the richness of parent–child interactions, may be overly descriptive (rather than predictive), and may restrict the search for mechanisms by which parents influence their children. Parenting style is not merely an additive combination of two clusters of parenting behaviors (i.e., responsiveness and demandingness). According to Darling and Steinberg (1993), parenting style is an environmental or "emotional climate" variable that is communicated by other aspects of parenting (in addition to demandingness and responsiveness), such as voice tone and body language. Thus, parenting style is likely an *inclusive* construct. It is also the case that there are other behaviors that are important components of the parenting task that are not part of "parenting style," regardless of how it is defined (Darling & Steinberg, 1993). For example, two authoritative parents may exhibit similar levels of demandingness and responsiveness, but may display these qualities in very different ways. Finally, demandingness and responsiveness are not necessarily manifested in the same way across different types of parenting styles. For example, the "demandingness" displayed by an authoritative parent probably differs from the "demandingness" displayed by an authoritarian parent, with the latter permitting less verbal give-and-take between parent and child. Thus, more specific parenting behaviors must be taken into account in order to explain differences in adolescent outcome (Darling & Steinberg, 1993).

Although the findings of the parenting style literature appear to be consistent across methodologies, adjustment outcomes, and developmental level, the bulk of the studies tells us little about the mechanisms through which parents' behaviors impact on their child's development. This section of the chapter reviews the literature on adolescent outcomes across the following parenting practices: (1) power-assertive and coercive control; (2) strictness, firm control, and consistency of discipline; (3) induction and democracy; (4) monitoring, supervision, and involvement; (5) warmth, responsiveness, and acceptance; (6) information provision and skill development; (7) constraining and enabling parenting behaviors; and (8) parenting behaviors that demonstrate connectedness and individuality. There is, of course, some overlap between the previous parenting style section and the current parenting practices section because some of the practices reviewed here have been discussed in reviews of the parenting style literature (e.g., Maccoby & J. Martin, 1983).

Power-assertive and coercive control. According to Patterson (1982, 1986), coercion is a family interactional process that is more common in families with antisocial offspring and occurs when family members reinforce and facilitate each others' aversive behaviors. Inept disciplinary practices that involve extreme punishment practices and lack of followthrough on consequences is also associated with antisocial behavior in children. Punishment appears to inhibit negative behavior in children without adjustment difficulties but has the opposite effect for antisocial children (Hetherington & B. Martin, 1986; Patterson, 1982).

In an 8-year longitudinal study of mothers of 1- to 10-year-olds (9–18 years at follow-up), Cohen and Brook (1987) found evidence for a positive association between power-assertive disciplinary techniques (defined as hitting, scolding, and threatening in this study) and several measures of child psychopathology. More specifically, they found that early levels of power-assertive techniques were associated with a subsequent increase in behavioral and affective problems. Similarly, increases in such disciplinary techniques were associated with concurrent increases in anxiety, immaturity, behavior problems, and affective problems. Thus, power-assertive disciplinary techniques are associated with conduct problems in children. Moreover, these effects tend to persist into adolescence and are found with observational and interview methodologies.

Strictness, firm control, and consistency of discipline. Power-assertive/coercive parenting techniques differ from parenting that is firm and strict. The former is more extreme, more dysfunctional, less consistent, and more damaging to the child (Maccoby & J. Martin, 1983; Patterson, 1986). Maccoby and J. Martin (1983, p. 42) argued that coercive parents "do not exercise firm control in the sense of establishing clear standards of expected behavior and maintaining consistent effective discipline." Although power-assertive parenting is often used interchangeably with authoritarian parenting (Maccoby & J. Martin, 1983), many studies use the term "power assertive" to refer to more punitive forms of parenting (e.g., Cohen & Brook, 1987) than is implied by the label "authoritarian." Thus, it is assumed here that authoritarian parents are firm, strict, and consistent, but are not necessarily power-assertive and coercive.

Whether strictness and firm control are associated with positive adolescent outcomes appears to depend on the context in which it occurs. The expectation that a child behave in accordance with a set of firmly set standards is more likely to have positive consequences for the adolescent if it is accompanied by verbal give-and-take between parent and child. Positive outcomes are also more likely if the child perceives the parents' rules as legitimate and if parents have respect for the individuality of the child (Maccoby & J. Martin, 1983). Of course, these latter qualities are defining characteristics of authoritative parenting (Maccoby & J. Martin, 1983). Baumrind (1991) referred to firm control in isolation as "directive/conventional control" (i.e., restrictiveness) and refers to firm control in the context of other authoritative characteristics as "assertive control" (i.e., firm but nonrestrictive). Firm control in isolation is not enough to produce positive outcomes; in fact, such control can undermine a child's feelings of self-reliance and intrinsic motivation (e.g., Deci, Driver, Hotchkiss, Robbins, & Wilson, 1993).

Induction and democracy. Authoritative parents differ from authoritarian parents not only in the level of warmth and affection that they display toward the child but also in their use of induction and democratic rearing techniques. Induction and democracy both require that parents acknowledge that their child's perspective may be different from their own. Induction involves a parent's attempt to explain assertions to the children by appealing to the child's concern for others or to their desire to be mature (Hoffman, 1970; Maccoby & J. Martin, 1983). Induction is an attempt by parents to legitimize their authority and help the child see an issue from the parents' perspective. Although induction appears to be associated with a host of positive outcomes in childhood (e.g., prosocial behavior, moral development; Maccoby & J. Martin, 1983), induction may be particularly important during adolescence because, as Hill (1988, p. 50) suggested, "in the face of greater cognitive sophistication on the part of the adolescent, naked assertion of parental power may delegitimate parental authority." Indeed, Hoffman (1975) found that induction by parents was only positively associated with prosocial behavior in the context of parenting characterized by low levels of power assertion (also see Elder, 1963).

Democratic rearing includes parenting practices that allow children to express their opinions about important family concerns and to question their parents' opinions. As was the case with induction, democratic rearing—with its characteristic encouragement of verbal give-and-take between parent and child—is associated with a host of positive outcomes (Baumrind, 1991). The degree to which parents are able to grant some degree of control to their children over important family issues appears to have implications for the child's level of self-esteem (Maccoby & J. Martin, 1983) and feelings of self-reliance (Steinberg, 1990). The degree to which parents can regulate the amount of give-and-take between them and their child as the child matures is an important task of parenting during the transition to adolescence (Fuligni & Eccles, 1993).

Monitoring, supervision, and involvement.   Whether or not parents are involved with their children (i.e., "the degree to which a parent is committed to his or her role as a parent," Maccoby & J. Martin, 1983, p. 48) and are able to consistently know their whereabouts appears to have implications for adolescent outcomes (Fuligni & Eccles, 1993; Maccoby & J. Martin, 1983; Patterson, 1986; Patterson, Bank, & Stoolmiller, 1990). Patterson (1986) found that parental involvement, as assessed with questionnaire and interview data, predicted higher levels of self-esteem in a study of antisocial behavior in preadolescents. In another study, maternal monitoring of adolescents' behavior proved to be the best predictor (negatively) of delinquent behavior (Patterson & Strouthamer-Loeber, 1984). In a 2-year longitudinal study of fourth graders (9-year-olds; sixth grade at follow-up) Patterson et al. (1990) found that inept disciplinary skills are associated with lack of monitoring, which is, in turn, associated with antisocial child behavior. Moreover, antisocial behavior at Time 1 was associated with lack of monitoring at Time 2—a circular homeostatic feedback loop. Using school-based samples rather than clinical samples, parental monitoring has been found to be associated with less extreme peer orientation and lower levels of susceptibility to peer pressure (Fuligni & Eccles, 1993; Steinberg, 1986).

Although the findings of this literature strongly suggest that greater degrees of parental involvement and supervision are beneficial for child development, some writers have been quick to caution that parents can be overly involved (Maccoby & J. Martin, 1983). Modifications in the degree and nature of supervision are necessary as the child makes the transition to adolescence. Moreover, such alterations in parenting are likely to facilitate development when built on a foundation of close relations with parents (Fuligni & Eccles, 1993; Grotevant & Cooper, 1985; Hill & Holmbeck, 1986).

Warmth, responsiveness, and acceptance.   Thus far, we have discussed a number of constructs related to parental control or the legitimization of parental control. A dimension of parenting that is orthogonal to parental control involves the degree of warmth and responsiveness that is present between parent and child. Unlike the "control" constructs where modifications in parenting practices are needed as the child matures (Fuligni & Eccles, 1993), similar changes in the "warmth" constructs are probably not necessary. That is, it is beneficial for parents to continue to be sources of support throughout the child's adolescent and adult years (Maccoby & J. Martin, 1983). Although there is some debate over operational definitions of various "warmth" constructs, it is clear that all are associated with a variety of positive adjustment outcomes in adolescence (including self-esteem, identity formation, prosocial behavior) and better parent–adolescent communication, as well as less depression, anxiety, and behavior problems (Armsden & Greenberg, 1987; Barnes & Olson, 1985; Dix, 1991; Hetherington & B. Martin, 1986; Maccoby & J. Martin, 1983; Papini, Micka, & Barnett, 1989; Papini & Roggman, 1992).

Although continuity of parental warmth during the transition to adolescence appears to facilitate development, this is not to say that levels of warmth and acceptance do not change during this developmental period. In fact, a number of studies suggest an increased emotional distance (Paikoff

& Brooks-Gunn, 1991) and perhaps less physical affection between parent and child during the peak of pubertal change (Hill, 1988). The task for parents, then, is to continue to provide warmth and acceptance during this period of disruption and realignment. Unfortunately, we know little about what level of warmth is optimal or what specific parenting behaviors are most likely to be experienced by the adolescent as indicative of warmth and responsiveness.

Information provision and skill development.   Little research has been conducted on parents' roles as information providers for their adolescent offspring. It is certainly the case that children vary in the degree to which they are open to information and socialization (Darling & Steinberg, 1993). It is also the case that children and adolescents are likely to imitate their parents' behaviors (Brooks-Gunn, 1993). For example, the manner in which parents model conflict resolution and negotiation skills may impact on the adolescent's ability to acquire these skills. It appears that parental socialization efforts and modeling have an impact on behaviors as diverse as academic achievement (Eccles, Jacobs, & Harold, 1990) and health promotion (Brooks-Gunn, 1993). Given that the health risks for adolescents have increased over the past two decades (Gans, 1990), parental information provision has taken on added importance, particularly in areas of sexual initiation, HIV and AIDS risk, and substance use. Future research will not only need to address ways in which parents provide information and guidance in these areas, but it will also need to focus on ways in which parents obtain the information they pass on to their child.

Constraining and enabling parenting behaviors.   Hauser and his colleagues conducted a number of studies on the effects of constraining and enabling family interaction behaviors during middle to late adolescence (Hauser, Powers, & Noam, 1991). How do such interaction patterns impact on the level of ego development in the parent and child generations? Hauser based his coding of constraining behaviors on Stierlin's (1974) theory of family interaction patterns and adolescent development. The notion here is that some (presumably less functional) families constrain the adolescent's adaptive attempts to differentiate by exhibiting devaluing, distracting, and withholding behaviors. Hauser also developed codes for "enabling" interactions that include behaviors such as empathy, acceptance, explaining, and curiosity (Hauser et al., 1984).

Hauser based his family interaction coding system on a theory that brings together a variety of parenting behaviors within one framework. His approach is relevant to the adolescent transition, given its focus on separation and autonomy strivings. The results of this research program suggest that there are predictable associations between constraining and enabling parenting behaviors and the adolescent's level of ego development (Hauser et al., 1984). At a more complex level, Hauser identified family interaction patterns associated with longitudinal pathways of ego development (Hauser, Powers, & Noam, 1991), as well as interaction patterns that differentiate various subgroups of adolescents and their families (e.g., psychiatric, nonpsychiatric). With regard to the latter, Hauser et al. (1987) found differences between psychiatric and nonpsychiatric adolescents with respect to the types of constraining and enabling sequences present in family interaction. For example, mothers and fathers of psychiatric patients were more likely to undermine each other's enabling behaviors with subsequent constraining behaviors. Finally, Hauser and his colleagues have begun to examine associations between *parental* level of ego development and *adolescent* outcomes (e.g., coping strategies; Hauser, Borman, Jacobson, Powers, & Noam, 1991).

Connectedness and individuality.   Grotevant and Cooper (1985; Cooper, Grotevant, & Condon, 1983) focused on outcomes of family interaction patterns during middle adolescence. Like Hauser, they based their investigations on a theoretical framework that is relevant to adolescent development, namely, a model of individuation. In particular, they are concerned with how communication patterns in the family facilitate or hinder the development of role-taking skills and identity development. With respect to family interaction patterns, they have been interested in behaviors that demonstrate individuality in family relationships. Individuality is operationally defined in terms of self-assertion (i.e., having a point of view and communicating it clearly) and separateness (i.e., expression of distinctness of self from others). They are also interested in communications that demonstrate connectedness, which is operationally defined in terms of permeability (i.e., expressions of openness to others' viewpoints) and mutuality (i.e., expressions of sensitivity and respect for others' viewpoints). It appears that in families where disagreements are permitted, adolescents demonstrate more advanced levels of identity exploration. More generally, expressions of both individuality and connectedness appear to be critical for adaptive adolescent development. Development is facilitated when adolescents are allowed to express their own unique point of view within a connected family environment (Cooper, 1988; Cooper et al., 1983).

Summary. Adolescents demonstrate more favorable outcomes when parents: (1) set clear standards for their child's behavior; (2) enforce rules and regulations with sanctions that are not overly punitive or facilitative of coercive cycles; (3) provide consistent discipline; (4) explain their assertions; (5) permit give-and-take between parent and child during family discussions; (6) remain involved in the adolescents' daily life and monitor their child's whereabouts without being overprotective; (7) provide a warm, responsive, and cohesive family environment; (8) provide information to the adolescent and aid the adolescent in developing useful skills, particularly in areas where risks are likely; and (9) encourage differentiation by allowing adolescents to develop their own opinions within a connected environment. Some of these parenting practices (e.g., firm control) probably have the most positive impact when they occur in the context of other adaptive parenting practices (e.g., allowing child to question parent's opinions). Considerable overlap exists between the types of parenting practices that facilitate development during childhood and those that facilitate development during the adolescent period. On the other hand, we would expect that one additional parenting practice that could be added to the previous list is the degree to which parents are flexible in altering their parenting approach as the child makes the transition to adolescence. It is to this issue that we turn our attention in the next section.

Changes in Parenting During the Transition to Adolescence

Earlier in this chapter, we discussed implications of developmental change for changes in the parenting task. This section examines the manner in which the task of parenting changes during the transition from childhood to adolescence and the consequences for the child when such changes in parenting are not forthcoming. Given the many changes that characterize the adolescent period, parents must continually fine-tune their parenting practices so as to be in line with the changing developmental needs of the child (Eccles et al., 1993; Holmbeck & Hill, 1991; Kidwell et al., 1983). The degree to which a parent is willing and/or able to adapt parenting approaches to such needs probably varies greatly (Hauser, Powers, & Noam, 1991). Parents who are more flexible may respond adaptively to developmental change (Holmbeck & Hill, 1991) and thus are more likely to facilitate development in their offspring (Kidwell et al., 1983). On the other hand, parents who discourage exploration and growth, preferring to maintain familial status quo, are likely to have children who fail to achieve a mature developmental status (Hauser, Powers, & Noam, 1991).

Along what parenting dimensions do parents find it necessary to modify their practices? It appears that one of the major tasks of parenting during adolescence is to be responsive to the adolescent's need for increasing responsibility and decision-making power in the family while at the same time maintaining a high level of cohesiveness and warmth in the family environment. That is, as children begin to assume more responsibilities and become more self-reliant (Hill & Holmbeck, 1986), favorable outcomes are more likely if parents continue to be sources of support for their child (e.g., Cooper, 1988; Cooper et al., 1983; Hauser, Powers, & Noam, 1991). Parent–child relationships prior to adolescence are characteristically asymmetrical with respect to the control dimension (Eccles et al., 1993). It is along this dimension that most of the alterations in parenting are likely to occur (Kidwell et al., 1983).

Eccles et al. (1993) described the transition to adolescence as a time when there are many challenges to the asymmetry in power that characterizes parent–child relations during the preadolescent period. They argued that there is a gradual movement away from asymmetry toward a state of asynchrony between the adolescent's need for autonomy and the parent's willingness to grant it (also see Holmbeck & O'Donnell, 1991). They identify several events that may serve as precursors for such asynchrony: increases in unsupervised contact with peers, exposure of the adolescent to relationships that are symmetrical in nature, and more exposure to their peer's family relationships (which may cause adolescents to question their own parents' authority). Such questioning may also be exacerbated by the advent of more sophisticated social cognitive skills during adolescence (Eccles et al., 1993).

Although there has been some theorizing about the changing parenting task during the transition to adolescence (Eccles et al., 1993; Holmbeck & Hill, 1991; Kidwell et al., 1983), little empirical work has so far focused on the consequences of a lack of change in parenting. In a 1-year longitudinal self-report study of sixth and seventh graders (11–12 years), Fuligni and Eccles (1993) investigated whether changes in parent–child relationships with respect to strictness and decision-making opportunity predicted peer advice seeking and extreme peer orientation. Extreme peer orientation was assessed by asking young adolescents if they would give up important responsibilities (e.g., schoolwork) in order to be popular with their friends. Findings revealed that adolescents who reported increases in parental strictness or decreases in their amount of decision-making power also reported higher levels of extreme peer orientation and an increased tendency to seek advice from peers. Lower levels of extreme peer orientation were found when adolescents reported that parents granted them more decision-making power and were less strict over time.

In summary, predictable changes in adolescent behavior seem to occur as a function of parents' efforts to modify their parenting strategies. The effects on adolescent behavior are particularly positive when parents alter their parenting practices in a manner that demonstrates sensitivity to the developmental needs of their maturing children. More generally, parental adaptability to developmental change may be another aspect of authoritative parenting that not only permits a smooth transition between developmental periods but may also maintain the adolescent's level of openness to socialization during such stressful transitions (Darling & Steinberg, 1993).

Discrepancies Between Parent and Adolescent Views of Family Issues

Incompatibilities between children's developmental needs and their mothers' or fathers' parenting behaviors are likely to emerge during periods of rapid intraindividual change (Paikoff, 1991). During the transition to adolescence, for example, parents and children renegotiate issues of autonomy and control, during which time family members are likely to be called on to manage differences of opinion in areas of importance to the adolescent.

Incongruities between parent and adolescent can exist in many forms (Collins, 1990; Holmbeck & O'Donnell, 1991): (1) incongruities *between* adolescents and parents with respect to *perceptions* (e.g., adolescents feel that they are in charge of deciding when it is bedtime versus a mother who feels that she is in charge of the decision); (2) incongruities *between* adolescents and parents with respect to *expectations* (e.g., adolescents expect that they will gain increasing autonomy in deciding when to come home at night versus a mother who expects to be making this decision until the child is a late adolescent); (3) discrepancies *within* the adolescent between perceptions and expectations (e.g., many adolescents come to see that the privileges they currently have—perceptions of "what is"—are discrepant with the privileges they feel they ought to have—expectations of "what should be"); and (4) discrepancies *within* the parent between perceptions and expectations (e.g., a mother may perceive that her child is beginning to demand more privileges but may not expect to have to make changes in her parenting for several more years).

What have we learned about the prevalence and outcomes of such discrepant viewpoints? As noted earlier, an apparent increase in parent–adolescent conflict during early adolescence is related to realignments in the parent–adolescent relationship, especially insofar as the boundaries of legitimate parental authority are reevaluated during adolescence (Smetana, 1988a, 1988b, 1989). Smetena (1988b) interviewed 5th through 12th graders (10–17 years) and their parents concerning their justifications regarding the legitimacy of parental authority across moral, conventional, and personal domains. Young adolescents increasingly come to treat conflictive issues as matters of personal jurisdiction, whereas parents tend to reason about the same issues from a social-conventional perspective. Parents and children maintain these differing viewpoints despite the fact that each is able to predict the others' perspective with considerable accuracy. These findings suggest that discrepant viewpoints do become more prevalent during the transition to adolescence, primarily due to the adolescents' tendency to view an increasing number of issues as falling within their own decision-making jurisdiction.

Collins (1990) also examined discrepant viewpoints, but from a somewhat different perspective. The notion here is that adolescence may be a time when parental expectancies for appropriate child behavior are violated with greater frequency than is the case in families with younger or older children. Put another way, it was anticipated that larger discrepancies would appear during early or middle adolescence than during middle childhood or late adolescence between parents' perceptions of their children's actual behavior and their views of what would be ideal for a child of that age. Similarly, larger discrepancies were expected during adolescence than at other times between children's perceptions of actual parent behaviors and their perceptions of ideal parent behaviors. In order to test these hypotheses, Collins and his colleagues examined parent and child self-report questionnaire data. Based on parent report, discrepancies between perceptions of actual and ideal child behavior were greater in families with 14-year-olds than in families with younger or older adolescents. Based on child report, discrepancies between perceptions of actual and ideal parent behavior were greater for the two older groups than for the younger group. Expectancies for child and parent behaviors were more likely to be violated during the transition to adolescence and, at least for parent report, these violations peaked during early and middle adolescence and then abated by late adolescence.

Combining these findings with those of Smetana (1988a, 1988b, 1989), we see that discrepancies emerge during early adolescence in at least two ways: between-person discrepancies, insofar as there are incongruities between parents' and adolescents' perceptions of important family matters; and within-person discrepancies, insofar as there are greater discrepancies between perceptions of actual and ideal behavior in both children's and parents' perceptions. Such violations in expectancies may occur for at least two reasons (Goodnow & Collins, 1990). Parents may be lulled into a false sense of stability during middle childhood, thus making it more likely that the dramatic changes of adolescence will produce violations of expectancies. In this case, parents continue to expect childlike behavior from their young adolescent despite evidence to the contrary. Alternatively, parents may alter their expectancies across a variety of domains based on changes in only one domain. Parents (and other adults) seem to expect more adultlike behavior from more physically mature adolescents (Goodnow & Collins, 1990). Another possibility is that some parents may be less inherently flexible than are other parents, again increasing the likelihood of discrepancies.

What are the outcomes of such discrepant viewpoints? Eccles et al. (1993) argued that when there is a poor fit between the developmental needs of the child and parenting practices, strained relations within the family are more likely. Recent research supports this argument (Paikoff, 1991). Holmbeck and O'Donnell (1991) examined discrepancies between maternal and child report on measures of decision making and desire for autonomy in a 6-month longitudinal study of adolescents age 10 to 18 years. Discrepancies in perceptions of who makes decisions in the family were associated with higher levels of conflict cross-sectionally and increases in conflict longitudinally. More conflict was also reported when adolescents desired more autonomy than mothers were willing to grant. Surprisingly, discrepancies in perceptions of decision making were also associated with *fewer* internalizing symptoms and *increases* in the level of mother–adolescent attachment. Thus, although discrepancies appear to be associated with increased parent–adolescent conflict, such increases in conflict may also indicate that adaptive transformations in parent–child relationships are occurring (Cooper, 1988; Steinberg, 1990).

From a somewhat different perspective, we have examined discrepancies in mothers' and daughters' perceptions of family cohesion and family conflict. More divergent perceptions (or discrepancies) regarding family cohesion were associated with increased dieting in daughters, whereas divergent perceptions of family conflict were associated with depressive affect. Thus, differing perceptions of the family may in some cases be linked to maladaptive outcomes in adolescence, although the meaning of these differences to parents and adolescents is not clear (Paikoff, Carlton-Ford, & Brooks-Gunn, 1993; also see Carlton-Ford, Paikoff, & Brooks-Gunn, 1991a).

In summary, the extent to which parents alter their behaviors during the transition to early adolescence and the discrepancies that emerge between child and parent perceptions seem to be linked. Such discrepancies appear to be linked, in turn, with increases in parent–adolescent conflict.

Parent–Adolescent Conflict

According to the early *Sturm und Drang* view of adolescent development (Freud, 1958; Hall, 1904), adolescence is inevitably a time of storm and stress and a period of conflictive detachment from parents, including a reorientation toward peers. One corollary of this view is that such turmoil is a necessary part of adolescent development—a disruptive phase that is necessary to ensure subsequent mental health. Although scholars (Blos, 1962; Erikson, 1968; Freud, 1958; Hall, 1904) disagree as to what underlies such disruption (Elmen & Offer, 1993), the notion of adolescent turmoil has worked its way into mainstream views of adolescence as well as public policy relating to adolescents (Holmbeck & Hill, 1988). Contrary to the beliefs of the general public (Holmbeck & Hill, 1988) and contrary to reports in the media, however, little empirical support exists for the contention that extreme levels of conflictive engagement characterize parent–adolescent relationships (Collins & Laursen, 1992; Laursen & Collins, 1994; Offer & Schonert-Reichl, 1992). Moreover, in those rare instances when high levels of conflict in the parent–adolescent relationship are found, they are predictive of poor early adolescent adjustment (Montemayor, 1983, 1986).

There are several reasons why parent–adolescent conflict has been subjected to so much empirical and theoretical scrutiny (e.g., Collins & Laursen, 1992):

(1) conflict is a natural component of any close relationship (Kelley et al., 1983).
(2) parent–adolescent conflict has psychological and clinical significance insofar as distressed families typically evidence more intense and higher levels of conflict than nondistressed families.
(3) "adolescence is a period in which conflict becomes ... more intricately embedded in social bonds that support development toward adult relationships and competencies" (Collins & Laursen, 1992, p. 236).
(4) parent–adolescent conflict serves an important role in signaling to parents that their parenting behaviors need to be modified in response to the changing developmental needs of their children.

Operational definitions of parent–adolescent conflict vary widely (Collins & Laursen, 1992; Laursen & Collins, 1994). Self-report of conflictive episodes (Robin & Foster, 1989), interview methodologies where parents and children are asked to discuss hypothetical and actual conflicts (e.g., Smetana, 1989), frequency counts of family interaction behaviors (Steinberg & Hill, 1978), and sequential analyses of behavioral interactions (Holmbeck & Hill, 1991) have all been employed. In future work in this area, it will be important to examine the self-report responses of both family members who are engaged in conflict (i.e., "insiders") and to use observational strategies where independent observers (i.e., "outsiders") code for the presence of dyadic conflictive sequences (Collins & Laursen, 1992; Holmbeck & Hill, 1991; Peterson, 1983). In addition, different aspects of conflictive interactions (e.g., conflict issues, incidence, initiation, intensity, resolution, and the outcomes of conflict; Collins & Laursen, 1992; Laursen & Collins, 1994) should be treated as distinct processes.

It appears that less than 10 percent of families endure serious relationship difficulties during adolescence (i.e., parent–adolescent relationships characterized by chronic and escalating levels of conflict and repeated arguments over serious issues; Paikoff & Brooks-Gunn, 1991; Steinberg, 1990), although we might expect higher percentages in lower social class environments (e.g., Edelman & Ladner, 1991; Hill, 1980a). Of these families, a sizeable proportion present with problems that are continuations of difficulties encountered in childhood—*before* the transition to adolescence (Collins, 1990; Collins & Laursen, 1992; Hill, 1985, 1987; Montemayor, 1983; Rutter, Graham, Chadwick, & Yule, 1976; Steinberg, 1990). As Hill (1985, p. 235) noted, although these percentages represent a sizeable number of families, the rates are "not large enough to be the basis for a general developmental theory." When there are conflicts between parents and adolescents, they tend to occur over rather mundane issues involving household responsibilities and privileges. Arguments over religious, political, or social issues are less common (Hill, 1985, 1987; Hill & Holmbeck, 1986; Montemayor, 1983, 1986; Steinberg, 1990). Arguments between parents and adolescents tend to occur at a rate of about one every 3 days (Montemayor, 1982), which is actually similar to the rate found in distressed marital dyads (Montemayor, 1986). It is unclear, however, whether the intensity and/or meaning of such conflicts is the same across these two populations.

When normative levels of conflict do occur between parents and adolescents, they typically do not undermine the quality of the attachment between parent and adolescent (Collins, 1990; Hill, 1980a, 1985, 1987; Hill & Holmbeck, 1986; Powers, Hauser, & Kilner, 1989; Steinberg, 1990). Value sharing is common between parents and adolescents, with adolescents tending to select as friends peers who have the same values as their parents (Collins, 1990; Hill, 1980a, 1985, 1987; Steinberg, 1990). Moreover, parental disapproval is anticipated to be more upsetting than peer disapproval by most adolescents (Hill, 1987). Thus, the bulk of the evidence suggests that discontinuities in the parent–child relationship during the transition to adolescence occur against a backdrop of relational continuity (Brooks-Gunn & Zahaykevich, 1989; Collins, 1990).

In the past, many reviewers maintained that "conflict [between parents and adolescents] is a situation that is best avoided" (Ellis, 1986, p. 156) and that level of conflict could be considered an indirect index of family dysfunction. More recently, some have speculated that the conflicts that occur in families of typically developing adolescents serve an adaptive role in the development of the adolescent and the overall functioning of the family (Cooper, 1988; Holmbeck & Hill, 1991; Steinberg, 1989, 1990). Tolerance of differences of opinion is associated with positive psychosocial outcomes (Collins & Laursen, 1982; Cooper et al., 1983). Conflicts may also aid the adolescent in learning conflict initiation and resolution skills (Holmbeck & Hill, 1991).

Holmbeck and Hill (1991) argued that parent–adolescent conflict can serve an adaptive function insofar as conflict is "an essential impetus to change, adaptation, and development" (Shantz, 1987, p. 284). They hypothesized that interpersonal/extrapsychic as well as intrapsychic processes allow conflict to play an adaptive role and make moderate levels of conflict normative in healthy families (Papini et al., 1989). With regard to the interpersonal/extrapsychic process, Holmbeck and Hill (1991) suggested that conflict may play an information-providing role. Conflicts may inform parents that the adolescents' needs and expectations have changed and that some sort of recalibration of the parent–child relationship is necessary. Behavioral change in response to development is not necessarily automatic (Kidwell et al., 1983); conflicts may bring about necessary changes in parenting as well as relational transformations. If, after a certain degree of conflict occurs, a poor fit still exists between the expectations of the adolescent and the parents' actual behaviors, further behavioral modifications may be necessary for there to be a realignment of the relationship (Collins, 1990; Eccles & Midgley, 1990; Holmbeck & O'Donnell, 1991; R. M. Lerner, 1987). Conflicts may also play a role in decreasing the discrepancies between parent and adolescent viewpoints (Holmbeck & O'Donnell, 1991; Smetana, 1988b).

Regarding intrapsychic processes, conflict may play a role in facilitating the individuation process that is triggered by reactions of the child and parents to developmental change (Holmbeck & Hill, 1991). The process of differentiation is believed to be particularly stressful for the mother–daughter dyad (Brooks-Gunn & Zahaykevich, 1989; Chodorow, 1978; Deutsch, 1944; H. Lerner, 1987; Rich, 1990), although a similar process appears to occur in other parent–adolescent dyads as well (Josselson, 1980; Kaplan, 1984). The strong bond that often exists between parent and child prior to adolescence must undergo some degree of change in order for the child to develop close relationships outside of the family. Psychoanalytic perspectives posit that adolescents come to experience themselves as overattached and undifferentiated and must, at some point, confront their "entanglement in family relationships" (Chodorow, 1978, p. 135). The point here is not that children must sever their relationship with their parents (Gilligan, Lyons, & Hanmer, 1990), but rather that parent–adolescent relationships must be renegotiated in such a way that children are able to maintain both a close relationship with their parents and close relationships with peers. The conflicts that occur during this renegotiation stage may promote such an individuation process (see Holmbeck, in press).

Whether or not conflicts serve an adaptive function in the life of the family (Cooper, 1988; Hill & Holmbeck, 1987; Holmbeck & Hill, 1991; Steinberg, 1990) probably depends in large part on how the individuals involved respond to the conflicts (Collins & Laursen, 1992). How disagreements are understood initially, how the conflicts are discussed, and how they are resolved all impact on the potential adaptiveness of a given conflict situation (Collins & Laursen, 1992). Parents may respond to conflicts in numerous ways. There may be a lack of responsiveness to the conflict, recognition of the conflict followed by an inappropriate or maladaptive response, or recognition of the conflict followed by an appropriate or adaptive response. The first two types of responses would be expected to produce a "stand-off" or an escalation in the level of conflict (Peterson, 1983; Robin & Foster, 1989) as well as an interruption of the conflict resolution process (Smetana, Yau, & Hanson, 1991). Such responses are probably more likely to occur in those families that experience a deterioration in parent–child relations during the transition to adolescence. Parents who respond to parent–adolescent conflict by employing a more severe authoritarian parenting style or by making no adjustments in their parenting practices may experience an exacerbation of the level of disruption during this transition. Parents who are more responsive to change in their offspring (i.e., those who are more "ego resilient"; J. H. Block & J. Block, 1980; Lewin, 1951) are probably most likely to provide an adaptive response to elevations in parent–adolescent conflict, although this hypothesis awaits empirical confirmation. Finally, with respect to adolescents' responses to parent–adolescent conflict, coercive responses to conflict (particularly on the part of boys) may also be associated with maladaptive outcomes, such as the inability of parents and adolescents to reach a compromise during an argument (Smetana et al., 1991).

In summary, although conflicts between parents and children over mundane issues appear to increase in frequency during the transition to adolescence, they appear to serve an adaptive role in most families. Cooper (1988) cautioned, however, that such conflicts can be facilitative of development only if they occur in a context of cohesive family relationships.

GENDER DIFFERENCES AND PARENTING PRACTICES

Although much of the research on parenting during adolescence has been conducted on mothers, enough data now exists to make more general statements about gender differences in the parenting of mothers versus fathers as well as more specific statements about dyadic differences (e.g., mother–son versus mother–daughter versus father–son versus father–daughter; Steinberg, 1987b). Mother–adolescent relationships differ from father–adolescent relationships in a number of important ways. Mothers tend to spend more time with their children than do fathers. Mothers are also more likely to be involved in caregiving, whereas fathers are more likely to engage in leisure activities with their children (Collins & Russell, 1991). Interactions with fathers tend to cover a less broad range of topic areas, being restricted mostly to instrumental issues (Youniss & Smollar, 1985). Despite these differences, Collins and Russell (1991) cautioned that, based on past theorizing, gender differences with respect to interactions are not as dramatic as one would expect.

The perturbations that have been found to occur in parent–child relationships shortly after the onset of pubertal development (Paikoff & Brooks-Gunn, 1991) appear to be more characteristic of mother–adolescent than father–adolescent dyads (Holmbeck & Hill, 1991; Steinberg, 1987a). Despite the higher prevalence of conflictive interaction in mother–adolescent dyads, mothers continue to be more important sources of support throughout adolescence than are fathers (Collins & Russell, 1991). Generally speaking, there is more closeness in mother–adolescent relationships than in father–adolescent relationships (Collins & Russell, 1991). Daughters perceive their fathers as authority figures with whom they interact little; Youniss and Smollar (1985, p. 51) characterized father–daughter relations as "nonrelations." Mother–daughter relationships are characterized by more mutuality than are father–daughter relationships; daughters and mothers report that they often rely on each other for help (Youniss & Smollar, 1985). Distance and asymmetry characterize father–son relationships. Sons turn to fathers for practical advice and recreational activities, but there is little intimate sharing. Sons are more open with their mothers than with their fathers, but they also tend to disagree over obedience and rule issues with their mothers more than with fathers. In addition, sons sometimes view their mothers as intrusive (Youniss & Smollar, 1985). More generally, mothers seem to be more in tune with their children than are fathers; Collins and Russell (1991) speculated that mothers become aware of their child's developmental changes before these changes are observed by fathers.

Whether the degree of congruence between mothers' and fathers' parenting styles has an impact on adolescent outcomes is a relatively unexplored area. The question here is whether the effects of the mother's parenting depends on the nature of the father's parenting. In what appears to be the first study of its kind, Johnson, Shulman, and Collins (1991) isolated four clusters of mother–father parenting combinations: two congruent patterns (authoritative congruent, permissive congruent) and two incongruent patterns (authoritative mother/rejecting father, authoritative father/rejecting mother). Findings revealed that adolescents were more likely to perceive parental incongruence than were preadolescents. Most importantly, adolescents coming from "incongruent" households exhibited more adjustment difficulties than did adolescents from "congruent" households.

CONCLUSIONS

The many developmental and contextual changes of early adolescence (biological, cognitive, social cognitive, emotional, and self-definitional changes, as well as changes in peer relationships and the school context) produce difficult challenges for parents as their children navigate the transition to the second decade of life. Parents are challenged to make modifications across a variety of parenting practices, while at the same time, demonstrating high levels of responsiveness. Parents often are additionally challenged to confront the changes in their offspring at the same time they are experiencing developmental concerns of their own.

What types of parenting styles and parenting practices are most likely to yield positive adolescent outcomes? At the most basic level, parents who are able to provide a responsive and warm parenting environment where there are clear expectations for mature behavior can expect to have the most well-adjusted offspring. Adolescents benefit from parents who enforce their rules, set clear standards, provide consistent discipline that is not overly punitive, remain involved without being intrusive, and permit independent thinking and behavior. Adolescents also thrive when parents are able to be flexible. Parents can demonstrate such flexibility by altering their parenting behaviors when appropriate (e.g., changing rules in the home, allowing the adolescent to have more decision-making responsibilities); allowing their adolescents more opportunities to express their own points of view (Cooper et al., 1983); and providing more explanations for their demands, which serve to legitimize their authority and acknowledge to the adolescent that they are aware of the adolescent's changing cognitive capacities (Hill, 1987). Many of these parenting practices form what has been referred to as the authoritative parenting style. Authoritative parenting (with its characteristically high levels of responsiveness, demandingness, and democracy) seems to be beneficial for adolescents across many outcomes and ecological niches.

Up until now, most research in this area has detailed the *types* of changes that do (and do not) occur in families during the transition to adolescence (Collins, 1990; Collins & Laursen, 1992). As yet, however, little is known about the *processes* that underlie these relational transformations (Paikoff & Brooks-Gunn, 1991). For example, we know what parents and adolescents argue about and how often they argue. We also know that these arguments tend to increase during early adolescence. On the other hand, we know far less about why puberty and parent–adolescent conflict are linked. Thus, it would be useful for investigators to move beyond providing general descriptions of effects (e.g., perturbations, increased conflict). Significant gains in our knowledge of relational transformations during the transition to adolescence are likely to be achieved by employing a process-oriented approach to the study of intraindividual developmental change and the manner in which such changes impact on the parenting task and parent–adolescent relationship (Petersen, 1988). By developing and evaluating models of underlying process, we will learn more about the mechanisms through which intraindividual change impacts on the task of parenting. One such model has recently been proposed by Holmbeck (in press), which integrates many of the themes discussed in the current chapter. Briefly, Holmbeck maintained that the developmental changes of adolescence produce changes in self-perceptions as well as changes in the perceptions of significant others. Given that adolescents' and parents' perceptions are most likely to be discrepant during early adolescence, a modest increase in parent–adolescent conflict is likely to occur during this period. Perceptions of conflict by the adolescent and parent and the manner in which the adolescent and parent manage the conflict determines whether the conflict will be facilitative of or detrimental to subsequent development.

Regardless of the model employed, it is clear that one focus of future research should be on ways in which the tasks of parenting change during the transition to adolescence and over the course of the adolescent period. Some have speculated that the degree to which parents are able to regulate their parenting behaviors based on the developmental needs of their offspring is a critical determinant of adolescent developmental outcome (Eccles et al., 1993; Holmbeck, in press; Holmbeck & Hill, 1991). Unfortunately, little research exists on the issue of "parental flexibility." Finally, little work has been done regarding the long-term consequences of different parenting strategies during early adolescence for outcomes during late adolescence and adulthood (Hauser & Greene, 1991; Holmbeck & Wandrei, 1993; Kobak & Sceery, 1988). In the same way that longitudinal investigations of early childhood have demonstrated significant associations between preschool relational adaptation and outcomes during middle childhood (e.g., Sroufe et al., 1990), it will be of interest to investigate whether the manner in which parents respond (or fail to respond) to the developing adolescent has a unique and distinct impact on adolescents' psychosocial functioning in later life.

ACKNOWLEDGMENTS

Completion of this chapter was supported in part by a Social and Behavioral Sciences Research Grant (No. 12-FY93-0621) from the March of Dimes Birth Defects Foundation and a grant from the National Institute of Mental Health (R01-MH50423).

REFERENCES

Achenbach, T. M., McConaughy, S. H., & Howell, C. T. (1987). Child/adolescent behavioral and emotional problems: Implications of cross-informant correlations for situational specificity. *Psychological Bulletin, 101*, 213–232.

Adelson, J. (Ed.). (1980). *Handbook of adolescent psychology*. New York: Wiley.

Adelson, J. (1985). Observations on research in adolescence. *Genetic, Social, and General Psychology Monographs, 111*, 249–254.

Amato, P. R., & Keith, B. (1991). Parental divorce and the well-being of children: A meta-analysis. *Psychological Bulletin*, *110*, 26–46.

Armsden, G. C., & Greenberg, M. T. (1987). The Inventory of Parent and Peer Attachment: Individual differences and their relationship to psychological well-being in adolescence. *Journal of Youth and Adolescence*, *16*, 427–454.

Barnes, H. L., & Olson, D. H. (1985). Parent–adolescent communication and the circumplex model. *Child Development*, *56*, 438–447.

Baumrind, D. (1968). Authoritarian vs. authoritative parental control. *Adolescence*, *3*, 255–272.

Baumrind, D. (1980). New directions in socialization research. *American Psychologist*, *35*, 639–652.

Baumrind, D. (1991). The influence of parenting style on adolescent competence and substance use. *Journal of Early Adolescence*, *11*, 56–95.

Becker, W. C. (1964). Consequences of different kinds of parental discipline. In M. L. Hoffman, & L. W. Hoffman (Eds.), *Review of child development research* (Vol. 1, pp. 169–208). New York: Russell Sage Foundation.

Belsky, J. (1984). The determinants of parenting: A process model. *Child Development*, *55*, 83–96.

Belsky, J., Steinberg, L., & Draper, P. (1991). Childhood experience, interpersonal development, and reproductive strategy: An evolutionary theory of socialization. *Child Development*, *62*, 647–670.

Berndt, T. J. (1979). Developmental changes in conformity to peers and parents. *Developmental Psychology*, *15*, 608–616.

Berndt, T. J. (1982). The features and effects of friendship in early adolescence. *Child Development*, *53*, 1447–1460.

Berndt, T. J. (1986). Children's comments about their friendships. In M. Perlmutter (Ed.), *Cognitive perspectives on children's social and behavioral development: The Minnesota Symposium on Child Psychology* (Vol. 18, pp. 189–212). Hillsdale, NJ: Lawrence Erlbaum Associates.

Berndt, T. J., & Perry, T. B. (1990). Distinctive features and effects of early adolescent friendships. In R. Montemayor, G. Adams, & T. Gullotta (Eds.), *Advances in adolescent development: From childhood to adolescence: A transitional period?* (Vol. 2, pp. 269–287). Beverly Hills, CA: Sage.

Block, J. H., & Block, J. (1980). The role of ego-control and ego-resiliency in the organization of behavior. In A. Pick (Ed.), *14th Minnesota symposium on child psychology* (pp. 39–101). Minneapolis: University of Minnesota Press.

Block, J. H., Haan, N., & Smith, M. B. (1969). Socialization correlates of student activism. *Journal of Social Issues*, *25*, 143–177.

Blos, P. (1962). *On adolescence: A psychoanalytic interpretation*. New York: Free Press.

Blos, P. (1979). *The adolescent passage*. New York: International Universities Press.

Brooks-Gunn, J. (1984). The psychological significance of different pubertal events to young girls. *Journal of Early Adolescence*, *4*, 315–327.

Brooks-Gunn, J. (1991). How stressful is the transition to adolescence for girls? In M. E. Colton & S. Gore (Eds.), *Adolescent stress: Causes and consequences* (pp. 131–149). New York: Aldine de Gruyter.

Brooks-Gunn, J. (1993). Why do adolescents have difficulty adhering to health regimes? In N. A. Krasnegor, L. Epstein, S. B. Johnson, & S. J. Yaffe (Eds.), *Developmental aspects of health compliance behavior* (pp. 125–152). Hillsdale, NJ: Lawrence Erlbaum Associates.

Brooks-Gunn, J., Graber, J., & Paikoff, R. L. (1993). Studying links between hormones and negative affect: Models and measures. *Journal of Research on Adolescence*, *4*, 469–486.

Brooks-Gunn, J., & Paikoff, R. L. (1992). Changes in self-feelings during the transition towards adolescence. In H. McGurk (Ed.), *Childhood social development: Contemporary issues* (pp. 63–97). Hillsdale, NJ: Lawrence Erlbaum Associates.

Brooks-Gunn, J., & Petersen, A. C. (1991). The emergence of depression in adolescence. *Journal of Youth and Adolescence*, *20*, 247–271.

Brooks-Gunn, J., & Reiter, E. O. (1990). The role of pubertal processes. In S. S. Feldman & G. R. Elliott (Eds.), *At the threshold: The developing adolescent* (pp. 16–53). Cambridge, MA: Harvard University Press.

Brooks-Gunn, J., & Ruble, D. N. (1982). The development of menstrual-related beliefs and behaviors during early adolescence. *Child Development*, *53*, 1567–1577.

Brooks-Gunn, J., Samelson, M., Warren, M. P., & Fox, R. (1986). Physical similarities of and disclosure of menarcheal status to friends: Effects of age and pubertal status. *Journal of Early Adolescence*, *6*, 3–14.

Brooks-Gunn, J., & Warren, M. P. (1988). The psychological significance of secondary sexual characteristics in nine- to eleven-year-old girls. *Child Development*, *59*, 1061–1069.

Brooks-Gunn, J., & Zahaykevich, M. (1989). Parent–daughter relationships in early adolescence: A developmental perspective. In K. Kreppner, & R. M. Lerner (Eds.), *Family systems and life-span development* (pp. 223–246). Hillsdale, NJ: Lawrence Erlbaum Associates.

Brown, B. B. (1990). Peer groups and peer cultures. In S. S. Feldman & G. L. Elliott (Eds.), *At the threshold: The developing adolescent* (pp. 171–196). Cambridge, MA: Harvard University Press.

Buchanan, C. M., Eccles, J. S., & Becker, J. B. (1992). Are adolescents the victims of raging hormones: Evidence for activational effects of hormones on moods and behavior at adolescence. *Psychological Bulletin*, *111*, 62–107.

Buchanan, C. L., Eccles, J. E., Flanagan, C., Midgley, C., Feldlaufer, H., & Harold, R. (1990). Parents' and teachers' beliefs about adolescence: Effects of sex and experience. *Journal of Youth and Adolescence*, *19*, 363–394.

Carlton-Ford, S. L., Paikoff, R. L., & Brooks-Gunn, J. (1991a). Methodological issues in the study of divergent views of the family. In R. L. Paikoff (Ed.), *New Directions for Child Development: Shared views in the family during adolescence* (No. 51, pp. 87–102). San Francisco: Jossey-Bass.

Carlton-Ford, S. L., Paikoff, R. L., & Brooks-Gunn, J. (1991b, July). *Depressive affect and daughters' and mothers' reports of family cohesion and conflict.* Paper presented at the International Society for the Study of Behavioral Development, Minneapolis, MN.

Chodorow, N. (1978). *The reproduction of mothering: Psychoanalysis and the sociology of gender.* Berkeley, CA: University of California Press.

Cohen, P., & Brook, J. (1987). Family factors related to the persistence of psychopathology in childhood and adolescence. *Psychiatry, 50,* 332–345.

Collins, W. A. (1990). Parent–child relationships in the transition to adolescence: Continuity and change in interaction, affect, and cognition. In R. Montemayor, G. Adams, & T. Gullotta (Eds.), *Advances in adolescent development: From childhood to adolescence: A transitional period?* (Vol. 2, pp. 85–106). Beverly Hills, CA: Sage.

Collins, W. A., & Laursen, B. (1992). Conflict and relationships during adolescence. In C. U. Shantz, & W. W. Hartup (Eds.), *Conflict in child and adolescent development* (pp. 216–241). New York: Cambridge University Press.

Collins, W. A., & Russell, G. (1991). Mother–child and father–child relationships in middle childhood and adolescence: A developmental analysis. *Developmental Review, 11,* 99–136.

Cooper, C. R. (1988). Commentary: The role of conflict in adolescent–parent relationships. In M. R. Gunnar & W. A. Collins (Eds.), *21st Minnesota symposium on child psychology* (pp. 181–187). Hillsdale, NJ: Lawrence Erlbaum Associates.

Cooper, C. R., Grotevant, H. D., & Condon, S. M. (1983). Individuality and connectedness in the family as a context for adolescent identity formation and role-taking skill. In H. D. Grotevant, & C. R. Cooper (Eds.), *Adolescent development in the family: New directions for child development* (No. 22, pp. 43–59). San Francisco: Jossey-Bass.

Damon, W., & Hart, D. (1982). The development of self-understanding from infancy through adolescence. *Child Development, 53,* 841–864.

Darling, N., & Steinberg, L. (1993). Parenting style as context: An integrative model. *Psychological Bulletin, 113,* 487–496.

Deci, E. L., Driver, R. E., Hotchkiss, L., Robbins, R. J., & Wilson, I. M. (1993). The relations of mothers' controlling vocalizations to children's intrinsic motivation. *Journal of Experimental Child Psychology, 55,* 151–162.

Deutsch, H. (1944). *The psychology of women.* New York: Grune & Stratton.

Dix, T. (1991). The affective organization of parenting: Adaptive and maladaptive processes. *Psychological Bulletin, 110,* 3–25.

Dix, T., Ruble, D., Grusec, J., & Nixon, S. (1986). Social cognition in parents: Inferential and affective reactions to children of three age levels. *Child Development, 57,* 879–894.

Dodge, K. A. (1990). Developmental psychopathology in children of depressed mothers. *Developmental Psychology, 26,* 3–6.

Dornbusch, S. M., Ritter, P. L., Leiderman, P. H., Roberts, D. F., & Fraleigh, M. J. (1987). The relation of parenting style to adolescent school performance. *Child Development, 58,* 1244–1257.

Duncan, G., Brooks-Gunn, J., & Klebanov, P. K. (in press). Economic deprivation and children's development. *Child Development.*

Durbin, D. L., Darling, N., Steinberg, L., & Brown, B. B. (1993). Parenting style and peer group membership among European-American adolescents. *Journal of Research on Adolescence, 3,* 87–100.

Eccles, J. S., Jacobs, J. E., & Harold, R. D. (1990). Gender role stereotypes, expectancy effects, and parents' socialization of gender differences. *Journal of Social Issues, 46,* 183–201.

Eccles, J. S., & Midgley, C. (1990). Changes in academic motivation and self-perception during early adolescence. In R. Montemayor, G. Adams, & T. Gullotta (Eds.), *Advances in adolescent development: From childhood to adolescence: A transitional period?* (Vol. 2, pp. 134–155). Beverly Hills, CA: Sage.

Eccles, J. S., Midgley, C., Wigfield, A., Buchanan, C. M., Reuman, D., Flanagan, C., & MacIver, D. (1993). Development during adolescence: The impact of stage-environment fit in young adolescents' experiences in schools and in families. *American Psychologist, 48,* 90–101.

Edelman, P. B., & Ladner, J. (Eds.). (1991). *Adolescence and poverty: Challenge for the 1990s.* Washington, DC: Center for National Policy Press.

Elder, G. H., Jr. (1963). Parental power legitimation and its effect on the adolescent. *Sociometry, 26,* 50–65.

Ellis, G. J. (1986). Societal and parental predictors of parent–adolescent conflict. In G. K. Leigh & G. W. Peterson (Eds.), *Adolescents in families* (pp. 155–178). Cincinnati, OH: South-Western.

Elmen, J., & Offer, D. (1993). Normality, turmoil, and adolescence. In P. H. Tolan, & B. J. Cohler (Eds.), *Handbook of clinical research and practice with adolescents* (pp. 1–19). New York: Wiley.

Erikson, E. (1968). *Identity: Youth and crisis.* New York: Norton.

Evelyth, P. B., & Tanner, J. M. (1976). *Worldwide variation in human growth.* London: Cambridge University Press.

Farrell, M. P., & Rosenberg, S. D. (1981). *Men at midlife.* Dover, MA: Auburn House.

Fauber, R., Forehand, R., Thomas, A. M., & Wierson, M. (1990). A mediational model of the impact of marital conflict on adolescent adjustment in intact and divorced families: The role of disrupted parenting. *Child Development, 61,* 1112–1123.

Freedman-Doan, C. R., Arbreton, A. J. A., Harold, R. D., & Eccles, J. S. (1993). Looking forward to adolescence: Mothers' and fathers' expectations for affective and behavioral change. *Journal of Early Adolescence, 13*, 472–502.

Freud, A. (1958). Adolescence. *Psychoanalytic Study of the Child, 13*, 231–258.

Fuhrman, T., & Holmbeck, G. N. (in press). A contextual-moderator analysis of emotional autonomy and adjustment in adolescence. *Child Development.*

Fuligni, A. J., & Eccles, J. S. (1993). Perceived parent–child relationships and early adolescents' orientation toward peers. *Developmental Psychology, 29*, 622–632.

Gaddis, A., & Brooks-Gunn, J. (1985). The male experience of pubertal change. *Journal of Youth and Adolescence, 14*, 61–69.

Gans, J. E. (1990). *Profiles of adolescent health series: Vol. 1. America's adolescents: How healthy are they?* Chicago, IL: American Medical Association.

Gilligan, C., Lyons, N. P., Hanmer, T. J. (Eds.). (1990). *Making connections: The relational worlds of adolescent girls at Emma Willard School.* Cambridge, MA: Harvard University Press.

Goodnow, J. J., & Collins, W. A. (1990). *Development according to parents: The nature, sources, and consequences of parents' ideas.* Hillsdale, NJ: Lawrence Erlbaum Associates.

Graber, J. A., Brooks-Gunn, J., & Warren, M. P. (in press). The antecedents of menarcheal age: Heredity, family environment, and stressful life events. *Child Development.*

Greif, E. B., & Ulman, K. J. (1982). The psychological impact of menarche on early adolescent females: A review of the literature. *Child Development, 53*, 1413–1430.

Grotevant, H. D., & Cooper, C. R. (1985). Patterns of interaction in family relationships and the development of identity exploration in adolescence. *Child Development, 56*, 415–428.

Grych, J. H., & Fincham, F. D. (1990). Marital conflict and children's adjustment: A cognitive-contextual framework. *Psychological Bulletin, 108*, 267–290.

Hall, G. S. (1904). *Adolescence: Its psychology and its relations to physiology, anthropology, sociology, sex, crime, religion, and education.* New York: Appleton.

Hammen, C., Burge, D., & Stansbury, K. (1990). Relationship of mother and child variables to child outcomes in a high risk sample: A causal modelling analysis. *Developmental Psychology, 26*, 24–30.

Harter, S. (1983). Developmental perspectives on the self–system. In E. M. Hetherington (Vol. Ed.) & P. H. Mussen (Series Ed.), *Handbook of child psychology: Vol. 4. Socialization, personality, and social development* (pp. 275–386). New York: Wiley.

Hartup, W. W. (1983). Peer relations. In E. M. Hetherington (Vol. Ed.) & P. H. Mussen (Series Ed.), *Handbook of child psychology: Vol. 4. Socialization, personality, and social development* (pp. 103–196). New York: Wiley.

Hartup, W. W. (1989). Social relationships and their developmental significance. *American Psychologist, 44*, 120–126.

Hauser, S. T., Borman, E. H., Jacobson, A. M., Powers, S. I., & Noam, G. G. (1991). Understanding family contexts of adolescent coping: A study of parental ego development and adolescent coping strategies. *Journal of Early Adolescence, 11*, 96–124.

Hauser, S. T., & Bowlds, M. K. (1990). Stress, coping, and adaptation. In S. S. Feldman, & G. L. Elliott (Eds.), *At the threshold: The developing adolescent* (pp. 388–413). Cambridge: MA: Harvard University Press.

Hauser, S. T., & Greene, W. M. (1991). Passages from late adolescence to early adulthood. In S. I. Greenspan, & G. H. Pollock (Eds.), *The course of life: Vol. 4. Adolescence* (pp. 377–405). Madison, WI: International Universities Press.

Hauser, S. T., Houlihan, J., Powers, S. I., Jacobson, A. M., Noam, G., Weiss-Perry, B., & Follansbee, D. (1987). Interaction sequences in families of psychiatrically hospitalized and nonpatient adolescents. *Psychiatry, 50*, 308–319.

Hauser, S. T., Powers, S. I., & Noam, G. G. (1991). *Adolescents and their families: Paths of ego development.* New York: Free Press.

Hauser, S. T., Powers, S. I., Noam, G. G., Jacobson, A. M., Weiss, B., & Follansbee, D. J. (1984). Familial contexts of adolescent ego development. *Child Development, 55*, 195–213.

Hetherington, E. M., & Anderson, E. R. (1988). The effects of divorce and remarriage on early adolescents and their families. In M. D. Levine & E. R. McAnarney (Eds.), *Early adolescent transitions* (pp. 49–67). Lexington, MA: Lexington Books.

Hetherington, E. M., & Clingempeel, W. G. (1992). Coping with marital transitions. *Monographs of the Society for Research in Child Development, 57* (Serial No. 227).

Hetherington, E. M., & Martin, B. (1986). Family factors and psychopathology in childhood. In H. C. Quay (Ed.), *Psychopathological disorders of childhood* (3rd ed., pp. 332–390). New York: Wiley.

Hibbs, E. D., Hamburger, S. D., Kruesi, M. J. P., & Rapoport, J. L. (1992). Parental expressed emotion and psychophysiological reactivity in disturbed and normal children. *British Journal of Psychiatry, 160*, 504–510.

Hill, J. P. (1980a). The family. In J. Johnson (Ed.), *Toward adolescence: The middle school years. The 79th yearbook of the National Society for the Study of Education* (pp. 32–55). Chicago: University of Chicago Press.

Hill, J. P. (1980b). *Understanding early adolescence: A framework.* Chapel Hill, NC: Center for Early Adolescents.

Hill, J. P. (1985). Family relations in adolescence: Myths, realities, and new directions. *Genetic, Social, and General Psychology Monographs, 111*, 233–248.

Hill, J. P. (1987). Research on adolescents and their families: Past and prospect. In C. E. Irwin (Ed.), *Adolescent social behavior and health: New directions for child development* (No. 37, pp. 13–31). San Francisco: Jossey-Bass.

Hill, J. P. (1988). Adapting to menarche: Familial control and conflict. In M. R. Gunnar, & W. A. Collins (Eds.), *21st Minnesota symposium on child psychology* (pp. 43–77). Hillsdale, NJ: Lawrence Erlbaum Associates.

Hill, J. P., & Holmbeck, G. N. (1986). Attachment and autonomy during adolescence. In G. J. Whitehurst (Ed.), *Annals of child development* (Vol. 3, pp. 145–189). Greenwich, CT: JAI Press.

Hill, J. P., & Holmbeck, G. N. (1987). Familial adaptation to biological change during adolescence. In R. M. Lerner & T. T. Foch (Eds.), *Biological-psychosocial interactions in early adolescence: A life-span perspective* (pp. 207–223). Hillsdale, NJ: Lawrence Erlbaum Associates.

Hill, J. P., Holmbeck, G. N., Marlow, L., Green, T. M., & Lynch, M. E. (1985a). Menarcheal status and parent–child relations in families of seventh-grade girls. *Journal of Youth and Adolescence, 14*, 314–330.

Hill, J. P., Holmbeck, G. N., Marlow, L., Green, T. M., & Lynch, M. E. (1985b). Pubertal status and parent–child relations in families of seventh-grade boys. *Journal of Early Adolescence, 5*, 31–44.

Hill, J. P. & Lynch, M. E. (1983). The intensification of gender-related role expectations during early adolescence. In J. Brooks-Gunn & A. C. Petersen (Eds.), *Girls at puberty: Biological and psychosocial perspectives* (pp. 201–228). New York: Plenum.

Hoffman, M. L. (1970). Moral development. In P. H. Mussen (Ed.), *Carmichael's manual of child psychology* (Vol. 2, pp. 261–360). New York: Wiley.

Hoffman, M. L. (1975). Altruistic behavior and the parent–child relationship. *Journal of Personality and Social Psychology, 31*, 937–943.

Holmbeck, G. N. (in press). A model of family relational transformations during the transition to early adolescence: Parent–adolescent conflict and adaptation. In J. A. Graber, J. Brooks-Gunn, & A. C. Petersen (Eds.), *Transitions through adolescence: Interpersonal domains and context.* Hillsdale, NJ: Lawrence Erlbaum Associates.

Holmbeck, G. N., & Hill, J. P. (1988). Storm and stress beliefs about adolescence: Prevalence, self-reported antecedents, and effects of an undergraduate course. *Journal of Youth and Adolescence, 17*, 285–306.

Holmbeck, G. N., & Hill, J. P. (1991). Conflictive engagement, positive affect, and menarche in families with seventh-grade girls. *Child Development, 62*, 1030–1048.

Holmbeck, G. N., & O'Donnell, K. (1991). Discrepancies between perceptions of decision-making and behavioral autonomy. In R. L. Paikoff (Ed.), *Shared views in the family during adolescence: New directions for child development* (No. 51, pp. 51–69). San Francisco: Jossey-Bass.

Holmbeck, G. N., & Wandrei, M. (1993). Individual and relational predictors of adjustment in first-year college students. *Journal of Counseling Psychology, 40*, 73–78.

Johnson, B. M., Shulman, S., & Collins, W. A. (1991). Systemic patterns of parenting as reported by adolescents: Developmental differences and implications for psychosocial outcomes. *Journal of Adolescent Research, 6*, 235–252.

Josselson, R. (1980). Ego development in adolescence. In J. Adelson (Ed.), *Handbook of adolescent psychology* (pp. 188–210). New York: Wiley.

Kandel, D. B., & Davies, M. (1986). Adult sequelae of adolescent depressive symptoms. *Archives of General Psychiatry, 43*, 225–262.

Kaplan, L. (1984). *Adolescence: The farewell to childhood.* New York: Simon & Schuster.

Keating, D. P. (1990). Adolescent thinking. In S. S. Feldman & G. L. Elliott (Eds.), *At the threshold: The developing adolescent* (pp. 54–89). Cambridge, MA: Harvard University Press.

Kelley, H. H., Berscheid, E., Christensen, A., Harvey, J. H., Huston, T. L., Levinger, G., McClintock, E., Peplau, L. A., & Peterson, D. R. (1983). *Close relationships.* New York: Freeman.

Kidwell, J., Fischer, J. L., Dunham, R. M., & Baranowski, M. (1983). Parents and adolescents: Push and pull of change. In H. I. McCubbin & C. R. Figley (Eds.), *Stress and the family: Vol. 1. Coping with normative transitions* (pp. 74–89). New York: Brunner/Mazel.

Kobak, R., & Sceery, A. (1988). Attachment in late adolescence: Working models, affect regulation, and representations of self and others. *Child Development, 59*, 135–146.

Lamborn, S. D., Mounts, N. S., Steinberg, L., & Dornbusch, S. M. (1991). Patterns of competence and adjustment among adolescents from authoritative, authoritarian, indulgent, and neglectful families. *Child Development, 62*, 1049–1065.

Lamborn, S. D., & Steinberg, L. (1993). Emotional autonomy redux: Revisiting Ryan and Lynch. *Child Development, 64*, 483–499.

Lapsley, D. K. (1990). Continuity and discontinuity in adolescent social cognitive development. In R. Montemayor, G. Adams, & T. Gullotta (Eds.), *Advances in adolescent development: From childhood to adolescence: A transitional period?* (Vol. 2, pp. 183–204). Beverly Hills, CA: Sage.

Laursen, B., & Collins, W. A. (1994). Interpersonal conflict during adolescence. *Psychological Bulletin, 115*, 197–209.

Lerner, R. M. (1987). A life-span perspective for early adolescence. In R. M. Lerner & T. T. Foch (Eds.), *Biological-psychosocial interactions in early adolescence* (pp. 9–34). Hillsdale, NJ: Lawrence Erlbaum Associates.

Lerner, H. (1987). Psychodynamic models. In V. B. Hasselt, & M. Hersen (Eds), *Handbook of adolescent psychology* (pp. 53–76). New York: Pergamon.

Lewin, K. (1951). *Field theory in social science.* New York: Harper.

Livesley, W. J., & Bromley, D. B. (1973). *Person perception in childhood and adolescence.* New York: Wiley.

Loeber, R. (1989). Natural histories of conduct problems, delinquency, and associated substance use: Evidence for developmental progressions. In B. B. Lahey & A. E. Kazdin (Eds.), *Advances in clinical child psychology* (Vol. 10, pp. 73–124). New York: Plenum.

Maccoby, E., & Martin, J. (1983). Socialization in the context of the family: Parent–child interaction. In E. M. Hetherington (Vol. Ed.) & P. H. Mussen (Series Ed.), *Handbook of child psychology: Vol. 4. Socialization, personality, and social development* (pp. 1–101). New York: Wiley.

Martin, B. (1975). Parent–child relations. In F. D. Horowitz (Ed.), *Review of child development research.* (Vol. 4, pp. 463–540). Chicago, IL: University of Chicago Press.

McLoyd, V. C. (1990). The impact of economic hardship on black families and children: Psychological distress, parenting, and socioemotional development. *Child Development, 61,* 311–346.

Moffitt, T. E., Caspi, A., Belsky, J., & Silva, P. A. (1992). Childhood experience and the onset of menarche: A test of a sociobiological model. *Child Development, 63,* 47–58.

Montemayor, R. (1982). The relationship between parent–adolescent conflict and the amount of time adolescents spend alone and with parents and peers. *Child Development, 53,* 1512–1519.

Montemayor, R. (1983). Parents and adolescents in conflict: All families some of the time and some families most of the time. *Journal of Early Adolescence, 3,* 83–103.

Montemayor, R. (1986). Family variation in parent–adolescent storm and stress. *Journal of Adolescent Research, 1,* 15–31.

Montemayor, R., & Eisen, M. (1977). The development of self-conceptions from childhood to adolescence. *Developmental Psychology, 13,* 314–319.

Offer, D. (1987). In defense of adolescents. *American Psychologist, 257,* 3407–3408.

Offer, D., & Schonert-Reichl, K. A. (1992). Debunking the myths of adolescence: Findings from recent research. *Journal of the American Academy of Child and Adolescent Psychiatry, 31,* 1003–1014.

Paikoff, R. L. (Ed.) (1991). *New Directions for Child Development: Shared views in the family during adolescence* (No. 51). San Francisco: Jossey-Bass.

Paikoff, R. L., & Brooks-Gunn, J. (1990). Physiological processes: What role do they play during the transition to adolescence? In R. Montemayor, G. Adams, & T. Gullotta (Eds.), *Advances in adolescent development: From childhood to adolescence: A transitional period?* (Vol. 2, pp. 63–81). Beverly Hills, CA: Sage.

Paikoff, R. L., & Brooks-Gunn, J. (1991). Do parent–child relationships change during puberty? *Psychological Bulletin, 110,* 47–66.

Paikoff, R. L., Brooks-Gunn, J., & Carlton-Ford, S. (1991). Effect of reproductive status changes on family functioning and well-being of mothers and daughters. *Journal of Early Adolescence, 11,* 201–220.

Paikoff, R. L., Carlton-Ford, S., & Brooks-Gunn, J. (1993). Mother–daughter dyads view the family: Associations between divergent perceptions and daughter well-being. *Journal of Youth and Adolescence, 22,* 473–492.

Papini, D. R., Datan, N., & McCluskey-Fawcett, K. A. (1988). An observational study of affective and assertive family interactions during adolescence. *Journal of Youth and Adolescence, 17,* 477–492.

Papini, D. R., Micka, J., & Barnett, J. (1989). Perceptions of intrapsychic and extrapsychic functioning as bases of adolescent ego identity statuses. *Journal of Adolescent Research, 4,* 460–480.

Papini, D. R., & Roggman, L. A. (1992). Adolescent perceived attachment to parents in relation to competence, depression, and anxiety: A longitudinal study. *Journal of Early Adolescence, 12,* 420–440.

Patterson, G. R. (1982). *Coercive family process.* Eugene, OR: Castalia.

Patterson, G. R. (1986). Performance models for antisocial boys. *American Psychologist, 41,* 432–444.

Patterson, G. R., Bank, L., & Stoolmiller, M. (1990). The preadolescent's contributions to disrupted family process. In R. Montemayor, G. R. Adams, & T. P. Gullotta (Eds.), *From childhood to adolescence: A transitional period?* (pp. 107–133). Newbury Park, CA: Sage.

Patterson, G. R., & Strouthamer-Loeber, M. (1984). The correlation of family management practices and delinquency. *Child Development, 55,* 1299–1307.

Petersen, A. C. (1988). Adolescent development. *Annual Review of Psychology, 39,* 583–607.

Petersen, A. C., Compas, B. E., Brooks-Gunn, J., Stemmler, M., Ey, S., & Grant, K. E. (1993). Depression in adolescence. *American Psychologist, 48,* 155–168.

Petersen, A. C., Sarigiani, P. A., & Kennedy, R. E. (1991). Adolescent depression: Why more girls? *Journal of Youth and Adolescence, 20,* 247–271.

Petersen, A. C., & Taylor, B. (1980). The biological approach to adolescence: Biological change and psychological adaptation. In J. Adelson (Ed.), *Handbook of adolescent psychology* (pp. 117–155). New York: Wiley.

Peterson, D. R. (1983). Conflict. In H. H. Kelley, E. Berscheid, A. Christensen, J. H. Harvey, T. L. Huston, G. Levinger, E. McClintock, L. A. Peplau, & D. R. Peterson (Eds.), *Close relationships* (pp. 360–396). New York: Freeman.

Powers, S. I., Hauser, S. T., & Kilner, L. A. (1989). Adolescent mental health. *American Psychologist, 44,* 200–208.

Preto, N. G., & Travis, N. (1985). The adolescent phase of the family life cycle. In M. P. Mirkin & S. L. Koman (Eds.), *Handbook of adolescents and family therapy* (pp. 21–38). New York: Gardner.

Rich, S. (1990). Daughters' views of their relationships with their mothers. In C. Gilligan, N. P. Lyons, & T. J. Hanmer (Eds.), *Making connections: The relational worlds of adolescent girls at Emma Willard School* (pp. 258–273). Cambridge, MA: Harvard University Press.

Robin, A. L., & Foster, S. L. (1989). *Negotiating parent–adolescent conflict: A behavioral-family systems approach.* New York: Guilford.

Robins, L. N. (1978). Sturdy childhood predictors of adult antisocial behavior: Replication from longitudinal studies. *Psychological Medicine, 8,* 611–622.

Ruble, D. N., & Brooks-Gunn, J. (1982). The experience of menarche. *Child Development, 53,* 1557–1566.

Rutter, M. (1990). Commentary: Some focus and process considerations regarding effects of parental depression on children. *Developmental Psychology, 26,* 60–67.

Rutter, M., Graham, P., Chadwick, O., & Yule, W. (1976). Adolescent turmoil: Fact or fiction? *Journal of Child Psychology and Psychiatry, 17,* 35–56.

Ryan, R., & Lynch, J. (1989). Emotional autonomy versus detachment: Revisiting the vicissitudes of adolescence and young adulthood. *Child Development, 60,* 340–356.

Savin-Williams, R. C., & Berndt, T. J. (1990). Friendship and peer relations. In S. S. Feldman & G. L. Elliott (Eds.), *At the threshold: The developing adolescent* (pp. 277–307). Cambridge, MA: Harvard University Press.

Savin-Williams, R. C., & Demo, D. H. (1984). Developmental change and stability in adolescent self-concept. *Developmental Psychology, 20,* 1100–1110.

Schaefer, E. S. (1959). A circumplex model for maternal behavior. *Journal of Abnormal and Social Psychology, 59,* 226–235.

Selman, R. L. (1980). *The growth of interpersonal understanding: Developmental and clinical analyses.* New York: Academic.

Shantz, C. U. (1987). Conflicts between children. *Child Development, 58,* 283–305.

Silverberg, S. B., & Steinberg, L. (1987). Adolescent autonomy, parent–adolescent conflict, and parental well-being. *Journal of Youth and Adolescence, 16,* 293–312.

Silverberg, S. B., & Steinberg, L. (1990). Psychological well-being of parents with early adolescent children. *Developmental Psychology, 26,* 658–666.

Simmons, R. G., & Blyth, D. A. (1987). *Moving into adolescence: The impact of pubertal change and school context.* New York: Aldine De Gruyter.

Simmons, R. G., Burgeson, R., & Reef, M. J. (1988). Cumulative change at entry to adolescence. In M. R. Gunnar & W. A. Collins (Eds.), *Development during the transition to adolescence: Minnesota Symposia on child psychology* (Vol. 21, pp. 123–150). Hillsdale, NJ: Lawrence Erlbaum Associates.

Small, S. A., Eastman, G., & Cornelius, S. (1988). Adolescent autonomy and parental stress. *Journal of Youth and Adolescence, 17,* 377–392.

Smetana. J. G. (1988a). Adolescents' and parents' conceptions of parental authority. *Child Development, 59,* 321–335.

Smetana, J. G. (1988b). Concepts of self and social convention: Adolescents' and parents' reasoning about hypothetical and actual family conflicts. In M. R. Gunnar & W. A. Collins (Eds.), *Minnesota Symposia on child psychology* (Vol. 21, pp. 79–122). Hillsdale, NJ: Lawrence Erlbaum Associates.

Smetana, J. G. (1989). Adolescents' and parents' reasoning about actual family conflict. *Child Development, 60,* 1052–1067.

Smetana, J. G., Yau, J., & Hanson, S. (1991). Conflict resolution in families with adolescents. *Journal of Research on Adolescence, 1,* 189–206.

Smolak, L., Levine, M. P., & Gralen, S. (1993). The impact of puberty and dating on eating problems among middle school girls. *Journal of Youth and Adolescence, 22,* 355–368.

Spencer, M. B., & Dornbusch, S. M. (1990). Challenges in studying minority children. In S. S. Feldman & G. L. Elliott (Eds.), *At the threshold: The developing adolescent* (pp. 123–146). Cambridge, MA: Harvard University Press.

Sroufe, L. A. (1983). Infant–caregiver attachment and patterns of adaptation in preschool: The roots of maladaptation and competence. In M. Perlmutter (Ed.), *Minnesota Symposia on child psychology* (Vol. 16, pp. 41–83). Hillsdale, NJ: Lawrence Erlbaum Associates.

Sroufe, L. A. (1985). Attachment classification from the perspective of infant–caregiver relationships and infant temperament. *Child Development, 56,* 1–12.

Sroufe, L. A., Egeland, B., & Kreutzer, T. (1990). The fate of early experience following developmental change: Longitudinal approaches to individual adaptation in childhood. *Child Development, 61,* 1363–1373.

Steinberg, L. (1986). Latchkey children and susceptibility to peer pressure: An ecological analysis. *Developmental Psychology, 22,* 433–439.

Steinberg, L. (1987a). Impact of puberty on family relations: Effects of pubertal status and pubertal timing. *Developmental Psychology, 23,* 451–460.

Steinberg, L. (1987b). Recent research on the family at adolescence: The extent and nature of sex differences. *Journal of Youth and Adolescence, 16,* 191–197.

Steinberg, L. (1988). Reciprocal relation between parent–child distance and pubertal maturation. *Developmental Psychology, 24,* 122–128.

Steinberg, L. (1989). Pubertal maturation and family relations: Evidence for the distancing hypothesis. In G. Adams, R. Montemayor, & T. Gullotta (Eds.), *Advances in adolescent development* (Vol. 1, pp. 71–92). Beverly Hills, CA: Sage.

Steinberg, L. (1990). Interdependence in the family: Autonomy, conflict, and harmony in the parent–adolescent relationship. In S. S. Feldman & G. L. Elliott (Eds.), *At the threshold: The developing adolescent* (pp. 255–276). Cambridge, MA: Harvard University Press.

Steinberg, L. (1993). *Adolescence.* New York: McGraw-Hill.

Steinberg, L., Dornbusch, S. M., & Brown, B. B. (1992). Ethnic differences in adolescent achievement: An ecological perspective. *American Psychologist, 47,* 723–729.

Steinberg, L., Elmen, J. D., & Mounts, N. S. (1989). Authoritative parenting, psychosocial maturity, and academic success among adolescents. *Child Development, 60,* 1424–1436.

Steinberg, L., & Hill, J. P. (1978). Patterns of family interaction as a function of age, the onset of puberty, and formal thinking. *Developmental Psychology, 14,* 683–684.

Steinberg, L., Lamborn, S. D., Dornbusch, S. M., & Darling, N. (1992). Impact of parenting practices on adolescent achievement: Authoritative parenting, school involvement, and encouragement to succeed. *Child Development, 63,* 1266–1281.

Steinberg, L., Mounts, N., Lamborn, S. D., & Dornbusch, S. M. (1991). Authoritative parenting and adolescent adjustment across varied ecological niches. *Journal of Research on Adolescence, 1,* 19–36.

Steinberg, L., & Silverberg, S. (1986). The vicissitudes of autonomy in early adolescence. *Child Development, 57,* 841–851.

Steinberg, L., & Silverberg, S. B. (1987). Influences on marital satisfaction during the middle stages of the family life cycle. *Journal of Marriage and the Family, 49,* 751–760.

Stierlin, H. (1974). *Separating parents and adolescents.* New York: Quadrangle.

Thomas, A., & Chess, S. (1977). *Temperament and development.* New York: Brunner/Mazel.

Youniss, J. (1980). *Parents and peers in social development: A Sullivan-Piaget perspective.* Chicago: University of Chicago Press.

Youniss, J., & Smollar, J. (1985). *Adolescent relations with mothers, fathers, and friends.* Chicago: University of Chicago Press.

5

Parent–Child Relationships in Adulthood and Old Age

Steven H. Zarit
David J. Eggebeen
Pennsylvania State University

INTRODUCTION

Parent–child relationships are a life-span issue. Rather than ceasing when children are launched from the family, these relationships endure with often complex patterns of interaction, support, and exchange that wax and wane around key transitions in the adult years. Indeed, family issues such as intergenerational conflict, mutual assistance, and inheritance have a timeless feel to them. Several trends in contemporary society, however, have made these issues different and more complex. Changes in mortality and morbidity have resulted in more people living longer and often with disabilities. Altered patterns of marriage and divorce have also meant more individuals entering old age without the support of a spouse. Finally, a stalled or unevenly growing economy has negatively affected the economic prospects of younger generations and caused a decline in confidence that extrafamilial institutions will help.

The purpose of this chapter is to review the most recent research on the nature of ties between aging parents and their adult children. Reflecting the basic premises of a life-span/life-course perspective, we assume that ties between aging parents and their adult children are a two-way street; for example, not only do children provide support and care to parents, but parents, even when children are adults, continue to support their children. We, then, in turn, examine issues of assisting the elderly, and of elderly parenting of adult children.

During recent years, a primary focus of research in gerontology has been on family caregiving and, specifically, the assistance provided to a disabled elder. The need for, and provision of, care to aging individuals by other family members is, in many ways, a focal issue in later life. With ever-increasing costs of medical and long-term care of the elderly, assistance by family members is often essential to the security and well-being of an older parent. Unfortunately, for many families this involvement is frequently stressful, with consequences that go beyond the immediate provision of care. Assisting a severely disabled parent may interfere with children's own employment, family life and/or well-being, or re-awaken long-standing conflicts with parents or siblings (Pearlin, Mullan, Semple, & Skaff, 1990).

Although critically important, many researchers are becoming convinced that caregiving is too narrow a focus to capture the reciprocal, contingent nature of parent–child ties across the life span. A life-course perspective implies that caregiving evolves from a long history of interactions and exchanges between parents and children. Parents provide many kinds of assistance to their adult children, including financial and emotional support. Even when children are assisting a disabled parent, the parent may still be returning some support as well. We believe that examination of these complimentary patterns of exchange contributes a fuller understanding of intergenerational relationships in later life than would a focus on caregiving alone, because care develops in the context of long-standing relationships with their unique histories of exchange, affection, and values.

We begin this chapter with an examination of the demographic changes that have dramatically altered the structure of the family and family relationships over the adult years. Based on these trends, critical issues in intergenerational relationships will be identified. We then briefly examine theoretical perspectives that illuminate the exploration of family relationships in adulthood. Turning to research, we consider what is known about patterns of assistance from parents to children during the adult years under routine circumstances, and then the types of assistance rendered from children to parents. We next review the extensive literature on caregiving, including who provides care, stresses associated with caregiving, and determinants and mediators of caregiving stress. We end this section with a discussion of the clinical implications of stresses and strains that are inevitably a part of caregiving situations. Finally, we speculate about the future of ties between the generations. As we look to the next century, should we be optimistic or pessimistic about the ability of families to support and care for each other across generational lines?

DEMOGRAPHIC CHANGES AND FAMILY TIES

The demographic revolution of the twentieth century has changed family structure in substantial ways. Increased life expectancy and decreased family size has resulted in an aging of the population and the family. Having an elder in the family had once been relatively rare; now, it is usual and expected.

Life expectancy has increased dramatically during the past 100 years. In the United States in 1900, life expectancy at birth was 46.4 years for men and 49 years for women. Currently, men have an expected life span of 72.0 years and women 78.9 years (National Center for Health Statistics, 1993). Life expectancy at age 65 shows a similar increase, from 11.5 years in 1900 to 15.2 years by 1989 for men, and from 12.2 years to 18.8 years for women for the same period (U.S. Bureau of the Census, 1992c). Thus, not only are people living longer, but old age now represents a greater proportion of the life span. The effect of these trends has been to increase the number and proportion of older people in the population. In 1900, only 4.1 percent of the population was age 65 or older. According to the 1990 census, 12.6 percent are currently 65 or older. This figure is expected to increase as the post-World War II baby boom reaches old age. By the year 2030, it is projected that 21.8 percent of the population will be over age 65 (Middle Projection Series; U.S. Bureau of the Census, 1992c).

Among non-Whites there is a smaller proportion of elderly than in the White population. This difference is due primarily to two factors: The non-White population has higher rates of mortality before age 65; and non-Whites, on average, have more children. In the coming decades, however, the numbers of non-White elderly are likely to increase somewhat faster than for White elderly.

These demographic trends also identify some other noteworthy characteristics of the older population. Of particular importance for family life is the growth of the number of "oldest-old," those people in their 80s and older. This age group has been growing at a faster rate than any other in the population. Currently, 2.8 percent of the United States population is age 80 and older, with the figure expected to rise to 5 percent by the year 2025 (Torrey, Kinsella, & Taeuber, 1987). Based on current mortality estimates, 30 percent of people in a birth cohort will live to 85 or more (U.S. Bureau of the Census, 1992a). The significance of this age group is that they are more likely to have disabilities that necessitate daily assistance with a variety of activities.

Another important trend is that the older population is predominantly female. Because women have greater life expectancies than men, they outnumber men by a 3:2 ratio among all people over age 65. This proportion increases with advancing age. Among people age 65 to 69, there are 81 men for every 100 women. By age 90, there are only 33 men for every 100 women (U.S. Bureau of the Census, 1992c). This trend has implications for marital status as well. Because women tend to marry men who are, on average, 4 years older than them, they are more likely to be widowed. According to the 1990 census, 42 percent of women age 65 and older and 77 percent of older men are married, whereas 49 percent of these older women and 14 percent of older men are widowed (U.S. Bureau of the Census, 1992c).

Most older people are healthy and live independently, but a substantial minority have limitations in functioning that require regular assistance. The proportion of those needing assistance increases with age. For example, over 45 percent of the community population over age 85 needs assistance with everyday activities, compared to only 2.4 percent of people under 65 years of age (U.S. Bureau of the Census, 1990). As would be expected, the proportion of individuals living in nursing homes rises in a similar way with advancing age, from 1.5 percent of those between 65 and 74 to 7 percent of those age 75 to 84, to 22 percent of people over 85 (U.S. Bureau of the Census, 1983).

Complicating the health care situation, Medicare during the mid-1980s began a systematic program to reduce the duration of inpatient hospital stays. Using a schedule of reimbursements based on diagnosis (diagnostically related groups, or DRGs), Medicare reimburses hospitals a fixed amount for a patient, rather than actual costs. This program creates an incentive to make inpatient stays as brief as possible, because hospitals must absorb the costs if the patient's expenses are more than Medicare's scheduled reimbursement. As a result, older people have been discharged "sicker and quicker."

The economic status of the elderly overall is probably better than at any time in history. The poverty rate for the elderly is 12.4 percent, with another 7.3 percent classified as "near-poor," that is, with incomes between 100 and 125 percent of the poverty level (U.S. Bureau of the Census, 1992b). The risk of poverty among the elderly varies considerably, however. Evidence from the 1991 Current Population Survey indicates that poverty rates are higher among the oldest old, single, divorced and widowed women, and minorities—groups that are increasingly characterizing the elderly population (U.S. Bureau of the Census, 1992b, 1992c).

Finally, the momentous changes in marriage and fertility are having a profound impact on later life families. Birth rates declined steadily from 1900 until the end of World War II, reversing during the 1950s and early 1960s, before falling to the current average of about 2 children born per woman (National Center for Health Statistics, 1993). Though the baby boom was characterized by a decline in childlessness, the proportion of large families (6 or more children) continued to fall. These fertility fluctuations have meant that current cohorts of elderly are comparatively advantaged in terms of availability of at least one child. This will change, however, as the baby boomers—whose rates of childbearing are substantially below that of their parents—begin to enter old age. High rates of marital dissolution are also changing the intergenerational family experiences of aging Americans. Divorced children often need help from their parents and are less able to provide caregiving assistance. In addition, a small, but growing proportion of elderly individuals are themselves divorced (Uhlenberg, Cooney, & Boyd, 1990). Available evidence suggests they are significantly worse off on a number of indicators, both economic and social, than elderly who are married or widowed (Uhlenberg, 1990).

These demographic trends have resulted in a situation in which multigenerational families are common. Adult children are likely to have elderly parents, who may provide occasional or regular assistance to them or their children. In turn, increased life expectancy means more people survive to ages when they will have chronic illnesses and need assistance. With smaller families, and potentially greater needs than resources among adult children, there may be fewer potential caregivers. As the population ages, caregivers themselves will be older. Thus, current trends suggest an increasing need for assistance on the part of aging adults. Unfortunately, this trend is occurring at the same time that there appear to be declining family resources to provide help.

CRITICAL ISSUES

Several critical issues emerge from examination of parent–child relationships across the adult years.

1. Demographic trends suggest that caregiving is becoming more common, as older generations live longer and are more likely to become disabled at some point in their lives. Correspondingly, younger generations also have increasing needs for assistance due to a variety of factors, including reduced economic opportunities and increased rates of teenage pregnancy and divorce. Because of increased survival and longevity of people with chronic mental or physical disabilities, parents may provide ongoing assistance to a child with special needs long into their own old age.

2. Although caregiving demands on the family are increasing, there is a diminishing capacity to provide assistance from both generations. Smaller family size and increased participation of women in the workforce means fewer people having less time to address emerging needs for assistance.

3. When care is needed, it emerges from long-standing patterns of interactions and exchanges. The configuration of assistance in families with grown children is complex, typically involving reciprocity rather than a transfer of resources and assistance in only one direction. Helping patterns that emerge in later life need to be understood in the context of ongoing patterns of reciprocity, rather than reduced to simple notions of "reverse parenting" or other such concepts.

4. The contributions of adult children to caring for elderly parents vary considerably, depending on family structure and their position in the family. Rather than one pattern, we find some children helping as secondary caregivers, assisting one parent in caring for another, or helping a sibling. Others may try to manage care while living at a distance from the parent, and some function as primary caregivers while receiving varying amounts of assistance from their own spouses, children, siblings, and other relatives.

5. Caregiving for a disabled elder is often very stressful for everyone involved. While the antecedents of caregiving stress have been described extensively, there is less agreement on what can be done to help families, or what the appropriate interface of family and formal services ought to be.

THEORETICAL APPROACHES TO PARENT–CHILD RELATIONSHIPS

Our examination of family relationships in the later years is guided by two main perspectives: a life-course perspective on changes in the family; and the application of stress theory to family caregiving.

A life-course perspective emphasizes that individuals and families develop over time and the course of development and change is influenced by social and historical context (Elder, 1974; 1978; 1985; Hagestad & Neugarten, 1985). This approach draws attention to variations both within cohorts or generations and between them. A major source of within-cohort heterogeneity is variations in the timing of transitional life events (e.g., marriage, childbirth, job, or career events). Parent–child relationships as well as flows of assistance are significantly moderated by life-course transitions— both the event and its timing. For example, the birth of a (grand)child is an important life event that triggers parental assistance to adult children. However, the timing and context of the birth are important determinants of the kinds and amount of assistance rendered. Equally important is the premise that change over time is ubiquitous, because people go through major transitional events. Needs of adult children change as they move through childbearing and as their children mature. Financial constraints of early adulthood may diminish for some as work careers stabilize. For others, however, unexpected changes or crises (such as divorce, job loss, or illness) may abruptly change ongoing patterns of parent–child relationships. Parents' experiences change as well. Retirement transitions, death of a spouse, changes in health, or residential changes are all transitions that affect relationships, the ability of parents to provide resources, and their own need for help.

A life-course perspective also assumes important variations between cohorts or generations. Historical events (economic depressions, wars), demographic changes (declining mortality, fluctuations in fertility), and cultural revolutions uniquely stamp successive cohorts. Thus, the life-span profile of parent–child relationships experienced by individuals who today are in their 70s was neither the same as that of cohorts before them, nor will it necessarily be typical of succeeding cohorts. Important cohort differences in contemporary society include increased participation of women in the workplace and decreased economic opportunities for young adults compared to their parents.

Finally, this perspective implies that life events in one generation have implications for life events in contiguous generations. It is not just the life-course transitions of children or their parents that matter, but how they interlock (Elder, 1985). For example, the ability or desire of parents to help their adult child cope with a newborn may be powerfully moderated by the timing of events in their own lives (e.g., work, health, and/or marital transitions). Complicating the picture further may be events in the lives of other siblings of the adult child (Eggebeen, Hogan, & Snaith, 1993) or even the caregiving needs of an aged parent of the parent (Brody, 1985; Eggebeen & Hogan, 1990). Parent–child relationships are a lifelong process of interchanges among individuals, influenced by their respective biographies and embedded in family, social, economic, and historical contexts.

Although the life-course perspective provides a broad framework for viewing family interactions, stress theory can illuminate the process of adaptation of families giving care to an elder (Cohler, Groves, Borden, & Lazarus, 1989; Kinney & Stephens, 1989; Vitaliano, Maiuro, Ochs, & Russo, 1989; S. H. Zarit, 1989, 1992). Caregiving involves chronic, long-term stressors that have cumulative and generally adverse effects over time. There are, however, considerable individual differences in how family members adapt to the caregiving role and in the degree of emotional distress and disruption they experience in their lives. Children assisting parents with very similar kinds of disabilities may show widely varying patterns of adaptation (e.g., Aneshensel, Pearlin, & Schuler, 1993; S. H. Zarit, 1992). The notion that a particular type of parent care consistently results in similar strains or adaptational patterns is not supported by the evidence.

Three key concepts are useful for understanding these individual differences. First is the notion of stress proliferation (Pearlin et al., 1990). Caregiving involves specific activities to assist a disabled parent that are stressful to varying degrees. With the cumulative demands of care over time, and as psychological, social, or economic resources may be used up, these primary care stressors can proliferate, interfering with functioning in other roles or with psychological and physical well-being. The degree of proliferation varies considerably, however, depending on the personal circumstances of the caregiver, as well as factors that may mitigate or lessen the impact of stressors. This stress buffering process is the second key point leading to individual differences in adaptation. Examples of factors that may lessen the impact of stressors include the caregiver's use of optimal coping strategies to manage everyday problems and pressures, and receiving timely social support and assistance from others. The third concept is that caregiving is a career with entry and exit points and key transitions around which expectations for behavior change (Pearlin, 1993). Caregivers are socialized to the role over time and learn different adaptive strategies. Critical transitions, such as nursing home placement, restructure key features of the caregiving role, but usually do not lead to the end of the family's involvement (Rosenthal, Sulman, & Marshall, 1993; S. H. Zarit & Whitlatch, 1992).

A central premise of this approach is that the experience of distress is not due to caregiving per se, but to the beliefs, meaning, resources, and coping strategies of families, as well as the larger family context in which care is given. It follows, then, that there may be modifiable aspects of many care situations, which will potentially reduce the stress caregivers experience. Even when it is not possible to change the elder's disability, changes in other aspects of the care situation can be very helpful for the caregiver.

In summary, stress theory provides a framework for understanding the caregiving experiences of family members. The explanatory power of this framework is considerably enhanced, however, when caregiving is viewed in context—something that a life-course perspective is particularly suited to do. This perspective sensitizes us to grapple with more than just the characteristics of a single caregiver. We need instead to consider the stresses and challenges of caregiving in the context of other family members, the cumulative history of the caregiver and recipient, including prior assistance between parent and child, and larger social and historical trends.

PARENT ASSISTANCE TO ADULT CHILDREN

The substance of parent–child relationships consists of what one does for another. How typical are exchanges between generations in contemporary American families? Is support from parents or children in times of need forthcoming? Is assistance effective? What patterns are evident over the life spans of children and parents? We address these questions in the next few sections by first reviewing research focused on parental help to adult children, including routine kinds of assistance, help to dependent adult children, and assistance in times of need. We then discuss research concentrating on adult children's assistance to parents, including both routine help and care in times of dependence or need.

What do parents give to their adult children? Most recent surveys that ask about routine assistance find that a majority of parents have given at least some form of help to at least one of their adult children in the recent past (e.g., within the past month). Estimates from the 1988 National Survey of Families and Households (NSFH) are that 62 percent of parents of adult children had given them some form of help (e.g., money, household assistance, advice or emotional support, or child care) within the past month. A recent Gallup (1991) survey of parents age 55 and older found essentially the same proportion (59 percent) had given help or money to at least one of their children (Gallup, 1992). Other surveys essentially corroborate the notion that routine help to children characterizes the majority of parent–child ties (A. S. Rossi & P. H. Rossi, 1990; Spitze & Logan, 1992).

The fact that more than half of parents are engaged in supporting their children should not necessarily be interpreted to mean that this support is either typical or responsive to needs. For example, data from the NSFH show that the proportion of parents giving a particular kind of assistance to any adult child never typifies the majority of parents. Parents are most likely to give advice (46 percent), while giving child-care, money, or household assistance characterize about a third of parents (Eggebeen 1992). Evidence from the Albany area survey of Spitze and Logan (1992), which focuses on help between parents and a particular child (rather than any child), finds routine giving of specific kinds of assistance never to typify more than one quarter of the parents. They also present some evidence on the frequency of giving each type of help and respondents' estimates of the amount of time spent in an average week helping a child. The median frequency of help given is about once a month, and the average number of hours per week is 1.22. Evidence of the responsiveness of parental support in times of need is also not very compelling. Data from the NSFH suggest that a child's poverty status, single-parenthood, poor physical health, or unemployment was not associated with a greater likelihood of parental support (Eggebeen & Wilhelm, 1993).

If needs do not necessarily spur parental giving, then what does? There are several strong predictors of parental giving, including the life-cycle stage of the child, the quality of the parent–child relationship, and how far apart parents and children live. Of particular importance, however, is parental resources. Parents with the most resources (married, highly educated, high income or wealth) are significantly more likely to help at least one of their children (Eggebeen, 1992; Eggebeen & Wilhelm, 1993; Hogan, Eggebeen, & Clogg, 1993). In short, the propensity to give to children appears to be driven more by the capacity of parents to give than children's needs.

Giving to children is moderated by both the life-course characteristics of children as well as parents. One of the surest ways to receive parental support is to have a child, and those with preschool-age children are the most likely to get help from their parents (Eggebeen, 1992; Eggebeen

& Hogan, 1990; Hogan, Eggebeen, & Clogg, 1993; Spitze & Logan, 1992). As grandchildren age, however, parental giving declines, even when parent's age is taken into account (Eggebeen & Hogan, 1990). This change occurs partly because aging parents are an important source of child care, which recedes in importance as grandchildren mature. Other forms of help—such as financial assistance, help with household chores, and even emotional support and advice—also decline as grandchildren age. By the time the last grandchild is 19 or older, aging parents tend to receive more assistance from their adult children than they give (Eggebeen & Hogan, 1990).

Evidence suggests that giving to children is also affected by changes in the life course of parents. Most significantly, as parents age, they tend to give less to their children (Cooney & Uhlenberg, 1992; Eggebeen, 1992). Much of the decline in giving as individuals age can be explained by factors associated with aging (e.g., declines in health, death of spouse, changing needs of children as they age). Yet, the monotonic decline in the likelihood of giving help to children by age persists even when these other factors are taken into account (Cooney & Uhlenberg, 1992; Eggebeen, 1992; A. S. Rossi & P. H. Rossi, 1990; Spitze & Logan, 1992).

Flows of assistance to adult children are also disturbed by changes in aging parents' marital status. There is some evidence that widowhood is associated with less support to children (Eggebeen, 1992; A. S. Rossi & P. H. Rossi, 1990). However, others have found that widowhood per se is not related to reduced assistance once changes in socioeconomic status and health are taken into account (Morgan, 1983; Spitze & Logan, 1992). Although less studied, divorce also appears to be associated with declines in giving support to children. There is some suggestion that this is more true for men than women (Cooney & Uhlenberg, 1990; Eggebeen, 1992).

An important, but often overlooked, transition in the lives of middle-age adults is the death of their parents (Winsbourgh, Bumpass, & Aquilino, 1991). The midlife transition to the top of the generational ladder has implications for assistance to children. As parents cope with the health declines and eventual death of their parents, they tend to give less assistance to children than when both their parents were alive or after both have died (Hogan, Eggebeen, & Snaith, 1993).

Finally, and inevitably, the death of the parent spurs a "final" intergenerational transfer. In general, social scientists have ignored this feature of the life course despite some suggestions that the potential for a bequest probably affects parent–child relationships (Bernheim, Shleifer, & Summers, 1985; Kotlikoff & Spivak, 1991). Economists, with their interest in intergenerational wealth transfers, however, have developed theories and models of bequests (see Eggebeen & Wilhelm, 1993). Available evidence suggests that parents typically treat their children equally in bequests (Menchik, 1980). Wilhelm (1993) also found substantial evidence of equal division, but those who did not give equally did not systematically give more to the child with lower earnings. Unfortunately, detailed information on the effects of future inheritance on current behavior and the determinants of patterns of bequests is difficult to come by.

This review is selective in that we have ignored subgroup variations in order to highlight overall patterns of assistance. We turn now to a brief discussion of differentials in support of children by the important features of race and gender. Ethnographic studies and specialized surveys document extensive social support networks among African-American families (Dilworth-Anderson, 1992; Stack, 1974; Taylor, 1986, 1988). These findings have led some researchers to conclude that African Americans have stronger kin networks than Whites (Stack, 1974; Wilson, 1986). Recent work based on nationally representative data, which systematically compare kin assistance of African Americans and Whites, have generally not found superior support networks among minority families even when socioeconomic differences are taken into account (Eggebeen, 1992; Hofferth, 1984; Hogan, Eggebeen, & Clogg, 1993; Hogan, Hao, & Parish, 1990).

There are two possible explanations for these discrepant findings. It may be that research based on small, nonrepresentative samples overestimated the significance of kin ties among minority families and that research based on more representative data can be interpreted as correcting the erroneous characterization that African-American families have exceptionally strong and effective kin networks. A more plausible explanation is that the plight of African Americans has worsened over the 1980s. The erosion of neighborhoods and communities within cities, the declining employment prospects of young African-American males, and the accelerating changes in family structure has meant that increasing numbers of African-American families are in situations where needs are many but resources are few (Wilson, 1987). The finding that by the early 1990s support networks among African-American families are comparatively weak probably says more about how much has changed in Black America in the past decade than about faulty conclusions drawn from ethnographic research.

A second well-documented source of variation in giving to children is that of gender. A number of studies show that women are more involved in kinkeeping activities (Eggebeen, 1992; A. S. Rossi & P. H. Rossi, 1990). There is also evidence of cross-generation gender differences in that mother–daughter ties are the strongest (A. S. Rossi & P. H. Rossi, 1990). When specific components of exchange are scrutinized, evidence suggests that giving tends to echo traditional sex-role expectations. Males are more likely to give financial help, and women tend to dominate in providing child-care and emotional support (Eggebeen, 1992).

Finally, small numbers of aged parents provide extensive assistance to children with special needs. Examples of these special groups include individuals with developmental disabilities, severe mental illness, and traumatic brain or spinal injuries. Aged parents assisting children with these types of disabilities may be providing extensive care that is physically and/or emotionally demanding (e.g., Friss, 1990; Smith & Tobin, in press). When parents are the primary support for these special needs individuals, the parents' own aging can underscore the fragility of the care arrangements.

Thus, our review of recent research on routine parental support of children show the following patterns: Most parents are routinely involved in support of at least one of their adult children. The likelihood of providing support appears to be influenced more by parental resources than children's need. However, support to children is strongly related to changes in their life course. Support of children lessens as parents age independent of disturbances caused by divorce or death, or health problems, although these transitions also have a major impact on giving to children. Recent work based on sample surveys indicate lower levels of support among African-American families relative to Whites. Finally, there is consistent evidence that support rendered to children differs by gender of the parent.

ADULT CHILDREN'S ASSISTANCE TO PARENTS

Next to spouses, adult children are the most important source of support for aging adults. Aging adults are two to three times more likely to pick children over anyone else as someone they would turn to in an emergency (Hogan & Eggebeen, in press). Children are also the first line of defense in times of illness recovery, or when elderly persons need a place to live. We begin with a discussion of relationships between children and their healthy normal parents, that is, patterns of routine assistance. Clearly, this is the dominant form of ties, yet the research on these exchanges is comparatively sparse. Following the discussion on routine ties, we review special literatures on assistance to dependent populations.

Routine Assistance

About 38 percent of aging American parents have received some routine help from their adult children (Eggebeen, 1992). Getting emotional support or advice is the most common form of assistance received by parents (28 percent) followed by help around the house (23 percent). Receiving financial help is very unusual; in the NSFH, less than 3 percent of parents report receiving a gift or loan of $200 or more from any of their children in the past 5 years (Eggebeen, 1992).

Several points need to be kept in mind when interpreting these numbers. First, parents are much more likely to give assistance to their children than to receive it. For example, evidence from the NSFH shows that parents are 1.7 times more likely to give than receive help from children (Eggebeen,

1992). Spitze and Logan (1992) reported an even greater imbalance in their data, with parents 2.6 times more likely to give than receive help. Thus, routine help from children is less frequent than assistance *to* children.

Second, the low rates of receipt of help do not necessarily reflect isolation or strained relationships. The average level of parent–child contact on a scale of 1 to 6 is 5.4 (Eggebeen, 1992). Indicators of the quality of the relationship between parents and children show overwhelmingly positive assessments on the part of parents (Snaith, Hogan, & Eggebeen, 1993). Also, when parents are asked whom they see as a potential source of support, they pick their children by a wide margin over friends, siblings, or other kin (Hogan & Eggebeen, 1994). These findings suggest that one should be careful about interpreting low levels of support from children as bad. Instead, it would seem that many middle-age parents have few needs that their children can help with, and therefore they do not solicit aid.

Third, low rates of financial assistance may be a recent development, reflecting changed circumstances of both older and younger cohorts. The relative financial situation of the elderly improved in the United States in the 1970s when increases in Social Security payments were tied to the Cost of Living Index. For significant segments of younger cohorts, the 1980s was a decade of reduced economic opportunities. It is possible, then, that financial aid to parents may have been more common in the past, but currently the opposite is more frequent.

Finally, these average amounts of assistance obscure considerable variation by age, family size, gender, and marital status. We turn to these patterns now. Even if the likelihood of giving help to children declines monotonically with age, receipt of assistance appears to slowly become more commonplace, accelerating in frequency after age 70 (Spitze & Logan, 1992). Much of this increase among the very old is related to growing dependence from increases in limitations on physical activities, poor health, or death of a spouse. It is these events that transform the kinds of support activities children have typically given their parents from routine help into caregiving. It should be noted, however, that increases in help occur even after controlling for decline in health or the death of a spouse (Eggebeen, 1992).

The strongest predictor of aging parents receiving routine help is number of children (Eggebeen, 1992). Even in modern industrialized societies, it appears that having many children is a reasonable strategy to ensure support in old age.

It has been argued that the greater investment on the part of women in kin relations throughout their life course results in their receiving more social support and assistance than men when they are old (Longino & Lipman, 1981; Spitze & Logan, 1989). Data from the NSFH show men are much less likely than women to receive help from children (Eggebeen, 1992). Some of this difference is accounted for by the different relationship—relative to women—that divorced men maintain with their children. Cooney and Uhlenberg (1990) found that mens's diminished contact with children after the divorce has implications into old age: They are significantly less likely than nondivorced men and women to have contact with their adult children. However, even when marital status is taken into account, women maintain a considerable advantage over men in receiving support from children (Eggebeen, 1992).

Divorce will become increasingly salient for future cohorts of elderly. Little research has investigated the plight of the divorced elderly, in part because, until recently, this group was a small proportion of the elderly (Uhlenberg, 1990). However, work using the NSFH, which examines either levels of interaction or tangible kinds of support, finds that neither divorced men nor women are especially supported by their children (K. A. Bulcroft & R. A. Bulcroft, 1991; Cooney & Uhlenberg, 1990; Eggebeen, 1992).

By comparison, there is considerable evidence that widowed aging parents receive more assistance from their children than do married parents (Eggebeen, 1992; Lopata, 1979; A. S. Rossi & P. H. Rossi, 1990; Stoller & Earl, 1983). Of course, the elevated levels of support are largely due to their greater tangible needs (Crimmins & Ingegneri, 1990; Morgan, 1983).

In summary, parents on balance give more assistance to their children than they receive, but this pattern probably reflects the comparatively fewer needs middle-age parents have relative to their children. As parents age, their needs grow and assistance from children appears responsive. Among the oldest old, where the need for support from children becomes more acute, patterns of routine care are transformed and many adult children face a period of intense caregiving.

Assistance to Dependent Parents

A rather extensive literature exists about assistance to dependent elderly, including who provides care and the stresses associated with caregiving. Helping patterns between children and their aged parents are characterized by considerable heterogeneity. The amount of help needed and assistance provided ranges from very minimal to extensive, around-the-clock responsibilities. At any single point in time, most elderly people need little or no regular assistance, so the amount of help being provided by children will be minimal. On occasion, however, even these minimal involvements can be very stressful, with children perceiving that their parents are making excessive demands on them. These kinds of interactions are probably best viewed as an extension of intergenerational conflict, where long-standing personal and family issues are more critical than caregiving involvement.

An important caregiving situation takes place when families mobilize resources around a particular event, such as a hospitalization or death. The transactions and decisions that occur during these events are of vital importance to the family, and include issues such as who provides assistance and who is perceived as not doing a fair share. The decisions made during these crisis events can, of course, have long-range consequences for everyone involved. Unfortunately, not much is known about how families mobilize and respond to these types of events, in part because they are difficult to anticipate and because the family's intensive involvement usually has a short duration.

The most typical caregiving situation, and the one that current research extensively addresses, involves providing long-term assistance. A parent's chronic disability can develop as the result of an acute problem, such as a sudden illness or accident. More typically, however, functional limitations associated with chronic disease accumulate gradually over a long period of time. Eventually, the older person and/or family recognize the need for regular assistance with everyday tasks.

Who becomes a caregiver?   When the need for assistance develops, help is most often provided by a family member. Social norms are strong not only about providing care, but also concerning who will be the caregiver. The belief that families are responsible for the care of their elderly relatives has long been a central tenet in many cultures (e.g., Habib, Sundström, & Windmiller, in press). With the emergence of modern nuclear families, concerns have often been expressed that the family will turn over care of the elderly to formal institutions. Although historical trends are difficult to determine, it appears that families remain highly involved, even when extensive formal services are available (Habib et al., in press). Indeed, given the increased probability of becoming a caregiver and assisting someone for a long period of time, families may be providing more help than ever before. One index of care is the proportion of older people in nursing homes and other institutional settings, which has remained constant at around 5 percent in the United States over the last 30 years.

Most people endorse attitudes of filial obligation, indicating their belief that children should be involved in their parents' lives and provide assistance when needed (e.g., Brody, Johnsen, & Fulcomer, 1984; Brody, Johnsen, Fulcomer, & Lang, 1983; Finley, Roberts, & Banahan, 1988). Many children, however, prefer not having to share a household with a parent. Correspondingly, many older people say they do not want to be a burden to their children, and also prefer not sharing a household with them (Brody et al., 1984). In one study of three generations of women, Brody and her associates (1983) found that the oldest generation was more accepting of receiving help from formal sources, whereas the youngest generation was the least accepting of this type of help.

When an elder needs assistance, one person typically assumes primary responsibility for care, with other family members playing a secondary or supplementary role, providing lesser amounts or intermittent assistance. On occasion, two children may share the care tasks relatively equally, or the elder may move from one household to another on a regular schedule.

The role of primary caregiver is more likely to be assumed by some family members than others. If an elder has a surviving spouse, that person would typically take on the primary caring responsibility. In those instances, children may play a secondary caregiving role, assisting their parents with some tasks. When the elder has no spouse, then a daughter is more likely to assume the primary caregiving role. Sons become primary caregivers when there are no daughters, performing similar tasks as daughters in those circumstances (Williamson & Schulz, 1990). When they are in a secondary role, sons often assume some traditional masculine tasks, such as managing finances and household repairs (Cantor, 1983). In the absence of any adult children or when adult children are unable to take on primary caregiving responsibilities, then other relatives or, in some instances, friends or acquaintances, may do so.

This pattern is borne out by data from a national survey of family caregivers (Stone, Cafferata, & Sangl, 1987). In this sample, caregivers were assisting with at least one activity of daily living. Figure 5.1 shows how the sample of caregivers were related to the care recipient, as well as whether they were the primary or secondary caregiver. Considering all caregivers, the most frequent relationship was spouse, either the husband or wife of the elder (35.5 percent of the sample of all caregivers). Daughters were the next most common group (28.9 percent). A small percentage (8.5 percent) were sons. Additionally, some daughters-in-law and sons-in-law, who were included in the "other" category, were providing care.

Nearly all of the spouses in this sample were primary caregivers, while 70 percent of daughters and slightly less than half of the sons had the main responsibility for their parent. If we consider only primary caregivers (Figure 5.1), the proportion of spouses among all caregivers is somewhat larger (48.8 percent), compared to daughters (28.6 percent) or sons (5.7 percent). Thus, adult children, and particularly daughters, may find themselves either in a primary care role, or, frequently, as secondary caregivers assisting a parent or a sibling.

The profile of characteristics of adult children caregivers that emerges in this survey is somewhat different from the media's image of a "sandwich generation" caught between the demands of parents and young children. Instead, consistent with the increased life expectancy of their parents' generation, most adult child caregivers are older, and their children are grown and out of the house. Daughters had an average age of 52.4 years, and sons an average of 48.6 years. It is noteworthy that 13 percent of daughters and 9 percent of sons were themselves over the age of 65. Three quarters of adult children did not have children under the age of 18 living in the household.

While we noted earlier that both parents and children prefer to live separately, the most common care arrangement when help is needed is for the older parent and adult child to share the same residence. This was the case for 61 percent of daughters and sons. Workforce participation was lower

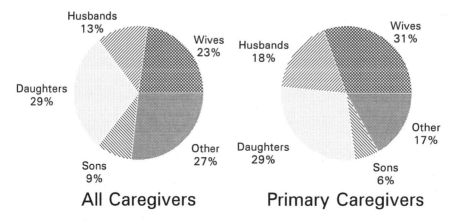

FIGURE 5.1. Relationship of family caregivers to the care recipient (adapted from Stone et al., 1987).

than one might expect. Forty-four percent of daughters and 55 percent of sons were currently employed (Stone et al., 1987).

These summaries do not, of course, reflect the full variation in patterns of family care. Of particular importance in coming years will be how single parenthood and high rates of divorce and remarriage will affect caregiving activities by adult children. There is some evidence from inner-city African-American families of a compression between generations, such that grandparents, who may be in their 30s and 40s, raise their grandchildren and perhaps also assist their own elderly parents and grandparents (Burton & Sörensen, 1993). These variations in family care will be important to examine.

Stresses of caregiving.   The point at which a parent begins to experience difficulty living independently is a critical transition for both elders and their children. Most elderly parents and adult children are unaware of the range of options available for specialized housing and community services to assist someone who is disabled, and they may not know where to find this type of information. Physicians are the professionals most people ask first in this situation, but many doctors, unfortunately, are ill-informed about aging services (MaloneBeach, S. H. Zarit, & Spore, 1992). Community-based services, such as a homemaker or nurse's aide who assists an elder in the home with specific tasks, or an adult day-care program, can be a valuable way of helping an elder remain at home. The availability, quality, and cost of these services can vary widely from one locale to another. Typically, however, family members perform the main tasks needed in caring for an elder.

A special set of circumstances, which arises frequently in modern society, is when children live at some distance from parents whose daily living skills are deteriorating. The child living at a distance faces the problem of obtaining reliable information about the parent's situation, identifying and assessing local resources that might help the parent, and deciding when to intervene. Because social services can vary so much from one region to another, finding out quickly what services are available and which agencies provide better quality home care can present a formidable task.

When it is difficult to arrange for or monitor services at a long distance, children may consider moving a parent closer to them or into their house. The choices in this type of situation are exceedingly difficult, and there are potential drawbacks associated with both moving and not moving the parent. Adult children who do not relocate a disabled parent may find themselves spending considerable time arranging for adequate care and supervision, as well as worrying about their parent's safety and well-being. They may receive frequent calls for help from their parent, other relatives who live near their parent, or from formal service providers who have become concerned or frustrated by the situation. Although moving the parent closer may give children more control over the parent's care and living arrangements, it can also undermine the parent's remaining social supports. A common problem is that adult children may unrealistically expect the parent to function independently in the new setting, but the unfamiliarity of a new place and new routine can overwhelm someone whose functioning is already compromised. The result may be greater dependency on children than they have expected. Parents may also unrealistically believe they could have maintained themselves in their own home and resent their children's efforts to relocate them.

Much of research literature has focused on how chronic stressors affect the caregiver's emotional well-being and health. The risks for caregivers as a group have been well-established. Being a caregiver is associated with decreased well-being, increased rates of depression, other types of emotional distress, and greater vulnerability to health problems (e.g., Anthony, Zarit, & Gatz, 1988; Gallagher, Rose, Rivera, Lovett, & Thompson, 1989; George & Gwyther, 1986; Kiecolt-Glaser, Dura, Speicher, Trask, & Glaser, 1991; Schulz, Williamson, Morycz, & Biegel, 1993).

Many studies combine caregivers into a single group and do not examine how kin relationship (i.e., being a child or a spouse) may affect emotional well-being and health. As a result, it is difficult to differentiate the specific problems of and risks to adult children. The available research suggests overall that adult child caregivers experience a similar degree of emotional distress as spouse caregivers, and report higher levels of distress than age-matched samples of noncaregivers. Two factors, however, temper these findings. First, gender is strongly related to reports of emotional distress. Wives and daughters who are caregivers report higher levels of distress than husbands or sons, even after controlling for severity of the parents' disease (e.g., Anthony-Bergstone et al., 1988; Schulz et al., 1993; Williamson & Schulz, 1990; S. H. Zarit & Whitlatch, 1992). Second, adult children appear quite similar to spouse caregivers in their vulnerability when sharing a household with their parent (Deimling, Bass, Townsend, & Noelker, 1989).

Some aspects of caregiving are more stressful than others. Caregivers are typically more distressed when a parent has behavior or emotional problems, than when only routine assistance with everyday tasks is required (e.g., Haley, Brown, & Levine 1987; Pruchno & Resch, 1989). Notably, people caring for an elder with a dementing illness, such as Alzheimer's disease, or with a mental disorder are more likely to experience emotional distress than caregivers of people with physical disabilities but only small degrees of behavioral or emotional disruption (Birkel, 1987; Pearson, Verma, & Nellett, 1988).

When considering how the stresses of caregiving can proliferate into other areas of the adult child's life, the most common problems are restriction of social and leisure activity, increased conflict with spouses and other family members, and increased difficulties at work (Brody, Hoffman, Kleban, & Schoonover, 1989; Deimling et al., 1989; Miller & Montgomery, 1990; Scharlach & Boyd, 1989; Semple, 1992; Stone et al., 1987; Suitor & Pillemer, 1993).

Conflict with other family members is fairly common (Brody et al., 1989; MaloneBeach & S. H. Zarit, in press). Semple (1992) examined three dimensions of family conflict: around definitions of the elder's illness and strategies for care, over family members' attitudes and behavior toward the patient, and over their behavior and attitudes toward the caregiver. All three types of conflict were more commonly reported by adult children than by spouse caregivers. In turn, higher levels of conflict were associated with feelings of depression and anger for the primary caregiver.

Other studies have found that the relationship between caregiving daughters and their siblings is a major source of interpersonal stress (Brody et al., 1989; Pillemer & Suitor, 1993). When the sisters of caregiving daughters were also interviewed, they reported high levels of guilt over not doing more (Brody et al., 1989). Many caregivers find that the advice and information they get from relatives is stressful, even though this type of help is often considered a form of social support (MaloneBeach & S. H. Zarit, in press). This counterintuitive finding may indicate that families do not listen to or find out what caregivers need, but instead push their own suggestions and agenda for handling the situation.

For many adult children caregivers, the increasing demands of caregiving can interfere with work. Many children leave the workforce when taking on responsibility for care of a parent (Stone et al., 1987). In one survey of caregivers of people with neurological disorders, about half the sample of daughters reported giving up their jobs (Petty & Friss, 1987). Among those people continuing to work, it is not uncommon to have absences, reduced work hours, or other disruptions of work that result from caregiving activities (Brody, Kleban, Johnsen, Hoffman, & Schoonover, 1987; Scharlach & Boyd, 1989; Stone et al., 1987). Having a child at home under the age of 18 adds to this pressure (Scharlach & Boyd, 1989).

Comparisons of daughters who are and are not employed and have shown, not surprisingly, that the former provide less overall care and are more likely to use formal services to assist the parent (Brody & Schoonover, 1986; Matthews, Werkner, & Delaney, 1989). Brody and her associates (1987) distinguished four groups of daughters who were caregivers: traditional homemakers, women who left employment to become caregivers, women who were employed and reported conflict over their continued employment, and women who were employed but had no conflict. Conflicted workers were those women who had reduced their work hours or were considering quitting their jobs as a result of caregiving. The women who left work or were conflicted over work were caring for mothers who were more severely disabled. They also reported higher levels of strain and disruption in their lives than the other two groups.

In addition to leading to role strain and conflict, the stresses of caregiving may proliferate in another way by threatening an individual's psychological sense of self (Pearlin et al., 1990). Examples of these types of changes include feeling trapped or feeling a loss of identity in the role of caregiver (Johnson & Catalano, 1983; Miller & Montgomery, 1990; Robinson & Thurnher, 1979). These factors have been found to be the strongest predictor of placing a disabled elder into a nursing home (Aneshensel et al., 1993).

Several mediating factors have been identified that lessen the adverse effects of chronic stress. One of the most important mediators is social support, either from one's informal network or from formal service providers. Siblings typically assist the primary caregiver with some caregiving tasks (Brody et al., 1989; Suitor & Pillemer, 1993), although, as noted earlier, there may also be conflict over this help. Friends may be a more important source of emotional support than siblings or other family members (Suitor & Pillemer, 1993).

Spouses provide critical support to caregivers. Brody and her colleagues (Brody, Litvin, Hoffman, & Kleban, 1992) compared married daughters who were caring for a parent with daughters who were not married (including separated or divorced, widowed, and never married). Married caregivers reported more support, less financial strain, and less depression than the unmarried daughters.

Formal help is a very important source of assistance for caregivers, and may be used more frequently by adult children caregivers than spouse caregivers (Johnson & Catalano, 1983). In general, however, rates of using services are fairly low for all caregivers (Mullan, 1993). Factors affecting utilization include the cost of care, difficulties in finding appropriate and good quality services, and reluctance by family caregivers to turn responsibilities over to someone else (MaloneBeach et al., 1992; Mullan, 1993). A major factor in caring for a parent is that Medicare and other third-party payers do not reimburse for long-term care, including nursing homes, under most circumstances. Another factor affecting service use is the caregiver's emotional state. Caregivers who are depressed and may thus have the most need for assistance use formal services the least (Mullan, 1993). Their depression and concomitant feelings of helplessness and hopelessness may act as barriers to obtaining assistance.

An important mediator of stress is how caregivers cope with daily stresses and challenges. It has generally been suggested that people with better problem-solving skills, who can distance themselves somewhat from problems and think about alternative courses of action, will function better than caregivers who respond emotionally to their situation (e.g., Johnson & Catalano, 1983; Niederehe & Funk, 1987; Vitaliano, Becker, Russo, Magana-Amato, & Maiuro, 1988–1989; S. H. Zarit, Orr, & J. M. Zarit, 1985). When coping with Alzheimer's disease or other long-term degenerative conditions, cognitive coping strategies, such as finding meaning in the situation, or seeking comfort in one's religious beliefs can be very helpful.

Caregiving activities may span several years, shifting in intensity as other circumstances in a caregiver's life also change. Only a few longitudinal studies have been conducted to date on the course of adult caregiving. These investigations suggest that caregivers can follow different trajectories, with some showing increased problems and stress-related symptoms, but others improving, even as the elder's condition worsens (e.g., Schulz et al., 1993; Townsend, Noelker, Deimling, & Bass, 1989; S. H. Zarit, Todd, & J. M. Zarit, 1986).

Probably the most momentous transition in caregiving is the decision to place a parent in a nursing home. Longitudinal investigation of placement suggests that adult children do not give up their role as caregivers when parents go to a nursing home. Instead, they typically remain involved, visiting their parent frequently, in some cases assisting their parent with daily activities (such as feeding or dressing), and interacting with staff to assure good care. Although placement is associated with some relief of emotional distress, many caregivers continue to experience high levels of guilt, depression and other problems after institutionalization (S. H. Zarit & Whitlatch, 1992). These feelings may persist as long as 2 years after placement (S. H. Zarit & Whitlatch, 1993).

Contemporary research on family caregiving has established a foundation for understanding the experience of adult children and the problems they encounter when caring for an elderly parent or parents. This research, however, is not without its limitations. An important limiting factor that is crucial for understanding the many different ways adult children can be involved in caregiving is that research has almost exclusively focused on people who are the primary or main providers of care. Much less is known about the problems and stresses of being in a secondary role, or how primary and secondary caregivers can interact effectively. The relationships between primary and secondary caregivers lend themselves to certain kinds of difficulties, for example, misunderstandings among the various helpers about the elder's disabilities and needs and about the type and schedule of assistance to the primary caregiver. As we have seen, conflict among siblings on these issues can be a major source of stress. Because many adult children are in a secondary helping role, either to a parent, or to a sibling who is the main provider of care to a parent, an understanding of the factors that lead to effective collaboration or to problems in these relationships would be very helpful.

CLINICAL IMPLICATIONS

Adult caregiving is a major event in family life. There are, however, many potential hazards as well as the possibility for fulfillment that comes from feeling one is meeting obligations to a parent. Many types of formal social services that provide part of the care to the disabled elder along with clinical interventions directed either at the elder, caregiver, or the wider family may be helpful to alleviate or prevent the development of excessive strain on caregivers.

Working with the elderly and their families requires some special skills in addition to basic clinical competencies. These skills are important for gaining an adequate understanding of the older person and the problems faced by the family and form a foundation for interventions with caregivers. Some of these skills include:

(1) *Assessment of Disorders of Aging*. Clinicians working with older people should be familiar with assessment procedures for disorders of aging. In particular, they need to be able to differentiate memory and cognitive problems due to dementia from problems of normal aging or reversible conditions such as depression (e.g., Kaszniak, 1990; S. H. Zarit et al., 1985). When families raise questions about the competency of an older individual, it is essential to be able to identify when there are real problems from situations where families may be using the parent's age to redress old grievances or to change the distribution of resources in the family.

(2) *Understanding of Diseases and Medications*. Working with the elderly requires an understanding of the course and consequences of major illnesses associated with aging and the effects of common medications. Clinicians need to be able to distinguish between what is and is not possible to achieve with treatment. As an example, rehabilitation for severe losses of vision is often possible, and older people can benefit from a variety of vision aids (Genensky & S. H. Zarit, 1993). In contrast, a person with Alzheimer's disease or another dementing disorder will be able to make only very limited functional gains. In those instances, more of the focus of treatment will be on how the family can change to cope effectively with the strains caused by the disease, rather than trying to improve the functioning of the "patient."

(3) *Awareness of One's Own Feelings About Aging*. Because aging is associated with many negative expectations and beliefs, clinicians should be aware of their own concerns and reactions. As in dealing with any other family situation, it is important not to side with one generation over another. Holding a negative bias against the elderly is one possibility. Clinicians can also err in the direction of taking the side of the elderly against children. Knight (1986) discussed these and other "counter-transference" issues that can arise when working with older people.

(4) *Knowledge of the Aging Service System*. Social resources are available to assist older people and their families. In critical situations, such as when a parent needs regular assistance, a social program like adult day care can be of enormous value. Programs, eligibilities, and costs, however, vary considerably from one part of the country to another. Clinicians working with the elderly should either familiarize themselves with these resources or collaborate with other clinicians or case managers who are aware of current programs and benefits.

A central issue is that Medicare does not cover many important services. As noted earlier, for example, Medicare does not pay for most nursing home stays. As a result, nursing home placement has significant financial consequences for families. Placement should never be suggested in a casual way, and planning should be undertaken with an understanding of the alternatives for paying for it.

Many different clinical strategies are useful when working with adult children and their aged parents (Smyer, S. H. Zarit, & Qualls, 1990). As indicated earlier, the starting point is a careful assessment of older persons and their family to clarify the problems and issues present. The following approaches are useful for addressing the stresses of caregiving:

(1) *Education.* Clinicians often play an educative role, helping families to understand the elder's problems and the consequences of those problems. Counseling sessions can be useful for clarifying families' goals and values regarding caregiving and helping them understand the alternatives available.

(2) *Improving Management of the Care Situation.* Many stressful aspects of care situations can be brought under better control by families. As an example, common behavioral disturbances associated with Alzheimer's disease, such as agitation, will often respond to behavioral management strategies (S. H. Zarit et al., 1985). Agitation may follow long periods of inactivity. By identifying inactivity as an antecedent of agitation, a family can plan activities to involve and stimulate the patient in order to head off the problem. Typically, a wide range of social and behavioral strategies can help improve the elder's mood and behavior, while lowering the strain on caregivers.

(3) *Change the Amount and Type of Help Provided by Family Members.* Although care usually falls primarily on one person in the family, assistance from other family members can often make the situation more manageable. They may not, however, understand the need for help or the type of help the primary caregiver would like. Family sessions that explore the elder's problems while addressing the caregiver's needs can be an effective way of mobilizing family resources (Mittelman et al., 1993; Whitlatch, S. H. Zarit, & von Eye, 1991; S. H. Zarit et al., 1985).

(4) *Bringing in New Resources.* In addition to mobilizing help within the family, clinicians can help caregivers obtain formal social services to provide care to the elder. Programs such as day care, overnight respite care, or home helpers who assist the elder with activities in the home can be quite valuable in reducing strain.

Families, however, may be reluctant to use formal services, believing either that someone else cannot do a good enough job, or that the elder will not accept help. Usually it is possible to work through these sorts of objections by examining them and suggesting alternative ways of thinking about using formal services (S. H. Zarit et al., 1985). Sometimes, however, the barriers are realistic, such as when a family cannot afford the cost of a program, or when services are not available or reliable.

Although an empirical literature on the effectiveness of treatment of family problems in later life is limited, some initial findings are available. In particular, a family systems approach that addresses patterns of interaction around caregiving and seeks to increase the amount of assistance being provided has shown promise (Mittelman et al., 1993; Niederehe & Frugé, 1984; Whitlatch et al., 1991; S. H. Zarit et al., 1985). A frequent source of help for caregivers is support groups. Although these groups may be very useful for helping family members understand their situation and the alternatives available to them, their role may be limited in addressing significant feelings of emotional distress or depression (S. H. Zarit & Teri, 1991).

One of the most unique interventions was conducted by Scharlach (1987). In this study, daughters who reported problematic relationships with their mothers were enrolled into either a support group or a group emphasizing cognitive behavioral skills. The evaluation of outcome focused both on the daughters and their mothers. The findings indicated the cognitive behavioral approach resulted in reduced stress among daughters and decreased loneliness among their mothers. This type of study, which examines the effects of treatment on both child and parent, is especially promising for identifying useful strategies for working with families.

FUTURE TRENDS

What will intergenerational support and family caregiving look like in the future? Should we be optimistic or pessimistic that current patterns will suffice to meet the needs of adult children and dependent, aging parents? Speculating about the future is always a risky prospect; unexpected historical events occur, the economy can move in unpredicted ways, political winds can abruptly shift. Yet, because of the demographic "momentum" of the social changes discussed earlier—changes that will have a direct bearing on the form and nature of current intergenerational support and caregiving—we can make some reasonable assertions.

The ongoing sociodemographic changes may make it difficult to be optimistic about the continued ability of families to bear a disproportionate burden of caregiving. Indeed, it is likely that a growing proportion of the elderly will be in need of care at the same time that the capacity of their children to provide support will be diminished.

At the same time, ever spiraling costs of medical care for society as a whole, and specifically for the elderly, mean that it is unlikely that there will be a large diversion of funds into social programs that provide assistance to family caregivers or to other approaches that encourage caring for older people in the community. Consensus reigns about the need for alternatives to institutionalization and the benefits of caring for older people in the community. Programs that share some portion of the care, such as adult day care, have been growing steadily in the United States. Coverage of supportive community-based services under Medicare or through special programs in some states has grown gradually. Additional increments can be expected, but it is unlikely that there will be any substantial increase of funds for these programs in the upcoming years.

As described earlier, some promising and relatively cost-effective approaches for addressing the problems of family caregivers and disabled elders have been identified. It is particularly important to examine benefits simultaneously both for the elders and their family at large. Service systems that are not unduly bureaucratic or confusing are also needed, ones that offer flexible solutions to the problems faced by the elderly. All too often, we try to fit people's problems into preexisting categories of services, rather than make programs responsive to specific needs.

At a more basic level, we need to consider what the role of the family ought to be. How much can adult children be expected to provide for disabled parents and what portion of assistance should come from the public sector, such as an enhanced Medicare program? In the Scandinavian countries, it is assumed that the state will take care of the needs of the elderly. Although families continue to provide substantial amounts of assistance, governments support high levels of formal care (e.g., Hokenstad & Johannson, 1990). As we examine our own circumstances, we need to ask what should the relative contributions be from families and from formal services, and how should the latter be funded. Unfortunately, there is little consensus either about the amount of formal help that should be available or how to pay for it.

Looking to the future, we can expect that families will continue to provide elderly adults extensive assistance. However, the unprecedented demands placed on adult caregivers by severely disabled elderly, the adult caregiver's other responsibilities, and their reduced economic and personal resources, mean that new forms of family care and new patterns of collaboration between formal and informal helpers need to be developed. The success of these approaches will have critical implications for the quality of family life in the next century.

CONCLUSIONS

Demographic changes in mortality, morbidity, marriage, and fertility have profoundly altered the context of intergenerational family ties. Declines in mortality means that adult child–aging parent ties are commonplace. On the other hand, greater survivorship has come partly at the expense of higher risks of chronic illness and dependency. Higher divorce rates among both adult children and their parents implies potentially more needs and fewer resources to share. Finally, the baby boom cohorts will face old age with comparatively fewer adult children than their parents had to rely on for support.

The majority of parents give assistance to their children on a routine basis. The strongest predictors of parental support are the birth of a (grand)child, the quality of the aging parent–adult child relationship, how far apart parents and children live, and parental resources. Also important are the age and marital status of the parents—parents give less as they age and married parents tend to give more than widowed or divorced parents. There is also evidence of substantial variations in patterns of routine assistance by race and gender. Surprisingly, recent research based on sample surveys find little evidence of more extensive aging parent–adult child ties among African Americans relative to Whites. Giving between generations differs for males and females. Women evidence stronger ties and engage in more extensive kin-keeping activities. Males are found to give financial help; women are more likely to provide emotional support and child care.

On balance, parents tend to give more than get routine help from adult children. Children are most likely to offer emotional support and advice, and least likely to provide financial help. Given the overall positive ratings of relationships and the high levels of contact, it appears that the low rates of support probably reflect the comparatively lower need of aging parents for routine assistance. While giving to adult children declines with age, reception of help from children becomes more common with the passing years.

Number of children, gender, and marital status considerably influence the extent of support given parents. Parents with large numbers of children receive much more assistance than parents of few adult children. Women receive more help from their children than men. Divorced men are particularly disadvantaged when it comes to assistance from adult children. Although considerable evidence shows that widowhood mobilizes support from children, preliminary work suggests that divorced parents are not especially supported by their children.

Disability of an elderly parent represents a major life transition for families. Adult children are involved in caring for parents in a variety of ways. Some children assist their other parent who has assumed the primary responsibility for care. In other instances, adult children take on the primary care role or help a sibling who has done so. Taking on long-term responsibilities of caring for an older person is often stressful and may be disruptive to other relationships and activities in one's life. Caregiving can become an all-consuming involvement, which quickly exceeds a caregiver's physical, emotional, and financial resources. Long-term caregiving has been found to be associated with several different kinds of negative consequences, including increased rates of depression and other emotional distress, increased risk of health problems, and increased strain or conflict with other family members and at work, as well as feelings of losing one's identity or being trapped in the role of caregiver.

Support from family and friends as well as good coping resources can lessen the negative impact on caregivers. Clinical interventions, which help families work more effectively together to support the primary caregiver while being sensitive to the needs of the elder, are a promising approach for reducing strain on everyone involved. Supportive services, such as adult day care, can also relieve some of the daily pressures for care from the family.

Despite the growing attention that family caregiving has received, it is difficult to be optimistic about future prospects. Demographic trends suggest that the number of disabled elderly will grow, while the resources of families to assist them will diminish. Increased rates of divorce, remarriage, and stepparent families complicate the picture of how much family care will be available in subsequent generations. New approaches are needed that support the efforts of family caregivers to assist parents or other elderly relatives. These approaches need to strike a balance among the interests of the elder, the family, and society, so that the last years of life can represent a fulfillment of family relationships, rather than a threat to the family's survival.

ACKNOWLEDGMENTS

Partial support for this chapter was provided by the Population Research Institute of the Pennsylvania State University, which has core support from the National Institute of Child Health and Human Development (Grant No. 1-HD28263-01); and by NICHD Grant No. 1 R01 HD26070, "Intergenerational Exchanges in Families with Children" (Dennis P. Hogan, principal investigator). Additional support was provided by NIA Grant No. 1 RO1 AG11354, "Mental Health of Caregivers of the Elderly: Day Care Use" (Steven H. Zarit, principal investigator).

REFERENCES

Adams, B. N. (1968). *Kinship in an urban setting*. Chicago: Markham.

Aneshensel, C. S., Pearlin, L. I., & Schuler, R. M. (1993). Stress, role captivity and the cessation of caregiving. *Journal of Health and Social Behavior, 34*, 54–70.

Anthony, C. R., Zarit, S. H., & Gatz, M. (1988). Symptoms of distress among caregivers of dementia patients. *Psychology and Aging, 3*, 245–248.

Becker, G. (1991). *A treatise on the family*. Cambridge: Harvard University Press.

Bernheim, B.D., Shleifer, A., & Summers, L. H., (1985). The strategic bequest motive. *Journal of Political Economy, 96*, 1045–1076.

Birkel, R. C. (1987). Toward a social ecology of the home-care household. *Psychology and Aging, 2*, 294–301.

Brody, E. M. (1985). Parent care as normative stress. *Gerontologist, 25*, 19–29.

Brody, E. M., Johnsen, P. T., Fulcomer, M. C., & Lang, A. M. (1983). Women's changing roles and help to the elderly: Attitudes of three generations of women. *Journal of Gerontology, 38*, 597–607.

Brody, E. M., Johnsen, P. T., & Fulcomer, M. C. (1984). What should adult children do for elderly parents? Opinions and preferences in three generations of women. *Journal of Gerontology, 39*, 736–746.

Brody, E. M., & Schoovoner, C. B. (1986). Patterns of parent-care when adult daughters work and they they do not. *Gerontologist, 26*, 372–381.

Brody, E. M., Kleban, M. H., Johnsen, P. T., Hoffman, C., & Schoonover, C. B. (1987). Work status and parent care: A comparison of four groups of women. *Gerontologist, 27*, 201–208.

Brody, E. M., Hoffman, C., Kleban, M. H., & Schoonover, C. (1989). Caregiving daughters and their local siblings: Perceptions, strains and interactions. *Gerontologist, 29*, 529–538.

Brody, E. M., Litvin, S. J., Hoffman, C., & Kleban, M. H. (1992). Differential effects of daughters marital status on their parent care experiences. *Gerontologist, 32*, 58–67.

Burton, L. M., & Sörensen, S. (1993). Temporal context and the caregiver role: Perspectives from ethnographic studies of multigeneration African-American families. In S. H. Zarit, L. I. Pearlin, & K. W. Schaie (Eds.), *Caregiving systems: Informal and formal helpers* (pp. 47–65). Hillsdale, NJ: Lawrence Erlbaum Associates.

Bulcroft, K. A., & Bulcroft, R. A. (1991). The timing of divorce. *Research on Aging, 13*, 226–243.

Cantor, M. H. (1983). Strain among caregivers: A study of experience in the United States. *Gerontologist, 23*, 597–604.

Cohler, B.J., Groves, L., Borden, W., & Lazarus, L. (1989). Caring for family members with Alzheimer's disease. In E. Light & B. Lebowitz (Eds.), *Alzheimer's disease treatment and family stress: Directions for research* (pp. 50–105). Washington, DC: U.S. Government Printing Office.

Cooney, T. M., & Uhlenberg, P. R. (1990). The role of divorce in men's relations with their adult children after mid-life. *Journal of Marriage and the Family, 52*, 677–688.

Cooney, T. M., & Uhlenberg, P. R. (1992). Support from parents over the life course. *Social Forces, 71*, 63–84.

Crimmins, E. M., & Ingegneri, D. G. (1990). Interaction and living arrangements of older parents and their children. *Research on Aging, 12*, 3–35.

Crimmins, E. M., Hayward, M. D., & Saito, Y. (1992, May). *Longer life but worsening health: The relationship between changing mortality and morbidity rates, and the prevalence of dependency in the older population*. Paper presented at the annual meeting of the Population Association of America, Denver, CO.

Dannefer, D. (1984). Adult development and social theory: A paradigmatic reappraisal. *American Sociological Review, 49*, 100–116.

Deimling, G. T., Bass, D. M., Townsend, A. L., & Noelker, L. S. (1989). Care-related stress: A comparison of spouse and adult–child caregivers in shared and separate households. *Journal of Aging and Health, 1*, 67–82.

Dilworth-Anderson, P. (1992). Extended kin networks in Black families. *Generations, 17*, 29–32.

Eggebeen, D. J. (1992). Family structure and intergenerational exchanges. *Research on Aging, 14*, 427–447.

Eggebeen, D. J., & Hogan, D. P. (1990). Giving between generations in American families. *Human Nature, 1*, 211–232.

Eggebeen, D. J., & Wilhelm, M. O. (1993, November.). *Patterns of support by older Americans and their children*. Paper presented at the annual meeting of Gerontological Society of America, New Orleans, LA.

Elder, G. H., Jr. (1974). *Children of the great depression*. Chicago: University of Chicago Press.

Elder, G. H., Jr. (1978). Family history and the life course. In T. Haraven (Ed.), *Transitions: The family and life course in historical perspective* (pp. 17–64). New York: Academic Press.

Elder, G. H., Jr. (1985). Perspectives on the life course. In G. H. Elder, Jr. (Ed.), *Life course dynamics, trajectories, and transitions, 1968–1980*. (pp. 23–49). Ithaca, NY: Cornell University Press.

Finley, N. J., Roberts, D., & Banahan, B. F., III (1988). Motivators and inhibitors of attitudes of filial obligation toward aging parents. *Gerontologist, 28*, 73–78.

Friss, L. (1990). A model state-level approach to family survival for caregivers of brain-impaired adults. *Gerontologist, 30*, 121–125.

Gallagher, D., Rose, J., Rivera, P., Lovett, S., & Thompson, L. W. (1989). Prevalence of depression in family caregivers. *Gerontologist, 29*, 449–456.

Genensky, S. M., & Zarit, S. H. (1993). Low-vision care in a clinical setting. In A. A. Rosenbloom, Jr. & M. W. Morgan (Eds.), *Vision and aging* (2nd ed., pp. 424–444). Boston: Butterworth-Heinemann.

George, L. K., & Gwyther, L. P. (1986). Caregiver well-being: A multidimensional examination of family caregivers of demented adults. *Gerontologist, 26*, 253–259.

George, L. K., & Gold, D. T. (1991). Life course perspectives on intergenerational connections. *Marriage and Family Review, 16*, 67–83.

Habib, J., Sundström, G., & Windmiller, K. (1993). Understanding the pattern of support for the elderly: A comparison between Israel and Sweden. *Journal of Aging and Social Policy, 5*, 187–206.

Hagastad, G. O., & Neugarten, B. L. (1985). Age and the life course. In R. H. Binstock & L. K. George (Eds.), *Handbook of aging and the social sciences* (2nd ed., pp. 35–61). New York: Academic Press.

Haley, W. E., Brown, S. L., & Levine, E. G. (1987). Family caregiver appraisals of patient behavioral disturbance in senile dementia. *Clinical Gerontologist, 6*, 25–34.

Hofferth, S. (1984). Kin networks, race, and family structure. *Journal of Marriage and the Family, 46*, 791–806.

Hogan, D. P., & Eggebeen, D. J. (in press). Sources of emergency help and routine assistance in old age. *Social Forces, 73*.

Hogan, D. P., Eggebeen, D. J., & Clogg, C. C. (1993). The structure of intergenerational exchanges in American families. *American Journal of Sociology, 98*, 1428–1458.

Hogan, D. P., Hao, L.-X., & Parish, W. L. (1990). Race, kin networks, and assistance to mother-headed families. *Social Forces, 68*, 797–812.

Hokenstad, M. C., & Johansson, L. (1990). Caregivers for the elderly in Sweden: Program challenges and policy initiatives. In D. E. Biegel & A. Blum (Eds.), *Aging and caregiving: Theory, research, and policy* (pp. 254–269). Newbury Park, CA: Sage.

Johnson, C. L., & Catalano, D. J. (1983). A longitudinal study of family supports to impaired elderly. *Gerontologist, 23*, 612–618.

Kaszniak, A. W. (1990). Psychological assessment of the aging individual. In J. E. Birren & K. W. Schaie (Eds.), *Handbook of the psychology of aging* (3rd ed., pp. 427–445). New York: Academic Press.

Kiecolt-Glaser, J. R., Dura, J. R., Speicher, C. E., Trask, O. J., & Glaser, R. (1991). Spousal caregivers of dementia victims: Longitudinal changes in immunity and health. *Psychosomatic Medicine, 53*, 345–362.

Kinney, J. M., & Stephens, M. A. P. (1989). Caregiving hassles scale: Assessing the daily hassles of caring for a family members with dementia. *Gerontologist, 29*, 328–332.

Knight, B. (1986). *Psychotherapy with older adults*. Newbury Park, CA: Sage.

Kotlikoff, L.J., & Spivak, A. (1991). The family as an incomplete annuities market. *Journal of Political Economy, 89*, 706–732.

Lancaster, J. B., & Lancaster, C. S. (1987). The watershed: Change in parental investment and family formation strategies in the course of human evolution. In J. B. Lancaster, J. Altmann, A. S. Rossi, & L. R. Sherrod (Eds.), *Parenting across the life span: Biosocial dimensions* (pp. 187–206). Hawthorne, NY: Aldine.

Longino, C. F., & Lipman, A. (1981). Married and spouseless men and women in planned retirement communities: Support network differentials. *Journal of Marriage and the Family, 43*, 169–177.

Lopata, H. Z. (1979). *Women as widows: Support systems*. Chicago: Elsevier.

MaloneBeach, E. E., & Zarit, S. H. (in press). Dimensions of social support and social conflict as predictors of caregiver depression. *International Psychogeriatrics*.

MaloneBeach, E. E., Zarit, S. H., & Spore, D. L. (1992). Caregivers' perceptions of case management and community-based services: Barriers to service use. *Journal of Applied Gerontology, 11*, 146–159.

Matthews, S. H., Werkner, J. E., & Delaney, P. J. (1989). Relative contributions of help by employed and nonemployed sisters to their elderly parents. *Journal of Gerontology: Social Science, 44*, S36–44.

Menchik, P. L. (1980). Primogeniture, equal sharing, and the U.S. distribution of wealth. *Quarterly Journal of Economics, 94*, 299–316.

Miller, B., & Montgomery, A. (1990). Family caregivers and limitations in social activities. *Research on Aging, 12*, 72–93.

Mittelman, M. S., Ferris, S. H., Steinberg, G., Shulman, E., Mackell, J. A., Ambinder, A., & Cohen, J. (1993). An intervention that delays institutionalization of Alzheimer's disease patients: Treatment of spouse-caregivers. *Gerontologist, 33,* 730–740.

Mullan, J. T. (1993). Barriers to the use of formal services among Alzheimer's caregivers. In S. H. Zarit, L. I. Pearlin, & K. W. Schaie (Eds.), *Caregiving systems: Informal and formal helpers* (pp. 241–260). Hillsdale, NJ: Lawrence Erlbaum Associates.

Morgan, L. A. (1983). Intergenerational economic assistance to children: The case of widows and widowers. *Journal of Gerontology, 38,* 725–731.

National Center for Health Statistics. (1993). Advance report for health statistics, 1991. *Monthly Vital Statistics Report, 42* (No. 2, supplement). Hyattsville, MD: Public Health Service.

Niederehe, G., & Frugé, E. (1984). Dementia and family dynamics: Clinical research issues. *Journal of Geriatric Psychiatry, 17,* 21–56.

Niederehe, G., & Funk, J. (1987, August). *Family interaction with dementia patients: Caregiver styles and their correlates.* Paper presented at the annual meeting of the American Psychological Association, New York.

Pearlin, L. I. (1993). The careers of caregivers. *Gerontologist, 32,* 647.

Pearlin, L. I., Mullan, J. T., Semple, S. J., & Skaff, M. M. (1990). Caregiving and the stress process: An overview of concepts and measures. *Gerontologist, 30,* 583–594.

Pearson, J., Verma, S., & Nellett, C. (1988). Elderly psychiatric patient status and caregiver perceptions as predictors of caregiver burden. *Gerontologist, 28,* 79–83.

Petty, D., & Friss, L. (1987, October). A balancing act of working and caregiving. *Business and Health ,* 22–25.

Pruchno, R. A., & Resch, N. L. (1989). Aberrant behaviors and Alzheimer's disease: Mental health effects on spouse caregivers. *Journal of Gerontology: Social Sciences, 44,* S177–182.

Robinson, B., & Thurnher, M. (1979). Taking care of aged parents: A family cycle transition. *Gerontologist, 19,* 586–593.

Rosenthal, C. J., Sulman, J., & Marshall, V. W. (1993). Depressive symptoms in family caregivers of long-stay patients. *Gerontologist, 33,* 249–257.

Rossi, A. S., & Rossi, P. H. (1990). *Of human bonding: Parent–child relations across the life course.* New York: Aldine de Gruyter.

Scharlach, A. E. (1987). Relieving feelings of strain among women with elderly mothers. *Psychology and Aging, 2,* 9–13.

Scharlach, A. E., & Boyd, S. L. (1989). Caregiving and employment: Results of an employee survey. *Gerontologist, 29,* 382–387.

Schulz, R., Williamson, G. M., Morycz, R., & Biegel, D. E. (1993). Changes in depression among men and women caring for an Alzheimer's patient. In S. H. Zarit, L. I. Pearlin, & K. W. Schaie (Eds.), *Caregiving systems: Informal and formal helpers* (pp. 119–140). Hillsdale, NJ: Lawrence Erlbaum Associates.

Semple, S. J. (1992). Conflict in Alzheimer's caregiving families: Its dimensions and consequences. *Gerontologist, 32,* 648–655.

Smith, G. C., & Tobin, S. S. (in press). Practice with older parents of developmentally disabled adults. In T. L. Brink (Ed.), *The forgotten aged: Ethnic, psychiatric and societal minorities.* New York: Haworth Press.

Smyer, M. A., Zarit, S. H., & Qualls, S. H. (1990). Psychological intervention with aging individuals. In J. E. Birren & K. W. Schaie (Eds.), *Handbook of the psychology of aging* (3rd ed., pp. 375–403). New York: Academic Press.

Snaith, S. M., Hogan, D. P., & Eggebeen, D. J. (1993, November). *Within family variations in support given to adult children.* Paper presented at the annual meeting of the Gerontology Society of America, New Orleans, LA.

Spitze, G., & Logan, J. (1989). Gender differences in family support: Is there a payoff? *Gerontologist, 29,* 108–113.

Spitze, G., & Logan, J. (1992). Helping as a component of parent–adult child relations. *Research on Aging, 14,* 291–312.

Stack, C. (1974). *All our kin: Strategies for survival in the black community.* New York: Harper & Row.

Stoller, E. P., & Earl, L. L. (1983). Help with activities of everyday life: Sources of support for the non-institutionalized elderly. *Gerontologist, 23,* 64–70.

Stone, R., Cafferata, G. L., & Sangl, J. (1987). Caregivers of the frail elderly: A national profile. *Gerontologist, 27,* 616–626.

Suitor, J. J., & Pillemer, K. (1993). Support and interpersonal stress in the social networks of married daughters caring for patients with dementia. *Journal of Gerontology: Social Sciences, 48,* S1–S8.

Sussman, M. (1965). Relationships of adult children with their parents in the United States. In E. Shanas & G. Strieb (Eds.), *Social structure and the family: Generational relations* (pp. 62–92). Englewood Cliffs, NJ: Prentice-Hall.

Taylor, R. J. (1986). Receipt of support from family among Black Americans. *Journal of Marriage and the Family, 48,* 67–77.

Taylor, R. J. (1988). Aging and supportive relationships among Black Americans. In J. Jackson (Ed.) *The Black American elderly.* New York: Springer-Verlag.

Townsend, A., Noelker, L., Deimling, G., & Bass, D. (1989). Longitudinal impact of interhousehold caregiving on adult children's mental health. *Psychology and Aging, 4,* 393–401.

Torrey, B. B., Kinsella, K., & Taeuber, C. M. (1987). An aging world. *International Population Reports Series P-95* (No. 78). Washington, DC: U.S. Department of Commerce.

Turke, P. W. (1989). Evolution and the demand for children. *Population and Development Review, 15,* 61–90.

Uhlenberg, P. R. (1990, October). *Implications of increased divorce for the elderly.* Paper presented at the United Nations International Conference on Aging Population in the Context of the Family, Kitakyushu, Japan.

Uhlenberg, P. R., Cooney, T. M., & Boyd, R. L. (1990). Divorce for women after midlife. *Journal of Gerontology: Social Sciences, 45*, S3–11.

U.S. Bureau of the Census. (1983). America in transition: An aging society. *Current Population Reports* (Series No. P23–128). Washington, DC: U.S. Government Printing Office.

U.S. Bureau of the Census. (1990). The need for personal assistance with everyday activities: Recipients and caregivers. *Current Population Reports* (Series No. P70–19). Washington, DC: U.S. Government Printing Office.

U.S. Bureau of the Census (1992a). Growth of America's oldest-old population. *Profiles of America's Elderly* (No. 2). Washington, DC: U.S. Government Printing Office.

U.S. Bureau of the Census. (1992b). Poverty in the United States: 1991. *Current Population Reports* (Series No. P60–181). Washington, DC: U.S. Government Printing Office.

U.S. Bureau of the Census. (1992c). Sixty-five plus in America. *Current Population Reports, Special Studies* (Series No. P23–178). Washington, DC: U.S. Government Printing Office.

Vitaliano, P. P., Becker, J., Russo, J., Magana-Amato, A., & Maiuro, R. D. (1988–1989). Expressed emotion in spouse caregivers of patients with Alzheimer's disease. *Journal of Applied Social Sciences, 13*, 216–250.

Vitaliano, P. P., Maiuro, R. D., Ochs, H., & Russo, J. (1989). A model of burden in caregivers of DAT patients. In E. Light & B. Lebowitz (Eds.), *Alzheimer's disease treatment and family stress: Directions for research* (pp. 267–291). Washington, DC: U.S. Government Printing Office.

Whitlatch, C. J., Zarit, S. H., & von Eye, A. (1991). Efficacy of interventions with caregivers: A reanalysis. *Gerontologist, 31*, 9–14.

Wilhelm, M. O. (1993). *Bequests and heirs' earnings: Testing the altruistic model of bequests.* Unpublished manuscript, Pennsylvania State University, University Park.

Williamson, G. M., & Schulz, R. (1990). Relationship orientation, quality of prior relationship, and distress among caregivers of Alzheimer's patients. *Psychology and Aging, 5*, 502–509.

Wilson, M. (1986). The Black extended family: An analytical consideration. *Developmental Psychology, 22*, 246–258.

Wilson, W. J. (1987). *The truly disadvantaged.* Chicago: University of Chicago Press.

Winsborough, H. H., Bumpass, L. L., & Aquilino, W. S. (1991). *The death of parents and the transition to old age* (NSFH Working Paper 39). Madison, WI: Center for Demography and Ecology, University of Wisconsin-Madison.

Zarit, S. H. (1989). Issues and directions in family intervention research. In E. Light & B. Lebowitz (Eds.), *Alzheimer's disease treatment and family stress: Directions for research* (pp. 458–486). Washington, DC: U.S. Government Printing Office.

Zarit, S. H. (1992). Concepts and measures in family caregiving research. In B. Bauer (Ed.), *Conceptual and methodological issues in family caregiving research* (pp. 1–19). Toronto: University of Toronto.

Zarit, S. H., Orr, N. K., & Zarit, J. M. (1985). *The hidden victims of Alzheimer's disease: Families under stress.* New York: New York University Press.

Zarit, S. H., Todd, P. A., & Zarit, J. M. (1986). Subjective burden of husbands and wives as caregivers: A longitudinal study. *Gerontologist, 26*, 260–270.

Zarit, S. H., & Teri, L. (1991). Interventions and services for family caregivers. *Annual Review of Gerontology and Geriatrics, 11*, 287–310.

Zarit, S. H., & Whitlatch, C. J. (1992). Institutional placement: Phases of the transition. *Gerontologist, 32*, 665–672.

Zarit, S. H., & Whitlatch, C. J. (1993). Short and long term consequences of placement for caregivers. *Irish Journal of Psychology, 14*, 25–37.

PART II

PARENTING VARIOUS KINDS OF CHILDREN

6

Parenting Siblings

Wyndol Furman
University of Denver

INTRODUCTION

Most families have two or more children. With the birth of a second child, the responsibilities and joys of parenting undergo marked changes. One no longer has a child, but instead one has two different children, usually of different ages, often of different gender, and each with a distinct personality. Parents may treat their latterborn children differently from their firstborn or from an only child. The birth of additional children may also lead to differences in the treatment of the others. Moreover, the degree of warmth, conflict, or other qualitative features of the children's relationships with one another may influence their parents' treatment of them.

This chapter is concerned with the potential influences that siblings have on parenting and parent–child relationships. Emphasis is placed on siblings who are not twins (see Lytton & Singh, in this *Handbook* for twin relationships). The first section presents a brief history of the field, outlining the central theories, research trends, and major conceptual issues. Then empirical literature on four relevant topics is discussed: how parent–child relationships may vary as a function of birth order, family size, and other family constellation variables; the changes that occur in childrearing with the birth of subsequent children; how the qualitative features or the characteristics of the sibling relationship may be related to parenting; and the degree of consistency in parental treatment of two children. Finally, future potential directions for the field are delineated.

A BRIEF HISTORY OF SIBLING RESEARCH

Little attention was paid to the role of siblings until the appearance of A. Adler's (1931) theory of individual psychology. Adler proposed that children's position in the family had a major influence on their experience growing up; like other psychodynamic theorists, he believed these childhood experiences shaped the nature of their personality (see also H. L. Ansbacher & R. R. Ansbacher, 1956). The following paragraphs provide brief summaries of his theory of how birth order affects childhood experiences and personality development.

Adler hypothezised that the oldest child has two distinct experiences. Early on, the oldest is the only child and receives considerable attention from parents. With the birth of the second child, however, the firstborn is "dethroned" and must suddenly share parents' attention and affection with a rival. Typically, the oldest child fights back for the mother's love. This struggle may foster a coercive pattern of interaction with the mother, or it may lead to a preference for the father. Adler thought that oldest children are the most likely to become "problem children." In particular, they may be prone to feeling insecure or hating people, particularly younger siblings. If, however, they feel certain of their parents' affection and are prepared for the transition by their parents, they may imitate their parents and take on a protective, nurturant role with younger siblings.

Adler observed that secondborns face the experience of always having had older siblings. Thus, they always share their parents' attention with other siblings and are expected to be more cooperative. Their older siblings often serve as "pacemakers" for them, which often leads to ambitiousness and competitiveness on the part of the secondborns. They too undergo dethronement if more children come into the family, although Adler thought this experience is less traumatic for them than firstborns because they had never been only children.

Youngest children are never displaced by other siblings. As a consequence, they are the babies in the families and are often pampered and spoiled. In some instances, the stimulation and chances for competition lead them to excel, but in other cases, such spoiling leads to feelings of inferiority, maladjustment, or neuroses.

Only children never have sibling rivals. Accordingly, feelings of competition are often directed toward fathers, and mothers often pamper them. Adler thought they often develop "mother complexes" in which they are "tied to their mothers' apron strings" and wish to have their fathers out of the picture. They desire to be the center of attention and feel it is their right.

Although Adler was primarily concerned with potential birth order effects, he pointed out that wide spacing of siblings would lead each child to have some of the features of an only child. Similarly, he briefly alluded to the impact of the sex of siblings. A boy who only has sisters may feel different and isolated in a family of mostly women. Similarly, an only girl among boys may become either very feminine or very masculine. Frequently, she feels insecure or helpless.

Adler's theory triggered a significant amount of research on the effects of birth order on personality, IQ, and adjustment. In fact, Ernst and Angst's (1983) review of the literature from 1946 to 1980 includes almost 1,500 references. Although prolific in nature, the work on ordinal position is not very systematic. It is easy to include birth order as a variable in a larger study. Many of the studies were not guided by theoretical propositions; often results were interpreted after the fact. The scientific yield of this research proved disappointing. In fact, many reviewers concluded that birth order or other family constellation variables are not major contributors to development and adjustment (Ernst & Angst, 1983; Schooler, 1972).

Perhaps as a result of the growing disenchantment with the family constellation research, in the 1980s investigators began to examine the features or characteristics of sibling relationships. That is, researchers began to look at the warmth, conflict, rivalry, or distribution of power in the relationships. Some of this work examines how birth order or other constellation variables might shape the features of sibling relationships, but the work differs from most past research by directly measuring the relationship features, rather than inferring them. Studies began to examine how the birth of a second child influences patterns of interactions and relationships among family members. In turn, the focus on relationship characteristics led to the important recognition that the relationship between two children cannot be characterized as just one relationship. Each participant has a different perspective and experience in the relationship, and outsiders or other family members have other views as well. Measures from different perspectives do not converge empirically, and theoretically they should not be expected to be identical (Furman, Jones, Buhrmester, & T. Adler, 1988).

Researchers also became interested in identifying the variables that might affect the nature of the sibling relationship. That is, empirical investigators wanted to determine why some siblings had close and harmonious relationships, whereas others had distant or conflictual ones. Quite naturally, parent–child relationships and parenting practices emerged as factors likely to shape the nature of sibling relationships. Although the general field of parenting had grown to recognize that children influence their parents and parenting (R. Q. Bell, 1968, 1971; Lewis & Rosenblum, 1974), it seems fair to say that most of the work in this particular area has been guided by an implicit model of parenting affecting siblings. As is discussed in this chapter, however, many of the findings concerning seeming parental influences could reflect the influences sibling relationships have on parents.

With the increased emphasis on the qualitative features of family relationships, investigators approached the topic of sibling relationships from a range of different theoretical perspectives. Attachment theory, social learning theory, role theory, and family systems theory have all guided work in the field. The empirical research on sibling research has not generated many new theoretical views, however. One noteworthy exception is Kreppner's theory, which integrates child developmental and family developmental perspectives in accounting for the changes in the family with the birth of a second child (Kreppner, 1989; Kreppner, Paulsen, & Schuetze, 1982).

Most recently, Plomin and his colleagues (Plomin & Daniels, 1987; Rowe & Plomin, 1981) observed that two siblings are no more alike than two unrelated children once one takes into account genetic influences. Thus, there seems to be little effect of any "shared" environmental influences that stem from being reared in the same house by the same parents. Instead, "nonshared" environmental influences seem to be more central determinants of development and adjustment. Rowe and Plomin (1981) proposed that such nonshared factors include family structural variables, differential parental treatment, differential sibling interactions, extrafamilial network influences, and accidental factors. Much recent work has focused on identifying the potential contribution nonshared environmental influences may have on development and adjustment.

Thus, the questions of interest and the methodological approaches have changed substantially over the course of the history of sibling research. The following sections review the research examining the links between siblings and parenting.

FAMILY CONSTELLATION VARIABLES

As noted previously, over 1,500 studies have examined the effects of birth order, spacing of siblings, family size, and other family constellation variables. Most of this literature, however, is not directly relevant to the question of how siblings may influence parenting. In the typical study, children or adults of different birth orders are compared on some individual characteristic, such as a personality trait. Observed differences are commonly interpreted in terms of differences in parent–child relationships, but the characteristics of parent–child relationships are rarely measured directly. Thus, one cannot determine from such studies if these particular features of parent–child relationships are responsible for any effect or, for that matter, even differ as a function of birth order. Moreover, one cannot even attribute any birth order effects to the parent–child relationship per se. For example, differences in firstborns' or latterborns' sibling relationships could also be responsible for any birth order effect. Adler often conceptualized the effects of birth order in terms of differences in sibling relationships as well as differences in parent–child relationships. For example, secondborns were thought to be envious of firstborns and struggled to surpass them. Because of the limitations of inferring relationship characteristics from family constellation variables, the review that follows focuses on studies that directly examine differences in family relationships.

Ordinal Position, Sex of Sibling, and Age Spacing Effects

Ernst and Angst (1983) conducted a systematic review of approximately 50 family constellation studies conducted between 1946 and 1980. This section summarizes the general pattern of results in these studies, and reports more recent investigations examining this topic.

A number of investigations have found that firstborns receive more attention and better care as infants and toddlers than latterborns (see Ernst & Angst, 1983; Grossman, Eichler, & Winickoff, 1980;

Parke & O'Leary, 1975). The differences may be more pronounced when the secondborn is a female or of the same gender as the firstborn (Dunn & Kendrick, 1981a; 1981b; Jacobs & Moss, 1976), or if the age spacing is between 19 and 30 months (Lewis & Kreitzberg, 1979).

In one of the more extensive studies on the topic, Belsky and his colleagues collected naturalistic observations of families at 1, 3, and 9 months after the birth of a firstborn or latterborn child (Belsky, Gilstrap, & Rovine, 1984; Belsky, Taylor, & Rovine, 1984). Compared to parents of firstborn children, those of latterborn children engaged, responded to, stimulated, and expressed positive affection less often. No differences were observed in first- and latterborn babies' behavior, indicating that the effects did not reflect responding to differences in infants' behavior. The differences in parents' behavior also tended to increase with time since the birth, perhaps reflecting the fact that 1-month-olds, regardless of ordinal position, demand a significant amount of time. Moreover, the differences in the treatment of first- and latterborn children were much greater for fathers than mothers. The investigators speculated that this finding may have occurred because mothers need to be with the newborns to breastfeed them and serve as primary caregivers, whereas fathers may take the responsibility for their older children.

Mothers are also more involved with firstborn toddlers than latterborn toddlers (Bradley & Caldwell, 1984). In a classic longitudinal study, however, Lasko (1954) reported that the first child enjoys a more child-centered environment in the first 2 years of life, but by 3 or 4 years of age the child is treated less warmly than secondborns at that age. These developmental trends probably reflect the fact that many of these families at that stage have a new child who needs their attention as well. Further support for this explanation comes from the literature, indicating that only children receive more parental attention throughout their development (see later).

Although the relative amount of attention may decline with age and the emergence of new siblings, differences remain in first- and latterborn preschool children's relationships with their parents. In particular, parents have higher expectations for their firstborns to achieve (Cushna, cited in Sutton-Smith & Rosenberg, 1970; Ersnt & Angst, 1983; Kammeyer, 1967). Firstborns are given more cognitively complex explanations and pressured more on an achievement task (Rothbart, 1971). Some of these expectations can be unrealistic. For example, parents with one child underestimate the age at which children begin to speak a complete sentence or sleep through the night (Waddell & Ball, 1980).

Perhaps because of the differences in expectations, mothers appear to be less tolerant and supportive and more controlling, demanding, intrusive and inconsistent with their firstborns (see Ernst & Angst, 1983; Ward, Vaughn, & Robb, 1988), especially when the firstborn is a daughter (Baskett, 1984; Rothbart, 1971). Similarly, independence training occurs earlier for firstborns (see Ernst & Angst, 1983). It is important to note that most of these studies were conducted with preschool children, and it is less clear if such differences occur later in development. In fact, many of Lasko's (1954) ordinal position effects were found only when the children were preschool age and not later when they were each in school.

Fathers are more likely to be the principal disciplinarian of adolescent firstborns than latterborns (Henry, 1957). Firstborn preadolescents and adolescents also report greater parental control than latterborns, but these differences may reflect differences in family size (see Ernst & Angst, 1983, and subsequent section). One study found that mothers with children close in age to each other treat them more rationally, democratically, and with more understanding than mothers with children who are widely spaced (Lasko, 1954). On the other hand, a study of adolescence found almost the opposite pattern (Kidwell, 1981).

The classic literature concerning parental favoritism or parental affection has yielded relatively inconsistent results (Ernst & Angst, 1983). Similarly, some recent investigators have reported that the youngest child is more likely to be favored (Furman & Buhrmester, 1985; Harris & Howard, 1985), but others have found firstborns to be favored (Neale, cited in N. M. Kiracofe & H. N. Kiracofe, 1990) or no differences among first-, middle-, or lastborns (Nardine & Zeidler, cited in N. M. Kiracofe & H. N. Kiracofe, 1990). Further complicating the picture, Koch (1960) reported that perceptions of favoritism vary as a function of genders of the children and the differences in their ages.

Firstborns appear to be more influenced by their parents and to be more parent- or adult-oriented (Baskett, 1984). In their review of the literature, Sutton-Smith and Rosenberg (1970) concluded that firstborns are more similar to their parents and identify more with their parents; such differences, however, may reflect differences in family size or social class (Ernst & Angst, 1983).

Finally, whereas most of the studies reviewed here have compared firstborns and latterborns of the same age, some other work has examined parents' behavior when the two children were different ages. Not surprisingly, parents display age-appropriate adjustments in their play or interaction with their two children (e.g., Stevenson, Leavitt, Thompson, & Roach, 1988). Mothers also direct more behavior toward younger siblings than older siblings in triadic interactions (Brody, Stoneman, & Burke, 1987; Brody, Stoneman, & McCoy, 1992). It is less clear if that difference reflects an age-appropriate adjustment or if the children construe it that way, even if it were. The issue of differential parental treatment is discussed further in a subsequent section.

Only Children

Another way to examine the influences of siblings on parenting is to look at the parent–child relationships of only children. Unfortunately, many studies on birth order have not distinguished between only children and firstborns who have siblings. In some instances, however, only children have been compared to firstborns or various categories of latterborns.

In a pair of metanalyses of approximately 20 studies, Falbo and Polit (1986) and Polit and Falbo (1987) reported that only children have more positive relationships with their parents. For example, mothers spend more time with their preschool-age only children than do mothers with two children (Falbo & Cooper, 1980). Similarly, parents with one child engage in more conversation with more information exchange during meals than do parents with two or three children (Lewis & Feiring, 1982). The magnitude of such differences, however, is relatively small (mean effect size $d = .20$ and mean effect size weighted by sample size $= .13$). Moreover, only children's relationships primarily differ from those of children from large families (5 children or more) and not from those in two-child families (mean ds $= .20$ vs. .08). Comparisons with firstborns have also yielded relatively small effects (mean $d = .08$). Together, these findings suggest that family size may be a stronger determinant of parent–child relationships.

Family Size

In a classic study of large families, Bossard and Boll (1956) reported that parenting in large families is "extensive" rather than "intensive." They argued that children in large families are loved, but their sheer number prohibits concentrated care on any one child. The emphasis is on the family as a whole rather than any particular individual. Children are expected to conform and cooperate with parents and elder siblings who have dominant roles. Similarly, obedience and discipline are stressed. Competition and rivalry are discouraged because of their divisive effects on the family. It is important to note that Bossard and Boll's conclusions were drawn from an in-depth study of 100 large families and not from direct comparisons of large and small families. Many of their observations, however, have been replicated in subsequent studies. For example, family size seems to decrease the amount of attention parents pay to any particular child or to each other (Lewis & Feiring, 1982). These inverse relations with family size are even found when education, SES, and mother's participation in the labor force are controlled for (Lindert, 1978).

As family size increases, parents are also more autocratic (Elder, 1962; Sears, Maccoby, & Levin, 1957). Fathers become more involved in childrearing (Lewis & Feiring, 1982) and are more likely to be the dominant decision maker (Elder & Bowerman, 1963; Sears et al., 1957). Parents with small families are less restrictive of their children's autonomy and more encouraging of their independence and self-direction than are parents with large families (Elder & Bowerman, 1963; Nye, Carlson, & Garrett, 1970). Similarly, family size is positively related to perceptions of parental punitiveness and rejection, and negatively related to perceptions of parental love and support (Kidwell, 1981; Nye et al., 1970; Peterson & Kunz, 1975; Scheck & Emerick, 1976). Recently, however, several investigators have reported that such sibsize effects are not present when parental education, occupation, race, intactness of the family, or social class are controlled for (N. J. Bell & Avery, 1985; Blake, 1989).

Methodological Problems in Family Constellation Research

Many investigators have pointed out that the interpretation of birth order or other family constellation effects is often flawed by a number of methodological problems (see Adams, 1972; Ernst & Angst, 1983; Kammeyer, 1967; Schooler, 1972). Even if one directly studies the associations between a family constellation variable and parent–child interactions or relationships, one cannot attribute any observed differences to the family constellation variable per se. Such limitations in inferring causality reflect the fact that these studies are inherently correlational. For example, family size may affect parenting, but it is just as plausible that parents' experiences rearing children may influence the likelihood of having more children.

The same line of reasoning applies in the case of birth order. Certainly, parenting behavior does not directly affect a child's birth order. After all, the child has already been born a firstborn or latterborn prior to the beginning of the parenting. Yet, prior parenting experiences can affect the likelihood that a child is of a certain ordinal position. That is, perhaps some parents decide to have fewer or only one child as a result of a positive experience with the firstborn, whereas those who have had negative experiences may decide to try again.

If negative (positive) experiences with one child are predictive of negative (positive) experiences with another child, then a higher proportion of secondborns than firstborns are likely to have a negative parent–child relationship. In those families where a positive experience with the secondborn was likely to have occurred (i.e., when the experience with the firstborn was positive), some parents may have chosen to not have another child, because they were content. Accordingly, in this hypothetical but plausible example, a finding that secondborn children have more negative relationships with parents actually reflects the effects of parenting the firstborn, rather than the effects of birth order on parenting.

More generally, family constellation variables are intercorrelated. In fact, the correlation between birth order and family size has been estimated to be as high as .70 (Eysenck & Cookson, 1970); even though all families with children must have a firstborn, only larger ones have fourth-, fifth-, or sixthborns. In turn, family size is associated with a wide range of variables, such as parental education, maternal IQ, likelihood of divorce, social class, religious affiliation, and population density (Barger & Hall, 1966; Blake, 1981; Ernst & Angst, 1983; Falbo, 1978b; Schooler, 1972; Udry, 1978). Consequently, firstborns are more likely to be from middle-class, non-Catholic, urban families than latterborns. Some investigators have tried to control for this problem by equating the number of children in studies of ordinal position, but such matching generates as many problems as it solves (discussed later).

In any case, controlling for sibship size does not eliminate the fact that other variables may be correlated with ordinal position, such as age of parent, family income, and childrearing expenses (see Adams, 1972; Ernst & Angst, 1983). Even comparisons of children within the same family may be confounded by these factors. In fact, the correlates may be quite subtle. For example, the mean age spacing between second- and thirdborn children is greater than that between first- and secondborn children; as a consequence, secondborns may not receive as much parental attention as their older or younger siblings, which may lead to greater dependency on their part (McGurk & Lewis, 1972). Although such a finding may appear as a birth order effect, it could actually reflect differences in spacing.

Similar difficulties exist in interpreting differences between only children and other children (see Falbo, 1978a). Only children are more likely to have a mother who works outside the home, and to come from single-parent families. The economic conditions of families of only children are not clear.

On the one hand, the childrearing expenses are less, but on the other hand, economic difficulties could lead some parents to have only one child. Moreover, some parents with only one child may have wished to have larger families. The proportion of voluntary and involuntary one-child families is not well known, and may be changing with the increase in women's participation in the labor force and changing attitudes about contraceptives and abortions.

Some investigators have tried to eliminate the effects of confounding variables by matching on the confounding variable or controlling for it statistically by partial correlation techniques or analysis of covariance. Even if one knew all the confounding variables (an obviously implausible assumption), such procedures would not permit us to make accurate causal inferences (Meehl, 1970). In particular, matching on one variable can lead to mismatching on another variable. For example, matching small and large families on social class may increase the likelihood that they differ in religious background. One solution is to determine if the results are the same when confounding variables are covaried or matched and when they are not. The inferences are strengthened if they are the same, but unfortunately they often are not (e.g., N. J. Bell & Avery, 1985).

Recently, investigators have begun to use structural modeling techniques to evaluate the plausibility of various models depicting the causal relations among a set of variables. Although such procedures have promise, it is not clear that they solve the problem of confounding variables because they too rely on partial correlation techniques. Moreover, accurate inferences are based on two vital assumptions: accurate specification of the time-lags (Gollob & Reichardt, 1987) and causal closure (i.e., all relevant variables are included in the model; James, Mulaik, & Brett, 1982). Unfortunately, one can confidently say that neither assumption is ever met.

Thus, the bottom line is that studies of birth order or other family constellation variables are inherently correlational. Stated simply, birth order is not experimentally manipulated, nor are subjects randomly assigned to different ordinal positions. These observations do not undermine the importance of such research. It is of value to know how parent–child interactions or other variables may be associated with birth order. At the very least, such work may provide clues about potential causal mechanisms, but conclusions about causality cannot be made from such data.

Finally, developmental psychologists face one other intractable methodological problem. It is not clear what the appropriate comparison is between first- and latterborn children's interactions with their parents. If first- and latterborn's interactions with their parents are observed at any one time, the children will differ in age as well as ordinal position. Needless to say, parents are likely to treat children of different ages differently regardless of their ordinal position. The alternative is to examine the parent–child interactions of first- and latterborns when the children are of the same age. Such comparisons, however, are confounded by potential cohort or time of observation effects—a classic instance of the problem of matching on one variable (age) and mismatching on another. Moreover, it is not clear what the phenomenologically relevant comparisons are. That is, if I am a 6-year-old secondborn child, do I compare how my parents treat me with how my parents treated the firstborn at age 6 or how they treat the firstborn now at age 8, for example? Children may make some adjustments for age, but anecdotal evidence clearly indicates that they also make comparisons of parents' contemporaneous behavior toward a sibling. What parent has not heard the refrain, "Why does [my sibling] get to do that and I don't?" Latterborn children perhaps feel they always have fewer privileges than their older siblings, even if their parents treat them identically when they are the same age.

Concluding Comments

The literature on family constellation variables has yielded some consistent patterns of results. The precise interpretation of these findings is not clear, however, because of the methodological problems inherent in this kind of work. Moreover, often these variables only account for less than 10 percent, or even less than 5 percent, of the variance. Although small effects can be interesting theoretically (Abelson, 1985), the documented explanatory power of these variables seems to stand in striking contrast to parents' and layperson's views of the importance of family constellation variables. How often have we heard someone say, "Of course, she's a firstborn," and then nod with understanding? Intuitively, it seems likely that individuals' experiences as a child would differ depending whether they had a sister or brother, if they were older or younger than a sibling, or if they came from a large family or one with no siblings.

Perhaps some important distinctions have been missed. Many studies have put all latterborns into a single category, a combination that may mask differences. For example, Kidwell (1981) found that middleborn adolescents reported more parental punitiveness and less parental support and reasonableness than either first- or lastborns. Similarly, middleborn children receive less caretaking than either first- or lastborns (Lindert, 1978). Perhaps greater progress would be made by using sufficiently large sample sizes to examine all the constellation variables simultaneously. Some work, for example, suggests that the effects of ordinal position are different for males and females (Miller & Maruyama, 1976; Paulhus & Shaffer, 1981). Although such efforts are important, the studies that have considered all the combinations of constellation variables have not yielded stronger or clearer effects. Often, in fact, the results of such studies are so complex that they baffle the most clever post hoc theorist.

Perhaps parents and laypeople are wrong and have simply confirmed their beliefs by only remembering the instances that meet their expectations. Before drawing that conclusion, however, we should entertain the possibility that a family constellation variable may lead to any number of different experiences, rather than any particular one. For example, some parents may think that older siblings should serve as caregivers and encourage such a role, but other parents may not think that older siblings should have that responsibility. The literature has shown that parents have expectations for what children of different ordinal positions are like (Baskett, 1985), but the size of those effects also indicates there is considerable variability in such expectations. Cultures vary in their expectations regarding sibling roles (see Zukow, 1988, in this *Handbook*), and it seems equally plausible to expect variation within cultures. This reasoning argues for examining family members' beliefs about role expectations directly, rather than inferring them from the family constellation variables. Greater progress was made in the field by assessing the characteristics of sibling relationships directly, rather than inferring them from the family constellation variables. Perhaps by directly examining expectations, the scientist's and layperson's view can be reconciled.

BIRTH OF A SIBLING

An alternative approach to determining the effects of siblings on parenting is to examine changes in the family after the birth of a second child. Many studies that have adopted this strategy have used longitudinal designs in which patterns of family interactions, particularly those with the firstborn, are observed before and after the arrival of a new sibling. This approach avoids some of the interpretive problems engendered by comparing one- and two-child families, which differ on variables other than simply having a second child. Of course, changes over time within a family could reflect the influence of other factors than the new birth. For example, one obvious concurrent change is that the firstborn child is getting older, although sometimes the time lag between pre- and postbirth observations is small enough to make this interpretation unlikely (Dunn & Kendrick, 1982).

In any case, a rather consistent pattern of results has emerged in these studies. First, most types of interaction between mothers and their firstborns occur less frequently after the birth of the second child than before (Dunn & Kendrick, 1980; Stewart, 1991; Stewart, Mobley, Van Tuyl, & Salvador, 1987). Second, it appears that mothers initiate fewer conversations and play, whereas firstborns initiate more after the birth than before (Dunn & Kendrick, 1980). Finally, the nature of the interactions between mothers and firstborns may also change. For example, both mothers and their firstborns display less warmth and more neutral affect subsequent to the birth of the second child (Taylor & Kogan, 1973). Similarly, confrontations between mother and firstborn occur more often; mothers make more prohibitions and firstborns are deliberately naughty more often (Dunn & Kendrick, 1980; Kendrick & Dunn, 1980). The confrontations primarily seem to occur when the mother is occupied with the newborn, and not when she is away from the baby. At the same time, though, the amount of positive interactions between firstborn and mother is greater when the mother is holding or feeding the newborn than when she is not with the baby. Thus, it appears that the birth of a sibling both changes the nature and the context of the interactions between mother and firstborn.

Individual differences in change have also been reported. Families in which there are higher levels of confrontation before the birth show greater increases in confrontation and maternal prohibition (Dunn & Kendrick, 1982). When the father and firstborn have a close relationship, the escalation in conflict with mother and decrease in joint attention after the birth is less marked (Dunn & Kendrick, 1983).

What might account for these changes? Certainly, the demands of a newborn could lead to significant changes in the mother's behavior toward the firstborn. Firstborns may also contribute to the changes. Many children show an increase in distress or behavior problems (Dunn, Kendrick, & MacNamee, 1981; Nadelman & Begun, 1982; Thomas, Birch, Chess, & Robbins, 1961). Young preschoolers, especially boys, are particularly likely to show such increases (Dunn et al., 1981; Nadelman & Begun, 1982), although toddlers do not seem to react as much (Thomas et al., 1961). Children who are "negative in mood" or have difficult temperaments prior to the birth are also more likely to show increases in problems subsequently (Dunn et al., 1981; Thomas et al., 1961). This "regressive" behavior may reflect an effort to actively maintain or regain the parents' attention and investment (Stewart, 1990). Some children, however, show no change or even a decrease in behavior problems (Nadelman & Begun, 1982). Over half begin to act with more mature manners, such as being more independent about feeding or toilet training (Dunn et al., 1981). In either case, it seems that children begin to view themselves differently and act differently as a consequence of the changes in their world.

Little is known about changes in father–child interactions. In the one existing study (Stewart, 1991; Stewart et al., 1987), talk between mother and firstborn decreased immediately after the birth and remained lower for a year, whereas talk between father and firstborn decreased gradually over the course of the secondborn's first year of life.

To date, studies have only examined changes from a month or two before the second birth to the first year afterward. Changes may have already begun during the second pregnancy. For example, Nadelman and Begun (1982) found differences in the interactions of firstborn children whose mothers were expecting a second child shortly and those whose mothers were not.

Equally important, little is known about how long changes associated with the birth of a sibling last or whether they change in nature over time. Kreppner et al. (1982) proposed a hermeneutic framework for conceptualizing the changes in the family from a triadic to tetradic system. The process involves three phases:

(1) Initial integration of the infant into the family (0–8 months). The central problem is the new structuring of family–home management; in particular, parents have to redistribute their efforts in light of the doubled responsibilities.

(2) Age of crawling and walking by the second child (9–16 months). The handling of sibling interactions becomes a central concern as the young one becomes more autonomous and involved with others.

(3) Differentiation within the family (17–24 months). The family establishes a generational differentiation as the parents change from becoming parents of an older child and infant to parents of two older children. Interactions become consolidated.

Kreppner et al. (1982) suggested that families use three strategies to integrate the new child. In some families, the father takes an increased amount of responsibility for the firstborn, thus permitting the mother to focus on the secondborn. In other families, the father takes more responsibility for household tasks, leaving the mother the responsibility for both children. Finally, a third group of parents is somewhat interchangeable in their roles. The first two groups have been found in some preliminary data (Kreppner, 1990). As yet, however, little is known about which kinds of families respond in each of these ways and why they do so.

Thus, further work is needed on individual differences in the adjustment to the birth of a sibling, changes in father–child interactions, and long-term changes in families. At the same time, research has shown that changes in parenting occur with the birth of a sibling. How these changes can be accounted for needs further explication, but it is clear that the presence of a sibling affects parenting.

SIBLING RELATIONSHIP CHARACTERISTICS

The preceding sections have examined the potential influence that birth order or other family constellation variables may have on parenting. That research suggests that the sheer existence of other siblings may have an influence on parenting. Not all siblings or sibling relationships are alike, however. The next sections examine how the characteristics of sibling relationships may be related to parenting or other facets of the family system.

Features of Sibling Relationships

Prior to examining the associations among different family relationships, it is important to consider how sibling relationships vary. Furman and Buhrmester (1985) interviewed children about the salient qualities in these relationships. Children commonly mentioned the following qualities: companionship, prosocial behavior, similarity, admiration of (or by) sibling, affection, nurturance by (or of) sibling, antagonism, quarreling, competition, dominance by (or over) sibling, parental partiality, and a general evaluation of the relationship. Based on these interviews, a questionnaire was developed to assess differences in sibling relationships. Factor analyses of children's questionnaire ratings yielded four dimensions: warmth/closeness, conflict, relative status/power, and rivalry. These dimensions (or subsets of them) have commonly appeared in other questionnaire and observational studies of sibling relationships (e.g., Minnett, Vandell, & Santrock, 1983; Stocker & McHale, 1992). In fact, it appears that these are manifestations of four dimensions common to most forms of personal relationships (T. F. Adler & Furman, 1988).

The study of relationship qualities provides us with a different picture from that obtained by examining family constellation variables. The characteristics of these relationships are not exclusively or even primarily determined by family constellation variables. In fact, although each of the qualitative factors is related to constellation variables, only status/power is strongly related to them (Furman & Buhrmester, 1985). As one might expect, the older sibling of the dyad is perceived to have more power and status than the younger one. Thus, sibling relationships vary considerably within any particular type of family constellation as well as between different family constellations. Accordingly, not only might family constellation variables be related to parenting, but the variation in sibling relationship quality may be related to parenting as well.

Parent–Child Relationships and Sibling Relationships

Several reasons can be given for expecting the characteristics of sibling relationships to influence parent–child relationships. First, according to family systems theory, the functioning of any one subsystem in the family is influenced by interactions within other subsystems (Minuchin, 1974). Second, the two may be linked through behavioral contagion effects. For example, conflicts between siblings could lead them to be readily angry with or irritated by their parents. Third, parents are likely to react to the tenor of the sibling relationship. If the siblings frequently fight, parents may feel less positively toward them and treat them with less affection. Finally, parents' disciplinary strategies and efforts may be influenced by the patterns of sibling interaction. For example, sibling conflicts may lead to more punitive discipline.

A number of investigators have examined the links between sibling relationships and parent–child relationships. Almost all the literature is correlational in nature, however, making it impossible to infer causality. In fact, most of the literature seems to stem from an implicit model that parenting affects sibling relationships. Still, this literature may provide some ideas about potential contributions of sibling relationships to parenting.

Links between sibling relationships and parent–child relationships exist even when one child is still an infant. When a preschool child and infant are both securely attached to their mother, they are most likely to have a nonantagonistic relationship with each other, whereas when both are insecurely attached, they are least likely to have such a relationship (Teti & Ablard, 1989). The evidence for links is particularly striking when one examines preschool and school-age sibling dyads. In one of the first studies on the topic, Bryant and Crockenberg (1980) reported that prosocial behavior between siblings is positively associated with maternal responsiveness, whereas antisocial behavior is negatively related. Similarly, verbal aggression and physical conflict are associated with parental physical punishment (Felson, 1983; Patterson, 1986). Stocker and McHale (1992) assessed sibling and parent–child relationships by interviewing family members and by a series of telephone calls about the day's interactions. Sibling hostility and rivalry was negatively related to warmth in relationships with both mothers and fathers. Sibling affection was positively related to paternal warmth.

In Furman and Giberson (in press), maternal perceptions of warmth in school-age children's relationships were positively associated with three indices of warmth in mother–child relationships. Maternal perceptions of sibling conflict were associated with perceptions of maternal power assertion. In a follow-up study, similar links were found with both mother–child and father–child relationships when assessed by either parent or child report. Additionally, observational ratings of sibling warmth were positively related with three observational indices of warmth in mother–child relationships and negatively related with power assertion. The reverse pattern of relations was found for sibling conflict. Similar patterns of relations were found in a third study of preschool sibling relationships (Katz, 1992).

Recently, several longitudinal studies have examined the links between sibling and parent–child relationships. Vandell and Wilson (1987) reported that 6- month-old infants' turn-taking with mothers was associated with the infants' interactions with their preschool siblings when the infants were 6 months and 9 months old, but the interactions with their siblings at 6 months of age were not predictive of their subsequent interactions with mothers when they were 9 months old. Similarly, Kendrick and Dunn (1983) found that maternal interventions in young siblings' conflicts was predictive of hostile interactions between siblings 6 months later, but hostile interactions between siblings were not predictive of their mothers' behavior subsequently. At least in early development when infants are just learning the rudimentary facets of interactions, the direction of effects may go from interactions with mother to interactions with siblings.

In a follow-up study of their research on early family interactions, Volling and Belsky (1992) collected home observations of 30 families when the older child was approximately 6 years old. Sibling conflict was concurrently associated with higher conflict between the mother and each child, but not between the father and the children. Sibling conflict was also associated with the firstborn having an insecure attachment to the mother at age 1 and maternal intrusiveness toward the firstborn at age 3. Paternal attachment was not related, but father support and facilitation of the the firstborn at age 3 was associated with prosocial behavior in the sibling dyad. Finally, in another longitudinal study (Brody, Stoneman, McCoy, & Forehand, 1992), ratings of low family harmony were associated with perceptions of sibling conflict and observations of negative interactions, both contemporaneously and 1 year later. Overcontrolling behavior by mothers and fathers was also associated with contemporaneous observations of sibling negative interactions, but was not predictive longitudinally. Unfortunately, the longitudinal links between sibling relationships and subsequent parent–child interactions have only been examined in studies of very young children (Kendrick & Dunn, 1983; Vandell & Wilson, 1987); therefore, any causal assertions about the direction of effects in the other studies must be considered tentative.

Differential Treatment

One can also expect the characteristics of sibling relationships to be associated with differences in parent–child relationships. For example, parents may hold one child more accountable for mutual misbehavior, and thus may punish that child more. In dysfunctional families, one child may acquire the role of the "bad child" and be treated differently from a sibling, the "good child." Alternatively, discrepancies in parental treatment could lead to resentment which is manifested through sibling conflict or rivalry.

The empirical literature provides clear support for these ideas. For example, when children are disparaging and discomforting to one another, mothers are more likely to attend to one's child's needs and not the other's than if the children are not disparaging (Bryant & Crockenberg, 1980). Similarly, low rates of various forms of positive sibling interactions and high rates of negative interactions are associated with differences in the degree to which mothers interact positively or communicate with their two children (Brody et al., 1987; Hetherington, 1988; Stocker, Dunn, & Plomin, 1989). Sibling relationships are also described less positively by mothers who are rated as being differentially responsive to their children (Stocker et al., 1989). Frequent sibling conflict and low sibling warmth are associated with differences in maternal warmth, when assessed by either questionnaires or observational measures (Furman & Giberson, in press). The ties with differences in the fathers' relationships with the two children are not as clear, as some studies have found such links (Brody, Stoneman, & McCoy, 1992), but others have not (Furman & Giberson, in press). Finally, maternal and paternal differential treatment are not only associated contemporaneously with perceptions of sibling conflict and ratings of negative behavior between siblings, but also predict such scores a year later (Brody, Stoneman, McCoy, & Forehand, 1982). Differential treatment is not associated with either the children's gender or ordinal position.

Differential treatment has not been examined directly in studies of very young sibling dyads, but the findings of several studies suggest similar patterns of relations may exist. For example, frequent maternal play and attention toward the firstborn shortly after the secondborn's birth is predictive of low rates of interaction between the two siblings when the younger child is 14 months old (Dunn & Kendrick, 1981b). Similarly, frequent mother–infant interaction and a high proportion of play with the infant are associated with negative social interactions between the siblings when the infant is 14 months old (Dunn & Kendrick, 1981a). Finally, maternal interaction with an infant is negatively related to positive interactions between the infant and preschool child (Howe & Ross, 1990).

Other research on differential treatment has found that adolescents who are better adjusted have more say in family decision making, feel closer to their parents, and have fewer conflicts with them than their less adjusted siblings (Daniels, Dunn, Furstenberg, & Plomin, 1985; Monahan, Buchanan, Maccoby, & Dornbusch, 1993). On the other hand, simple differences in personality are not very related to differences in parental treatment (Daniels, 1986). Finally, greater differences in parental treatment occur in sibling dyads in which one child had a disability than in dyads in which neither did, suggesting that the children's characteristics may contribute to such differences in parental treatment (McHale & Pawletko, 1992).

Indirect Links

The quality of children's siblings relationships may also be associated with the quality of the marital relationship and so may have an impact on the sibling relationship. As noted previously, family system theorists expect all of the subsystems to be interrelated (Minuchin, 1974). In both married and divorced families, more positive sibling interactions are linked to more positive spousal/ex-spousal relationships (MacKinnon, 1989). Similarly, perceived sibling conflict is positively related to perceived marital conflict, whereas perceived warmth is negatively related (Furman & Giberson, in press).

Concluding Comments

It is clear that characteristics of sibling relationships are associated with similar characteristics of parent–child relationships. The links between differential parental treatment and disharmony in sibling relationships are particularly well documented. It also appears that the characteristics of the parents' marriage and the children's sibling relationship may be related to one another, although that issue has received less empirical attention.

Although the links are evident, what is less clear is the direction of effects among the various family relationships. One might intuitively expect bidirectional effects, but the existing work has not provided any evidence of such bidirections. Moreover, little is known about the mechanisms or processes that might link the different relationships. For example, do the characteristics of sibling relationships have direct effects on marriages, or do they have indirect effects by influencing parent–child relationships, which in turn influence marriages? In either case, should the links be explained in terms of imitation, behavioral contagion, working models, or some other process? The question of process is discussed later.

CONSISTENCY IN PARENTS' RELATIONSHIP WITH THEIR CHILDREN

A final consideration is the consistency in parents' behavior. Evidence that different children are treated differently would be consistent with the idea that children's characteristics influence parenting. Consistency across children would suggest, although by no means prove, that such characteristics do not matter. To some degree, investigators studying family constellation variables, the birth of a second child, and the qualitative features of relationships have all examined these questions in their studies of mean differences within or across families. A statistically significant difference, however, does not neccessarily mean that parents are not relatively consistent. As noted earlier, the magnitude of many effects are not very high. Moreover, basic statistics tell us that questions of mean differences and correlations are independent of one another.

How consistent are parents? An early investigation on the topic found relatively low levels of consistency in mothers' affective relationships toward her children, but relatively high levels of consistency in childrearing (Lasko, 1954). In a study of first- and secondborn infants, mothers were somewhat consistent in their social, affectionate, and caregiving behavior toward each, although the magnitude of consistency varied markedly across specific variables (Jacobs & Moss, 1976). Similarly, consistency occurs in mothers' rates of playful and attentive behavior toward their first and second children when each is 1 year old (Dunn & Kendrick, 1982). Mothers' behaviors toward their 2-year-olds and their 4- to 6-year-olds is relatively consistent, especially when the children are of the same sex (Abramovitch, Pepler, & Corter, 1982).

Maternal attachment classifications are relatively concordant for firstborn and secondborns; in particular, 57 percent of the siblings are classified the same, whereas one would expect only 34 percent to be the same by chance (Ward et al., 1988). The similarity or concordance is particularly striking in light of the fact that stability of attachment classification over time for the same child is only 60 percent. Significant relations also exist between mothers' supportive and helpful behavior toward their firstborn and toward their secondborn when each child is 2 years old (Ward et al., 1988). Interestingly, these relations remain significant when similarity in the children's behaviors is controlled for, but the two children's behaviors are no longer correlated when the similarities in mothers' behavior is controlled for.

In a pair of studies, the Colorado Adoption Project team examined the consistency of maternal behavior toward first- and secondborns when each child was 1 year of age (Dunn, Plomin, & Nettles, 1985) and when each was 2 years old (Dunn, Plomin, & Daniels, 1986). At both ages, relatively high levels of consistency exist in maternal affection and verbal responsiveness (rs = .45 to .66). Controlling behavior is somewhat consistent at 1 year of age (r = .37), but less so at age 2 (r = .19).

Mothers' behavior toward the same child at 1 and 2 years of age is less consistent! Apparently, the developmental changes in the children elicit different behaviors from mothers.

The Stanford Adolescent Custody Study examined parenting and parent–child relationships in divorced families (Monahan et al., 1993). The parenting of different children was less related than studies have found the parenting of different children in intact families to be, especially to the degree that the children in the divorced families lived apart.

Plomin and his colleagues' recent emphasis on the importance of nonshared environmental influences has triggered work on the issue of consistencies and differences in parental treatment (Plomin & Daniels, 1987; Rowe & Plomin, 1981). Daniels and Plomin (1985) developed an inventory, the *Sibling Inventory of Differential Experiences*, to assess differential experiences. Although comparisons across scales must be made cautiously, it appears that adolescents and young adults perceive greater differences in their sibling and peer interactions than in their interactions with their parents. In fact, 56.5 percent reported they receive similar treatment, 34.5 percent reported "a bit" of difference, and only 9 percent indicated "much" difference. In a follow-up study, Daniels et al. (1985) asked mothers and fathers to rate their closeness toward their two children and their two children's "say" in decisions. Relatively high levels of consistency across children exist, but when the two children are asked similar questions, their reports are only modestly correlated with one another. Similar patterns exist in children of divorced families (Monahan et al., 1993). Children who live apart after their parents' divorce differ more than children who live together, however, suggesting there are shared as well as nonshared family influences (Monahan et al., 1993).

Not surprisingly, the literature reviewed here provides evidence of both consistency and inconsistency in parenting behavior. The findings that different children are treated somewhat differently is certainly consistent with the idea that children's characteristics influence parenting. Such variability could, however, reflect changes in the parents as well. Additionally, comparisons of the different studies do not lead to obvious conclusions about which facets of parenting are and are not consistent across children. Similarly, little is known about the factors that contribute to consistencies and inconsistencies. Accordingly, further work is needed before one can conclude if and how siblings may influence the consistency of parenting.

FUTURE DIRECTIONS

Evidence exists that parenting behavior is related to family constellation variables, the birth of a second child, and the quality of sibling relationships. Whether family constellation variables, the birth of a sibling, or the nature of the relationship affects or causes changes in parenting behavior is less clear. Because most studies are correlational in nature, the causal influences could be from parent to child. Although the task of identifying the direction of causality will always be formidable, several types of studies may prove useful.

First, studies examining genetic influences on parents' interactions with their children can give clues about the direction of influence. A series of studies from the Colorado Adoption Project has shown that mothers interact more similarly toward their two biological children than toward two adopted children (Dunn et al., 1986; Dunn et al., 1985; Dunn & Plomin, 1986; Rende, Slomkowski, Stocker, Fulker, & Plomin, 1992). Twin studies of adolescents' perceptions of parental treatment have also found evidence of genetic influences (Rowe, 1981, 1983). The similarity in biological children's behavior that stems from shared genes seems to lead to more similar treatment by their mothers. It is possible that mothers expect that genetically related children are more similar and treat them accordingly, although past twin studies have found that mothers are responding to actual similarities rather than creating them (Lytton, 1977; Lytton & Singh, in this *Handbook*).

A second strategy is to compare a mother's and stranger's behavior toward a child. If the mother and stranger treat the child similarly, then one would infer that they are responding to some facet of the child's behavior. Differences in maternal and stranger treatment would reflect the contributions the adults bring to the interactions or the contributions of the existing relationship between adult and child. For example, Thoman, Barnett, and Liederman (1971) found that primiparous mothers took more intervals to feed their infant than multiparous mothers did, but nurses took equal amounts of time. These findings suggest that the primiparous mothers' inexperience is responsible for the difference between their feeding of first- and latter borns, rather than some infant characteristic.

A third strategy is to observe a parent interacting with their two children. If no differences are observed in the parent's behavior toward the two children, then any differences in the children's behavior would be a reflection of the children's contribution to the interaction. If the children's behavior is similar, then any differences in the parent's behavior would be attributed to the parent. For example, Belsky and his colleagues found that parents of firstborns responded to their children more than parents of secondborns did, but the first- and secondborn children did not differ in their behavior (Belsky, Gilstrap, & Rovine, 1984; Belsky, Taylor, & Rovine, 1984); thus, the differences could be attributed to the parents. Such interpretations must be made cautiously, however, as it is possible that the children or parents differed on some other variable that was not measured. After all, one is left with the question of why the parents (children) responded differently if there were no differences in the other's behavior.

More generally, Kenny and La Voie's (1984) social relations model can be used to separate out the contributions of different individuals. Using a round robin procedure, each person is observed interacting with every other family member. One can then estimate actor effects (i.e., the consistency of a person's behavior in different dyads), partner effects (i.e., the extent to which one's behavior is elicited by a particular partner), and relationship effects (i.e., behavior specific to that dyad). One can also estimate the degree to which behaviors are reciprocated. In one such study of preschoolers, infant siblings, and their parents (Stevenson et al., 1988), the adjustments individuals made to one another (relationship effects) far outweighed either actor effects or partner effects. Some actor effects were found for children, but not parents. Parents were more likely to adjust to their partner, suggesting that they were primarily responsible for the structuring that occurred in their interactions with their children. Although this methodological strategy has great promise, it does leave open the question of where relationship effects come from. That is, how did the past characteristics of the parent and child contribute to the relationship that currently exists?

A related strategy is to gather detailed observational data on the patterns of interaction between parents and children. Sequential analyses could reveal how the behavior of one person affects the subsequent responses of others. Such an approach would not, however, provide information about the long-term impact of behavior.

Another strategy for identifying potential causal links between parent and child is to conduct longitudinal studies. Unfortunately, almost all of the existing work in this field has collected data at only one point in time. Moreover, the few longitudinal studies have primarily focused on comparisons of mean levels across time, rather than examining correlations across time. When correlations have been examined, most investigators have only looked at the links between parent–child and subsequent sibling interactions, and not the reverse. Without knowing the ties from past sibling interactions to current parent–child interactions, it is hard to make causal inferences of any type. Although the longitudinal strategy has advantages over the collection of data at only one point, the limits of structural modeling techniques discussed previously should be kept in mind. Structural modeling is designed to rule out particular causal models, rather than document causal links (Breckler, 1990).

Finally, one could manipulate the two children's behavior toward one another and observe the parent's response. This strategy has been commonly used to isolate the short-term effects of one child's behavior on a parent (or vice versa; see Bell & Harper, 1977), but it does not appear to have been used in studies of sibling relationships.

Even when studies using these different strategies suggest that the children may be affecting parenting, one should not necessarily conclude that it is something about a sibling or having a sibling that is responsible. For example, many investigators have reported differences in the treatment of male and female siblings (Fagot, in this *Handbook*). Although it is clear the gender of the child has an impact on parenting, it is not as clear that the gender of the sibling matters. That is, differences between boys and girls in the same family may be the same as the differences between families of only girls and families of only boys. Thus, one would need to compare differences in the treatment of a child when the sibling is the same or opposite gender. Such comparisons exist for studies of personality characteristics (see Sutton-Smith & Rosenberg, 1970), but are relatively rare in the study of parent–child interaction. One exception is that mothers seem to interact less with secondborns when they are of the same gender as the firstborns (Kendrick & Dunn, 1982).

Similar problems exist in interpreting the literature on the differences in the personality characteristics of siblings (see Brody et al., 1987; Furman & Lanthier, in press; Stocker et al., 1989). That is, the child's temperament seems to have an impact, but it is not as clear that the relative temperament of the child versus that of a sibling matters as well. Once again, one would need to determine whether variations in a sibling's temperament affect the parental treatment of a child.

Although the existing work sheds some light on the potential links between parenting and sibling relationships, further work is needed to specify the mechanisms responsible for such links (Furman & Giberson, in press). One of the problems with family constellation constructs is that they are not direct indices of any family processes. At most, they are associated with or predictive of certain family processes. Thus, identifying a significant effect of birth order does not tell us how or why there are birth order differences. Do such effects reflect differences in parent–child relationships, sibling relationships, or other effects on family processes? Similarly, if parenting of the firstborn changes as a result of the birth of a sibling, is it because of the economic changes in the family, the extra parenting demands, or the older child's feelings of rivalry? Directly measuring the characteristics of parent–child and sibling relationships has led to progress, but even here much work remains. For example, imagine that warmth in sibling relationships has been demonstrated to affect warmth in parent–child relationships. How does one explain that? Numerous theoretical mechanisms, such as contagion effects or system effects, could account for it. Investigators need to develop means of ruling out alternative explanations. Finally, it is important to remember that our measures are snapshots of a system of variables that have a history of influence on one another. Moreover, they may have reached some state of relative homeostatis. It is not clear how well static pictures—even repeated ones—capture the process of change. Thus, progress has been made, but the future presents some challenging problems to address.

CONCLUSIONS

This chapter addresses the question of how sibling relationships affect parenting and parent–child relationships. Four different approaches have been used to examine this question. First, A. Adler's (1931) theory of individual psychology triggered an extensive amount of research on how parent–child relationships may vary as a function of birth order, family size, and other family constellation variables. These studies have found some differences, particulary when the children are young. Specifically, parents appear to be more involved and perhaps warmer in their relationships with their firstborns. At the same time, parents also have higher expectations for and are more controlling of their first borns. Only children also seem to have more positive relationships with their parents than other children, particularly children in large families. Family size may, in fact, be one of the more important variables as it seems that relationships are more autocratic and less intensive in larger families. Although parent–child relationships vary as a function of family constellation variables, it is important to remember that these differences are modest in size. Moreover, it is difficult to interpret these effects as they are inherently confounded with a number of other variables, such as SES. Perhaps as a result, relatively little work is now done on family constellation variables.

A second way to look at the influence of siblings on parenting is to examine the changes that occur in childrearing with the birth of subsequent children. Although relatively few such studies have been conducted, they have found that interactions between the firstborn and mothers are less frequent, less warm, and more conflictual after the birth of a sibling than before. Changes in father–child interactions seem similar, but they have been studied less frequently. It is also unclear how long the changes in parenting last after the birth of the siblings and whether they change in nature over time.

The third approach is to examine how the qualitative features or characteristics of sibling relationships are related to parenting. Warmth and positive interactions in sibling relationships are associated with warmth and positive interactions in parent–child relationships. Similarly, sibling conflict and hostility are linked with conflict and hostility between parents and children. Sibling warmth is also associated with similar treatment of the children by parents, whereas sibling conflict is associated with differential treatment by parents. The quality of the sibling relationships also seems related to the marital quality, although how the two relationships are linked is less clear. For that matter, it is not clear what processes are responsible for any of the observed relations between sibling relationships and other family relationships.

A fourth and final approach has been to examine the degree of consistency in the parental treatment of two children. Research indicates that children are treated somewhat differently, which is consistent with the idea that children's characteristics may influence parenting. Unfortunately, such inconsistencies could also stem from changes in parents' behaviors that are caused by other factors.

Each of these four different approaches has led to a better appreciation of the links between siblings and parenting. At the same time, it is still difficult to draw firm causal inferences or to be able to specify the processes or theoretical mechanisms that are responsible for any observed links. Attention to those issues may lead to a greater understanding of exactly how and when siblings affect parenting.

REFERENCES

Abelson, R. P. (1985). A variance explanation paradox: When a little is a lot. *Psychological Bulletin, 97*, 129–133.

Abramovitch, R., Pepler, D., & Corter, C. (1982). Patterns of sibling interaction among preschool-age children. In M. E. Lamb & B. Sutton-Smith (Eds.), *Sibling relationships: Their nature and significance across the life span* (pp. 61–86). Hillsdale, NJ: Lawrence Erlbaum Associates.

Adams, B. N. (1972). Birth order: A critical review. *Sociometry, 35*, 411–439.

Adler, A. (1931). *What life should mean to you.* Boston: Little, Brown.

Adler, T. F., & Furman, M. (1988). A model for children's relationships and relationship dysfunctions. In S. W. Duck (Ed.), *Handbook of personal relationships* (pp. 211–229). New York: Wiley.

Ansbacher, H. L., & Ansbacher, R. R. (1956). *The individual psychology of Alfred Adler.* New York: Basic Books.

Barger, B., & Hall, E. (1966). The interrelationships of family size and socio-economic status for parents of college students. *Journal of Marriage and the Family, 28*, 186–187.

Baskett, L. M. (1984). Ordinal position differences in children's family interactions. *Developmental Psychology, 20*, 1026–1031.

Baskett, L. M. (1985). Sibling status effects: Adult expectations. *Developmental Psychology, 21*, 441–445.

Bell, N. J., & Avery, A. W. (1985). Family structure and parent–adolescent relationships: Does family structure really make a difference? *Journal of Marriage and the Family, 47*, 503–508.

Bell, R. Q. (1968). A reinterpretation of the direction of effects in studies of socialization. *Psychological Review, 75*, 81–95.

Bell, R. Q. (1971). Stimulus control of parent or caretaker behavior by offspring. *Developmental Psychology, 4*, 63–72.

Bell, R. Q., & Harper, L. V. (1977) *Child effects on adults.* Hillsdale, NJ: Lawrence Erlbaum Associates.

Belsky, J., Gilstrap, B., & Rovine, M. (1984). The Pennsylvania infant and family development project, I: Stability and change in mother–infant and father–infant interaction in a family setting at one, three, and nine months. *Child Development, 55*, 692–705.

Belsky, J., Taylor, D., & Rovine, M. (1984). The Pennsylvania infant and family devleopment project, II: The development of reciprocal interaction in the mother–infant dyad. *Child Development, 55*, 706–717.

Blake, J. (1981). The only child in America: Prejudice versus performance. *Population and Development, 1*, 43–54.

Blake, J. (1989). *Family size and achievement.* Berkeley, CA: University of California Press.

Bossard, J.H.S., & Boll, E. S. (1956). *The large family system.* Philadelphia: University of Pennsylvania Press.

Bradley, R. H., & Caldwell, B. M. (1984). The HOME inventory and family demographics. *Developmental Psychology, 20*, 315–320.

Breckler, S. J. (1990). Applications of covariance structure modeling in psychology: Cause for concern? *Psychological Bulletin, 107*, 260–273.

Brody, G., Stoneman, Z., & Burke, M. (1987). Child temperaments, maternal differential behavior, and sibling relationships. *Developmental Psychology, 23*, 354–362.

Brody, G., Stoneman, Z., & McCoy, J. K. (1992). Associations of maternal and paternal direct and differential behavior with sibling relationships: Contemporaneous and longitudinal analyses. *Child Development, 63*, 82–92.

Brody, G., Stoneman, Z., McCoy, J. K., & Forehand, R. (1992). Contemporaneous and longitudinal associations of sibling conflict with family relationship assessments and family discussions about sibling problems. *Child Development, 63*, 391–400.

Bryant, B. K., & Crockenberg, S. B. (1980). Correlates and dimensions of prosocial behavior: A study of female siblings with their mothers. *Child Development, 51*, 529–544.

Daniels, D. (1986). Differential experiences of siblings in the same family as predictors of adolescent sibling personality differences. *Journal of Personality and Social Psychology, 51*, 339–346.

Daniels, D., Dunn, J., Furstenberg, F. F. Jr., & Plomin, R. (1985). Environmental differences within the family and adjustment differences within pairs of adolescent siblings. *Child Development, 56*, 764–774.

Daniels, D., & Plomin, R. (1985). Differential experience of siblings in the same family. *Developmental Psychology, 21*, 747–760.

Dunn, J., & Kendrick, C. (1980). The arrival of a sibling: Changes in patterns of interaction between mother and firstborn child. *Journal of Child Psychology and Psychiatry, 21*, 119–132.

Dunn, J., & Kendrick, S. (1981a). Interaction between young siblings: Association with the interaction between mother and firstborn. *Developmental Psychology, 17*, 336–343.

Dunn, J., & Kendrick, C. (1981b). Social behavior of young siblings in the family context between same-sex and different-sex dyads. *Child Development, 52*, 1265–1273.

Dunn, J., & Kendrick, S. (1982). *Siblings: Love, envy, and understanding.* Cambridge, MA: Harvard University.

Dunn, J., Kendrick, C., & MacNamee, R. (1981). The reaction of firstborn children to the birth of a sibling: Mothers' reports. *Journal of Child Psychology and Psychiatry, 22*, 1–18.

Dunn, J., & Plomin, R. (1986). Determinants of maternal behavior towards 3-year-old siblings. *British Journal of Developmental Psychology, 4*, 127–137.

Dunn, J. F., Plomin, R., & Daniels, D. (1986). Consistency and change in mothers' behavior toward young siblings. *Child Development, 57*, 348–356.

Dunn, J. F., Plomin, R., & Nettles, M. (1985). Consistency of mothers' behavior toward infant siblings. *Developmental Psychology, 21*, 1188–1195.

Elder, G. H., Jr. (1962). Structural variations in the child rearing relationship. *Sociometry, 25*, 241–262.

Elder, G. H. Jr., & Bowerman, C. E. (1963). Family structure and child-rearing patterns: The effects of family size and sex composition. *American Sociological Review, 28*, 891–905.

Ernst, C., & Angst, J. (1983). *Birth order: Its influence on personality.* New York: Springer-Verlag.

Eysenck, H. J., & Cookson, D. (1970). Personality in primary school children: family background. *British Journal of Educational Psychology, 40*, 117–131.

Falbo, T. (1978a). Reasons for having an only child. *Journal of Population, 1*, 181–184.

Falbo, T. (1978b). Sibling tutoring and other explanations for intelligence discontinuities of only and last borns. *Journal of Population, 1*, 349–363.

Falbo, T., & Cooper, C. R. (1980). Young children's time and intellectual ability. *Journal of Genetic Psychology, 173*, 299–300.

Falbo, T., & Polit, D. (1986). Quantitative review of the only child literature: Research evidence and theory development. *Psychological Bulletin, 100*, 176–189.

Felson, R. B. (1983). Aggression and violence between siblings. *Social Psychology Quarterly, 46*, 271–285.

Furman, W., & Buhrmester, D. (1985). Children's perceptions of the qualities of sibling relationships. *Child Development, 56*, 448–461.

Furman, W., & Giberson, R. S. (in press). Identifying the links between parents and their children's sibling relationships. In S. Shulman (Ed.), *Close relationships in social–emotional development.* Norwood, NJ: Ablex.

Furman, W., Jones, L., Buhrmester, D., & Adler, T. (1988). Children's, parents' and observers' perspectives on sibling relationships. In P. G. Zukow (Ed.) *Sibling interaction across culture* (pp. 165–183). New York, Springer-Verlag.

Furman, W., & Lanthier, R. (in press). Personality and sibling relationships. In G. Brody (Ed.) „Sibling relationships—causes and consequences: Advances in applied developmental psychology.* Norwood, NJ: Ablex.

Gollob, H. F., & Reichardt, C. S. (1987). Taking account of time lags in causal models. *Child Development, 58*, 80–92.

Grossman, F., Eichler, L., & Winickoff, S., with Anzalone, M., Gofseyeff, M., & Sargent, S. (1980). *Pregnancy, birth, and parenthood.* San Francisco: Jossey-Bass.

Harris, I., & Howard, K. (1985). Correlates of perceived parental favoritism. *Journal of Genetic Psychology, 146*, 45–56.

Henry, A. F. (1957). Sibling structure and perception of the disciplinary role of parents. *Sociometry, 20*, 67–85.

Hetherington, E. M. (1988). Parents, children, and siblings: six years after the divorce. In R. A. Hinde & J. Stevenson-Hinde (Eds.), *Relationships within families* (pp. 311–331) Oxford, England: Oxford University Press.

Howe, N., & Ross, H. S. (1990). Socialization, perspective-taking, and the sibling relationship. *Developmental Psychology, 26*, 160–165.

Jacobs, S. M., & Moss, H. A. (1976). Birth order and sex of sibling as determinants of mother–infant interaction. *Child Development, 47,* 315–322.

James, L. R., Mulaik, S. A., & Brett, J. M. (1982). *Causal analysis: Assumptions, models, and data.* Beverly Hills, CA: Sage.

Kammeyer, K. (1967). Birth order as a research variable. *Social Forces, 46,* 71–80.

Katz, T. (1992). *Parents and siblings: Family relationships of young children.* Unpublished doctoral dissertation, University of Denver, Denver, CO.

Kendrick, C., & Dunn, J. (1980). Caring for a second baby: Effects on the interaction between mother and firstborn. *Developmental Psychology, 16,* 303–311.

Kendrick, C., & Dunn, J. (1982). Protest or pleasure: The response of firstborn children to interactions between their mothers and infant siblings. *Journal of Child Psychology and Psychiatry, 23,* 117–129.

Kendrick, C., & Dunn, J. (1983). Sibling quarrels and maternal responses. *Developmental Psychology, 19,* 62–70.

Kenny, D. A., & La Voie, L. (1984). The social relations model. In L. Berkowitz (Ed.) *Advances in experimental social psychology* (Vol. 18, pp. 141–182). New York: AcademicPress.

Kidwell, J. S. (1981). Number of siblings, sibling spacing, sex, and birth order: Their effects on perceived parent–adolescent relationships. *Journal of Marriage and the Family, 43,* 315–332.

Kiracofe, N. M., & Kiracofe, H. N. (1990). Child-perceived favoritism and birth order. *Individual Psychology, 46,* 74–81.

Koch, H. L. (1960). The relation of certain formal attributes of siblings to attitudes held toward each other and toward their parents. *Monographs of the Society for Research in Child Development, 25*(4, Serial No. 78).

Kreppner, K. (1989). Linking infant development-in-context reserach to the investigation of life-span family development. In K. Kreppner & R. M. Lerner (Eds.), *Family systems and life-span development* (pp. 33–64). Hillsdale, NJ: Lawrence Erlbaum Associates.

Kreppner, K. (1990, October). *Differences in parents' cooperation patterns after the arrival of a second child.* Paper presented at the 21st Baby International Conference, Lisbon, Portugal.

Kreppner, K., Paulsen, S., & Schuetze, Y. (1982). Infant and family development: From triads to tetrads. *Human Development, 25,* 373–391.

Lasko, J. K. (1954). Parent behavior toward first and second children. *Genetic Psychology Monographs, 49,* 97–137.

Lewis, M., & Feiring, C. (1982). Some American families at dinner. In L. M. Laosa & I. E. Sigel (Eds.), *Families as learning environments for children* (pp. 115–145). New York: Plenum.

Lewis, M., & Kreitzberg, V. (1979). The effects of birth order and spacing on mother–infant interactions. *Developmental Psychology, 15,* 617–625.

Lewis, M., & Rosenblum, L. (Eds.). (1974) *The effect of the infant on its caregiver: The origins of behavior* (Vol. 1). New York: Wiley.

Lindert, P. H. (1978). *Fertility and scarcity in America.* Princeton, NJ: Princeton University Press.

Lytton, H. (1977). Do parents create, or respond to, differences in twins? *Developmental Psychology, 13,* 456–459.

MacKinnon, C. E. (1989). An observational investigation of sibling interactions in married and divorced families. *Developmental Psychology, 25,* 36–44.

McGurk, H., & Lewis, M. (1972). Birth order: A phenomenon in search of an explanation. *Developmental Psychology, 7,* 366.

McHale, S. M., & Pawletko, T. M. (1992). Differential treatment of siblings in two family contexts. *Child Development, 63,* 68–81.

Meehl, P.E. (1970). Nuisance variables and the *ex post facto* design. In M. Radner & S. Winokur (Eds.) *Minnesota studies in the philosophy of science* (Vol. 4, pp. 373–402). Minneapolis, MN: University of Minnesota.

Miller, N., & Maruyama, G. (1976). Ordinal position and peer popularity. *Journal of Personality and Social Psychology, 33,* 123–131.

Minnett, A. M., Vandell, D. L., & Santrock, J. W. (1983). The effects of sibling status on sibling interaction: Influence of birth order, age spacing, sex of child, and sex of sibling. *Child Development, 54,* 1064–1072.

Minuchin, S. (1974). *Families and family therapy.* Cambridge, MA: Harvard University Press.

Monahan, S. C., Buchanan, C. M., Maccoby, E. E., & Dornbusch, S. M. (1993). Sibling differences in divorced families. *Child Development, 64,* 152–168.

Nadelman, L., & Begun, A. (1982). The effect of the newborn on the older sibling: Mother questionnaires. In M. E. Lamb & B. Sutton-Smith (Eds.), *Sibling relationships: Their nature and significance across the life span* (pp. 13–38). Hillsdale, NJ: Lawrence Erlbaum Associates.

Nye, I., Carlson, J., & Garrett, G. (1970). Family size, interaction, affection, and stress. *Journal of Marriage and the Family, 32,* 216–226.

Parke, R. D., & O'Leary, S. (1975). Father–mother–infant interaction in the newborn period: Some findings, some observations and some unresolved issues. In K. Riegel & J. Meacham (Eds.), *The developing individual in a changing world: Vol. 2. Social and environment issues.* The Hague, Netherlands: Mouton.

Patterson, G. (1986). The contribution of siblings to training for fighting: A microsocial analysis. In D. Olweus, J. Block, & M. R. Radke-Yarrow (Eds.) *Development of antisocial and prosocial behavior: Research, theories, and issues* (pp. 235–261). New York: Academic Press.

Paulhus, D., & Shaffer, D. R. (1981). Sex differences in the impact of number of older and number of younger siblings on scholastic aptitude. *Social Psychology Quarterly, 44,* 363–368.Peterson, E. T., & Kunz, P. R. (1975). Parental control over adolescents according to family size. *Adolescence, 10,* 419–427.

Plomin, R., & Daniels, D. (1987). Why are children in the same family so different from one another? *Behavavioral and Brain Sciences, 10,* 1–22.

Polit, D. F., & Falbo, T. (1987). Only children and personality development: A quantitative review. *Journal of Marriage and the Family, 49,* 309–325.

Rende, R. D., Slomkowski, C. L., Stocker, C., Fulker, D. W., & Plomin, R. (1992). Genetic and environmental influences on maternal and sibling interaction in middle childhood: A sibling adoption study. *Developmental Psychology, 28,* 484–490.

Rothbart, M. K. (1971). Birth order and mother–child interaction in an achievement situation. *Journal of Personality and Social Psychology, 17,* 113–120.

Rowe, D. C. (1981). Environmental and genetic influences on dimensions of perceived parenting: A twin study. *Developmental Psychology, 17,* 203–208.

Rowe, D. C. (1983). A biometrical analysis of perceptions of family environment: A study of twin and singeleton sibling kinships. *Child Development, 54,* 416–423.

Rowe, D. C., & Plomin, R. (1981). The importance of nonshared (E_1) environmental influences in behavioral development. *Developmental Psychology, 17,* 517–531.

Scheck, D. C., & Emerick, R. (1976). The young male adolescent's perception of early child-rearing behavior: The differential effects of socioeconomic status and family size. *Sociometry, 39,* 39–52.

Schooler, C. (1972). Birth order effects: Not here, not now! *Psychological Bulletin, 78,* 161–175.

Sears, R. R., Maccoby, E. E., & Levin, H. (1957). *Patterns of child rearing.* Evanston, IL: Row & Peterson.

Stevenson, M. B., Leavitt, L. A., Thompson, R. H., & Roach, M. A. (1988). A social relations model analysis of parent and child play. *Developmental Psychology, 24,* 101–108.

Stewart, R. B., Jr. (1991). *The second child: Family transition and adjustment.* Newbury Park, CA: Sage.

Stewart, R., Mobley, L., Van Tuyl, S., & Salvador, M. (1987). The firstborn's adjustment to the birth of a sibling: A longitudinal assessment. *Child Development, 58,* 341–355.

Stocker, C., Dunn, J., & Plomin, R. (1989). Sibling relationships: Links with child temperament, maternal behavior, and family structure. *Child Development, 60,* 715–727.

Stocker, C. M., & McHale, S. M. (1992). The nature and family correlates of preadolescents' perceptins of their sibling relationships. *Journal of Social and Personal Relationships, 9,* 179–195.

Sutton-Smith, B., & Rosenberg, B. G. (1970). *The sibling.* New York: Holt, Rinehart & Winston.

Taylor, M., & Kogan, K. (1973). Effects of birth of a sibling on mother–child interaction. *Child Psychiatry and Human Development, 4,* 53–58.

Teti, D. M., & Ablard, K. E. (1989). Security of attachment and infant–sibling relationships: A laboratory stduy. *Child Development, 60,* 1519–1528.

Thoman, E. B., Barnett, C. R., & Leiderman, P. H. (1971). Feeding behaviors of newborn infants as a function of parity of mother. *Child Development, 42,* 1471–1483.

Thomas, A., Birch, H. G., Chess, S., & Robbins, A. (1961). Individuality in responses of children to similar environmental situations. *American Journal of Psychiatry, 117,* 798–803.

Udry, J. R. (1978). Differential fertitility by intelligence: The role of birth planning. *Social Biology, 25,* 10–14.

Vandell, D. L., & Wilson, K. S. (1987). Infants' interactions with mother, sibling, and peer: Contrasts and relations between interaction system. *Child Development, 58,* 176–186.

Volling, B. L., & Belsky, J. (1992). The contribution of mother–child and father–child relationships to the quality of sibling interaction: A longitudinal study. *Child Development, 63,* 1209–1222.

Waddell, K. J., & Ball, F. L. (1980, August). *Parental knowledge questionnaire: The first two years.* Paper presented at the meetings of the American Psychological Association, Montreal, Quebec, Canada.

Ward, M. J., Vaughn, B. E., & Robb, M. D. (1988). Social–emotional adaptation and infant–mother attachment in siblings: Role of the mother in cross-sibling consistency. *Child Development, 59,* 643–651.

Zukow, P. G. (Ed.). (1988). *Sibling interaction across culture.* New York: Springer-Verlag.

7

Parenting Boys and Girls

Beverly I. Fagot
University of Oregon
and Oregon Social Learning Center

INTRODUCTION

The idea that there is something unique and different about rearing children—parenting—is a recent construct. The word *parent* comes to us from the Latin root meaning to give birth, but today the word parent and the process we call *parenting* means far more. It entails not only giving birth, but providing for children up to their adult years and beyond. It entails providing not only for the child's physical well-being, but also providing warmth and security to insure good psychological adjustment, discipline for moral development, and stimulation for intellectual growth. Society is harsh in its judgment of those who fail in any of these domains, yet dictionaries do not even define the word, and our society requires no special training for parenting. We provide even less information concerning differences in parenting boys and girls, yet if a child shows cross-sex behaviors, most laypersons and many professionals assume the parents have been derelict in their parenting duties (Zucker & Green, 1992).

No child in our society is born into a gender-free world. Children are wrapped from birth in sex-differentiated information. Snugly tucked into pink or blue blankets, they are enfolded in gender as well. As infants strive to understand all they see and hear, they begin to form categories that help organize the flood of information that inundates them. The distinction between female and male, feminine and masculine, provides a readily available organizing principle relevant to the child's own self (Martin & Halverson, 1981). Clearly the sex of the child is an important factor in rearing children. Several studies suggest that, when asked to describe infants, individuals used the stated sex of the infant to organize their descriptions (J. Condry & S. Condry, 1976; Rubin, Provenzano, & Luria, 1974). However, two major reviews (Lytton & Romney, 1991; Maccoby & Jacklin, 1974) have concluded that there is little evidence to suggest that boys and girls are treated differently. Despite the importance of sex and gender, there is little agreement on the extent to which boys and girls receive different socialization, on whether they should, and on whether it makes any difference.

In this chapter, *sex* is defined as the biological difference between boys and girls, and *gender* as the construction that society has imposed on sex. Thus, when speaking of males and females, the term *sex* is used, whereas masculinity and femininity are discussed as *gender*. The terms *sex role* and *sex typing* have been traditionally used in psychology, so many older instruments and articles use these terms. Rather than attempting to rewrite psychological literature, we use the terminology of the author whenever necessary.

This chapter is organized in the following way: First, one of the major issues in the field—the influence of parents on gender-role socialization—is discussed. Next, historical views of parenting are considered along with a discussion of theories of parenting in relation to gender-role socialization. One of the points of interest is how parenting style relates to child outcome. Next, the components of parenting are examined, and family management variables, scaffolding or instruction variables, and attachment or relationship building are considered. The next section focuses on more specific research on parenting boys and girls and discusses gender-role socialization and gender-role adoption by children. This section also includes a discussion of the relation of parenting to the failure of the children to adopt a gender identity consonant with their biological sex. The next section of the chapter examines situations where either the parent or the child encounter difficulties. Finally, new directions for research and an evaluation of whether boys and girls receive or need different types of parenting are discussed.

CENTRAL ISSUES

For many parents and professionals, a central issue about rearing boys and girls is the reason they turn out so different. This is a continuation of the nature versus nurture question that has been a central theme in many biological and social sciences. Work from anthropology has long been used to describe the way that different cultures ascribe roles to the two sexes that are then seen within that culture as natural. Mead (1935) described sex and temperament in three cultures to illustrate how cultural socialization influenced both the attitudes and behaviors attributed to each sex as well as the modal temperament within the society. Whiting and Edwards (1988) studied the rearing of boys and girls across several cultures in an attempt to examine rearing differences and similarities. They presented a strong case for cultural influences on rearing constrained by the child's maturational period. From this study, it is clear that boys and girls are quite capable of taking almost any role prescribed by the culture, but that the roles prescribed by the cultures are determined to some extent by the reproductive roles the children will play when adults. By describing the lives of children at several different ages, Whiting and Edwards also showed that gender expectations are increasingly powerful from early toddlerhood through adolescence. In most societies, *lap children* (their term), both boys and girls, live in similar worlds, but their paths diverge sometime during childhood. By adolescence in many cultures, the knowledge and activities of boys and girls show very little overlap.

Within a clinical framework, Money and Ehrhardt (1972) presented powerful evidence that the child's basic definition of self as boy or girl—gender identity—was influenced by the sex in which the child was being reared. Whereas evidence from the last 20 years has suggested that many gender-role behaviors (particularly those determining sexual behaviors) are more highly organized through hormonal influences than previously thought (Meyer-Bahlburg, 1984), the evidence for the influence of early socialization as male or female remains strong. As becomes evident when we review historical and current theories of childrearing, there is no clear-cut answer to just how much influence the culture and parenting styles have on the developmental paths of boys and girls.

In developmental psychology literature, the influence of differential socialization by parents on determining the different roles taken by boys and girls has been a subject of continuing debate for the past 20 years (Block, 1983; Lytton & Romney, 1991; Maccoby & Jacklin, 1974). Maccoby and Jacklin (1974) reviewed the literature for all studies they could find on gender-role socialization. They found that most studies were biased or limited in several ways, both in terms of subject population and interpretation of studies. There were few studies with direct data on fathers; the studies dealt mostly with children before the age of 5; and most of the samples were of well-educated middle-class parents. Many studies implied causality between parental socialization and child sex differences where only correlational findings existed. Both the method of data collection and the reporting agent influenced the results of these studies. It was not that the studies failed to show differential socialization, but that there was little consistency in the direction of differences. Maccoby and Jacklin concluded that, beyond shaping obvious sex-typed play and the fact that boys received more physical punishment than girls, there were few consistent differences in the socialization of boys and girls.

Block (1976) questioned this conclusion. Specifically, she agreed that few of the studies dealt with fathers, who might be expected to provide stronger gender-role socialization than mothers, and that the studies were biased toward younger children. Block felt that both of these biases worked against findings of gender-related differences in socialization. Block (1983) suggested several areas in which parental treatment might make a difference, such as in providing models for girls' behaviors versus allowing trial-and-error exploration for boys. Several subsequent attempts to examine parental differences in the treatment of boys and girls have consistently found evidence for reinforcement of sex-typed toy play, particularly from fathers (Caldera, Huston, & O'Brien, 1989; Langlois & Downs, 1980), but these studies were not designed to test Block's more broad-reaching hypotheses.

Huston's (1983) review of the literature on sex typing devoted just one short paragraph to differential treatment of boys and girls during the first year of life. Huston noted that, within the overall similarity of caregiving, a few consistent differences could be seen, but like Maccoby and Jacklin, she concluded that patterns of parental interaction are similar for boys and girls. Lytton and Romney (1991) completed a meta-analysis of 172 studies examining the socialization differences of boys and girls and also found few consistent differences across studies. On the other hand, Bem (1983, 1993) argued that the lenses of gender unnecessarily restrict both males and females. Her belief is that biology is relatively limited in determining the behaviors we come to know as "gender role," and that if the society, including socialization within the family, were less structured by gender, both men and women would profit.

Ample data exist to suggest that the differentiation process by which infants are exposed to gender information begins in the newborn period and is consistent at a very broad level. Differential treatment by sex starts as soon as the infant's sex is known. The newborn nursery provides color-coded blankets, identification bracelets, and diapers. Gifts to the child are carefully selected by sex, with girls receiving pastel outfits, sometimes beruffled, when boys are given tiny jeans and bold colors. Although parents seldom mention sex-appropriateness when asked about clothing choices for their infants, most infants are dressed in sex-typed clothing (M. Shakin, D. Shakin, & Sternglanz, 1985). Older children and adults are also readily discriminable on the basis of clothing and hair style, which, in conjunction with body type, voice cues, and any number of sex-differentiated behaviors, proclaim the sex of nearly everyone in sight.

There is no lack of information with which to identify or discriminate the sexes, and one side of the puzzle of understanding the development of gender is to understand the process by which infants first come to recognize males and females as categorically distinct. Fagot and Leinbach (1993a) reviewed this early recognition process in detail with particular attention to the child's developing cognitive capacities to construct gender. Children are seen as taking in and organizing environmental input schematically by "chunking" or categorizing information as best they can (Bem, 1981; C. L. Martin & Halverson, 1981). In the ordinary course of events, this process leads to associative rather than piecemeal retention of information, so that related pieces of information will ultimately tend to be recognized and recalled together. These networks of associations are the basis of schema that help the child organize and interpret new experience and regulate behavior (C. L. Martin, 1993). Because children live in a sex-typed world, this process results in schema concerning gender that guide the choice of "sex-appropriate" behaviors and the knowledge of the action patterns necessary for carrying them out within this framework. Fagot and Leinbach (1993) concluded that the interplay between environmental input from family and cultural sources, the child's interest in understanding gender, and the child's developing cognitive system are all important in construction of the gender system. However, the mechanisms by which this process occurs remain difficult to untangle. This chapter points out that the evidence for different parenting styles early in the child's life is reasonably strong and these early differences in parenting play an important part in promoting children's gender-role development.

HISTORICAL CONSIDERATIONS

Modern-day child specialists sometimes speak as if children and parenting were recent inventions. Yet for every culture about which we have any information, we have bits of information about parenting. Even for the cave painters of France (about whose culture we know so little save the visual images left on the wall), we have tiny handprints left in the same caves, to remind us that these too were people who cared for their children and who kept them with them during important periods of their lives. As we review theories of parenting, it is important to remember that the process of parenting is old; only the study of that process is new.

At least in Western society, however, the most recent invention appears to be daughters. A large historical literature exists on the care of sons, but there is little written on the care of daughters. And if the tenor of biblical childrearing quotes is any indication of practice, the role of the son does not fare well. Most early treatises on parenting were written by men, and they were concerned with the upbringing of boys. Although the necessity for providing love and warmth for the young child is occasionally mentioned, most information on parenting emphasizes the importance of the child's mind, either in terms of what we call intellectual abilities or what we now call moral values. Most discussion concerns training the upper-class child, and we have little information concerning the rearing of the large majority of children.

One of the most complete treatises on childrearing in modern Western culture was Locke's (1693/1964) *Some Thoughts Concerning Education*, which is basically a practical guide to a father about rearing a son. As might be expected from the culture of the seventeenth century, much of the essay concerns the necessity of establishing early authority over the child. There are warnings about too much love, about the problems of material rewards, and the concern that children might be spoiled by servants. Yet there are surprisingly modern recognitions of individual differences in children, of the superiority of discipline through reasoning as opposed to corporal punishment, of the importance of parental role models, and the recognition that the best motivator for the child is the esteem of parents. As might be expected, Locke presented a very rational view of childrearing, remaining above much of the turmoil of actual parenting, perhaps because Locke was a bachelor and himself had no children. Girls are not mentioned in Locke's treatise.

In the late 1700s, Wollstonecraft (1975; Todd, 1990) wrote extensively on parenting and, in particular, on the education of daughters. Her works are heavily influenced by Locke's rational approach, but also touch on early care. There is a concern that mothers nurse their own infants, that young children, both boys and girls, need a warm, loving environment, but most of her writings reflect a concern for the rearing of girls. Her *Thoughts on the Education of Daughters* expressed a concern that girls were not taught to discipline their minds, but allowed to grow without intellectual skills or moral discipline. Wollstonecraft's essays were very popular in her day, suggesting some influence and some concern on the part of parents that childrearing was not simply the intellectual process suggested by Locke. Within the feminist literary tradition, Wollstonecraft's ideas were commented upon; however, most essays concerning the history of parenting and children have ignored her works, and it is only within the last 20 years that it has become widely available.

The views on parenting and children have changed greatly in the 200 years since Wollstonecraft, yet it is interesting to note that she identified the two main themes that have emerged within the parenting literature of the last 50 years: the necessary balance and the inevitable tension between parental warmth and parental control.

THEORIES OF PARENTING IN RELATION
TO GENDER-ROLE SOCIALIZATION

Modern-day theories of parenting have their roots in Freud's description of the family. Freud articulated very clearly the family roles that mirrored the upper middle-class European family structure during the late 1800s, with the mother providing love and warmth and the father rules and discipline. It is likely that such families were relatively rare, as upper middle-class children were cared for by servants, and for the most part the poor did not have the time to follow such strict roles. However accurate this characterization was in reality, it has had a profound effect on our thinking about parenting, about the roles of the mother and father within the family, and about the gender-role identification of boys and girls. Prior to Freud, most treatises on parenting emphasized the education and moral development of the child. With Freud's emphasis on the satisfaction of drives came a clearer articulation that the quality of early care would influence later development. Freud's influence on the modern mind should not be underrated, for we cannot really understand the theoretical and empirical literature on parenting since 1900 without understanding how Freud's views permeate our thinking. Our emphasis on providing a sensitive caregiving environment during early childhood, as well as our articulations of family roles, are influenced, either directly by or in opposition to, Freudian thinking.

Freud's (1905/1972) view of sex-role development plays out as a function of the biological sex of the child, not in terms of socialization differences. Freud proposed two types of identification. The first he called *anaclitic* (leaning upon), which is somewhat parallel to what is now called attachment, although Freud believed it occurred because the caregiver satisfied the infant's basic needs, and this type of identification, usually with the mother or some substitute female caregiver, was not differentiated for boys and girls. The second type of identification occurred during the *phallic* period, at around 4 years of age. According to Freud, during this time the child comes to have active sexual desires directed toward the opposite-sex parent. However, it soon becomes clear to the child that the same-sex parent is more powerful than the child, and that the situation must be resolved.

The resolution of this conflict and its outcome are very different for boys and girls. The terms *Oedipal* and *Electra complex* have become almost "pop psychology" in some ways, but the far-reaching implications of the differential resolutions of boys' and girls' conflicts cannot be overstated. The boy—from fear of the father (whom he fears as the aggressor, in general) and through his own fear of castration—resolves his conflict by identifying with the aggressor, and by doing so internalizes the attitudes, behaviors, and moral standards of the male parent. In this way, the boy develops a strong superego and a complete identification with all that is male. For the girl, who has already identified with her mother through anaclitic attachment, the situation is somewhat different. Her phallic identification, which Freud claimed is less complete than that of the boy, takes place through fear of loss of the mother's love. To Freud, the girl never would internalize the female role as completely as males did the male role, because the paralyzing fear of castration, said to be felt by all small boys, was never there. In fact, many male and female differences in Freud's eye came from the differences in resolution of the identification process. From Freud's theory we gain the picture of the girl as incomplete, because she has not gone through the male identification process. This scenario has had a profound influence on psychological thinking about males and females, far beyond the scientific support available for the theory.

The next major influence came from the field of sociology with T. Parsons and Bales (1955), who described the traits they felt characterized male and female family roles. In their view, women are more expressive, nurturant, and emotionally sensitive, and thus should be in charge of management of relationships, of children, and the home. Men are more instrumentally competent, and should therefore be in charge of setting rules, and be employed outside the home. According to Parsons and Bales, such roles are necessary for family life and childrearing. A good deal of empirical work on family relations and parenting has been done to refute the necessity or the benefits of such rigid role structure. In fact, in Terman's (1925) long-term study of successful men and women of the very generation most influenced by these ideas, regrets were expressed in old age by women because they had not used their talents in the world and by men because they had not spent enough time with their families in building relationships (P. S. Sears & Barbee, 1977; R. R. Sears, 1977). Most studies suggest that both men and women have expressive and instrumental qualities and that they are happier when both are expressed.

Sears and his colleagues (R. R. Sears, Maccoby, & Levin, 1957; R. R. Sears, Rau, & Alpert, 1965) reworked Freudian theory within the framework of learning theory. For the first time in one theory, two qualities to parenting, *warmth* and *control*, were made explicit. However, R. Sears' concepts of parenting, influenced by Freud and Parsons, still made the assumption that mothers would provide warmth and emotional support, and fathers discipline and control. Sex-role identification would take place through modeling and reinforcement. In fact, R. Sears' work, like most studies of the time, concentrated mostly on the mother as informant, rendering a view of the father filtered through the eyes of the mother. Throughout the 1950s and 1960s, there were tests of this supposedly optimal family role division, most of which found, first, that such families were in actuality few and far between. And, second, when they existed, they did not appear to function as well as families in which both parents shared expressive and instrumental qualities.

In 1966, two major views of sex-role development were presented. Mischel (1966) updated social learning theory, emphasizing the importance of situational variables in determining the meaning of specific activities. The social learning history of the child was expected to influence cognitive as well as social processes. The social learning history of the child was to influence the child's attitudes as well as behaviors, so that both internal and external processes would contribute to sex-role development. Kohlberg (1966) presented a cognitive developmental view of sex-role development. Kohlberg's work rejuvenated research on sex-role development. Emphasis shifted from the socialization of sex-role by parents to the child's own attempts to understand gender as constructed by society. The child's growing cognitive capacities allowed the construction of increasingly sophisticated gender categories. Although the environment still provided information concerning sex and gender, the primary focus of Kohlberg's theory was the universality of the stages children go through in attempting to understand gender differentiation. In Kohlberg's view, the individual differences in parenting styles and their relation to children's adoptions of gender roles were not so interesting as the underlying stages of cognitive development that led children to adopt society's definitions of sex and gender.

PARENTING STYLES AND CHILD OUTCOMES OTHER THAN GENDER ROLE

Much of the parenting literature in the past 30 years has not dealt with sex-role socialization, but has instead been a search for typologies of parenting. Baumrind (1971) published an extensive and influential reappraisal of parenting in which she concentrated the dimension of parental control to characterize three parenting styles. In Baumrind's work, parental control referred to the attempts of parents to socialize the child into the family and society. All parents do this with more or less success. Baumrind found that children require a balance of control and warmth and are better off when both mothers and fathers give both. She described three styles of parenting in which the types of control varied. The first style of parenting she called *authoritarian*, in which the parent attempts to shape and control the child in accordance with a set standard of conduct. Such parents value obedience, believe in punitive measures to curb the child's self-will, and do not allow discussion about the correctness of the standard. *Authoritative* parents also believe the child should behave in accordance with their rules and standards, but within a context of rational discussion. Such parents encourage communication and share reasons for conduct with the child. Authoritative parents do not see themselves as infallible and are open to change as circumstances change. *Permissive* parents do not place as much emphasis on the child conforming to a set of rules; instead, the child is consulted, and self-regulation by the child is emphasized. The parent is seen as a resource but not necessarily as the final word in setting external standards for the child's behavior. Within each of these parenting types, the parent can vary on warmth, and both the type of control and the use of warmth can influence the child's development. Baumrind argued strongly that authoritative parenting appeared to be a most effective style, in that it gave the child structure but was open to change. However, Baumrind and Black (1967) showed an early recognition that boys and girls may react differently to parenting styles; in conditions of low structure with high emotional warmth, girls appeared to be very competent, whereas boys appeared to be much less competent.

Much of the parenting research of the 1970s consisted of attempts to validate Baumrind's categories and her suggestion that authoritative parenting would be the most effective style of parenting. There has been a great deal of support for this within the well-functioning, middle-class families favored by Baumrind for her research. Recent work also suggested that in high-risk situations, such as urban ghettos, boys in particular might benefit from authoritarian parenting. One problem with using Baumrind's typologies is that many parents do not fit the definitions, and variations within each type are often greater than the differences between types.

Maccoby and J. A. Martin (1983) used R. Sears' initial formulation of warmth and control and Baumrind's emphasis on style of control to attempt a reformulation of parenting, which takes into account all these different components of parenting. Maccoby (1980, 1992) used the *social learning* approach to reformulate parenting into two major divisions: *demandingness* and *responsiveness*. Parents can vary in their demandingness (i.e., the number and types of demands they make on the child) and in their responsiveness to the child's bids for attention. This framework has allowed Maccoby and other researchers to move beyond the types of families studied by Baumrind, into families of divorce, of differing ethnic groups, and so forth. In addition, families are no longer forced into categories that may not fit their individual styles. In more recent writings, Baumrind used the categories of demandingness and responsiveness to define parental characteristics. Present-day theorists often sound very similar to Locke in their call for parents to demand standards of behavior of the child while responding to the individual needs of the child.

In some ways, theorizing about parenting has come full circle. We came from a period in which little attention was paid to socialization differences of boys and girls to one in which a great deal of attention was paid and now are back to theories paying little attention to socialization differences. The reasons for this emphasis are probably multiply determined. Later in the chapter, when we review empirical findings, it becomes clear that the results have been mixed. However, there has also been a paradigm shift in the field of psychology. In the 1960s and early 1970s, social learning theory was very popular, but in the late 1970s and 1980s, cognitive psychology became the dominant paradigm and the emphasis shifted to understanding the capacity of the child to interpret the world. This paradigm shift is mirrored within the literature of gender-role development, with a change from socialization studies to those of the cognitive development underlying gender knowledge. Currently there is an emerging emphasis on neuroscience and the beginnings of a return to biological explanations for gender differences. By the end of this century, the emerging theories concerning parenting may look very different from those espoused today. One thing is certain, researchers must enlarge the theoretical work on parenting beyond the two-parent biological family and examine the multitude of family structures in which children are now being reared.

COMPONENTS OF PARENTING

Broad theoretical approaches provide an outline to try to understand parenting and, in particular, how the sex of the child influences parenting style. However, in order to do the research, it is necessary to define constructs through processes. Three constructs that have been used to study parenting are discussed: family management, scaffolding, and attachment. In addition, differences in the ways each has been applied to the parenting of boys and girls are examined.

Family Management

Patterson (1982; Patterson, Reid, & Dishion, 1992) suggested that four variables are crucial to effective parenting. He called these *family management* variables. First, some parents apply consistent and effective controls on problem behavior; other parents frequently threaten, scold, and natter, but seldom back up their threats with effective action. The variable measuring this family management skill is called *discipline*. Second, some parents carefully track the whereabouts of their children, whereas others do not note any but the most obvious changes in their children's behavior. The variable constructed to measure this skill is called *monitoring*. Third, some parents can negotiate, can solve problems, and can cope with crises arising inside and outside the family; others cannot do these things. The variable that assesses these skills is *problem solving*. A fourth variable is *positive reinforcement*, by which parents reinforce the child for those behaviors they wish to maintain. By employing certain techniques in their own lives, parents inevitably foster these same techniques in their children, well or ill. Children learn to relate to others in part by watching adults relate, to help themselves by watching parents fend for themselves, and to work or learn by watching others do so. Patterson's theory focuses more on the control or demand aspects of parenting, but has the advantage of very clearly defining what processes are behind the general concept of control.

Patterson's concepts were developed within a clinical setting and have been tested mostly on boys. There are clear predictions for boys between lack of monitoring, inept discipline (particularly harsh and abusive discipline), and lack of problem solving to antisocial behavior, delinquency, school failure, and lack of self-esteem (Capaldi & Patterson, 1991; Reid & Patterson, 1989). The dimension of warmth or positive reinforcement has not had a major effect in Patterson's findings. Only recently, however, has this model considered that girls may elicit different management practices than boys. Trying to predict oppositional problem behaviors in children from age 2 to 5, Fagot and Leve (1994) found that, for boys, both parental coercive interactions and the child's own aggressive and non-compliant behaviors at age 2 predicted teachers' ratings of externalizing problem behaviors as the child entered kindergarten at age 5. However, these factors were not predictive for girls, suggesting that a different process must be taking place even though teacher ratings of externalizing problems were very similar for boys and girls. Dishion, Patterson, and Kavanagh (1992) found that a prevention program for young adolescents designed with the family management variables was effective for boys, but not for girls. It is clear that some variable other than discipline and monitoring is important in preventing girls' antisocial behavior. Kavanagh and Hops (1994) examined gender differences in developmental paths to problem behaviors. They found that girls appeared to be more affected by lack of positive behaviors, particularly from the mother. There is some evidence that girls from families that use inept discipline and lack of positive reinforcement provide the same treatment to their own children (Laub & Sampson, 1988). McCord (1988) spoke of such young women as the carriers for the next generation of delinquents.

Scaffolding

Vygotsky (1978) attempted to create a psychology that included the social origins and influences on human cognitive functioning. For Vygotsky, the social world of the child channels development. He emphasized that development occurs in situations where the child's problem solving is guided by an adult who structures and models ways to solve a problem, a process he called *scaffolding*. Adults can arrange the environment so that children can reach a level beyond their present capabilities when working on their own. This is called the *zone of proximal development*, defined as the "distance between the actual developmental level as determined by independent problem solving under adult guidance or in collaboration with more capable peers" (p. 86). The child's individual mental functioning develops through experience in the zone of proximal development. The structure provided serves as a scaffold for learning, providing contact between old and new knowledge. Thus, to understand development, we must attend to formal and informal instruction provided by the parents in the course of the child's daily activities.

Considerable work has been done in this area. Sigel and Cocking (1977) examined the effects of what they labeled *distancing techniques* on the child's competence. Distancing techniques within this model are cognitive strategies parents use to help a child understand a problem. They can range from concrete (such as asking a child to label) to abstract (such as synthesizing new structures for the child). More recently, Rogoff (1990) applied Vygotsky's principles to adults' attempts to provide scaffolds for children's problem solving, a technique described by Rogoff as *guided participation*. Again, the techniques studied constitute cognitive strategies to increase the child's understanding of the problem and to help the child move to a new level of thinking. The work on scaffolding has focused on the responsiveness aspect of parenting. The role of the parent as teacher is recognized, and the dimensions that go into this aspect of parenting have been more carefully defined, so that we have a better idea of the process behind this dimension of parenting.

Rogoff did not concentrate on sex-role behaviors, but she provides examples of ways in which parents teach gender roles as they attempt to teach the child needed skills. Clearly, children learn much about the gender expectations of their cultural role as a function of parents' guided participation. For example, Rogoff (1986) gave a detailed analysis of a Mayan mother guiding her daughter in the process of learning to weave, in which the mother provided the child with gradually increased portions of the whole process. Boys in the Mayan culture receive similar guided learning from their fathers. Rogoff (1990) noted that parents seem to use similar principles in teaching boys and girls, but the content of what they teach is very different. It is often not possible to appreciate guided participation in today's complicated technological environment. However, Fagot observed in rural families in Baja California that both boys and girls received ample amounts of affection and guidance from both parents, and indeed many family tasks were shared, so that all children, from age 2 to 16, participated in the arduous tasks of watering the garden and helping to herd the goats. However, the children were also guided by each parent toward the roles defined by their gender. Girls were helped with kitchen tasks and participated in making the goat cheese, a major source of family income, and boys were introduced to the maintenance of pack animals because guiding is another major source of family income. Children as young as age 2 already had individual tasks within the family. Although they shared in the social work and play of the family, there was no doubt that work roles and hence social roles were defined by sex.

Gauvain and Fagot (1993) examined mothers' attempts to guide toddlers' performance of three problem-solving tasks and found that child characteristics measured by temperament scales influenced the degree of responsiveness and control provided by the mother, but that the sex of the child at this age did not affect the mother's style of interaction. Gauvain, Fagot, and Cupp (1993) examined the teaching styles used by parents in the cognitive laboratory tasks with 5-year-old children. The child came in once with the mother and once with the father and was asked to solve two tasks: copying a puzzle and delivering materials along a route that called for reverse order delivery. The tasks had similar rules but different materials. Mothers and fathers showed more similarity than differences in most dimensions of instruction. Mothers provided more positive emotional support for the child during the task, and fathers provided more rules, but the mean differences were very small and the ranges very wide. Boys and girls were treated in a very similar fashion by both parents. Girls were slightly more likely to be given directions, and boys were slightly more likely to receive negative feedback. For both boys and girls, those who did best on the task had parents who tried to explain the rules and who were supportive of their child's efforts. If the first parent was one who tried to make sure the child understood the underlying rules of the tasks, then the child often explained the task to the second parent rather than waiting for instructions. For both boys and girls, having one parent who explained the rules was sufficient—because they were as competent as children who had both parents explaining rules—as long as both parents were positive and supportive.

Mothers and fathers appear to use very similar teaching styles with boys and girls when given the structure of the laboratory, but the arenas in which they teach in the home may well be very different. Mothers tend to spend more time teaching girls about household tasks (cooking, sewing), but this sort of training is not given to boys as often. In this society, outside of sports, it may be that boys do not receive as much guided participation as do girls, and this may be one of the reasons behind differences in academic and social competencies seen throughout childhood.

Attachment

The third component of parenting that has received a great deal of attention has been that of emotional support, but as noted in the historical review, this component of parenting does not have a long history. The Freudian point of view emphasized the importance of satisfaction of children's drives, but the discussion was mostly in terms of satisfaction of physical rather than emotional needs. This began to change in the 1960s. Harlow and Zimmerman (1959) published their work with infant monkeys and their surrogate mothers. Harlow paired a warm, soft surrogate mother who did not feed the infant monkey with a wire surrogate who fed the infant. If the Freudian view were correct, infants should identify with the nurturant surrogate; but instead, infants went to the warm, soft, cloth mother when they were distressed. Bowlby (1969, 1973) argued that social responsiveness was necessary for development and, without a caregiver who provided warmth and security but also opportunities for social interaction, the child could not develop normally. Bowlby's second important point was that the child developed an internal working model of social relationships from the early caregiving relationship. He called this process *attachment*.

Recent literature in the field of the child and family has emphasized the importance of the attachment relationship. Ainsworth, Blehar, Waters, and Wall (1978) developed the Strange Situation to test individual differences in the patterning of infants' attachment behaviors. This procedure allows the researcher to classify the child's security and reaction patterns toward the mother. Work in this area has related the child's attachment relationship to maternal sensitivity, warmth, and intrusiveness.

There are few reported differences in boys' and girls' attachment classifications or in maternal sensitivity toward boys and girls. However, reports are emerging that there are different antecedents and consequences for boys and girls of different attachment styles. Van den Boom (1989) found that irritable babies, particularly males, were more likely to be classified as insecure and to have problems later on in their development. Fagot and Kavanagh (1993) found differences in parental socialization practices in the home directed toward secure and insecure boys and girls. Boys who were insecure received very little instruction from either the mother or father, whereas girls who were insecure received more instruction from fathers than secure girls, but much less from mothers. Clearly this finding has implications for the predicted effects within different family compositions. Fagot and Kavanagh (1990) found that teachers rated girls who had been classified as insecure-avoidant as having more problems with both the teacher and peers in toddler playgroups. Using the Cassidy and Marvin (1990) preschool measure of attachment, Turner (1991) found that boys who were insecure were more aggressive and disruptive, but insecure girls were more dependent than secure children. With the same group of children, Turner (1993) also found that insecure children directed more dependency requests toward teachers. Insecure boys' requests were ignored, whereas insecure girls were given more help than secure children. Both children and teachers used the sex of the child to influence their behaviors toward boys and girls, even when the boys and girls were engaging in similar behaviors.

Summary

Most of the research described in this section on the components of parenting has come from work done in the United States, and not much attention has been paid to social class, ethnic, or religious differences. The exception to this has been the work on scaffolding, which has always used cross-cultural data to illustrate guided participation. There has been a recent increase in studies examining parenting processes within different groups in the United States, and perhaps 5 years from now our knowledge concerning the components of parenting will be expanded. In addition to the lack of information beyond white middle-class families, there has not really been an examination of different pathways for boys and girls. This makes it difficult to draw too many conclusions on similarities and differences in these basic components in parenting, because we simply do not have enough information. Most researchers look at mean differences and, if they find none, analyze all data together; however, they may be overlooking important interactions between the sex of the child and the type of parenting that manifests in terms of different pathways.

PARENTING AND GENDER-ROLE SOCIALIZATION

There are numerous anecdotes in the developmental literature on the strength of societal stereotypes concerning gender. Any parent who has tried to raise a child to feel free to sample broad ranges of activities knows the deadening effect of the peer group, the media, and the way that society is structured on children's attempts to try. The daughter of one of my graduate students announced that women could not fix things around the house even though she knew her mother had made her living as a carpenter prior to returning to graduate school, and my son came home after 2 days in preschool to announce that he could not grow up to teach seminars (previously his lifelong ambition, because he knew from personal observation that everyone at seminars got to eat cookies) because only women could be teachers; these examples make clear the limitations placed on development by societal gender rules. The next section addresses the ways parenting relates to our stereotypical views of what mothers and fathers do and what boys and girls are like.

Differences in Parenting by Mothers and Fathers

The traditional view of the family is one of the mother providing warmth and caregiving and the father providing discipline and support (T. Parsons & Bales, 1955). These characterizations of family life do not appear to describe parenting today and probably never did. Although mothers do spend more time with their children than fathers, and this is as true of mothers who work outside the home as those who spend their days at home with the children (Pederson, 1980), the roles of present day-mothers and fathers appear to have evolved somewhat differently. Mothers do most of the routine caregiving, but the father's role is not that of the abstract disciplinarian; instead, the father appears to have taken over many of the qualities of playmate. Lamb (1977, 1981) found that it was play time when fathers spent time with toddler-age children. Children were returned to the mother whenever they needed some type of care.

Block (1976) suggested that fathers will be more important to the sex-role development of children than mothers and they will interact with boys and girls in very different ways, whereas mothers will react in similar ways to boys and girls. She based this suggestion in part on Johnson' *reciprocal role theory* (1963, 1975), which predicts that the father's behavior will promote typically sex-typed behavior in both boys and girls. Whereas both mothers and fathers are expected to encourage traditional sex typing, fathers will make greater distinctions between sons and daughters. Boys will be sought out by the father and will be encouraged to take on an instrumental, independent style of behavior, whereas girls will be encouraged to seek help and to be more dependent.

Siegel (1987) examined 39 studies on differential socialization and concluded that some support exists for the uniqueness of the father's role. Fathers were more likely to show sex-specific differences than mothers; however, the direction of the effects was contradictory among the studies, so it is difficult to interpret the findings. For example, with 1- and 2-year-old children, Weinraub and Frankel (1977) reported fathers talking more to sons, whereas Stoneman and Brody (1981) reported that fathers spoke more to daughters. These studies suggest that fathers may be more variable than mothers in responses to their children. Thus, researchers are more likely to find that fathers differ in their responses to boys and girls, but this may be a statistical artifact of greater variability, rather than a finding based on a consistent paternal mode of responding.

Mothers spend far more time with their children, do most of the caregiving, and if the family breaks up, are far more likely to rear children as single parents. There is some movement within the middle class for more involvement of the father within the family. But even in families choosing an egalitarian type of childrearing in which both parents are employed outside the home, mothers continue to do most of the caregiving (Fagot & Leinbach, in press). Consequently, when one looks at parenting variables that predict future performance of the child either in the social or cognitive realm, mother variables in most studies tend to be stronger predictors than father variables. Father absence does predict problems for the child, but studies of this phenomenon tend to be highly confounded with lack of economic well-being and increased social stress, so it is difficult to know whether it is father absence or other variables that predict negative outcome. More research is necessary with fathers (Phares & Compas, 1992); but maternal variables tend to show stronger relations to children's problem behaviors than do paternal variables (Patterson et al., 1992).

Much of our information concerning the role of fathers comes from mothers. What we know directly from fathers is biased toward well-educated fathers and concerns interactions in infancy and early childhood. Recent articles from several researchers have found minimal support for the uniqueness of the father's role. Whereas fathers in some studies played physically with boys more frequently than with girls and were more consistent in their encouragement of sex-typed toys, there was only modest support for a differential effect on other sex-role variables. Differences, when they were found, were more likely to occur with respect to reported attitudes about the differences between boys and girls than in differences in behavior toward boys and girls. The role of the father in the child's life after school entry and on into adolescence and adulthood has not been studied.

Block (1976) suggested that, because preschool-age children were overrepresented in the literature reviewed by Maccoby and Jacklin (1974), the role of parental socialization might be underestimated; she hypothesized that sex-role socialization should increase with age. Lytton and Romney (1991) found that there were more studies showing parent treatment differences in the younger ages. In addition, mother and father differences were found more often in higher quality studies, particularly those involving observations of parent-child interactions. Lytton and Romney also found that the only consistent sex-differentiated parental reaction was in encouragement of sex-typed behaviors.

The Child's Input to Gender-Role Socialization

Some of the variability in early gender knowledge may be due to differences in children's rates of cognitive development, but social influences, including the father's responses, are also implicated. Fagot and Leinbach (1989) studied gender labeling and children's adoption of sex-typed behaviors in a longitudinal study of gender labeling, behavior, and parenting variables. At the 18-month observations (prior to acquisition of gender labeling), boys and girls did not differ on any of five behavior patterns for which sex differences have often been found (large motor activity, male-typed toy play, female-typed toy play, communication attempts, aggression). At 27 months, when half the children could label gender, the early labeling children of both sexes played more with sex-typical toys, and early labeling girls spent more time in communication with adults and showed less aggression than late-labeling girls or either group of boys.

When the children were 18 months old, prior to label acquisition or observed sex differences in the five behaviors, both fathers and mothers of the children who would become early labelers responded to sex-typical behavior with both more positive and more negative reactions; that is, they were giving more emotionally charged feedback when the child was engaged in sex-typical behavior. Fathers of early-labeling children gave more traditionally sex-typed responses on both the Attitude Toward Women Scale (Spence, Helmrich, & Stapp, 1973) and the Traditionality Scale of the Child Rearing Practices Report (Block, 1965). Fagot, Leinbach, and O'Boyle (1992) investigated the extent to which gender labeling and gender stereotyping in 24-, 30-, and 36-month-old children related to each other and to the mothers' sex-role attitudes and responses to sex-typed behavior in a free-play situation with their children. It was first established that children who understood labels for boys and girls displayed more knowledge of gender stereotypes than children who did not. Mothers whose children had mastered labels for boys and girls endorsed more traditional attitudes toward women and toward sex roles within the family. The same mothers also initiated and reinforced more sex-typed toy play with their children.

Weinraub et al. (1984) investigated several aspects of early sex typing, including gender identity, gender labeling, sex-typed toy preferences, and awareness of sex-role stereotypes in children between 26 and 36 months of age, and intercorrelations among the various forms of early gender knowledge and a number of family variables. Gender labeling (identifying pictures of two men, two women, two boys, and two girls by producing appropriate labels and by sorting) and sex-role stereotyping (sorting eight pictures representing sex-typed occupational activities and eight pictures of adults' clothing and possessions) were seen in 26-month-old children (the youngest age tested) and found in the majority of 36-month-olds. Stereotypic sorting of eight pictures of children's toys was not found before 31 months. Children as young as 26 months showed sex-typed toy preferences, with those who could label themselves correctly spending more time with sex-typed toys. Fathers' sex-typed personality traits, their attitudes about sex roles, and their records of their own activities in their children's presence were correlated with several of the indices of gender knowledge in their children, but mothers' attitudes and activities were not correlated.

Whether parents provide differential socialization for boys and girls is a question that has been debated for a number of years. The other side of the question is whether boys and girls respond differently to parents' attempts to socialize them. The results of the Maccoby and Jacklin (1974) review, as well as the Lytton and Romney (1991) meta-analysis, convince us that looking for sex-differentiated socialization in all parent reactions will not help us understand sex-role development or differences in boys and girls. The Lytton and Romney analysis strongly suggests that age is a crucial variable and that the way we define and measure parent reactions and child behaviors will affect the outcome of our studies. The question also needs to be asked within an interactive framework. A model for this is found in J. A. Martin (1981) and in J. A. Martin, Maccoby, and Jacklin (1981), in which there are careful attempts to define both the child's behavior and the nature of the parental response.

As mentioned earlier, the process by which infants are exposed to gender information begins at birth; differential treatment by sex starts as soon as the infant's sex is known—with color-coded blankets in the nursery and presents that very clearly designate the sex of the child. The so-called Baby-X studies are often cited as showing that parents begin to show sex-differentiated attitudes from an early age (Rubin et al., 1974). When parents are asked to describe their newborns, they do so in very sex-stereotyped terms. In a variation of these studies, a baby is dressed in unisex clothes; individuals are told that the child is either a boy or girl and asked to describe the child. In another variation, individuals are shown the same baby dressed as a boy or a girl and asked to describe the child. The findings across these studies are quite consistent. Babies thought to be boys are described as tough and sturdy, whereas those thought to be girls are described as frail and sweet (J. Condry & S. Condry, 1976).

In contrast to these studies are the inconsistent findings from laboratory studies. In a series of studies examining mother–infant interaction prior to 6 months of age, Bornstein and his colleagues found little indication of sex differences in either the infants' behaviors or the mothers' behaviors directed to the infants. These studies examined language interaction as well as other types of stimulation (Bornstein & Tamis-LeMonda, 1990; Bornstein et al., 1992), and found they were similar for boys and girls. On the other hand, in studies of emotional responsiveness, mothers of babies and toddlers were reported to be more emotionally responsive to daughters (Cherry & Lewis, 1976; Maccoby, Snow, & Jacklin, 1984; Maletesta, Culver, Tesman, & Shepard, 1989). Yet in the attachment studies using the Strange Situation, which is certainly emotionally arousing, no maternal sex-determined differences in response to boys and girls were found. Nor have attachment studies found differences in attachment classifications between boys and girls. The interaction of attitudes and actual behaviors as they impinge on rearing boys and girls remains a rich area to study.

In an attempt to examine sex-determined socialization within a broader age group, Fagot and Hagan (1991) examined behavioral differences in mothers' and fathers' reactions toward boys and girls at three different ages (12 months, 18 months, and 5 years) in a study of actual behaviors, not parent attitudes. Home observations were chosen as the best method to look at socialization differences for several reasons. Lytton and Romney found that observational studies of parental socialization showed the greatest differences between mothers and fathers. Home observations allow both the children and the parents to react more naturally than do more tightly controlled laboratory studies. Although it is true that boys and girls have different sets of toys, as shown by Rheingold and Cook (1975), male- and female-typed behaviors were defined very broadly in this study, and there was no home in which it would have been impossible for the child to engage in both types of behaviors.

To examine differential socialization of boys and girls by mothers and fathers, home observations were completed for families of 92 12-month-old children, 82 18-month-old children, and 172 5-year-old children. In this study, parents' reactions to boys and girls' behaviors were examined, particularly those found to be sex-typed in previous studies. Differences in mothers' and fathers' styles of interaction emerged; for instance, mothers gave more instructions and directions than did fathers, and fathers spent more time in positive play interaction. There were also differences in parents' reactions to 12- and 18-month-old boys and girls; most differences were quite expected, with the exception that boys received more negative comments for attempts to communicate than did girls. It has been suggested in the literature that fathers would be more involved in sex typing than mothers, but that was not confirmed in this study, with the one significant exception that fathers gave fewer positive reactions to boys engaged in female-typical toy play at 18 months. Sex-role socialization, as defined by differential reactions to sex-typed behaviors, appears to be more prevalent when parents are reacting to very young children.

Parenting and Gender Deviancy

Early studies of boys who showed extremely feminine behaviors simply assumed the Freudian influenced model of identification within a pathogenic family (Bieber et al., 1962). Indeed, much of the research assumes that the boy must learn to denigrate the female, to downplay the competence of the mother, and to take on parts of the masculine role that are not really very admirable (Green, 1987). In some other approaches, this is much more explicit and done in more punative fashion (Rekers, 1982). The long-term prospective study by Green (1987), comparing a group of boys identified as very feminine with a nonfeminized control group, found almost no consistent differences in parental treatment between the clinical and control groups. Zucker and Green (1992) made it clear that gender deviancy is a process that appears to be interrelated with the child's temperament, appearance, physical health, and parental treatment rather than resulting from some specific parenting practices.

Summary

Summarizing the findings concerning differences in mothers' and fathers' socialization of boys and girls is difficult, as we are still working with a very small sampling of parenting behaviors. However, some findings are emerging. First, it is clear that gender stereotypes are applied to children as soon as they are born; that is, the perception of appearance, behavior, personality, and temperament are influenced by the supposed sex of the child. In the absence of other information, gender is used as a category to generate descriptive statements about the child. Parents and others will provide an environment for the child that is gender proscriptive from birth on; that is, choice of clothes, toys, and playmates will be influenced by the child's sex. However, the more familiar one is with the child, the more the individual child's own appearance, behavior, personality, and temperament will influence the response of others to that child. Therefore, mothers, and probably fathers, when placed in a situation where they are called on to react to their infant or young child, will use the child cues to guide their behaviors. Few consistent sex differences in infants' and young children's behaviors have been found, so there are few consistent sex-determined socialization practices by their parents. Sex of the child does influence socialization, especially during transitions, and the very structure of the child's physical environment will be determined by the child's sex. As the child grows older, work and play roles will be further differentiated by sex, but parents will continue to react in structured situations in ways more determined by the child's own individuality than by the child's sex. As with most questions in psychology, the old question of whether boys and girls are treated differently by their parents cannot be answered with a yes or no, for it depends on the age of the child, the method of study, the social class, and all those other variables that make the study of social development so difficult, but also so interesting.

FAILURES OF PARENTING FOR BOYS AND GIRLS

There is great concern today about the failure of the family and hence the failure of parenting. We have reports of differential rates and types of abuse of young boys and girls. Straus, Gelles, and Steinmetz (1980) reported that boys are more likely to be physically abused and girls are more likely to be sexually abused.

There is also a good deal of information concerning boys' and girls' developmental paths of adjustment, particularly after the age of 4. During childhood, boys are seen to have more adjustment problems (Earls, 1987; Eme, 1979). By adolescence, however, girls show increasing adjustment problems (McGee et al., 1990), and by adulthood, prevalence rates for affective disorders are 2:1, females to males (Nolen-Hoeksema, 1987). Although there is some indication that boys do not respond as well to attempts to parent, behavioral studies find fewer differences than do attitude studies. Stronger relations between temperament and problems have been reported for males (Prior, Smart, Sanson, & Oberklaid, 1993), and parenting variables have predicted problems in boys but not girls (Dishion et al., 1992; Fagot, 1993). Girls' adjustment in childhood has been widely ignored, because they appear to have fewer problems. Throughout childhood, more boys than girls are referred for treatment, but by middle adolescence, boys and girls are encountering difficulties at equal rates, although girls are more likely to be internalizing and referred to mental health facilities, whereas boys are seen for externalizing problems both in mental health facilities and through juvenile justice services. It is only very recently that there has been a call for understanding the complicated relations between parenting variables and psychopathology for both sexes (Zahn-Waxler, 1993).

TRANSITIONS IN THE FAMILY: EFFECTS ON BOYS AND GIRLS

The literature on family transitions (divorce and remarriage) is itself in transition. The early literature on divorce suggested that girls were more buffered than boys against change (Hetherington, M. Cox, & R. Cox, 1978, 1982). After an initial period of conflict, mothers and daughters settled into supportive relationships, but mothers and sons remained more conflicted. In turn, the early adjustment of girls of divorced families appeared to be no different from that of girls in two-parent families, but boys continued to have problems. Hetherington, Anderson, and Hagan (1989) reported that individual characteristics of the child were as important to adjustment as the sex of the child, and that some of the reported sex differences may have been overstated. Early divorce studies examined young children. Once adolescents were studied, the whole picture of family transitions began to change (Hetherington, 1987, 1989). Hetherington and Clingempeel (1992) found that young adolescent girls in divorced and step-parent families were having many difficulties adjusting to the new family environment, although the pattern of their problems was somewhat different from boys, showing less of the disruptive behaviors associated with boys and more internalizing problems. Hetherington (1993) found complicated relations between gender and family type in children's adjustment to transition. She found that stepfathers and early adolescent girls did not mix well, with high conflict in such families and stepfathers seeing the girl as quite disturbed. Teachers tended to see boys from nontraditional families as having more problems, but parents saw girls as equally problematic. This literature suggests that our understanding of family processes in nontraditional families is quite limited.

FUTURE DIRECTIONS

In the late 1970s and early 1980s, there were serious discussions of how one might free the child from gender restrictions. Greenberg (1978) wrote a practical guide to nonsexist childrearing, suggesting to parents that gender roles were extremely confining and that childrearing should be directed toward the interests and skills of the particular child rather than dictated by sex. Bem (1983) discussed rearing a gender aschematic child in a gender schematic world. At that point, there appeared to be a genuine trend toward unisex clothes for children and a de-emphasis on sex-typed toys. However, in the world of the 1990s, sex typing has returned. There are now pink and blue diapers, and woe to the parent who runs out of one and uses the wrong color diaper on the wrong sex child. Does this backlash in the world of advertising mean that children are being reared in the more sex-typed fashion of the 1950s? Apparently not, if we look at career choices among girls or participation in sports; however, there certainly has been a backlash against feminism (Faludi, 1991). Young college women and men will insist that they are not feminists, but they often turn out to be very liberal in their gender-role attitudes, particularly the women. For many of these women, there is simply no question that they will have careers or at least jobs, and they fail to endorse the double standard in every mode of life. If we compare their attitudes with those of feminists in the 1970s, they appear very similar. What might this mean for the socialization of the next generation of children? These are the children of the first generation of feminists. These are the children of mothers and fathers who have tried to practice nonsexist childrearing. In some ways this appears to have been successful; their children accept the idea that men and women will have similar roles in society. But how they will transmit gender knowledge to the next generation is unknown.

The next decade promises to be fascinating in terms of understanding the underlying processes of individual differences in parenting. We suddenly have many new technologies available to study process. First, the availability of new methods to study brain functions should permit a view of some underlying biological processes that may lead to different parenting styles. Second, the availability of good, inexpensive video facilities has increased the chance of understanding behavioral processes. Third, computer graphics have reached the point where it is possible to simulate situations and present standard stimuli to both parents and children to study parenting processes. Finally, the statistical tools necessary to study complex interactional processes have been developed within the last decade so that it is possible to handle the complex data that come from the multimethod designs that are becoming more common in studying family socialization. The study of parenting boys and girls should particularly benefit from these new technologies for there is the opportunity to understand just what both the child and the parent contribute to the process at several different levels.

In addition to new technologies, our understanding of normative development has grown so that it is now possible to see how environmental stimuli affect a known ongoing process. One of the real difficulties with many older studies is that one was never sure whether the research manipulations were appropriate for the age of children being tested. One example of this was the use of rather complicated questions with young children concerning their gender-role knowledge. The results of these studies made it appear that 2- and 3-year-olds were quite naive in terms of cultural knowledge concerning gender. Once age-appropriate tests were designed that did not ask for abstract verbal performance, it became clear that even 2-year-old children are quite sophisticated about some components of the cultural gender schema (Fagot & Leinbach, 1993).

The increasing ability to do good empirical work and the emphasis on components of parenting—such as family management, scaffolding, and attachment—should contribute to the development of new theories of parenting and family socialization. At this point, the field is quite scattered, with a number of small mini-theories being tested. There has been a tendency by people working within each paradigm to ignore work in other paradigms, a situation that has not been helpful for understanding family processes. At this point, some rapprochement is beginning among the different paradigms.

In addition, depending on the type of statistical approach used, the findings may vary within the same sample. For example in a recently completed study by Fagot and Leve (1994), we found no mean differences in girls' and boys' behavior at age 2 and 5 on several methods used to measure oppositional behaviors, and we found few mean differences in parents' behavior directed toward the children. However, when we employed regression techniques to predict teacher ratings of boys' and girls' oppositional behaviors at age 5 from the parents' and children's behaviors at age 2, we found very different patterns. Despite the lack of mean differences in boys' and girls' behaviors at age 5, teacher ratings of boys' oppositional behavior was highly correlated with poor academic progress, off-task behavior in problem-solving tasks, and problems with peers. For girls who are rated oppositional by the teachers, none of the academic, peer, or problem-solving behaviors were relevant, but they scored lower on self-esteem. Future studies need to investigate the interaction between sex of the child and predictor and outcome variables, and examine mean differences.

CONCLUSIONS

Traditional gender differences are perhaps summed up by the nursery rhyme that girls are made of "sugar and spice and everything nice," whereas boys are "snips and snails and puppy dog tails." How much has changed in the last 30 years? In the everyday lives of men and women, things are quite different. The nuclear family in which both biological parents live with their offspring is now in the minority. The family where the father works outside the home while the mother is not employed outside the home is even more rare, yet over the past 30 years children show little change in their gender stereotypes (Leinbach & Hort, 1989). Will this next generation of children begin to reflect cultural changes in their thinking about what it means to be a boy or girl? This question can be answered only if we believe that parenting of boys and girls has changed, and the evidence for such change is very slim. In fact, with the advent of knowing the sex of the child prior to birth have come studies showing that mothers apply gender stereotypes to movement patterns in utero (Beal, 1993).

Although good parenting is similar for both sexes, transitions and variations in parenting styles and family styles may have different consequences for boys and girls. It may be more difficult at certain ages to be a boy or girl, and the culture may push in different directions, but all indications are that the same authoritative, reasoned, controlled, and responsive parenting is most effective for both boys and girls. Parents should also realize they can provide a good start for children, but society and changing times can interfere with the best laid plans. A parent may prefer that a child not be gender stereotyped, but the effects of peer groups, television, school, and all the other influences will push toward gender stereotyping. As a parent, it is perhaps best to retain one's sense of humor and remember that research shows that, in the long run, children tend to adopt the values, attitudes, and beliefs that parents instill in them.

Has the central question concerning the role of parents in creating differences between boys and girls been answered? No, it is alive and well, and perhaps Bem's (1993) The Lenses of Gender will rekindle the whole debate. However, we know more about parenting in several domains, and perhaps with careful examination of methods and terminology, some sense may be made of the contradictory findings. One prototype for this research might be the work on math achievement done by J. E. Parsons, Adler, and Kaczala (1982), who found that, for girls, math achievement appeared to be predicted by parental attitudes rather than parental behaviors. It may be that some child outcomes are best predicted by attitudes, whereas others are best predicted by behaviors. More careful work defining both predictors and outcomes is needed. More attention also needs to be paid to cultural differences within societies, as well as cross-cultural differences. Goodnow (in this Handbook) argues that boys and girls are given different tasks and activities and that the action of doing or practicing these tasks in effect defines roles, including gender roles. Finally, the last 15 years have brought a welcomed emphasis on the contribution of the child to the socialization process. With much of the work emphasizing gender as a cognitive variable, we can now appreciate that gender differentiation, once begun, needs very little input from the environment to maintain differentiation between the sexes.

We continue to find that similar treatment of boys and girls does not necessarily lead to similar outcomes. We know that deviations from balanced warmth and control in parent–child relationships have different consequences for boys and girls. We also know that boys and girls have reacted quite differently to the changing family norms of the last half century. Parenting is never an easy task, and the guidelines of yesterday are not as relevant for childrearing today. This may be a blessing or a curse, for both boys and girls, as we move to different definitions of family and parenting; only time will tell. The next decade should be an exciting time for researchers, as new technologies and integrated knowledge from different paradigms provide a rich environment to study the parenting process and to better understand the similarities and differences in the ways that parents rear their boys and girls.

ACKNOWLEDGMENTS

Research and preparation of this chapter were supported by grant MH 37911 from the Behavioral Sciences Research Branch, Family Processes Division, NIMH, and grant HD 19739 from the Center for Research for Mothers and Children, NICHD.

REFERENCES

Ainsworth, M.D.S., Blehar, M. C., Waters, E., & Wall, S. (1978). *Patterns of attachment: A psychological study of the Strange Situation*. Hillsdale, NJ: Lawrence Erlbaum Associates.

Baumrind, D. (1971). Current patterns of parental authority. *Developmental Psychology Monograph, 4*(1, Pt. 2).

Baumrind, D., & Black, A. E. (1967). Socialization practices associated with dimensions of competence in preschool boys and girls. *Child Development, 38*, 291–327.

Beal, C. R. (1993). *Boys and girls: The development of gender roles*. New York: McGraw-Hill.

Bem, S. L. (1981). Gender schema theory: A cognitive account of sex typing. *Psychological Review, 88*, 354–364.

Bem, S. L. (1983). Gender schema theory and its implications for child development: Raising gender-aschematic children in a gender-schematic world. *Signs: Journal of Women in Culture and Society, 8*, 598–616.

Bem, S. L. (1993). *The lenses of gender: Transforming the debate on sexual inequality*. New Haven, CT: Yale University Press.

Bieber, I., Dain, H., Dince, P., Drellich, M., Grand, H., Gundlach, R., Kremer, M., Rifkin, A., Wilbur, C., & Bieber, T. (1962). *Homosexuality: A psycholoanalytic study of male homosexuals*. New York: Basic Books.

Block, J. H. (1965). *Child rearing practices report: A set of items for the description of parental socialization and values*. (Available from Institute of Human Development, University of California, Berkeley, CA 94720).

Block, J. H. (1976). Issues, problems, and pitfalls in assessing sex differences: A critical review of the psychology of sex differences. *Merrill-Palmer Quarterly, 22*, 283–308.

Block, J. H. (1983). Differential premises arising from differential socialization of the sexes: Some conjectures. *Child Development, 54*, 1335–1354.

Bornstein, M. H., Tal, J., Rahn, C., Galperin, C. A., Pecheux, M. G., Lamour, M., Toda, S., Azuma, H., Ogino, M., & Tamis-Lemonda, C. S. (1992). Functional analysis of the contents of maternal speech to infants of 5 and 13 months in four cultures: Argentina, France, Japan, and the United States. *Developmental Psychology, 28*, 593–603.

Bornstein, M. H., & Tamis-LeMonda, C. S. (1990). Activities and interactions of mothers and their firstborn infants in the first six months of life: Covariation, stability, continuity, correspondence, and prediction. *Child Development, 61*, 1206–1217.

Bowlby, J. (1969). *Attachment and loss: Vol. 1. Attachment*. London: Hogarth.

Bowlby, J. (1973). *Attachment and loss: Vol. 2. Separation: Anxiety and anger*. London: Hogarth.

Caldera, Y. M., Huston, A. C., & O'Brien, M. (1989). Social interactions and play patterns of parents and toddlers with feminine, masculine, and neutral toys. *Child Development, 60*, 70–76.

Capaldi, D., & Patterson, G. R. (1991). Relation of parental transitions to boys' adjustment problems: I. A linear hypothesis. II. Mothers at risk for transitions and unskilled parenting. *Developmental Psychology, 27*, 489–504.

Cassidy, J., & Marvin, R. (1990). *Attachment organization in preschool children: Coding guidelines*. Seattle: MacArthur Working Group on Attachment.

Cherry, L. J., & Lewis, M. (1976). Mothers and two-year olds: A study of sex-differentiated aspects of verbal interaction. *Child Development, 46*, 532–535.

Condry, J., & Condry, S. (1976). Sex differences: A study of the eye of the beholder. *Child Development, 47,* 812-819.

Dishion, T. J., Patterson, G. R., & Kavanagh, K. (1992). An experimental test of the coercion model: Linking theory, measurement, and intervention. In J. McCord & R. Trembley (Eds.), *The interaction of theory and practice: Experimental studies of interventions* (pp. 253–282). New York: Guilford.

Earls, F. (1987). Sex differences in psychiatric disorders: Origins and developmental influences. *Psychiatric Developments, 1,* 1–23.

Eme, R. F. (1979). Sex differences in psychopathology: A review. *Psychological Bulletin, 86,* 574–595.

Fagot, B. I. (1993, February). *Prediction of behavior problems at age 5 from age 2: Should we identify children or parents?* Paper presented at the Society for Research in Child and Adolescent Psychopathology, Santa Fe, NM.

Fagot, B. I., & Hagan, R. (1991). Observations of parent reactions to sex–stereotyped behaviors: Age and sex effects. *Child Development, 62,* 617–628.

Fagot, B. I., & Kavanagh, K. (1990). The prediction of antisocial behavior from avoidant attachment classifications. *Child Development, 61,* 864–873.

Fagot, B. I., & Kavanagh, K. (1993). Parenting during the second year: Influences of age, sex of child, and attachment classification. *Child Development, 63,* 258–271.

Fagot, B. I., & Leinbach, M. D. (1989). The young child's gender schema: Environmental input, internal organization. *Child Development, 60,* 663–672.

Fagot, B. I., & Leinbach, M. D. (1993). Gender-role development in young children: From discrimination to labeling. *Developmental Review, 13,* 203–224.

Fagot, B. I., & Leinbach, M. D. (in press). Gender knowledge in egalitarian and traditional families. *Sex Roles.*

Fagot, B. I., & Leve, L. S. (1994). *Prediction of oppositional behavior from early childhood to school entry.* Manuscript under review.

Fagot, B. I., Leinbach, M. D., & O'Boyle, C. (1992). Gender labeling, gender stereotyping, and parenting behaviors. *Developmental Psychology, 28,* 225–230.

Faludi, S. (1991). *Backlash: The undeclared war against American women.* New York: Crown.

Freud, S. (1972). *Three essays on the theory of sexuality* (J. Strachey, Ed.). New York: Avon Books. (Original work published 1905)

Gauvain, M., & Fagot, B. I. (1993). *Child temperament as a mediator of mother–toddler problem solving.* Unpublished manuscript.

Gauvain, M., Fagot, B. I., & Cupp, R. (1993). *Guidance and support by mothers and fathers during problem solving with 5-year olds.* Unpublished manuscript.

Green, R. (1987). *The "sissy boy syndrome" and the development of homosexuality.* New Haven, CT: Yale University Press.

Greenberg, S. (1978). *Right from the start: A guide to nonsexist child rearing.* Boston: Houghton Mifflin.

Harlow, H. F., & Zimmerman, R. R. (1959). Affectional responses in the infant monkey. *Science, 130,* 421–423.

Hetherington, E. M. (1987). Family relations six years after divorce. In K. Pasley & M. Ihinger-Tallman (Eds.), *Remarriage and stepparenting: Current research and theory* (pp. 185–205). New York: Guilford.

Hetherington, E. M. (1989). Coping with family transitions: Winners, losers, and survivors. *Child Development, 60,* 1–14.

Hetherington, E. M. (1993). An overview of the Virginia longitudinal study of divorce and remarriage with a focus on early adolescence. *Journal of Family Psychology, 7,* 39–56.

Hetherington, E. M., Anderson, S. R., & Hagan, M. S. (1989). Marital transitions: A child's perspective. *American Psychologist, 44,* 303–312.

Hetherington, E. M., & Clingempeel, W. G. (1992). Coping with marital transitions: A family systems perspective. *Monographs of the Society for Research in Child Development, 57* (2–3, Serial No. 227).

Hetherington, E. M., Cox, M., & Cox, R. (1978). The aftermath of divorce. In J. H. Stevens & M. Matthews (Eds.), *Mother–child, father–child relations* (pp. 110–155). Washington, DC: National Association on Education of Young Children.

Hetherington, E. M., Cox, M., & Cox, R. (1982). Effects of divorce on parents and children. In M. E. Lamb (Ed.), *Nontraditional families* (pp. 233–288). Hillsdale, NJ: Lawrence Erlbaum Associates.

Huston, A. C. (1983). Sex-typing. In E. M. Hetherington (Vol. Ed.) & P. H. Mussen (Series Ed.), *Handbook of child development: Vol. 4: Socialization, personality, and social development* (pp. 387–467). New York: Wiley.

Johnson, M. M. (1963). Sex role learning in the nuclear family. *Child Development, 34,* 315–333.

Johnson, M. M. (1975). Fathers, mothers, and sex typing. *Sociological Inquiry, 45,* 15–26.

Kavanagh, K., & Hops, H. (1994). Good girls? Bad boys? Gender and development as contexts for diagnosis and treatment. In T. M. Ollendick & R. J. Prinz (Eds.), *Advances in clinical child psychology* (Vol. 16, pp. 41–79). New York: Plenum.

Kohlberg, L. A. (1966). A cognitive developmental analysis of children's sex-role concepts and attitudes. In E. E. Maccoby (Ed.), *The development of sex differences* (pp. 82–172). Stanford, CA: Stanford University Press.

Lamb, M. E. (1977). Father–infant and mother–infant interaction in the first year of life. *Child Development, 48,* 167–181.

Lamb, M. E. (1981). The development of father–infant relationships. In M. E. Lamb (Ed.), *The role of the father in child development* (rev. ed., pp. 459–488). New York: Wiley.

Langlois, J. H., & Downs, C. (1980). Mothers, fathers, and peers as socialization agents of sex-typed play behavior in young children. *Child Development, 51,* 1217–1247.

Laub, J. H., & Sampson, R. J. (1988). Unraveling families and delinquency: A reanalysis of the Glueck's data. *Criminology*, *26*, 355–379.

Leinbach, M. D., & Hort, B. (1989, April). *Bears are for boys: "Metaphorical" associations in the young child's gender schema.* Paper presented at Biennial Meeting of the Society for Research in Child Development, Kansas City, MO.

Locke, J. (1964). *Some thoughts concerning education* (abridged ed.; F. W. Garforth, Ed.) Woodbury, NJ: Barron's Educational Series. (Original work published 1693)

Lytton, H., & Romney, D. M. (1991). Parents' sex-related differential socialization of boys and girls: A meta-analysis. *Psychological Bulletin, 109*, 267–296.

Maccoby, E. E. (1980). *Social development: Psychological growth and the parent–child relationship.* New York: Harcourt Brace.

Maccoby, E. E. (1992). The role of parents in the socialization of children: An historical overview. *Developmental Psychology, 28*, 1006–1017.

Maccoby, E. E., & Jacklin, C. N. (1974). *The psychology of sex differences.* Stanford, CA: Stanford University Press.

Maccoby, E. E., & Martin, J. A. (1983). Socialization in the context of the family. In E. M. Hetherington (Vol. Ed.) & P. H. Mussen (Series Ed.), *Handbook of child development: Vol. 4. Socialization, personality, and social development* (pp. 1–101). New York: Wiley.

Maccoby, E. E., Snow, M. E., & Jacklin, C. N. (1984). Children's dispositions and mother–child interaction at 12 and 18 months: A short-term longitudinal study. *Developmental Psychology, 20*, 459–472.

Malatesa, C. Z., Culver, C., Tesman, J. R., & Shepard, B. (1989). The development of emotion expression during the first two years of life. *Monographs of the Society for Research in Child Development, 54*(1–2, Serial No. 219).

Martin, C. L. (1993). New directions for investigating children's gender knowledge. *Developmental Review, 13*, 184–204.

Martin, C. L., & Halverson, C. F. (1981). A schematic processing model of sex typing and stereotyping in children. *Child Development, 52*, 1119–1134.

Martin, J. A. (1981). A longitudinal study of the consequences of early mother interaction: A microanalytic approach. *Monographs of the Society for Research in Child Development, 46*(Serial No. 190).

Martin, J. A., Maccoby, E. E., & Jacklin, C. N. (1981). Mothers' responsiveness to interactive bidding and nonbidding in boys and girls. *Child Development, 52*, 1064–1067.

McCord, J. (1988). Parental behavior in the cycle of aggression. *Psychiatry, 51*, 14–23.

McGee, R., Feehan, M., Williams, S., Partridge, F., Silva, P. A., & Kelly, J. (1990). DSM-III disorders in a large sample of adolescents. *Journal of the American Academy of Child and Adolescent Psychopathology, 29*, 611–619.

Mead, M. (1935). *Sex and temperament in three primitive cultures.* New York: William Morrow.

Meyer-Bahlburg, H.F.L. (1984). Psychendocrine research on sexual orientation: Current status and future options. In G. J. De Vries (Ed.), *Progress in brain research* (Vol. 6, pp. 375–398). Amsterdam: Elsevier Science.

Mischel, W. (1966). A social-learning view of sex differences in behavior. In E. Maccoby (Ed.), *The development of sex differences* (pp. 56–81). Stanford, CA: Stanford University Press.

Money, J., & Ehrhardt, A. A. (1972). *Man & woman; boy & girl.* Baltimore, MD: Johns Hopkins University Press.

Nolen-Hoeksema, S. (1987). Sex differences in unipolar depression: Evidence and theory. *Psychological Bulletin, 101*, 405–422.

Parsons, J. E,, Adler, T., & Kaczala, C. (1982). Socialization of achievement attitudes and beliefs: Parental influences. *Child Development, 53*, 310-321.

Parsons, T., & Bales, R. (1955). *Family socialization and interactive process.* Glencoe, IL: Free Press.

Patterson, G. R. (1982). *Coercive family process.* Eugene, OR: Castalia.

Patterson, G. R., Reid, J. B., & Dishion, T. J. (1992). *Antisocial boys.* Eugene, OR: Castalia.

Pederson, F. A. (1980). *The father–infant relationship: Observational studies in the family setting.* New York: Praeger.

Phares, V., & Compas, B. E. (1992). The role of fathers in child and adolescent psychopathology: Make room for Daddy. *Psychological Bulletin, 111*, 387–412.

Prior, M., Smart, D., Sanson, A., & Oberklaid, F. (1993). Sex differences in psychological adjustment from infancy to eight years. *American Academy of Child and Adolescent Psychiatry, 32*, 291–304.

Rekers, G. A. (1982). *Shaping your child's sexual identity.* Grand Rapids, MI: Baker Book House.

Reid, J. B., & Patterson, G. R. (1989). The development of antisocial behavior patterns in childhood and adolescence. *European Journal of Personality, 3*, 107–119.

Rheingold, H. L., & Cook, K. V. (1975). The contents of boys' and girls' rooms as an index of parent behavior. *Child Development, 46*, 459–463.

Rogoff, B. (1986). Adult assistance in children's learning. In T. E. Raphael (Ed.), *The context of school based literacy* (pp. 27–40). New York: Random House.

Rogoff, B. (1990). *Apprenticeship in thinking: Cognitive development in a social context.* New York: Oxford University Press.

Rubin, J. Z., Provenzano, F. J., & Luria, Z. (1974). The eye of the beholder: Parents' views on sex of newborns. *American Journal of Orthopsychiatry, 44*, 512–519.

Sears, P. S., & Barbee, A. (1977). Career and life satisfaction among Terman's gifted women. In J. C. Stanley, W. D. George, & C. H. Solano (Eds.), *The gifted and the creative: A fifty-year perspective.*(pp. 28–65). Baltimore, MD: Johns Hopkins University Press.

Sears, R. R. (1977). Sources of life satisfaction of the Terman gifted men. *American Psychologist, 32,* 119–128.

Sears, R. R., Maccoby, E. E., & Levin, H. (1957). *Patterns of childrearing.* Evanston, IL: Row Peterson.

Sears, R. R., Rau, L., & Alpert, R. (1965). *Identification and child rearing.* Stanford, CA: Stanford University Press.

Shakin, M., Shakin, D., & Sternglanz, S. H. (1985). Infant clothing: Sex labeling for strangers. *Sex Roles, 12,* 955–963.

Sigel, I. E., & Cocking, R. R. (1977). *Cognitive development from childhood to adolescence: A constructivist perspective.* New York: Holt, Rinehart & Winston.

Siegel, M. (1987). Are sons and daughters treated more differently by fathers than by mothers? *Developmental Review, 7,* 183–209.

Spence, J. T., Helmrich, R., & Stapp, S. (1973). A short version of the Attitudes Toward Women Scale. *Bulletin of Psychonomic Science, 2,* 219–220.

Stoneman, Z., & Brody, G. H. (1981). Two's company, three makes a difference: An examination of mothers' and fathers' speech to their young children. *Child Development, 52,* 705–707.

Straus, M. A., Gelles, R. J., & Steinmetz, S. K. (1980). *Behind closed doors: Violence in the American family.* Grand City, NY: Doubleday/Anchor.

Terman, L. M. (1925). *Genetic studies of genius.* Stanford, CA: Stanford University Press.

Todd, J. (Ed.). (1990). *A Wollstonecraft anthology.* New York: Columbia Press.

Turner, P. J. (1991). Relations between attachment, gender, and behavior with peers in preschool. *Child Development, 62,* 1475–1488.

Turner, P. J. (1993). Attachment to mother and behaviour with adults in preschool. *British Journal of Developmental Psychology, 11,* 75–89.

van den Boom, D. C. (1989). Neonatal irritability and the development of attachment. In G. A. Kohnstamm, J. E. Bates, & M. K. Rothbart (Eds.), *Temperament in childhood* (pp. 299–318). New York: Wiley.

Vygotsky, L. S. (1978). *The mind in society: The development of higher psychological processes.* Cambridge, MA: Harvard University Press.

Weinraub, M., Clements, L. P., Sockloff, A., Ethridge, T., Gracely, E., & Myers, B. (1984). The development of sex role stereotypes in the third year: Relationships to gender labeling gender identity, sex typed toy preferences. *Child Development, 55,* 1493–1503.

Weinraub, M., & Frankel, J. (1977). Sex differences in parent–infant interaction during free play, departure, and separation. *Child Development, 48,* 1240–1249.

Whiting, B. B., & Edwards, C. P. (1988). *Children of different worlds: The formation of social behavior.* Cambridge: Harvard University Press.

Wollstonecraft, M. (1975). *A vindication of the rights of women* (C. H. Posten, Ed.). New York: Norton. (Original work published 1792)

Zahn-Waxler, C. (1993). Warriors and worriers: Gender and psychopathology. *Developmental Psychopathology, 5,* 79–90.

Zucker, K. J., & Green, R. (1992). Psychosexual disorders in children and adolescents. *Journal Child Psychology and Psychiatry, 33,* 107–151.

8

Parenting Twins

Hugh Lytton
Jagjit K. Singh
Lin Gallagher
University of Calgary

INTRODUCTION

Litters of offspring among animals must have been a familiar phenomenon to our nomadic and agricultural ancestors, hence multiple births among humans cannot have been a surprising or mysterious occurrence. Nevertheless, twins figure as special human beings in myth and literature, and interest in them goes back as far as recorded history. The Bible tells of Jacob and Esau, who presumably were fraternal, because they displayed different physical characteristics (Esau being hairy, and Jacob smooth). Greek mythology tells of Castor and Pollux, who form the Gemini constellation in the sky. Rome had its mythical twin founders, Romulus and Remus. Twins also figure in much of literature, from a Plautus comedy to Shakespeare to Thornton Wilder's (himself a twin) "Bridge of San Luis Rey."

Sometimes twin gods provide benefits (e.g., the Indian twin gods Acvin look after the weak and oppressed), but often twins are regarded as products of evil spirits, especially in Africa. In that continent (and among American Indians, too), one of a twin pair was sometimes killed (particularly the female partner), perhaps out of a fear of incest, or the belief that incest had already occurred in utero. But for some African tribes, a twin birth also is the occasion of a special joyous ceremony of welcome. So it appears that there is no universal attitude to twins, either as omens of good or ill (see Scheinfeld, 1973).

Certainly by the late nineteenth century it was known how identical or "one-egg" (monozygotic or MZ) twins and fraternal or "two-egg" (dizygotic or DZ) twins were created, and hence their different genetic relatedness was appreciated. The idea of using twins in genetic analyses probably stems from Sir Francis Galton, who in 1875 wrote about twins as a criterion of the relative powers of nature and nurture. Since the days of Galton—and Gesell, McGraw, and Newman around the turn of the century—innumerable investigations have compared MZ and DZ twins' intrapair correlations for height, weight, physiological, and autonomic nervous system measures, and additive and

185

socioemotional characteristics, to determine the relative importance of environmental and genetic factors in development (see Mittler, 1971). Indeed, twins have been the footsoldiers of nature–nurture battles throughout this century.

More recently the development of twins has been studied in its own right because their relationships to parents and to each other are marked by unique circumstances that make them different from those of singletons. Rearing twins—and *a fortiori* other multiple birth sets—subjects their parents to stresses that singleton parents are not subject to and tests, as it were, the limits of childrearing skills. Hence a comparison of twins' and singletons' experiences in their interactions with their parents throws light not only on the problems of rearing two children of the same age, but also on the processes involved in parent–child interaction and socialization in general. In the case of MZ twins, moreover, the impact of differential parental treatment in shaping twins' personalities is supposedly discernible and can theoretically be derived from any differences between the twin partners.

Psychoanalysts have found twins especially attractive and have used child observation of twins as the canvas on which analytic reconstruction then paints a rich picture in order "to advance psychoanalytic understanding of individuation, identification, self-image, identity, and psychopathology" (Dibble & Cohen, 1981, p. 45). Burlingham (1952), for instance, presented a detailed psychoanalytic study of the development of three pairs of identical twins.

The occurrence of MZ twinning (due to the splitting of a single ovum) is thought to be a random event, and, indeed, the MZ twinning rate is nearly constant at about 3.5 per thousand confinements all over the world. The occurrence of DZ twinning, on the other hand (due to double ovulation), is more frequent at later maternal ages (peak at about 37 years), and is due to greater secretion of pituitary gonadotrophin at those ages (Bulmer, 1970). The DZ twinning rate also varies widely across races; in the earlier part of this century, it was about 8 per thousand confinements in Whites—a level it has now roughly recaptured—but it was approximately twice as large in Africans and about half as large in Mongoloid-Asians. The rate is also about one and a half times as large for African Americans as for White Americans. The reasons for the differential DZ twinning rates are not known, but the ratios among races do not seem to have varied much in recent times (Bulmer, 1970; Inouye & Imaizumi, 1981).

Prior to 1970, DZ twinning rates were declining in a number of industrialized countries. It is thought this was attributable to a changing age distribution of mothers, plus other factors (e.g., social class changes). But between 1974 and 1990 multiple birth (MB) rates in Canada, for example, increased from 912 to 1,058 per 100,000 population. The rate of triplet and higher order births grew by a remarkable 250 percent, but the twinning rate also rose. These increases are probably due to the use of ovulation-inducing drugs (fertility drugs); similar trends have been found in the United States and Great Britain. There is, in fact, a narrow margin between a dose of fertility hormones leading to a conception and one that produces multiple conceptions; so it is not surprising that 36 percent of mothers of triplets and 70 percent of mothers of quadruplets between 1982 and 1985 were reported to have received ovulation-inducing hormones.

In the 1980s, the proportion of twins born to women under 25 declined, but the proportion of twins born to women over 30 increased, and the MB rate out of all births to mothers over 40 was 22 percent. A shift of childbearing to higher ages among women in general, plus access to assisted conception are thought to have contributed to these increases in MB rates among women over 30 in the 1980s (Millar, Wadhera, & Nimrod, 1992).

The following is a brief overview of the central issues and topics discussed in detail in later sections: We discuss the potential handicap that low birthweight and preterm children—and twins are generally among them—may suffer from. Another section deals with the special problems that face parents in raising two children of the same age. Then we examine the way in which the development of social characteristics, language, and intelligence is affected by the "twoness" of the twin situation. In particular, we assess the evidence for the importance of biological versus environmental (parental childrearing) effects on twins' language and intelligence, and discuss this question in the context of the more general question of what influence parents have on their children overall.

Discussions of differences between twins and singletons and between their respective parents apply to both MZ and DZ twins, and also to same-sex and opposite-sex twins, unless one twin type (MZ or DZ) is specified.

BIOLOGICAL HANDICAPS IN TWINS AND THEIR CONSEQUENCES

Twins' fetal development takes place in a more crowded womb and they are born, on average, 3 weeks earlier than are singletons. Hence their average birthweight (which increased slightly between 1974 and 1990) is about 2,400 g, versus the average singleton birthweight of around 3,500 g. Indeed, obstetric risk is naturally high for twins. They are at greater risk for congenital impairments and abnormalities than singletons, owing to very premature birth and very low birthweight in a proportion of twins. Such impairments, which could include cerebral palsy and congenital heart defects, have also been linked to stress in the uterus, because multiple pregnancies are at greater risk of complications, such as toxaemia, placenta praevia, or fetal growth restriction.

Perinatal mortality in twins is about 4.5 times higher than in singletons, with prematurity being related to the cause of death in three quarters of the cases. Mortality is also often due to the twin–twin transfusion syndrome, which occurs in some MZs. In those cases, the twins' fetal circulation systems are connected, because they share a single chorion (membrane) in the womb, and then one twin sometimes donates blood to the other twin, with the blood donor becoming anemic and malnourished (Simonoff, 1992). In fact, MZ twins overall suffer from greater prenatal handicapping conditions, and a higher mortality rate and lower birthweight than DZ twins (Allen, 1955; Benirschke & Kim, 1973).

Low-birthweight children in later life tend to have more diseases, engage in less activity, and lose a greater number of school days to illness and poorer health status, though social factors may moderate this risk (see later) (Millar et al., 1992). (For attempts at remedying these adverse effects see Goldberg & DiVitto, in this *Handbook*.) However, up to a point "preterm," as normally defined, is not an adverse factor for twins, as the lowest risk for twins exists when gestation lasts 38 weeks rather than 40 weeks as in singletons (Rutter & Redshaw, 1991). Effects of biological adversities are always mediated by the social environment. This means that effects of low birthweight are particularly pronounced in lower social classes, whereas in more privileged social environments low-birthweight children are hardly more at risk than normal-birthweight children (Kopp, 1983).

But, whatever their social class status, parents of MB babies must cope with many physical, mental, economic, and social stressors that can have adverse effects on family life. High demands are made on their time and efforts in looking after the twins—feeding, washing, and diapering them—with breast-feeding presenting special difficulties; and, in addition, they have to put up with more than the usual interruptions of their nightly sleep. There is also considerable cost involved in caring and transporting twins. These difficulties are compounded when there are older siblings. All this means greater demands on parents' patience, efforts, time, and understanding (see "Quality of the Environment for Twins Versus Singletons," "Development of Language and Intelligence," and "Voices of Twin Mothers" later.)

PROBLEMS IN REARING TWINS

The following section deals with the special problems and challenges in childrearing that the "twoness" of the twin situation creates for parents.

Demands on Twin Versus Singleton Parents

Mothers of twins are generally much more involved with their offspring than mothers of singletons. A detailed observational investigation of a few sets of MB families in Israel (Goshen-Gottstein, 1979) reports that mothers of twins spent 35 percent of their time on infant-centered activities during a 3-hour home visit versus 25 percent for mothers of singletons. Care of the newborn babies was the most time-consuming task. Interestingly, Corter and Stiefel (1983) reported that mothers of twins do *not* treat the pair as a unit more often than mothers of a sibship treat their children; in other words, they do not achieve economies of scale.

Lytton (1980) used naturalistic home observations to study the interactions of twins and singletons with their parents, in a sample of 46 sets of male twins and 44 male singletons, 2 to 3 years of age. Behavior counts and impressionistic ratings for various kinds of behavior were derived from the observations. Not only are parents under greater time pressure when they have twins, but they are also under greater stress. There often are inevitable conflicts between the twins—one twin biting the other as a method of attack or defense was reported by a number of parents of these 2-year-olds, and parents naturally found this difficult to deal with—and then there are the twins' and other siblings' competing demands directed at the parents. But, transcending the conflicts, twins also acquire relative cohesion as a pair who often act and play together. Such intimacy may often mean that language becomes less important as a means of communication, and speech evolves into inarticulate grunts or monosyllables, unintelligible to others (the so-called secret language of twins). In general, their self-sufficiency will lead twins to seek less contact with others and hence to relative social isolation from adults. Nevertheless, their cohesion as a unit often fails to translate into a flow of chatter among themselves (e.g., in Lytton's, 1980, study the mean number of utterances by one twin to the other over about 4 or 5 hours of observation was only 22).

Fathers are inevitably much more involved in child care when twins arrive than with singletons. But even in MB families, Goshen-Gottstein (1979) reported that fathers helped only about 10 percent of the time—sometimes they were not at home during observations—and they spent more time on older children and general household duties than on infants. Siblings were also called on to help for longer hours in homes of twins than of singletons. Moreover, energy-saving devices, such as propping up bottles, and confining children to cribs or playpens, were more in evidence in twin than singleton households.

Three months after the twins' birth many mothers in an Australian study reported they were exhausted (76 percent), had no time to themselves (79 percent), and were depressed (30 percent)—these are much higher percentages than found with singleton mothers (Hay & O'Brien, 1984). Many American twin mothers stressed the fatigue associated with caring for two babies simultaneously, especially the difficulties of feeding the two of them. Mothers also underlined the importance of help from fathers and even grandmothers (Vandell, 1990). Only 16 percent of Australian parents had another child after the twins, although this was partly the result of the twins tending to be the later children in the family. However, 32 percent of the sample only had twins, where there would have been an opportunity to have other children (Hay & O'Brien, 1984). The stresses associated with twin rearing are illustrated by the fact that there is a higher incidence of child abuse among twins than singletons (Vandell, 1990).

Quality of Environment for Twins Versus Singletons

Does the quality of the environment differ between twin and singleton households, and if so, how does this affect the twins' development?

Zajonc's confluence theory.   The outstanding theory bearing on twins' cognitive development—almost the only one in this area—is Zajonc's "confluence model." This model posits that children's cognitive development is very largely influenced by the intellectual climate in the family of rearing, and this will be a function of the number of children and their spacing. That is, the family's intellectual climate will be diluted the larger the number of children and the smaller the time gap between them, because the intellectual contribution of young children to newborns is bound to be small relative to that of parents or older siblings, something that will exert an adverse influence on the younger children in a sibship, and on twins in particular. Zajonc and Markus (1975) provided some confirmatory data for their theory from large-scale studies, and particularly cited the lower IQs of twins and triplets as examples and corroboration of this effect. However, as we see here, the theory, as it relates to twins, has not remained uncontested. Many issues of parenting twins that we discuss focus on the quality of the environment that parents are able to provide for two children of the same age—an issue that is central to this theory.

Observations of twin families. As several studies (e.g., Bornstein & Ruddy, 1984; Lytton, 1980) have demonstrated, the presence of two children of the same age in the home is likely to alter quite dramatically the climate of the relationships between children and parents; that is, this presence modifies the environmental contingencies to which children are exposed as well as the self-perceptions and family perceptions of the twins themselves.

The more important differences between twin and singleton groups that emerged in Lytton's study are shown in Table 8.1. (The twin and singleton groups did not differ significantly in level of mothers' education, and the Table indicates where controlling for mothers' education nevertheless has an effect on the twin–singleton difference.) The influence of the "twin situation" is clearly quite pervasive in this study. It is particularly noticeable in *parent* behavior, where it is not swamped by social class effects. Twins experience fewer verbal interchanges with their parents overall, and they receive fewer directions, either by way of commands or of suggestions, fewer verbal justifications and generalizations of rules, and commands or prohibitions are less consistently followed through. Twins, too, meet with less praise and receive fewer overt expressions of affection, although this should not be interpreted as meaning that parents love their twins less than singleton parents love their children— they simply have less time to show their affection. Twin mothers, however, also display less appropriate sensitivity in responding to their children's distress or demands, verbally or nonverbally, than do singleton mothers—very probably, they cannot afford to show the same sensitivity to their children's needs that singleton mothers do. Twin parents also are far less verbally responsive to their children's initiations than are singleton parents.

TABLE 8.1
Some Important Twin–Singleton Differences at Age 2

Singletons Higher Than Twins Child Variables			
Child Variables			
	$p <$		$p <$
Number of actions	.001	Rate positive actions	.001
Vocabulary IQ (PPVT)	.05[a]	Rate negative actions	.001
Comply ratio	.05[a]	Speech maturity (ratg)	.01
Instrumental indep'ce (ratg)	.05[a]	Rate child speech	.001
Internalized standards (ratg)	.001	Speech—% of actions	.001
Mother Variables		*Father Variables*	
Command-prohibition— % of actions[b]	.001	Command-prohibition— % of actions	.001
Use of reasoning %	.001	Use of reasoning %	.001
Affection %	.001	Affection %	.001
Consistency of enforc't (ratg)	.01	Consistency of enforc't (ratg)	.01
Suggestion %	.001	Suggestion %	.001
Positive action %	.001	Positive action %	.01
Love withdrawal %	.05	Rate father–child speech	.001
Rate mother–child speech	.001		
Child Variables		*Mother Variables*	
Attachment behavior— % of actions	.01	Number of actions	.02
Walking %	.01		
Expression of displeasure %	.001		

Note. Adapted from Lytton (1980). Differences significant at the .05 level in two-tailed *t* tests are shown.

[a]When the contribution of the mother's education was allowed for as a prior predictor, twinship no longer added significantly to the prediction for this variable in a multiple-regression analysis, indicating no significant twin–singleton difference (*p* .05).

[b]"% of actions" and "%" denote percentage of the given agent's total actions.

In general, the greater pressure on twin parents' time—and, possibly also, the relative cohesion of the twin pair—seems to lead to parents' being less involved with their children, and, although this may indeed have some positive effects, it also means an impoverishment of the children's environment. The effects this has on twins' speech and language skills are discussed later.

The decreased quantity of mother–twin interaction compared with singletons is not due to twins interacting more with each other—they tend to do little of this, as noted earlier. They are more likely to initiate interactions with their mothers and to respond to mothers' initiations than to each other. Savic (1980) noted that not only the quantity, but also the nature of interactions differs in twin households from that in singleton households. Thus, twins have more choice concerning whether or not to respond to mothers' initiations. Common occurrences, for instance, are that mother addresses the pair, but only one twin responds, or that mother starts an interaction with Twin A, but Twin B takes over the interaction in the middle.

One of the disadvantages of being brought up as a twin is that twins have less prolonged uninterrupted interactions with their mothers than singletons do. This may arise because parents try to divide their attention equally between the two competing sets of demands, or because of interruptions and demands from the other twin. In fact, sustained dyadic interaction and attention to one twin are rare. When mother is with both twins, many instances of shifts of attention between the two twins occur, and sometimes mother would attempt to deal with both twins at the same time (e.g., handing a toy to Twin A, while talking to Twin B, telling him what to do) as mothers frequently do with siblings. In fact, mothers and twins rarely interact as triads, but are most likely to do so when they are brought together round a toy (Clark & Dickman, 1984; Lytton, 1980; Rutter & Redshaw, 1991; Savic, 1980; Vandell, 1990).

Father–mother differences.   Differences between mothers' and fathers' behavior toward their boys were noted in Lytton's (1980) study, but they were not analyzed separately for twins and singletons. Hence the following applies to both groups. When it comes to seeking nurturance—either proximity or attention or help—the child clearly turns to mother on the whole rather than to father; that is, both twins and singletons communicate their needs and demands, as well as their signals of distress, more to mother than to father, even allowing for his shorter presence in the home. (Attachment behavior per se—in which twins and singletons differ—is discussed later.)

When it comes to play, however, the situation is reversed: Father engages in far more play, and particularly rough-and-tumble play, with the boys than mother does, even relative to his shorter time in the home (see Parke, in this *Handbook*). Part of the reason why play is such a salient activity for father in this study is no doubt the fact that the observations took place around supper time. When father comes home at this time, these mostly homemaker mothers, after a long tiring day with two lively twins, are glad to let him take over "play duty," and he is usually pleased to have this opportunity. Father, generally, also exhibits more affection and positively toned actions, partly, perhaps, because of his extensive play with the children.

Mother enters into far more verbal communications of all kinds with the children than father does in both twin and singleton families. Furthermore, mother plays a far more prominent role than father in attempting to change the children's behavior by commands, suggestions, or providing rationales for her directions. She considers this part of her duty as she goes through the day with the children. She evidently feels more reponsible for the children's behavior and welfare and hence intervenes more in the children's doings—that is, on their behalf, as well as to restrain and change their behavior. The children sometimes react to this by turning a selectively deaf ear to her and comply less with her than with father's requests (Lytton, 1980).

In a questionnaire study of parents of 377 twin pairs, 1 to 6 years old, Cohen, Dibble, and Grawe (1977) found that mothers also tend to be less peremptory, and overwhelmingly more "child-centered" than fathers in the sense that they monitor their children's welfare and activities more.

Effect of arrival of twins on older siblings.   The impact on a sibling, perhaps 1 to 3 years old, is one important aspect of the arrival of twins that parents often have to contend with. Whereas toddlers usually feel displaced in their parents' attention and affection by the arrival of a baby, this effect is exacerbated when twins arrive on the scene, as was noted in several families in Lytton's (1980) study. (It is noteworthy that 64 percent of older siblings reacted negatively to twins' arrival in an Australian study; Hay & O'Brien, 1984). Not only do twins, because of their more urgent needs, demand and get far more of the parents' attention than the older child, but by the time they are 2½, they also tend to form a unit who play and act together (excluding the older child in the process) even though verbal interchanges between twins are sparse. In these cases, the older children, perceiving themselves isolated or downgraded by the twins, would develop intense feelings of rivalry. They would become the classical "difficult children," interfering with the interlopers and their play, or throwing temper tantrums. It is a hard fact that, when three young children compete for parents' attention and time, it is the older singleton who gets the short end of the stick. Further, it is notable that older brothers harbor more negative feelings toward new twin arrivals than do older sisters (Hay & O'Brien, 1984).

When mothers were more attentive and involved in joint play with elder daughters for about a year before the sibling's birth, and when their firstborns had a secure rather than insecure attachment to them, the older sibling's interaction with the newborn tends to be especially hostile and unfriendly, and sib conflict, at slightly older ages, is particularly sharp. The reason may be that children with a history of supportive parent–child relationships experience a severe sense of loss when the parent now directs attention and affection that once was solely theirs to a younger sib (J. Dunn & Kendrick, 1982; Volling & Belsky, 1992). These conclusions are based on studies of singletons, but they are likely to apply equally to the arrival of twins.

Equal Versus Differentiated Treatment

The essential question that twin parents, in particular, quite often consciously ask themselves is: How can we combine equal and fair distribution of resources with our desire to emphasize individuality and meet individual needs? It is clear from several reports that far more parents claim that they try to treat twins alike than say the opposite. Only rarely is one twin reported as receiving some kind of experience that differs from that accorded the other twin (Loehlin & Nichols, 1976). In self-ratings, too, parents report very high consistency of treatment between twin partners ($r = .80$ or more). In fact, they do not differentiate their behaviors toward twin partners as much as they differentiate the twins' perceived personalities (Cohen et al., 1977). Such similarity of treatment is attempted in the service of equal and fair distribution of resources (qualifications discussed later). Where differences do occur, the correlations between differences in parental treatment and differences in children's abilities, personality, and interests are very small. Overall, differential treatment, measured in a variety of ways, can account for only a tiny fraction of variance in personality; hence, parental treatment differences do not explain twins' behavioral differences (Loehlin & Nichols, 1976).

Behavior-genetic analyses attempt to estimate genetic and environmental components of variance in human characteristics by comparisons between MZ and DZ within-pair correlations or variances (see Plomin, DeFries, & McClearn, 1990). For these analyses to be valid, it has been claimed that the "equal environments assumption" has to be met. The argument goes like this: Suppose parents accorded more similar treatment to a pair of twins simply because of their knowledge that their twins are MZ, and not because they present very similar needs and demands, arising out of their genetic identity. Such an attitude, it has been thought, might give rise to spuriously greater similarity in these twins, which, in a behavior-genetic analysis, would inflate the genetic component relative to the environmental component emerging from the analysis of a given characteristic (but see the previous paragraph about lack of effects of parental differential treatment).

MZs have repeatedly been found to receive more similar treatment in several respects than DZs (e.g., Cohen et al., 1977; Loehlin & Nichols, 1976; Rowe, 1981). Lytton (1980) found the same thing, but he also found that parents' do not introduce systematically greater similarity of treatment for MZs in actions that they initiate themselves and that are not contingent on the child's immediately preceding behavior; and when parents hold a mistaken belief about the twins' zygosity (i.e., think actual MZs to be DZs and vice-versa), their treatment of the twins is more in line with the twins' actual than their perceived zygosity. It seems that regardless of parental expectations in regard to degree of behavioral similarity (MZ or DZ), young children with identical genetic endowment are likely to elicit somewhat similar parental behavior. In other words, parents respond to rather than create twins' genetic similarity or differences (see also Cohen et al.,1977, and Scarr & Carter-Saltzman, 1979).

Hence the somewhat greater similarity of treatment of MZ than of DZ twins does not invalidate behavior-genetic analyses. Nor does the existence of undoubted differences in socialization experiences between twins and singletons, in our opinion, invalidate the use of twins in behavior genetics because there is no evidence that twins, as a group, differ systematically from singletons in genetic endowment or the structure of the genome, and technically the differences in environment between twins and singletons are not relevant, as classical behavior-genetic analyses compare only variances of MZ and DZ twins, and no singleton variances enter into the calculations.

The conclusion that parents tend to accommodate their behavior to each twin's individuality—within the context of the goal of fair treatment—has also received support from the mothers' responses in the interview at age 2, when they were asked whether they made differences between the twins and why (Lytton, 1980). Many mothers acknowledged they treated the twins—both MZ and DZ—differently, but always attributed such differential treatment to the differing needs and personalities of the children. Typically, one child would be seen as needing more attention or warmth, or as more mischievous, less easygoing, and less docile than the other. In two cases, differences in treatment were directly related to the fact that one twin suffered respiratory distress at birth and had to be kept in an incubator for some weeks, whereas the other one did not. The following are some of the interviewer's notes for an MZ twin pair:

> Mother doesn't think of them as twins—J has been behind. Their personalities warrant their being treated differently. The differences that mother makes are those they demand, or events produce. J is ten times worse than D in climbing on cupboards and tables and is usually spanked. Mother often has to spank J for things that D does not have to be spanked for. D is more sensitive—reponds to a look or being sent to his room. Mother spends about half an hour holding and cuddling D, and about 15 minutes with J or as much time as he'll allow.

Allowances were still being made for J at age 9 (at follow-up), because of his handicaps, namely a hearing defect and speech difficulties. In the follow-up phase of this investigation (Lytton, Watts, & B. E. Dunn, 1984), the problem of developing individuality and meeting individual needs within the context of overall equal and fair treatment elicited comments from a number of parents. In general, parents stressed that the rules were the same for both children, and their overall aim was one of fairness, but within the limits of this general principle they made differences in response to the children's differing personalities and needs.

The principle of equality of basic rights, but differing responses to different personalities was spelled out by this DZ mother:

> Basically I try to treat them all equally in what I'm buying for them, getting for them. They may all get the same thing—different colors or sizes—so there's no fights. ... I want them to be different, to have their own personalities, their own group of friends. When they started school I made it most definite that I wanted them in separate classrooms, from Kindergarten on.

The reasons for making differences was clearly put by this mother of DZ twins:

> If there's differences, it's not because I make them. It's because they make them. ... So the differences are because of their needs, not because of anything I figure I should change.

Another DZ mother stressed that "They're so unalike that you would never treat them the same." The husband also said that he tends to baby one twin more, because he does not do as well as the other one academically, and he places more demands on the second twin because he responds more to that.

Parents of MZ twins are aware of the temptation to treat them as one and consciously force themselves to treat them as individuals. One MZ mother commented:

> I tend to treat them alike which is a pitfall with twins. It's easier to think of them as your third child. That was one of the problems when they went to Grade 1. Suddenly I had four children, and I always felt I had three. Because suddenly I had two teachers to see, two field trips to go on. ... It's important to treat them differently, but it's very easy to fall into the habit of saying "the twins" and "they." And they speak that way, too. They say "we don't like him," or "Billy doesn't like us." You want them to enjoy being twins, but you also want them to be individuals. That's the biggest challenge of twins.

Another MZ mother said:

> I think we've tried to build up the difference because it's so slight. ... Many times neighbors have discounted the fact that they are two different people— they call them the same name, etc. So we try to say "You don't have to dress alike, can have different toys, etc." ... I try to make them stand on their own. They have a hard time doing that. ... If they are in trouble, they are in trouble together, and if they were doing something well, they're doing it together.

The questionnaires sent to twin parents by Hay and O'Brien (1984) also shed light on the question of equal versus differentiated attitudes to, and treatment, of twin partners. To most questions (e.g., "To which twin do you feel closer?") the vast majority of parents answered "Both." But there were exceptions where "both" was the answer offered only by a minority of parents, and these questions were: "Which twin required more attention?" "Which twin was easier to manage?" "Which twin was fussier?" and "Which twin was more active and alert?" These questions clearly refer to aspects that might well be considered part of the twins' temperamental make-up that forced differentiation on parents (cf. Sanson & Rothbart, in this *Handbook*).

It is of interest to note that mothers differentiate between children within a pair of DZ twins more than fathers do in areas like consistency, monitoring, and parental temper and detachment. Mothers also differentiate more between partners in MZ pairs, perhaps because they are more intimately familiar with the individuality of each twin (Cohen et al., 1977).

Favorites.   Do parents have favorites among their children? Having children of the same age highlights contrasts as well as similarities between them. In an attempt to distinguish between what appear to be very similar personalities, parents may sometimes seek differences and accentuate preferences, rather than emphasize equality of treatment (Rutter & Redshaw, 1991). They may, for instance, emphasize different sets of skills for each twin, as did one family that rewarded and stressed mathematical skills for one twin and verbal skills for the other (Ainslie, 1985, cited in Vandell, 1990).

Indeed, if twins differ in nature, it is natural for mother (or father) to feel closer to one or the other. In the study of 9-year-old twins, therefore, Lytton et al. (1984) made a subjective judgment as to the favorite status of one twin, in cases where this seemed warranted on the basis of parents' interview responses and impressions of especially close relationships, observed during a structured family interaction task. There were no significant differences between the reported treatment of "favorites" versus "nonfavorites" by parents, but then parents would not be likely to admit such differential treatment in self-reports.

But there were some suggestive differences in children's characteristics. The favorite twins slightly exceeded the nonfavorite twins in verbal ability, and the latter had an edge over the former in nonverbal ability (neither difference was significant). It may be that the favorite twin's superiority in verbal communication made for closer ties with mother and that the nonfavorite twin compensated for this by more practical activities.

Favorite twins were rated as more attached to their mothers, as slightly more compliant, and, above all, as exhibiting fewer antisocial problems than their nonfavorite partners. These differences were all plausible in that they provided explanations *why* one twin was more favored by his mother than the other. It is naturally easier to love the child who is more compliant or less deviant in behavior. On the other hand, the possibility exists that greater attachment and compliance, and fewer behavior problems flowed from the favorite status. We have no means of distinguishing between these hypotheses, but here, as so often, bidirectional influences are likely to be operating.

Sex-typed rearing.   This topic is a narrower part of the larger question of equal versus individually tailored treatment. Very little is known about the sex-typed treatment of opposite-sex twins. Where this aspect of parenting has been examined, few significant differences in behavior toward sons versus daughters have been found, strikingly fewer than differences between the behavior of mothers and fathers, for instance in Cohen et al.'s (1977) study. Mothers were the more child-centered parent (shown in concern for children's welfare and in their close supervision), but they were more child centered for boys than for girls.

A unique observational study of a few twin, triplet, and quadruplet families has been carried out in Israel (Goshen-Gottstein, 1981). What emerges is a picture of a mix of unconscious, or at least nondeliberate, sex-equal treatment and of conscious, sex-typed socialization. The results are somewhat counterintuitive. Mothers permitted more proximity seeking (dependence) in boys, encouraged more helping in girls, reinforced boys' and girls' aggression equally, and placed no emphasis on sex-typed toy play. Conscious sex-differentiating practices were differential hairstyle and clothing (e.g., skullcaps for boys), which came only in the third year of life. In strictly religious families, a very conscious and high degree of sex segregation in religious and school activities occurred (i.e., boys attended an all-male nursery school from 2½ years, and had reading lessons in the fourth year of life, whereas girls attended a girls' nursery school from 3 years, and took reading lessons from age 6 on). Apart from this strict segregation in religious activities, the general trend of absence of systematic sex-typed treatment coincides with Lytton and Romney's (1991) findings, except that these authors found one aspect of significant differential socialization, namely, the encouragement of same-sex-typed toy play. Overall, we see how having twins poses some special problems that are, however, not insoluble for parents, and how it makes parents walk a thin line between fair and equal distribution of resources and treatment tailored to each twin's individual needs.

DEVELOPMENT OF SOCIAL CHARACTERISTICS

Attachment (usually, to mother), as a developmental function of the child, is a concept and topic that, following Bowlby's conceptualization (e.g., Bowlby, 1958), has found wide acceptance among developmental psychologists. It attained especial popularity as an experimental paradigm with the development of a measurement tool, the Strange Situation, by Ainsworth, which provided a usable instrument for categorizing children as showing secure or insecure attachment (the latter being subdivided into avoidant or anxious) (Ainsworth, Blehar, Water, & Wall, 1978; see also previous chapters in this *Handbook*).

Security of Attachment in Twins

One might expect twins to display a higher incidence of insecure attachment than singletons do because the excessive demands placed on mother's care and attention by twins may lead some mothers to give them less than optimal maternal care. Following the reasoning of, for instance, Klaus and Kennell (1982), it has been suggested by some that a mother can form a successful intimate relationship with only one baby at a time, and that mothers of twins may therefore encounter difficulty in meeting the needs of two infants simultaneously. Both Vandell et al. (1988) and Goldberg and Minde and their associates (Goldberg, Perrotta, Minde, & Corter, 1986; Minde, Corter, & Goldberg, 1986) investigated the question of whether security of attachment in twins differed from that in singletons. Minde and Goldberg's sample consisted of 26 twin pairs and 25 singleton controls, all of whom had birthweights of less than 1,500 g, studied over the first year of life. The outcome was unusually clear: Neither low birthweight nor twinship imperiled security of attachment. The distribution of attachment categories in both the Vandell study of twins and the Minde and Goldberg study of low birthweight babies did not differ significantly from those in other studies of normal term babies (about 70 percent secure, 10 percent avoidant, 20 percent resistant). Twins were no more likely than singletons to be insecurely attached, and the processes contributing to attachment security in twins were found to be the same as those in singletons (Goldberg et al., 1986). However, a number of twins were in a "marginally secure" category, and the mothers of these marginally secure infants were rated lower on responsivity and sensitivity (rated from observations) than all mothers of all other attachment categories. Such behavior would normally be expected to lead to insecure attachment in the infants. Goldberg et al. (1986) made the interesting suggestion that it is precisely the presence of a same-age peer that may be a protective factor, contributing to security of attachment, so that it pushes these twins into at least the marginally secure category.

The same category of attachment security (A, B, or C) seems to have been allotted to DZ as often as to MZ twin partners, a fact consistent with the theory that attachment quality is primarily a matter of maternal/paternal environment and relationships, not a matter of temperament (Vandell, 1990). Plomin and Rowe's (1979) behavior-genetic analyses came to similar conclusions, namely that relationships with—and social behavior toward—mother were mainly shaped by experiences with mother.

In the Minde et al. study, mothers showed a slight preference for one of the twins, manifested by more positive statements about that twin, and more caregiving and visual and vocal attention—although the tendency was slight, not overpowering, and was hardly ever admitted to by the mother. The preference was demonstrably related to the medical status of the infant (i.e., to the child's robustness and visual attention and responsiveness to the mother). But preferences fluctuated over the first year, and a shift in preference occurred particularly when the initially nonpreferred infant was more attentive and sociable later on. The existence of a preference enhanced the probability of secure attachment, not only for the preferred, but, interestingly, also for the nonpreferred infant—it may even be a necessary condition for secure attachment, since all twin pairs in this study whose mothers showed no preference were later insecurely attached. Having a preference, according to the authors, may indicate that the mother is sensitive to the individualities of the twins and committed to their individual needs, whereas apparent egalitarian treatment could be indicative of lesser interest and of lower intensity and rate of interactions (Minde et al., 1986).

Lytton (1980) quantified the *amount* of attachment behavior displayed by 2-year-old boys, expressed as a rate per unit time, rather than classifying infants by categories of attachment security. He found that twins engage in greater amount of attachment behavior to their parents, than singletons do. This result might be traced to parents' lesser display of affection, since the twins may feel the need to reassure themselves of their parents' love. But, since it was mainly the nonverbal attachment behaviors of the younger twins (i.e., proximity-seeking), that manifested themselves, the result may also be a consequence of twins' greater general immaturity.

At age 2, attachment behavior was indexed by amount of such behavior shown to each parent, and at the follow-up at age 9 by asking mothers and fathers to whom the child was more attached. At both 2 and 9 years, the majority of children (about 60 percent) displayed more attachment to mother than to father. This was so despite the fact that fathers did a lot of romping and rough-housing with the children. Father, it seems, was the playmate, whereas mother was the comforter in distress overall.

There was one difference between the twins and the singletons at 2: Relatively more twins than singletons were "father attached," in that they displayed more attachment behavior to fathers than mothers. Why did these children buck the general trend? It may be that some of the twins were seeking an available attachment figure as a protective device against the lesser availability of the mother; indeed, in many twin pairs each partner appropriated his own attachment object. But Lytton also found that the father-attached group had mothers who tended to exhibit less desirable qualities (e.g., a high propensity to physical punishment). Dibble and Cohen (1981) also found a frequent tendency for twins to attach themselves to separate parents.

Going by mothers' and fathers' reports on twins' attachment object at age 9, it appears that there was a developmental shift from unilateral attachment to one parent at 2 to greater equality of attachment at 9. Equal attachment was observed for 19 percent of the twins at age 2, but it was reported for an average of 59 percent at age 9, a change that can well be thought of as due to the growth of greater independence and maturity. However, it might also be attributable to parents' wish to be "fair" to each other in their reports (Lytton, Watts, & Dunn, 1988).

Overall then, it would appear that security of attachment relationships is not affected by the fact of twinship, that is, the fact that two children of the same age are being reared together.

Twin–Twin Relations

Although twins share the same home and the same parents, each twin has many unique experiences. It is sometimes said that this "nonshared" environment, which encompasses extrafamilial encounters—such as in the classroom or with different friends—as well as differential treatment by parents, is a more influential factor for the twins' personality development than is the environment that they share. However, as noted earlier, Loehlin and Nichols (1976) found essentially no relation between individualized parental practices and twins' personalities.

Interactions between the co-twins at the younger ages are not as frequent or intense as one might expect. If one compares the interactions of single-born sibs about 1½ and 2½ years old, with those of 1½-year-old twins, one finds more interaction in singleton dyads, because of the greater social activity by the older sib. Younger sibs also give to, or share with, or imitate older sibs almost 3 times as much as twins do with one another (Corter & Stiefel, 1983).

As Savic (1980) found, an adult's presence can sometimes be the catalyst for bringing about twin–twin interaction. Both twins, for instance, might try to engage mother, and if she was non-responsive, they would slide into interaction with each other instead; or, in an alternative scenario, one twin would interject himself in an ongoing interaction between mother and the other twin. However, twins do not compensate for an insecure attachment to mother by more interaction with their co-twins: on the contrary, twins who are insecurely attached to mother are less likely to interact with their co-twins than are securely attached twins (Vandell, 1990).

Let us turn to competition between co-twins. In Lytton's observations of 2-year-old twins, competition for mother's attention occurred fairly regularly. Thus, if mothers or fathers held Twin A on their knee, Twin B would cry "up, up," clamoring for the same privilege; or if one twin showed off a drawing to the mother, or was "cleaning" a chair, the other twin would want to do the same thing.

In one longitudinal study of twins' interactions, at age 2 to age 3, 25 percent of the time was taken up by joint play, such as sharing toys or run–chase games. When there was disharmony, the single most common theme was a struggle about objects. But, by age 5, almost no conflict was observed. The most common pattern was for shared play to occur, but some twins kept a wary distance from each other. In fact, it was those twins who had many conflicts at 2 who were more likely to ignore the other twin at 5, in this way finding a conflict-free solution to their relationship (Wilson, 1987).

In Lytton et al.'s (1984) follow-up of twins at age 9, a structured family task provided the opportunity of noting competitiveness and cooperation between the twin partners: In only one third of the twin pairs did competitiveness predominate, and with them it tended to be pervasive and to extend into the twins' general interactions. The competitive twins were, for the most part, fraternal twins with obvious physical and behavioral differences and frequently with a marked discrepancy in skills in an area. But among the competitive twins there were also some MZ twins with poor social skills, who interacted intensely because they had difficulty making other friends.

Being close to each other and joining in shared activities was a more salient trait in these twins than having outgoing relationships with peers. Most twins found comfort and support in such a close relationship, which held over and above temporary petty squabbles. Indeed, twins often prefer each other's company to being separate, and they worry about each other when they are separated. One of the pervasive fears and dislikes of the twins, as the authors found in recruiting twins for their follow-up, was being compared with each other in an evaluative (school) context, presumably because this might lead to feelings of inferiority, rivalry, and hostility.

Common identity versus individuation?   One perennial question is: Should twins be placed in different classrooms at school to enhance individuality, or should they be kept together for mutual support, or other reasons? According to Koch (1966), separation of same-sex twins at school occurs about one third of the time, but opposite-sex twins are separated about half the time. At least in part the separation or togetherness is the fulfilment of the twins' own wishes (see "Voices of Twin Mothers" at the end of this chapter). More male than female twins wish to be separated, but as many same-sex DZs as MZs (about two thirds of twins) wish to be together. The more vigorous, older, and aggressive twin pairs are more frequently separated, whereas the closer, more conforming, and scholastically able twins tend to be kept together—for obvious reasons. Typically, boys are much more likely to be separated than girls, partly as the outcome of their own wishes and partly because of their more vigorous and sometimes obstreperous natures (as Koch thought). Schools may often feel this to be in the twins' own, as well as in the class's interests. Research seems to show that better speech form and more freedom from stuttering are associated with placement of twins in different classes (Koch, 1966), with the obverse of the coin being that twins who are closer to each other (e.g., interact more) have more speech and articulation problems than others (Hay & O'Brien, 1984).

Constant companionship and similar needs and satisfactions for co-twins may result in great closeness and assimilation of behavior and traits, or it may have as its outcome deliberate attempts at "de-identification" (as in a striving for separate identities: Schacter, Gelutz, Shore, & Auler, 1978). MZs report, as one might expect, that they are closer; DZs say they are more concerned with their own individual rights and show greater rivalry. Adult twins, in general, successfully develop separate identities (Vandell, 1990). However, extremes of common identity can sometimes be seen in older adult twins who not only have similar occupations and preferences, but who, at Twin Conferences, delight in showing themselves dressed in identical costume and jewelery.

In young twins, closeness may manifest itself by secret language, or "cryptophasia," as it has been called. It may be that closeness relieves twins of the necessity of developing more intelligible means of communication, as understanding between them is facilitated by context, gestures, and common intention.

Dominance.   Seventy-five percent of the mothers of 2-year-old male twins studied by Lytton (1980) identified one twin as the more dominant, but many also qualified this by mentioning fluctuations in dominance according to situation and over time. Examining potential correlates of dominance in child characteristics, Lytton found no significant correlations with birthweight, vocabulary IQ, degree of compliance or attachment, or with maternal practices. The only variable that showed a near-significant relation (at the .10 level) was the child's rate of speech. Confirmation of this finding comes from the fact that several mothers mentioned that the dominant twin talked more.

These findings suggest that the child's fluency is related to competence in dealing with the environment and hence to being perceived as a leader: This relation again highlights the importance of speech. In this sense, it is understandable that, in many twin pairs, one twin becomes the "Secretary for External Affairs," whereas the other one keeps the twin relationship going.

In the follow-up of twins at age 9 conducted by Lytton and his colleagues, the question of whether there is a leader and a follower among the twin partners was again raised. Only 57 percent of mothers identified one twin as the more dominant at this age: With age and more contact with others outside the family circle, a certain shift toward greater equality between the twins had emerged. However, in two thirds of the pairs, the dominance or equality relationship remained unchanged over the 7-year time span, and in only three pairs was there a switch in the identity of the dominant partner. It seems, therefore, that such relationships between twin partners are fairly enduring (Lytton et al., 1988).

Koch (1966), who studied 90 pairs of twins of varying zygosity, from age 5 to 7 years, also reported dominance–submission relationships in 61 percent of twin pairs and found the relationship to be rather stable. Dominance in school-age twins, it appears, depends on many factors: intellectual ability , physical prowess, and interpersonal skills. In DZ opposite-sex pairs, it was the girl who predominated mostly, probably because of her advanced social skills.

Peer and Adult Relations

One might think that the pair situation among twins provides practice in interactional skills that might transfer to later peer relationships, but there is no evidence for such helpful generalization. On the contrary, infant twins spent one third the time that singletons do in peer interaction in comparable playroom situations (Vandell, Owens, Wilson, & Henderson, 1988). Also, Kim, Dales, Connor, Walters, and Witherspoon (1969), observing twins and singletons in nursery school, found twins to be less affectionate and less aggressive, as well as more solitary, than singletons at age 3, but none of these differences remained significant by age 5. Zazzo (1976) claimed that twins suffer from greater social isolation than singletons, because of the inward-turning nature of the "couple effect." And Hay and O'Brien (1984) also found persistent problems in peer relationships for girl twins. These negative findings mainly come from preschool children.

However, there are also some more optimistic reports—generally about older twins—in the literature: According to Koch (1966), twins' close relationships with each other do not interfere with their relationships with other children at school, where twins are as involved with other children and with adults as singletons. Often twins' relationships with peers have proved to be excellent, and teachers have reported that twins were less selfish, more friendly, and more helpful than singletons (Hay & O'Brien, 1984; Koch, 1966).

In Lytton, Watts, and B. F. Dunn's (1987) follow-up of 9-year-old twins and singletons, none of the teacher ratings of social characteristics (e.g., compliance, independence, teacher dependence, peer relations) showed any difference between twins and singletons that even approached statistical significance, nor did the ratings on a maladjustment questionnaire. Twins' peer relationships were rated as being even slightly better than those of singletons, so twins, it seems, are not necessarily less sociable than singletons, as some authors have claimed.

Which characteristics of twins predict the nature of peer relationships? First, involvement with other children is correlated with intelligence test scores. Second, security of attachment seems to predict good sibling/peer interactions: In Vandell's and colleagues' study, if at least one co-twin had a secure attachment relationship to mother, the pair played more with each other and more with unfamiliar peers than did those where only insecure attachments prevailed. Hence the relation between security of attachment and good peer relations seems confirmed. But dyads composed of securely attached twins (assessed at 12 months) spent more time in peer interaction as early as 6 months. Perhaps both peer interaction and secure attachment are mediated by dispositional characteristics that predate both attachment and peer competence—and may be of biological origin (Vandell et al., 1988)?

Psychopathology

There are also no differences in rated maladjustment or in psychopathology between twins and singletons in smaller samples selected from the population at large (Hay & O'Brien,1984, 1987; Lytton et al., 1987). However, more conduct disorders have been diagnosed in twins, both in a clinic-referred sample of children and in large British national cohorts (see Rubin, Stewart, & Chen, in this *Handbook*). The higher incidence of conduct disorder might be explained by parental discipline being less effective, or affection being manifested to a somewhat lesser degree in twin than in singleton families. (Lytton, 1980, found less internalization of behavioral standards in 2-year-old twins than singletons, although this need not lead to conduct disorder.) Perhaps a twin is more in danger of developing behavior difficulties by being exposed to a misbehaving twin partner at close quarters. Also, lower reading level and language delay may be risk factors for twins, since marked language delay is associated with high risk of socioemotional and behavioral problems in singletons. However, these are speculations only (Simonoff, 1992).

In summary, the relationships of twins to each other involve some special problems: How intensely do they want to achieve a common identity and to what degree do they want to develop a separate individuality? Twins will solve such problems according to their own inclinations. Twins vary in interpersonal skills, and hence in quality of peer relationships, just like singletons, and, apart from their slight immaturity in the early school years, overall it seems that their twinship itself poses no special threat to their peer interactions.

As regards behavior problems, we find that twin–singleton differences in their incidence on national cohorts and in referral rates to clinics (twins higher) are much smaller than twin–singleton differences in language, reading, and IQ and hence likely to be of little practical importance (Rutter & Redshaw, 1991).

DEVELOPMENT OF LANGUAGE AND INTELLIGENCE

Twins' slight lag in language skills and verbal intelligence compared with singletons has always held a special fascination for psychologists because its explanation was in doubt: It could be attributable to twins' biological vulnerabilities or to the fact that they grow up as a pair (the latter explanation would exemplify Zajonc's confluence theory), or of course to a combination of these two factors.

The Facts

There is consensus in the research literature that, on average, twins score 5 to 7 points lower on verbal intelligence tests than singletons (Mittler, 1971; Myrianthopoulos, Nichols, & Broman, 1976; Record, McKeown, & Edwards, 1970). Moreover, among twins, MZs lag behind DZs on verbal tests (Koch, 1966). Language has also generally been found to be delayed in twins compared with singletons (Day, 1932; Hay, Prior, Collett, & Williams, 1987; Mittler, 1971), and, consequently, so has reading skill (Johnston, Prior, & Hay, 1984). Bornstein and Ruddy (1984), investigating a small sample in detail, reported that twins from infancy were lower than singletons on all measures of language development, and so did Tomasello, Mannle, and Kruger (1986). The effects are greater for male twins where the negative consequences of being a twin are exacerbated by the greater vulnerability of males (Hay & O'Brien, 1984). The 2-year-old male twins in Lytton's (1980) study spoke less and their speech was marked by greater immaturity of construction and articulation than that of singletons, matched for age and maternal education (see Table 8.1). They also had lower scores on the Peabody Picture Vocabulary Test. In addition, Conway, Lytton, and Pysh (1980) found that the complexity of twins' speech was less than that of matched singletons.

Much is sometimes made of twins' so-called secret language (autonomous language or cryptophasia), as if this was a systematically invented secret code. Bakker (1987), examining twins' actual speech, found at least 90 percent of twins' vocabulary was traceable to parents' vocabulary. The secret language consisted of phonological distortions and sounds that were simplified and made easier. Informal observations in Lytton's (1980) study also did not reveal any evidence for the existence of cryptophasia at age 2, only of the use of immature, badly formed speech, such as Bakker (1987) described. This would sometimes be intelligible to co-twins, whose intentions and notions it expresses, and who are in constant contact with each other, and not to the mother, in the same way that some children's unformed speech may be intelligible to mother when it is not to outsiders. As twins spend more time with others—in preschool and school, where they may often receive speech therapy—distortions and grammatical inaccuracies disappear. Hence the notion of a systematically invented "secret language" is probably a myth.

When the twins in Lytton's sample were compared with a fresh, matched group of singletons during a follow-up at age 9, the twins had significantly lower *verbal* intelligence test scores than the singletons (see Table 8.2), even after removing the effects of maternal education, and the same applied to math achievement. But the inferiority in verbal scores was entirely due to the MZ twins, as the DZ

TABLE 8.2
Twin–Singleton Differences on Cognitive Measures (Age 9)—Singletons Higher

	p[a]
Verbal intelligence[b]	.05
Nonverbal intelligence[c]	.70
Math achievement[d]	.04
Reading comprehension achievement[d]	.06
Total achievement score[d]	.05[e]
Academic competence—teacher rating	.50
Speech maturity—teacher rating	.95

Note. Adapted from Lytton, Watts, and Dunn (1987).
[a]Two-tailed t tests, $df = 34$.
[b] Crichton Vocabulary Scale—Percentiles.
[c]Raven's Colored Progressive Matrices—Percentiles.
[d]Peabody Individual Achievement Test—Percentiles.
[e]When mothers' education was covaried, no significant twin–singleton difference remained for this variable.

twins' scores were indistinguishable from those of the singletons. In *nonverbal* intelligence, the twins as a whole practically equalled the singletons, nor did they have significantly lower scores in tests of reading comprehension or in teachers' ratings of academic and speech competence (Lytton et al., 1987).

Although there has been repeated confirmation from a number of studies (e.g., Benirschke & Kim, 1973; Lytton et al., 1987; Mittler, 1971; Record et al., 1970) that twins are exposed to greater pre- and perinatal hazards than singletons are, it should be noted that the 9-year-old twins in Lytton and his colleagues' follow-up had fully overcome these initial handicaps in their physical development, as their height and weight at age 9 were indistinguishable from those of singletons.

Research is also quite consistent in showing that parents have fewer verbal interchanges with each twin than singleton parents do with their children. Bornstein and Ruddy (1984) reported that at 4 months of age, mothers of twins encouraged attention to the environment less, and that at 12 months they were less likely to talk to their children than mothers of singletons. Twelve-month-old twins then showed lower language skills than their singleton controls, and the authors assumed this was the effect of earlier maternal behavior, since twins were the equals of singletons in maturity and habituation rate at 4 months (which generally predicted 12-month vocabulary).

Tomasello et al. (1986) similarly found, from another small sample, that although twin mothers spoke as much overall as did singleton mothers, on average, individual twins had less speech specifically directed to them than did singleton children. Twins participated in fewer and shorter episodes of joint attentional focus, and had fewer and shorter conversations with their mothers, who also exhibited a more directive style of interaction. These are important indicators, because joint attentional episodes and the number of maternal utterances and questions were positively correlated, but the number of directives was negatively correlated, with children's vocabulary in the sample as a whole. The slower language growth of twins, the authors concluded, is associated with the special pragmatic constraints on social and linguistic interactions in triadic situations (the twin situation) that form the postnatal family environment.

The Effects of Biological and Postnatal Family Environment on Twins' Language

In general, at the toddler stage, if one added parents' speech to both twins' together, it would no doubt exceed in quantity the speech addressed to singletons. However, what affects the child is how much speech each twin receives, and twins experience fewer verbal interchanges of all kinds with their parents than singletons. Parents of twins in their socialization practices also, on average, are less psychologically minded and child centered than parents of singletons. These kinds of socialization experiences might suffice to explain the twins' well-documented language deficit.

However, other possible explanations exist. One is the fact that twins tend to form a cohesive unit. The delay in using "I," for instance, it has been thought, may be due to merged, undifferentiated identities in twins (Zazzo, 1982). On the other hand, as Savic (1980) claimed, it may simply be due to the complexity of the language task involved.

An alternative hypothesis would be to attribute twins' verbal deficit to their undoubtedly more adverse prenatal and perinatal experiences (e.g., lower birthweight, more pregnancy complications, and so forth). Conway et al. (1980) examined the contributions of both biological and postnatal environmental factors to the twin–singleton language differences, and found that at age 2 biological prenatal factors explained about 8 percent of variance in the speech measures, but maternal speech measures explained 15 percent of variance. The simple amount of mother's speech was, in fact, the best predictor of children's speech ability. In other words, at age 2 the "twoness" of the twin situation seems a more powerful determinant of twins' lag in linguistic competence than are biological pre- and perinatal difficulties. Such a conclusion is reinforced by the findings of an earlier study of twins who survived the death of their twin partners and were brought up as singletons, and which reported that at age 11 these surviving twins had a mean IQ at the singleton level, 5 points higher than that of twin pairs (Record et al., 1970).

These outcomes would also be in line with Breland's (1974) finding from large-scale studies of older children and adolescents that the close spacing of siblings results in more adverse effects on the intellectual development of the younger one than more generous spacing. Twinship is, of course, the extreme instance of close spacing and shows the same results for both twins. It is findings such as these that inspired—and corroborated—Zajonc's confluence model of intellectual development (see earlier, and Zajonc & Markus, 1975).

However, evidence counter to the theory also exists. Lytton et al. (1987), in their follow-up study (see Table 8.2), tried to unravel the effects of biological birth hazards from the environmental effects of the twin situation and the effects of maternal education. Their analysis demonstrated that mothers' educational level and birth difficulties were significant influences on verbal ability at age 9, and when these factors were held constant, the twin–singleton difference in verbal ability was no longer significant. All these aspects together explained only 18.7 percent of the variance in verbal ability, but other factors that were not measured in the investigation (e.g., aspects of the home environment not captured by mothers' education or the twin–singleton dichotomy) must be operating, too. It should be noted that the MZ performance in verbal ability and achievement remained significantly lower than either that of DZ twins or of singletons in this study. The essential point about these results is that by age 9 the twins' lag in verbal competence can no longer be explained by the "twin situation," in view of the fact that this lag was confined entirely to MZ twins and was no longer present in DZ twins. Thus, these findings disconfirm Zajonc's confluence hypothesis, discussed earlier, as did Brackbill and Nichols' (1982) findings, which failed to confirm the importance of birth interval in the intellectual status of 7-year-old children. Moreover, neither these authors nor a large scale study on the twins of the Collaborative Perinatal Project (Myrianthopoulos et al., 1976) found any differences in IQ between single survivor twins, after their partner had died, and other twin pairs. It is not clear how the differences in outcomes between these and other studies, which support Zajonc's model, arose.

The change in explanatory factors from age 2 to age 9 in Lytton's investigations does not invalidate the earlier finding. When children are 9 years old, parents no longer play such a predominant and near-exclusive role in their children's cognitive development because at that age the children will also derive a great deal of stimulation from the wider world of friends and school. The fact of being twins therefore recedes into the background as a determinant of verbal ability, but the effects of mothers' educational level and of possible perinatal handicapping conditions to some extent persist. In the final analysis, therefore, our data seem to indicate that social class/education differences are more influential for verbal and cognitive development than the mere fact of being twins.

Although these findings confirm those of other investigations in showing that twins, and particularly MZ twins, still lag somewhat behind singletons in verbal ability and school achievement, the gap between twins and singletons narrows between age 2 and 9. The twins also cannot be distinguished from singletons in nonverbal ability or in social development. The lag in verbal skills, therefore, has to be seen in perspective. From the history of many twins, it is evident that most individual twins overcome any initial handicap, with the large majority growing into fully competent adults.

CONCLUSIONS

What are the implications of multiple births for the quality of life of individuals? Medical profession-als are developing a growing awareness of the medical, social, and economic problems caused by multiple births. Given recent developments in infertility treatment that lead to smaller numbers of ova or embryos being transferred to the uterus, it is possible to achieve both high rates of pregnancy and a triplet rate of only 1 percent. Monitoring estrogen levels, and choosing a carefully adapted fertility treatment method can therefore reduce the incidence of multiple births, and concern over the health implications of such births may, in fact, lead to changes in fertility treatments (Millar et al., 1992).

What are the main problems in rearing twins? It is by no means clear yet what the differences in psychological development, including language and cognitive development, between twins and singletons are due to. But maybe the fact that parents have to divide their attention and resources between two children of the same age plays at least some part. If this is the case, parents may perhaps be able to mitigate some of the adverse effects by ensuring that each twin has a parent's undivided attention for a given time, thus making interaction more exclusive. They may do this by each parent allotting some time to each twin individually, or by sharing care and attention with willing supporters, such as grandparents, in their social network (see the Postscript in this chapter, "Voices of Twin Mothers.")

Having written a great deal about the influence of parental environment on twins' development, our final question is: What influence do parents have on their children anyhow? Twins who were found to be securely attached at 12 months spent more time in peer interaction already at 6 months of age, compared with insecurely attached pairs (Vandell et al., 1988; see discussion earlier). Perhaps some dispositional characteristics, possibly of biological origin, are responsible for both peer competence and secure attachment. Parents' childrearing practices do not operate in a vacuum. They work in interaction with, and often as a reaction to, the child's predisposition. Reciprocal, recurrent interactions—called "transactions"—in which children's and parents' predispositions and mutual relationships are interwoven, occur continuously between parents and children, and they will have a large, cumulative effect on the development of ordinary children. Lytton (1980), in a microanalysis of home observations, identified such transactions in concrete detail; examples are that mother's negative actions (criticism) increased the child's positive ones over time, and the child's positive actions eventually tended to reduce mother's negative ones. In this way, mother and child actions constituted a feedback loop.

In some aspects of socialization parents' influence seems to predominate, whereas in others the child's predisposition appears to play the larger role. In the area of control-compliance, the influence seems to run mainly from parent to child: This was so in Lytton's (1980) investigation. And, in confirmation, Rowe's (1983) genetic study of older twins found that parental control behavior is not influenced by *offspring* genetic characteristics. On the other hand, in the area of attachment and warmth, influence runs mainly from child to parent (Lytton, 1980), and Rowe (1983) similarly detected substantial influence from offspring genotype on parental acceptance/rejection—which is closely related to attachment—again confirming the finding of the behavioral study. Perhaps in the area of attachment and acceptance/rejection, the child is the dominant force, because parents do not set out on a purposeful program to create or direct attachment to them, and acceptance is also largely a matter of the child's disposition and relationship with the parent. On the other hand, most parents do engage in a conscious, purpose-driven program of shaping and controlling the child's behavior— hence it is their dispositions and goals that count here.

For the creation of the ordinary characteristics of the ordinary child, parents' socializing efforts seem to be the predominant influence overall. Thus, less dictatorial techniques by parents may well elicit more cooperation from the child, and parents can, indeed, by appropriate procedures and attitudes promote such things as more voluntary compliance with house rules, good "manners," or consideration for others. But parents are influenced by the child's nature and accommodate their actions to the child's individuality and needs (e.g., by reacting to MZ twins more similarly than to DZ twins). They may also adapt their influence techniques to the degree of the child's person orientation or temperament (Bell, 1977; Kochanska, 1991), or encourage play with certain (sex-typed) toys when that is the child's preference (Lytton & Romney, 1991; Snow, Jacklin, & Maccoby, 1983).

Moreover, there are limits to parental influence. Severe psychopathology is not likely to arise from poor childrearing practices alone. Serious disorders, be they schizophrenia or conduct disorder, generally fit the "vulnerability-stress" model—a predisposition to a disorder is inherited and this liability is then turned into reality by stressors in family life (e.g., poor parental discipline techniques) or rendered less likely by buffering factors (e.g., maternal affection; Goldstein, 1988). In the case of pathological conditions, the children's own predispositions may even be the stronger force that parental influence can sway only so much (see Lytton, 1990). However, twins' as well as other children's later personalities, in general, are best explained as outcomes of reciprocal and recurrent interactions over time between the organism and the environment.

POSTSCRIPT: VOICES OF TWIN MOTHERS

The First Year
By Lin Gallagher

As the proud mother of four children, I have earned the privilege of being realistic regarding the finer points of parenting. Strangers often stop me and exclaim "Oh twins, you are so lucky!" Depending on the day, or rather the night, I may offer the stranger their pick for a week or respond lovingly in agreement.

The first few months since the birth of the twins have been a challenge. The beginning of any baby's life is sleepless and busy, but this is multiplied times two with twins. For the last six months the longest stretch of sleep I have had at one time is 3 hours, and this is rare. Even my husband is called into the act. I breast-fed for the first several months, which allowed him the opportunity to sleep through individual crying, but when a harmonious duet occurred we were both awakened. He at least could do pacifier duty until I was ready for number two.

Time has mellowed things around here. Both babies have begun smiling, playing with their older brothers, and even sleeping in longer stretches (occasionally). But I have resigned myself to the fact that my life right now revolves around my children's needs. In our house, there always seems to be too little time and energy and too much chaos and too many demands.

But like anything in life, there is the good and the bad. Fortunately, with twins there is a lot more of the good. I particularly enjoy watching them play together. They are a study in motion with eight little hands and feet whirling in the air. To them it really doesn't matter whose fingers or whose toes end up in whose mouth. Each will as contentedly suck on the other's fingers as their own. As they get older, their interest in the other's antics increases and the beginnings of a very close relationship is unfolding before us.

Although I have raised two other children, parenting twins has brought a new set of issues. I used to worry about giving equal amounts of attention to each of the babies. But, as they grow, I realize I can relax and just try and meet the demands of each individual. Although Colin will sit and play by himself happily and is less demanding throughout the day, he makes sure he gets his time in other ways. He very often will awaken earlier in the morning for extra cuddles, or will smile and gyrate so invitingly when you walk by you can't help but pick him up.

The twins also seem continuously to change who is the more contented and easier to care for. Right after birth, Kelsey was almost 2 pounds larger than Colin, and seemed to be more relaxed and easier to settle. After a few months, Colin became the more contented baby. He enjoyed his own company, whereas Kelsey seemed to need constant reassurance that mom was around. This is changing again, as Colin is demanding more and more stimulation and Kelsey is becoming very interested in developing her fine motor skills. Kelsey can now spend long stretches carefully examining a toy, her toes, or whatever is handy.

One thing reassuring about parenting twins is how different they are in personalities, needs, and responses. Colin is constantly in motion. His arms and legs are always going and his eyes open wide sponging up any action around. He is quick to smile with a twinkle in his eye to attract the attention of any passers-by. He is a baby who is ready and willing to experience new situations.

Kelsey is the opposite, preferring quieter surroundings. She is cautious with new faces and surroundings, preferring the comfort of mom's arms. Although she is less active, she seems to spend more time taking in her surroundings. It is this difference that makes me realize that perhaps babies have a more important role to play in how they respond to the world around them than we acknowledge.

One thing for sure is the role they play in my response to them. My family may have doubled, but so have the smiling, laughing faces to love. And on most days I think my luck has doubled times two.

Creating or Responding to Gender Differences at 8 Months of Age?

Our babies are starting to master many new feats and we are amazed by the difference in their abilities and interests. Colin continues to be constantly on the go. He has started to crawl at 7½ months, he is curious about everything around him, and when you play peek-a-boo he just cannot wait for you to pull off the blanket. Kelsey is the opposite. She has no interest in crawling yet and is content to sit and watch the action. When you play peek with her she waits patiently and greets you with a big smile as the blanket comes off.

Kelsey is the first girl in the family, and it is hard not to compare the twins with respect to gender. For the most part, both the babies are encouraged in the same play and games. But we do treat Kelsey a little differently from Colin. She responds much more to gentle play or cradling in our laps. Although Colin enjoys being held and cuddled, he is much happier crawling around. Colin really likes action; the louder the toy bangs, the happier he is. When we play with Colin there is a lot more tickling and wrestling.

Kelsey also has a much higher level of separation anxiety than Colin. She will scream in outrage when mom leaves the room. Around strangers Colin will become anxious if mom strays too far, but isn't too bothered at home.

Being the only daughter in a family of four children does give Kelsey special status. For her first Christmas I felt compelled to give her a doll. We have decided that we will provide her with the opportunity to play with "girl" toys such as dolls and tea sets. But we plan to follow her lead whether she enjoys Barbies or Tonka trucks.

As a tomboy myself, I have no urge to push Kelsey into any particular play. Most childhood pursuits are very unisex, like tricycle riding, modeling clay, and so on. But there is no problem if Colin ends up playing dolls with Kelsey or Kelsey plays cars with Colin. Because of their interest in each other, I suspect there will be a lot of compromise on both their parts. I think what is most important to me is that Kelsey and Colin direct their own interests. The twins reinforce for me how children differ right from birth, and as their parent I feel the need to be sensitive to what makes each child special.

2 Years Old and Later
By Jagjit K. Singh

2-Year-Olds

In the first years it seems to be time continuously to change diapers, nurse, clean, sleep, burp, rock, and change diapers all over again. When does mom get to sleep and eat and exercise? What about time to think, to wonder, to relax?

So it is essential to hire a helper to do the physical chores around the house while mother looks after the babies. Doctors must educate fathers to help in whatever way they can. Too often, the mother appears very preoccupied with the babies, and the father feels left out and helpless. This is another reason for the father to be involved. Help from other family members must also be sought. Moreover, it is essential to receive such help so that the mother can go out without the twins once in a while.

The joys of having twins are surely more than double the joys of having singletons because of the jubilant interactions between the two. Twins seem to need each other when sleeping, having a bath, eating, walking, crawling. Physical closeness seems to be what they need. Some twins greet each other with hugs and kisses when they get up in the morning. But twins also quarrel. They can surprise their parents by having nasty hand fights, kicking, biting, and yelling at each other. And they do reinforce each other's mischief.

This all applies to the first couple of years. Does it change when the twins are 2 years old? "Wonderful age," is how one mother describes it. "They spread things all over the room."

What does mom have to contend with at this age? Temper tantrums! All mothers have to contend with these. However, if both the members of the twin pair resort to temper tantrums, it can be nerve wracking. Very often, when one is having a temper tantrum, the other is quiet and almost fearful of the crying. But, sometimes the other one decides to cry, too (maybe because the first one is upset), and this is very hard on the parents.

What is really amazing is that by the time the twins are about 1½ to 2½ years old, they seem to be scheming all the time. Some mothers wonder whether "as soon as the twins get up in the morning they plan to collaborate on the exciting agendas for the day. It appears as though one distracts mother, while the other spills the shampoo on the living room carpet. They also keep a straight face and blame the other."

Visits to the Doctor's Office and Other Challenges.   Visits to the doctor's office can be quite a chore. Both babies are crying to be picked up by mother and hence they are red and sweaty; the mother gets embarrassed. So what should the mother do the next time? If possible, she should bring dad or a friend along. Mothers of twins almost never leave home without another adult, especially when visiting the doctor!

There is a possibility that infections pass quickly from one to the other. The sheer physical nearness promotes this mutual infection. Doctors sometimes prescribe the medicine for both twins, as a preventative measure, even when only one comes in for an infection.

Taking twins out is much more draining, psychologically and physically, than taking a singleton out. Whether it is going for walks, or drives, for structured play, or to a friend's house, parents seem to think twice before taking twins out. When the mother goes for walks in the park or in the mall, she feels she does not have enough control—one of the twins walks into that fashion store, loving the feel of those expensive blouses hanging on the racks, while the other runs off to the candy store! Rather than an enjoyable outing, it becomes a stressful event. Should mom be advised to let the 2-year-olds enjoy themselves? Should she teach them limits? Or should she just avoid going out, especially if she is alone? But then, wouldn't the twins miss out on something?

Sharing occurs on good days. On bad days, even if there are two identical toys or milk bottles or shirts, both will cry for the one toy/milk bottle or shirt. One wonders whether the twins have decided, "Let's drive mom crazy!" It is important for mom to understand that at this age any scheming is unlikely.

At this age, it seems that children are always dumping things: dumping clothes from drawers, dumping cereal, dumping shampoo, dumping toys. And to top it all, they love to walk on the mess. It seems that when twins are about 2 years old, they are no longer as sweet and well-behaved as they used to be; they become explorers and collaborators. It is as if "they suddenly decided that what they wish to do is worth getting into trouble for" or that "they like the challenge of getting mom upset and of getting a rap on the hand."

Alternate care.   What are the considerations when parents think of alternate care for twins of this age? What if the mother has had enough at home and really wishes to get out, even if for a part-time job? Day care for twins is obviously more expensive than for a single child. Moreover, every morning, two children would have to be dressed instead of one. If one gets sick, who would look after that one? Would the other one still go to day care? Who would drop the other one aff at the day care? Would mom have to stay at home with the sick one? Would mom hire a nanny for the few days? So, in fact, having a nanny come in to babysit is a preferred mode of alternate child care for most working parents of twins.

4- to 6-Year-Olds

Mothers see a definite competition between twins that is not there in singletons. Mothers sometimes find that "by 3 or 4 years twins start telling on each other, demand attention from parents, undermine you by manipulating you and tattling on the other twin, and acting as if he/she is mum's favorite."

"We don't like to look the same."   By this age, twins have had enough of being exclaimed at and compared. They do not like to be compared and do not like to look the same. They are very offended when people call them by the other twin's name accidentally. Parents of twins have to remember not to accept clothes that are identical, especially if the twins have expressed a dislike for the sameness. Mothers have to be careful when buying outfits or accessories that both get equivalent, but not identical, things.

Of course, twins *are* different from each other. Yet parents cannot help but compare the two in terms of almost everything: height, weight, motor development, language development, teething, and skills in school-related activities. They get anxious, especially if one twin is left behind the other in several respects. This helps neither the parents nor the twins. In fact, hearing about such comparisons, rivalry between the two may start and escalate as time goes on.

Preschool.   By this age (4 to 5 years), the twins are sent to preschool and playschool. There are many issues that parents of twins at these ages have to consider:

1. Be prepared to face stereotypical responses from teachers regarding expectations, especially of twin boys.
2. Educate teachers on the differences between the twins: the names, the likes and dislikes, the personalities.
3. Be ready for different and varied friendships, and
4. The possibility of splitting the twins into two different classes. Many teachers feel that because of their and others' tendencies to compare twins, it is for the good of the twins to be placed in different classes.

Memories and reflections.   By the time the twins are this age and are going to preschool or Grade 1, mother has time to reflect on the past. Mothers often feel they have missed their children's childhood. Because of the sheer busy-ness of life, mothers do not remember the cuddles, the hugs, and the simple joys. One mother remembers seeing a home video of their Christmas celebrations from 2 years ago. She found herself nagging at the twins all the time and observed: "Life was so mechanical and so tiring."

Parents have resorted to many strategies for quality bonding between them and the twins. For instance, each parent takes turns taking one of the twins out to do an errand or to spend some special time with. This way, attention is devoted to each twin by each parent. The next time, the parents switch twins. It does work well for most parents of twins, especially for this 4- to 6-year-old group.

8- to 9-Year-Olds

The issues change from baths and diapers to temper tantrums to the *taxi stage.* As twins and singletons grow older, they develop different interests, and likes and dislikes. The only difference is that, whereas a singleton would be enrolled in two (or three) activities, if the twins are allowed to be enrolled in two activities each (and if interests are different), this would make a total of four activities for the parent to be the driver for!

In school.   When they are 6 or 7 years old, twins can tell parents whether or not they wish to be together in class. A mother remembers that at the end of Grade 1, her twins asked to be separated in the next grade. She says they did not experience any trauma because, as the twins said, "We do get to meet each other after class, anyway."

Sameness exploited!   In spite of the resistance to looking the same and being compared, twins can exploit this sameness for some fun. As one mother recalls, her 8-year-old twins decided it would be a great idea to dress up identically and sit in the other twin's class on April Fool's Day—to confuse the teacher.

Yet another little anecdote: As one mother with a pair of twins wandered into a ladies' dress store, one put on a dress and showed herself off. The other twin said: "Oh, I think I should buy that dress; it does look good on me!"

These anecdotes express the wonderfulness of twins and the joys of parenting them. One cannot help but realize that although there are similarities, parenting twins brings with it issues, concerns, and practices that are different from those of parenting a singleton child. One cannot help but be amazed at the unique stories being told, witnessing some interesting episodes, and being a part of the most exhilarating experiences of twins and their parents.

ACKNOWLEDGMENTS

We thank Barbara Sack, Elizabeth Kelly, Carol Cameron, and Kim Van Steenbergen for sharing their experiences in parenting twins in interviews with Jagjit K. Singh. Some of the anecdotes and excerpts in the last section of the chapter are taken from these interviews.

REFERENCES

Ainsworth, M.D.S., Blehar, M. C., Waters, E., & Wall, S. (1978). *Patterns of attachment: A psychological study of the strange situation.* Hillsdale, NJ: Lawrence Erlbaum Associates.

Allen, G. (1955). Comments on the analysis of twin samples. *Acta Geneticae Medicae et Gemellologiae, 4,* 143–159.

Bakker, P. (1987). Autonomous language in twins. *Acta Geneticae Medicae et Gemellologiae, 36,* 233–238.

Bell, R. Q. (1977). Socialization findings re-examined. In R. Q. Bell & R. V. Harper (Eds.), *Child effects on adults* (pp. 53–84). Hillsdale, NJ: Lawrence Erlbaum Associates.

Benirschke, K., & Kim, C. (1973). Multiple pregnancy (Part 1). *New England Journal of Medicine, 288,* 1278–1284.

Bornstein, M., & Ruddy, M. G. (1984). Infant attention and maternal stimulation: Prediction of cognitive and linguistic development in singletons and twins. In H. Bouma & D. G. Bouwhuis (Eds.), *Attention and performance X: Control of language processes* (pp. 433–445). Hillsdale, NJ: Lawrence Erlbaum Associates.

Bowlby, J. (1958). The nature of the child's tie to his mother. *International Journal of Psychoanalysis, 39,* 350–373.

Brackbill, Y., & Nichols, P. L. (1982). A test of the confluence model of intellectual development. *Developmental Psychology, 18,* 192–198.

Breland, H. M. (1974). Birth order, family configuration and verbal achievement. *Child Development, 45,* 1011–1019.

Bulmer, M. G. (1970). *The biology of twinning in man.* London: Oxford University Press.

Burlingham, D. (1952). *Twins: A study of three pairs of identical twins.* London: Imago.

Clark, P. M., & Dickman, Z. (1984). Features of interaction in infant twins. *Acta Geneticae Medicae et Gemellologiae, 33,* 165–171.

Cohen, D. J., Dibble, E. D., & Grawe, J. M. (1977). Parental style. *Archives General Psychiatry, 34,* 445–451.

Conway, D., Lytton, H., & Pysh, F. (1980). Twin-singleton language differences. *Canadian Journal of Behavioural Sciences, 12,* 264–271.

Corter, C., & Stiefel J. (1983). *Sibling interaction and maternal behaviour with young premature twins.* Paper presented at the Biennial Meeting of the Society for Research in Child Development.

Day, E. (1932). The development of language in twins. *Child Development, 3,* 179–199.

Dibble, E. D., & Cohen, D. J. (1981). Personality development in identical twins: The first decade of life. *Psychoanalytic Study of the Child, 36,* 45–70.

Dunn, J., & Kendrick, C. (1982). *Siblings: Love, envy and understanding.* Cambridge, MA: Harvard University Press.

Goldberg, S., Perrotta, M., Minde, K., & Corter, C. (1986). Maternal behavior and attachment in low-birth-weight twins and singletons. *Child Development, 57,* 34-46.

Goldstein, M. (1988). The family and psychopathology. *Annual Review of Psychology, 39,* 283–299.

Goshen-Gottstein, E. R. (1979). Families of twins: A longitudinal study in coping. *Twins: Newsletter of the International Society for Twin Studies* (4–5), 2.

Goshen-Gottstein, E. R. (1981). Differential maternal socialization of opposite-sexed twins, triplets, and quadruplets. *Child Development, 52,* 1255–1264.

Hay, D. A., & O'Brien, P. J. (1984). The role of parental attitudes in the development of temperament in twins at home, school and in test situations. *Acta Geneticae Medicae et Gemellologiae, 33,* 191–204.

Hay, D. A., & O'Brien, P. J. (1987). Early influences on the school adjustment of twins. *Acta Geneticae Medicae et Gemellologiae, 36,* 239–248.

Hay, D. A., Prior, M., Collett, S., & Williams, M. (1987). Speech and language development in preschool twins. *Acta Geneticae Medicae et Gemellologiae, 36,* 213–222.

Inouye, E., & Imaizumi, Y. (1981). Analysis of twinning rates in Japan. In L.Gedda, P. Parisi, & W.E. Nance (Eds.), *Twin research 3, Part A* (pp. 21–33) New York: Alan R. Liss.

Johnston, C., Prior, M., & Hay, D. A. (1984). Prediction of reading disability in twin boys. *Developmental Medicine and Child Neurology, 26,* 588–595.

Kim C. C., Dales, R. J., Connor, R., Walters, J., & Witherspoon, R. (1969). Social interaction of like-sex twins and singletons in relation to intelligence, language, and physical development. *Journal of Genetic Psychology, 114,* 203–214.

Klaus, M., & Kennell, J. (1982). *Parent–infant bonding.* St. Louis: C. V. Mosby.

Koch, H. (1966). *Twins and twin relations.* Chicago: University of Chicago Press.

Kochanska, G. (1991). Socialization and temperament in the development of guilt and conscience. *Child Development, 62,* 1379–1392.

Kopp, C. B. (1983). Risk factors in development. In P. H. Mussen (Series Ed.) & M. M. Haith & J. J.Campos (Vol. Eds.), *Handbook of child psychology: Vol. 2. Infancy and developmental psychobiology* (pp. 1081–1188). New York: Wiley.

Loehlin, J. C., & Nichols, R. C. (1976). *Heredity, environment, and personality.* Austin, TX: University of Texas Press.

Lytton, H. (1980). *Parent–child interaction: The socialization process observed in twin and singleton families.* New York: Plenum.

Lytton, H. (1990). Child and parent effects in boys' conduct disorder: A reinterpretation. *Developmental Psychology, 26,* 683–697.

Lytton, H., & Romney, D. M. (1991). Parents' differential socialization of boys and girls: A meta-analysis. *Psychological Bulletin, 109*, 267–296.

Lytton, H., Watts, D., & Dunn, B. E. (1984). *Cognitive and social development from 2 to 9: A twin longitudinal study.* Unpublished manuscript, University of Calgary, Canada.

Lytton, H., Watts, D., & Dunn, B. E. (1987). Twin–singleton differences in verbal ability: Where do they stem from? *Intelligence, 11*, 359–369.

Lytton, H., Watts, D., & Dunn, B. E. (1988). Continuity and change in child characteristics and maternal practices between ages 2 and 9: An analysis of interview responses. *Child Study Journal, 18*, 1–15.

Millar, W. J., Wadhera, S., & Nimrod, C. (1992). Multiple births: Trends and pattern in Canada, 1974–1990. *Health Reports 1992, 4*, No. 3, Ottawa: Statistics Canada.

Minde, K., Corter, C., & Goldberg, S. (1986). The contribution of twinship and health to early interaction and attachment between premature infants and their mothers. In J. D. Call (Ed.), *Frontiers of infant psychiatry* (Vol. 2, pp. 160–175). New York: Basic Books.

Mittler, P. (1971). *The study of twins.* London: Penguin Books.

Myrianthopoulos, N. C., Nichols, P. L. & Broman, S. H. (1976). Intellectual development of twins - comparison with singletons. *Acta Geneticae Medicae et Gemellologiae, 25*, 376–380.

Plomin, R., DeFries, J. C., & McClearn, G. E. (1990). *Behavioral genetics: A primer* (2nd ed.). New York: Freeman.

Plomin, R., & Rowe, D. C. (1979). Genetic and environmental etiology of social behavior in infancy. *Developmental Psychology, 15*, 62–72.

Record, R. G., McKeown, T., & Edwards, J. H. (1970). An investigation of the difference in measured intelligence between twins and single–births. *Annals of Human Genetics, 34*, 11–20.

Rowe, D. C. (1981). Environmental and genetic influence on dimensions of perceived parenting: A twin study. *Developmental Psychology, 17*, 203–208.

Rowe, D. C. (1983). A biometrical analysis of perceptions of family environments: A study of twin and singleton sibling kinships. *Child Development, 54*, 416–423.

Rutter, M., & Redshaw, J. (1991). Growing up as a twin: Twin–singleton differences in psychological development. *Journal of Child Psychology and Psychiatry, 32*, 885–895.

Savic, S. (1980). *How twins learn to talk.* New York: Academic Press.

Scarr, S., & Carter-Saltzman, L. (1979). Twin method: Defense of a critical assumption. *Behavior Genetics, 9*, 527–542.

Schacter, F. F., Gelutz, G., Shore, E., & Auler, M. (1978). Sibling deidentification judged by mothers. *Child Development, 49*, 543–546.

Scheinfeld, A. (1973). *Twins and supertwins.* London: Pelican Books.

Simonoff, E. (1992). Comparison of twins and singletons with child psychiatric disorders: An item sheet study. *Journal of Child Psychology and Psychiatry, 33*, 1319–1332.

Snow, M. E., Jacklin, C. N., & Maccoby, E. E. (1983). Sex-of-child differences in father–child interaction at one year of age. *Child Development, 54*, 227–232.

Tomasello, M., Mannle, S., & Kruger, A. C. (1986). Linguistic environment of 1- to 2-year-old twins. *Developmental Psychology, 22*, 169–176.

Vandell, D. L. (1990). Development in twins. *Annals of Child Development, 7*, 145–174.

Vandell, D. L., Owen, M. T., Wilson, K. S., & Henderson V. K. (1988). Social development in infant twins: Peer and mother–child relationships. *Child Development, 59*, 168–177.

Volling, B. L., & Belsky, J. (1992). The contribution of mother–child and father–child relationships to the quality of sibling interaction: A longitudinal study. *Child Development, 63*, 1209–1222.

Wilson, K. S. (1987). *Social interaction in twins: Relations between the second and fifth years of life.* Unpublished doctoral dissertation, University of Texas, Dallas.

Zajonc, R. B., & Markus, G. B. (1975). Birth order and intellectual development. *Psychological Review, 82*, 74–88.

Zazzo, R. (1976). The twin condition and the couple effect on personality development. *Acta Geneticae Medicae et Gemellologiae, 25*, 343–352.

Zazzo, R. (1982). The person: Objective approaches. In W. Hartup (Ed.), *Review of child development research* (Vol. 6, pp. 247–290). Chicago: University of Chicago Press.

9

Parenting Children Born Preterm

Susan Goldberg
The Hospital for Sick Children, Toronto
Barbara DiVitto
North Shore Children's Hospital, Salem

INTRODUCTION

Each year from 2 percent to 9 percent of newborn babies require specialized care in a neonatal intensive care unit (NICU). The majority of these are babies born prematurely (before 37 weeks of gestation) and weigh less than 2,500 g (5 lbs) at birth. The techniques of modern medical technology have doggedly pushed back the frontiers of viability so that in the 1990s even babies as young as 23 to 24 weeks gestation with weights as low as 500 g may survive. The parents of these babies confront unique problems engendered by the early timing of the birth, a prolonged hospital stay, and distinctive patterns of behavior and development during their infant's early years. In this chapter, we consider these problems and the ways in which they affect parents. In doing so, we summarize research on parent–infant interaction and relationships in the first year of life and consider the practical implications of the research. We do not attempt a comprehensive in-depth review, but concentrate on more recent work and try to tell a story, citing illustrative examples in more or less detail as they are relevant to the themes we develop. We chose to focus on the first year of life because it has been most intensively studied and it is the time when children born prematurely are most different from others and most challenging for their parents.

This chapter includes five main sections. It begins with a history of changes in hospital care for preterm infants and the way this impinged on parents. The second major section outlines considerations that make caring for a preterm infant unique: the time when birth occurs, the nature of the hospital experience, and the preterm infant's different developmental and behavioral patterns. The third part outlines theories concerning parent–child relationships and their respective interpretations of prematurity. The fourth reviews research on parent–child relationships and the fifth considers clinical interventions aimed at improving parent–child relationships. Throughout the chapter we use the terms *preterm* and *premature* interchangeably.

HISTORY OF PRETERM CARE: ITS EFFECTS ON PARENTS

Interest in preterm birth was first evidenced in Paris in the late 1800s by the physician Pierre Budin. He pioneered research on pre- and postnatal growth and on prematurity as a special disorder of the newborn and authored the first text in neonatology (the care of the newborn). In it, he described the use of incubators designed for preterm infants (Budin, 1907). His invention was the predecessor of today's incubators, which control temperature, oxygen, and humidity within glass-walled containers. At the same time, others in Berlin and Helsinki were also investigating solutions for the problems of preterm infants: poor temperature control, feeding difficulties, and vulnerability to disease (Avery, 1983).

In this era, preterm infants were separated from their parents, and parents were excluded from their care. Budin's techniques were brought to the United States by his student, Martin Cooney, who exhibited preterm infants in incubators at fairs and expositions in the United States and Europe as a commercial venture. It is difficult to imagine doctors or parents supporting this activity, but these infants were not expected to live. Parents had to be coaxed into taking "survivors" home after they had been on tour. On the positive side, demonstrating the success of these techniques led to their adoption in North American hospitals.

The introduction of hospital-based care improved preterm survival rates but also increased the isolation of parents from infants. The cause of respiratory problems in preterm infants was thought to be "germs," and parents were potential carriers. Early care stressed cleanliness and sterility. The practice of banning contact between infants and parents continued even after the discovery of hyaline membrane disease (functional immaturity of the lungs) in 1949 as the primary cause for these respiratory problems. Complications from treatment procedures began to be recognized in the 1940s and 1950s. These included retrolental fibroplasia (the abnormal increase of fibrous tissue behind the lens of the eye), which can cause blindness. This condition was found to be the result of excessive concentrations of oxygen in the incubator. Similarly, hearing problems in children born prematurely were related to antibiotics administered to ward off infection (Harrison, 1983).

Despite these discoveries, there was little change in preterm care until the 1960s, when neonatology became a recognized medical specialty. At this time, new techniques for reducing the incidence and severity of the problems associated with prematurity were developed. These included refined techniques for assisted breathing, equipment and laboratory tests to detect physiological problems, new surgical techniques, feeding methods, and drugs. The highly trained staff, specialized techniques, and machines were expensive, and needed for only a few births, so they were housed in NICUs in regional medical centers rather than local hospitals.

The unintended consequence of this change was further separation of families and babies, as at this time babies were transported by plane or specially equipped vans to regional centers for early care. Mothers usually remained in local hospitals, and fathers had to divide their visiting time between mother and baby. Furthermore, the "high-tech" environment of the neonatal intensive care unit, which was designed to support life functions and promote survival, was intimidating to frightened and anxious parents. Amidst the special technology, equipment, and trained staff, parents often felt overwhelmed, isolated, and unimportant to their baby's care. Through the 1960s, NICU care continued to emphasize maintenance of a sterile environment to prevent infection. Parents continued to be viewed as another source of infection whose presence should be minimized. Furthermore, handling was considered stressful to these babies, so affectionate and nurturant handling were kept to a minimum; invasive painful procedures were infants' primary human contacts.

A daring experiment was reported from Stanford University Medical Center in the early 1970s that marked a major transition . Mothers had been allowed into the NICU to handle and care for their premature infants. During this time, rates of infection were compared to periods when parents were not allowed into the nursery. The expected increase in infection rates did not occur (Barnett, Leiderman, Grobstein, & Klaus, 1970). A replication at Case Western Reserve Medical Center in Cleveland produced similar results (Kennell, Trause, & Klaus, 1975). These data, which showed conclusively that parent contact was not dangerous for preterm babies, led caregivers to question the traditional policy of separation. Research was then undertaken to investigate the effects of increased contact between mothers and babies. As a result of this research, hospital practices shifted toward allowing and encouraging parents to come into the NICU to handle and care for their infants. However, even in the most supportive nurseries, parents' visits are different experiences from those of parents of full-term infants.

Much has been written over the past 20 years on the NICU as an environment for development (Eyler, Woods, Behnke, & Conlon, 1992; Goldberg & DiVitto, 1983; Goldson, 1992b), and researchers have examined effects of holding, cuddling, massage, and skin-to-skin contact on even very fragile babies. Based on data showing benefits of affectionate handling, hospitals further expanded the role of parents by instituting unrestricted visiting and encouraging parental participation in care. Such changes have had positive effects. As well as removing physical barriers (i.e., separation of infants and parents), efforts were made to remove psychological barriers. These include more privacy for parents and infants, opportunities to be involved in the infant's care (which may increase parents' self-confidence and self-esteem), and opportunities for parents to participate in support groups while infants are still in isolettes in the nursery (Minde, Shosenberg, Thompson, & Marton, 1983; Paludetto, Fággiano-Perfetto, Asprea, DeCurtis, & Margara-Paludetto, 1981).

Possibly the most recent dramatic changes in care have evolved out of necessity in developing countries like Colombia. Because of severe economic constraints, hospitals lack the equipment and bed space to accommodate the number of premature infants born each day. Premature infants in satisfactory clinical condition, no matter how small, go directly to their mothers as early as 2–3 hours after birth (Anderson, Marks, & Wahlberg, 1986). Mothers breast-feed and carry them in an upright position on their chests in slings, hence the name "kangaroo care." Small infants who do well go home to their parents as early as 12 hours after birth. Dramatic reductions in mortality, morbidity, and parental abandonment have been reported under these conditions. This practice of "putting touch into tech" contrasts with traditional practices in the United States and Europe, where preterm infants with no complications are kept in incubators for several weeks (Anderson et al., 1986). Reflecting on these improvements, Anderson et al. (1986, p. 808) pointed out that nourishment, warmth, and nurturance, seem "to provide the ideal environment for premature infants." This course may also enhance parental self-confidence and investment in child care.

Some changes have occurred in the care and treatment of premature infants in the United States over the past 10 to 15 years. A comparison of NICU care in 1976 versus 1990 showed that nurses were the adults involved in the majority of interactions at both times. An average of 2½ hours was devoted to medical intervention both in 1976 and in 1990. However, amount of social interaction changed in the 14 years. The average amount of social interaction in 1976 was less than 5 minutes per day compared to 1 hour daily in 1990. It was also noted that social interaction by parents was related to accessibility of infant (i.e., type of bed) rather than illness (i.e., oxygen requirements). Thus, parents were unlikely to remove babies from isolettes for interaction even when the infants were on room air and could have been taken out. The increase in talking and playing reflects changing attitudes regarding the importance of social interaction for premature babies. Thus, in some ways, practices have come full circle: from a very early time when preterm infants were largely cared for by parents if they survived, through a period of increasing isolation during the development of the primary technology that improved survival with a gradual return to increasing parent involvement. The modern challenge is to provide the benefits of the best medical technology while simultaneously supporting developing parent–infant relationships.

UNIQUE FEATURES OF PRETERM BIRTH

There are three aspects of parenting experience that are unique to prematurity: The first is the timing of birth; the second, the nature of the initial hospital experience; and the third, the behavioral and developmental features of prematurity. This section considers how each of these can affect infants, parents, and their relationship.

Birth and Its Timing

In the course of normal development, 38 to 42 weeks from conception is the optimal time for birth. Were the infant to stay in the womb longer, growth would be hampered by lack of space; the infant could become too large to pass through the birth canal, and the mother might be physiologically unable to meet increased needs for nourishment. However, the fetus requires the support and protection of the uterine environment while major organs and organ systems (e.g., heart, lung, nervous system) are being formed and until capable of functioning outside. Early births produce infants who are well-adapted for life in the womb but not prepared for the external environment. The earlier a baby is born, the more physiological functions are compromised and require artificial support and management. At one time, even with artificial support, infants under 28 weeks from conception were not considered viable. Modern technology has continued to push back the limits of viability so that more aggressive interventions and long hospital stays of small fragile babies are now routine. There is disagreement as to whether the outcome for these babies has improved (Goldson, 1992a). Because they are not well adapted for life outside the womb, preterm infants are vulnerable to failures in basic maintenance systems, infections, and iatrogenic problems (negative side effects of treatment intended to remediate problems). Some of these have long-term consequences for development. In discussing the age of preterm babies, we refer to both chronological age (time from birth) and corrected age (age from expected date of birth) because preterm babies of a given chronological age are at an earlier phase of development than term peers with the same birthdate.

Parents also undergo a developmental process during pregnancy. For the mother, part of the process is experiencing physical changes associated with support of a developing life. Both parents experience complex psychological changes as they form expectations for their new infant, engage in preparation for infant care and prepare for new roles (Zeanah & McDonough, 1989). This process is interrupted when birth occurs prematurely. There may be concrete concerns about missing childbirth classes, not yet having a crib, bassinet, or baby clothes. The crisis aspect of preterm birth and its psychological impact have long been recognized. Parents' expectations for a normal delivery and a healthy infant are violated, and they must come to terms with disappointment and loss (Pederson, Bento, Chance, Evans, & Fox, 1987; Zeanah, Canger, & Jones, 1984) as well as fears for the infant's health and future. The normal joy and rituals surrounding birth are absent and the discomfort of family and friends can isolate new parents from needed social support.

A second issue for parents is the realization that they cannot care for their baby on their own, which is reinforced if the infant is removed to special facilities in another hospital. Instead of looking forward to bringing their baby home in a few days, they anticipate a prolonged hospital stay of unknown length, the possibility of life-threatening complications, and compromised development. The resulting sense of failure may be especially strong for mothers (Jeffcoate, Humphrey, & Lloyd, 1979).

A third issue is that preterm births are more common among families with limited resources. Mothers who are very young, have had little or inadequate prenatal care, and experience the stresses of poverty and social disadvantage have a higher rate of premature births than those in more advantaged circumstances. These families may be particularly overwhelmed and lacking in resources to alleviate the crisis of preterm birth. The financial costs of intensive care are well beyond the resources of most families. Even where insurance or a universal health care system covers the primary cost, there are unexpected expenses (e.g., costs of travel, food, and possibly lodging for long-distance trips to the hospital). These are not unique to premature birth, but they do exacerbate the stresses already mentioned.

The Hospital Environment

Given the precarious ability of the preterm infant to maintain normal body functions, the primary agenda of neonatal intensive care is maintaining and enhancing the physical well-being of the infant by artificial means—surgical, chemical, or mechanical. Studies of the ecology of the NICU concur in indicating high noise levels, high illumination, large numbers of caregivers and caregiving interventions, and lack of relation between infant behavior and environmental events. The extent to which these conditions directly affect development is unknown because it is impossible to disentangle specific features of care from effects of the medical conditions that require them. The NICU is neither a good approximation to the womb nor a normal home environment. It was never designed to be either of these things, but rather to deal with life-threatening medical crises. When effects of NICU care on the infant have been measured, studies usually focus on alterations designed to provide a more developmentally appropriate environment (e.g., Field, 1990).

To the extent that the preterm infant experiences human contact, it is primarily for medical and nursing procedures, many of which are invasive and stressful. A recent study suggests that such procedures account for approximately 2 hours of contact daily (Eyler et al., 1992). It has been demonstrated that most of these interventions result in irregularities of heart rate and breathing, skin color change, and disorganized behavior (Blackburn & Barnard, 1985), with the infant requiring time to recover. Thus, the traditional approach has been to protect infants by interacting as little as possible. However, these are interventions designed to monitor or improve physiological functioning rather than to comfort or soothe the infant. There is increasing evidence that interventions designed to comfort and soothe, whether mechanical (e.g., rocking) or human, are effective in improving the infant's physiological condition (Field, 1990). Furthermore, nurses do form attachments to babies in their care and engage in play, talk, and holding beyond the routine care (Corter et al., 1978).

However attentive and engaging, nursing care is not an approximation of parental care. From the point of view of the parent–infant relationship, the most salient feature of prolonged hospital care for the preterm infant is the limitation of social experiences with parents. Of course, if the infant were still in utero, these experiences would not be available. Nevertheless, parents have the expectation of establishing a social relationship with their infant and want to do so in spite of the noncondusive surroundings and the limitations of the infant. As infants grow older, even while still in hospital care, they become more alert and responsive. Most hospitals now encourage parents to visit preterm infants from the beginning, but several factors conspire to limit the potential satisfaction of these visits. If the baby is moved from the hospital where the birth occurred, the infant is less accessible to parents. Even if the infant is in a unit reasonably close to the mother's, mothers may not be able to visit until their own hospital stay terminates. We have already noted the psychological barriers for parents in this highly technical environment. Many poignant accounts by parents effectively capture the emotional turmoil of this experience.

A number of empirical studies asked parents to reflect on salient aspects of their baby's hospitalization (Affleck, Tennen, & Rowe, 1990; Jackson & Gorman, 1988; Miles, 1989; Pederson et al., 1987). When parents are interviewed or questioned during the hospital stay or at the time of discharge, they report that the appearance and behavior of the baby and fears about health and survival are the most stressful aspect of the experience (Miles, 1989; Pederson et al., 1987), followed by unexpected alterations in the parental role (Miles, 1989). However, when looking back on the hospital experience, parents whose infants are in good health at 1 year of age minimize the stresses of the early experience and respond no differently than those of term babies (Jackson & Gorman, 1988). Mothers and fathers agree on which experiences are stressful, but they use different coping strategies (Affleck et al., 1990). Mothers seek social support and use escape strategies; fathers minimize and use instrumental approaches. Choice of different coping strategies may lead to marital conflict, but may also bring couples closer together if they perceive their strategies as complementary (Affleck et al., 1990).

In recognition of the difficulties faced by parents during the period of intensive care, there have been efforts to provide extra support and enhance parenting skills (see Patteson & Barnard, 1990, for a recent review) and to train and support professionals to work with parents (see Marshall, Kasman, & Cape, 1982). An increasing number of hospitals have support groups run by parents with the help of professionals. With one exception (Minde et al., 1983), such groups have not been evaluated in a systematic way. Nevertheless, they fill important needs of parents during the hospitalization and following discharge (Boukydis, 1982).

Going Home: Preterm Infant Behavior and Development

The transition from hospital to home, much as it is eagerly anticipated, brings new stresses. If a baby is transferred from a regional unit to a local hospital, parents encounter new staff, new routines, and new policies. When babies go home, whether directly from intensive care or from a community hospital, parents who have spent weeks or months watching professionals care for their baby may feel overwhelmed by the new responsibility and isolated from the psychological supports of hospital staff and other parents.

The age of preterm infants at birth and discharge varies. Of course, term infants are also born at different ages and therefore return home at different ages from conception, but these variations are small. The best evidence suggests that many aspects of development proceed on a time-table that is not altered by the time of birth, but is anchored by the time of conception (Hunt & Rhodes, 1977). Thus, parents of term infants look for developmental milestones on the basis of age from birth, but parents of preterm infants have to wait that much longer to see the expected accomplishments.

For example, babies born at term usually begin social smiles at 6 to 8 weeks of age. Preterm infants first show social smiles in the second month *past term* (Anisfeld, 1982). Thus, a preterm infant born 10 weeks early may be from 16 to 18 weeks chronological age before engaging in social smiles. If we remember that care of any newborn is exhausting and demands parent sacrifices, delay in reaching rewarding milestones can be seen as a frustration for parents, particularly when the potential for permanent handicaps is of concern.

In addition to doing things later than term infants, preterm infant behavior and appearance may differ qualitatively from that of term peers. The normal physical features of infants are unique in ways that appeal to adults; a flattened nose, broad cheeks, large head, and relatively large eyes characterize infants of many species. Preterm infants often lack these features (Maier, Holmes, Slaymaker, & Reich, 1984) and are judged less attractive than term infants, although experience caring for a preterm baby modifies these judgments (Corter, Trehub, Boukydis, Ford, Celhoffer, & Minde, 1978). The cries of babies who experienced stressful medical conditions differ acoustically from those of healthy infants, differences recognizable by naive adults (Friedman, Zahn-Waxler, & Radke-Yarrow, 1982; Lester & Zeskind, 1979). Although initially preterm infants may cry very little, particularly if they have respiratory complications (Molitor & Eckerman, 1992), their cries are more physiologically arousing to adults (Frodi et al., 1978) and at later ages they are observed to be relatively fussy and irritable (Brachfeld, Goldberg, & Sloman, 1980; Crawford, 1982; Field, 1977a; Steifel, Plunkett, & Meisels, 1987) more difficult to soothe (Friedman, Jacobs, & Werthmann, 1982), and are described as temperamentally difficult by parents (Field, 1979). Differences between term and preterm infants have also been noted in alertness, responsiveness (Anders & Keener, 1985; Davis & Thorman, 1987; Lawson, Ruff, McKCarton-Down, Kurtzberg, & Vaughan, 1984; Telzrow, Kang, Mitchell, Ashworth, & Barnard, 1980), and ability to maintain behavioral organization in response to complex social stimulation (McGehee & Eckerman, 1983). This is not a chapter on preterm infants per se, and so we do not review research on preterm behavior. Rather, we emphasize the different nature of the preterm infant as a social partner and note that parental adjustments and compensatory maneuvers may be required. Indeed, one issue that has been raised is the extent to which high levels of parent interaction with preterm infants are intrusive (Field, 1977a, 1977b) versus compensatory (Goldberg, 1982), an issue considered in a later section.

Recently, Stern and her associates (summarized in Stern & Karraker, 1990) studied adult expectations of preterm infants described as a prematurity stereotype. In this research, adults shown videotapes of an infant labeled "premature" (even though actually term) rated the baby less "developed, sociable, active, competent and liked" than the same infant labeled "full term." When interacting with an unfamiliar infant, mothers behaved differently toward a baby labeled "premature" by touching less and offering more immature toys. Furthermore, labeling a baby "premature" affected the infant's behavior, presumably as a consequence of the altered behavior of the adult partner. It has been suggested that such stereotypes have a negative influence on parents of preterm infants. However, even if mothers of premature infants stereotype an unfamiliar baby labeled "premature," the actual beliefs of mothers concerning their own premature infant have not been well studied. One study using the Neonatal Perception Inventory (NPI) found that mothers' perceptions of preterm infants become more positive over time and exceeded those of term infants at 1 month (Alfasi et al., 1985). In general, stereotypes are engaged in unfamiliar situations; concrete information and experience decreases use of stereotypes. On the one hand, this suggests that prematurity stereotypes are less likely to influence impressions of one's own baby than an unfamiliar one. On the other hand, the prolonged period of limited involvement with a baby during hospitalization may be fertile ground for formation of stereotypes, which may indeed account for some aspects of parental behavior with preterm infants.

In summary, parents of preterm babies face a daunting task. They take on the role of parenthood before they or their baby are ready for it. They do so under highly stressful hospital conditions with limited opportunities for normal interactions, and their babies may be behaviorally more difficult to manage. What are the implications of these circumstances for the formation of parent–child relationships?

THEORETICAL PERSPECTIVES ON RELATIONSHIPS WITH PRETERM INFANTS

Most theoretical approaches to the study of parent–infant relationships emphasize the influences of parents on infants. Traditionally, infants are perceived as passive recipients of parents' socialization. As research techniques enabled us to investigate infants' perceptual, cognitive, and learning skills, conceptions of infants changed dramatically and ideas about parent–infant relationships changed with them. Indeed, there was increasing interest in the ways in which children, including infants, influenced parents. The 1970s were marked by an increase in studies of "reciprocity" and detailed analysis of the structure of adult–infant interactions.

Within this framework, studies of preterm infants and parents focused on ways in which the behavior and appearance of preterm infants elicited unique responses from parents. For example, Goldberg (1977) articulated a model of parent–infant interaction that emphasized clarity and consistency of infant cues and infant responsiveness as determinants of parent feelings of competence. Subsequently, she argued that preterm infants would provide less clarity and consistency of behavior than their term counterparts and would therefore be more challenging for parents (Goldberg, 1979). In addition, limits in the perceptual and cognitive skills of preterm infants could modify the impact of parent behaviors on infants. Thus, Field (1982) conceptualized the young preterm infant as having a relatively high threshold to respond to adult social stimulation coupled with a low tolerance for stimulation. The challenge for adult caregivers of preterm infants is to maintain social interactions within the narrow intensity band that elicits infant response without exceeding the infant's tolerance level. Adults have more latitude when interacting with term infants.

A different approach to parent–infant relationships was spearheaded by Klaus and Kennell (1976, 1982) under the rubric of "bonding." Bonding was described as the process by which parents come to feel an emotional investment in individual offspring. Although the later formulation (Klaus & Kennell, 1982) considered bonding to be a lifelong process, the early work focused on effects of initial contacts of parents and infants, particularly mothers. It was suggested that optimal mother–infant relationships were fostered by close contact during a brief period after delivery thought to be "critical" or "sensitive" for bonding. A large number of studies were conducted to explore this phenomenon, and reviews of these studies proliferated (e.g., Goldberg, 1983; Myers, 1984). Although the majority concluded the evidence was unconvincing, the concept of early bonding achieved great popularity, and parents and professionals pressed hospitals to change patterns of care to allow early contact. A side effect of this popular enthusiasm was that it left parents who could not experience early contacts with feelings of failure. The routine procedure of removing preterm babies to special nurseries, possibly in another hospital, deprived parents of these important opportunities to bond. Thus, when this approach is applied to the experience of preterm infants and their parents, the primary focus is on detrimental effects of early separation.

A third approach to parent–infant relationships that has gained currency in the last 25 years is that of attachment theory, rooted in concepts advanced by Bowlby (1969). Bowlby emphasized the protective function of the caregiver as the foundation for formation of infants' emotional ties to parents. Because the human infant cannot survive without intensive adult care, Bowlby argued, our evolutionary history biases infants to look and behave in ways that elicit adult proximity and care. Over the first year of life, these attachment behaviors become organized into a goal-corrected system focused on a specific caregiver, usually, but not necessarily, the mother. The conditions under which this system is activated reflect the infant's experiences of care from that figure. Ainsworth, Blehar, Waters, and Wall, (1978) elaborated the concept of the caregiver as protector to emphasize the importance of providing a "secure base" for exploratory behavior and developed a standardized laboratory observation that allows infants to reveal their expectations of the caregiver. This procedure, known as the Strange Situation, is considered to provide a measure of the quality of the infant–parent relationship as perceived by the infant.

Within this framework, the effects of preterm birth can be approached in a number of ways. First, because Bowlby emphasized an evolutionary history that selected infants for ability to engage adults in caregiving, the survival of infants who would not have been viable in the "environment of evolutionary adaptiveness" clearly poses problems for ensuing parent–child relationships. Second, attachment theory places great weight on the ability of parents to provide consistent and responsive care. Although the theory emphasizes experiences of being parented as the primary contributor to parental abilities, unexpected burdens, lack of early opportunities for caregiving, and poor social support in the instance of prematurity may also disrupt parents' responsiveness.

Although it is primarily a methodological rather than a theoretical contribution, the development of the Strange Situation procedure had an important effect on the study of preterm infants and their parents. In the Strange Situation, infant and caregiver participate in a standard series of separations and reunions. Ainsworth and her colleagues (1978) demonstrated that infants' reactions to the parent's return after separation were a good marker of the type of care infants had experienced in the home over the first year of life. Many researchers who do not subscribe to attachment theory have used the Strange Situation as an outcome measure in studies of preterm infants because it is one of the few well-standardized validated measures of early social development. Thus, there is a consistent body of data on behavior of preterm infants in the Strange Situation as well as extensive normative data for comparison. Because infant behavior in the Strange Situation is used to make inferences about the caregiver's prior responsiveness, we can also think of the Strange Situation as revealing infants' perspectives on their relationships with specific caregivers.

These theoretical approaches do not differ in predicted outcomes. All agree that preterm infants and the circumstances that surround their birth present parents with unique challenges. All agree that parent–infant relationships will be more vulnerable to problems than those of healthy term infants. They differ primarily in attributions about the reasons for this vulnerability—which aspects of the preterm experience are most influential in creating potential problems. Social interaction approaches emphasize limitations of the infant per se; bonding theory emphasizes the effects of prolonged initial separations; and attachment theory emphasizes parent ability to provide responsive care. These are not seen as mutually exclusive approaches and studies have not been designed to discriminate among them.

In recent years, research has been shaped by an integrative approach that espouses "transactional" models (Sameroff & Chandler, 1975). As a further step beyond the notion of mutual regulation, the transactional approach emphasizes dynamic aspects of development whereby the outcome at any one stage (whether for parent, infant, or the relationship) becomes the input or shapes response to input at the next stage. No single feature is expected to exercise influence over a prolonged developmental period without itself reflecting the effects of the developmental process. From this perspective, we can consider the theories described earlier to emphasize different aspects of an ongoing process.

OBSERVATIONS OF PARENT–INFANT RELATIONSHIPS

Background

Empirical research on preterm infants and their parents is a recent phenomenon. In the early part of this century, research on preterm infants was concerned with survival and health statistics. Subsequent interest was in global functioning of the child: measures of IQ, school performance, and needs for special services were common outcomes. Although there were occasional reports concerning child social functioning, temperament, and behavior problems, parent experience was largely ignored. It was not until the development of neonatology as a discipline (and the medical technology that came with it) brought large numbers of preterm infants, their parents, and health professionals together for extended periods that understanding and interest in parents' experiences developed.

Earlier we referred to the innovative experiments that first brought parents into NICUs. With convincing evidence that parent visiting did not compromise infant health and concern about early bonding opportunities, more facilities allowed and encouraged parent visiting. Thus, for the first time there were opportunities to observe interactions of parents with infants in incubators. Evaluation of these changes led to interest in parent–child interactions and parent experiences after hospital discharge. A further development, the formation of parent support groups, created organized "consumers" eager for practical information and scientific research about parents and preterm infants.

These were practical developments that drew researchers toward the study of early social experiences of preterm infants and their families. There were also scientific issues that created the impetus for these studies. Premature birth was increasingly recognized as a "natural experiment" in the study of parent–infant relationships, providing conditions that could not be ethically manipulated (e.g., extended separation during a hypothesized critical period), for reasonably large numbers of families with ready access through hospital units. The next section summarizes research on preterm infants and their parents, with an emphasis on observational studies concerned with the nature of early parent–child interactions and relationships.

Parents and Infants in Hospital

Two kinds of studies provide information about parent–infant relationships during hospitalization. The first is concerned with the general ecology of the NICU and includes information about parent visiting patterns. These studies report frequency and length of visits and may include information about type of interactions (e.g., caregiving, social interaction, conversation with others). They do not attempt detailed analysis of parent–infant interactions. The second type of study is concerned exclusively with parent–infant relationships and focuses on detailed observations of what parents and infants do during hospital visits. We consider information from each of these types.

Reports of frequency and length of parent visits vary widely, reflecting historical changes and local differences in hospital policies as well as factors accounting for individual differences between families. In the initial studies that introduced parents into the NICU (Fanaroff, Kennell, & Klaus, 1972; Leifer, Leiderman, Barnett, & Williams, 1972), "low" rates of visiting were reported (once every 6 days and less than twice in 3 weeks, respectively). Several years later, at the start of an intervention study, presumably after NICU visiting was routine, similar rates were reported (Rosenfield, 1980). In contrast, among parents who volunteered for a longitudinal study of parent–infant relationships in Boston in the mid-1970s, the majority of parents reported visiting daily (DiVitto & Goldberg, 1979). Thus, simple permission for parents to enter the NICU can still lead to large differences in amount of visiting. Other factors must contribute substantially to parent visiting patterns.

The most detailed study of hospital visiting patterns was undertaken in the mid-1970s in Exeter, England (Hawthorne, Richards, & Callon, 1978). In the first week that the infant was in the hospital, the primary determinant of visiting was whether or not the mother was in the same hospital. When the mother was in the same hospital, she usually visited at least daily. After discharge, she visited less often. If the mother was in another hospital, the infant was likely to be visited no more than twice in the first week and more often after the mother's discharge. Mother visiting was more consistent than father visiting. Fathers were likely to visit more often if they were middle class and had been present at the birth. "Long stay" babies (those who stayed more than 2 weeks) were primarily low- birthweight babies transferred from other hospitals and were visited less often than babies with shorter stays. For these babies, distance from home, presence of other children at home, and social class affected visiting patterns.

It is also clear that overt and covert messages from unit staff can affect parent visiting. In an effort to increase maternal visiting, Zeskind and Iacino (1984) had NICU staff schedule weekly "appointments" for mothers with babies in the NICU during which they visited their baby with a supportive staff member. Mothers in the appointment group made more spontaneous visits than those in the control group. Although increased visiting was associated with less positive current perceptions of the baby, it was also associated with more positive long-term expectations.

One of the most intriguing findings concerning visiting patterns is the incidental observation of increased visiting among mothers of babies receiving supplemental stimulation (Rosenfield, 1980). The investigator suggested two reasons: First, increases in alertness in the experimental group babies may have made visits more pleasurable for mothers and increased their interest in visiting. Second, knowledge that their babies had been singled out for "special treatment" may have motivated mothers to visit more often. A recent effort to compare the ecology of neonatal units over the span of a decade noted that social interactions with infants in intensive care have increased over that period with parents contributing some of that increase (Eyler et al., 1992).

Nevertheless, parents account for only 14 percent of the human contacts an infant in NICU experiences (Gottfried & Gaiter, 1985), and this may account for the general lack of information about *parent* experiences in NICU. In a commentary evaluating contributions to a volume on infants in intensive care, Kennell and Klaus (1985) marked the absence of such information and emphasized the need to examine the impact of NICU experience on parents as well as infants.

A number of studies interviewed or obtained questionnaire surveys from parents (see earlier), but few attempts have been made to observe what happens when parents visit infants in hospital. The primary source of information is a series of studies conducted by Minde and his colleagues. In these studies, an electronic event recorder provided continuous recording of infant and parent behaviors during two visits for each week of hospitalization. Over the course of the hospital stay, mothers increased the duration of visits as well as the proportion of time they were actively engaged with the infants. Furthermore, some mothers were consistently more active than others. These mothers called and visited more and were more actively involved with their infants at later home observations. This was not related to the infants' medical condition. Instead, mothers who reported better relationships with their families of origin and spouses and had fewer social risk factors in their histories were more likely to be in the active group (Minde, Marton, Manning, & Hines, 1980). However, when detailed behavior sequences were analyzed, mothers' behavior was related to infant behavior particularly in the high activity group. In a later study, a detailed index was used to assess the medical condition of 184 low-birthweight preterm infants daily and showed that infant behavior was related to illness scores (infants who were seriously ill were less active than healthier counterparts) and maternal activity was related to the infant's medical course (infants with a short hospital course became more active and their mothers correspondingly increased their vocalization, touching, and looking, whereas infants with a long hospital stay remained inactive for a long time and their mothers showed low activity rates). These differences persisted even after infants had been home several months (Minde, Whitelaw, Brown, & Firzhardinge, 1983). A second study demonstrated that mothers of preterm twins were more active with the healthier of twins (Minde, Perrota, & Corter, 1982).

In a small pilot study that observed both fathers and mothers of 12 preterm infants, few differences were found between fathers and mothers during nursery visits (Marton, Minde, & Perrotta, 1981). However, a more recent study (Levy-Shiff, Sharir, & Mogilner, 1989) reported consistent differences in mother and father behavior. Like the Minde group, these investigators found that duration of visits and amount of activity increased from the initial observation (when the infant left intensive care) to the discharge observation. Mothers were more active than fathers, but fathers surpassed mothers in play and stimulation. These differences are consistent with reports of general mother–father differences in behavior with infants. In explaining the differences between the two studies, it is important to note differences in sample size, cultural settings (Canada and Israel), and the fact that the Israeli sample included older, heavier, and probably healthier babies.

In summary, a variety of factors affects the extent to which parents visit and become actively engaged with their preterm babies. There is some suggestion that active engagement is related to subsequent parent involvement and could be increased by supportive hospital policies and practices.

Parents and Infants at Home

In contrast to the few studies of parent–infant interaction in hospital, studies of parents and infants after discharge are numerous. With few exceptions, these studies focus on mothers. The majority entail comparison with term dyads. The initial wave in this research emerged from the studies introducing parents to the NICU and were strongly influenced by the coalescence of ideas leading to the formulation of the bonding concept. Research in the animal literature has shown that maternal behavior can be extinguished by separation of infants and mothers for a brief period immediately after birth (Klaus & Kennell, 1976). The expectation, based on the animal studies, was that maternal behavior would be depressed or difficult to establish if mothers were not exposed to the appropriate initiating stimuli (i.e., the infant) during this critical or sensitive period. Indeed, none of these studies reported infant behavior, but focused on differences between *mothers* of preterm and term infants to test for separation effects. Such effects were, in fact, observed. Later, other reports confirmed these findings but also studied infant behavior (DiVitto & Goldberg, 1979; Minde et al., 1983). These later studies included observations in the hospital, but also followed dyads home in the early weeks. Preterm infants were found to be less alert and responsive than their term peers (DiVitto & Goldberg, 1979), and preterm babies who were medically more compromised were less active than their healthier counterparts (DiVitto & Goldberg, 1979; Minde et al., 1983). Maternal behavior paralleled that of infants: Preterm babies were afforded less body contact, touch, and vocalization than term babies (DiVitto & Goldberg, 1979) and those who were more seriously ill had less active mothers than did healthier peers (DiVitto & Goldberg, 1979; Minde et al., 1983). Only one report of relatively early observations (Beckwith & Cohen, 1978) was inconsistent with theories about bonding, but it suggested that depressed behavior of infants might also make a contribution. Beckwith and Cohen (1978) reported that, in a large heterogeneous sample of preterm dyads, babies who had experienced more neonatal complications received *more* rather than *less* caregiving from mothers at 1 month corrected age.

As studies of older preterm infants began to accumulate, it became clear that certainly from 3 months (corrected age) onward, the pattern reported by Beckwith and Cohen (1978) predominated. Although these studies differed widely in the age and physical status of the preterm babies sampled, the situations observed, the recording procedures, methods, and coding schemes, and the geographic and socioeconomic environments in which infants were being raised, there was remarkable concordance in findings. The studies are now more numerous, but our summary description in earlier reviews remains unchanged (Goldberg, 1978; Goldberg & DiVitto, 1983). Being the parent of a prematurely born infant is "more work and less fun" (Goldberg & DiVitto, 1983).

Where differences between preterm and term infants are reported, preterm infants are found to be less attentive (Barnard, Bee, & Hammond, 1984; Brachfeld et al., 1980; Crnic, Greenberg, Ragozin, Robinson, & Basham, 1983a; Field, 1977a; Greene, Fox, & Lewis, 1983; Malatesta, Grigoryev, Lamb, Albin, & Culver, 1986), less initiating (Brown & Bakeman, 1979), less responsive (Alfasi et al., 1985; Barnard et al., 1984), show less positive affect (Crnic et al., 1983a), and to be more irritable (Brachfeld, Goldberg, & Sloman, 1980; Crawford, 1982; DiVitto & Goldberg, 1979; Field, 1977; Stevenson, Roach, Ver Haeve, & Leavitt, 1990). In turn, their mothers are described as taking a more active role than that taken by mothers of term infants. That is, they stay closer (Crnic et al., 1983; Greene et al., 1983), hold and touch more (Brachfeld, Goldberg, & Sloman, 1980; Crawford, 1982; Crnic et al., 1983a), provide more tactile and kinesthetic stimulation (Brachfeld et al., 1980; Crnic et al., 1983a), direct attention more (Barnard et al., 1984; Field, 1977a; 1979), and are judged to be less sensitive to their infants (Alfasi et al., 1985; Field, 1977a, 1977b; Zarling, Hirsch, & Landry, 1988). Although several reports suggest that these observed differences diminish with age (Alfasi et al., 1985; Brachfeld et al., 1980; Brown & Bakeman, 1979; Crawford, 1982; DiVitto & Goldberg, 1983), others note differences as late as 1 (Crnic et al., 1983b) or 2 years of age (Barnard et al.,1984).

Because this phenomenon has been widely documented and discussed, it seems less useful to review the studies than to consider explanations for this pattern. In doing so, we examine studies that emphasize similarities between preterm and term dyads and that chose unique approaches to understanding mother–infant relationships.

Prematurity, Immaturity, and Illness

The first explanation focuses on differences in infant behavior and factors that influence infant capacity for interactive behavior. The way in which research designs match preterm and term dyads for age has been controversial, although more recent studies usually match on time from conception. However, this means that matches are confounded by interactive experience—in general, at the same postconception age, term dyads have had more time in "normal" interactive environments. Other studies therefore matched dyads for "time from discharge" so that all dyads had the same amount of home experience (e.g., Brown & Bakeman, 1979), although infants are not matched for either age from conception or age from birth. Still others matched on chronological age (e.g., DiVitto & Goldberg, 1979) to match amount of experience, although type of experience varied (a larger proportion of the experience of preterm dyads is in hospital rather than home), and some studies have used more than one matching strategy (e.g., Crawford, 1982). It is these latter studies that provide information on the relative effects of prematurity (the timing of the birth) and immaturity (the infant's developmental status) on dyadic interactions.

When data are compared for chronological versus postconception-matched groups, postconception matches yield fewer preterm–term differences in dyadic interactions (Alfasi et al., 1985; Brachfeld et al., 1980; Crawford, 1982). However, some differences remain, and the majority of studies that use postconception matching are consistent with the description of preterm dyads as having less socially competent infants and more highly active mothers. Therefore, infant immaturity does not account for all differences in infant or maternal behavior.

Although severity of neonatal complications is usually related to gestational age and birthweight, examination of preterm groups that differ in illness status, but are well matched on gestational age and birthweight can assess the contribution of severity of illness to early dyadic interactions. Because such matches are difficult to make, few researchers undertake such designs. However, in one recent study (Jarvis, Myers, & Creasey, 1989), three groups of preterm infants were compared: those who were healthy (HP), those with respiratory distress syndrome (RDS), and those whose respiratory problems had led to more lasting problems with breathing, bronchopulmonary dysplasia (BPD). These three groups were relatively well matched for gestational age (31–32 weeks on average) and birthweight (1,200–1,600 g). Mothers and infants were videotaped in teaching tasks at 4 and 8 months. There were no differences in observed infant behaviors, but mothers in the BPD group were scored lower than the others on sensitivity, response to distress, and growth-fostering activities, suggesting that severity of illness contributes to observed differences.

An alternative approach is illustrated in a study by Greene et al. (1983), which included four groups of infants: term and preterm with subgroups of healthy and sick infants within birth status. Although the preterm subgroups differed in the expected direction (the "sick" infants were smaller and born younger than the healthy ones), the term groups did not. In the newborn period, differences in infant behavior as measured on Brazelton's Neonatal Behavioral Assessment Scales (1973) revealed effects of both maturity and health status. The same was true of behavior in free play at 3 months, primarily in maternal behavior. Furthermore, scores on the neonatal assessment predicted maternal responsiveness. Thus, this study suggests that early infant behavior is affected by both health and birth status and maternal behavior is responsive to these early differences, even later when differences in infant behavior are less observable. Although their data confound health and prematurity, Minde and his colleagues (1983) also reported persistent effects of the infant's hospital course on maternal behavior within a low-birthweight preterm group several months after discharge when infant differences were no longer evident.

A more complex view focuses not on how prematurity and immaturity influence interactive behavior but on which aspects of interaction are affected by each. Bendersky and Lewis (1992) used factor analysis to parse maternal interactive behavior into three components: affect, stimulation, and education. Evidence of each component was found at each of 5 ages in a sample of 121 low-birthweight preterm dyads: 3, 12, 18, 28, and 36 months. Neither the affective component nor the education component were affected by parameters of medical history. However, in the early observations, infants with more medical problems received more stimulation; the reverse was true by 36 months: Children whose early histories reflected more medical problems were receiving less stimulation.

Thus, there is evidence that prematurity, immaturity, and illness affect interactions of preterm infants with their parents. Furthermore, in addition to the direct effects on infant behavior, there are indirect effects on parent behavior because differences in parent behavior can be observed even in the absence of infant differences. These indirect effects may be the residue of earlier adjustments to infant behavior or they may reflect a prematurity stereotype, as suggested by Stern and Karraker (1990).

Explaining Maternal Behavior: Overstimulation or Compensation?

A second explanation for observed differences between preterm and term dyads is concerned with the *appropriateness* of maternal behavior to the infant's behavior or developmental needs. Appropriateness clearly incorporates value judgments about what is and is not "good" for infants and preterm infants in particular. A pattern of behavior "good" for one purpose may compromise other potential parental goals, and such relationships may differ for preterm and term infants. For example, we assume that young infants should be held close during feedings and that affectionate social interactions during feeding are beneficial to social development. However, experimental study of the behavior of young preterm infants suggests that this "normal" amount of physical contact and social exchange may be too much for preterm babies (Field, 1977b; McGehee & Eckerman, 1983) and may disrupt feeding. Thus, a parent feeding a preterm baby makes decisions regarding the relative importance of nutrition and social development, decisions that do not concern parents of healthy term babies.

How then are we to decide what is appropriate behavior? Two general approaches have been taken. The first relies on objective scoring schemes that reflect judgments widely accepted in the field as to appropriate childrearing practices or interactive goals. The second relies on infant outcomes either behavior in the context of observation or subsequent developmental outcome. These approaches are by no means "value free." Rather they are "value explicit" in that they provide a clear operational measure, albeit one that incorporates values. These approaches do not always concur in arriving at definitions of appropriate behavior either. Earlier, we noted that a number of studies included reports that mothers of preterms were less sensitive or more intrusive than mothers of term infants (Alfasi et al., 1985; Field, 1977a, 1977b; Zarling et al., 1988) or that mothers of sicker babies were less sensitive (Jarvis et al., 1989) than those of healthy infants. All of these studies reflect reliable observation scoring procedures. However, in some cases, a different observational approach yields a different interpretation.

An example of this is seen in a study by Field (1977b) regarding feeding behavior of mothers of 3- to 4-month-olds. Field reported that mothers of both preterm and term infants restricted activity with their infants to periods when the nipple was out of the infants' mouth. This is similar to earlier reports that the "normal" pattern during feedings is for mothers to confine stimulation to times when the infant is not sucking on the nipple. Field (1977b) found that mothers in the preterm group were more likely than those in the term group to be active during "nipple in" periods. In a later study, DiVitto and Goldberg (1983) amplified the findings of Field (1977b). First, they observed four groups of infants (three preterm groups with different levels of health and neonatal complications and one term group) over four occasions: hospital, 10 days postdischarge, and twice at 4 months. Second, they examined infant patterns of sucking and pausing and found that as infants got older, they spent more of the "nipple in" time sucking and less time pausing. Preterm infants did more pausing during "nipple in" times than terms. Finally, all groups of mothers gradually decreased their stimulation during infant sucking over time, but this happened most rapidly in the term group. Thus, preterm and term dyad achieved similar organization of maternal behavior around the infants' sucking pattern but it developed more slowly in preterm dyads.

Studies focusing on organization of behavior highlight similarities of preterm and term dyads rather than differences. This is true of studies by Landry (e.g., Landry, 1986) of joint attention in toy play and those by Censullo (1992) and Mann and Plunkett (1992) of mutual responsivenss. In these studies, preterm and term dyads achieved the same goals, albeit in different ways. For example, at 3 months of age, mothers of preterms were scored lower than term dyads on responsiveness, and preterm dyads were generally less positive and had fewer episodes of repeated turntaking. However, there were no group differences in scores on mutual responsiveness (Censullo, 1992). In addition, there were no differences between groups in infant fussing. These findings are reinforced by those of Mann and Plunkett (1992) with a more compromised preterm group (restricted to those with birthweights less than 1,250 g). Preterm and term groups did not differ in the amount of mutual gaze at 4 months of age but differed in the context in which it occurred. These extremely low-birthweight infants engaged in more mutual gaze when being held than did term infants and they were also held significantly more than their term counterparts. Thus, by holding infants more, mothers in the preterm group succeeded in achieving as much mutual gaze as mothers in term dyads. These differences in strategy were no longer evident at 8 months, when preterm dyads engaged in more mutual gaze than the term group. In fact, mutual gaze in the preterm dyads was described at 8 months as being like that in the term group at 4 months, again suggesting that different strategies may reflect accommodation to developmental needs of preterm infants. Thus, although the low-birthweight babies were less responsive than the term infants, the two groups did not differ in amount of mutual engagement, nor were there differences in infant negative behaviors such as fussing, crying, and squirming. The investigators concluded that this pattern was more consistent with the "compensation" than the "overstimulation" view.

Parent–Infant Relationships: Infant Attachment

The appropriateness of maternal behavior may also be evaluated by examining subsequent developmental outcome. There are numerous studies relating mother–infant interaction in preterm dyads to later cognitive and social outcomes in the preschool years (e.g., Cohen & Parmelee, 1983; Greenberg & Crnic, 1988), and as late as 8 and 12 years of age (Beckwith & Parmelee, 1986; Beckwith, Rodning, & Cohen, 1992). Within the scope of this chapter, we confine ourselves to the quality of the relationship that develops between infants and their parents. For this purpose, we turn to examine studies using Ainsworth's Strange Situation to assess quality of attachment. In this procedure, coding criteria developed by Ainsworth and her colleagues are used to classify infant–adult pairs who have experienced two laboratory separations and reunions into three or sometimes four patterns; one considered optimal (secure), the remaining categories representing different forms of less optimal, (insecure) attachment. As noted earlier, infant behavior in this context is considered to reflect the infants' expectation that the caregiver will respond to these needs. The validity of this assumption is based on studies showing that these reunion behaviors reflect the consistency of maternal response to infant needs over the first year of life (Ainsworth et al., 1978).

Thus, in reviewing the studies of preterm infants observed in the Strange Situation, we make the assumption that the data inform us about the infants' perceptions of the relationship: Secure infants have experienced consistent and responsive care and are confident that the caregiver will meet their needs. Insecure infants have experienced different forms of inconsistent or unresponsive care and have developed strategies for behaving accordingly: to "hide" needs for the caregiver by engaging in other activities (avoidant group); to emphasize needs for attention by escalating expressions of distress and/or helplessness (ambivalent/resistant group); or, if they have not developed an effective strategy, to show abrupt shifts in strategy and odd inexplicable behaviors (disorganized/disoriented group).

All of the theoretical approaches we reviewed would predict that preterm infants are less likely than term infants to be securely attached. It is well established that in low stress samples in North America, as well as a substantial number of samples from other continents, approximately 65 percent of infants are securely attached (van Ijzendoorn & Kroonenberg, 1988). Studies of attachment in preterm infants that made direct comparisons with a term group generally did not find the proportion of securely attached infants to differ between those groups (Brown & Bakeman, 1980; Easterbrooks, 1989; Field, Dempsey, & Shuman, 1981; Frodi, 1983; Frodi & Thompson, 1985; Rode, Chang, Fisch, & Sroufe, 1981; Rodning, Beckwith, & Howard, 1989). Comparison of distributions of attachment patterns in preterm dyads with published norms also indicates no shift to insecure patterns of attachment (Goldberg et al., 1986). Two studies are notable for diverging from this pattern.

First, Wille (1991), with a socially disadvantaged sample of 18 term infants, 18 healthy preterm, and 18 sick preterm infants, reported no differences between the two preterm groups, but only 44 percent of the preterms were securely attached compared to 83 percent of term infants, a statistically significant difference. This effect reflects both a decrease in secure attachment in the preterm group (although probably not below the levels typically reported for socially disadvantaged samples) and an increase in the term group. Indeed, a recent meta-analysis of attachment data from a variety of clinical samples notes that "normative" comparison groups typically include substantially more secure babies than expected (van Ijzendoorn, Goldberg, Kroonenberg, & Frenkel, 1992). The second discordant study (Plunkett, Meisels, Stiefel, Pasick, & Roloff, 1986) reported that within a preterm sample those with more serious early medical complications were more likely to be in the ambivalent/resistant group than their healthier peers. This difference did not reflect differences in frequency of secure attachments, but differences in relative frequency of different forms of insecurity. The most useful way of explaining these divergent studies is to turn to the meta-analyses of van Ijzendoorn and his colleagues (van Ijzendoorn et al., 1992). Meta-analysis is a statistical way of combining data from similar studies to yield a quantitative summary. In these analyses, data from six studies of preterm infants, including most of those already cited, were aggregated and compared with aggregated data from normative studies. As the authors argued, relatively small samples selected for research may show shifts in attachment distributions that are, in fact, chance occurrences. The aggregation of data presumably overcomes this problem and is therefore more reliable as individual samples have only minimal influence on the pooled data. The meta-analyses show that although the Plunkett et al. (1986) data are somewhat deviant from the normative comparison data, this is not a statistically significant deviation. Analyses that included the two preterm samples that used the disorganized category (Goldberg, Lojkasek, Gartner, & Corter, 1989; Rodning et al., 1989) showed some shift in the preterm group toward including more disorganized cases than expected. However, these were not statistically significant shifts.

Thus, the bulk of the data indicates that by the end of the first 12 to 18 months of life, preterm infants and their parents have developed a relationship that, with respect to attachment security, does not differ from that of term infants and parents. If we consider the formation of a secure attachment to indicate appropriate care in the first year of life, these data on attachment suggest that in spite of observed differences in mother–infant interaction in the first year of life, preterm and term infants are equally likely to form secure attachments with parents (i.e., to perceive their parents as providing responsive care). Thus, we can infer that the observed differences are adaptive. Mothers treat their preterm babies in ways that are appropriate to their needs and support normal development.

One caution is in order. Attachment only reflects one aspect of parent–child relationships, though a very important one. The finding that term and preterm groups do not differ in attachment patterns does not mean there are no differences, only that there are no differences in attachment per se.

NEW DIRECTIONS IN CLINICAL CARE

Research documents both the vulnerability of preterm infants to developmental difficulties and the heavier demands placed on caregivers. Attachment data suggest that the majority of infants and parents do well, but there remains a sense of greater challenge and burden for parents rearing a preterm infant than that experienced in families with term babies. In an effort to reduce such burdens, intervention programs have been implemented both in hospital and after discharge. Interventions may concentrate primarily on infants, primarily on parents, or on parent–child interactions. This section describes the theories behind interventions and the evolution in thinking about appropriate intervention strategies for infants and parents.

Because the preterm infant is not well adapted to extrauterine life, one strategy is to bring the baby as quickly as possible to readiness for independent life. This strategy promises to reduce length of hospitalization and hence parent–infant separation, as well as to produce an infant who is more responsive to parent efforts.

Initially, interventions carried out in the NICU were based on the premise that the preterm infant is an extrauterine fetus and the developmentally appropriate experience should be womblike, that is, provide experiences that resemble those of the fetus in utero. Thus, motorized hammocks (Neal, 1968), rockers (Barnard, 1972), and waterbeds (Korner et al., 1975) were used to simulate maternal movement and tape-recordings of heartbeats and the maternal voice (Kraemer & Pierpont, 1976) were used to simulate fetal auditory experience. These approaches may have been appropriate for the baby, but made no effort to consider parental needs.

A second approach viewed the infant as an immature newborn and assumed the appropriate environment should approximate the home. Interventions based on this reasoning included stroking, massaging, and handling (Freedman, Boverman, & Freedman, 1966; Hasselmeyer, 1964; Solkoff & Matusak, 1975; Solkoff, Yaffe, Weintraub, & Blase, 1969), hanging mobiles on cribs (Scarr-Salapatek & Williams, 1973), playing tape-recorded voices, exercise programs (Rosenfeld, 1980), and regular play (Scarr-Salapatek & Williams, 1973). In these studies, the extra handling, play, and stimulation was usually carried out by research staff or nurses. Only a few studies considered maternal handling. Powell (1974) found that "handled" infants regained their birthweights faster than control infants, but there were no differences between mother and nurse-handled groups in hospital or at follow-up. However, on average, mothers visited only once every 4 days, whereas nurses participated daily. Thus, mothers "accomplished" as much as the nurses with fewer contacts. When the mother does the handling, there may be benefits to the parent–child relationship as well as direct effects on infant development. Thus, although not particularly intended to do so, studies in which parents participated in stimulating the infant may have inadvertently met some parental needs.

The importance to parents of opportunities to handle and care for their preterm infant in the NICU has been discussed in previous sections. Such opportunities increase parental feelings of self-confidence and competence in reading infant cues, making decisions, and responding appropriately to infant behavior. Caretaking opportunities also help parents feel that the baby belongs to them and not to the hospital staff. Having parents feel more invested in the relationship with the infant also enhances the care that the infant receives both before and after discharge, which, in turn, facilitates infant development.

Despite differences in methodology, subjects and results, most intervention studies reported some benefits of early stimulation to infants (Korner, 1987). An important aspect is that stimulated infants became more alert, reponsive, and thus were more rewarding for parents to interact with. This was reflected in increased parental visiting to the NICU as compared with control subjects (Rosenfeld,

1980). Thus, whether or not intervention affected infant development directly, it improved infant responsiveness and parents' perceptions of their infants. More alert and responsive infants are likely to receive more parental attention and stimulation.

A second general intervention strategy is to provide parents with additional skills that will compensate for their infant's interactive limitations. Whereas the interventions discussed earlier were restricted to in-hospital programs, those that target parents often offer at-home components following discharge (Bromwich & Parmelee, 1979; Rice, 1977; Scarr-Salapatek & Williams, 1973). One study taught mothers a massage and rocking procedure (Rice, 1977); another taught activities to enhance infant development and provided developmentally appropriate toys (Scarr-Salapatek & Williams, 1973); a third focused on mothers' interaction with babies in ways that matched infant skills and temperament (i.e., individualized intervention; Bromwich & Parmelee, 1979). In this last, study parents in the intervention group were later more likely to provide appropriate activities for their infants and were more sensitive observers of their babies than those in the control group. In general, longer term benefits occurred when programs included ongoing parental involvement and support following discharge (Barnard & Bee, 1983; Field, Widmayer, Stringer, & Ignatoff, 1980; Patteson & Barnard, 1990; Scarr-Salapatek & Williams, 1973).

There has been less systematic intervention explicitly directed to parents than to infants. The early work at Stanford encouraged mothers to touch and care for their preterm infants in the NICU (Barnett et al., 1970). There and elsewhere, experience enhanced parent self-confidence at discharge and later on, as well as leading to more positive and affectionate social interactions (Kennell et al., 1974; Klaus et al., 1972; Leiderman & Seashore, 1975; Seashore, Leifer, Barnett, & Leiderman, 1973). Hospitals increasingly recognize the need to provide emotional support to parents during the NICU experience and after discharge. Social service personnel and translators for non-English-speaking parents are often available for support and help in obtaining concrete services like housing, transportation, food, medical care, and financial assistance. Further opportunities to practice infant care are available in hospitals that provide rooming-in arrangements before discharge.

Parent education about preterm infants' development and behavior also helps parents to be more informed and realistic about their babies (Blackburn, 1983; Harrison, 1983). Educational interventions include use of video and discussion (Harrison & Twardosz, 1986) intensive parent teaching programs (Brooten et al., 1986; Nurcombe et al., 1983), and home-based teaching through the infant's first year (Field et al., 1980; Ross, 1984). These programs help parents recognize infant cues and provide an understanding of health and daily care. Outcome measures for evaluation include infant health and development, length of hospitalization, parent–child interaction, and quality of the home environment. Despite differences in the methodology, the majority of studies report some positive outcomes. The common factor seemed to be repeated contact with a consistent supportive figure over time (e.g., 1 year; Heinieke, Beckwith, & Thompson, 1988). Thus, a relationship with a supportive figure overshadowed the specific content of the interventions (Patteson & Barnard, 1990).

One valuable source of information and support is "veteran" parents who share experiences with new parents at small group meetings or in individual sessions. In a study of one such program, mothers who attended the group sessions visited their infants more often and were more active during visits than a comparison group of mothers. At the time of discharge, "group" mothers also reported more satisfaction with the medical and nursing care their child received. They had a better understanding of their child problems, were more confident in their ability to provide care, and were more familiar with community resources than those who did not have a group experience. At a 1-year follow-up, group parents were found to be more socially stimulating and promoted independence in their children more than comparison families (Minde et al., 1983). Thus, the opportunity to meet with veteran parents is a useful support for parents of preterm infants. It reduces stress, offers support, and fosters more positive parental attitudes. It is likely too, if one adheres to a transactional model (Sameroff & Chandler, 1975), that there are indirect benefits to parent–child interactions and parental involvement that affect the child's development.

Most recently, attention has focused on tailoring caregiving and medical procedures to the needs, states, and responses of the infant. By recognizing each baby as an individual, programs are designed to be appropriate to each infant's condition, reactions, and needs. One innovative application of this type involved placing a breathing teddy bear, set to match the infant's breathing rate, in the isolette, and allowing the infants to regulate their interaction with it. In fact, preterm infants (32–34 weeks gestational age) spent more time in contact with the breathing bear than with a nonbreathing bear and showed more neurobehavioral maturation in the form of quiet sleep both in the hospital and 5 weeks later at home (Thoman & Ingersoll, 1989).

The work of Als and colleagues (e.g., 1986) has been instrumental in protecting premature infants in the NICU from inappropriate, intrusive, and unnecessary stimulation. Her work has emphasized the characteristics of the infant prior to intervening, rather than applying a standard, routine procedure or program. These studies are having an impact on caregiving practices in the NICU and on the involvement of the family in the infant's care. The first step is to identify, on an individual basis for each child and family, opportunities and experiences to support the infant's current level of development without undue stress. When parents observe an assessment of their infant's capabilities, they have a more realistic perception of their infant; fathers report less anxiety, and mothers are more aware of infant cues for overstimulation (R. E. Culp, A. M. Culp, & Harmon, 1989). Furthermore, infants in individualized care show improved medical outcomes (e.g., shorter stays on the respirator, fewer days on supplemental oxygen, earlier oral feeds, improved weight gain, lower incidence of intraventricular hemorrhage or bleeding into the brain, and less severe levels of bronchopulmonary dysplasia or abnormal changes in the lung tissue). Developmental outcomes also show infants receiving individualized care to have better behavioral regulation and better developmental scores at 3, 6, and 9 months corrected ages (Als et al., 1986). Such results would indicate that the goal in intervention should be to make it more appropriate to each infant's special needs and to "listen to the baby."

One implication of this approach is that parent needs are part of each infant's unique situation and are therefore to be considered in the intervention design. A second is that parents who are focused on their own baby may be an important source of information for hospital staff who must consider needs of many infants. This emphasis on identifying each infant's strengths and needs, as well as teaching the family how to read cues and to respond appropriately supports both the infant's development and the parents' feelings of competence in caring for their preterm infant. Educating parents and supporting their involvement in caring for their infant from the earliest days in the NICU helps to increase self-confidence in parenting skills and investment in their infant's development.

Thus, a variety of interventions have been shown to have beneficial effects on preterm infants and their families. Although most interventions were focused exclusively on enhancing infant development, they may have had the beneficial "side effect" of engaging parents. More recent work has been more likely to include parents in planned interventions and to view support for parents as an important ingredient in an intervention program.

CONCLUSIONS

Significant medical and technical advances in neonatal intensive care have markedly increased the survival rates of low-birthweight premature infants. As techniques for reducing incidence and severity of problems associated with prematurity were developed, isolation of parents from infants increased. However, in the last 20 years, hospitals have moved toward allowing and encouraging parents to handle and care for their infants in hospital. Nevertheless, the experience remains stressful and significantly different from that of parents of term infants. Recent changes in the care of preterm infants acknowledge the need to support not only the infant's physical well-being, but the emotional functioning of the family and infant.

For both the infant and parent, unique features associated with preterm birth (the timing, the NICU experience, and the initial and developing capacities of the infant) affect parent–child relationships.

We have focused on how these difficulties can persist over the first year. Infants are dependent on adults for survival, and preterm infants are more vulnerable to effects of inadequate care than their term peers. Because preterm infants are qualitatively different from term infants in physical appearance and behavior, and take longer to attain milestones like smiling and reaching for a toy, adjustments and compensatory maneuvers by parents are required.

Few studies have observed preterm infants and their parents in the hospital, but those that have indicated a variety of factors that affect the extent to which parents are able to visit and to become actively engaged. Active engagement is related to subsequent parental involvement, and can be facilitated by supportive hospital policies and practices.

There have been numerous studies of preterm infants and their parents in the year following hospital discharge. These studies are notably limited in focusing on mothers; there are few data on fathers and preterm infants. In the first 3 months, infants with more medical problems are less active and receive less maternal contact, but after 3 months, mothers take a more active role. A number of explanations have been offered for this pattern. Studies that have examined infant behavior and factors that influence infant capacity for interactive behavior have found that early infant behavior is affected by both health and birth status, and maternal behavior was responsive to these early differences. Furthermore, mothers of preterms may continue to behave differently from those of term infants even when the differences in infant behavior have disappeared. However, these differences may best be interpreted as adaptations of parents to the developmental skills and needs of the infant. This is confirmed by studies showing that the majority of preterm infants are securely attached to their mothers by 12 to 18 months of age (corrected).

New directions in hospital and home care for preterm infants are moving to include parents as involved partners in their infant's care from the early days and to individualize care for infants and parents. Research has played a major role in changing patterns of care for preterm infants and changes in clinical practice have raised new questions for research. Although the developments in medical technology that enabled these infants to survive originally did so with a loss of parent–infant contact, the current wave of innovations includes efforts to make early care more humane for both infants and parents. Early evidence suggests these innovations will not be at the expense of physical health and growth, but will also enhance physical well-being.

REFERENCES

Affleck, G., Tennen, H., & Rowe, J. (1990). Mothers, fathers, and the crisis of newborn intensive care. *Infant Mental Health Journal, 11*, 12–25.

Ainsworth, M.D.S., Blehar, M., Waters, E., & Wall, S. (1978). *Patterns of attachment.* Hillsdale, NJ: Lawrence Erlbaum Associates.

Alfasi, A., Schwartz, F. A., Brake, S. C., Fifer, W. P., Fleischman, A. R., & Hofer, M. (1985). Mother–infant feeding interactions in preterm and full term infants. *Infant Behavior and Development, 8*, 167–180.

Als, H., Lawhorn, G., Brown, E., Gibes, R., Duffy, F., McAnulty, G., & Blickman, J. (1986). Individualized behavioral and environmental care for the very low birth weight preterm infant at high risk for bronchopulmonary dysplasia: Neonatal intensive care unit and developmental outcome. *Pediatrics, 78*, 1123–1131.

Anders, T., & Keener, M. (1985). Developmental course of nighttime sleep–wake patterns in full term and preterm infants during the first year of life. *Sleep, 8*, 173–192.

Anderson, G., Marks, E., & Wahlberg, V. (1986). Kangaroo care for premature infants. *American Journal of Nursing*, 807–809.

Anisfeld, E. (1982). The onset of social smiling in preterm and full-term infants from two ethnic backgrounds. *Infant Behavior and Development, 5*, 387–395.

Avery, M., & Litwack, G. (1983). *Born early: The story of a premature baby.* Boston: Little, Brown.

Bakeman, R., & Brown, J. V. (1980). Early interaction: Consequences for social and mental development at 3 years. *Child Development, 51*, 437–447.

Barnard, K. E. (1972). *The effect of stimulation on the devotion and amount of sleep and wakefulness in the premature infant.* Unpublished doctoral thesis, University of Washington, Seattle.

Barnard, K., & Bee, H. (1983). The impact of temporally patterned stimulation on the development of the preterm infant. *Child Development, 54*, 1156–1167.

Barnard, K. E., Bee, H. L., & Hammond, M. A. (1984). Development of changes in maternal interactions with term and preterm infants. *Infant Behavior and Development*, *7*, 101–113.

Barnett, C., Leiderman, P., Grobstein, R., & Klaus, M. (1970). Neonatal separation: the maternal side of interactional deprivation. *Pediatrics*, 197–205.

Beckwith, L., & Cohen, S.E. (1978). Preterm birth: Hazardous obstetrical and postnatal events as related to caregiver–infant behavior. *Infant Behavior and Development*, *1*, 403–411.

Beckwith, L., & Parmelee, A. H. (1986). EEG patterns of infants, home environment and later IQ. *Child Development*, *47*, 579–588.

Beckwith, L., Rodning, C., & Cohen, S. (1992). Preterm children at early adolescence and continuity and discontinuity in maternal responsiveness from infancy. *Child Development*, *63*, 1198–1208.

Bendersky, M., & Lewis, M. (1992, May). *Patterns of maternal interactive behavior over age.* Paper presented at International Conference of Infant Studies, Miami Beach, FL.

Blackburn, S. (1983). Fostering behavioral development of high risk infants. *Journal of Obstetrics and Gynecological Nursing,* Supplement, May/June, 76–86.

Blackburn, S., & Barnard, K. (1985). Analysis of caregiving events related to preterm infants in the special care unit. In A. Gottfried & J. Gaiter (Eds.), *Infant stress under intensive care* (pp. 113–129). Baltimore: University Park Press.

Boukydis, C.F.Z. (1982). Support groups for parents with premature infants in NICUs. In R. E. Marshall, C. Kasman, & L. S. Cape (Eds.), *Coping with care for sick newborns* (pp. 215–238). Philadelphia: Saunders.

Bowlby, J. (1969). *Attachment* (Vol. 1). New York: Basic Books.

Brachfeld, S., Goldberg, S., & Sloman, J. (1980). Prematurity and immaturity as influences on parent–infant interaction at 8- and 12 months. *Infant Behavior and Development*, *3*, 289–306.

Brazelton, T. B. (1973). *Neonatal Behavioral Assessment Scale: Clinics in Developmental Medicine.* No. 50. London: William Heineman Medical Books, Ltd.

Bromwich, R., & Parmelee, A. H. (1979) An intervention program for preterm infants. In T. M. Field, A. M. Sostek, S. Goldberg, & H. H. Shuman (Eds.), *Infants born at risk* (pp. 389–412). Jamaica NY: Spectrum.

Brooten, S., Kumar, S., Brown, L., Butts, P., Finkler, S., Bakewell-Sachs, S., Gibbons, A., & Delworia-Papadopoulos, M. (1986). A randomized clinical trial of early hospital discharge and home follow-up of very low birth weight infants. *New England Journal of Medicine*, *315*, 934–939.

Brown, J. V., & Bakeman, R. (1979). Relationships with human mothers with their infants during the first year of life: Effects of prematurity. In R. W. Bell & W. P. Smotherman (Eds.), *Maternal influences and early behavior* (pp. 353–374). Jamaica, NY: Spectrum.

Budin, P. (1907). *The nursling.* London: Caxton.

Censullo, M. (1992, May). *Relationship of early responsiveness to one-year outcomes in preterm and full-term infants.* Paper presented at the International Conference on Infant Studies. Miami, FL.

Cohen, S., & Parmelee, A. H. (1983). Prediction of five-year Stanford Binet scores in preterm infants. *Child Development*, *54*, 1242–1253.

Corter, C., Trehub, S., Boukydis, C.F.Z., Ford, L., Celhoffer, L., & Minde, K. (1978). Nurse's judgments of the attractiveness of preterm infants. *Infant Behavior and Development*, *1*, 373–380.

Crawford, J. W. (1982). Mother–infant interaction in premature and full term infants. *Child Development*, *53*, 957–962.

Crnic, K. A., Greenberg, M. T., Ragozin, A. S., Robinson, N. M., & Basham, R. B. (1983a). Effects of stress and social support on mothers of premature and full-term infants. *Child Development, 54*, 209–217.

Crnic, K. A., Ragozin, A. S., Greenberg, M. T., Robinson, N. M., & Basham, R. B. (1983b). Social interaction and developmental competence of preterm and full term infants during the first year of life. *Child Development*, *54*, 1199–1210.

Culp, R. E., Culp, A. M., & Harmon, R. J. (1989). A tool for educating parents about their premature infants. *Birth*, *16*(1), 23–26.

Davis, D., & Thoman, E. (1987). Behavioral states of premature infants: Implications for neural and behavioral development. *Developmental Psychology*, *20*(1), 25–38.

DiVitto, B. A., & Goldberg, S. (1979). The development of early parent–infant interaction as a function of newborn medical status. In T. M. Field, A. M. Sostek, S. Goldberg, & H. H. Shuman (Eds.), *Infants born at risk* (pp. 311–332). Jamaica, NY: Spectrum.

DiVitto, B., & Goldberg, S. (1983). Talking and sucking: Infant-feeding behavior and parent stimulation in dyads with different medical histories. *Infant Behavior and Development*, *6*, 157–165.

Easterbrooks, M. (1989). Quality of attachment to mother and father: Effects of perinatal risk status. *Child Development*, *60*, 825–831.

Eyler, F. D., Woods, N. S., Behnke, M., & Conlon, M. (1992, May). *Changes over a decade: Adult–infant interaction in the NICU.* Paper presented at the International Conference on Infant Studies, Miami.

Fanaroff, A. A., Kennell, J. H., & Klaus, M. H. (1972) Followup of low birthweight infants–the predictive value of maternal visiting patterns. *Pediatrics*, *49*, 287–290.

Field, T. M. (1977a). The effects of early separation, interactive deficits and experimental manipulations on infant–mother face-to-face interaction. *Child Development*, *48*, 763–771.

Field, T. M. (1977b). Maternal stimulation during infant feeding. *Developmental Psychology*, *13*, 539–540.

Field, T. M. (1979). Interaction patterns of preterm and full term infants. In T. M. Field, A. M. Sostek, S. Goldberg, & H. H. Shuman (Eds.), *Infants born at risk* (pp. 333–356). Jamaica, NY: Spectrum.

Field, T. M. (1982). Affective displays of high risk infants during early interactions. In T. M. Field & A. Fogel (Eds.), *Emotion and early interaction* (pp. 101–126). Hillsdale, NJ: Lawrence Erlbaum Associates.

Field, T. M. (1990). Neonatal stress and coping in intensive care. *Infant Mental Health Journal*, *11*(1), 57–65.

Field, T. M., Dempsey, J., & Shuman, H.H. (1981). Developmental followup of preterm and postterm infants. In S. Friedmans & M. Sigman (Eds.), *Preterm birth and psychological development* (pp. 299–312). New York: Academic Press.

Field, T., Widmayer, S., Stringer, S., & Ignatoff, E. (1980). Teenage, lower class mothers and their preterm infants: an intervention and developmental followup. *Child Development*, *51*, 426–436.

Freedman, D. H., Boverman, H., & Freedman, N. (1966). *Effects of kinesthetic stimulation on weight gain and smiling in premature infants*. Paper presented at American Orthopsychiatric Association, San Francisco.

Friedman, S. L., Jacobs, B. S., & Werthman, M. W. (1982). Preterms of low medical risk: Spontaneous behaviors and soothability at expected date of birth. *Infant Behavior and Development*, *5*, 3–10.

Friedman, S. L., Zahn-Waxler, C., & Radke-Yarrow, M. (1982). Perception of cries of full term and preterm infants. *Infant Behavior and Development*, *5*, 161–174.

Frodi, A. (1983). Attachment behavior and sociability with strangers in premature and full term infants. *Infant Mental Health Journal*, *4*, 13–22.

Frodi, A., Lamb, M., Leavitt, L., Donovan, C., Neff, C., & Sherry, D. (1978). Father's and mother's response to the faces and cries of normal and premature infants. *Developmental Psychology*, *14*, 490–498.

Frodi, A., & Thompson, R. A. (1985). Infant responses in the Strange Situation: Effects of prematurity and of quality of attachment. *Child Development*, *56*, 1280–1290.

Goldberg, S. (1977). Social competence in infancy: A model of parent–infant interaction. *Merrill-Palmer Quarterly*, *23*, 163–178.

Goldberg, S. (1978). Prematurity: Effects on parent–infant interaction. *Pediatric Psychology*, *3*, 137–144.

Goldberg, S. (1979). Premature birth: Consequences for the parent–infant relationship. *American Scientist*, *67*, 214–220.

Goldberg, S. (1983). Parent–infant bonding: Another look. *Child Development*, *54*, 1355–1385.

Goldberg, S., & DiVitto, B. (1983). *Born too soon*. San Francisco: Freeman.

Goldberg, S., Lojkasek, M., Gartner, G., & Corter, C. (1989). Maternal responsiveness and social development in preterm infants. In M. Bornstein (Ed.), *Maternal responsiveness: characteristics and consequences* (pp. 89–104). San Francisco: Jossey-Bass.

Goldberg, S., Perrotta, M., Minde, K., & Corter, C. (1986). Maternal behavior and attachment in low birthweight twins and singletons. *Child Development*, *57*, 34–46.

Goldson, E. (1992a). Follow-up of low birthweight infants: A contemporary review. In M. L. Wolraich, & D. Routh (Eds.), *Advances in developmental and behavioral pediatrics* (Vol. 10, pp. 159–180). Philadelphia: Jessica Kingsley Publishers.

Goldson, E. (1992b). The neonatal intensive care unit: Premature infants and parents. *Infants and Young Children*, *4*(3), 31–42.

Gottfried, A. W., & Gaiter, J. (1985). *Infant stress under intensive care*. Baltimore: University Park Press.

Greenberg, M., & Crnic, K. (1988). Longitudinal predictors of developmental status and social interaction in premature and full-term infants at age two. *Child Development*, *59*, 554–570.

Greene, J. G., Fox, N. A., & Lewis, M. (1983). The relationship between neonatal characteristics and three-month mother–infant interaction in high-risk infants. *Child Development*, *54*, 1286–1296.

Harrison, H. (1983). *The premature baby book: A parent's guide to coping and caring in the first years*. New York: St. Martin's Press.

Harrison, L., & Twardosz, S. (1986). Teaching mothers about their preterm babies. *Journal of Obstetric and Gynecological Nursing*, *15*(2), 165–172.

Hasselmeyer, E. (1964). The premature neonate's response to handling. *American Nurses Journal*, *11*, 25–24.

Hawthorne, J. T., Richards, M.P.M., & Callon, M. (1978). A study of parental visiting of babies in a special care unit. In F.S.W. Brimblecombe, M.P.M. Richards, & N.R.C. Roberton (Eds.), *Separation and special care baby units* (pp. 33–54). London: Heineman Medical Books.

Heinicke, C., Beckwith, L., & Thompson, A. (1988). Early intervention in the family system: a framework and review. *Infant Mental Health Journal*, *9*(2), 111–141.

Hunt, J. V., & Rhodes, L. (1977). Mental development in preterm infants during the first year. *Child Development*, *48*, 204–210.

Jackson, A., & Gorman, W. A. (1988). Maternal attitudes to preterm birth. *Journal of Psychosomatic Obstetrics and Gynecology*, *8*, 119–126.

Jarvis, P. A., Myers, B. J., & Creasey, G. L. (1989). The effects of infants' illness on mothers' interaction with prematures at 4 and 8 months. *Infant Behavior and Development*, *12*, 25–35.

Jeffcoate, J., Humphrey, M., & Lloyd, J. (1979). Disturbance in parent–child relationship following preterm delivery. *Developmental Medicine and Child Neurology*, *21*, 344–352.

Kennell, J. H., & Klaus, M. H. (1985). Commentary 2. In A. W. Gottfried & J. L. Gaiter (Eds.), *Infant stress under intensive care* (pp. 271–277). Baltimore: University Park Press.

Kennell, J. H., Trause, M., & Klaus, M. H. (1975). Evidence for a sensitive period in the human mother. In *Parent–infant interaction. CIBA Foundation Symposium,* No. 33, Amsterdam: Elsevier, 87–101.

Klaus, M. H., Jerauld, R., Kreger, N., McAlpine, W., Steffa, M., & Kennell, J. H. (1972). Maternal attachment: Importance of the first postpartum days. *New England Journal of Medicine, 286,* 460–463.

Klaus, M. H., & Kennell, J. (1976). *Maternal–infant bonding.* St. Louis: Mosby.

Klaus, M. H., & Kennell, J. H. (1982). *Parent–infant bonding.* St. Louis: Mosby.

Korner, A. (1987). Preventive intervention with high risk newborns–theoretical, conceptual, and methodological perspectives. In J. Osofsky (Ed.), *Handbook of infant development* (pp. 1006–1036). New York: Wiley.

Korner, A., Kraemer, M., Faffuer, M., & Casper, L. (1975). Effects of waterbed flotation on premature infants: A pilot study. *Pediatrics, 56,* 361–367.

Kraemer, H. C., & Pierpoint, M. E. (1976). Rocking, waterbeds, and auditory stimula to enhancegrowth of preterm infants. *Journal of Pediatrics, 88,* 297–299.

Landry, S. H. (1986). Preterm infants' responses in early joint attention interactions. *Infant Behavior and Development, 9,* 1–14.

Lawson, K. R., Ruff, H. A., McKCarton-Down, C., Kurtzberg, D., & Vaughan, H. G. (1984). Auditory-visual responsiveness in full-term and preterm infants. *Developmental Psychology, 20,* 120–127.

Leiderman, P., & Seashore, M. (1975). Mother–infant separation: Some delayed consequences. In *CIBA Foundation Symposium 33 : Parent–infant interaction* (pp. 213–239). Amsterdam: Elsevier.

Leifer, A. D., Leiderman, P. H., Barnett, C. R., & Williams, J. A. (1972). Effects of mother–infant separation on maternal attachment behavior. *Child Development, 43,* 1303–1318.

Lester, B. M., & Zeskind, P. S. (1979). The organization and assessment of crying in the infant at risk. In T. M. Field, A. M. Sostek, S. Goldberg, & H. H. Shuman (Eds.), *Infants born at risk* (pp. 121–144). Jamaica, NY: Spectrum.

Levy-Shiff, R., Sharir, H., & Mogilner, M. B. (1989). Mother–and father–preterm infant relationship in the hospital preterm nursery. *Child Development, 60,* 93–102.

Maier, R. A., Holmes, D. L., Slaymaker, F. L., & Reich, J. N. (1984). The perceived attractiveness of preterm infants. *Infant Behavior and Development, 7,* 403–414.

Malatesta, C. Z., Grigoryev, P., Lamb, C., Albin, M., & Culver, C. (1986). Emotion socialization and expressive development in preterm and full term infant. *Child Development, 57,* 316–330.

Mann, J., & Plunkett, J. (1992, May). *Home observations of extremely low birthweight infants: Maternal compensation or overstimulation.* Paper presented at the International Conference on Infant Studies, Miami Beach, FL.

Marshall, R. E., Kasman, C., & Cape, L. S. (1982). *Coping with caring for sick newborns.* Philadelphia: Saunders.

Marton, P., Minde, K., & Perrotta, M. (1981). The role of the father for the infant at risk. *American Journal of Orthopsychiatry, 51,* 672–678.

McGehee, L. J., & Eckerman, G. O. (1983). The preterm infant as a social partner: Responsive but unreadable. *Infant Behavior and Development, 6*(4), 461–470.

Miles, M. S. (1989). Parenting needs with premature infants: Sources of stress. *Critical Care Nursing Quarterly, 12*(3), 69–74.

Minde, K. K, Ford, L., Celhoffer, & Boukydis, C. Z. (1975). Interactions of mothers and nurses with preterm infants. *Canadian Medical Association Journal, 113,* 741–745.

Minde, K. K., Marton, P., Manning, D., & Hines, B. (1980). Some determinants of mother–infant interaction in the premature nursery. *Journal of the American Academy of Child Psychiatry, 19,* 1–21.

Minde, K., Perrotta, M., & Corter, C. (1982). The effect of neonatal complications in premature twins on their mother's preference. *Journal of the American Academy of Child Psychiatry, 21,* 446–452.

Minde, K. K., Shosenberg, N., Thompson, J., & Marton, P. (1983). Self-help groups in a premature nursery—followup at one year. In J. Call, E. Galenson, & R. Tyson (Eds.), *Frontiers of infant psychiatry* (pp. 264–272). New York: Basic Books.

Minde, K. K., Whitelaw, A., Brown, J., & Fitzhardinge, P. (1983). Effect of neonatal complications in premature infants on early parent–infant interactions. *Developmental Medicine and Child Neurology, 25,* 763–777.

Molitor, A. E., & Eckerman, C. O. (1992, May). *Behavioral cues of distress/avoidance in preterm infants.* Paper presented at the International Conference on Infant Studies, Miami, FL.

Neal, M. (1968). Vestibular stimulation and developmental behavior of the small premature infant. *Nursing Research Reports, 3,* 2–5.

Nurcombe, B., Rauh, V., Howell, D., Teti, D., Rudoff, P., Murphy, B., & Brennan, J. (1983). An intervention program for mothers of low birth weight infants: Outcomes at 6 and 12 months. In J. Call, E. Galenson, & R. Tyson (Eds.), *Frontiers of infant psychiatry* (pp. 201–210). New York: Basic Books.

Paludetto, R., Faggiano-Perfetto, M., Asprea, A., DeCurtis, M., & Margara-Paludetto, P. (1981). Reactions of 60 parents allowed unrestricted contact with infants in the NICU. *Early Human Development, 5,* 401–409.

Patteson, D. M., & Barnard, K. E. (1990). Parenting of low birthweight infants. *Infant Mental Health Journal, 11*(1), 37–56.

Pederson, D. R., Bento, S., Chance, G. W., Evans, B., & Fox, A. M. (1987). Maternal emotional responses to preterm birth. *American Journal of Orthopsychiatry, 57,* 15–21.

Plunkett, J., Meisels, S., Stiefel, G., Pasick, P., & Roloff, D. (1986). Patterns of attachment among infants of varying biological risk. *Journal of the American Academy of Child Psychiatry, 25,* 794–800.

Powell, L. (1974). The effect of extra stimulation and maternal involvement on the development of low birth weight infants and on maternal behavior. *Child Development, 45,* 106–113.

Rice, R. (1977). Neurophysiological development in premature infants following stimulation. *Developmental Psychology, 13,* 69–76.

Rode, S., Chang, P., Fisch, R., & Sroufe, L. A. (1981). Attachment patterns of infants separated at birth. *Developmental Psychology, 17,* 188–191.

Rodning, C., Beckwith, L., & Howard, J. (1989). Characteristics of attachment organization in prenatally drug-exposed toddlers. *Development and Psychopathology, 1,* 277–289.

Rosenfield, A. G. (1980). Visiting in the intensive care nursery. *Child Development, 51,* 939–941.

Ross, G. (1984). Home intervention for premature infants of low-income families. *American Journal of Orthopsychiatry, 54*(2), 263–270.

Sameroff, A. K., & Chandler, M. J. (1975). Reproductive risk and the continuum of caretaking casualty. In F. D. Horowitz, E. M. Hetherington, S. Scarr-Salapatek, & G. Siegel (Eds.), *Review of child development research* (Vol. 4, pp.187–244). Chicago: University of Chicago Press.

Scarr-Salapatek, S., & Williams, M. (1973). The effects of early stimulation on low birth weight infants. *Child Development, 44,* 94–101.

Seashore, M., Leifer, A., Barnett, C., & Leiderman, P. (1973). The effects of denial of early mother–infant interaction on maternal self-confidence. *Journal of Personality and Social Development, 26,* 369–373.

Solkoff, N., & Matusak, D. (1975). Tactile stimulation and behavioral development among low birthweight infants. *Child Psychiatry and Human Development, 6,* 33–37.

Solkoff, N., Yaffe, S., Weintraub, D., & Blase, B. (1969). Effects of handling on the subsequent development of premature infants. *Development Psychology, 1,* 765–768.

Stern, M., & Karraker, K. H. (1990). The prematurity sterotype: Empirical evidence and implications for practice. *Infant Mental Health Journal, 1,* 3–11.

Stevenson, M. B., Roach, M. A., Ver Haeve, J. N., & Leavitt, L. A. (1990). Rhythms in the dialogue of infant feeding: Preterm and term infants. *Infant Behavior and Development, 13,* 51–70.

Stiefel, G. S., Plunkett, J. W., & Meisels, S. J. (1987). Affective expression among preterm infants of varying levels of biological risk. *Infant Behavior and Development, 10,* 151–164.

Thoman, E. B., & Ingersoll, E. W. (1989). The human nature of the youngest humans: Prematurely born babies. *Seminars in Perinatology, 13*(6), 482–494.

Telzrow, R., Kang, R., Mitchell, S., Ashworth, C., & Barnard, K. (1980). *An assessment of the behavior of the premature infant at forty weeks conceptual age.* Unpublished manuscript, University of Washington, Seattle.

Van Ijzendoorn, M., Goldberg, S., Kroonenberg, P., & Frenkel, O. (1992). The relative effects of maternal and child problems on the quality of attachment: A meta-analysis of attachment in clinical samples. *Child Development, 63,* 840–858.

Van Ijzendoorn, M., & Kroonenberg, P. (1988) Cross cultural patterns of attachment: A meta-analysis of the strange situation. *Child Development, 59,* 147–156.

Wille, D. E. (1991). Relation of preterm birth with quality of infant–mother attachment at one year. *Infant Behavior and Development, 14,* 227–240.

Zarling, C. L., Hirsch, B. J., & Landry, S. (1988). Maternal social networks and mother–infant interactions in full term and very low birthweight preterm infants. *Child Development, 59,* 178–185.

Zeanah, C., Canger, C., & Jones, J. (1984). Clinical approaches to traumatized parents. Psychotherapy in the intensive care nursery. *Child Psychiatry and Human Development, 14,* 158–169.

Zeanah, C., & McDonough, S. (1989). Clinical approaches to families in early intervention. *Seminars in Perinatology, 13*(6), 513–522.

Zeskind, P. S., & Iacino, R. (1984). Effects of maternal visitation to preterm infants in the neonatal intensive care unit. *Child Development, 55,* 1887–1893.

10

Parenting Children With Down Syndrome and Other Types of Mental Retardation

Robert M. Hodapp
UCLA Graduate School of Education

INTRODUCTION

Rearing a child with mental retardation challenges any parent. Besides the child's cognitive difficulties, children with Down syndrome and other types of retardation often have associated motor, medical, psychopathological, and other handicaps. One must also consider the parents' emotional reactions and concerns. Parents of children with retardation must cope with having produced a "defective" child, a child who looks and acts differently from agemates. Such parental concerns re-occur throughout the child's life, culminating in the issue of how the adult with Down syndrome or other mental retardation syndrome will live when parents can no longer provide in-home care.

And yet, difficult as such parenting issues are, many parents cope successfully with rearing a child with retardation. Different families vary in their styles of coping, specific child characteristics influence parental and familial reactions, and many formal and informal supports protect parents from depression and hopelessness. These parents continue to need external support, but they often cope reasonably well.

Before reviewing issues involved in parenting a child with retardation, three issues must be addressed. First, it is necessary to note the area's ties to the parenting of children without retardation. Theories of parenting derive from those used to conceptualize parenting of nonretarded children, and most studies compare parents of children with retardation to parents of nonretarded children. Resultant intervention efforts have generally taken differences in behavior in nonretarded and retarded groups and have attempted to make the parents of children with retardation more "like normal." Although such direct links to parenting nondisabled children might be criticized, the benchmark for theory, research, and intervention has always been the parent–nonretarded child pair.

Second, this chapter discusses parenting of children with Down syndrome and other types of mental retardation. There are many causes of mental retardation, but this chapter focuses primarily on Down syndrome, while mentioning two other genetic disorders, fragile X syndrome and Prader-Willi syndrome. Down syndrome, the most common genetic form of mental retardation, is usually caused by a trisomy (or third chromosome) at the 21st pair. Fragile X syndrome, the second most common genetic form of retardation, is an X-linked disorder that "breaks the rules" of sex-linked genetic disorders: Males are more often and more severely affected, but females can be either affected or unaffected carriers (Dykens, Hodapp, & Leckman, 1994). Prader-Willi syndrome is a less common genetic disorder caused by a small deletion on chromosome 15. Individuals with Prader-Willi syndrome are often extremely obese and are obsessed with eating and hoarding food. As described later, Down syndrome, fragile X syndrome, and Prader-Willi syndrome each present parents with different childrearing issues.

A third issue concerns the studies themselves. Many studies—particularly those of the 1960s and 1970s—examined parents and families of children who are "handicapped" or "mentally retarded." The prevailing view has been that parents react in a similar way to a child with any disability. Only recently have studies examined parents of children with specific disability conditions to examine whether parents of children with mental retardation differ from those with motor, visual, hearing, or emotional impairments. Even in studies examining parents of children with retardation, most studies continue to examine parents of children who are more versus less severely retarded, as opposed to children with one or another genetic cause of mental retardation (Hodapp & Dykens, 1994). As a result, the subjects of parenting studies vary widely: Some studies examine parents of children with disabilities, others of children with retardation, still others of children with Down syndrome or other genetic cause of mental retardation.

HISTORY OF PARENTING STUDIES

Parents of Children with Retardation

Parents of children with any type of disability have traditionally been considered to be prime candidates for emotional disorders. In studies of parents of children with mental retardation, with emotional disorders, and with no impairments, Cummings, Bayley, and Rie (1966) found that mothers of 4- to 13-year-old retarded children were more depressed, more preoccupied with their children, and had greater difficulty in handling their anger toward their children than mothers of nonretarded children. Fathers, too, have been considered prone to suffer from emotional problems. Cummings (1976) found that, compared to fathers of nonretarded children, fathers of children with retardation were more likely to show increased rates of depression; these fathers also scored lower in dominance, self-esteem, and enjoyment of their (retarded) children (see also Erickson, 1969; W. L. Friedrich & W. N. Friedrich, 1981). Cummings (1976) characterized this constellation of fathers' increased depression and lower dominance, self-esteem, and enjoyment of their children as "neuroticlike constriction."

The marital couple is also affected by the presence of a child with disabilities. Families with children who are mentally retarded or otherwise disabled have generally been thought to follow a "classic" pattern: Mothers become overinvolved with the child with retardation, whereas fathers withdraw from the situation, either emotionally or physically (Levy, 1970). In some families, this pattern escalates until marital difficulties predominate: Not all studies show increased levels of divorce in families with children who are retarded, but many do. In both Gath's (1977) study of children with Down syndrome and Tew, Payne, and Lawrence's (1974) study of children with cerebral palsy, families with disabled children were less likely to be intact than were families with same-age nonretarded children. Presumably, difficulties in dealing with the birth and increased demands of the child with disabilities lead to an increased prevalence of parental breakup (Hagamen, 1980).

Studies of parental pathology and marital breakups form one strand in the history of research on parents of children with retardation. A second strand more specifically examines why parents are affected and which psychological mechanisms are involved in their reactions. For the most part, such studies involve mothers, the parent who usually cares for the child with retardation.

The orientation of most of these studies involves the so-called maternal mourning reaction. Solnit and Stark (1961), drawing on Freud's work on mourning and melancholia, proposed that mothers mourn the birth of any type of "defective" infant. This mourning was thought to be akin to the grieving that occurs in response to a death, with the "death" being the loss of the mother's fantasy of the idealized, perfect infant. Solnit and Stark felt that maternal mourning occurs in response to the birth of a child with any cognitive, motor, social, or physical defect. These researchers were aware that their application of the grief-mourning model was not perfect, in that maternal mourning (as opposed to the actual death of the baby) is complicated by the presence of an actual, live child. This model did, however, imply the time-bound nature of the mourning process, the idea that one "works through" one's mourning reaction over the first few years of the child's life.

Influenced by Solnit and Stark's (1961) model, later workers examined mothers of children with various types of handicaps to determine the nature and course of maternal mourning. Although the number and names of stages have varied with the author, most workers hypothesized that there are essentially three stages of maternal mourning (see Blacher, 1984, for a review). Directly after birth (or diagnosis), mothers experience shock, involving the dissociation of their knowledge from their feelings about having given birth to a child with disabilities. Mothers say things like "I found myself repeating 'It's not real' over and over again" (Drotar, Baskiewicz, Irvin, Kennell, & Klaus, 1975, p. 712). The second stage involves "emotional disorganization." This disorganization predominantly manifests itself as either anger toward others or depression (i.e., anger toward oneself). During this stage, mothers blame doctors, God, or themselves for their child's disability. This period of emotional disorganization may last from months to years, and differs from the first period in that mothers are much more in touch with their emotions and have begun to integrate their intellectual and emotional reactions toward rearing the child with retardation. The third and final stage involves "emotional re-organization." Having worked through their initial feelings of shock and anger-depression, mothers come to realistically appreciate and love their child with disabilities. Parents now realize that the birth of the child with disabilities was "nothing I had done" and that their child is "very special" (Drotar et al., 1975, p. 713). Parents set about to act in the child's best interests, as mothers increasingly accept the child's strengths and limitations.

In both the original Solnit and Stark study and in later studies, no specific time constraints were placed on maternal mourning. Researchers noted only that mothers (and, presumably, fathers) proceed in order from dissociation to emotional disorganization to emotional re-organization over the early childhood years. For the most part, though, emotional reactions to having a child with disabilities were thought to be worked through during the early childhood years.

In contrast to this stage model of maternal mourning, Olshansky (1962, 1966) noted that the metaphor of working through a grief reaction is inadequate, that parents continue having strong emotional reactions as the child gets older. He noted that "most parents of a mentally defective child suffer chronic sorrow throughout their lives. ... The intensity of this sorrow varies from time to time for the same person, from situation to situation, and from one family to the next" (1962, pp. 190–191). Olshansky asked that mental retardation workers change their clinical practices to accommodate long-term reactions that can occur at various points over the child's lifetime. He noted that the Solnit and Stark (1961) view "appears to be an attempt to define the afflicted parents as neurotic" (1966, p. 22), when the problem of parenting a child with retardation "is clearly both in and outside of the [parents'] psyche" (p. 21).

Parent–Child Dyads

Given this background of either stagelike or recurrent maternal mourning, researchers during the 1970s searched for differences in various parental behaviors between dyads with children who did and did not have mental retardation. As a rule, the earliest studies found such differences. Buium, Rynders, and Turnure (1974) and Marshall, Hegrenes, and Goldstein (1973) found that mothers of children with Down syndrome provided less complex verbal input and were more controlling in their interactive styles than were mothers of same-age nonretarded children. Although these authors noted only that the two groups of mothers differed in their behaviors, later workers citing these studies referred to the "verbal deprivation" (Mahoney, 1975) encountered by children with mental retardation.

Not all studies find such differences in maternal input. Rondal (1977) and Buckhalt, Rutherford, and Goldberg (1978), for example, observed that mothers of children with retardation behaved similarly to mothers of nonretarded children. Rondal (1977) noted that, when children with Down syndrome and nonretarded children were matched on the child's mean length of utterance (MLU), "None of the comparisons of mothers' speech to normal and to Down Syndrome children led to differences that were significant or close to significant" (p. 242) between the two groups. Additionally, both groups of mothers adjusted their language upward (i.e., longer MLUs, type-token ratios) as the children's language levels increased. Rondal (1977, p. 242) concluded that "the maternal linguistic environment of DS children between MLU 1 and 3 is an appropriate one."

What could lead to such divergent findings from one study to another? Most differences were undoubtedly caused by methodological differences across studies. In general, when the child with retardation has been matched to the nonretarded child on chronological age (CA), mothers of children with mental retardation have been found to interact differently. But children with retardation are, by definition, functioning below nonretarded agemates; CA-matching may thus not be appropriate. A more appropriate strategy might be to match mother–child dyads on the child's mental age (MA) or the child's level of language (MLU). The issue of what constitutes an appropriate matching variable continues to be debated.

Family Characteristics

A final area of investigation has been the characteristics of families of children with disabilities, the ways in which these families are similar to or different from families of children without mental retardation. In a classic work, Farber (1959) identified several differences between families with and without retarded children. He noted, for example, that the child with retardation increasingly violates the family's "rules" concerning appropriate family roles. Whereas the infant with retardation plays the "infant role," at later ages the child with retardation continues always being "a little kid." The rights and responsibilities typical of middle childhood or the teen years are not passed on to the child with retardation.

Several implications arise from this lack of movement in the roles undertaken by the child with retardation. First, nonimpaired siblings assume different roles than would normally be expected. Farber (1959) identified the "role tensions" experienced by nonretarded siblings, particularly by the oldest daughter. As older girls are the traditional caregivers in Western society, oldest daughters more often perform household jobs and supervise younger children, thereby freeing their mothers to care for the child with retardation (Harkness & Super, in this *Handbook*). Probably due to their inability to enjoy their childhood years, these oldest daughters more often display depression and other psychopathology (see Lobato, 1983).

The retarded child's social role stagnation also does not allow these families to move through a normal family life cycle. Like individual children, families too "develop," undergoing changes in dynamics from the couple's early years of marriage, to the 3, 4, or more person family rearing young children, to dealing with one or more child's growing independence, to the children's "breaking away" and parental negotiation of the "empty nest syndrome," to grandparenthood for the parents and a new family cycle for the now married children (Carter & McGoldrick, 1988; Combrinck-Graham, 1985; Duvall, 1957). But Farber (1959) noted that, when rearing children with more severe levels of retardation (i.e., IQs below 50), parents are never allowed to "grow up" along with their children, thus parents are forced to become stuck in issues of parenting younger children.

Alongside Farber's work on family roles, early (and subsequent) studies delineated basic demographic differences between families with and without retarded children. The differences, although expectable, are nonetheless interesting. Families who are more affluent cope better with rearing a child with disabilities than do those making less money (Farber, 1970; Hoff-Ginsburg & Tardif, in this *Handbook*); two-parent families cope better than one-parent families (Beckman, 1983; Weinraub & Gringlas, in this *Handbook*); and women in better marriages cope better than those in troubled marriages (Beckman, 1983; Friedrich, 1979; Wilson & Gottman, in this *Handbook*). In addition, families are less likely to use social supports when children are older (Suelzle & Keenan, 1981), even as the child-care needs of such children increase due to the child's becoming taller, heavier, and (oftentimes) more difficult to manage.

As the initial work of a new field, studies of parents, interactions, and familial integration set the stage for the explosion of parenting work over the past decade or so. These earlier studies provided basic information about how parents react emotionally and how they interact with their children, as well as how families respond both dynamically and demographically to the child with retardation. More importantly, this early work provided the themes that continue to organize parenting research.

THEORETICAL AND METHODOLOGICAL ISSUES
IN PARENTING THE CHILD WITH RETARDATION

Four central themes cut across both earlier and later work on parents, interactions, and the larger family unit. These issues include a move from pathology to stress-coping perspectives, the influences of familial meaning systems on parental and familial adaptation, group versus individual differences approaches, and the entire issue of how one best studies parenting in children with Down syndrome and other types of mental retardation.

From Pathology to Stress-Coping: Examining
the Models Used to Conceptualize Parenting

The earliest work on families of children with retardation considered parents, interactions, and families as a whole in terms of psychopathology. Parents were examined for psychiatric problems, and for expressed or latent anger and other negative emotions (e.g., as on the MMPI; Erickson, 1969). Interactions between parents and children with retardation were examined to determine how such interactions differed from interactions between mothers and nonretarded children, and differences were considered as evidence of deficient interactions. Divorce, role tensions, and stuck family cycles for families as a whole all reflect the dominant "pathology focus" of parenting research during the 1960s and 1970s.

Gradually, however, researchers have shifted from considering the child as a cause of psychopathology to a stressor on the family system (Crnic, Friedrich, & Greenberg, 1983). This change in perspective is important, for although stressors can be detrimental, they are not always so. In some situations, stressors can strengthen mothers and fathers—as individuals or couples—and families as groups. This perspective allows for a more positive, albeit realistic, orientation toward the problems and strengths of these families.

The stress-coping perspective has also led to borrowing models from other areas. Specifically, McCubbin and Patterson's (1983) "ABCX model" has been adapted by family researchers to help explain potential variations among families of children with mental retardation. This model, which McCubbin and Patterson modified (from Hill, 1949) to explain the effects of father–absence in families during the Vietnam war, has been further adapted for retarded children into a "Double ABCX" model. Briefly stated, the Double ABCX model hypothesizes that the effects of the "crisis" of having a child with retardation ("X" in the model) is due to specific characteristics of the child (the "stressor event," or A), mediated by the family's internal and external resources (B) and by the family's perceptions of the child (C). But compared to father absence or other relatively unchanging situations, children with retardation and their effects on families change over time: Characteristics of the child change as the child gets older, the family's internal and external resources may change, and so too may the family's perceptions of the child. Hence, the "Double" in the Double ABCX model.

Although it is an overly broad framework, the Double ABCX model has nevertheless served researchers well. Most importantly, the model helps explain both negative and positive consequences of rearing a child with retardation (Minnes, 1988). For all families, children displaying fewer emotional problems and requiring less physical caretaking may help parents and families to adjust more positively. In the same way, families with few internal or external resources are more likely to be negatively affected by the child with retardation; families with more resources should do better.

The Child's Meaning to the Parents

As psychologists in many fields are discovering, human beings are "meaning-makers," creatures obsessed with deriving meaningful understandings of human events (e.g., Bruner, 1990). Yet until recently, the role of meaning—of what the child with retardation means to the parents—has rarely been examined. This recent focus on meaning can best be seen in examinations of interactions between children with retardation and their parents. A common finding is that such interactions are both "the same and different" from interactions between nonretarded child–mother dyads (see next section). Many interactive differences appear due to the different meanings of the child with mental retardation to the mother.

Consider the following vignette from Jones' (1980, p. 221) study of mothers of children with Down syndrome:

> There was a strong tendency for the mothers of the Down syndrome children to refer repeatedly to "teaching" their children when in verbal interaction with them. This was in contrast to the descriptions given by the mothers of the normal children, who felt that although their children probably learned from these "chats" together, it was the children's company they appreciated most at these times. ... As one mother of a Down syndrome child explained, "It's sit him on your knee and talk to him, that's the main object. Play with him, speak to the child, teach him something."

In addition to the role of meaning in mother–child interactions, families have complex meaning systems for both the family overall and for each individual member. Employing an ecological perspective on the family, Gallimore, Weisner, Kaufman, and Bernheimer (1989) described the different "social constructions" held by families of children with retardation. They noted that some families feel that the child with retardation needs intensive intervention, whereas others feel that the other, nonretarded children should receive more time and attention. Families then change their day-to-day lifestyles to accommodate their prevailing values. To Gallimore et al., the meaning of the child with retardation—and how the child with retardation fits within the overall family's meaning system—is the most important influence on the family's behaviors and how these behaviors are interpreted by each family member.

Group Versus Individual Difference Approaches

All families of children with retardation are not alike. Individual mothers and fathers, siblings, families as a unit, and children with retardation themselves all display individual characteristics that may affect parenting. Yet most research on parenting children with Down syndrome and other retardation syndromes has compared parents, interactions, and families of children with retardation to parents, interactions, and families of nonretarded children. Such studies have sought to determine if behaviors are "the same or different" relative to behaviors occurring in response to nonretarded children. Although such a "group differences" approach has been useful in many areas, it needs to be complemented by studies examining intragroup variation among families of children with retardation.

A complementary focus on individual differences has begun to affect the parenting literature, somewhat as a result of the Double ABCX and other stress-coping models. If any one family's reaction is due to a combination of child characteristics and the family's internal and external resources and perceptions, then individual differences—in the child with retardation, the parents, and the entire family system—become important foci of research and intervention. Indeed, families differ on a host of factors: in the degree to which they are warm or cold, open or closed, harmonious or unharmonious. Personal characteristics of—and relationships among—mothers, fathers, sisters, brothers, and extended family members all vary from one family to another, and all potentially influence parenting. In the same way, there are many characteristics of children themselves that affect parental and familial reactions. The child's CA, MA, IQ, degree and types of associated handicap, personality, and interests might all be important. Most of these characteristics have so far received little attention.

Another important factor may be the child's type of mental retardation. Studies of behavior in Down syndrome (e.g., Cicchetti & Beeghly, 1990) and fragile X syndrome (Dykens et al., 1994) reveal that behavioral strengths–weakness and trajectories of development may differ based on the child's type of mental retardation. Specific maladaptive behaviors may also differ based on the child's specific cause of retardation (Dykens, 1994); the life-threatening obesity, food preoccupations, and temper tantrums of children with Prader-Willi syndrome are good examples in this regard (Dykens, Hodapp, Walsh, & Nash, 1992). These child characteristics, in turn, affect the nature of familial adaptation. Yet studies of parenting often include in a single subject group families of children with many different types of mental retardation (Hodapp & Dykens, 1991). More work is needed on many aspects of the parents, families, and children to see which factors differentially affect parental and familial reactions.

Methodological Issues

Since the late 1960s, workers in mental retardation have debated how best to conceptualize behavior in children with mental retardation. On one side have been the many defect theorists, researchers who believe that mental retardation is caused by one or another specific defect (for a review, see Zigler & Balla, 1982). On the other side are developmental workers who propose that children with certain types of mental retardation—particularly those demonstrating no specific organic cause—show more general delays across many different domains of functioning (Zigler & Hodapp, 1986).

One key aspect of this debate concerns CA- versus MA-matching, whether it is better to compare children with retardation to nonretarded children of the same chronological age (CA-matching) or mental age (MA-matching). Defect theorists have long advocated CA-matching, arguing that this strategy directly demonstrates a child's deficiencies in a particular area. Defect theorists also note that MA is a composite measure, allowing different children to achieve the identical mental age in different ways (Baumeister, 1967). Developmentalists respond that, in order to show that a child is "deficient" in a particular area, delayed performance below overall mental age must be established. Performance that is deficient to CA-matches shows only that a particular task is one of many performed poorly by the child with retardation (Cicchetti & Pogge-Hesse, 1982).

Whatever one's views concerning CA- versus MA-matching, this debate has revolved around the retarded child's own behavior. How should one study the more complicated issues of parents, or maternal behaviors within interactions, or the family systems of children with retardation? It would seem that research strategies need to be tailored to the question of interest. For example, studies of maternal language input should employ children with and without mental retardation who are of the same language-age (e.g., Conti-Ramsden, 1989). Because language is the issue, equating the two groups of children on overall linguistic functioning would seem most sensible. But even this strategy is problematic, in that oftentimes children with Down syndrome or other specific retardation syndromes do not show "flat" or "across-the-board" functioning levels, even within a single domain like language. For instance, children with Down syndrome demonstrate relatively poor grammatical versus pragmatic abilities (Beeghly & Cicchetti, 1987) and poor expressive as opposed to receptive language (Miller, 1987). Furthermore, in several etiological groups, strengths-weaknesses become more pronounced as the child gets older. Thus, for example, boys with fragile X syndrome become relatively more impaired in sequential processing—a particular type of intellectual functioning—with increasing chronological age (Hodapp, Dykens, Ort, Zelinsky, & Leckman, 1991), just as a specific weakness in the grammatical abilities of children with Down syndrome may become more pronounced as the child gets older (Miller, 1992).

In contrast to examinations of input language, CA-matching might be more appropriate for studies of family functioning. As Stoneman (1989) noted, families with 10-year-old children are in a particular family stage, even if the child functions at a 5-year-old level. To examine issues such as divorce rates, quality of marriage, sibling reactions, and other family dynamics, CA-matching may be the most appropriate strategy. In line with this reasoning, most family studies have compared families of children with and without mental retardation when the children are matched on CA.

At the same time, however, not every family question may be best addressed with a CA-match. Specifically, many of the changes of family dynamics involve reactions based on the children's immaturity, on the idea that children with retardation—although they may be 10-year-olds—in fact act like a much younger children. For example, if families of a child with retardation are indeed "stuck" in their development (Farber & Rowitz, 1986), then a match to a group of families of nonretarded children of the same MA might be indicated. Better yet, both CA- and MA-matching might be useful to address such questions. Such a dual-matching strategy would reveal not only the ways in which these families differ from others at similar "family stages" (i.e., when children are of particular ages), but it would also show the degree to which such families actually are stuck in development due to parenting a child of a particular developmental level. Until now, few parenting studies have employed such "dual matching" procedures.

The discussion so far concerns group differences, but an additional methodological issue relates to individual differences, the idea that there are wide individual differences from one family to another. But here, too, many important variables have not yet been examined. We know little, for example, about the family development of families who are more versus less successful in parenting the child with retardation, and only generally why some marriages break up whereas others become stronger. How familial adaptation might differ based on the family's SES, ethnicity, and parental education levels remains almost totally unexplored. Furthermore, even those variables that have been studied are generally examined in a piecemeal fashion, making more difficult the determination of each variable's contribution to individual differences among families. Change may be occurring, however, as more researchers use larger, family-systems frameworks to conceptualize their findings. More attention is needed to the ways of doing research from the group-difference versus the individual-difference perspective and what each implies.

MODERN RESEARCH ON PARENTING
THE CHILD WITH RETARDATION

The four issues just discussed can be found within much of the modern research in maternal and paternal reactions, mother–child interactions, and the reactions of the family as a whole to rearing the child with Down syndrome and other types of retardation. Much of this research combines recent theories and methodologies with the perspectives and findings of the 1960s and early 1970s.

Factors Affecting Maternal and Paternal Reactions

Much modern research has examined both the Solnit and Stark and the Olshansky perspectives to delineate further when and how parents react to the child with retardation. When closer, more fine-grained examinations have been performed, researchers have found that a host of factors affect parental emotional reactions.

Child's chronological age.   The first of these factors concerns the age of the child. Several researchers have attempted to determine when emotional reactions and concerns are most likely to occur for mothers of children with handicaps. For example, Emde and Brown (1978) noted that parents of children with Down syndrome undergo several waves of depression over the child's first year of life (Field, in this *Handbook*). After the extreme depression at the baby's birth and diagnosis, parents generally do better until approximately 4 months of age, when strong feelings of sadness reappear. This second wave of depression occurs as parents realize the behavioral implications of Down syndrome, as their infants show more dampened affect and less consistent social smiles than do same-age nonretarded children. Considering the preschool period as a whole, mothers are generally most concerned about milestones appearing during the earliest years (e.g., walking, talking), although certain later-occurring milestones (e.g., toilet training, writing) also bring about high levels of maternal concern (Hodapp, Dykens, Evans, & Merighi, 1992).

Such recurrent emotional reactions continue throughout the childhood years. Wikler (1986) noted that parents experience stress during puberty (age 11–15) and during the onset of adulthood (age 20–21). Compared to responses from these same mothers 2 years before or after these periods, lesser amounts of stress were reported (Wikler, 1986). In a more general sense, Minnes (1988) described a "pile-up" of stressors on mothers as the child gets older, even as mothers less often use formal and informal social supports (Suelzle & Keenan, 1981).

In considering Solnit and Stark's formulation, it seems that, although parental emotions may be most intense directly after birth, later events and milestones also evoke strong reactions. As Wikler (1981, p. 284) noted, "The accepted view that a crisis occurs following the diagnosis because of the general disruption of expectancies is probably correct; but the conclusion that the gradually gained equilibrium is permanent is probably incorrect."

Nature of disability.   A second factor affecting maternal reaction is the child's type of disability. Holroyd and MacArthur (1976) found that mothers of children with autism were more upset and disappointed than were mothers of children with Down syndrome; the former group was also more concerned about the autistic child's dependency and the child's effects on the remainder of the family (see also Goldberg, Marcovitch, MacGregor, & Lojkasek, 1986). Furthermore, the developmental milestones to which mothers react differ from one handicapping condition to another; for example, mothers of children with Down syndrome show concern over different sets of milestones than do mothers of children with cerebral palsy (Hodapp et al., 1992). In short, characteristics of the child's disability condition influence maternal emotional reactions.

Maternal personality characteristics.   So too may differences in the mothers themselves sometimes lead to different maternal reactions. For example, mothers who carry the fragile X gene have been found to more often be shy, anxious, and withdrawn compared to mothers of children with other types of disabilities (see Dykens et al., 1994). Such personality characteristics—which appear specific to female carriers of the fragile X gene—contribute to difficulties that professionals often have in interacting with these women, and in the problems these women have in making use of clinical, educational, and other supportive services (Dykens & Leckman, 1990).

Paternal reactions.   Just as the reactions of mothers may differ due to several factors, so too may maternal reactions differ from reactions of fathers. Few studies have examined paternal compared to maternal reactions, but mothers and fathers do appear to vary. Damrosch and Perry (1989) asked mothers and fathers to retrospectively describe their emotional reactions since the birth of their children with Down syndrome. Two graphs were provided. The first graph, consistent with Solnit and Stark's mourning model, showed strong emotional reactions early and then gradual acceptance of the child with disabilities. The second graph featured a series of wide emotional swings that was more consistent with the repeated "up and down" pattern of Olshansky's recurrent reactions model. Mothers and fathers differed in their reactions: Mothers more often described their feelings as repeatedly up and down (i.e., the recurrent reactions pattern), whereas fathers reported early emotional reactions then later acceptance (i.e., the "maternal mourning" model).

Mothers and fathers may also differ in how they conceptualize the child and the child's problems. Many studies have found that mothers experience more stress and feel themselves less in control of the situation than fathers (Bristol, Gallagher, & Shopler, 1988; Damrosch & Perry, 1989; Goldberg et al., 1986). Mothers may also react more to specific stressors than fathers: for example, mothers much more than fathers express needs for more social and familial support, information to explain the child's handicap to others, and help with child care (Bailey, Blasco, & Simeonsson, 1992).

In contrast, fathers seem more affected by the instrumental and pragmatic aspects of the child with retardation, as well as by specific aspects of the child's disability. Fathers are particularly concerned about the costs of caring for a child with disabilities and what the child will mean to the family as a whole (Price-Bonham & Addison, 1978). Comparing factors affecting mothers versus fathers of young children with retardation, Krauss (1993, p. 401) noted that "mothers reported more difficulty than did fathers in adjusting to the personal aspects of parenting and parenthood (parental health, restrictions in role, and relations with spouse). ... Fathers reported more stress related to the child's temperament (e.g., child's mood and adaptability) and their relationship to the child (such as feelings of attachment and of being reinforced by the child)."

Given these differences, factors that support mothers may not support fathers. Frey, Greenberg, and Fewell (1989) found that the presence of supportive social networks promotes better coping on the part of mothers of children with retardation, whereas fathers cope better when there is a minimal amount of criticism from extended families. Both mothers and fathers cope best if the other spouse is coping well and if each feels a strong measure of personal control in rearing the child with retardation.

In considering the research on parental emotional reactions, much progress has occurred since the original Solnit–Stark and Olshansky formulations. Increasingly, researchers are developing a taxonomy of child and family characteristics that affect parental reactions, a taxonomy that should promote more effective parental coping strategies throughout the childhood years.

Mother–Child Interactions

Starting with Rondal's (1977) study showing that mothers of children with Down syndrome provide similar levels of language input as mothers of nonretarded children of the same level of language (i.e., MLU), many studies have examined interactions between mothers and children with a variety of disability conditions. These studies converge on a basic theme: Maternal interactive behaviors with their children with disabilities appear both the same as and different from maternal behaviors with nondisabled children of the same level of language.

With few exceptions, the similarities have occurred when one examines what might be called the structural properties of input language. Mothers provide language that is of the same grammatical complexity, has the same amount of information per sentence, and appears much like the language provided by mothers of nonretarded children of the same language or mental age. As in Rondal's (1977) study, mothers of children who are higher in language provide higher level input, thereby providing the child with the "developmental scaffold" or Language Assistance Support System (Bruner, 1983) considered important by developmental psycholinguists.

Yet at the same time, these mothers appear very different in their styles of interaction. Even when children with and without retardation are equated on overall mental or linguistic age, mothers of children with Down syndrome and other types of retardation are often more didactic, directive, and intrusive compared to mothers of nonretarded children (see Marfo, 1990). Such stylistic differences between mothers of children with and without mental retardation are seen on a number of levels. Tannock (1988) found that, compared to mothers of nonretarded children, mothers of children with Down syndrome took interactive turns that were longer and more frequent; in addition, these mothers more often "clashed"—or spoke at the same time as—their children (see also Vietze, Abernathy, Ashe,

& Faulstich, 1978). Mothers of children with Down syndrome also switched the topic of conversation more often, and less often silently responded to the child's utterance. Children with Down syndrome thus participated in "asymmetrical" conversations with their mothers, conversations in which the mother more often controlled the topic, the child's response, and the nature of the back-and-forth conversation.

Although many studies have now found this stylistic difference, why mothers in the two groups differ remains unclear. The most common explanation is that mothers of children with retardation inject their parenting concerns into the interactive session. Greater numbers of mothers of children with retardation consider interactions as "teaching sessions," as moments not to be squandered in the nonstop effort to intervene effectively (Cardoso-Martins, & Mervis, 1984; Jones, 1980). In contrast, mothers of nonretarded children display fewer fears and concerns; they may simply desire to play—in a more spontaneous and less directive manner—with their nonretarded children.

Less often considered is the possibility that children with Down syndrome and other types of retardation may actually require more intensive, intrusive interactions for optimal development in cognition, language, or other domains. Cicchetti and Sroufe (1976) noted that infants with Down syndrome often show hypotonicity, or weakened muscle tones. Further, those infants and young children who are the most hypotonic are the most impaired, both intellectually (Cicchetti & Sroufe, 1976) and adaptively (Cullen, Cronk, Pueschel, Schnell, & Reed, 1981). The latency between the timing of the mother's utterance and the child's response may also be longer in the child with Down syndrome (Maurer & Sherrod, 1987), making asymmetrical interactions more likely. In addition, following Baumrind's (1972) work on nonretarded child–mother interactions, Crawley and Spiker (1983) distinguished between maternal directiveness and maternal responsiveness. Crawley and Spiker concluded that "an optimal combination of sensitivity, elaborativeness, and directiveness may provide the environment most conducive to development in these children" (p. 1321). In short, more lethargic and more hypotonic children might require more intensive, more didactic interactions.

Complicating things even more is the entire issue of infant cues and readability. As they are often more lethargic and more hypotonic, infants and young children with Down syndrome may provide fewer and less clear interactive cues, at least in the months directly prior to intentional communication (Hyche, Bakeman, & Adamson, 1992). These infants may therefore be less "readable" (Goldberg, 1977) to the mother, even as mothers gradually learn to interpret their child's vague or slight communicative behaviors (Sorce & Emde, 1982; Yoder, 1986). To date, it remains unclear why interactions between mothers and children with Down syndrome differ in style (but not in structure) from interactions between mothers and same-level nonretarded children; most likely, some combination of maternal and child factors seems implicated.

A third issue concerns the goals of mother–child interaction. As noted earlier, mothers of children with Down syndrome may feel a greater need to teach as opposed to play with their children, whereas mothers of nonretarded children may often merely play with and enjoy their young offspring (Cardoso-Martins & Mervis, 1984; Jones, 1980). This sense comes from maternal reports of interaction, but also from observations of these mothers' styles of interaction. Mothers of children with retardation are much more likely to request higher-level behavior from their children than mothers of nonretarded children. Indeed, Mahoney, Fors, and Wood (1990) found that mothers of children with Down syndrome (CA = 30 months; MA = 17 months) requested behavior at approximately the 15-month level, whereas mothers of MA-matched nonretarded children requested behavior at an average level of 10 months. In Vygotskian terms, requesting the highest level behavior should aid the child's development, but such optimally demanding requests fit with the more didactic, directive, and intrusive style of interactions often noted for mothers of children with handicaps.

In line with most work in this area, the previous review focuses on studies examining differences between maternal behaviors of children with and without mental retardation. But several studies have now examined variation in maternal behaviors within retarded (usually Down syndrome) samples. The main finding is that not all mothers of children with Down syndrome behave identically.

In the first direct examination of this issue, Crawley and Spiker (1983) rated maternal sensitivity and directiveness of mothers in their interactions with their 2-year-old children with Down syndrome. They found wide individual differences from one mother to another. Some mothers were highly directive, whereas others followed the child's lead; similarly, mothers varied widely in their rated degrees of sensitivity to their children. Because the two dimensions of sensitivity and directiveness were somewhat orthogonal, mothers could be high or low on either sensitivity or directiveness. All four combinations were demonstrated in this study. Just as mothers of nonretarded children vary widely on both directiveness and sensitivity, so too do mothers of children with Down syndrome.

More recently, Mahoney et al. (1990) described two groups of mother–child dyads in children with Down syndrome: those who were "turn balanced" versus "turn imbalanced." Turn-balanced mothers produced 52 percent of turns, whereas the child with Down syndrome produced 48 percent of turns (i.e., one or more interactive behaviors with less than a 1-second pause). In contrast, turn-imbalanced mothers produced 60 percent of turns in the interactive session, allowing children only 40 percent of turns. Although turn-balanced and turn-imbalanced mothers were similar on some measures (e.g., asking for high-level behaviors from their children), many differences between the two groups were also noted. For example, turn-imbalanced mothers requested actions more often from their children, and their requested actions often differed from the child's focus of attention. The Mahoney et al. (1990) study highlights the ways that mothers of children with Down syndrome differ one from another.

Mother–child interactions, then, are interesting from the perspective of both group differences and intragroup variation. As a group, mothers of children with mental retardation are "the same but different" in their interactions from mothers of nonretarded children at similar mental ages. They are the same in the structural aspects of their input—such things as MLU, type-token ratio, and other measures of communicative complexity. At the same time, these mothers appear more intrusive, didactic, and "pushy." It remains unclear whether such stylistic differences are due to maternal emotional reactions or to child factors; so too do the effects of such stylistic differences on child functioning remain unknown. Complicating the picture further is the increasing evidence that not all mothers of children with retardation are intrusive or didactic; like mothers of typically developing children, these mothers too vary widely in their styles of interaction.

Family Characteristics

Modern research on families continues the historic tradition of delineating the characteristics of families of children with retardation. In recent years, however, the conceptual frameworks have shifted from family pathology to family stress and coping. As with parents and mother–child interaction, research emphasizes both differences of these families from families with nonretarded children, and intragroup variation across families with a retarded member.

A good example of the change to a stress-coping perspective comes from work on family support. Earlier research noted that families of children with retardation were often isolated, with few formal and informal supports. Wikler, Wasow, and Hatfield (1981) even noted a divergence of perception on the part of the families themselves and the social service workers who aid them. Whereas parents were concerned about child milestones occurring both earlier and later (e.g., child reaches adulthood) during the child's life, social service personnel identified the early years as the period of most difficulty for parents and other family members. Such professional perspectives may exacerbate the "front-loading" of services for families of children with retardation, the tendency of services to more often be provided during the earliest years, even as these families may require more help—and become less connected to formal support services—as the child gets older (Suelzle & Keenan, 1981).

And yet, although these families may receive less formal support later on, they are not quite as isolated as earlier hypothesized. In work with families of children with retardation and with chronic illness, Kazak and Marvin (1984; also Kazak, 1987) noted that families of children with both conditions possess strong informal social networks, but these networks differ from those of families without a disabled member (Cochran & Niego, in this *Handbook*). Specifically, Kazak and Marvin

(1984) found that parents of children with disabilities have smaller social networks, but networks that are more dense. These mothers thus receive a fair amount of informal support, but the support comes from the mother's own mother, sister, or a few close family friends. Such networks are denser in that each member of the network interacts with every other.

As Byrne and Cunningham (1985) noted, the presence of smaller but denser social networks is both good and bad. These families are not isolated, in that they often receive support, encouragement, and respite from day-to-day responsibilities from a small circle of loving friends and relatives. But as the networks are smaller, parents of children with handicaps have fewer contacts with a wider, more diffuse network of friends and associates. Families are often enmeshed in a tightly organized, intimate circle of social support that at times can feel suffocating.

In addition to such group-differences research, recent years have featured more work on how families with retarded members differ one from another. Through cluster analysis, for example, Mink, Nihira, and Meyers (1983) identified five types of families of children with severe retardation: cohesive, harmonious families; control-oriented, somewhat unharmonious families; low disclosure, unharmonious families; child-oriented, expressive families; and disadvantaged, low morale families. Similar though not identical family clusters have been found for families of children with mild and borderline mental retardation (Mink, Nihira, & Meyers, 1984). More and more, then, variation among different families is being characterized.

Such work helps explain which child, individual member, or family variables lead to different family styles. One intriguing possibility is that the child's type of mental retardation contributes to different family styles. In Mink et al. (1983), for example, almost two thirds of "cohesive harmonious" families were of children with Down syndrome, a much higher percentage than might be expected by chance. In the same way, much of the earlier work (e.g., Holroyd & MacArthur, 1976) revealed that parents of children with Down syndrome experienced less stress than did parents of children with autism. Similar findings may hold even in families of adults with Down syndrome. Seltzer, Krauss, and Tsunematsu (1993) found that mothers (mean age = 65 years) of middle-age adults with Down syndrome report less caregiving stress and burden, less family conflict, fewer unmet service needs, and more satisfying support networks than do aging mothers of adults with retardation from other causes. Seltzer et al. emphasized that the reasons for such differences remain unknown: Compared to many other disorders of mental retardation, Down syndrome features readily accessible support groups and a more researched, more understood clinical syndrome. Or it may be that, as Mink et al. (1983, p. 495) noted, "Taking into consideration the effects of children on their caretakers, we may speculate that Down syndrome children [or adults] will have a positive effect on the climate of the home."

Recent family work, then, shows a move in emphasis from pathology to stress and coping. Such research also shows the complexity of familial reactions, and the strong influences of factors associated with both the child (age, type of retardation) and the family (size and nature of family network).

PRACTICAL INFORMATION

Like the larger field of child development (Sears, 1975), the field of parenting children with retardation is not purely a scientific enterprise. Instead, the field has strong and enduring ties to practical concerns. Many family researchers consult with or direct intervention services, others write practical books and manuals for parents of children with various types of mental retardation. This chapter therefore discusses the practical implications of classical and modern research for parents, interactions, and families overall.

Mothers and Fathers

Compared to only two decades ago, parents of children with mental retardation are now much more visible, playing the role of active decision makers in their children's services. These parents are simultaneously members of parent organizations, advocates for their individual children and for children with disabilities in general, and recipients of professional services (A. P. Turnbull & H. R. Turnbull, 1986). Professional services themselves have also increased dramatically. Only 30 years ago, many children with Down syndrome were institutionalized; nowadays, children and families are served through a variety of services, ranging from services supporting parents in performing in-home care to part- or full-time residential services for children with the most severe and multiple handicaps. This "continuum of services" for individuals with retardation gives parents both more rights and more responsibilities.

Many of these expanded rights and responsibilities concern schools, the most important service provided throughout the childhood years. Federal laws such as Public Law 94-142, the Education for All Handicapped Children Act of 1975, now provide as a right a free, appropriate public school education for all children with retardation. The hallmark of this legislation is that all children be educated in the *least restrictive environment* (LRE). This term, often equated with education within a mainstreamed classroom, actually entails a host of alternatives. LRE allows for full-time mainstreaming, part-time mainstreaming with a resource room or specialist, special classes within a public school, and even special classes or special residential schools when necessary to meet the child's educational needs. Integral to decisions concerning the best educational alternative are the child's Individualized Educational Plan (IEP) and the series of legal hearings and appeals that are the right of all parents of children with disabilities. Compared to the days when school systems refused to educate children with retardation, the years since PL 94-142 feature major societal advances for children with retardation and their families.

Residential services have also changed enormously over the past 30 years. As recently as the 1960s, parents had two choices: provide in-home care or institutionalize their child with retardation. In contrast, families now enjoy a continuum of residential alternatives. In-home care is the option of most parents, and many are aided in this choice by parent training programs and part-time child-care aid. Respite care, summer camps, and other services allow parents and other family members a break from their parenting duties. Group home and residential care services are also available, particularly for multiproblemed families and for parents of children with the most profound retardation, multiple handicaps, or severe behavior problems.

Although the range of educational and residential services has expanded tremendously over the past decade, more services are needed. The numbers of respite care homes and other parental supports remain distressingly small in many communities. In addition, these services need to be flexible to the needs of particular parents and families. Further, such services are not always first-rate; an over-concern with the setting of services needs to be replaced by more attention to what occurs *within* the different service settings (Zigler, Hodapp, & Edison, 1990).

In addition to formal educational and residential services, parents also benefit from the many parent support groups that have become prominent over the past several decades. These run the gamut from large to small, from emphases on all handicaps to a focus on a single handicap, and from national organizations (often with local chapters) to local groups. The largest and most well-known of the national organizations is the National Association for Retarded Citizens (NARC). Founded in 1950, NARC is a nationwide parent organization with high visibility. Besides providing supportive and informational services, NARC was instrumental in passing PL 94–142 and other federal disability legislation.

Besides organizations concerned with all children with retardation, there are also numerous groups for parents of children with different types of mental retardation. The National Down Syndrome Society, National Fragile X Foundation, Prader-Willi Syndrome Association, and other organizations are particularly good sources of support and information for parents of children with each type of mental retardation. Most of these groups organize national conferences annually. Parents, researchers, and service providers all attend these conferences, providing interchanges of needs, experiences, and information rarely available in other contexts. If parents, researchers, and service providers are to be linked in a common partnership, more such forums are necessary.

Mother–Child Interactions

In addition to the many behavior modification and training programs available to help caregivers to parent their children with retardation (Baker, 1989), several programs have focused on mother–child interactions. Two deserve notice, one focused on early parenting in general, the second on improving specific behaviors within mother–child interaction.

The first program, the Parent–Infant Interaction Model, was developed by Bromwich (1976, 1990) in the late 1970s. Designed for mothers of children with a variety of handicaps, this program involves 10 general steps that are individualized to the specific, individual needs of each child, caregiver, and family. The preliminary steps focus on enhancing the quality of parent–infant interaction by improving the caregiver's (usually the mother's) self-esteem, making her feel more comfortable with the child, and teaching her to become a sensitive observer of, and interactor with, her baby. Later steps involve strategies to understand each family's stresses and supports, and to help each member of the family deal with rearing a child with retardation.

Although not specific to mothers of children with Down syndrome or with retardation, Bromwich's program provides a good general model for mother–child interactions. The hope is that such programs can help to foster productive mother–child interactions, maternal perceptions, and familial responses—all of which can be started early and then continue on as the child with retardation grows older. Bromwich (1990) acknowledged that her program works best with mothers who suffer only from the special strains and emotional reactions felt by any mother of a child with disabilities. She cautioned that mothers who have psychiatric disorders or mental retardation might have trouble benefiting from the Parent–Infant Interaction Model, and more intensive therapy for the caregiver might be necessary (as described by Fraiberg, 1980). Even considering these limitations, Bromwich's model provides intervention strategies that seem helpful to most parents of children with retardation.

A second intervention approach is more specific, focusing on the behaviors of mothers of children with retardation within the interaction setting. Based on studies showing that mothers of children with retardation are often more didactic and controlling in their interactive styles, Mahoney (1988) advocated the Transactional Intervention Program (TRIP). This model features instructions to help mothers become more balanced in their turn-taking and to imitate the child's behavior. While reaching these two goals, mothers observe the infant and allow the child opportunities to initiate interactions. Preliminary findings show that infants with Down syndrome develop faster in cognition and in language when provided these "low directive" as opposed to "high directive" maternal interactive behaviors. Although focused on only one aspect of parenting, Mahoney's (1988) model may help to produce better, more productive interactions. The model may, however, overemphasize the interactional differences between mothers of children with and without retardation. In addition, the TRIP model, unlike Bromwich (1990) and more "family-support" models for mothers of at-risk children (e.g., Provence & Naylor, 1983), gives less weight to individual differences among mothers and families of children with retardation (Marfo, 1992). Nor does the model emphasize maternal emotions and perceptions (Hodapp, 1988), or the different needs of mothers of children with different types of handicaps (Hodapp & Dykens, 1991). Still, as one of the few intervention programs specifically tied to the growing literature on mother–child interactions, the TRIP and other such models help to improve mother–child interactions with children with Down syndrome and other forms of mental retardation.

Families

As service-delivery systems change and the prevalence of in-home care increases, families of children with retardation are increasingly the object of attention. This attention has even begun to infiltrate federal legislation. The recently enacted federal law, PL 99-457, expands educational and support services to the 0- to 3-year-old group, allowing a bridging of services from birth until adulthood. A major component of PL 99-457 is its provision of an individualized family service plan (IFSP), thereby recognizing that the family more than the child alone needs services during these early years (Krauss & Hauser-Cram, 1992).

But even as some federal laws are including families, many issues remain unresolved. For example, families with children who are severely profoundly retarded or who have multiple handicaps face severe financial hardships. In addition to documenting the medical costs of caring for such children, Barenbaum and Cohen (1993) noted how simple changes in health care coverage could benefit these families enormously. They suggested that changes can be as easy as considering as a medical-habilitative service the costs of babysitting a child with a shunt.

Other concerns relate to when and how services are provided. As noted by Suelzle and Keenan (1981), families of children with retardation receive most services early on, even as they often need more services as the child gets older. Other difficult issues revolve around how care is provided for children with multiple impairments, or for those who are "dually diagnosed"—that is, who have both mental retardation and psychiatric impairments. How fathers are reached is another major issue, as is the question of how paternal needs can be addressed as families change (to the extent that they do) as the child with handicaps gets older.

FUTURE DIRECTIONS

With both a research and interventionist bent, research on parenting has advanced rapidly over the past few decades. Yet a few major areas and problems remain to be addressed in future research.

Research with Better Theoretical Grounding

The three subareas of parenting children with mental retardation feature a wide, some might say bewildering, array of theoretical orientations. Studies of maternal and paternal emotional reactions often show a psychoanalytic—or at least a clinical—perspective, focusing on the loss of the idealized child and maternal and paternal depression and psychopathology. Mother–child interaction studies employ Bell's (1968) interactional theory, and comparisons of dyads with and without retarded children usually focus on MA or other, level-of-functioning matching (e.g., MLU) as used in the developmental approach to mental retardation (Zigler & Hodapp, 1986). Family work has used sociological role theory (Farber & Rowitz, 1986), models such as the Double ABCX (Minnes, 1988), and, at times, little or no theories, as when delineating basic family characteristics of families of a child with retardation. Yet to this day, few studies have joined these different perspectives and different bodies of knowledge.

Part of the problem involves the "ownership" of different research questions by researchers in different disciplines or research traditions. For the most part, maternal and paternal reactions have been the province of child psychiatry and child clinical psychology; mother–child interactions the focus of developmental psychologists and special educators; and families the work of family researchers and social workers. Each research community works in relative isolation, with little attempt to join these different, but mutually influential, levels.

In addition to the gaps and lack of coordination in the areas of parental reactions, interactions, and familial adaptation, other areas also require attention. Three areas in particular deserve note.

Individual differences.   With the exception of the few studies cited earlier, little research has been devoted to the issue of individual differences in the parenting field. There is also a need to simultaneously examine group differences (whether parenting is the same or different when parenting children with and without retardation) and individual differences (how and why individual parents of children with retardation differ one to another).

Life span.   Apart from the work of Krauss, Seltzer, and their colleagues (e.g., Seltzer et al., 1993), few researchers have systematically examined the family functioning of older individuals with retardation. Indeed, reviews of family work (e.g., Stoneman, 1989) show that the large majority of studies on parental emotional reactions, mother–child interaction, and family reactions focus on children, often during the preschool years. Fewer studies have examined the families of older children with retardation, fewer still of adults with retardation.

Methodologies. In addition to the many gaps in our information about parenting, more attention needs to be paid to how one performs family research in mental retardation. The issue of matching—of whether MA- or CA-matches are best (described earlier)—is one unresolved methodological issue, but there are many others. For example, it remains unresolved whether parenting studies should examine parents of children who are disabled, have mental retardation, or have a particular form of mental retardation. At the very least, subject groups need to be better described.

Ties to the Practice of Intervention and to Policy

Even though many family researchers are interested in practical issues, research on parenting in mental retardation connects only marginally with the common practice of intervention or policy. Only a few research findings have been integrated within the majority of intervention programs, and even some obvious concepts rarely become incorporated in intervention work. For example, Olshansky's (1962, 1966; Wikler, 1986) recurrent maternal reactions model continues to be ignored in most service systems; to this day, many services continue to be "front-loaded," with fewer services for parents and families of older individuals with mental retardation. In the same way, few concerted efforts have been made to link family research to public policy. Barenbaum and Cohen (1993) highlighted just how minor such changes need to be to help parents and families, but rarely are such changes made. One can only hope that the tie between research and practice—on both intervention and policy levels—will soon become stronger.

CONCLUSIONS

In summarizing the work on parenting children with Down syndrome and other forms of mental retardation, one can envision the glass as either half empty or half full. If judged by the amount of unknown information, the glass is half empty. Even after a decade or more of intense work, we still do not know how parents, interactions, and families "go together," how each level changes over time, how each is affected by many child characteristics, and other interesting issues. The parenting field also continues to be dominated by research on White, middle-class families, leaving understudied essential questions relating to SES and ethnicity.

And yet, compared to what was known only 30 years ago, the glass is more than half full. From the early days of Farber, of Solnit and Stark, and of Olshansky, we now know much more about these families, their interactions with their children, and the child's affects on siblings and the family as a whole. More importantly, what we know has been fit into more interesting, less detrimental frameworks, as parents, interactions, and families are now seen as coping under stressful circumstances. Such stress may help or hinder adaptation, but these stress-coping perspectives seem both more accurate and more humane.

In effect, research on parenting children with retardation might be considered as a discipline that has only recently begun to reach its stride. Indeed, probably more has been learned about parenting children with retardation in the past 10 to 15 years than was known in all the years up until this time. The next 10 to 15 years promise continued, near exponential growth. With an increased joining of different perspectives and more fully considered research paradigms, such work will hopefully be more integrated, more useful to service providers and policymakers. This knowledge should also, ultimately, help parents face the many difficult challenges in parenting the child with Down syndrome or other forms of mental retardation.

ACKNOWLEDGMENTS

I thank Marc Bornstein and Elisabeth Dykens for comments on earlier versions of this chapter.

REFERENCES

Bailey, D., Blasco, P., & Simeonsson, R. (1992). Needs expressed by mothers and fathers of young children with disabilities. *American Journal on Mental Retardation, 97,* 1–10.

Baker, B. (1989). *Parent training and developmental disabilities. Monograph of the American Association on Mental Retardation.* Washington, DC: AAMR.

Barenbaum, A., & Cohen, H.J. (1993). On the importance of helping families: Policy implications from a national study. *Mental Retardation, 31,* 67–74.

Baumeister, A. (1967). Problems in comparative studies of mental retardates and normals. *American Journal of Mental Deficiency, 71,* 869–875.

Baumrind, D. (1972). Socialization and instrumental competence in young children. In W. W. Hartup (Ed.), *The young child: Reviews of research* (Vol. 2, pp. 202–224). Washington, DC: National Association for the Education of Young Children.

Beckman, P. (1983). Influence of selected child characteristics on stress in families of handicapped children. *American Journal of Mental Deficiency, 88,* 150–156.

Beeghly, M., & Cicchetti, D. (1987). An organizational approach to symbolic development in children with Down Syndrome. In D. Cicchetti & M. Beeghly (Eds.), *Symbolic development in atypical children. New Directions for Child Development* (No. 36, pp. 529). San Francisco: Jossey-Bass.

Bell, R.Q. (1968). A reinterpretation of the direction of effects in studies of socialization. *Psychological Review, 75,* 81–95.

Blacher, J. (1984). Sequential stages of parental adjustment to the birth of the child with handicaps: Fact or artifact? *Mental Retardation, 22,* 55–68.

Bristol, M., Gallagher, J., & Shopler, E. (1988). Mothers and fathers of young developmentally disabled and nondisabled boys: Adaptation and spousal support. *Developmental Psychology, 24,* 441 –451.

Bromwich, R. (1976). Focus on maternal behavior in infant interaction. *American Journal of Orthopsychiatry, 46,* 439–446.

Bromwich, R. (1990). The interaction approach to early intervention. *Infant Mental Health Journal, 11,* 66–79.

Bruner, J. (1983). *Child's talk.* New York: Norton.

Bruner, J. (1990). *Acts of meaning.* Cambridge, MA: Harvard University Press.

Buckhalt, J.A., Rutherford, R., & Goldberg, K. (1978). Verbal and nonverbal interactions of mothers with their Down Syndrome and nonretarded infants. *American Journal of Mental Deficiency, 82,* 337–343.

Buium, N., Rynders, J., & Turnure, J. (1974). Early maternal linguistic environment of normal and Down syndrome language learning children. *American Journal of Mental Deficiency, 79,* 52–58.

Byrne, E., & Cunningham, C. (1985). The effects of mentally handicapped children on families: A conceptual review. *Journal of Child Psychology and Psychiatry, 26,* 847–864.

Cardoso-Martins, C., & Mervis, C. (1984). Maternal speech to prelinguistic children with Down Syndrome. *American Journal of Mental Deficiency, 89,* 451–458.

Carter, B., & McGoldrick, M. (Eds.). (1988). *The changing family life cycle: A framework for family therapy* (2nd ed.). New York: Gardner Press.

Cicchetti, D., & Beeghly, M. (Eds.). (1990). *Children with Down Syndrome: A developmental perspective.* New York: Cambridge University Press.

Cicchetti, D., & Pogge-Hesse, P. (1982). Possible contributions of the study of organically retarded persons to developmental theory. In E. Zigler & D. Balla (Eds.), *Mental retardation: The developmental-difference controversy* (pp. 277–318). Hillsdale, NJ: Lawrence Erlbaum Associates.

Cicchetti, D., & Sroufe, L.A. (1976). The relationship between affective and cognitive development in Down Syndrome infants. *Child Development, 47,* 920–929.

Combrinck-Graham, L. (1985). A developmental model for family systems. *Family Process, 24,* 139–150.

Conti-Ramsden, G. (1989). Parent–child interaction in mental handicap: An evaluation. In M. Beveridge, G. Conti-Ramsden, & I. Levdar (Eds.), *Language and communication in mentally handicapped people* (pp. 218–225). London: Chapman & Hall.

Crawley, S., & Spiker, D. (1983). Mother–child interactions involving two-year-olds with Down Syndrome: A look at individual differences. *Child Development, 54,* 1312–1323.

Crnic, K., Friedrich, W., & Greenberg, M. (1983). Adaptation of families with mentally handicapped children: A model of stress, coping, and family ecology. *American Journal of Mental Deficiency, 88,* 125–138.

Cullen, S., Cronk, C., Pueschel, S., Schnell, R., & Reed, R. (1981). Social development and feeding milestones of young Down Syndrome children. *American Journal of Mental Deficiency, 85,* 410–415.

Cummings, S. (1976). The impact of the child's deficiency on the father: A study of fathers of mentally retarded and chronically ill children. *American Journal of Orthopsychiatry, 46,* 246–255.

Cummings, S., Bayley, H., & Rie, H. (1966). Effects of the child's deficiency on the mother: A study of mentally retarded, chronically ill, and neurotic children. *American Journal of Orthopsychiatry, 36,* 595–608.

Damrosch, S., & Perry, L. (1989). Self-reported adjustment, chronic sorrow, and coping of parents of children with Down Syndrome. *Nursing Research, 38,* 25–30.

Drotar, D., Baskiewicz, A., Irvin, N., Kennell, J., & Klaus, M. (1975). The adaptation of parents to the birth of an infant with congenital malformation: A hypothetical model. *Pediatrics, 56,* 710–717.

Duvall, E. (1957). *Family development.* Philadelphia: Lippincott.

Dykens, E. (in press). Measuring behavioral phenotypes: Provocations from the "New Genetics." *American Journal on Mental Retardation.*

Dykens, E.M., Hodapp, R.M., & Leckman, J.F. (1994). *Behavior and development in fragile X syndrome.* Newbury Park, CA: Sage.

Dykens, E.M., Hodapp, R.M., Walsh, K.K., & Nash, L. (1992). Adaptive and maladaptive behavior in Prader–Willi Syndrome. *Journal of the American Academy of Child and Adolescent Psychiatry, 31,* 1131–1136.

Dykens, E.M., & Leckman, J.F. (1990). Developmental issues in fragile X syndrome. In R.M. Hodapp, J.A. Burack, & E. Zigler (Eds.), *Issues in the developmental approach to mental retardation* (pp. 226–245). New York: Cambridge University Press.

Emde, R., & Brown, C. (1978). Adaptation to the birth of a Down syndrome infant: Grieving and maternal attachment. *Journal of the American Academy of Child Psychiatry, 17,* 299–323.

Erickson, M. (1969). MMPI profiles of parents of young retarded children. *American Journal of Mental Deficiency, 73,* 727–732.

Farber, B. (1959). The effects of the severely retarded child on the family system. *Monographs of the Society for Research in Child Development, 24*(Serial No. 2).

Farber, B. (1970). Notes on sociological knowledge about families with mentally retarded children. In M. Schreiber (Ed.), *Social work and mental retardation* (pp. 118–124). New York: John Day.

Farber, B., & Rowitz, L. (1986). Families with a mentally retarded child. *International Review of Research in Mental Retardation, 14,* 201–224.

Fraiberg, S. (Ed.). (1980). *Clinical studies of infant mental health: The first year of life.* New York: Basic Books.

Frey, K., Greenberg, M., & Fewell, R. (1989). Stress and coping among parents of handicapped children: A multidimensional perspective. *American Journal on Mental Retardation, 94,* 240–249.

Friedrich, W.L., & Freidrich, W. N. (1981). Psychosocial assets of parents of handicapped and nonhandicapped children. *American Journal of Mental Deficiency, 85,* 551–553.

Friedrich, W.N. (1979). Predictors of coping behavior of mothers of handicapped children. *Journal of Consulting and Clinical Psychology, 47,* 1140–1141.

Gallimore, R., Weisner, T., Kaufman, S., & Bernheimer, L. (1989). The social construction of ecocultural niches: Family accomodation of developmentally delayed children. *American Journal on Mental Retardation, 94,* 216–230.

Gath, A. (1977). The impact of an abnormal child upon the parents. *British Journal of Psychiatry, 130,* 405–410.

Goldberg, S. (1977). Social competence in infancy: A model of parent–infant interaction. *Merrill-Palmer Quarterly, 23,* 163–177.

Goldberg, S., Marcovitch, S., MacGregor, D., & Lojkasek, M. (1986). Family responses to developmentally delayed preschoolers: Etiology and the father's role. *American Journal on Mental Retardation, 90,* 610–617.

Hagamen, M.B. (1980). Family adaptation to the diagnosis of mental retardation in a child and strategies of intervention. In L.S. Syzmanski & P.E. Tanguay (Eds.), *Emotional disorders of mentally retarded persons* (pp. 149–171). Baltimore: University Park Press.

Hill, R. (1949). *Families under stress.* New York: Harper & Row.

Hodapp, R.M. (1988). The role of maternal emotions and perceptions in interactions with young handicapped children. In K. Marfo (Ed.), *Parent–child interaction and developmental disabilities* (pp. 32–46). New York: Praeger.

Hodapp, R.M., & Dykens, E.M. (1991). Toward an etiology-specific strategy of early intervention with handicapped children. In K. Marfo (Ed.), *Early intervention in transition: Current perspectives on programs for handicapped children* (pp. 41–60). New York: Praeger.

Hodapp, R.M., & Dykens, E.M. (1994). The two cultures of behavioral research in mental retardation. *American Journal on Mental Retardation, 98,* 675–687.

Hodapp, R.M., Dykens, E.M., Evans, D.W., & Merighi, J.R. (1992). Maternal emotional reactions to young children with different types of handicaps. *Journal of Developmental and Behavioral Pediatrics, 13,* 118–123.

Hodapp, R.M., Dykens, E.M., Ort, S.I., Zelinsky, D.G., & Leckman, J.F. (1991). Changing patterns of intellectual strengths and weaknesses in males with fragile X syndrome. *Journal of Autism and Developmental Disorders, 21,* 503–516.

Holroyd, J., & MacArthur, D. (1976). Mental retardation and stress on parents: A contrast between Down syndrome and childhood autism. *American Journal of Mental Deficiency, 80,* 431–436.

Hyche, J., Bakeman, R., & Adamson, L. (1992). Understanding communicative cues of infants with Down Syndrome: Effects of mothers' experience and infants' age. *Journal of Applied Developmental Psychology, 13,* 1–16.

Jones, O. (1980). Prelinguistic communication skills in Down Syndrome and normal infants. In T. Field, S. Goldberg, D. Stern, & A. Sostek (Eds.), *High-risk infants and children: Adult and peer interaction* (pp. 205–225). New York: Academic Press.

Kazak, A. (1987). Families with disabled children: Stress and social networks in three samples. *Journal of Abnormal Child Psychology, 15,* 137–146.

Kazak, A., & Marvin, R. (1984). Differences, difficulties, and adaptation: Stress and social networks in families with a handicapped child. *Family Relations, 33,* 67–77.

Krauss, M. (1993). Child-related and parenting stress: Similarities and differences between mothers and fathers of children with disabilities. *American Journal on Mental Retardation, 97,* 393–404.

Krauss, M. W., & Hauser-Kram, P. (1992). Policy and program development for infants and toddlers with disabilities. In L. Rowitz (Ed.), *Mental retardation in the year 2000* (pp. 184–196). New York: Springer-Verlag.

Levy, D. (1970). The concept of maternal overprotection. In E.J. Anthony & T. Benedek (Eds.), *Parenthood* (pp. 387–409). Boston: Little, Brown.

Lobato, D. (1983). Siblings of handicapped children: A review. *Journal of Autism and Developmental Disorders, 13,* 347–364.

McCubbin, H., & Patterson, J. (1983). Family transitions: Adaptations to stress. In H. McCubbin & C. Figley (Eds.), *Stress and the family. Vol. 1: Coping with normative transitions* (pp. 5–25). New York: Brunner/Mazel.

Mahoney, G. (1975) . Ethological approach to delayed language acquisition. *American Journal of Mental Deficiency, 80,* 139–148.

Mahoney, G. (1988). Enhancing the developmental competence of handicapped infants. In K. Marfo (Ed.), *Parent–child interaction and developmental disabilities* (pp. 203–219). New York: Praeger.

Mahoney, G., Fors, S., & Wood, S. (1990). Maternal directive behavior revisited. *American Journal on Mental Retardation, 94,* 398–406.

Marfo, K. (1990). Maternal directiveness in interactions with mentally handicapped children: An analytical commentary. *Journal of Child Psychology and Psychiatry, 31,* 531–549.

Marfo, K. (1992). Correlates of maternal directiveness with children who are developmentally delayed. *American Journal of Orthopsychiatry, 62,* 219–233.

Marshall, N., Hegrenes, J., & Goldstein, S. (1973). Verbal interactions: Mothers and their retarded children versus mothers and their nonretarded children. *American Journal of Mental Deficiency, 77,* 415–419.

Maurer, H., & Sherrod, K. (1987). Context of directives given to young children with Down syndrome and nonretarded children: Development over two years. *American Journal of Mental Deficiency, 91,* 579–590.

Miller, J.F. (1987) . Language and communication characteristics of children with Down Syndrome. In S.M. Pueschel, C. Tingey, J. Rynders, A. Crocker, & D. Crutcher (Eds.), *New perspectives on Down Syndrome* (pp. 233–262). Baltimore: Brookes.

Miller, J.F. (1992). Lexical development in young children with Down Syndrome. In R. Chapman (Ed.), *Processes in language acquisition and disorders* (pp. 202–216). St. Louis: Mosby.

Mink, I., Nihira, C., & Meyers, C. (1983). Taxonomy of family life styles: I. Homes with TMR children. *American Journal of Mental Deficiency, 87,* 484–497.

Mink, I., Nihira, C., & Meyers, C. (1984). Taxonomy of family life styles: II. Homes with slow-learning children. *American Journal of Mental Deficiency, 89,* 111–123.

Minnes, P. (1988). Family stress associated with a developmentally handicapped child. *International Review of Research on Mental Retardation, 15,* 195–226.

Olshansky, S. (1962). Chronic sorrow: A response to having a mentally defective child. *Social Casework, 43,* 190–193.

Olshansky, S . (1966). Parent responses to a mentally defective child. *Mental Retardation, 4,* 21–23.

Price-Bonham, S., & Addison, S. (1978). Families and mentally retarded children: Emphasis on the father. *The Family Coordinator, 27,* 221–230.

Provence, S., & Naylor, A. (1983). *Working with disadvantaged parents and their children: Scientific and practical issues.* New Haven, CT: Yale University Press.

Rondal, J. (1977). Maternal speech in normal and Down syndrome children. In P. Mittler (Ed.), *Research to practice in mental retardation. Vol. 3. Education and training* (pp. 239–243). Baltimore: University Park Press.

Sears, R.R. (1975). *Your ancients revisited: A history of child development.* Chicago, IL: University of Chicago Press.

Seltzer, M., Krauss, M., & Tsunematsu, N. (1993). Adults with Down Syndrome and their aging mothers: Diagnostic group differences. *American Journal on Mental Retardation,97,* 496–508.

Solnit, A., & Stark, M. (1961). Mourning and the birth of a defective child. *The Psychoanalytic Study of the Child, 16,* 523–537.

Sorce, J.F., & Emde, R. (1982). The meaning of infant emotional expression: Regularities in caregiving responses in normal and Down syndrome infants. *Journal of Child Psychology and Psychiatry, 23,* 145–158.

Stoneman, Z. (1989). Comparison groups in research on families with mentally retarded members: A methodological and conceptual review. *American Journal on Mental Retardation, 94,* 195–215.

Suelzle, M., & Keenan, V. (1981). Changes in family support networks over the life cycle of mentally retarded persons. *American Journal of Mental Deficiency, 86,* 267–274.

Tannock, R. (1988). Mothers' directiveness in their interactions with children with and without Down Syndrome. *American Journal on Mental Retardation, 93,* 154–165.

Tew, B., Payne, H., & Lawrence, K. (1974). Must a family with a handicapped child be a handicapped family? *Developmental Medicine and Child Neurology, 16,* Supplement 32, 95–98.

Turnbull, A.P., & Turnbull, H.R. (1986). *Families, professionals, and exceptionality: A special partnership.* Columbus, OH: Merrill.

Vietze, P., Abernathy, S., Ashe, M., & Faulstich, G. (1978). Contingency interaction between mothers and their developmentally delayed infants. In G.P. Sackett (Ed.), *Observing behavior* (Vol. 1, pp. 115–132). Baltimore: University Park Press.

Wikler, L. (1981) . Chronic stresses in families of mentally retarded children. *Family Relations, 30,* 281–288.

Wikler, L. (1986). Periodic stresses in families of mentally retarded children: An exploratory study. *American Journal of Mental Deficiency, 90,* 703–706.

Wikler, L., Wasow, M., & Hatfield, E. (1981). Chronic sorrow revisited: Attitudes of parents and professionals about adjustment to mental retardation. *American Journal of Orthopsychiatry, 51,* 63–70.

Yoder, P. (1986). Clarifying the relation between degree of infant handicap and maternal responsivity to infant communicative cues: Measurement issues. *Infant Mental Health Journal, 7,* 281–293.

Zigler, E., & Balla, D. (Eds.). (1982). *Mental retardation: The developmental-difference controversy.* Hillsdale, NJ: Lawrence Erlbaum Associates.

Zigler, E., & Hodapp, R.M. (1986). *Understanding mental retardation.* New York: Cambridge University Press.

Zigler, E., Hodapp, R.M., & Edison, M. (1990). From theory to practice in the care and education of retarded individuals. *American Journal on Mental Retardation, 95,* 1–12.

11

Parents of Aggressive and Withdrawn Children

Kenneth H. Rubin
Shannon L. Stewart
Xinyin Chen
University of Waterloo

All children are essentially criminal.
—Diderot

A child is a curly, dimpled lunatic.
—Ralph Waldo Emerson

Having children is like having a bowling ball installed in your brain.
—Martin Mull, cited in Byrne (1988)

INTRODUCTION

A quick glance at the quotations offered above would lead one to assume that parenting is not a simple matter. For hundreds of years, writers of philosophy, fiction, and comedy have portrayed the child as a significantly stressful addition to the family unit. Nevertheless, it is also the case that the arrival of an infant brings with it, to most parents, a great deal of joy and enthusiastic anticipation. Or to offer yet another observation: "My mother had a great deal of trouble with me, but I think she enjoyed it" (Mark Twain, cited in Byrne, 1988, p. 301).

Most people would agree that children represent a challenge to their parents. Yet, these challenges are most often met by parents with acceptance, warmth, sensitivity, and responsivity. At times, however, for reasons we are only beginning to understand, the challenge of childrearing is met by parents with coldness, unacceptance, neglect, and/or hostility. Perhaps there are ecologically based stressors that produce such rearing behaviors (e.g., lack of financial resources, parental separation and divorce, lack of social support); or, perhaps there are infant and child characteristics that lead parents to interact negatively with and to feel negatively about their offspring. Perhaps too, parents themselves have experienced particularly negative childrearing histories and model the behaviors of their own parents and family culture or norms in the rearing of their children (Rogosch, Cicchetti,

Shields, Toth, in this *Handbook*; Main, Kaplan, & Cassidy, 1985). It is our belief that when parents think about childrearing and child developmental trends in ways that deviate from cultural norms, and/or when they interact and respond to their children in psychologically inappropriate ways, they will develop negative relationships with their children. We believe also that when parent–child relationships and parent–child interactions within the family are negative, it does not auger well for normal child development.

It is the purpose of this chapter to describe the parenting histories of two types of children who deviate from their agemates vis-à-vis their social behavioral and emotional profiles; typically these children have been referred to as (1) socially withdrawn and anxious, and (2) aggressive and interpersonally hostile. Our focus is on childhood aggression and withdrawal because these behaviors reflect the two most commonly described behavioral disorders in childhood (Moskowitz, Schwartzman, & Ledingham, 1985).

Aggression in Childhood

Aggression is a behavioral reflection of psychological *undercontrol*; it is also one of the major reasons for treatment referral in childhood. This is the case, not only because the child's behavior is out-of-control, but also because it is interpersonally destructive and longitudinally stable (e.g., Olweus, 1979). Furthermore, aggression in childhood forecasts later maladaptive outcomes such as delinquency and criminality (Farrington, 1991; Huesmann, Eron, Lefkowitz, & Walder, 1984). Finally, aggression and other behavioral markers of undercontrol are associated with a plethora of other difficulties. For example, children who have conflicts with the environment (heretofore referred to as children with *externalizing* disorders) have deficits in understanding the perspectives, feelings, and intentions of others (Dodge, 1986; Rubin, Bream, & Rose-Krasnor, 1991). They bully their classmates and quickly establish negative reputations amongst their peers (e.g., Coie & Kupersmidt, 1983). Given the potential danger of hostile, unthinking aggressive behavior for its victims, it is not surprising that the phenomenon of aggression in childhood has attracted voluminous and compelling conceptual and empirical treatments (see Pepler & Rubin, 1991, for recent reviews).

There is growing evidence that the quality of the children's relationships with parents and the experience of particular forms of parenting practices contribute significantly to the development of undercontrolled, aggressive behavioral profiles. One purpose of this chapter , therefore, is to review the relevant literature concerning the associations between "parenting," parent–child relationships, and childhood aggression.

Social Withdrawal in Childhood

The study of childhood aggression has a broader, richer conceptual and empirical history than that of psychological *overcontrol* and its behavioral manifestation, social withdrawal. The predominant interest in externalizing disorders most likely stems from a variety of significant factors. First, from the very earliest years of childhood, aggression is more salient and likely to evoke some form of negative affect (e.g., anger) in the perceiver than social withdrawal (Mills & Rubin, 1990). Second, children in Western cultures are attending group care and educational settings at earlier ages for longer periods of the lifespan than in earlier generations. As such, control in these group settings is an important agendum item for caregivers and educators, and children who are out of control are viewed as serious challenges to the delivery of appropriate group care and/or education. Consequently, children who demonstrate aggressive, impulsive, or overactive symptomatology are targeted early and often for ameliorative attention (e.g., Pepler, King, & Byrd, 1991). Quiet, affectively over-controlled young children on the other hand often represent veritable models of proper school decorum. As a result, they are less likely to be disruptive, and their difficulties may go undetected or ignored by the typically harried caregiver or educator.

Nevertheless, it is the case that professionals have persisted in regarding psychological overcontrol and its behavioral manifestations in childhood as comprising a major category of disorder (e.g., Achenbach & Edelbrock, 1981) and as warranting intervention (e.g., Conger & Keane, 1981). Moreover, the primary behavioral manifestation of overcontrol, social withdrawal, becomes increasingly salient to caregivers and peers with increasing age (e.g., Bacon & Ashmore, 1985; Bugental & Cortez, 1988; Bugental & Shennum, 1984; Younger & Boyko, 1989). As such, the social reticence of withdrawn children makes interaction effortful for others and contributes to the development of distant and sometimes difficult relationships (Hymel, Rubin, Rowden, & LeMare, 1990). Further, from a developmental perspective, it has been proposed that peer interaction represents a social context within which children learn to consider the perspectives of others and coordinate them with their own (e.g., Mead, 1934; Piaget, 1926). Thus, children who consistently demonstrate behaviors that are paradigmatically "driven by" problems within the self (heretofore referred to as internalizing problems), may be at major risk for failing to develop those social and social-cognitive skills that purportedly result from peer interactive experiences. Not only are socially withdrawn children lacking in social-cognitive and social competence (LeMare & Rubin, 1987; Rubin & Krasnor, 1986), but with increasing age they come to recognize their shortcomings and express strong feelings of loneliness and negative self-regard (Hymel, Woody, & Bowker, 1993; Parkhurst & Asher, 1992). Moreover, social withdrawal in childhood is both developmentally stable (Olweus, 1984; Rubin, Hymel, & Mills, 1989) and predictive of internalizing difficulties in adolescence (e.g., Olweus, 1993; Rubin, 1993).

As is the case with aggression, researchers are now asking whether or not the quality of parent–child relationships and the experience of particular parenting styles contribute significantly to the development of social withdrawal in childhood. However, unlike the relatively extensive parenting literature concerning childhood aggression, studies of the parent–child relationships and the socialization experiences of children who may be described as psychologically overcontrolled are scant to nonexistent. What is known, however, is addressed here.

In summary, it is our intention to examine the extant literature concerning the parents of children who suffer from two of the most serious impediments to a normal, happy, and adaptive life—aggression and social withdrawal. We begin by defining and contrasting the constructs of social competence and incompetence; as one might expect, aggression and withdrawal are viewed as manifestations of social incompetence. Then, we describe briefly a number of theories that have drawn parents into the developmental equation in which pathways to behavioral undercontrol and overcontrol in childhood are predicted. Thereafter, we describe research in which the quality of the parent–child relationship, parental beliefs or ideas about the development of social competence and both aggression and withdrawal, and parenting practices are associated with the expression of aggression and social withdrawal in childhood. In a final section, we examine factors that may influence the types of parent–child relationships, parental beliefs, and parenting behaviors associated with the development of aggression and social withdrawal.

DEFINITIONS AND THEORY OF SOCIAL COMPETENCE AND INCOMPETENCE

Given that the expression of both aggression and social withdrawal have been considered clear manifestations of a lack of social competence, this chapter begins with some working definitions. It is highly probable that there are as many definitions of social competence as there are students of it; as such, the definitions offered must be taken as reflecting the personal biases of the present authors. We begin by making three assumptions: First, it seems reasonable to assume that social competence is both *desirable* and *adaptive*. Second, an equally reasonable assumption is that both *aggressive and socially wary and withdrawn children are lacking in social skills*. Third, drawing on the first two assumptions, we believe that *the demonstration of childhood aggression and/or social withdrawal is maladaptive and not conducive to normal social and emotional growth and well-being.*

In order to better understand these assumptions, it seems essential that we arrive at a reasonable definition of *social competence*. McFall (1982) characterized social competence as a "judgment call" based on an audience's view of an actor's behavioral repertoire. Social competence is the ability to successfully achieve personal goals in social interaction while simultaneously maintaining positive relationships with others over time and across settings (Rubin & Rose-Krasnor, 1992). Thus, the consistent demonstration of friendly, cooperative, altruistic, successful, and socially acceptable behavior over time and across settings is likely to lead one to judge the actor as socially competent. Furthermore, the display of socially competent behavior in childhood results in peer acceptance and in successful adolescent outcomes. Recent empirical research supports these contentions (e.g., Morison & Masten, 1991).

On the other hand, the demonstration of unfriendly, agonistic, hostile behavior, even if directed to very few individuals within a limited number of settings, and even if the behavior results in personally successful outcomes, is likely to be unacceptable and judged as incompetent (e.g, Coie, Dodge, & Kupersmidt, 1990). Moreover, the reasonably consistent demonstration of social reticence, of unassertive social strategies to meet social goals, and of relatively high rates of unsuccessful social outcomes has been judged as incompetent (Rubin & Krasnor, 1986). Thus, children who have been identified by peers, teachers, and/or parents as aggressive or socially withdrawn cannot be characterized as socially competent.

If one believes the attainment of social competence is adaptive, then aggressive or withdrawn children display behaviors, emotions, and probably cognitions that must be considered maladaptive, thereby placing these children at risk for the development of psychological difficulties. Childhood aggression predicts the expression of externalizing disorders, school drop-out, and criminality in adolescence (Farrington, 1991; Kupersmidt & Coie, 1990). Social withdrawal in childhood predicts adolescent problems of an internalizing nature (Rubin, 1993).

Having reached these three conclusions, we can ask how it is that children acquire social competence (or in the case of aggressive and withdrawn children, social incompetence). The development of social competence and incompetence is likely a function of factors *internal* to the child, such as cognitive ability (e.g., Green, Forehand, Beck, & Vosk, 1980), temperament (e.g., Bates, Bayles, Bennett, Ridge, & Brown 1991), and physical appearance (Langlois & Stephan, 1981), as well as of factors *external* to the child, such as the reinforcement of specific behaviors by peers (Patterson, Littman, & Bricker, 1967).

Parents and Social Competence: Developmental Theory

Another likely source of the development of socially adaptive and maladaptive behaviors is the child's parents. According to Hartup (1985), parents serve at least three functions in the child's development of social competence: First, parent–child interaction is a context within which many competencies necessary for social interaction develop. This relationship furnishes the child with many of the skills required to initiate and maintain positive relationships with others, such as language skills, the ability to control impulses, and so on. Second, the parent–child relationship constitutes emotional and cognitive resources that allow the child to explore the social and nonsocial environments. It is a safety net permitting the child the freedom to examine features of the social universe, thereby enhancing the development of problem-solving skills. Third, the early parent–child relationship is a forerunner of all subsequently formed extrafamilial relationships (Bornstein, in this *Handbook*; Edwards, in this *Handbook*). It is within this relationship that the child begins to develop expectations and assumptions about interactions with other people and to develop strategies for attaining personal social goals and protecting the self.

In keeping with these functions, both classical theorists and contemporary researchers have implicated parents and the quality of parent–child relationships in the development of adaptive and maladaptive social behaviors. For example, early *psychoanalytic* theorists (e.g., Freud, 1973) noted that parents were both directly and indirectly responsible for the resolution of the Oedipus complex

(Hetherington & Martin, 1986). Of particular relevance were the ego defence mechanisms that were thought to underlie the display of undercontrolled behaviors. For example, to those of the psychoanalytic persuasion, resolution of the Oedipus complex resulted, in part, from identification with the aggressor. In order to avoid the threat of castration (or, for girls, the threat of whatever the Freudians believed to be worse than castration), the child identified with the parent who posed the perceived threat. If the parent with whom the child identified was hostile and authoritarian, the child would be predicted to exhibit angry, aggressive behaviors in both familial and extrafamilial settings. Similarly relevant was the ego-defense mechanism of *displacement*; in this case, the child displaced affect onto a person other than the appropriate one. Thus, if the child's anger was parent driven, hostility was directed to less threatening targets, such as siblings or peers. Also relevant was the development of the *superego*; this was viewed by psychoanalysts as yet another offshoot of Oedipus complex resolution. Thus, in classic psychoanalytic theory, identification with a given parent allowed the child to internalize the social and moral standards of the parent. Accordingly, the development of the superego was thought to provide children with the ability to control aggressive impulses and with the motivation to perform altruistic acts that would benefit others.

Ethological adaptations of psychoanalytic models also have provided the rationale for a strong association between "parenting" and both adaptive and maladaptive child functioning (Ainsworth, 1973). The connection between attachment theory and the production of under- and overcontrolled behavior is best understood by referring to Bowlby's (1973) construct of "internal working models." For example, Bowlby proposed that the early mother–child relationship lays the groundwork for the development of internalized models of familial and extrafamilial relationships. These internal working models were thought to be the product of parental behavior—specifically, parental sensitivity and responsivity (Spieker & Booth, 1988). Given an internal working model that the parent is available and responsive, it was proposed that the young child would feel confident, secure, and self-assured when introduced into novel settings. Thus, *felt security* has been viewed as a highly significant developmental phenomenon that provides the child with sufficient emotional and cognitive sustenance to allow the active exploration of the social environment. *Exploration* is purported to result in play (LaFreniere & Sroufe, 1985; Pastor, 1981), which, in turn, leads to the development of problem-solving skills and competence in both the impersonal and interpersonal realms (Rubin & Rose-Krasnor, 1992). From this perspective, then, the association between security of attachment in infancy and the quality of children's social skills is attributed, indirectly, to maternal sources (Sroufe, 1983).

Alternatively, the development of an insecure infant–parent attachment relationship has been posited to result in the child's developing an internal working model that interpersonal relationships are rejecting or neglectful. In turn, the social world is perceived as a battleground that must either be attacked or escaped from (Bowlby, 1973). Thus, for the insecure and angry child, opportunities for peer play and interaction are nullified by displays of hostility and aggression in the peer group. Such behavior, in turn, results in the child's forced (by the peer group) lack of opportunities to benefit from the communication, negotiation, and perspective-taking experiences that typically will lead to the development of a normal and adaptive childhood. For insecure and wary/anxious children, opportunities for peer play and interaction are nullified by the children themselves. Consequently, social and emotional fearfulness prevails to the point at which the benefits of peer interaction are practically impossible to obtain. Empirical support for connections between security of attachment and the display of aggressive or socially fearful and withdrawn behavior is described later.

Finally, *behaviorists* have suggested that parents shape children's social behaviors through processes of conditioning and modeling. Children's tendencies to directly imitate adult communicative, prosocial, aggressive, and even socially anxious and withdrawn behaviors have been reported consistently in the literature; in addition, social behaviors have been described as responsive to reinforcement principles (Radke-Yarrow & Zahn-Waxler, 1986). A strong link between parental socialization techniques and the display of child behavior in nonfamilial settings has been central to proponents of social learning theory (Sears, 1961).

In summary, almost all major psychological theories that deal with the development of children's social and emotional development in general, and more specifically with the development of competent and adaptive versus incompetent and maladaptive behaviors (aggression and social withdrawal), place a primary responsibility on parental attributes and behaviors, as well as on the quality of the parent–child relationship. These theories have provided, historically, the undercarriage for a quickly growing corpus of data concerning the nexus of parent–child relationships, "parenting" behaviors, and child "outcomes." We review the literature here, as it pertains to the parents of children who exhibit overcontrolled and undercontrolled emotions and social behaviors.

ATTACHMENT RELATIONSHIPS, SOCIAL COMPETENCE, AND AGGRESSION AND SOCIAL WITHDRAWAL

One theoretically driven research stream is focused on the purported effects of the *quality of the parent–child relationship*. This focus derives primarily from ethological theory and the constructs of secure and insecure attachment and internal working models of the self in relation to others. The methodologies employed are drawn mainly from the classic Strange Situation (Ainsworth, Blehar, Waters, & Wall, 1978), which allows distinctions to be made between parent–child partners who have secure or insecure attachment relationships. Concurrent and predictive associations between varying attachment classifications and the expression of competent, aggressive, and passive–withdrawn behavior are subsequently examined.

Social Competence and Security of Attachment

The inability to regulate one's emotions and, relatedly, to control one's behavioral impulses "marks" the child as "at risk" for psychological dysfunction. Given the risk status of children who have emotion and behavior regulation difficulties, researchers have raised questions about the etiology of these phenomena. As it happens, it has been common for researchers, parents, and childcare professionals to turn to the quality of the child's relationships with primary caregivers as possible explanatory starting points.

During infancy, responsive and sensitive parenting leads to the development of a secure internal working model of relationships (Spieker & Booth, 1988). Thus, the sensitive and responsive parent is able and willing to recognize the infant's or toddler's emotional signals, to consider the child's perspective, and to respond promptly and appropriately according to the child's needs. In turn, the child develops a working belief system that incorporates the parent as one who can be relied on for protection, nurturance, comfort, and security; a sense of trust in relationships results from the secure infant/toddler–parent bond. Furthermore, the child forms a belief that the self is competent and worthy of positive response from others.

This internal working model allows the child to feel secure, confident, and self-assured when introduced to novel settings, and this sense of felt security fosters the child's active exploration of the social environment (Sroufe, 1983). In turn, exploration of the social milieu allows the child to address a number of significant "other-directed" questions such as "What are the properties of these other people?" "What are they like?" and "What can and do they do?" Once these exploratory questions are answered, the child can begin to address "self-directed" questions such as "What can *I* do with this person?" This is the question that defines peer *play*.

It is during play with peers that children experience the interpersonal exchange of ideas, perspectives, roles, and actions. From social negotiation, discussion, and conflict with peers, children learn to understand others' thoughts, emotions, motives, and intentions (e.g., Doise & Mugny, 1981). In turn, armed with these new social understandings, children are able to think about the consequences of their social behaviors, not only for themselves but also for others. The development of these social-cognitive abilities has long been thought to result in the production of socially competent behaviors (e.g., Selman, 1985).

Support for these conjectures emanates from research in which it has been demonstrated that securely attached infants are likely to be well adjusted and socially competent in the early and midyears of childhood. For example, researchers have reported consistently that securely attached infants are more able than their insecurely attached counterparts to produce numerous acceptable and flexible solutions to hypothetical social dilemmas presented to them in an interview format (Arend, Gove, & Sroufe, 1979; Goldberg, Lojkasek, Gartner, & Corter, 1989). In the one published study of observed social problem-solving skills to date, Booth, Rose-Krasnor, and Rubin (1991) reported significant differences between preschool-age children, who, as infants, were classified as securely versus insecurely attached to their mothers. The securely attached children were less likely to use *aggressive* means to achieve their social goals than were their insecurely attached agemates. Furthermore, the problem-solving strategies used by securely attached children from middle-class, low-risk families were more likely to meet with successful outcomes than were the strategies employed by insecurely attached children from low-risk backgrounds. Taken together with the data produced by children's responses to hypothetical–reflective interviews, the observational data indicate that secure infant attachment relationships predict adaptive cognizing about resolving interpersonal dilemmas, adaptive production and enactment of adaptive strategies, and the experience of successful social problem-solving outcomes. A secure infant attachment relationship has also been found to predict, at 4 years of age, more elaborate and flexible play styles, more positive social engagement, greater empathy in peer play, and greater ego resilience (an index of response flexibility, persistence, and resourcefulness), than insecure attachment relationships. Securely attached infants are also more popular and more likely to develop friendships at age 4 than their insecure counterparts (Sroufe, 1983).

Aggression, Withdrawal, and Insecurity of Attachment

According to Bowlby, attachment behavior that is not met with comfort or support arouses anger and anxiety. A baby whose parent has been inaccessible and unresponsive is frequently angry because the parent's unresponsiveness is painful and frustrating. At the same time, because of uncertainty about the parent's responsiveness, the infant is apprehensive and readily upset by stressful situations. To protect against these intolerable emotions, it is postulated that the infant develops ego defense strategies. These strategies involve excluding from conscious processing any information that, when processed in the past, aroused anger and anxiety (Bowlby, 1980; Case, 1991). In situations that could arouse these emotions, infants block conscious awareness and the processing of thoughts, feelings, and desires associated with their need of the parent. This information-processing blockage leads to the deactivation of the behavioral system mediating attachment behavior, such that the behavioral expression of attachment-related thoughts and emotions are inhibited.

When stressful situations arouse the infant's need for contact with the parent, different coping strategies are activated depending on the nature of the infant's expectations and assumptions about the parent (Bowlby, 1973). Moreover, attachment theorists have suggested that the expectations and assumptions that infants build up about others and the means by which they cope with these cognitions are internalized and carried forward into subsequent relationships (Bowlby, 1973). Thus, it has been proposed that, in their subsequent peer relationships, insecure-avoidant infants (A babies) are guided by previously reinforced expectations of parental rejection; hence, they are believed to perceive peers as potentially hostile and tend to strike out proactively and aggressively (Troy & Sroufe, 1987). Indeed, researchers have reported that A babies do exhibit more hostility, anger, and aggressive behavior in preschool settings than their secure counterparts (LaFreniere & Sroufe, 1985; Sroufe, 1983; 1988; Troy & Sroufe, 1987). Insecure-ambivalent infants (C babies), on the other hand, are thought to be guided by a fear of rejection; consequently, in their extrafamilial peer relationships they are postulated to attempt to avoid rejection through passive, adult-dependent behavior and withdrawal from the prospects of peer interaction (Renken, Egeland, Marvinney, Mangelsdorf, & Sroufe, 1989). Researchers have indicated that C babies are more whiney, easily frustrated, and socially inhibited at

2 years than their secure agemates (Fox & Calkins, 1993; Matas, Arend, & Sroufe, 1978). At 4 years of age, children who had been classified at 1 year as C babies have been described as lacking in confidence and assertiveness (Erickson, Sroufe, & Egeland, 1985), and at 7 years as passively withdrawn (Renken, Egeland, Marvinney, Sroufe, & Mangelsdorf, 1989).

In summary, it would appear that a secure attachment relationship sets the stage for the development of social competence and positive peer relationships. Insecure attachment relationships in infancy, on the other hand, seem to set in motion developmental processes that have been shown to predict the expression of undercontrolled, aggressive behavior and overcontrolled, wary, inhibited, and passively withdrawn behavior in childhood. Thus, early developing internal working models that apply to issues of interpersonal trust and security, empathy, reciprocity, self-worth, and self-assuredness (Elicker, Englund, & Sroufe, 1992), and that result from the development of attachment relationships with parents, appear to guide the subsequent expression of emotion and behavior in children.

The internal working models previously described as guiding the expression of competent and incompetent, adaptive and maladaptive emotional and behavioral expressions are generally construed as residing within the minds of children. It is important to note, however, that parents, too, have internal working models of relationships. These models have been framed recently within the constructs of parental beliefs, ideas, and cognitions about the development, maintenance, and dissolution of relationships and about the behaviors that might contribute to the quality of relationships. We next review this literature, as it pertains to social competence, withdrawal, and aggression.

PARENTS' BELIEFS ABOUT ADAPTIVE AND MALADAPTIVE BEHAVIORS

A second major research stream linking parental and child domains consists of studies concerning *parents' cognitions or ideas about development* and the socialization goals and socialization strategies they believe to be most appropriate for promoting child development. Studies in this stream have focused, for example, on how parents' attributions about their children's behaviors influence their strategic and affective responses to those behaviors (e.g., Bugental & Shennum, 1984; Sameroff & Feil, 1985). Recent reviews of parental beliefs and ideas (e.g., Goodnow, 1988, in this *Handbook*; McGillicuddy-DeLisi & Sigel, in this *Handbook*; Miller, 1988) have highlighted the significance of this domain for understanding the socialization process; and these authors collectively have emphasized the need to clarify relations among parental belief structures, parenting behaviors, and child "outcomes."

There is emerging evidence that parents' ideas, beliefs, and perceptions concerning child development, in general, and the development and maintenance of adaptive and maladaptive behavioral and emotional styles, in particular, contribute to, predict, and partially explain the development of socially competent and incompetent behaviors in childhood. The conceptual underpinnings of this research are drawn from *researchers'* beliefs that parents' childrearing practices represent a behavioral expression of parental notions about how children become socially competent, how family contexts should be structured to shape children's behaviors, and how and when children should be taught to initiate and maintain relationships with others (Laosa & Sigel, 1982). To this end, research concerned with parents' ideas about children's socioemotional development represents an examination of their own "inner working models" of the relations among social skills, emotion regulation, and social relationships. Thus, many researchers believe that parenting behaviors are cognitively "driven" and that these cognitions are themselves influenced by sociocultural forces such as parental educational and socioeconomic status and ethnicity; the gender, age, and developmental level of their child, and their own history of parent–child relationships (Bacon & Ashmore, 1986; Dix, Ruble, & Zamborano, 1989). In this section, therefore, we consider whether parenting attitudes and beliefs are associated with children's social competencies and behavioral disturbances (specifically, aggression and social withdrawal).

Parents' Beliefs About Social Competence

It seems reasonable to conclude that the more parents think it is important for their children to be socially competent, the more likely it is for them to be involved in promoting it. Indeed, Cohen (1989) reported that the more mothers valued and felt responsible for their children's sociability, the more they tended to be involved in promoting their children's peer relationships. Furthermore, Rubin et al. (1989) found that mothers who considered the development of social skills to be very important had children who were observed to demonstrate social competence in their preschools. These children more frequently initiated peer play, used appropriate kinds of requests to attain their social goals, were more prosocial, and were more successful at gaining peer compliance than their agemates whose mothers did not place a high priority on the development of social competence. In general, parents tend to view their children optimistically and forecast healthy developmental outcomes for them. Parents of socially competent children believe that, in early childhood, they should play an active role in the socialization of social skills via teaching and providing peer interaction opportunities. They also believe that when their children display maladaptive behaviors, it is due to transitory and situationally caused circumstances (Dix & Grusec, 1985; Goodnow, Knight, & Cashmore, 1985).

Parents whose preschoolers display socially incompetent behaviors (such as social reticence, hostility, aggression) are less likely to endorse strong beliefs in the development of social skills (Rubin et al., 1989). Furthermore, they are more likely to attribute the development of social competence to internal factors ("children are born that way"), to believe that incompetent behavior, once attained, is difficult to alter, and to believe that interpersonal skills are best taught through direct instructional means (Rubin et al., 1989).

These findings give insights about how parents' ideas about social development may influence their socialization behaviors. Thus, external attributions for the development of social competence may be conducive to the use of constructive means to teach social skills. Internal attributions about how children develop competent and incompetent social skills may lead to one of two potential childrearing styles (Rubin, Rose-Krasnor, Bigras, Mills, & Booth, in press). On the one hand, the belief that social behavior is "internally" caused can lead to parental feelings of hopelessness and helplessness; in this case, parental neglect or a laissez-faire, permissive approach to socializing social skills or dealing with maladaptive social behavior may ensue. On the other hand, parents may adopt a "spoil the rod, spare the child" rearing style. In this case, parents may "try harder" to counter the influence of factors perceived to be internally caused, thereby adopting an authoritarian, high power assertive socialization belief system. These speculations have received initial support (see Rubin & Mills, 1992, and Rubin et al., in press).

One conclusion that may derive from these findings is that parental involvement in the promotion of social competence is mediated by strong beliefs in the importance of social skills. When a socially competent child demonstrates poor social performance, parents who place a relatively high value on social competence are likely to be the most involved and responsive. Over time, such involvement may be positively reinforced by the child's acquisition of social skills. At the same time, parents are likely to value social skills displayed by their children, and these children will be perceived as interpersonally competent and capable of autonomous learning. Hence, parental beliefs and child characteristics will influence each other in a reciprocal manner (Mills & Rubin, 1993a).

Parental Beliefs About Aggression and Withdrawal

Recently, researchers have begun to explore how parents feel about, think about, and consequently deal with childrens' aggression and social wariness and withdrawal. To a large extent, this research is guided by information-processing approaches to the study of parenting problems (e.g., Bugental, 1992; Rubin & Mills, 1992).

According to Bugental (1992), for example, parenting may be a source of considerable stress, especially if the child is viewed as a "problem." The "problematic" child who demonstrates difficult behaviors at a given point in time may evoke rather different parental emotions and cognitions than the "normal" child who demonstrates the identical maladaptive behaviors, but only rarely. In the case of normal children, the production of aggression or social withdrawal and wariness may activate parental feelings of concern, puzzlement, and in the case of aggression, anger. These affects are regulated by the parent's attempts to understand, rationalize, or justify the child's behavior and by the parent's knowledge of the child's social skills history and the known quality of the child's social relationships at home, at school, and in the neighborhood. Thus, in the case of nonproblematic children, the evocative stimulus produces adaptive, solution-focused parental ideation that results in the parent's choice of a reasoned, sensitive, and responsive approach to dealing with the problem behavior (Bugental, 1992). In turn, the child views the parent as supportive and learns to better understand how to behave and feel in similar situations as they occur in the future. As such, a reciprocal connection is developed between the ways and means of adult and child social information processing.

In the case of aggressive children, any hostile behavior—whether directed at peers, siblings, or parents—may evoke strong parental feelings of anger and frustration. Such emotions are often difficult to regulate given that they are accompanied by significant physiological responses (e.g., increases in heart rate and electrodermal activity; Obrist, 1982). As a consequence, parents may be unable to control their expressive behavior and the socialization strategy provoked is one that may be best regarded as undercontrolled, power assertive, and coercive (Bugental, 1992). Needless to say, this parental response, mediated by affect and beliefs/cognitions about the intentionality of the child behavior, the historical precedence of child aggression, and the best means to control child aggression, is likely to evoke negative affect and cognitions in the child; the result of this interplay between parent and child beliefs, affects, and behavior may be the reinforcement and extension of family cycles of hostility (Patterson & Bank, 1989; Patterson, Capaldi, & Bank, 1991).

In the case of socially wary and withdrawn children, any expression of social fearfulness in the peer group may evoke parental feelings of concern, sympathy, and perhaps, with increasing child age, a growing sense of frustration. The parent may be overcome by a strong belief that the child must be helped in some way. Such a "read" of the situation and of the child may be guided by a developing belief system that social withdrawal is dispositionally based, that it is accompanied by strong and debilitating child feelings of fear and social anxiety, and by child behaviors that evoke, in peers, attempts to be socially dominant. The resultant parental behavior, guided by the processing of affect and historically and situationally based information, may be of a "quick fix" variety for parent and child. That is, to release the child from social discomfort, the parent may simply "take over," telling the child what to do and how to do it. Alternatively, the parent may simply solve the child's social dilemmas by asking other children for information desired by the child, obtaining objects desired by the child, or requesting that peers allow the child to join them in play. Needless to say, these direct parenting activities are likely to reinforce the child's feelings of insecurity, resulting in the mainte- nance of a systemic cycle of child hopelessness/helplessness and parent overcontrol/overprotection (see Mills & Rubin, 1993a, for an elaboration of this latter scenario).

Parents' Beliefs About Aggression and Withdrawal: Normative Studies

Students of developmental psychopathology generally agree that an understanding of normalcy and normal development is prerequisite to understanding deviations from the norm (Sroufe & Rutter, 1984). Thus, knowing how parents of "normal" and competent children respond to questions concerning their feelings about, attributions for, and preferred means of dealing with their children's displays of aggression and/or social withdrawal is a starting point. These beliefs are examined also insofar as they are related to the age of the child. This latter perspective provides the reader with an appreciation of the significance of child-based factors (such as age), on the parental belief system. Following this review, we contrast the beliefs of parents of aggressive, withdrawn, and "aver- age"/competent children.

Not surprisingly, parents have very different ideas about the derivation of aggression and withdrawal and how they might go about reacting behaviorally to them. For example, parents of preschoolers (age 4) and early elementary schoolers (age 6) express great concern when asked how they would feel if they were to observe their own child behaving consistently in an aggressive or withdrawn fashion. However, parents report that aggressive behavior elicits anger and disappointment, whereas withdrawal is more inclined to evoke surprise and puzzlement (Mills & Rubin, 1990). Given these reported affective reactions, it is not surprising that parents are more likely to suggest the use of high power assertive strategies to deal with their children's aggression than with their social withdrawal (Mills & Rubin, 1990). These parental reactions to hostility with hostility point aptly to the importance of accepting a bidirectional influence vis-à-vis the development and maintenance of aggression in childhood. It is also of interest to note that parents of preschoolers report that children's expressions of hostile aggression and wary withdrawal may be attributed to transient states such as a passing development stage (Mills & Rubin, 1990).

The previous findings apply to parents of relatively young children. Obviously, parents' beliefs, perceptions, and attitudes change as their children grow older (McNally, Eisenberg, & Harris, 1991; Mills & Rubin, 1992). Parents recognize that advances in social skill occur with age and, therefore, they think that older children must be held more responsible than younger children for their negative behaviors. For example, mothers tend to react to socially inappropriate behaviors with increasing negative affect with increasing child age (Dix et al., 1989). Dix and Grusec (1985) proposed that changes in disciplinary beliefs are associated with changes in parental attributions about the causes of specific child behaviors as children grow older.

In accordance with principles of attribution theory, behaviors that are very discrepant from normative standards tend to be attributed to stable traits or internal dispositions. These attributions, in turn, influence parental perceptions. Consistent with this analysis, mothers consider negative behaviors as more intentional and dispositional in older than in younger children. Furthermore, the more intentional and/or dispositional parents believe negative behaviors to be, the more upset they get when these behaviors are expressed (Dix, Ruble, Grusec, & Nixon, 1986; Dix et al., 1989). These affective reactions may lead some parents to respond in anger to their children's behaviors and others to respond by "moving away" from, or neglecting, the producer of these negative behaviors.

In support of these arguments, Mills and Rubin (1992) found, in a longitudinal study, a number of changes in the ways that mothers appraised displays of aggression and withdrawal, in the strategies they chose to deal with these behaviors, and in the beliefs that they had about how children learn social skills. For example, from 4 to 6 years, displays of aggression and withdrawal become less easily excused as reflecting immaturity or as being caused by sources external to the child (e.g., "Other children began the fight." "Other children would not allow my child to join them in play"). Instead, there was an increase in the extent to which mothers attributed these behaviors to internal dispositional characteristics. For withdrawal, these trait attributions were associated with an increase, on the part of mothers, not to respond to the behavior. These findings suggest that, during early childhood, parents may make active efforts to deal with the child's social wariness and withdrawal; however, in time, if parents judge that their efforts have fallen short, they may choose to ignore or to avoid the problem.

Interestingly, no such developmental change in behavioral response obtained for aggression; thus, aggression, despite being attributed to dispositional causes, seemed more difficult to excuse than the continued expression of withdrawal. Perhaps this finding resulted from the salience of aggression and from its clear negative consequences for children, their parents, their teachers, and their peers.

In summary, it seems likely that parents' feelings about, attributions for, and behavioral reactions to the expression of aggression and withdrawal change with child age. The extant data are descriptive of parental beliefs for children who are of preschool and early elementary school age; thus, further developmental data are presently required. Moreover, there have been few, if any, studies in which the beliefs of mothers about the development of social competence have been compared with the beliefs of fathers. And, mother versus father beliefs for sons versus daughters have rarely been compared. Consequently, it would appear as if this is an area in need of further investigation.

Parents of Aggressive and Withdrawn Children: Parental Beliefs

The research reviewed concerning parental beliefs about the development of social skills and of aggression and withdrawal derives from parents who had children who were socially and emotionally normal. Researchers who have followed a social information-processing model in their studies of parental beliefs have posited a number of ways in which parents of socially "different" children might think about social and emotional development (Bugental, 1992; Mills & Rubin, 1993a, 1993b).

Parents of aggressive children.   Mothers of aggressive children appear to hold beliefs about social development that vary from those of nonaggressive, normal children (Rubin & Mills, 1990, 1992). For example, when asked to indicate how a variety of social skills (e.g., making friends, sharing with peers) might best be learned by their preschoolers, they were more likely than mothers of average children to suggest they would take a highly direct approach. Parents of aggressive preschoolers believed more strongly than mothers of average children in the use of "low distancing" teaching styles (Sigel, 1982) that provide children with minimal opportunities to think about alternative perspectives, consequences of interactive behaviors for themselves and for others, and social "planning." Given that low distancing strategies have been associated with incompetent performance vis-à-vis the development of impersonal problem-solving skills (McGillicuddy-DeLisi, 1982), it would not seem to be a far stretch to suggest a nonoptimal social outcome for those children of parents who believe social skills can be taught through direct instruction.

Although their children are highly aggressive and they indicate that aggression makes them angry, mothers of aggressive preschoolers are nevertheless more inclined than mothers of average preschoolers to choose very indirect strategies or no strategies at all to deal with their children's aggressive behavior. Thus, for mothers of aggressive preschoolers there seems to be some disparity between their proactive beliefs, which suggest a preference for highly directive parenting styles, and their choice of reactive strategies, which indicate a preference for a laissez-faire style. This disparity may stem from their attribution of aggressive behavioral displays to age-related dispositional factors. Thus, it may be that these mothers' attempts to teach social skills directively are unsuccessful; moreover, they may be somewhat intimidated by their child's aggressiveness. Perhaps they attribute preschooler's behavior and their own lack of success to short-lived age-related factors and choose less direct strategies in order to lessen their anxiety, avoid confrontation, and wait out what they hope will be a passing phase. It may be, then, that these mothers attempt to normalize their children's behavior despite the fact that it makes them feel angry. Such conflicting emotions and attributions could perpetuate a high level of aggression in the child in precisely the way described by Patterson (1982, 1986); that is, by initiating an erratic pattern of behavioral interchanges in which undesirable behavior is sometimes rewarded or ignored as the parent attempts to avoid confrontation, and desirable behavior is sometimes, out of frustration, dealt with in an authoritarian fashion.

Interestingly, the mothers of aggressive elementary school-age children attribute the attainment of social skills and the consistent expression of aggressive behavior to internal, dispositional sources (Rubin et al., in press). Given the stability of aggressive behavior in childhood (Olweus, 1979), this finding is hardly surprising. Furthermore, with increasing age, mothers of aggressive children report not only that their children's hostility causes them to feel angry, but they also express less surprise and puzzlement than mothers of average children when their children demonstrate aggressive behavior. In short, these mothers appear to be getting used to their children's maladaptive behavioral styles. Acceptance of the causes of aggression and the lack of surprise when it occurs, do *not* engender a laissez-faire attitude in reaction to elementary school-age children's aggressive behavior. Rather, mothers of aggressive children are more inclined than mothers of average children to suggest the use of high-powered, punitive strategies to deal with aggression. It is likely, then, that with increasing age parents find it increasingly difficult to accept the hostile behavior of their children, despite believing that their behavior is dispositionally based. Perhaps the belief in a dispositional basis for aggressive behavior is merely defensive and expressive of parental frustration. Perhaps, too, the child's behavior results in negative reports to parents by teachers, schoolmates, and neighborhood parents.

Such information may not prove to be surprising, and the parent may attempt to explain the behavior by implicating biology in the development of aggression. But the end result is that the behavior must be brought under control. As a consequence, power assertive techniques become highly favored.

Parents of socially withdrawn children.   Rubin and Mills (1990, 1992) found that mothers of extremely withdrawn preschoolers, like mothers of aggressive children, think about children's social development in ways that differ considerably from mothers of average children. For example, like mothers of aggressive children, when they were asked to indicate how a variety of social skills might best be learned by their preschooler, mothers of withdrawn children were more likely to suggest that they would *tell* their children directly how to behave and less likely to believe that their children learn best by being active participants in and processors of their social environments. Thus, as is the case for aggressive children, the suggested use of "low distancing" socialization techniques (Sigel, 1982) minimizes opportunities to think about alternative perspectives, consequences of interactive behaviors for themselves and for others, and social "planning." As with aggressive children, social incompetence in withdrawn children may result, in part, from parental use of low distancing socialization strategies (McGillicuddy-DeLisi, 1982). Although the mothers of socially withdrawn preschoolers believe more strongly than the mothers of average children that social skills can be taught directly, mothers of *elementary school-age* withdrawn children believe more strongly than mothers of average children that it would be difficult to alter social skills deficiencies (Mills & Rubin, 1993b). Thus, on the one hand, these parents express a strong belief in low distancing strategies to aid in the initial development of social skills, but on the other hand, they do not think strongly of a positive prognosis for parental intervention when skills fail to develop.

Insofar as reactive parental beliefs are concerned, it has been shown that when mothers of socially withdrawn preschoolers were asked about their reactions to hypothetical incidents of their child's expression of peer directed aggression and withdrawal, they indicated that (1) they would feel more guilty and embarrassed; (2) they would more likely attribute such behaviors to internal, dispositional sources; and (3) they would react to such displays of maladaptive behavior more often in coercive, high-powered assertive ways than mothers of average/competent preschoolers (Rubin & Mills, 1990).

Taken together, the results described previously paint a portrait of mothers of socially withdrawn preschoolers as overprotective. Such an overcontrolling behavioral style would assuredly be detrimental to the child's developing senses of autonomy and social efficacy in the peer milieu; furthermore, such parenting beliefs are probably not conducive to the healthy development of social competence or positive self-regard. Indeed, early research has shown that an overprotective, overly concerned parenting style is associated with submissiveness, dependency, and timidity in early childhood (discussed later); these characteristics are descriptive of children who are socially withdrawn in the peer culture (Olweus, 1993).

The causal attributions and reported emotional reactions of these mothers were also indicative of overdirection. Mothers of socially withdrawn prechoolers not only expressed more anger, disappointment, guilt, and embarrassment about their children's maladaptive social behaviors than other mothers, they are also more inclined to blame them on traits in their child. This constellation of emotions and attributions suggests that these mothers may be somewhat unable to moderate their affective reactions to problematic behaviors. Perhaps in an attempt to regulate their own emotions about their children's behaviors, these mothers choose to "keep their house in order" by overregulating their children's activities. In summary, the extant data provide an initial empirical hint that socially withdrawn preschoolers are exposed to a rather complex mix of conflicting maternal emotions and attributions, and that mothers of socially inhibited children may feel overidentified with and somewhat ambivalent toward their children (Levy, 1943; Parker, 1983).

Interestingly, these observations appear to change with the increasing age of the withdrawn child. For example, during elementary school (age 5–9), mothers of withdrawn children described their affective reactions to social withdrawal as involving less surprise and puzzlement than mothers of normal children. These data are themselves unsurprising given the stability of withdrawal from the early to midyears of childhood (e.g., Asendorpf, 1993). Furthermore, although mothers of withdrawn elementary schoolers continued to attribute withdrawal to internal, personality traits in their children, they no longer suggest that they would react to displays of withdrawal in a power assertive manner (Mills & Rubin, 1993b).

In summary, parents of aggressive and withdrawn children appear to differ from those of average children in the ways in which they think about socializing social skills and in the ways they report reacting to their children's displays of social withdrawal and/or aggression. It is plausible that these parental beliefs have some bearing on the ways in which parents actually behave with their children. Although there are virtually no data available on this topic (Miller, 1988), there is a literature in which the behaviors of parents of aggressive and withdrawn children have been described. We turn to this literature in the next section.

PARENTING BEHAVIORS AND CHILDREN'S AGGRESSION AND SOCIAL WITHDRAWAL

If parents' *cognitions* about the development of social competence, aggression, and withdrawal are implicated in the expression of parental behavioral "styles," then the socialization practices of parents whose children are aggressive or withdrawn ought to differ from those of parents whose children are socially competent and normal. One means by which such parenting differences have been examined has involved the conceptualization of two basic dimensions of parenting—*warmth/responsiveness* and *control/demandingness* (Baumrind, 1971; Maccoby & Martin, 1983). The first dimension concerns the *affective* continuum of parenting; it ranges from warm and sensitive behavior on the one hand to cold or hostile behavior on the other hand. The second dimension deals with issues of *power assertion*. At one end of the continuum is the frequent use of restrictive demands and high control; at the opposite end of the continuum is frequent lack of supervision and low control. The interaction of the two continua constitutes an oft-referred to, fourfold scheme that includes *authoritative* parenting (high warmth, high control), *authoritarian* parenting (low warmth, high control), *indulgent/permissive* parenting (high warmth, low control), and *indifferent/uninvolved* parenting (low warmth, low control) (see Baumrind, 1971).

These different parenting classifications may mesh well with notions concerning the development of social competence, aggression, and social withdrawal in childhood. Indeed, researchers have shown that the children of *authoritative* parents tend to be socially responsible and competent, friendly and cooperative with peers, and generally happy (Baumrind, 1967, 1971). The authoritative and democratic parenting style is both concurrently and predictively associated with the development of mature moral reasoning and prosocial behavior (Eisenberg & Murphy, in this *Handbook*; Hoffman, 1970; Yarrow, Waxler, & Scott, 1971), high self-esteem (Loeb, Horst, & Horton, 1980), and academic achievement (Lamborn, Mounts, Steinberg, & Dornbusch, 1991; Steinberg, Lamborn, Dornbusch, & Darling, 1992). In contrast, parents who provide insufficient or imbalanced responsiveness and control (authoritarian, permissive, and uninvolved) are likely to have children who are socially incompetent, aggressive, and/or socially withdrawn (Baumrind, 1967, 1971, 1991; Dishion, 1990; Lamborn et al., 1991). The following sections document in greater detail the particular forms of parenting behavior that distinguish between parents of aggressive, withdrawn, and socially competent children. It should be noted that, regardless of its theoretical strength, Baumrind's fourfold paradigm of parenting has not been used frequently in empirical research. Thus, our discussion in the following section is related to, but not restricted to, Baumrind's classification scheme.

Parenting Behavior and Aggression in Childhood

One parenting variable that is frequently reported as a correlate of childhood aggression is parental *rejection*. Rejecting parents frequently and inappropriately apply power-assertive techniques and punishment. In general, it has been found that parents who are cold and rejecting, physically punitive, and who discipline their children in inconsistent manners have aggressive children (e.g., R. D. Conger et al., 1992, 1993; Dishion, 1990; Eron, Huesmann, & Zelli, 1991; Olweus, 1980; Weiss, Dodge, Bates, & Pettit, 1992). For example, Olweus (1980) found that childhood aggression could be predicted by mothers' negative affect vis-à-vis their sons and by their use of high power-assertive techniques when disciplining them. These maternal variables continued to predict aggressive behavior even after child temperament and mothers' permissiveness for aggression were controlled. Similarly, Weiss et al. (1992) recently found that harsh parental discipline predicted child aggression in school. This relation remained significant after child temperament, SES, and marital violence were controlled. The results reported for the influences of parental hostility and rejection on children's social adjustment and aggression appear to be generalizable across cultures (Chen & Rubin, 1993; Whiting & Edwards, 1988).

The process by which parental hostility, coldness, and rejection results in childhood aggression is not difficult to understand. For one, such a parenting style creates a familial environment that elicits feelings of frustration among its constituents. Frustration, in turn, may result in feelings of anger and hostility; these feelings, if left unchecked or unregulated, likely produce hostile and aggressive interchanges between children and their parents (Dollard, Doob, Miller, Mowrer, & Sears, 1939). Second, parental rejection and punishment serve as a model of hostility and inappropriate forcefulness for the child (Bandura, 1977). Third, as noted earlier, it is also possible that parental hostility and rejection constitute a basis for the child to develop an internal working model of the self as unworthy and of the social world as cold, distrustful, and hostile (Bowlby, 1969, 1973). These negative perceptions of and feelings about the world may contribute to the child's lack of expressed consideration of others in social interactions and to the development of an unfriendly and hostile behavioral repertoire.

It is important to note that parents of aggressive children are not *always* cold and punitive; rather, it appears that they apply power-assertive techniques and punishments in an *inconsistent* fashion (Parke & Slaby, 1983). Thus, at times, these parents punish their child's deviant behaviors, but at other times, they choose to ignore or even encourage them (Katz, 1971; Martin, 1975). For example, parents may punish and discourage deviant, hostile behavior in the home, but may actually encourage hostility and aggression in the peer group. Moreover, parents of aggressive children have been found to use power-assertive techniques proactively when or where it is actually inappropriate to do so (e.g., during parent–child free play), but fail to provide appropriate control and support in situations where they are called for (e.g., in a highly structured situation). Finally, some researchers have reported that parents of aggressive children actually respond *positively* to deviant child behavior, but aversively to nondeviant behavior (Lobitz & Johnson, 1975; Patterson, 1982; Snyder, 1977). Parents' encouragement of a child's aggressive behavior may result from an aspiration for the child to be dominant in the peer group. It is also possible that these parents actually believe that aggression and violence are appropriate means by which to solve interpersonal problems. Thus, it can be concluded safely that relatively frequent, but inconsistent use of parental high power assertion fosters aggressive behavior in childhood.

In addition to parental rejection and high power-assertive strategies, parental permissiveness, indulgence, and lack of supervision have often been found to correlate with children's aggressive behavior. For example, in Baumrind's original studies (1967, 1971), permissive parents who failed to exercise necessary control and to make demands for mature behavior tended to have impulsive, acting-out, and immature children. Olweus (1980) also found that maternal permissiveness of aggression was the *best* predictor of child aggression. Parental neglect, and lack of monitoring and supervision, also have been found to be related to truancy, drinking problems, precocious sexuality, and deliquency in adolescence and adulthood (Lamborn et al., 1991; Patterson, 1982; Pulkkinen, 1982). It may not be difficult to understand these associations, given that parental tolerance and neglect of the child's aggressive behavior may actually have the implication of legitimization and encouragement of aggression.

Although an overview of the extant literature would paint a picture of the parent of an aggressive child as being a harsh disciplinarian, as using such punitive measures inconsistently, as not monitoring and providing necessary supervision in situations that require them, and as behaving in a cold, rejecting manner, it is nevertheless the case that not all data are supportive of this portrait. From time to time, researchers fail to report a contemporaneous association between "negative" parenting and children's aggression (see Hart, DeWolf, Wozniak, & Burts, 1992). Furthermore, even if one were to argue that the corpus of data is largely supportive of the associations already noted, one could not argue, with much conviction, that negative indices of parenting "caused" childhood aggression. For example, in several recent longitudinal studies (e.g., Eron, Huesman, Dubow, Romanoff, & Yarmel, 1987; Vuchinich, Bank, & Patterson, 1992), *predictive relations* between parental discipline and child antisocial behavior were found to be nonsignificant, although *contemporaneous reciprocal relations* between them were statistically significant. It should be noted that researchers have recently attempted to aggregate scores of parenting skills, including parental nurturance and rejection, monitoring, and inconsistent parenting (e.g., R. D. Conger et al., 1992, 1993; Dishion, 1990). It appears as if these more global indices of parental effectiveness demonstrate reliable results in predicting childhood aggression.

In summary, much research exists in which parental hostility, rejection, and lack of warmth have been associated with the expression of aggressive behavior in childhood. It is important to note, however, that parenting practices do not represent the best long-term predictors of aggression, delinquency, and criminality. For example, Eron and colleagues (Eron et al., 1987; Lefkowitz, Eron, Walder, & Huesmann, 1977) reported that whereas parental behavior could reliably predict aggression in childhood, it was childhood aggression, not parental behavior, that best predicted aggression and criminality in adolescence and adulthood. The long-term effects of parental variables on later aggression and criminality, through the mediation of childhood aggression, have been documented also in other research programs (e.g., Farrington, 1983). Thus, it would appear that negative parental behavior helps establish and maintain a pattern of *childhood* aggression, which, itself, provides a strong foundation for the development of undercontrolled, externalizing problems in later life.

Parenting Behavior and Social Withdrawal in Childhood

In comparison with the literature concerning the parents of aggressive children, what is known about the behaviors of parents of socially withdrawn children is negligible. The general lack of information in this regard may stem from several factors. As aforementioned, the phenomenon of social withdrawal was viewed as neither a "risk variable" nor as a "marker" of psychological maladaptation. To the extent that these beliefs dominated the clinical literature, there was little reason to study the etiology of the phenomenon (see Rubin & Asendorpf, 1993). Further inhibiting the study of parenting influences was the notion that significant elements of the construct of social withdrawal (e.g., shyness, behavioral reticence) were biologically based and relatively unaffected by socialization beliefs and behavior (e.g., Kagan, Reznick, & Snidman,1987; Plomin & Daniels, 1986).

The emergence of studies in which social withdrawal has been demonstrated as a variable reflective of psychological maladaptation and predictive of internalizing difficulties (e.g., Achenbach & Edelbrock, 1981; Hymel et al., 1990; Rubin, Chen, & Hymel, 1993) has led to the search for parenting associations and predictors. The "construct" of social withdrawal includes the demonstration of social wariness and anxiety, the virtual nonexistence of exploration in novel social situations, social deference, submissiveness, and sad affect during encounters with peers, and negative self-regard concerning one's own social skills and relationships (Hymel et al., 1993; Rubin, 1982, 1985). With these defining properties in mind, it is noteworthy that Baumrind (1967) found that the parents of socially anxious, unhappy children who were insecure in the company of peers were more likely to demonstrate *authoritarian* socialization behaviors than the parents of more socially competent children. Other researchers have reported that children whose parents use authoritarian childrearing practices tend to have low self-esteem and lack spontaneity and confidence (Coopersmith, 1967;

Lamborn et al., 1991; Lempers, Clark-Lempers, & Simons, 1989). Furthermore, MacDonald and Parke (1984) found that boys perceived by teachers as socially withdrawn, hesitant, and as spectators in the company of peers tend to have fathers who are highly directive and less engaging and physically playful in their interactions with their sons. Their mothers were described as being less likely than mothers of nonwithdrawn sons to engage them in verbal exchange and interaction. The findings were less clear-cut for socially withdrawn daughters. In general, however, the researchers reported that during parent–child play, the parents of socially withdrawn children were less spontaneous, playful, and affectively positive than parents of more sociable children.

Other researchers have found that children's social timidity, withdrawal, and adult dependency is associated with parental *overprotection* (Eisenberg, 1958; Kagan & Moss, 1962; Martin, 1975; Parker, 1983), a practice that is conceptually related to the constructs of power assertion and intrusion. Overprotective parents tend to restrict their child's behavior and actively encourage dependency. For example, overprotective parents encourage their children to maintain close proximity to them and they do not reinforce risk-taking and active exploration in unfamiliar situations. And, Hinde, Tamplin, and Barrett (1993) reported that preschoolers who are often observed to be alone in school make and receive frequent initiations with their mothers. These data suggest that the influence between parenting and social withdrawal is bidirectional. In the case of Hinde et al.'s study, the interaction sequences between mothers and their children were described as brief, suggesting dependency bids on the part of the children and protectiveness and oversolicitation on the part of the mothers.

Taken together, the extant data concerning the parenting behaviors and styles associated with social withdrawal focus clearly on two potential socialization contributors—overcontrol and overprotection. Parents who use high power-assertive strategies and who place many constraints on their children tend to rear shy, reserved, and dependent children. Thus, the issuance of parental commands combined with constraints on exploration and independence may hinder the development of competence in the social milieu. Restrictive control may also deprive the child of opportunities to interact with peers. As such, it should not be surprising that children who are socially withdrawn are on the receiving end of parental overcontrol and overprotection.

The findings described previously, however, stem from very few databases. Moreover, the children were studied across a wide variety of ages. Furthermore, the contexts within which parents of socially withdrawn children display overcontrol and overprotection have not been well specified. Thus, unlike the literature on the parents of aggressive children, it must be concluded that, at this time, the socialization correlates and causes of social withdrawal are not well known.

FACTORS INFLUENCING THE PARENTS OF AGGRESSIVE AND WITHDRAWN CHILDREN

It has long been argued that the development of maladaptive social behavior derives principally from the quality of the children's relationships with their parents and from experience with particular parenting practices such as rejection, neglect, overprotection, and/or the inappropriate and incompetent use of harsh disciplinary techniques. Despite these traditional perspectives, it is the case that researchers are now able to demonstrate that parental affect, cognition, and behavior may be a function of *child* characteristics (Bell & Chapman, 1986; Kuczynski & Kochanska, 1990; Lytton, 1990; Sanson & Rothbart, in this *Handbook*). That is, parents respond differently to children who are dispositionally "easy," "wary," and "difficult" (or *perceived* by parents to be dispositionally "easy," "wary," and "difficult"). Furthermore, researchers have reached the conclusion that parenting emotions, cognitions, and behaviors must be examined within a broad context of background variables, including family resources, positive and negative life experiences, the quality of the spousal relationship (if one exists), and the availability to parents of social support (e.g., Belsky, 1984; Cox, Owen, Lewis, & Henderson, 1989; Minuchin, 1985). In the following sections, we describe these contextual influences on parents and children, keeping in mind child "outcomes" of social competence, aggression, and/or social withdrawal.

Stress, Parenting, and Child Behavior

In recent years, researchers have attempted to understand how the experience of stress, the availability of social and emotional support, and parental psychopathology interact and conspire to influence parenting behaviors known to predict child maladjustment (Belsky, 1984; R. D. Conger et al., 1992, 1993; Patterson et al., 1991). For example, *economic stress*, brought on by the lack of financial resources, makes scarce the availability of necessary goods. It also creates feelings of frustration, anger, and helplessness that can be translated into less than optimal childrearing styles. Stressful economic situations predict parental negativism and inconsistency (Elder, Van Nguyen, & Caspi, 1985; Lempers et al., 1989; Weiss et al., 1992). Thus, parents who are financially distressed tend generally to be more irritable and moody than parents who have few financial difficulties. They are less nurturant, involved, child centered, and consistent with their children (R. D. Conger, McCarty, Young, Lahey, & Kropp, 1984; Elder et al., 1985; Patterson, 1983, 1986). These latter parenting behaviors are associated with the development and display of maladaptive child behaviors. Thus, it should not be surprising that a positive association has also been reported between economic stress and children's affectively underregulated social behavior (aggression, e.g., Dooley & Catalano, 1988; Weiss et al., 1992; Windle, 1992). These results mirror those reported earlier for those children whose families experienced the Great Depression (Elder, 1974; Elder et al., 1985).

Interspousal conflict is another stressor that predicts parenting behaviors associated with child maladjustment (Wilson & Gottman, in this *Handbook*). Researchers have reported consistently that spousal discord and marital dissatisfaction predict negative parental attitudes about childrearing as well as insensitive, unresponsive parenting behaviors (Cox et al., 1989; Emery, 1982; Jouriles et al., 1991). As outlined earlier, these parenting cognitions and behaviors are associated with both aggression and withdrawal in childhood. Spousal hostility can also affect children directly by providing them with models of aggressive behavior. Thus, it is not surprising to find that child aggression is predicted by interspousal conflict (Dadds & Powell, 1991; Jouriles et al., 1991). It is important to note, however, that marital conflict is more predictive of child aggression in boys than in girls (J. H. Block, J. Block, & Morrison, 1981).

Yet another family-based stressor is *parental psychopathology*. For example, maternal depression is associated with a lack of parental involvement, responsivity, spontaneity, and emotional support in childrearing (Downey & Coyne, 1990; Field, in this *Handbook*; Kochanska, Kuczynski, & Maguire, 1989; Zahn-Waxler et al., 1988). Given that depression is associated with maternal feelings of hopelessness and helplessness (Gurland, Yorkston, Frank, & Stone, 1967), the pattern of parenting behaviors noted earlier is not surprising. Furthermore, families in which one or both parents is depressed are found to be less cohesive and emotionally expressive than families in which the parents are psychologically well (Billings & Moos, 1985).

Given previous findings, it should not be surprising that parental depression is associated with social inhibition, wariness, and withdrawal in early childhood (Kochanska, 1991; Rubin, Both, Zahn-Waxler, Cummings, & Wilkinson, 1991; Z. Welner, A. Welner, McCrary, & Leonard, 1977). Moreover, given that social withdrawal is viewed as reflecting psychological problems of an internalizing nature, it is likewise unsurprising that parental depression is associated with, and predictive of, depression and anxiety in childhood (McKnew, Cytryn, Efron, Gershon, & Bunney, 1979).

Parental depression, however, is not only associated with parental uninvolvement and withdrawal from childrearing repsonsibilities. When depressed parents attempt to gain some element of control in their lives, they resort to highly authoritarian patterns of childrearing (e.g., Gelfand & Teti, 1990; Hammen, 1988; Kochanska & Radke-Yarrow, 1992). This mix of parental uninvolvement and overinvolvement is likely responsible for reports that parental depression is associated not only with social withdrawal in childhood, but with aggression as well (see Downey & Coyne, 1990, for a review). How it is that some children of depressed parents develop social behavioral patterns of social withdrawal and wariness, whereas others become aggressive is not known.

Finally, it is important to note that the effects of stress on parenting behaviors can be moderated, or buffered, by the availability of *social support* (Cohen & Wills, 1985; Compas, 1987; Crnic, Greenberg, Ragozin, Robinson, & Basham, 1983). For example, in a study by Jennings, Stagg, and Conners (1991), a group of mothers was interviewed extensively about their social networks; they were also observed during a play session with their children. It was found that mothers who were more satisfied with their personal social support networks were more likely to praise their children and less likely to intrusively control them. Social support systems and good marital relationships also serve as protective factors in parenting behavior (Cohen & Wills, 1985; Rutter, 1990). For example, Rutter and Quinton (1984) found that institution-reared women who had supportive spouses were more competent parents than those who had the same childhood experiences but lacked spousal support. It has been argued that supportive social networks may be sources of emotional and affective strength and of information that enhance feelings of competence in coping with stresses, including those concerned with parenting.

Parenting: A Mediator and Moderator of Family Stress and Resources

Parenting behavior has been conceived of as both mediating and moderating the direct effects of stress on the child. Thus, in most conceptually driven models in which the development of aggression and withdrawal are described (see Pepler & Rubin, 1991; Rubin & Asendorpf, 1993, for extensive reviews), variables such as stress and support are viewed as *distal* influences on child behavior. These distal variables are seen as influencing parental beliefs and behavior (Mills & Rubin, 1990), the more *proximal* influences on child outcomes. To this end, parental behavior has been considered a factor that mediates between distal ecological variables and children's adaptive and maladaptive behavior (Belsky, 1984).

Recent advances in statistical technology have allowed the examination of the mediational role of parental beliefs and behavior. For example, a typical procedure in hierarchical regression analysis is to enter first into the equation a given parenting variable (or variables), and then subsequently to enter the conceptually distal, ecological "influences" in the prediction of some child outcome. The significantly reduced power of ecological variables in predicting child behavior after partialling out parenting variables allows the implication that parenting behavior plays a mediational role. Path analysis and more complicated structural equation modeling analysis also have been applied to obtain a more complete description of the relations among family stresses, resources, parenting, and child behavior (e.g., R. D. Conger et al., 1992, 1993). For example, Lempers et al. (1989) found that economic hardship had a significant and negative direct effect on parental nurturance and a positive direct effect on inconsistent discipline. In turn, parental nurturance had a negative direct effect on children's depression and loneliness; inconsistent parenting had a positive direct effect on children's depression/loneliness and delinquency. Finally, economic stress had a positive indirect effect on depression–loneliness and delinquency through the mediation of parenting practices. R. D. Conger et al. (1992, 1993) examined the relations among economic stress, parental depression, marital conflict, parenting, and adolescent adjustment and maladjustment. Economic stress had a *positive* direct effect on parental depression; in turn, depression had a *negative* direct effect on parental nurturance and involvement. Finally, parental nurturance and involvement were found to contribute *positively* to the prediction of adolescent adjustment and *negatively* to adolescent maladjustment problems (antisocial behavior and depression).

Parents can also *moderate*, or buffer, their children from stressful life circumstances. The notion of moderation derives from findings that not all children who are exposed to stress or risk factors exhibit problems associated with abnormal development; some *protective* factors attenuate or "buffer" the negative effects of the risk factors. Simply put, "good parenting" serves the function of protecting the child from the negative influences associated with family stress (Masten, Morison, Pellegrini, & Tellegen, 1990; Rutter, 1979, 1990). For example, Rutter (1979) reported that children from high-risk environments in which there was relatively high marital discord, and yet who received warmth and nurturance from at least one parent, were less likely to exhibit conduct disorder than children who did not have such a qualitively warm and nurturant parent–child relationship. Similarly, Masten et al. (1990) found that children who experienced many stressful life events, but who had family support and nurturance, tended to be less aggressive and disruptive and less disengaged in social situations than those who experienced stress and did not have supportive parents.

FUTURE DIRECTIONS

In this chapter we have attempted to describe the family as a complex system that is influenced, not only by its constituent members, but also by external, socioecological forces. Interactions between family members are bidirectional and mutually influential (Minuchin, 1985; Sameroff, 1983). This conceptualization of the family *as a transactive system* represents an evocative starting point for future studies of the development of aggression and social withdrawal in childhood.

What we know about the *parents* of aggressive and withdrawn children fails to capture some of the very simplest tenets of a transactional model of family systems. For example, it is safe to conclude that virtually nothing is known about *paternal* contributions to problems of psychological undercontrol and overcontrol in children. And, although we indicated an association to exist between the quality of the parent–infant/child attachment relationship and the later expression of competent and incompetent social behavior in childhood, the *relative* contributions of the quality of father–son versus father–daughter attachment relationships and mother–son versus mother–daughter attachment relationships to the prediction of internalizing and externalizing forms of behavior problems in boys and girls is unknown. Also unknown are the relative contributions of paternal versus maternal beliefs and parenting behaviors to the prediction of internalizing and externalizing forms of behavior problems in boys and girls. In short, a plethora of questions remain to be addressed vis-à-vis the contributions of father–son/daughter and mother–son/daughter relationships and interactive patterns to the etiology of behavioral maladjustment in children.

Another relative unknown is the degree to which parents can influence the development, maintenance, and amelioration of child behavior problems at different points in the span of childhood. Are parents better able to influence child behavior during the early rather than mid-to-late years of childhood? Parents believe they are more influential in contributing to social developmental outcomes in early than in late childhood (e.g., Mills & Rubin, 1992). Moreover, with increasing child age, parents increasingly attribute child maladjustment to internal, dispositional characteristics of the child (Mills & Rubin, 1993a). These data hint at the possibility that parents think about and interact with their children in different ways at different points in childhood (see also Rubin et al., in press). A catalogue of beliefs and behaviors, within and across situations (e.g., at home or in public; free play or during structured activities), for parents of socially competent, aggressive and withdrawn children during the early, middle, and later years of childhood would be invaluable. This "mapping" of within and across group, cross-age parental characteristics should be on the agendum of those interested in the developmental course of behavioral maladaption and the intervention and prevention thereof.

We have described the results of many studies, almost all of which were completed in North America and Western Europe. The fact is, we do not know whether the characteristics of the parents of competent, aggressive, and withdrawn children vary from culture to culture or whether the etiologies of behavioral disorders are identical from one culture to another. In fact, we do not even know whether behaviors viewed as abnormal in Western cultures are similarly evaluated in other cultures! The importance of this latter issue is illustrated by a recent study by Chen, Rubin, and Sun (1992). In this study, aggression, but not withdrawal, was evaluated negatively by peers and teachers in a sample of elementary school-age children residing in Shanghai, China. Further, parents of aggressive Chinese children were found to lack warmth and to be authoritarian, just as in Western samples; but, parents of withdrawn children were not different behaviorally from parents of socially competent children (Chen & Rubin, 1993). This study, and others like it, raise a large question mark vis-à-vis the universality and generalizabilty of the findings we have reported herein. We would do well to be aware that cultural values play an enormous role in determining the "meanings" of behavioral adaptation and normalcy, and within cultures parental beliefs and behaviors are likely to be associated with child "outcomes" in meaningful ways. We face the task of determining the meanings of normalcy and maladaptation in the the context of culture.

We know much more about the parents of aggressive children than about the parents of children who are socially withdrawn. Recently, researchers have reported that there are many different forms of social solitude, each of which carries different psychological meanings (e.g., Coplan, Rubin, Fox, Calkins, & Stewart, 1994; Rubin & Mills, 1988). Some forms of solitude reflect inner feelings of social wariness and anxiety; other forms reflect preferential interest in objects rather than people; still others seem to reflect immaturity. In the present review, we have focused on children who are socially withdrawn because of their social wariness and anxiety. However, the research reviewed has rarely, if ever, distinguished the different meanings of solitude. There is a wealth of opportunity to discover the characteristics of the parents of withdrawn children. It may well be, for example, that parents of socially anxious, wary, withdrawn children have very different types of relationships with, beliefs about, and interactions with their children than parents of children who are not fearful but who choose to play with objects rather than with peers.

In summary, there are many questions remaining to be addressed in future studies of parents of aggressive and socially withdrawn children. We have provided above some initial "leads" concerning where we think the immediate research "action" may be.

CONCLUSIONS

It is not easy being a parent. In this chapter, we have attempted to demonstrate that it is at least equally difficult to be a child of an insensitive, unresponsive parent. Psychologically undercontrolled (aggression) and overcontrolled (social withdrawal) behavior problems in childhood derive from a complex mix of ecological factors, child characteristics, parent–child relationships, and parental beliefs and behaviors. In our concluding commentary, we attempt to put the pieces of the developmental puzzle together by suggesting two conceptually based pathways that may serve as models for the future study of the relations between parent–child relationships, parenting, and the development of aggression and withdrawal in childhood.

A Developmental Pathway to Aggression in Childhood

We begin by positing that babies who are viewed by their parents as difficult and overactive *and* who are born into less than desirable situations, may be at risk for the receipt of less than optimal care. Temperamentally difficult infants do tend to have mothers who are more aggressive, less nurturant, more anxious, and less responsive than mothers of nondifficult babies (Egeland & Farber, 1984; Spieker & Booth, 1988). Ecological conditions may be critical mediating factors; for example, Crockenberg (1981) reported that mothers of temperamentally difficult babies who have social and financial support are less negative in their interactions with their infants than high-risk mothers. Thus, for some families, the *interaction* between infant dispositional characteristics and stressful setting conditions may promote parental socialization practices that produce qualitatively poor early parent–child relationships that can be characterized as *insecure*, and perhaps hostile, in nature (Engfer, 1986).

As we noted earlier, an insecure attachment relationship has been thought to conjur up, in children, an internal working model of a comfortless and unpredictable social universe. These cognitive representations may lead some insecurely attached children to behave in the peer group "by ... doing battle with it" (Bowlby, 1973, p. 208). Indeed, as described earlier, there is a group of babies who, having established insecure attachment relationships with their primary caregivers by 12 or 18 months, direct hostility, anger, and aggression to their peers during the preschool years (Sroufe, 1983).

And, once expressed in a relatively consistent manner, aggression, from very early in childhood, is an unforgiving and highly salient, determining cause of peer rejection (Coie et al., 1990). Thus, it follows logically (and, indeed, empirically) that children who are rejected by their peers because of their proactive hostility may soon become precluded from the very sorts of activities that supposedly aid in the development of social skills—peer interaction, negotiation, and discussion. Furthermore, aggressive children are unlikely to trust their peers; it has been shown, for example, that aggressive children believe that negative social experiences are usually caused intentionally by others (Dodge & Frame, 1982). This mistrust and misattribution to others of hostile intention suggests that the aggressive child's peer relationships can be characterized as hostile and "insecure."

Given the salience of externalizing behaviors, it is not surprising that children's peers and their teachers tend to agree about whom it is that can be characterized as hostile and aggressive (e.g., Hymel et al., 1990; Ledingham et al., 1982). Moreover, given that aggression is highly disruptive when produced on school grounds and at school time, it is not surprising that teachers often request meetings with the parents of aggressive perpetrators. These school-based external appraisals are assuredly discomforting to parents, especially to those parents who have not enjoyed a secure and pleasant relationship with their child or to those experiencing a good deal of stress. One may posit at least two possible outcomes from such school-based teacher–parent "confrontations": (1) Parents may attribute their child's maladaptive behavior to dispositional or biological factors, thereby alleviating themselves of the responsibility of having to deal with aggressive displays. This type of attributional bias may lead to parental feelings of helplessness in the face of child aggression, and thus, predict a permissive or laissez-faire response to aggressive behavior. (2) Parents may attribute their child's behaviors to external causes and utilize overly harsh, power-assertive techniques in response to their children's maladaptive behavior. Both the neglect of aggression and the harsh treatment of it, especially in an environment lacking warmth, are likely to create even more problems for child, parents, and for their relationships (Forgatch, 1991; Patterson, 1979).

In summary, social incompetence of an *externalizing* nature may be the product of "difficult" temperament (Bates et al., 1991), of insecure parent–child relationships (Sroufe, 1983), of authoritarian *or* laissez-faire parenting (Baumrind, 1967), of family stress (Brunk & Henggeler, 1984), and most likely of the joint interactions between "all of the above." It is extremely important to note, however, that despite beginning this first pathway with a description of temperamentally "difficult" infants, many such children do not develop insecure attachment relationships and do not behave in an abnormally aggressive fashion during the preschool and elementary school years. Indeed, in most studies of predictive relations between infant "difficult" temperament and the subsequent development of attachment relationships, no clear predictive picture emerges (e.g., Bates et al., 1991). Thus, it may be posited that skilled parenting, under conditions of limited stress and optimal support, can buffer the effects of potentially "negative" biology. Basically, this is the classic argument of "goodness of fit" between parental characteristics and infant dispositional characteristics offered originally by Thomas and Chess (1977).

A Developmental Pathway to Social Withdrawal in Childhood

This pathway begins with newborns who may be biologically predisposed to have a low threshold for arousal when confronted with social (or nonsocial) stimulation and novelty. Studies of temperamental inhibition show that, under conditions of novelty or uncertainty, some babies demonstrate physical and physiological changes suggesting that they are "hyperarousable" (e.g., Fox & Calkins, 1993; Kagan, Reznick, & Snidman, 1987; Miyake, Chen, & Campos, 1985)—a characteristic that may make them extremely difficult for their parents to soothe and comfort. Indeed, some parents find infantile hyperarousability aversive (Kagan, Reznick, Clarke, Snidman, & Garcia Coll, 1984). Consequently, under some circumstances, parents may react to easily aroused and wary babies with hostility, insensitivity, lack of affection, nonresponsivity, and/or neglect. Each of these parental variables also predicts the development of insecure parent–infant attachment relationships and they can be significantly accounted for by environmental and personal stressors. Thus, as with the first pathway, an interplay of endogenous, socialization, and early relationships factors, as they co-exist under the "umbrella" of negative setting conditions, will lead to a sense of felt insecurity. In this way, the internal working models of insecurely attached, temperamentally inhibited children may lead them to "shrink from" rather than "do battle with" (Bowlby, 1973, p. 208) their social milieu.

Children who are socially inhibited, and who, in fact "shrink anxiously away" from their peers, preclude themselves from the positive outcomes associated with social exploration and peer play. Thus, one can predict a developmental sequence in which inhibited, fearful, insecure children withdraw from their social world of peers, fail to develop those skills derived from peer interaction, and, because of this, become increasingly anxious and isolated from the peer group. With age, social reticence or withdrawal becomes increasingly salient to the peer group (Younger & Boyko, 1989; Younger, Schwartzman, & Ledingham, 1986). This deviation from age-appropriate social norms is associated with the establishment of negative peer reputations. Thus, by the mid-to-late years of childhood, social withdrawal and anxiety are as strongly correlated with peer rejection and unpopularity as is aggression (French, 1988; Rubin et al., 1993; Rubin, Hymel, LeMare, & Rowden, 1989).

Unlike their aggressive counterparts, however, anxiously withdrawn children rarely get into trouble by "acting out" at home or school. Given their reticence to explore their environments, these children may demonstrate difficulties in getting social "jobs" done or social problems ameliorated. Sensing the child's difficulties and perceived helplessness, parents may try to aid them very directly by either manipulating their child's social behaviors in a power assertive, highly directive fashion (e.g., telling the child how to act or what to do) or by actually intervening and carrying out the child's social interchanges by themselves (e.g., directly intervening during object disputes). Such over-controlling, overinvolved socialization strategies have long been associated with social withdrawal in childhood (e.g., Brunk & Henggeler, 1984; Hetherington & Martin, 1986). Parental overdirective-ness is likely to maintain rather than to ameliorate postulated problems associated with social inhibition. Overdirectiveness will not help the child deal firsthand with social interchanges and dilemmas; it probably prevents the development of a belief system of social self-efficacy; and it likely perpetuates feelings of insecurity within and outside of the family.

In summary, social incompetence of an overcontrolled nature may be the product of "inhibited" temperament, of insecure parent–child relationships, of overdirective, overprotective parenting, of family stress, and most likely of the joint interactions between "all of the above." A fearful, wary inhibited temperament may be "deflected" to a pathway toward the development of social competence by responsive and sensitive caregiving and by a relatively stress-free environment. Similarly, inhibited temperament is unnecessary for the development of an incompetent behavioral style of an internalizing nature. Parental overcontrol and overinvolvement, especially when accompanied by familial stress and a lack of social support, are hypothesized to deflect the temperamentally easy-going infant to a pathway of internalizing difficulties.

The pathways just described represent useful heuristics for the study of the etiology of aggression and social withdrawal in childhood. They are also suggestive of the indirect and direct ways that parents may contribute to the development and maintenance of these phenomena. However, they should certainly not be taken as the only routes to the development of over- and undercontrolled psychological disorders in childhood. Thus, we welcome the research community's support in providing alternative perspectives, as well as empirically derived information, concerning the relations between parent–child relationships, parenting cognitions and behaviors, and the ontogeny of aggression and social withdrawal in childhood.

REFERENCES

Achenbach, T. M., & Edelbrock, C. (1981). Behavioral problems and competencies reported by parents of normal and disturbed children aged four through sixteen. *Monographs of the Society for Research in Child Development, 46* (Serial No. 188), 1–82.

Ainsworth, M.D.S. (1973). The development of infant–mother attachment. In B. Caldwell & H. Ricciuti (Eds.), *Review of child development research* (Vol. 3, pp. 1–94). Chicago: University of Chicago Press.

Ainsworth, M., Blehar, M., Waters, E., & Wall, S. (1978). *Patterns of attachment*. Hilldale, NJ: Lawrence Erlbaum Associates.

Arend, R., Gove, F., & Sroufe, L. A. (1979). Continuity of individual adaptation from infancy to kindergarten: A predictive study of ego-resiliency and curiosity in preschoolers. *Child Development, 50,* 950–959.

Asendorpf, J. B. (1993). Beyond temperament: A two-factorial coping model of the development of inhibition during childhood. In K. H. Rubin & J. B. Asendorpf (Eds.), *Social withdrawal, inhibition and shyness in childhood* (pp. 265–289). Hillsdale, NJ: Lawrence Erlbaum Associates.

Bacon, M. K., & Ashmore, R. D. (1985). How mothers and fathers categorize descriptions of social behavior attributed to daughters and sons. *Social Cognition, 3,* 193–217.

Bacon, M. K., & Ashmore, R. D. (1986). A consideration of the activities of parents and their role in the socialization process. In R. D. Ashmore & D. M. Brodzinsky (Eds.), *Thinking about the family: Views of parents and children* (pp. 3–34). Hillsdale, NJ: Lawrence Erlbaum Associates.

Bandura, A. (1977). *Social learning theory*. Englewood Cliffs, NJ: Prentice-Hall.

Bates, J. E., Bayles, K., Bennett, D. S., Ridge, B., & Brown, M. M. (1991). Origins of externalizing behavior problems at eight years of age. In D. J. Pepler & K. H. Rubin (Eds.), *The development and treatment of childhood aggression* (pp. 93–120). Hillsdale, NJ: Lawrence Erlbaum Associates.

Baumrind, D. (1967). Child care practices anteceding three patterns of preschool behavior. *Genetic Psychology Monographs, 76,* 43–88.

Baumrind, D. (1971). Current patterns of parental authority. *Developmental Psychology Monographs, 4.*

Baumrind, D. (1991). To nurture nature. *Behavioral and Brain Sciences, 14,* 386.

Bell, R. Q., & Chapman, M. (1986). Child effects in studies using experimental or brief longitudinal approaches to socialization. *Developmental Psychology, 22,* 595–603.

Belsky, J. (1984). The determinants of parenting: A process model. *Child Development, 55,* 83–96.

Billings, A. G., & Moos, R. H. (1985). Children of parents with unipolar depression: A controlled 1 year follow-up. *Journal of Abnormal Child Psychology, 14,* 149–166.

Block, J. H., Block, J., & Morrison, A. (1981). Parental agreement–disagreement on child-personality correlates in children. *Child Development, 52,* 965–974.

Booth, C. L., Rose-Krasnor, L., & Rubin, K. H. (1991). Relating preschoolers' social competence and their mothers' parenting behaviors to early attachment security and high risk status. *Journal of Social and Personal Relationships, 8,* 363–382.

Bowlby, J. (1969). *Attachment and loss: Vol. 1. Attachment.* New York: Basic Books.

Bowlby, J. (1980). *Attahment and loss: Vol. 2. Loss.* New York: Basic Books.

Bowlby, J. (1973). *Attachment and loss: Separation, anxiety, and anger.* New York: Basic Books.

Brunk, M. A., & Henggeler, S. W. (1984). Child influences on adult controls: An experimental investigation. *Developmental Psychology, 20,* 1074–1081.

Bugental, D. B. (1992). Affective and cognitive processes within threat-oriented family systems. In I. E. Sigel, A. V. McGillicuddy-DeLisi, & J. J. Goodnow (Eds.), *Parental belief systems: The psychological consequences for children* (pp. 219–248). Hillsdale, NJ: Lawrence Erlbaum Associates.

Bugental, D. B., & Cortez, V. (1988). Physiological reactivity to responsive and unresponsive children—as modified by perceived control. *Child Development, 59,* 686–693.

Bugental, D. B., & Shennun, W. A. (1984). "Difficult" children as elicitors and targets of adult communication patterns: An attributional-behavioral transactional analysis. *Monographs of the Society for Research in Child Development, 49* (1, Serial No. 205).

Byrne, R. (1988). *1,911 best things anybody ever said.* New York: Ballantine.

Case, D. (1991). *The mind's staircase.* Hillsdale, NJ: Lawrence Erlbaum Associates.

Chen, X., & Rubin, K. H. (July, 1993). *Family capital and psychological resources, parental behavior, and children's social competence.* Paper presented at the 12th biennial meetings of the International Society for the Study of Behavioral Development, Recife, Brazil.

Chen, X., Rubin, K. H., & Sun, Y. (1992). Social reputation and peer relationships in Chinese and Canadian children: A cross-cultural study. *Child Development, 63,* 1336–1343.

Cohen, J. S. (1989). *Maternal involvement in children's peer relationships during middle childhood.* Unpublished doctoral dissertation, University of Waterloo, Waterloo, Ontario, Canada.

Cohen, S., & Wills, T. A. (1985). Stress, social support, and the buffering hypothesis. *Psychological Bulletin, 98,* 310–357.

Coie, J. D., & Kupersmidt, J. B. (1983). A behavioral analysis of emerging social status in boys' groups. *Child Development, 54,* 1400–1416.

Coie, J. D., Dodge, K. A., & Kupersmidt, J. B. (1990). Peer group behavior and social status. In S. R. Asher & J. D. Coie (Eds.), *Peer rejection in childhood* (pp. 17–59). New York: Cambridge University Press.

Compas, B. E. (1987). Coping with stress during childhood and adolescence. *Psychological Bulletin, 101,* 393–403.

Conger, J. C., & Keane, S. P. (1981). Social skills in the treatment of isolated or withdrawn children. *Psychological Bulletin, 90,* 478–495.

Conger, R. D., Conger, K. J., Elder, G. H. Jr., Lorenz, F., Simons, R., & Whitbeck, L. (1992). A family process model of economic hardship and adjustment of early adolescent boys. *Child Development, 63*, 526–541.

Conger, R. D., Conger, K. J., Elder, G. H. Jr., Lorenz, F., Simons, R., & Whitbeck, L. (1993). Family economic stress and adjustment of early adolescent girls. *Developmental Psychology, 29*, 206–219.

Conger, R. D., McCarty, J. A., Young, R. K., Lahey, B. B. & Kropp, J. P. (1984). Perception of child, child-rearing values and emotional distress as mediating links between environmental stressors and observed maternal behavior. *Child Development, 55*, 2234–2247.

Coopersmith, S. (1967). *The antecedents of self-esteem*. San Francisco: Freeman.

Coplan, R. J., Rubin, K. H., Fox, N. A., Calkins, S. D., & Stewart, S. L. (1994). Being alone, playing alone, and acting alone: Distinguishing among reticence,and passive- and active-solitude in young children. *Child Development, 65*, 129–137.

Cox, M. J., Owen, M., Lewis, J. M., & Henderson, V. K. (1989). Marriage, adult adjustment and early parenting. *Child Development, 60*, 1015–1024.

Crnic, K. A., Greenberg, M. T., Ragozen, A. S., Robinson, M. M., & Basham, R. B. (1983). Social interaction and developmental competence of preterm and full term infants during the first year of life. *Child Development, 54*, 1199–1210.

Crockenberg, S. B. (1981). Infant irritability, mother responsiveness, and social support influences on the security of mother–infant attachment. *Child Development, 52*, 857–865.

Dadds, M. R. & Powell, M. B. (1991). The relationship of interparental conflict and global marital adjustment to aggression, anxiety, maturity in aggressive and nonclinic children. *Journal of Abnormal Child Development, 19*, 553–567.

Dishion, T. J. (1990). The family ecology of boys' peer relations in middle childhood. *Child Development, 61*, 874–892.

Dix, T. H., & Grusec, J. E. (1985). Parent attribution processes in the socialization of children. In I. E. Sigel (Ed.), *Parental belief systems: The psychological consequences for children* (pp. 201–233). Hillsdale, NJ: Lawrence Erlbaum Associates.

Dix, T. H., Ruble, D. N., & Zambarano, R. J. (1989). Mothers' implicit theories of discipline: Child effects and the attribution process. *Child Development, 60*, 1373–1391

Dix, T. H., Ruble, D., Grusec, J. E., & Nixon, S. (1986). Social cognition in parents: Inferential and affective reactions to children of three age levels. *Child Development, 57*, 879–894.

Dodge, K. A. (1986). A social information processing model of social competence in children. In M. Permutter (Ed.) *Minnesota Symposia on Child Psychology: Vol. 18. Cognitive perspectives on children's social and behavioral development* (pp. 77–125). Hillsdale, NJ: Lawrence Erlbaum Associates.

Dodge, K. A., & Frame, C. L. (1982). Social cognitive biases and deficits in aggressive boys. *Child Development, 53*, 620–635.

Doise, W., & Mugny, G. (1981). *Le développement social de l'intelligence*. Paris: Inter Editions.

Dollard, J., Doob, L. W., Miller, N. E., Mowrer, O. H., & Sears, R. R. (1939). *Frustration and aggression*. New Haven, CT: Yale University Press.

Dooley, D., & Catalano, R. (1988). Recent research on the psychological effects of unemployment. *Journal of Social Issues, 44*, 1–12.

Downey, G., & Coyne, J. C. (1990). Children of depressed parents: An integrative review. *Psychological Bulletin, 108*, 50–76.

Egeland, B., & Farber, E. A. (1984). Infant–mother attachment: Factors related to its development and changes over time. *Child Development, 55*, 753–771.

Eisenberg, L. (1958). School phobia: A study in the communication of anxiety. *American Journal of Psychiatry, 114*, 712–718.

Elder, G. H. Jr. (1974). *Children of the Great Depression*. Chicago: University of Chicago Press.

Elder, G. H. Jr., Van Nguyen, T., & Caspi, A. (1985). Linking family hardship to children's lives. *Child Development, 56*, 361–375.

Elicker, J., Englund, M., & Sroufe, L. A. (1992). Predicting peer competence and peer relationships in childhood from early parent–child relationships. In R. Parke & G. Ladd (Eds.), *Family–peer relationships: Model of linkage* (pp. 77–106). Hillsdale, NJ: Lawrence Erlbaum Associates.

Emery, R. (1982). Interparental conflict and the children of discord and divorce. *Psychological Bulletin, 92*, 310–330.

Engfer, A. (1986). Antecedents of behavior problems in infancy. In G. A. Kohnstamm (Ed.), *Temperament discussed: Temperament and development in infancy and childhood* (pp. 155–180). Amsterdam: Stwets & Zeitlinger.

Erickson, M. F., Sroufe, L. A., & Egeland, B. (1985). The relationship between quality of attachment and behavior problems in preschool in a high risk sample. In I. Bretherton & E. Waters (Eds.), Growing points of attachment theory and research. *Monographs of the Society for Research in Child Development, 50* (1–2, Serial No. 209).

Eron, L. D., Huesmann, L. R., Dubow, E., Romanoff, R., & Yarmel, P. W. (1987). Aggression and its correlates over 22 years. In D. H. Crowell, I. M. Evans, & C. R. O'Donnell (Eds.), *Childhood aggression and violences* (pp. 249–262). New York: Plenum.

Eron, L. D., Huesmann, L. R., & Zelli, A. (1991). The role of parental variables in the learning of aggression. In D. J. Pepler & K. H. Rubin (Eds.), *The development and treatment of childhood aggression* (pp. 169–188). Hillsdale, NJ: Lawrence Erlbaum Associates.

Farrington, D. P. (1983). Randomized experiments on crime and justice. In M. Ronry & N. Morris (Eds.), *Crime and justice* (Vol. 4, pp. 257–308). Chicago: University of Chicago Press.

Farrington, D. P. (1991). Childhood aggression and adult violence: Early precursors and later life outcomes. In D. J. Pepler & K. H. Rubin (Eds.), *The development and treatment of childhood aggression* (pp. 5–29). Hillsdale, NJ: Lawrence Erlbaum Associates.

Forgatch, M. S. (1991). The clinical science vortex: A developing theory of anti-social behavior. In D. J. Pepler & K. H. Rubin (Eds.), *The development and treatment of childhood aggression* (pp. 2291–316). Hillsdale, NJ: Lawrence Erlbaum Associates.

Fox, N. & Calkins, S. (1993). Relations between temperament, attachment, and behavioral inhibition: Two possible pathways to extroversion and social withdrawal. In K. H. Rubin & J. Asendorpf (Eds.), *Social withdrawal, inhibition, and shyness in childhood* (pp. 81–100). Hillsdale, NJ: Lawrence Erlbaum Associates.

French, D. C. (1988). Heterogeneity of peer rejected boys: Aggressive and nonaggressive subtypes. *Child Development, 59,* 976–985.

Freud, S. (1973). *An outline of psychoanalysis.* London: Hogarth. (Original work published 1938)

Gelfand, D. M., & Teti, D. M. (1990). The effects of maternal depression on children. *Clinical Psychological Review, 10,* 329–353.

Goldberg, S., Lojkasek, M., Gartner, G. M., & Corter, C. (1989). Maternal responsiveness and social development in preterm infants. *New Directions for Child Development, 43,* 89–103.

Goodnow, J. J. (1988). Parents' ideas, actions, and feelings: Models and methods from developmental and social psychology. *Child Development, 59,* 286–320.

Goodnow, J. J., Knight, R., & Cashmore, J. (1985). Adult social cognition: Implications of parents' ideas for approaches to development. In M. Perlmutter (Ed.), *Cognitive perspectives and behavioral development: Vol. 18. The Minnesota symposia on child psychology* (pp. 287–329). Hillsdale, NJ: Lawrence Erlbaum Associates.

Green, K., Forehand, R., Beck, S., & Vosk, B. (1980). An assessment of the relationship among measures of children's social competence and children's academic achievement. *Child Development, 51,* 1149–1156.

Gurland, B., Yorkston, N., Frank, L., & Stone, A. (1967). *The structured and scaled interview to assess maladjustment.* Mimeographed booklet, Biometric Research, Department of Mental Hygiene, New York.

Hammen, C. (1988). Self-cognitions, stressful events and the prediction of depression in children of depressed mothers. *Journal of Abnormal Child Psychology, 16,* 347–360.

Hart, G. H., DeWolf, D. M., Wozniak, P., & Burts, D. C. (1992). Maternal and paternal disciplinary styles: Relations with preschoolers' playground behavioral orientations and peer status. *Child Development, 63,* 879–892.

Hartup, W. W. (1985). Relationships and their significance in cognitive development. In R. A. Hinde, A. Perret-Clermont, & J. Stevenson-Hinde (Eds.), *Social relationships and cognitive development* (pp. 66–82). Oxford, England: Clarendon.

Hetherington, E. M., & Martin, B. (1986). Family factors and psychopathology in children. In H. C. Quay & J. S. Werry (Eds.), *Psychopathological disorders of childhood* (3rd ed., pp. 332–390). New York: Wiley.

Hinde, R. A., Tamplin, A., & Barret, J. (1993). Social isolation in 4 year olds. *British Journal of Child Psychology, 11,* 211–236.

Hoffman, M. L. (1970). Moral development. In P. H. Mussen (Ed.), *Handbook of child psychology* (Vol. 2, pp. 211–236). New York: Wiley.

Huesmann, L. R., Eron, L. D., Lefkowitz, M. M., & Walder, L. O. (1984). Stability of aggression over time and generations. *Developmental Psychology, 20,* 1120–1134.

Hymel, S., Rubin, K. H., Rowden, L., & LeMare, L. (1990). A longitudinal study of sociometric status in middle and late childhood. *Child Development, 61,* 2004–2121.

Hymel, S., Woody, E., & Bowker, A. (1993). Social withdrawal in childhood: Considering the child's perspective. In K. H. Rubin & J. B. Asendorpf (Eds.), *Social withdrawal, inhibition and shyness in childhood* (pp. 237–262). Hillsdale, NJ: Lawrence Erlbaum Associates.

Jennings, K. D., Stagg, V., & Conners, R. E. (1991). Social networks & mothers interactions with their preschool children. *Child Development, 62,* 966–978.

Jouriles, E. N., Murphy, C. M., Farris, A. M., Smith, D. A., Richlers, J. E., & Waters, E. (1991). Marital adjustment, parental disagreements about child rearing and behavior problems in boys: Increasing the specificity of the marital assessment. *Child Development, 62,* 1424–2433.

Kagan, J. & Moss, H. A. (1962). *Birth to maturity: A study in psychological development.* New York: Wiley.

Kagan, J., Reznick, J. S., & Snidman, N. (1987). The physiology and psychology of behavioral inhibition in children. *Child Development, 58,* 1459–1473.

Kagan, J., Reznick, J. S., Clarke, C., Snidman, N., & Garcia Coll, C. (1984). Behavioral inhibition to the unfamiliar. *Child Development, 55,* 2212–2225.

Katz, R. C. (1971). Interactions between the facilitative and inhibitory effects of a punishing stimulus in the control of children's hitting behavior. *Child Development, 42,* 1433–1446.

Kochanska, G. (1991). Patterns of inhibition to the unfamiliar in children of normal and affectively ill mothers. *Child Development, 62,* 250–263.

Kochanska, G., Kuczinski, L., & Maguire (1989). Impact of diagnosed despression and self-reported mood on mothers' control strategies: A longitudinal study. *Journal of Child Psychology, 17,* 493–511.

Kochanska, G., & Radke-Yarrow, M. (1992). Inhibition in toddlerhood and the dynamics of the child's interaction with an unfamiliar peer at age five. *Child Development, 63,* 325–335.

Kuczynski, L., & Kochanska, G. (1990). Development of children's noncompliance strategies from toddlerhood to age five. *Developmental Psychology, 26,* 398–408.

Kupersmidt, J. B., & Coie, J. D. (1990). Preadolescent peer status, aggression, and school adjustment as predictors of externalizing problems in adolescence. *Child Development, 61,* 1350–1362.

LaFreniere, P., & Sroufe, L. A. (1985). Profiles of peer competence in the preschool: Interrelations between measures, influence of social ecology, and relation to attachment history. *Developmental Psychology, 17,* 289–299.

Lamborn, S. D., Mounts, N. S., Steinberg, L., & Dornbusch, S. M. (1991). Patterns of competence and adjustment among adolescents from authoritative, authoritarian, indulgent and neglectful families. *Child Development, 62,* 1049–1065.

Langlois, J. H. & Stephan, C. W. (1981). Beauty and the beast: The role of physical attraction in peer relationships and social behavior. In S. S. Brehm, S. M. Kassin, & S. X. Gibbans (Eds.), *Developmental social psychology: Theory and research* (pp. 152–168). New York: Oxford University Press.

Laosa, M., & Sigel, I. E. (1982). *Families as learning environments for children.* New York: Plenum.

Lefkowitz, M. M., Eron, L. D., Walder, L. O., & Huesmann, L. R. (1977). *Growing up to be violent: A longitudinal study of the development of aggression.* New York: Pergamon.

LeMare, L., & Rubin, K. H. (1987). Perspective-taking and peer interactions: Structural and developmental analyses. *Child Development, 58,* 306–315.

Lempers, J. D., Clark-Lempers, D., & Simons, R. L. (1989). Economic hardship, parenting and distress in adolescence. *Child Development, 60,* 25–39.

Levy, D. M. (1943). *Maternal overprotectiveness.* New York: Columbia University.

Lobitz, W. C. & Johnson, J. (1975). Normal versus deviant children: A multi-method comparison. *Journal of Abnormal Psychology, 3,* 353–374.

Loeb, R. C., Horst, L., & Horton, P. J. (1980). Family interaction patterns associated with self-esteem in preadolescent girls and boys. *Merrill-Palmer Quarterly, 26,* 205–217.

Lytton, H. (1990). Child and parent effects in boys' conduct disorder: A reinterpretation. *Developmental Psychology, 26,* 683–697.

Maccoby, E. E., & Martin, J. A. (1983). Socialization in the context of the family: Parent–child interaction. In E. M. Hetherington (Vol. Ed.) & P. H. Mussen (Series Ed.), *Handbook of child psychology: Vol. 4. Socialization, personality, and social development* (pp. 1–101). New York: Wiley.

Main, M., Kaplan, N., & Cassidy, J. (1985). Security in infancy, childhood, and adulthood: A move to the level of representation. In I. Bretherton, & E. Waters (Eds.), Growing points of attachment theory and research. *Monographs of the Society for Research in Child Development, 50,* (Serial No. 209) pp. 66–104.

Martin, B. (1975). Parent–child relations. In F. Horowitz (Ed.), *Review of child development research* (pp. 463–540). Chicago: University of Chicago Press.

Masten, A. S., Morison, P., Pelligrini, D., & Tellegen, A. (1990). Competence under stress: Risk and protective factors. In J. Rolf, A. S. Masten, D. Cicchetti, K. H. Nuechterlein, & S. Weintraub (Eds.), *Risk and protective factors in the development of psychopathology* (pp. 236–256). New York: Cambridge University Press.

Matas, L., Arend, R. A., & Sroufe, L. A. (1978). The continuity of adaptation in the second year: Relationship between quality of attachment and later competence. *Child Development, 49,* 547–556.

McFall, R. M. (1982). A review and reformulattion of the concept of social skills. *Behavioral Assessment, 4,* 1–33.

McGillicuddy-DeLisi, A. V. (1982). Parental beliefs about developmental processes. *Human Development, 25,* 192–200.

McKnew, D. H., Cytryn, L., Efron, A. M., Gershon, E. S., & Bunney, W. E. (1979). Offspring of parents with affective disorders. *British Journal of Psychiatry, 134,* 148–152.

McNally, S., Eisenberg, N., & Harris, J. D. (1991). Consistency and change in maternal child-rearing practices: A longitudinal study. *Child Development, 62,* 190–198.

Mead, G. (1934). *Mind, self and society.* Chicago: University of Chicago Press.

Miller, S. A. (1988). Parents' beliefs about children's cognitive development. *Child Development, 59,* 259–285.

Mills, R.S.L., & Rubin, K. H. (1990). Parental beliefs about problematic social behaviors in early childhood. *Child Development, 61,* 138–151.

Mills, R.S.L., & Rubin, K. H. (1992). A longitudinal study of maternal beliefs about children's social behavior. *Merrill-Palmer Quarterly, 38,* 494–512.

Mills, R.S.L., & Rubin, K. H. (1993a). Socialization factors in the development of social withdrawal. In K. H. Rubin & J. Asendorpf (Eds.), *Social withdrawal, inhibition and shyness in childhood* (pp. 117–148). Hillsdale, NJ: Lawrence Erlbaum Associates.

Mills, R.S.L., & Rubin, K. H. (1993b). Parental ideas as influences on children's social competence. In S. Duck (Ed.), *Learning about relationships* (pp. 98–117). Newbury Park, CA: Sage.

Minuchin, P. (1985). Families and individual development: Provocations from the field of family therapy. *Child Development, 56,* 289–302.

Miyake, K., Chen, C., & Campos, J. (1985). Infant temperament, mother's mode of interaction, and attachment in Japan: An interim report. In I. Bretherton & E. Waters (Eds.), Growing points of attachment theory and research. *Monographs of the Society for Research in Child Development, 50* (Serial No. 209), 276–297.

Morison, P., & Mastin, A. (1991). Peer reputation in middle childhood as a predictor of adaptation in adolescence: A seven year follow-up. *Child Development, 62,* 991–1007.

Moskowitz, D. S., Schwartzman, A. E., & Ledingham, J. E. (1985). Stability and change in aggression and withdrawal in middle childhood and early adolescence. *Journal of Abnormal Psychology, 94,* 30–41.

Obrist, P. A. (1982). Cardiac-behavioral interactions: A critical appraisal. In J. T. Cacioppo & R. E. Petty (Eds.), *Perspectives in cardiovascular psychophysiology* (pp. 265–291). New York: Guilford.

Olweus, D. (1979). Stability of aggressive reaction patterns in males: A review. *Psychological Bulletin, 86,* 852–875.

Olweus, D. (1980). Familial and temperamental determinants of aggressive behavior in adolescent boys: A causal analysis. *Developmental Psychology, 16,* 644–660.

Olweus, D. (1984). Stability in aggressive and withdrawn, inhibited behavior patterns. In R. M. Kaplan, V. J. Konecni, & R. W. Novaco (Eds.), *Aggression in children and youth* (pp. 104–136). The Hague: Nijhoff.

Olweus, D. (1993). Victimization by peers: Antecedents and long-term outcomes. In K. H. Rubin & J. B. Asendorpf (Eds.), *Social withdrawal, inhibition and shyness in childhood* (pp. 315–341). Hillsdale, NJ: Lawrence Erlbaum Associates.

Parke, R. D., & Slaby, R. G. (1983). The development of aggression. In P. H. Mussen (Series Ed.) & E. M. Hetherington (Vol. Ed.), *Handbook of child psychology: Vol. 4. Socialization and personality processes* (pp. 547–642). New York: Wiley.

Parker, G. (1983). *Parental overprotection: A risk factor in psychosocial development.* New York: Grune & Stratton.

Parkhurst, J. T., & Asher, S. R. (1992). Peer rejection in middle school: Subgroup differences in behavior, loneliness and interpersonal concerns. *Developmental Psychology, 28,* 231–241.

Pastor, D. L. (1981). The quality of mother–infant attachment and its relationship to toddler's initial sociability with peers. *Developmental Psychology, 17,* 323–335.

Patterson, G. (1982). *Coercive family process.* Eugene, OR: Castilia.

Patterson, G. R. (1979). A performance theory for coercive family interaction. In R. Cairns (Ed.), *The analysis of social interactions* (pp. 119–161). Hillsdale, NJ: Lawrence Erlbaum Associates.

Patterson, G. R. (1986). Maternal rejection: Determinant or product for deviant child behavior? In W. Hartup & Z. Rubin (Eds.), *Relationships and development* (pp. 73–94). Hillsdale, NJ: Lawrence Erlbaum Associates.

Patterson, G.R. (1983). Stress: A change agent for family process. In N. Garmezy & M. Rutter (Eds.), *Stress, coping, and development in children* (pp. 235–264). New York: McGraw-Hill.

Patterson, G. R. & Bank, L. (1989). Some amplifying mechanisms for pathologic process in families. In M. Gunnar & E. Thelen (Eds.), *Systems and development: The Minnesota symposia on child psychology* (Vol. 22, pp. 167–209). Hillsdale, NJ: Lawrence Erlbaum Associates.

Patterson, G. R., Capaldi, D., & Bank, L. (1991). An early starter model for predicting delinquency. In D. J. Pepler & K. H. Rubin (Eds.), *The development and treatment of childhood aggression* (pp. 139–168). Hillsdale, NJ: Lawrence Erlbaum Associates.

Patterson, G. R., Littman, R. A., & Bricker, W. (1967). Assertive behavior in children: A step toward a theory of aggression. *Monographs of the Society for Research in Child Development, 35* (No. 5).

Pepler, D., & Rubin, K. H. (1991). *The development and treatment of childhood aggression.* Hillsdale, NJ: Lawrence Erlbaum Associates.

Pepler, D., King, G., & Byrd, W. (1991). A social cognitively based social skills training program for aggressive children. In D. J. Pepler & K. H. Rubin (Eds.), *The development and treatment of childhood aggression* (pp. 361–379). Hillsdale, NJ: Lawrence Erlbaum Associates.

Piaget, J. (1926). *The language and thought of the child.* London: Routledge & Kegan Paul.

Plomin, R., & Daniels, D. (1986). Genetics and shyness. In W. H. Jones, J. M. Check, & S. R. Briggs (Eds.), *Shyness: Perspectives on research and treatment* (pp. 63–80). New York: Plenum.

Pulkkinen, L. (1982). Self control and continuity from childhood to late adolescence. In P. B. Baltes & O. G. Brim, Jr. (Eds.), *Life-span development and behavior* (Vol.4, pp. 63–105). New York: Academic Press.

Radke-Yarrow, M., & Zahn-Waxler, C. (1986). The role of familial factors in the development of prosocial behavior: Research findings and questions. In D. Olweus, J. Block, & M. Radke-Yarrow (Eds.), *Development of antisocial and prosocial behavior* (pp. 207–234). Orlando, FL: Academic Press.

Renken, B., Egeland, B., Marvinney, D., Sroufe, L. A., & Mangelsdorf, S. (1989). Early childhood antecedents of aggression and passive-withdrawal in early elementary school. *Journal of Personality, 57,* 257–281.

Rubin, K. H. (1982). Social and social-cognitive developmental characteristics of young, isolate, normal and sociable children. In K. H. Rubin & H. S. Ross (Eds.), *Peer relationships and social skills in childhood* (pp. 353–374). New York: Springer-Verlag.

Rubin, K. H. (1985). Socially withdrawn children: An –at risk" population? In B. H. Schneider, K. H. Rubin, & J. E. Ledingham (Eds.), *Peer relationships and social skills in childhood: Issues in assessment and training* (pp. 125–139). New York: Springer-Verlag.

Rubin, K. H. (1993). The Waterloo Longitudinal Project: Correlates and consequences of social withdrawal from childhood to adolescence. In K. H. Rubin & J. Asendorpf (Eds.), *Social withdrawal, inhibition and shyness in childhood* (pp. 291–314). Hillsdale, NJ: Lawrence Erlbaum Associates.

Rubin, K. H., & Asendorpf, J. (1993). *Social withdrawal, inhibition, and shyness in childhood.* Hillsdale, NJ: Lawrence Erlbaum Associates.

Rubin, K. H., Both, L., Zahn-Waxler, C., Cummings, M., & Wilkinson, M. (1991). The dyadic play behaviors of children of well and depressed mothers. *Development and Psychopathology, 3,* 243–251.

Rubin, K. H., Bream, L., & Rose-Krasnor, L. (1991). Social problem solving and aggression in childhood. In D. J. Pepler & K. H. Rubin (Eds.), *The development and treatment of childhood aggression* (pp. 219–248). Hillsdale, NJ: Lawrence Erlbaum Associates.

Rubin, K. H., Chen, X., & Hymel, S. (1993). The socio-emotional characteristics of extremely aggressive and extremely withdrawn children. *Merrill-Palmer Quarterly, 39,* 518–534.

Rubin, K. H., Hymel, S., & Mills, R.S.L. (1989). Sociability and social withdrawal in childhood: Stability and outcomes. *Journal of Personality, 57,* 237–255.

Rubin, K. H., Hymel, S., LeMare, L., & Rowden, L. (1989). Children experiencing social difficulties: Sociometric neglect reconsidered. *Canadian Journal of Behavioural Science, 21,* 94–111.

Rubin, K. H., & Krasnor, L. R. (1986). Social cognitive and social behavioral perspectives on problem-solving. In M. Perlmutter (Ed.), *Minnesota symposia on child psychology* (Vol. 18, pp. 1–68). Hillsdale, NJ: Lawrence Erlbaum Associates.

Rubin, K. H., & Mills, R.S.L. (1990). Maternal beliefs about adaptive and maladaptive social behaviors in normal, aggressive, and withdrawn preschoolers. *Journal of Abnormal Child Psychology, 18,* 419–435.

Rubin K. H., & Mills, R.S.L. (1992). Parent's thoughts about children's socially adaptive and maladaptive behaviors: Stability, change and individual differences. In I. Sigel, J. Goodnow, & A. McGillicuddy-deLisi (Eds.), *Parental belief systems* (pp. 41–68). Hillsdale, NJ: Lawrence Erlbaum Associates.

Rubin, K. H., & Rose-Krasnor, L. (1992). Interpersonal problem-solving and social competence in children. In V. B. van Hasselt & M. Hersen (Eds.), *Handbook of social development: A lifespan perspective* (pp. 283–323). New York: Plenum.

Rubin, K. H., Rose-Krasnor, L., Bigras, M., Mills, R.S.L., & Booth, C. (in press). Predicting parental behavior: The influences of setting conditions, psychosocial factors and parental beliefs. In R. Tessier, C. Bouchard, & G. M. Tarabulsy (Eds.), *Child and family: Contexts for development.* Laval University Press.

Rutter, M. (1979). Protective factors in children's responses to stress and disadvantage. In M. W. Kent & J. E. Rolf (Eds.), *Primary prevention of psychopathology: Vol. 3. Social competence in children* (pp. 49–74). Hanover, NH: University Press of New England.

Rutter, M. (1990). Psychosocial resilience and protective mechanisms. In J. Rolf, A. S. Masten, D. Cicchetti, K. H. Nuechterlein, & S. Weintraub (Eds.), *Risk and protective factors in the development of psychopathology* (pp. 181–214). New York: Cambridge University Press.

Rutter, M., & Quinton, E. (1984). Parental psychiatric disorder: Effects on children. *Psychological Medicine, 14,* 853–880.

Sameroff, A. J. (1983). Developmental systems: Contexts and evolution. In W. Kessen (Ed.), *Handbook of child psychology: Vol. 1. History, theory and methods* (pp. 238–294). New York: Wiley.

Sameroff, A. N., & Feil, L. A. (1985). Parental concepts of development. In I. Sigel (Ed.), *Parental belief system: The psychological consequences for children* (pp. 83–105). Hillsdale, NJ:Lawrence Erlbaum Associates.

Sears, R. R. (1961). Relation of early socialization experiences to aggression in middle childhood. *Journal of Abnormal and Social Psychology, 63,* 466–492.

Selman, R. L. (1985). The use of interpersonal negotiation strategies and communicative competences: A clinical-developmental exploration in a pair of troubled early adolescents. In R.A. Hinde, A. Perret-Clermont, & J. Stevenson-Hinde (Eds.), *Social relationships and cognitive development* (pp. 208–232). Oxford, England: Clarendon.

Sigel, I. E. (1982). The relationship between parental distancing strategies and the child's cognitive behavior. In L. M. Laosa & I. E. Sigel (Eds.), *Families as learning environments for children* (pp. 47–86). New York: Plenum.

Snyder, J. J. (1977). Reinforcement analysis of interaction in problem and non-problem families. *Journal of Abnormal Psychology, 86,* 528–535.

Spieker, S. J., & Booth, C. L. (1988). Maternal antecedents of attachment quality. In J. Belsky & T. Nezworski (Eds.), *Clinical implications of attachment* (pp. 95–135). Hillsdale, NJ: Lawrence Erlbaum Associates.

Sroufe, L. A. (1983). Infant–caregiver attachment and patterns of adaptation in preschool: Roots of maladaptation and competence. In M. Perlmutter (Ed.), *Minnesota symposia on child psychology* (Vol. 16, pp. 41–81). Hillsdale, NJ: Lawrence Erlbaum Associates.

Sroufe, L. A. (1988). The role of infant–caregiver attachment in development. In J. Belsky & T. Nezworski (Eds.), *Clinical implication of attachment* (pp. 18–38). Hillsdale, NJ: Lawrence Erlbaum Associates.

Sroufe, L. A., & Rutter, M. (1984). The domain of developmental psychopathology. *Child Development, 55,* 17–29.

Steinberg, L., Lamborn, S. D., Dornbusch, S. M., & Darling, N. (1992). Impact of parenting practices on adolescent achievement: Authoritative parenting, school involvement and encouragement to succeed. *Child Development, 63,* 1266–1281.

Thomas, A., & Chess, S. (1977). *Temperament and development.* New York: Brunner/Mazel.

Troy, M., & Sroufe, L. A. (1987). Victimization among preschoolers: Role of attachment relationship history. *Journal of the American Academy of Child and Adolescent Psychiatry, 26*, 166–172.

Vuchinich, S., Bank, L., & Patterson, G. R. (1992). Parenting, peers and the stability of antisocial behavior in preadolescent boys. *Developmental Psychology, 28*, 510–521.

Weiss, B., Dodge, K. A., Bates, J. E., & Pettit, G. S. (1992). Some consequences of early harsh discipline: Child aggression and maladaptive social information processing study. *Child Development, 63*, 1321–1335.

Welner, Z., Welner, A., McCrary, M. D., & Leonard, M. A. (1977). Psychopathology in children with depression: A controlled study. *Journal of Nervous and Mental Disease, 164*, 408–413.

Whiting, B. B., & Edwards, C. P. (1988). *Children of different worlds: The formation of social behavior.* Cambridge, MA: Harvard University Press.

Windle, M. (1992). A longitudinal study of stress buffering for adolescent problem behaviors. *Developmental Psychology, 28*, 522–530.

Yarrow, M. R., Waxler, C. Z., & Scott, P. M. (1971). Child effects on adult behavior. *Developmental Psychology, 5*, 300–311.

Younger, A. J., Boyko, K. A. (1989). Aggression and withdrawal as social schemas underlying children's peer perceptions. *Child Development, 58*, 1094–1100

Younger, A. J., Schwartzman, A. E., & Ledingham, J. E. (1986). Age-related differences in children's perceptions of social deviance: Changes in behavior or perspective? *Developmental Psychology, 22*, 531–542.

Zahn-Waxler, C., Mayfield, A., Radke-Yarrow, M., McKnew, D. H., Cytryn, L., & Davenport (1988). A follow-up investigation of offspring of parents with bipolar disorder. *American Journal of Psychiatry, 145*, 506–509.

12

Parenting Talented Children

David Henry Feldman
Tufts University
Jane Piirto
Ashland University

INTRODUCTION

Although few would sympathize with parents who find themselves trying to rear a child with exceptional intellectual talent, it is in fact one of the most daunting and often discouraging challenges that family life has to offer. It is not simply the fact that parenting children who are at the extremes of ability requires substantially greater resources of all sorts, although that is certainly the case. Contrary to conventional wisdom—which would have it that the more talented the children, the easier it should be to care for them—based on recent findings it appears that the reverse is actually the case (Albert, 1990 a,1990b; Bloom, 1981, 1985; Feldman, with Goldsmith, 1991; Howe, 1982; Radford, 1990; Sears, 1979). In addition, rearing children who have extraordinary abilities sometimes engenders negative responses from others in the community, ranging from mild ambivalence to downright hostility.

This chapter discusses some of the issues that confront parents who must try to meet the unique challenges associated with trying to develop the full potential of their talented children. Of course, *all* parents want to do the best to bring forth and nurture the abilities and interests of their children, but not all parents feel the burden of responsibility that comes from a realization that a child may have exceptional potential. This awareness alone makes the parenting situation quite unlike that which faces most typical parents. Of course, the old saying that, "all children are gifted" may be true, but those with outstanding talent demand special efforts from all the systems with which they come into contact—the family, the school, the society.

Parents must identify the specific nature of the child's talent and decide how to respond. In some instances, the talents may be multiple, compounding both the identification and the response problems. It may seem obvious that there is not one form of giftedness, but several, and these several kinds of giftedness may have different sorts of implications for parenting (Morelock & Feldman, 1991, 1993; Piirto, 1992, 1994). And yet, the field that investigates and tries to serve those with exceptional abilities has tended to focus its efforts on one kind of talent, namely the kind that equips a child to do well in a traditional school curriculum. Academic talent is most often identified by using standardized IQ tests or achievement tests.

In fact, the very term *gifted* has come, in the minds of some researchers and to the consternation of others, to be synonymous with having a high IQ (Gagné, 1985; Gardner, 1982, 1983; Piirto, 1994; Smutny & Eby, 1990; Sternberg, 1985; Tannenbaum, 1983, 1986). In recent years there has been increasing pressure to move toward a more diverse and inclusive notion of *talent*; it is fair to say that the field is currently in a state of transition (Feldman, 1992; Piirto, 1994). The shift from a focus on more general academic talent to an emphasis on multiple specific gifts is a major one that will affect theory, research, and practice with talented children (Feldman, 1992; Gardner, 1983; Treffinger, 1991). If so, there will be major shifts in definitions, policies, and practices aimed at meeting the needs of talented children. For parents, a shift in the underlying conceptualization of the field may well mean a rapidly changing environment within which decisions must be made.

It is beyond the scope of this chapter to provide a review of all of the known forms of talent and giftedness and their consequences for issues of parenting. At best we can provide an overview of the variety of the many forms that talents and gifts might take, and then try to suggest what these forms of talent and giftedness might mean for parents and for those who work with parents of talented children.

The chapter is divided into five main sections. The first deals with general family systems theory and its relationship to talent development. The second deals with extreme talent such as that manifested in prodigies and students of very high IQ, more than three standard deviations above the mean (a frequency of fewer than 5 students per 1,000) or students in the top 1 percent of achievers on the Scholastic Aptitude Test (SAT) and the American College Test (ACT). The third deals with the kinds of gifts and talents that have received the greatest amount of attention from the scholarly and applied fields during the past half century. These have been of two sorts: *general academic talent* beyond that of most peers, but not at the far extreme, and some *specific* kinds of talents. The fourth deals with underachievement as a phenomenon recognized by therapists and educators of academically talented students. The fifth deals with the influence of pressure toward achievement on talent development.

General academic talent means that the child has the ability to do unusually well in standard academic settings embracing traditional curricula and teaching methods. Academic talent of this sort is usually discovered through testing, although other means of identification such as teacher or parent observations, or peer or self-nomination, are occasionally used, particularly at younger ages. More specific talents (such as artistic, scientific, or leadership talent) tend to be discovered through children's activities, observations by parents and/or teachers, and performance in organized activities. Occasionally, special testing programs are aimed at the discovery of specific kinds of talent (e.g., the talent searches of Johns Hopkins University, Northwestern University, Duke University, and others, or such programs as the Westinghouse Talent Search in science).

There have been more efforts to respond to the needs of academically talented children than to any other form of talent, and so the available options from which parents may choose are both more numerous and better established within most public school systems than are options for the development of extreme academic talent (or very high IQ), or in more specific talent areas. This is not to suggest that resources available are likely to be sufficient, because even in the most active communities with the longest traditions of support for "gifted education," programs are rarely available for children at all age levels, and are especially rare for younger children (Alvino, 1985, 1989; Lewis, 1979; Passow, 1979; Tannenbaum, 1983). Most formal programs begin during the later elementary school years. By then, patterns of underachievement may have set in (Piirto, 1994; Roedell, 1989).

When we turn to the more specific kinds of talents, we will see that these talents are on the one hand, more numerous and, on the other hand, less systematically served than general academic talent. This means the challenges facing parents of children with powerful talents directed toward more specific domains (such as music, dance, sports, or computers) are at once more difficult to meet and less likely to be met through well-established channels of support, information, or guidance.

THE FAMILY SYSTEM AND THE DEVELOPMENT OF TALENT

There is a saying that talent seems to "run in families." Actors breed actors (the Fondas, the Redgraves, the Sheens); professors breed professors (Margaret Mead); race car drivers breed race car drivers (the Unsers, the Pettys); athletes breed athletes (the Ripkens, the Roses); artists breed artists (the Wyeths, the Renoirs); writers breed writers (the Cheevers, the Updikes); musicians breed musicians (the Graffmans, the Bachs) (Albert, 1990a, 1990b; Brophy & Goode, 1988; V. Goertzel & M. G. Goertzel, 1962; V. Goertzel, M. G. Goertzel, & T. Goertzel, 1978; Simonton, 1984, 1988, 1991). Family systems theory has been developed to explain this phenomenon of "like father, like son" (Fine & Carlson, 1992). In family systems theory, a child's talent is viewed as an adaptation of the child to the entire family's interactions. This includes parents, grandparents, siblings, and takes into account birth order, labeling, and gender (Jenkins-Friedman, 1992). The notion that there is something in the family's interactions that produces talented behaviors takes into account the environment within which a child is reared and that child's responses to the environment.

Simonton (1984) found that the age of the parents matters, and younger parents who are able to interest their children in their own passions seem to be better able to excite their children to follow in their footsteps. An example from novelist and essayist Susan Cheever's memoir *Home Before Dark* (1984, p. 107) illustrates how interest was developed in the children of a writer:

> Every Sunday after dinner, we each recited a poem for the rest of the family. It began with sonnets and short narrative verse, Shakespeare and Tennyson, but soon we were spending whole weekends in competitive feats of memory. My father memorized Dylan Thomas' "Fern Hill," my mother countered with Keats' "Ode to a Nightingale," I did "Barbara Fritchie," my father did "The Charge of the Light Brigade," and so forth. Ben, who was eight, stayed with shorter poems.

Age of parents also takes into account the high level of energy it takes to keep up with a talented child.

There are a number of factors that determine how parents will react to the presence of great talents in their children. The birth position of the child is one factor. Simonton (1984, 1988) noted that firstborns tend to reach eminence or to be considered geniuses more often than their younger siblings, but there is some evidence that laterborns whose births have been spaced several years apart have similar opportunities. Much seems to depend on parental will and energy to nurture that talent (Kulieke & Olszewski-Kubilius, 1989.

Family values may place particular importance on certain talents, such as music or mathematics, and provide traditions that create a context within which the responsibility to talent takes place. For these reasons, children with the same set of talents, manifesting themselves in the same ways, but reared in different families may provoke strikingly different responses to their talents depending on one or more of the factors just listed (Benbow, 1992; Feldman, 1992; Feldman, with Goldsmith, 1991; Morelock & Feldman, 1991).

There are a number of studies that converge on the idea that a responsive set of parents, and a family that values achievement (particularly in the target domain), are critical catalysts in cases of extreme potential (Bloom, 1981, 1985; Feldman, with Goldsmith, 1991; V. Goertzel & M. G. Goertzel, 1962; V. Goertzel et al., 1978; Goldsmith, 1987, 1990; Kulieke & Olszewski-Kubilius, 1989; Radford, 1990; VanTassel-Baska, 1989). This is not to say that children whose homes have been turbulent, fractionated, or even pathological have not sometimes attained eminence or remarkably high achievement, especially achievement in artistic domains (Albert, 1980; Piirto, 1992).

Many family systems operate on what has been called a dysfunctional level, and these interactions, too, have enhanced talent development. In fact, Van Tassel-Baska and Olszewski-Kubilius (1989, p. 8) noted that "some form of adversity or a seemingly inhibiting or detrimental factor which exists within the family structure or happens to the individual can and does somehow work in a beneficial, generative manner." Among such factors are cultural and economic disadvantage, physical deformity, rejection by parents or peers, tension in the family, and parental loss.

Simonton (1988) called the latter "the orphanhood effect." For many children, a parent's death is a provocation for achievement. The mother of Jane and Peter Fonda committed suicide, as did the father of Jane's husband, Ted Turner. So did the mother of the surrealistic painter Magritte. Edgar Allen Poe's mother died, and he and his sister were in the room with her body for several days. Terr (1990) speculated that this resident precipitated Poe's fascination with death and horror. The poet Robert Frost's father died when he was 11 years old. The writer William Styron's mother died when he was 13, and in his award-winning memoir, *Darkness Visible,* he attributed a depression at 60 to "incomplete mourning" (1990, p. 81). This "orphanhood effect" may also have affected Abraham Lincoln, who was an only child whose mother died young.

High achievement after childhood trauma is an area that is not fully explored. The psychoanalyst Miller (1981, 1990) postulated that adult achievement in creative domains takes place when there has been childhood trauma with warmth present, whereas childhood trauma without warmth present can produce destructive adult behavior. Albert (1980) called it "wobble," the presence in the families of creative people of tension and dissent. The implications for parents with talented children seem to be that troubles should be faced, dealt with, and that children should be encouraged to express themselves not only in therapy, but through metaphoric media such as the arts (Piirto, 1992).

There is some belief that eminence is achieved more readily by people who have had childhood adversity, but that general well-being and a supportive home environment in a safe economic environment is more conducive to more ordinary gifted individuals, such as those in the Terman study (Piirto, 1992; Van Tassel-Baska & Olszewski-Kubilius, 1989). The preponderance of the evidence, however, suggests that the more valued a particular form of talent tends to be within a family, and the greater the amount of support the talent is given, the greater the degree to which those talents will be expressed in significant achievement.

The family's lifestyle is a great influence on a child's and a teenager's talent development and school achievement. Nontraditional lifestyles do not seem to affect achievement as much as one would think. Rather, it is the closeness of the family and the degree to which the family considers itself a family that is important. A 12-year longitudinal study of nontraditional families by Weisner and Garnier (1992, p. 621) showed that academic achievement is not negatively affected when a child is in a one-parent family, a low-income family, or a family with "frequent changes in mates or in household composition" if one particular factor was present: If the family chose the lifestyle because it had an intelligible and clear meaning—for instance, a religious choice leading to home schooling— but if the nonconventional family emphasized achievement as important, the children did not experience a lowered achievement pattern.

Even though the parents may have been "highly experimental" in such arenas as diet or health care, they saw that their children had inoculations and medical and dental checkups. They thought it was important for their children to do well in school. Indeed, the researchers found that "some nonconventional lifestyles can protect children against possible difficulties in school," where others can put children at risk. The variable that was important was that the parents were committed to the lifestyle and to the importance of school achievement. One thinks of the "aging hippies," the "bohemian actors," and the "poor struggling artists in garrets" as being in this category. Although poor, or in unconventional living arrangements, their children are often high achievers who follow in their parents' footsteps, just as children from families with more conventional lifestyles.

As evidence that family systems have differential effects on genetically similar members, there is some confirmation that siblings reared within the same family often turn out to be remarkably different (e.g., the eminent beat poet Allen Ginsberg and his older brother, Eugene, who was a lawyer; both were sons of a mother who was a schizophrenic and a father who was a high school teacher and poet). Louis Ginsberg, their father, said of Allen's choice of career: "Is he a poet by nature or nurture? I think both" (Miles, 1989, p. 29). The writer Graham Greene was a middle child in a large and nurturing family, and his father was a headmaster. Greene viewed his world with such great sensitivity that he attempted suicide in boarding school during his teenage years; he had to go into psychoanalysis while his older brothers thrived and were school leaders (Sherry, 1989).

Piechowski's interpretation of Dabrowski's "overexcitability" theory may be in operation here; that is, the intensity with which each child perceives events may differ, and what may send one child into extreme reactions, may just roll off another child's back (Piechowski, 1979, 1989, 1991). In fact, the children's temperament and personality may be most important in the development of their talents, and even in the case of multitalented children, in the family's choice of which talent to develop. A passive, dreamy personality and temperament may lend itself to the quiet, endless reading that seems to have been evident in the childhoods of most adult writers; an aggressive, dominating personality and temperament may lend itself to the cutthroat world of childhood chess or athletics (Piirto, 1994).

It is relatively easy for children to do something their parents approve of and value, and for which they provide teachers, tutors, and materials. The biographical literature is rife with stories of people whose parents pointed them in the right direction and then who stood back and watched them develop. "My son the doctor" is often pointed to medicine by parental desire and will. In her study of world-class research neurologists, Sosniak (1985, cited in Bloom, 1985) found that even in college, when some of them thought they would change majors, their parents expressed disapproval and the neurologists stayed on the premed track. One said he thought his parents were not that involved in his choice of career until he threatened not to pursue medicine; then he found out how adamant they were about his career. This illustrates the strong influence of the family system on a child's interaction with the world.

Other traumas that tear apart the traditionally intact family system are divorce; illness; frequent moving; physical, verbal, and sexual abuse; and the like. Talented youth who become scientists, mathematicians, and classical musicians seem often to come from families that were more stable than the families of actors, writers, popular musicians, visual artists, and dancers, that is, people in the arts (Kulieke & Olszewski-Kubilius, 1989; Piirto, 1992, 1994). Perhaps the long schooling necessary for functioning as an adult scientist, mathematician, or musician is a result of the time a family continually spent striving together to develop the school-related career potential of a talented child.

The fact that many talented adults come from family situations that are less than ideal illustrates that even the most laissez-faire parenting (or absence thereof) has an impact on talent development. Two interesting phenomena are operant. One is the "stage mother" or "Little League father" situation. In this case the parent is obsessed, even to the point of destructive narcissism, with the development of the children's talent whether or not they want their talent developed. The other is the "I don't care what you do just so long as you're happy" situation. In this scenario, busy parents do what is necessary for safety and health, but little beyond that. Both situations can produce talented adults. Judy Garland is an example of the former; her mother was so obsessed with Judy's career as a child actress that she even permitted the use of amphetamines and tranquilizers so that Judy could work longer hours in the studio (Edwards, 1975). An example of the latter is the mother of the actor and comedian Steve Allen, who permitted him to move—alone—from Chicago to the southwest at the age of 16 in order to take a job as a radio announcer. Allen came from a theatrical family where hard drinking was part of the lifestyle.

Other parents move with their children to pursue the talent. The mother of the dancer Suzanne Farrell moved Suzanne and her two sisters from Cincinnati to New York City at the offer of an audition with Balanchine; they lived in one room while their mother worked as a private nurse (Farrell & Bentley, 1990). However, Farrell said her mother was not a "stage mother" because she always worked to support them, and never hovered in the practice room antechambers with the other mothers to gossip. The parents of Albert Einstein moved to Italy when he was a teenager, leaving him to board with a local family and attend the gymnasium by himself. He soon quit, went to join his family, and never graduated (Clark, 1971). Einstein's father, like Edward Teller's (Blumberg & Panos, 1990), saw his mathematical talent and provided him with a college student tutor. The concert pianist Gary Graffman's father was a violinist, and he frequently sat with Gary while he practiced his lessons (Graffman, 1981). Graffman gave a concert at Carnegie Hall during his early teenage years. The strong influence of family interests is especially operant in the pursuit of musical talent. According to Graffman (1981, p. 47):

Even though my father was dead set against turning me into a child performer, daily practicing came first: I practiced every morning from 7:20 to 8:20 before school (in addition to two or three hours afterward). Whether or not I wanted to do this was never a consideration. My parents brought me up in a loving, but strict, European manner. I was not consulted in such matters. One went to school, one ate what was set before one; one practiced. It was as simple as that.

Thus the families of talented children cope with the talent in remarkably different ways; some focus on it and some ignore it. On balance, though, those that focus on their children's talent development are more likely to see the child's talent fulfilled.

Baumrind (1971) indicated that there are three parenting styles: authoritarian, authoritative, and permissive. All three environments have produced talented adults, although the authoritarian style tends to produce resentment and stifling that forces talented students to sneak, hide, and sublimate the expression of their talent so that it takes place outside the home or surfaces later in life. For example, the social reformer Margaret Sanger was forced to leave home to gain the freedom to finish school; her mother had 18 pregnancies and died of cervical cancer at age 49. Margaret's alcoholic father wanted her to be his housekeeper. Gray (1979, p. 25) reported that: "she let their run-down house deteriorate even more. Realizing she could never get enough money to return to Claverack to graduate, she decided to leave Corning for good."

Another example is the actor Marlon Brando, who was sent to military school by parents who did not know what to do with his rebelliousness. He was asked to leave the school because of his behavior, and he came to New York City to live with his sisters who were studying the arts. He wanted to study acting, but his father disapproved. As Thomas (1973, p. 20) pointed out, "Marlon would not be dissuaded by his father's scorn." Although he had considered many careers, including the ministry, acting appealed to him. He began to study with Stella Adler at the New School for Social Research. The rest is history.

There is also some evidence that gender of the child and parent influence the development of various kinds of talent. Male writers, for example, seem to have had what Miller (1987, p. 114) called ineffectual fathers: "It would strike me years later how many male writers had fathers who had actually failed or whom the sons had perceived as failures." He noted that this was the case for Faulkner, Fitzgerald, Hemingway, Wolfe, Poe, Steinbeck, Melville, Whitman, Chekhov, Hawthorne, Strindberg, and Dostoevsky. The same may be true for female writers (Piirto & Battison, 1994). Mothers' attitudes toward mathematics have greatly influenced both their sons' and daughters' achievement. If mothers say, "Well, I wasn't any good at math either," daughters especially might view mathematics as not being a gender-appropriate field to pursue (Eccles & Harold, 1992). Highly academically talented students who participated in the talent searches conducted among seventh graders also had differential influence by fathers and mothers (Benbow, 1992; Kulieke & Olszewski-Kubilius, 1989; VanTassel-Baska, 1989). Academically talented youth who participated in the talent searches tend to have strong, highly educated fathers as well as mothers who are also highly educated, but who do not work full time outside the home. These are tendencies, however. Helson (1983) noted that creative female mathematicians were often only children whose fathers treated them like sons.

PARENTING CHILDREN WITH EXTREME TALENTS

The following types of extreme talents are discussed here: cases of extremely high IQ; cases of extreme talents in specific areas, with or without notable high IQs to go along with them; and genius or eminence, an outcome that has been extensively studied in relation to parenting.

Extremely high IQ has been a topic of study for nearly a century. It most notably began with Terman's massive *Genetic Studies of Genius* begun in the 1920s (Sears, 1979), and continues to the present day (Tomlinson-Keasey & Little, 1990). Studies of extreme talents in specific have been more recent and still more sporadic phenomena, falling into two categories: extreme talent in (usually) mathematical or verbal abilities such as shown by a very high score on the SAT s (e.g., Benbow, 1992; Benbow & Minor, 1990; Hunt, Lunneborg, & Lewis, 1975) or on the ACTs (Colangelo & Kerr, 1990).

One cognitive difference Colangelo and Kerr found in these extremely high scorers was that high mathematics scorers had superior short-term memory and high verbal scorers had superior long-term memory. High verbal scorers often use their verbal ability in fields that are less specific to their ability than do high mathematics scorers. For example, high verbal talent is necessary in academe, in business, in leadership and politics, in law, and in most high-level professions. In fact, high verbal talent never hurt anyone. On the other hand, the lack of high mathematical ability does not mean a person cannot reach eminence. High mathematical ability is much more specific to achievement in science and in mathematics (and possibly in invention).

A second area in which extreme talent has been examined have been the studies of child prodigies in various specific fields (e.g., Deakin, 1972; Feldman, with Goldsmith, 1991; Radford, 1990). Studies of genius and eminence go back at least to Sir Francis Galton (1869), and have been carried on in recent years by Albert (1983, 1990a, 1990b; Albert & Runco, 1986) and Simonton (1984, 1988, 1992), among others. Here too, family variables have often been found to play a significant role in determining the degree of expression of talent. Biographical studies have produced a substantial amount of information about family influence on the achievement of eminence (V. Goertzel & M. G. Goertzel, 1962; V. Goertzel et al., 1978).

It should also be noted that, with the exception of Simonton's work (1984, 1988, 1991) on historical movements and, to some extent, Bloom's (1985) on world-class performers, virtually all of the available information from observations of parenting, family structure, and the like is based on the study of individuals or relatively small groups of cases. This means that the database is quite small on the one hand, but on the other hand such studies often produce rich and extensive information about each situation. There have been few studies of extreme talent that have examined relations among parenting variables and outcomes in children. There have been still fewer studies that attempt to control or manipulate variables, thus limiting the generalizability of findings.

Because the topic of study is so specific to individuals, that is, how their talents were nurtured and developed, this limitation of the research does not look to be easily remedied. Longitudinal studies such as Terman's; Subotnik and Steiner's (1993) study of Westinghouse winners; Arnold's (1993) study of Illinois valedictorians (Subotnik & Arnold, 1993); the work by the Study of Mathematically Precocious Youth (SMPY; Benbow, 1992); or snapshot studies such as Harris' (1990) of the students at the Hollingworth experimental schools in New York City; and the follow-up studies of high-IQ students who attended the Hunter College Elementary School in New York City (Subotnik, Karp, & Morgan, 1989; Subotnik, Kasson, Summers, & Wasser, 1993) are imperfect but valuable ways of looking at high IQ and high achieving students. Most of the students in the Hunter and Hollingworth studies had very high IQs. The Hunter studies found that few, if any, of these students who had a special elementary education targeted for their abilities reached eminence, although most were professionals and most of the women had attained advanced degrees (PhD, MD, LD). A typical graduate reflected on the outcomes of his life: "The quality of my life? Economic comfort. Lovely apartment, nice car, beautiful son, house in the country, take a vacation. Successful in business. [Male, age 49]" (Subotnik et al., 1993, p. 88). These high-IQ students generally came from professional families, and they became professionals themselves. Comparison studies of the achievement of students from similar socioeconomic backgrounds who have lower IQs have not been done, and this is a concern of researchers (Baird, 1985).

Case studies are often the method of choice when an area of investigation is just beginning. This technique is better suited to exploring unknown psychological terrain; Freud's work on the unconscious, Piaget's studies of babies, and Darwin's observations of his son Doddy (Kessen, 1965) were all based on case study research. This should alert the reader to the fact that work in the area of very high potential, or giftedness, is still in its early phases, and that whatever patterns of parent behavior have been observed should be taken as provisional.

Those who have studied parenting in cases of extreme giftedness have found that there are many similarities between these situations and the situation of parenting children with handicaps (Albert & Runco, 1986; Bloom, 1982, 1985; Borland, 1989; Clark, 1992; Feldman, with Goldsmith, 1991;

Hall & Skinner, 1980; Tannenbaum, 1983; Vail, 1987). One difference between the two kinds of extreme situations is that impediments to functioning are quite naturally seen as a higher priority for support, and consequently the allocation of resources tends to be much more substantial, whereas, in all but a few countries, talents are typically seen as the responsibility of the individual children and their family. This makes the likelihood of successfully rearing talented children often as dependent on parents' abilities to generate adequate material resources as on their parenting skills. We consider three issues about parenting extremely talented children: recognizing extreme talents and gifts, responding to identified talents and gifts, and sustaining optimal conditions for the development of talents and gifts.

Recognizing Extreme Gifts and Talents

The first task that faces parents who may think they have a child of unusual potential is to try to identify what the nature and strength of that talent might be. For some talents this is a relatively straightforward matter, even during the first few years of life. For other talents and gifts, the signs may be more subtle, or not evident until after the child is much older.

For the 120 subjects in Bloom's (1985) study of world-class performers—mathematicians, research neurologists, concert pianists, sculptors, Olympic swimmers, and tennis champions—the talents that were to lead to such high levels of achievement before age 35 were evident before the age of 5 for some fields, not others. For the research neurologists, mathematicians, and to some extent the sculptors, there were few early signs of the children's extreme potential. However, the swimmers and tennis players as well as the pianists were identified as having a special inclination toward the particular field before the age of 5 (Bloom, 1981, 1985; Gustin, 1985; Sloan & Sosniak, 1985; Sosniak, 1985a, 1985b). The identified talent was not always exactly a match for the future field of excellence; for example, a child might have intense interest in all ball games before 5, but focus on tennis during the succeeding 5 years.

The 1985 research of Bloom, Sosniak, Gustin, and Sloan also revealed that few of the children, across fields, were thought to be child prodigies, that is, to have prodigious talents that leaped full blown into existence. The growth trajectory was more gradual, and tended to follow a pattern of expression that depended on the presence of attentive and active parental support, direction, and encouragement. It was also true that in all fields there was an early need to involve other people who could offer specialized instruction in the target field. In explicit contradiction to the oft-believed view that extreme talent will somehow express itself, Bloom and his coworkers found that sustained efforts to identify and nurture talents in their children was a distinguishing feature of the families in the study.

Parenting Children with Extreme Talent: General and Specific

Although the data are less plentiful, it has been found that the more extreme the talents of children, the more extreme will be the qualities and characteristics of their parents (Deakin, 1972; Feldman, with Goldsmith, 1991; V. Goertzel & M. G. Goertzel, 1962; V. Goertzel et al., 1978). For example, Feldman and Goldsmith in their study of child prodigies found that in each of the six families at least one of the parents essentially devoted their life to providing optimal support for a child's emerging talent. The families also tended to see themselves as different from other families, to isolate themselves from the rest of the community, and to create a kind of cocoonlike structure to nurture their child's early development (Feldman, 1993). These prospective findings tend to be confirmed by retrospective data on those who have achieved eminence in their lives and careers (V. Goertzel & M. G. Goertzel, 1962; V. Goertzel et al., 1978).

Parents who were highly opinionated, actively involved in causes or movements, and sometimes unstable were common in the families of those who were to become eminent. On the other hand, it appears that the families in Bloom's (1985) sample of world-class performers provided a more stable and tranquil context, albeit one highly focused on the particular domain to be mastered. The cocoonlike quality that Feldman found in the prodigy families seemed to be present as well in the Bloom sample, but with a somewhat different emotional characteristic. The families of the prodigies seemed more fortresslike, and the latter seemed open, but protective and focused on the task at hand.

In a longitudinal study of six male child prodigies in fields ranging from chess to music to science to writing, Feldman (Feldman, with Goldsmith, 1991) found that even among these very extreme cases it was not obvious for three of the children in what field they would become a prodigy before age 5. For one of the musicians and the two chess players in the sample, their talents were strikingly obvious, whereas for the writer, the scientist, and one child whose gifts were so diverse that it was impossible to guess in what direction he would go, the specific focus of talent was not apparent that early. These results tend to confirm Bloom's conclusion that identifying the specific field of talent expression is not essential for later excellence, although music and chess tend to show themselves earliest, often before age 5. What seems necessary is a commitment to identify talents early and systematically to develop those talents.

Both Bloom's and Feldman's research shows that early identification and valuing of talents tend to occur in homes where there is already a tradition of involvement in a relevant field. In other words, if a child with musical talent is born into a family that values and enjoys music and where music is an important part of family life, the chances are much better that this talent will be recognized and developed than in a family with different values.

There are few, if any, performers at the top of their fields in music or chess who began playing later than age 10, and beginning the process by age 3 or 4 confers a distinct advantage. Whether or not there is a "critical period" in the strict sense of the term (i.e., a period of time during which it is essential to be exposed to a particular kind of stimulation) is not known, but it is true that the later a talent for chess or music is discovered, the less likely it is to be fully expressed. If not discovered and responded to before age 10, the likelihood of full expression of potential is greatly reduced (Feldman, with Goldsmith, 1991).

In other fields (such as writing, art, mathematics, dance, and most sports), identifying a strong talent and responding to it can occur several years later. Most writers, artists, and mathematicians, for example, do not begin serious preparation until after age 12, although the interests, predispositions, and predictive behaviors are evident earlier (Piirto, 1994). For example, the mathematician and philosopher Bertrand Russell and the theoretical physicists Albert Einstein and Edward Teller all demonstrated their passion for mathematics and logical thought before they were 10. Russell (1967, p. 38) wrote:

> At the age of eleven, I began Euclid, with my brother as my tutor. This was one of the great events of my life, as dazzling as first love. I had not imagined that there was anything so delicious in the world. After I had learned the fifth proposition, my brother told me that it was generally considered difficult, but I had found no difficulty whatever. This was the first time it had dawned upon me that I might have some intelligence. From that moment until Whitehead and I finished *Principia Mathematica*, when I was thirty-eight, mathematics was my chief interest, and my chief source of happiness.

For the most part, however, students who pursue natural science and philosophical studies tend to begin later, often well into the teens (Feldman, with Goldsmith, 1991; Lehman, 1953).

If a child is a girl and girls are not encouraged to pursue particular fields, or if a child is laterborn and only firstborn children tend to be seen as especially talented, the chances of noticing a talent are certainly reduced. Or, if a family's history is focused on one domain, such as theater or medicine or music, but the child's talent happens to be in a different domain, again the chances are diminished that an extraordinary talent will be recognized (Feldman, with Goldsmith, 1991). As more is known about the relation between a child's natural areas of talent and a family's match or mismatch with those talents, it may be possible to equip parents to better recognize talent in areas other than those to which they are naturally predisposed. Once recognized and responded to, it then falls to parents to decide how to sustain the development of a talent that has emerged in their child.

When we shift our focus to the more general academic abilities, there are many studies of early identification of high IQ in children. This literature shows that it is difficult to determine the degree of general intellectual giftedness earlier than 3 years (Roedell, Jackson, & Robinson, 1980). Some recent studies have used experimental procedures during early infancy to predict IQs at later ages, but these procedures are not available to parents, and are in any case still in the early phases of development (Bornstein, 1989; Rose, 1989).

Sustaining the Development of Exceptional Talents in Young Children

It is now well-established that a talent, however extreme it may be, requires sustained, coordinated, and effective support from parents and others for a period of at least 10 years to have a chance of fulfilling its promise (Bloom, 1985; Feldman, with Goldsmith, 1991; Hayes, 1981; Piirto, 1994). Having great talent does not guarantee great achievement, nor is talent capable of expressing itself without substantial resources external to the child.

Therefore, the decision to try to develop even an extreme talent has profound implications for every member of the target child's family. It is unlikely that a family will have the resources to sustain more than one process at the same time (Bloom, 1985; Feldman, with Goldsmith, 1991; VanTassel-Baska & Olszewski-Kubilius, 1989). This means that siblings of the target child are likely to receive a great deal less, proportionally, of the family's resources, a reality often difficult to accept and live with (Rolfe, 1978). The need to focus or refocus resources makes it in some ways not surprising that there is rarely more than one prodigy in a family and that families historically have tended to concentrate on the firstborn (usually male) child when it comes to talent development (Feldman, with Goldsmith, 1986; Goldsmith, 1990; Radford, 1990). There is also a folk wisdom (however objectionable within contemporary contexts) to withhold support and assistance from talented girls. In most cultures it is less likely that a daughter will be able to fulfill her talent because of lack of opportunity, prejudice, and established networks and institutions, so it follows that an investment in her talent would be not as likely to bear full fruit (Goldsmith, 1987, 1990; Greer, 1979; Piirto, 1991b). In global context, two thirds of the world's illiterates are female.

How is a parent to know if the sacrifices necessary to develop a child's talent are worth making? This is a question that may seem to have an obvious answer, but in truth does not. Of course most parents would say that they want to develop a child's talents to their fullest, whatever the cost. But few families have the resources to develop every child's talents to their fullest expression, and that often makes it necessary to choose one child's talents over another's, to focus on, or to insist that all the children develop talents in the same domain, that is, the domain valued by the parents. Thus we have the establishment of salons, dynasties, or teams. "Going into the family business" is a common practice in the development of all talents, not just extreme talent. If a family with a child who has great musical talent, for example, lives in a rural area far from the next level of teacher, and the lessons must be taken weekly or semiweekly, the family is faced with a decision: Shall we move to be nearer to the teacher? Moves such as this were documented by Feldman and Goldsmith (1986) in the case of one of the prodigies studied, who moved from another state to the Boston area to find a suitable school, but moves to develop the talent are more common in cases of athletics (especially tennis, ice skating, and gymnastics) or in musical talent. The decision to develop a talent is one that requires reflection as to parents' values, goals, and priorities as well as a realistic assessment of the strength of the child's talent and the effect developing that talent will have on the family system, especially the siblings.

To help with the decision about whether or not to pursue full talent development, it is often wise to consult with individuals who are knowledgeable about the domain in question and who have had experience in what it means to go through a rigorous, protracted training process. This is especially true for parents who find themselves trying to reckon the strength of a child's talent in a field with which they themselves are unfamiliar. Even when parents are experienced in the domain in question, there are reasons to seek advice from outside experts or consultants. First, it is difficult for parents to assess accurately the potential in their own children because of their close attachment to them. Second, coaches, master teachers, trainers, and high-level practitioners generally have much more experience than parents in assessing and developing talent. Parents have themselves and their children to use as a primary basis for judgment. An active coach or teacher may have worked with hundreds of students (Bloom, 1985; Feldman, with Goldsmith, 1991).

In most instances, the advice given by experienced people within a domain will not be definitive with respect to the course of the talent's development. This is true for several reasons, the most important of which is that it is not possible to predict with confidence what will happen to a talent over time. There are too many uncertainties in the process to assert with confidence what the course of a child's progress will be. Indeed, parents would be wise to question too positive a prediction, particularly if the person giving that prediction is trying to recruit the child into a program, school, or relationship.

The earlier the prediction about the strength and distinctiveness of a given talent, the less confidence can be placed in its accuracy. This is not so much because it is impossible to detect and assay talent early; in some fields (such as chess, music, and certain athletic domains) talent can be assessed at very early ages, often younger than 5. The uncertainty in making predictions is that there are many things involved in bringing even a very extreme talent to full expression, and these simply cannot be guaranteed to occur. Even if they do occur, they must be sustained over several years as well as transformed when necessary. The children's chess coach Sunil Weeramantry has indicated that high-IQ children in kindergarten all demonstrate a rudimentary ability to play chess, but that prodigious talent begins to differentiate children as early as second grade, at the end of their primary tournament playing years (S. Weeramantry, personal communication, May 1988).

The kinds of supports that must be put into place and sustained include the right teachers teaching the right kinds of lessons for child performers, the right integration of the target activity with other priorities for the child and the family, the right level of challenge in terms of competition and public performance, and a context that encourages continued involvement in the activity in question. To summarize, a number of other factors that may be beyond the control of the child and the child's family are involved in talent development. These are sufficient financial resources, proximity to appropriate facilities, and the availability of appropriate teachers.

Another less documented but certainly essential component in talent development is freedom from cultural proscriptions against certain activities. Gender proscriptions are the most common. For example, in the United States young males experience disapproval if they want to use their psychomotor talent in dance, especially classical ballet. Jacques D'Amboise, the former Balanchine dancer who now conducts school-based classes in New York City, is especially eloquent on the topic of attracting psychomotor-talented males to dance, and has even set up special classes for them during the school day, but the battle against cultural proscription is an uphill one. Even world-class dancers such as Nureyev had to confront a disapproving father in order to seriously pursue a career in dance. Percival (1975, p. 21) wrote that Nureyev's father "was none too pleased to find that his only son had grown up to be interested only in something as 'unmanly' as dancing and told the boy to forget the whole thing." Young females experience disapproval if they want to use their logical-mathematical talent in chess. Few female chess talents continue playing tournament chess beyond the elementary tournament years, even though they have the ability to do so. Reasons given for this are a diversity of other interests and special lessons, a lack of female role models at the higher stratosphere of the chess world, and a lack of understanding by the home schools of the necessity for constant practice and competition all over the country and the world (S. Weeramantry, personal communication, March 1987).

In some fields where talent development begins early, a phenomenon labeled the "midlife crisis" in music performers has been observed to occur with some frequency (Bamberger, 1982). Usually occurring some time between the 12th and 18th years, this so-called midlife crisis refers to a breakdown in the child's ability to perform and an accompanying emotional crisis in the child's confidence in being able to perform at a high level. Many promising careers have come to an early end because of the debilitating effects of this crisis. The description of an adolescent crisis for performers has been well documented in only one field—music—though informal observations have been made in the field of chess (Feldman, with Goldsmith, 1991) and in writing (Piirto, 1992). It should also be stressed that this phenomenon has been observed only in U.S. culture; it may or may not occur in other cultural contexts. It could also be that the so-called midlife crisis is in part precipitated by the highly professionalized and competition-oriented schools of music where most of the students with extreme talent pursue their chosen field. How such schools are organized, how they respond to and develop talent, and what they see as in their interest in terms of public visibility all play a significant part in how they impact the process of talent development.

PARENTING ACADEMICALLY TALENTED CHILDREN AND CHILDREN WITH SPECIFIC TALENTS

Alvino (1985) listed common issues faced by parents of talented and gifted students. Some were home related and some were school related. Among the home-related issues were awe and fear of the children and their talents, denial of the children's talents, the burden of supporting the talent (e.g., books, trips, teachers, lessons, equipment), equating verbal maturity with social maturity, sibling issues, stress (both for the child and for the family), friendships and peer relationships, the nature of the interests, and self-esteem. School-related issues included finding programs and schools that supported the child's talent, defining reasonable and unreasonable expectations by the school and the home, apathy of schools to talent development, the potential for social mobility of the child because of the presence of the talent, and being perceived by the school as "pushy."

Shore, Cornell, Robinson, and Ward (1991, p. vii) surveyed recommended practices in gifted education and noted 10 commonly cited parenting practices for parents of gifted youth:

(1) Be sensitive to potential sibling adjustment problems;
(2) Avoid excessive emphasis on developing the child's giftedness;
(3) Avoid stereotypes and misconceptions about the gifted label;
(4) Be aware of how personal needs and feelings influence the relationship with the child;
(5) Encourage social as well as academic development;
(6) Foster potential for giftedness through preschool intervention;
(7) Participate in and lobby for programs;
(8) Facilitate social development through ability–peer contact;
(9) Discourage children's perfectionism and excessive self-criticism; and,
(10) Emotional support from parent groups and counselors should be available.

They found some research support for the first three recommended practices. Numbers 4, 5, and 6 had limited support. Numbers 7, 8, 9, and 10 had been studied little, if at all, in populations of gifted students with suitable comparison groups.

Even though it is apparent that eminent individuals often come from parenting situations that are not ideal, nevertheless, there are many ways parents can provide optimal environments for the nurture of creative talent. Piirto (1992) listed the following:

(1) Provide a private place for creative work to be done;
(2) Provide materials (e.g., musical instruments, sketchbooks);
(3) Encourage and display the child's creative work and avoid evaluating it overly;
(4) Do your own creative work and let the child see you doing it;
(5) Value the creative work of others, attend museums, theater, movies, and talk about books and events;

(6) Pay attention to what your family background, your family mythology, your family system is teaching the child;

(7) Avoid emphasizing sex-role stereotypes;

(8) Provide private lessons and special classes;

(9) If hardship comes into your life, use the hardship positively, to encourage the children to express themselves through the arts;

(10) Emphasize that talent is only a small part of creative production and that discipline and practice are important;

(11) Allow the child to be "odd"; avoid emphasizing socialization at the expense of creative expression; and

(12) Enjoy your child.

Cornell (1983, 1989) and Cornell and Grossberg (1986, 1987) supplied some evidence in their studies of gifted students and their siblings that how parents treat the gifted child in relation to siblings is important. Comparisons of siblings should be carefully made, if at all. Parents' reactions to having their children labeled as "gifted" are often problematic within the family system. Some parents develop an especially intense relationship with the labeled child, and are sometimes overinvolved in the child's education and development. Such overinvolvement can lead to underachievement and disabling perfectionism, both widely cited problems of talented students. Underachievement deserves special attention here because it is one of the most common problems for which parents of academically talented youth seek professional help.

PARENTING WHEN ACADEMICALLY TALENTED YOUTH UNDERACHIEVE

Several writers and researchers have made important contributions to our knowledge of underachievement. Among these are Delisle (1992), Richert (1991), Rimm (1986), Supplee (1990), and Whitmore (1980). Underachievement continues to plague parents and educators of the talented as one of the most recalcitrant problems that high-IQ youth continue to have. By now we know that each underachiever is different, and that each case must be looked at individually to determine the reason for the underachievement and thus to be better able to reverse it.

What is underachievement? The quick answer most people would give is that underachievement is not receiving the grades that IQ would indicate are possible. Another quick definition is that underachievement is receiving high scores on standardized achievement tests but low grades in school. Another definition of underachievement targets causes. For example, underachievement is caused by learning disabilities, or by the social climate of the school, or by affective characteristics in the child, or by passive–aggressive parenting patterns.

The emerging paradigm in the field of talent development, as described earlier, features achievement as being predictive for certain manifestations of talent. If a child underachieves, the talent will not be developed: Here is a child with a high IQ who refuses to do the work in the classroom. Here is a child with high achievement test scores who refuses to turn in the projects. The educators and parents beg, cajole, compliment, and harangue the child. "You have such potential! You should be doing better! You won't get into a good college with grades like these! You could do so well; why won't you produce?" The child is the powerful force in these dynamics, both with the parents and with the school, and that is why Rimm (1986) insisted there must be a *tri-focal* approach to reversing underachievement, and that is that the school, the parents, and the child must all take responsibility for the reversal or the underachievement will continue. The child is the key figure in this triangle. Gallagher (1991, p. 225) wrote that "until the child essentially agrees" with the parent's and the school's noticing that the child is an underachiever, "it will be very difficult to persuade him/her to change."

It is often assumed that children want to do well in school, and schools and parents are often quick to blame themselves for underachievement. It is also often assumed that the evils of the society—racism, classism, prejudice against the handicapped—are to blame for underachievement. It is often assumed for these that children are feckless victims of "the system." Then why do some children from lower social classes, of various races, with learning disabilities and physical handicaps achieve despite the "system," and others do not? The quality of resiliency that is just beginning to be explored seems operational here.

What are the personality traits of people who underachieve? For underachieving males at least, Terman and Oden (1947) found that those who did not meet the potential their IQ scores indicated, were unable to persevere, unable to formulate goals, preferred to drift rather than to take action, and had low self-confidence. These problems were chronic: That is, they continued from childhood to adolescence to adulthood. Underachievement, Delisle (1982, 1992) reminded us, is often in the eyes of the beholder.

Whitmore's (1980) work, reported in *Giftedness, Conflict, and Underachievement*, was a milestone in that she specifically studied children who were put into a special program in 1970 that sought to remedy underachieving behavior. This program, called the Cupertino Project, focused on second and third graders with very high IQs who were underachieving. Individualized instruction was offered and results showed that students' achievement generally improved over the long term.

Rimm (1986) used a behavioral approach to the reversal of underachievement. She described four different categories of underachievers: the dependent conformers, the dependent nonconformers, the dominant conformers, and the dominant nonconformers. Underachievers were grouped into dependent children and dominant children, conformers and nonconformers. Dependent children manipulate adults and others in their environment by such plaintive pleas as "help me," "nag me," "protect me," "feel sorry for me," "love me," and "shelter me." The difficulty is in determining when these pleas are manipulative and when they are genuine. Rimm (1986, p. 148) said that parents and teachers "must assure yourselves that these children can build self-confidence and competence only through effort and perseverance, and that it is indeed a true kindness to permit these children to experience some stress."

For each of these groups, there are suggested steps in remediation. Rimm was quick to point out that family patterns often foster or encourage underachievement. Passive-aggressive children often have one passive-aggressive parent and one who is made the bad guy; likewise, with aggressive children, there is often aggression in the family. Patterns in the family can be both positive and negative for achievement. Piirto (1992) called it the "family mythology." Rimm (1986) reported that potentially harmful family models were these: "I didn't like school either"; having a home that is disorganized; having passive-aggressive parenting; having parents who are overworked who come home exhausted, complaining, and failing to provide models that work is satisfying, challenging, and life enhancing. Rimm's work was criticized for being too negative to parents (Baum, 1990). However, proponents of clinical interventions utilizing behavioral approaches such as Rimm's would say that drastic measures are often needed in reversing underachievement, which is often entrenched, insidious, and a hallmark of dysfunction in the family or school.

Richert (1991) presented a refreshingly different definition of underachievement. Pointing out the obvious but often overlooked question: What if the IQ is not a good measure of potential after all? What if the IQ test that puts the child in people's minds into "underachieving status" was inaccurate? Richert noted that "underachievement is most often defined in terms of academic achievement" measured by school-related methods such as grades, standardized test scores, and teacher-made test results. What if these are not good ways of assessing underachievement? What if the tests themselves are the problem?

The children's lives as a whole should be assessed. Do the children who get low grades and who have high test scores have an intense life of achievement at home? Do they read 7 books a week? Do they program computers and participate in a wide network of computer friends throughout the area? Do they have sketchbooks and do intensive drawing and artwork? Do they practice their music for 7 hours a day? How are these children underachieving? Richert (1991, p. 139) pointed out that "repeated studies have revealed no correlation, or sometimes even a small negative correlation, between academic achievement (good grades) and adult giftedness in a wide range of fields."

The childhoods of creative people often show that many of them had intense lives at home, away from school, and that their adult achievements were foreshadowed by their childhood activities, many of which were not school related (Piirto, 1991a, 1992, 1994). Many people with arts-related achievements were underachievers in school: Suzanne Farrell (1990), the world-class dancer from Cincinnati, Ohio, never finished high school, and when she did go to school she was too restless to concentrate; the architect Frank Lloyd Wright in his autobiography could not remember a single thing he learned in school in Madison, Wisconsin, but could remember every invention he and his friends made out of school (Wright, 1932/1977); the visual artist Georgia O'Keeffe (Robinson, 1989) called every teacher she had a fool, except for the ones in a convent school in Wisconsin she attended for a year; she consciously got bad grades and disobeyed what she regarded as dumb rules during her last year in a Virginia high school.

Richert (1991) in questioning the definition of underachievement, posed an interesting conundrum: If many high achievers in later life found the schools stifling, boring, and the teachers and rules worse, the role of the schools in talent development in the various domains is diminished and the role of parents and family are probably enhanced. People in the arts do not have the necessity, as do people in mathematics and the sciences, of taking one course following another course in order to make their mark. The attainment of the PhD is *de rigueur* for mathematicians and scientists, and this means reading many textbooks, conforming, and taking more advanced courses. Such educational attainment is not necessary for visual artists or performers—actors, dancers, or musicians—or for writers, although the schools encourage writers more than they do other types of creatively talented people.

Supplee (1990) used Tannenbaum's conception of giftedness to define underachievement. Tannenbaum (1983), in *Gifted Children*, proposed that giftedness emerges if all five arms in a "starfish" are present. These are the necessary conditions for giftedness to materialize: general intellectual ability (the "G" factor), specific academic abilities (such as math ability or reading ability), non-intellective factors (such as persistence, self-esteem, or creativity), environmental factors (family, school), and chance (proximity, knowing the right people). Supplee (1990) found that the under-achievers she studied were missing one or more of the starfish arms; some had high IQs but did not have other factors; some had fantastic special abilities but did not have persistence; some were very poor, a negative environmental factor, although they had all four other factors; some had physical or learning disabilities, which fall into the chance arm.

Supplee found success in reversing underachievement by beginning with improving the students' self-esteem and proceeding to the improvement of their attitudes, school behaviors, and academic growth. There was also a component that helped parents to understand the causes of the child's underachievement, as well as to examine their expectations for their child, to be positive communicators with their child, and to examine familial patterns and familial dynamics. A support group of parents was formed to discuss common concerns. Small positive gains in achievement were reported. Nevertheless, underachievement has been and remains a thorny problem for the parents and educators of gifted and talented students.

PRESSURES TOWARD HIGH ACHIEVEMENT
AND THEIR IMPACT ON TALENTED YOUTH

Another situation that merits attention for the parents of talented youth is the influence of affluence and parental success on such children. It is a fact that most students in formal school programs for the gifted and talented have average or above-average socioeconomic status. This discrepancy has led to concerted efforts by the federal government, through the Jacob C. Javits Gifted and Talented Education Act of 1988, to identify and serve students from disadvantaged backgrounds. As Coles

(1977), Elkind (1987), Vail (1987), Brooks (1989), and others have pointed out, children of high-achieving parents often face particular problems around the issue of talent development and achievement. Noting that the qualities needed to be a high achiever in the world are sometimes directly opposite to the qualities needed to be nurturing parents, Brooks (1989, p. 29) pointed out that difficulties among children with high-achieving parents may be provoked by parents who have succeeded in the workplace. The workplace often demands perfection, efficiency, a concern about image, firmness, selfishness, long work hours, and a top priority that success should come first. Children often need to have their errors tolerated, patience and gentleness, special times for family activities, and an understanding that failure promotes growth.

Fast-track, high-achieving parents often made it the hard way, attending public schools and state universities, and they want their children not to have to do it that way, attitudes that may put undue pressure on these children to conform to newly acquired lifestyles in affluent surroundings. Brooks also pointed out that such parents often seek to maintain control to the extent that even their children's achievements should be attributable to the parents' efforts: Brooks cited Henry Ford's behavior with his son Edsel as an example. Whenever Edsel began to achieve on his own, Ford would cut him down and humiliate him, often publicly. The parent who uses connections to get an interview at a prestigious school or an audition with a coveted teacher may thwart a fragile young person's self-esteem, that is, the child's ability to feel proud of accomplishing things by dint of hard work or talent. Such parenting behaviors point out that talented children may be viewed as their parents' products, much as their degrees, prestigious jobs, promotions, and possessions.

Amy Tan, in *The Joy-Luck Club* (1989), dramatized this situation among Asian mothers who had immigrated and had reared American daughters. The mothers competed among themselves for evidence of whose daughter had the most achievements. One forced her daughter to become a chess player, another forced piano lessons on a decidedly uninterested child. Payant (1993, p. 73) stated that in contemporary fiction, as in contemporary life, females especially have difficulty in separating themselves from their mothers, and mothers have difficulty in seeing their children as whole human beings: "It does not take Freudian–Lacanian theory to tell us of a mother's difficulty in seeing her children as separate people."

The "chance" factors of ethnicity, socioeconomic status, and geographical location can also affect the development of talent. Parents have primary influence on all of these factors. In studying highly academically talented students from disadvantaged backgrounds, VanTassel-Baska (1989) found that the parents' attitudes toward their situations were primary in the development of talent. If parents viewed their socioeconomic status as temporary, and if they provided enrichment through public libraries, special programs, and involvement in the schools, the students' talents were likely to be developed. Likewise, Ford (1993) and Ford and Harris (1992) noted that academically talented African-American youth took their achievement motivation from their parents, but that especially for males in junior high school and high school, the peer group was often a strong deterrent to the development of that talent.

Thus, it can be seen that the optimal development of talent is inextricably related to family variables that may or may not be under the control of the parents. Such variables as death, divorce, or other trauma may hit a family unawares, and such events can have minimal or maximal effect on talent development. Other variables such as passive–aggressive parenting, underachievement or perceived underachievement, providing opportunities and situations where children's talent can be encouraged, and the chance to be with peers who are similar are under the control of the parents and awareness of options can enhance such development.

CONCLUSIONS

To summarize, several points can be made. First, parents often have difficulty in identifying a child's talent and in formulating responses to the presence of talent. The problem is magnified when a child or children have multiple talents, or multiple potentialities. Second, general academic talent as identified by having high test scores on IQ tests or standardized achievement tests, is often developed in the school and in special programs for the gifted and talented; however, outstanding special talent (such as that in athletics, chess, or the arts) needs responses that may not be developed in the school, and that may affect the whole family system. Third, talent development is often the product of the whole family's interests, occupations, and heritage. Talent often seems to run in families. Whether this is heredity or environment is not the point; the point is that there are families of actors, artists, athletes, businesspersons, academics, and the like, where the talent is nurtured by the efforts of the whole family system. Fourth, research on children with extremely high IQs or children who are prodigies reveals that there is a cocoonlike quality that the parents engender in the families. The families see themselves as different from the norm, and they often expend extreme amounts of energy in talent development for the prodigy. The talents of siblings are often undernoticed in such extreme family dynamisms toward a child's talent development. Fifth, underachievement is a phenomenon that affects families with academically talented students. Responses to underachievement ranging from school-based special programs to individual behavioral and family therapy are common. Sixth, a difficult parenting situation for talented children can arise in families of achievement, especially where there is recent affluence, where parents who have moved up in social status often unduly ignore the emotional needs of their children in order to satisfy their own needs for status.

It should be clear from what has been said that early identification of talent, creating an appropriate response and sustaining an optimal process of talent development, are highly complex and subtle matters. Although much more is known about these issues than was true even a decade ago, the knowledge base remains spotty, thin, and fragmented. It seems reasonable to predict that, a decade hence, the processes of extreme talent development and general talent development will be much better understood than they are at this juncture, to the great benefit of the children who depend on that knowledge to sustain them through the long period of preparation for their chosen calling.

REFERENCES

Albert, R. S. (1980). Family positions and the attainment of eminence: A study of special family positions and special family experiences, *Gifted Child Quarterly, 24,* 87–95.

Albert, R. S. (1983). *Genius and eminence: The social psychology of creativity and exceptional achievement.* Oxford, England: Pergamon.

Albert, R. S. (1990a). Family position and the attainment of eminence. *Gifted Child Quarterly, 24,* 87–95.

Albert, R. S. (1990b). Identity, experiences, and career choice among the exceptionally gifted and eminent. In M. Runco & R. Albert (Eds.), *Theories of creativity* (pp. 14–34). Newbury Park, CA: Sage.

Albert, R. S., & Runco, M. (1986). The achievement of eminence: A model based on a longitudinal study of exceptionally gifted boys and their families. In R. J. Sternberg & J. E. Davidson (Eds.), *Conceptions of giftedness* (pp. 332–359). New York: Cambridge University Press.

Alvino, J. (1985). *Parents' guide to raising a gifted child.* Boston: Little, Brown.

Alvino, J. (1989). Parents' guide to raising a gifted toddler. Boston: Little, Brown.

Arnold, K. D. (1993). The Illinois Valedictorian Project: Academically talented women in the 1980s. In D. T. Schuster & K. D. Hulbert (Eds.), *Women's lives through time: Educated American women of the twentieth century* (pp. 85–94). New York: Jossey-Bass.

Baird, L. L. (1985). Do grades and tests predict adult accomplishment? *Research in Higher Education, 23* (1), 3–85.

Baum, S. (1990). Review of *How to parent so children will learn. Gifted Child Quarterly, 34* (4), 169–170.

Bamberger, J. (1982). Growing up prodigies: The midlife crisis. In D. H. Feldman (Ed.), *Developmental approaches to giftedness and creativity* (pp. 61–77). San Francisco: Jossey-Bass.

Baumrind, D. (1971). Current patterns of parental authority. *Developmental Psychology Monograph, 4* (2, series No. 1).

Benbow, C. P. (1992). Mathematical talent: Its nature and consequences. In N. Colangelo, S. G. Assouline, & D. L. Ambroson (Eds.), *Talent development: Proceedings from the 1991 Henry B. and Jocelyn Wallace national research symposium on talent development* (pp. 95–123). Unionville, NY: Trillium.

Benbow, C. P., & Minor, L. L. (1990). Cognitive profiles of verbally and mathematically precocious students: Implications for the identification of the gifted. *Gifted Child Quarterly, 34,* 21–26.

Bloom, B. S. (1981, November). Talent development. *Educational Leadership,* 86–94.

Bloom, B. S. (1982). The master teachers. *Phi Delta Kappan, 63,* 664–667.

Bloom, B. S. (Ed.). (1985). *The development of talent in young people.* New York: Ballantine.

Blumberg, S. A., & Panos, L. G. (1990). *Edward Teller: Giant of the golden age of physics.* New York: Macmillan.

Borland, J. H. (1989). *Planning and implementing programs for the gifted.* New York: Teachers College Press.

Bornstein, M. (1989). Stability in early mental development: From attention and information processing in infancy to language and cognition in childhood. In M. Bornstein & N. Krasnegor (Eds.), *Stability and continuity in mental development* (pp. 147–171). Hillsdale, NJ: Lawrence Erlbaum Associates.

Brooks, A. A. (1989). *Children of fast-track parents: Raising self-sufficient and confident children in an achievement-oriented world.* New York: Viking.

Brophy, B., & Goode, E. E. (1988, Dec. 12). Amazing families. *U.S. News & World Report,* 78–87.

Cheever, S. (1984). *Home before dark.* Boston: Houghton Mifflin.

Clark, B. (1992). *Growing up gifted* (4th ed.). Columbus, OH: Merrill.

Clark, R. (1971). *Einstein: The life and times.* New York: World Publishing.

Coles, R. (1977). *Privileged ones. Children of crisis* (Vol. 5). Boston: Little, Brown.

Colangelo, N., & Kerr, B. A. (1990). Extreme academic talent: Profiles of perfect scorers. *Journal of Educational Psychology, 82,* 404–409.

Cornell, D. G. (1983). Gifted children: The impact of positive labeling on the family system. *American Journal of Orthopsychiatry, 53,* 322–335.

Cornell, D. G. (1989). Child adjustment and parent use of the term "gifted." *Gifted Child Quarterly, 33,* 63–64.

Cornell, D. G., & Grossberg, I. N. (1986). Siblings of children in gifted programs. *Journal for the Education of the Gifted, 9,* 253–264.

Cornell, D. G., & Grossberg, I. N. (1987). Family environment and personality adjustment in gifted program children. *Gifted Child Quarterly, 31,* 59–64.

Deakin, M. (1972). *The children on the hill.* Indianapolis: Bobbs-Merrill.

Delisle, J. (1982). Striking out: Suicide and the gifted adolescent. *Gifted/Creative/Talented, 24,* 16–19.

Delisle, J. (1992). *Social and emotional needs of the gifted.* Boston: Longman.

Eccles, J., & Harold, R. D. (1992). Gender differences in educational and occupational patterns among the gifted. In N. Colangelo, S. G. Assouline, & D. L. Ambroson (Eds.), *Talent development: Proceedings from the Henry B. and Jocelyn Wallace national research symposium on talent development* (pp. 2–30). Unionville, NY: Trillium.

Edwards, A. (1975). *Judy Garland: A biography.* New York: Simon & Schuster.

Elkind, D. (1987). *Miseducation: Preschoolers at risk.* New York: Knopf.

Falk, G. (1987). Gifted children's perception of divorce. *Journal for the Education of the Gifted, 11*(1), 29–43.

Farrell, S. W., & Bentley, T. (1990). *Holding on to the air.* New York: Summit.

Feldman, D. H. (1979). The mysterious case of extreme giftedness. In H. Passow (Ed.), *The gifted and the talented* (pp. 335–351). Chicago: University of Chicago Press.

Feldman, D. H. (1992). Has there been a paradigm shift in gifted education? In N. Colangelo, S. G. Assouline, & D. L. Ambroson (Eds.), *Talent development: Proceedings from the 1991 Henry and Jocelyn Wallace national research symposium on talent development* (pp. 89–94). Unionville, NY: Trillium.

Feldman, D. H. (1993). Cultural organisms in the development of great potential: Referees, termites and the Aspen Music Festival. In R. Wozniak & K. Fischer (Eds.), *Development in context: Acting and thinking in specific environments* (pp. 225–251). Hillsdale, NJ: Lawrence Erlbaum Associates.

Feldman, D. H., with Goldsmith, L. (1991). *Nature's gambit: Child prodigies and the development of human potential.* New York: Teachers College Press.

Fine, M. J., & Carlson, C. (Eds.). (1992). *The handbook of family–school intervention: A systems perspective.* Needham Hts., MA: Allyn & Bacon.

Ford, D. Y. (1993). Black students' achievement orientation as a function of perceived family achievement orientation and demographic variables. *Journal of Negro Education, 62*(1), 47–66.

Ford, D. Y., & Harris, J. J. (1992). The American achievement ideology and achievement differentials among preadolescent gifted and nongifted African American males and females. *Journal of Negro Education, 61*(1), 45–64.

Gagné, F. (1985). Giftedness and talent: Reexamining a reexamination of the definition. *Gifted Child Quarterly, 29,* 103–112.

Gallagher, J. J. (1991). Personal patterns of underachievement. *Journal for the Education of the Gifted, 14,* 221–233.

Galton, F. (1869). *Hereditary genius: An inquiry into its laws and consequences.* London: Macmillan.

Gardner, H. (1982). *Art, mind, & brain.* New York: Basic Books.

Gardner, H. (1983). *Frames of mind.* New York: Basic Books.

Goertzel V., & Goertzel, M. G. (1962). *Cradles of eminence.* Boston: Little, Brown.

Goertzel, V., Goertzel, M. G., & Goertzel, T. (1978). *Three hundred eminent personalities: A psychosocial analysis of the famous.* San Francisco: Jossey-Bass.

Goldsmith, L. (1987). Girl prodigies: Some evidence and some speculations. *Roeper Review, 10,* 74–82.

Goldsmith, L. (1990). The timing of talent: The facilitation of early prodigious achievement. In M.J.A. Howe (Ed.), *Encouraging the development of exceptional skills and talents* (pp. 17–31). Leicester, England: British Psychological Society.

Goldsmith, L. T., & Feldman, D. H. (1988). Idiot savants: Thinking about remembering. *New Ideas in Psychology, 6*, 15–23.

Graffman, G. (1981). *I really should be practicing.* New York: Avon.

Gray, M. (1979). *Margaret Sanger: A biography of the champion of birth control.* New York: Richard Marek.

Greer, G. (1979). *The obstacle race: The fortune of women painters and their work.* New York: Farrar, Straus, & Giroux.

Gustin, W. C. (1985). The development of exceptional research mathematicians. In B. Bloom (Ed.), *Developing talent in young people* (pp. 270–331). New York: Ballantine.

Hall, E. G., & Skinner, N. (1980). *Somewhere to turn: Strategies for parents of the gifted and talented.* New York: Teachers College Press.

Harris, C. R. (1990). The Hollingworth longitudinal study: Follow-up, findings, and implications. *Roeper Review, 12*(3), 216–221.

Hayes, J. (1981). *The complete problem solver.* Philadelphia: Franklin Institute Press.

Helson, R. (1983). Creative mathematicians. In R. Albert (Ed.), *Genius and eminence: The social psychology of creativity and exceptional achievement* (pp. 211–230). London: Pergamon.

Hunt, E., Lunneborg, C., & Lewis, J. (1975). What does it mean to be high verbal? *Cognitive Psychology*, 194–227.

Jenkins-Friedman, R. (1992). Families of gifted children and youth. In M. J. Fine & C. Carlson (Eds.), *The handbook of family–school intervention: A systems perspective* (pp. 175–186). Needham Hts., MA: Allyn & Bacon.

Kessen, W. (1965). *The child.* New York: Wiley.

Kulieke, M. J., & Olszewski-Kubilius, P. (1989). The influence of family values and climate on the development of talent. In J. VanTassel-Baska & P. Olszewski-Kubilius (Eds.), *Patterns of influence on gifted learners: The home, the self, and the school* (pp. 40–59). New York: Teachers College Press.

Lehman, H. (1953). *Age and achievement.* Princeton, NJ: Princeton University Press.

Lewis, D. (1979). *How to be a gifted parent.* New York: Norton.

McGuffog, C., Feiring, C., & Lewis, M. (1987). The diverse profile of the extremely gifted child. *Roeper Review, 10*, 82–87.

Miles, B. (1989). *Ginsberg: A biography.* New York: Simon & Schuster.

Miller, A. (1981). *Drama of the gifted child.* New York: Doubleday.

Miller, A. (1989). *The untouched key: Tracing childhood trauma in creativity and destructiveness.* New York: Doubleday.

Miller, A. (1987). *Timebends: A life.* New York: Harper & Row.

Morelock, M., & Feldman, D. H. (1991). Extreme precocity. In N. Colangelo & G. Davis (Eds.), *Handbook of gifted education* (pp. 347–364). Boston: Allyn & Bacon.

Morelock, M., & Feldman, D. H. (1993). Prodigies and savants: What they have to tell us about giftedness and human cognition. In K. Heller, F. Monks, & H. Passow (Eds.), *International handbook for research on giftedness and talent* (pp. 161–181). Oxford, England: Pergamon Press.

Payant, K. B. (1993). *Becoming and bonding: Contemporary feminism and popular fiction by American women writers.* Westport, CT: Greenwood Press.

Percival, J. (1975). *Nureyev.* New York: Popular Library.

Piechowski, M. M. (1979). Developmental potential and the growth of self. In J. VanTassel-Baska & P. Oliszewski-Kubilius (Eds.), *Patterns of influence: The home, the self, and the school* (pp. 87–101). New York: Teachers College Press.

Piechowski, M. M. (1991). Emotional development and emotional giftedness. In N. Colangelo & G. A. Davis (Eds.), *Handbook of gifted education* (pp. 285–306). Needham Hts., MA: Allyn & Bacon.

Piirto, J. (1991a). Encouraging creativity in adolescents. In J. Genshaft & M. Bireley (Eds.)., *Understanding gifted adolescents* (pp. 104–122). New York: Teachers College Press.

Piirto, J. (1991b). Why are there so few? Creative women: Mathematicians, visual artists, musicians. *Roeper Review, 13*(3), 142–147.

Piirto, J. (1992). *Understanding those who create.* Dayton: Ohio Psychology Press.

Piirto, J. (1994). *Talented children and adults: Their development and education.* New York: Macmillan.

Piirto, J., & Battison, S. (1994). Successful creative women writers at midlife. In N. Colangelo, S. Assouline, & D. L. Ambroson (Eds.), *Talent development* (Vol. 2, pp. 461–466). Dayton: Ohio Psychology Press.

Radford, J. (1990). *Child prodigies and exceptional early achievers.* New York: Macmillan.

Richert, E. S. (1991). Patterns of underachievement among gifted students. In M. Bireley & J. Genshaft (Eds.), *Understanding the gifted adolescent* (pp. 139–162). New York: Teachers College Press.

Rimm, S. (1986). *The underachievement syndrome.* Apple Valley, WI: Apple Valley Press.

Robinson, R. (1989). *Georgia O'Keeffe: A life.* New York: Harper & Row.

Roedel, W. (1989). Early development of gifted children. In J. VanTassel-Baska & P. Olszewski-Kubilius (Eds.), *Patterns of influence on gifted learners: The home, the self, the school* (pp. 13–28). New York: Teachers College Press.

Roedell, W., Jackson, N., & Robinson, H. (1980). *Gifted young children.* New York: Teachers College Press.

Rolfe, L. M. (1978). The Menuhins: A family odyssey. San Francisco: Panjandrum/Aris Books.

Rose, S. (1989). Measuring infant intelligence: New perspectives. In M. Bornstein & N. Krasnegor (Eds.), *Stability and continuity in mental development* (pp. 171–188). Hillsdale, NJ: Lawrence Erlbaum Associates.

Russell, B. (1967). *The autobiography of Bertrand Russell, 1872–1914.* Boston: Little, Brown.

Sears, P. S. (1979). The Terman studies of genius, 1922–1972. In A. H. Passow (Ed.), *The gifted and talented: Their education and development. The 78th yearbook of the national society for the study of education* (pp. 75–96). Chicago: University of Chicago Press.

Sherry, N. (1989). *The life of Graham Greene.* New York: Viking.

Shore, B. M., Cornell, D. G., Robinson, A., & Ward, V. S. (1991). *Recommended practices in gifted education: A critical analysis.* New York: Teachers College Press.

Simonton, D. K. (1984a). *Genius, creativity and leadership: Historiometric inquiries.* Cambridge, MA: Harvard University Press.

Simonton, D. K. (1988). *Scientific genius.* Cambridge, MA: Harvard University Press.

Simonton, D. K. (1992). The child parents the adult: On getting genius from giftedness. In N. Colangelo, S. G. Assouline, & D. L. Ambroson (Eds.), *Talent development: Proceedings from the 1991 Henry and Jocelyn Wallace national research symposium on talent development* (pp. 278–297). Unionville, NY: Trillium.

Sloan, K. D., & Sosniak, L. A. (1985). The development of accomplished sculptors. In B. Bloom (Ed.), *Developing talent in young people* (pp. 298–347). New York: Ballantine.

Smutny, J., & Eby, J. (1990). *A thoughtful overview of gifted education.* New York: Longman.

Sosniak, L. A. (1985a). Becoming an outstanding research neurologist. In B. Bloom (Ed.), *Developing talent in young people* (pp. 348–408). New York: Ballantine.

Sosniak, L. A. (1985b). Learning to be a concert pianist. In B. Bloom (Ed.), *Developing talent in young people* (pp. 19–66). New York: Ballantine.

Stanley, J., & Benbow, C. (1986). Youths who reason exceptionally well mathematically. In R. J. Sternberg & J. E. Davidson (Eds.), *Conceptions of giftedness* (pp. 361–387). New York: Cambridge University Press.

Sternberg, R. (1985). *Beyond IQ: A triarchic theory of human intelligence.* New York: Cambridge University Press.

Styron, W. (1990). *Darkness visible: A memoir of madness.* New York: Random House.

Subotnik, R. F., & Arnold, K. D. (Eds.). (1993). *Beyond Terman: Longitudinal studies in contemporary gifted education.* Norwood, NJ: Ablex.

Subotnik, R. F, Karp, D. E., & Mortan, E. R. (1989). High IQ children at midlife: An investigation into the generalizability of Terman's *Genetic Studies of Genius. Roeper Review, 11* (3), 139–145.

Subotnik, R. F., Kasson, L., Summers, E., & Wasser, A. (1993). *Genius revisited: High-IQ children grown up.* Norwood, NJ: Ablex.

Subotnik, R. F., & Steiner, C. (1993). Adult manifestations of adolescent talent in science: A longitudinal study of 1983 Westinghouse Science Talent Search winners. In R. F. Subotnik & K. D. Arnold (Eds.), *Beyond Terman: Longitudinal studies in contemporary gifted education* (pp. 117–139). Norwood NJ: Ablex.

Supplee, P. (1990). *Reaching the gifted underachiever: Program strategy and design.* New York: Teachers College Press.

Tan, A. (1989). *The joy-luck club.* New York: G. Putnam's.

Tannenbaum, A. (1983). *Gifted children.* New York: Macmillan.

Tannenbaum, A. (1986). Giftedness: a psychosocial approach. In R. J. Sternberg & J. E. Davidson (Eds.), *Conceptions of giftedness* (pp. 21–51). New York: Cambridge University Press.

Terman, L. M., & Oden, M. H. (1947). *The gifted child grows up, twenty-five years follow up of a superior group: Genetic studies of genius* (Vol. 3). Stanford, CA: Stanford University Press.

Terr, L. (1990). *Too scared to cry.* New York: Basic Books.

Thomas, B. ((1973). *Marlon: Portrait of the rebel as an artist.* New York: Random House.

Tomlinson-Keasey, C., & Little, T. D. (1990). Predicting educational attainment, occupational achievement, intellectual skill, and personal adjustment among gifted men and women. *Journal of Educational Psychology, 82*(1) 442–455.

Treffinger, D. (1991). Future goals and directions. In N. Colangelo & G. A. Davis (Eds.), *Handbook of gifted education* (pp. 441–449). Needham Hts., MA: Allyn & Bacon.

Vail, P. L. (1987). *Smart kids with school problems: Things to know and ways to help.* New York: Dutton.

Van Tassel-Baska, J. (1989). The role of the family in the success of disadvantaged gifted learners. In J. Van Tassel-Baska & P. Olszewski-Kubilius (Eds.), *Patterns of influence on gifted learners: The home, the self, and the school* (pp. 60–80). New York: Teachers College Press.

Van Tassel-Baska, J., & Olszewski-Kubilius, P. (Eds.). (1989). *Patterns of influence on gifted learners: The home, the self, and the school.* New York: Teachers College Press.

Weisner, T. S., & Garnier, H. (1992). Nonconventional family life-styles and school achievement: A 12-year longitudinal study. *American Educational Research Journal, 29*(3), 605–632.

Whitmore, J. (1980). *Giftedness, conflict, and underachievement.* Boston: Allyn & Bacon.

Wright, F. L. (1932/1977). *An autobiography.* New York: Horizon Press.

Author Index

Bandstra, E. S., **IV**, 109, *121*
Banducci, R., **IV**, 211, *221*
Bandura, A., **I**, 269, *278*; **II**, 247, *256*; **III**, 34, *56*; **IV**, 35, 52, 229, 230, *251*, 327, 328, 338, *346*
Bane, M. J., **III**, 137, *139*
Bank, L., **I**, 76, *87, 89*, 102, *116*, 264, 270, 272, *282*; **III**, 237, *251*; **IV**, 7, 10, *27*, 212, *221*, 248, 248, *251, 256*
Bank, P. B., **III**, 178, *203*
Banks, E. M., **II**, 66, *79*
Banner, C. N., **III**, 374, *386*
Bar, O., **III**, 213, *231*
Baradaran, L. P., **IV**, 249, *255*
Barajas, N., **III**, 197, *206*
Baran, A., **III**, 211, 214, 216, 217, 227, *229, 232*
Baranowski, M., **I**, 91, 94, 97, 104, 105, 108, *115*
Baranowski, M. D., **III**, 371, *386*
Barash, D., **III**, 153, *171*
Barbee, A., **I**, 168, *183*
Barber, B. L., **III**, 315, *330*
Barber, L., **III**, 35, *63*
Barbour, N. G., **IV**, 334, 340, 341, 342, *351*
Barclay, M. S., **IV**, 217, *225*
Barclay-McLaughlin, G., **III**, 423, *434*
Barcus, E. E., **IV**, 331, 335, 338, 339, *346*
Bard, K., **II**, 47, *58*
Bard, K. A., **II**, 29, 31, 32, 33, 34, 35, 36, 41, 44, 47, 50, 52, 53, 54, 55, 56, 58
Bare, J. E., **II**, 15, *23*, 59, *83*
Baren, M., **III**, 218, *230*
Barenbaum, A., **I**, 248, 249, *250*
Barer, B. M., **III**, 101, *109*
Barfield, R. J., **II**, 19, *21*
Barger, B., **I**, 148, *159*
Bargh, J. A., **III**, 325, *329*
Barglow, P., **II**, 151, *156*; **III**, 122, *139*, 152, *171*
Barham, L. J., **III**, 160, *175*
Barker, D. J., **II**, 65, *79*
Barker, D. J. P., **IV**, 19, *23*
Barker, R., **IV**, 176, *181*
Barker, R. G., **II**, 244, *256*; **IV**, 60, *79*
Barling, J., **II**, 146, *156*, 148, 149, *156*; **IV**, 35, *54*, 284, 285, *296*
Barnard, D. E., **III**, 13, *24*
Barnard, K., **I**, 213, 214, 225, *227, 228, 231*
Barnard, K. B., **III**, 122, 123, 124, 127, 129, *146*
Barnard, K. E., **I**, 14, *31*, 56, *60*, 213, 219, 220, 224, 225, *227, 228, 230*; **III**, 13, 14, 16, 17, 18, 21, *22, 23, 24*
Barnes, B. A., **IV**, 173, 174, *185*
Barnes, H. L., **I**, 102, *112*
Barnes, K., **IV**, 338, *348*
Barnes, S., **III**, 200, *203*
Barnes, W. S., **II**, 218, *234*; **III**, 197, *206*
Barnett, B., **IV**, 105, *119*
Barnett, C., **I**, 210, 225, *228, 231*; **II**, 104, *115*
Barnett, C. R., **I**, 157, *162*, 217, *230*; **II**, 96, 104, *115*
Barnett, D., **IV**, 128, 130, 131, 139, 145, 146, 149, *153, 154, 159*, 388, *402*
Barnett, J., **I**, 102, 108, *116*
Barnett, K., **I**, 74, *83*
Barnett, L. A., **IV**, 355, *372*
Barnett, R. C., **II**, 144, 145, *156*; **III**, 29, 34, 35, *56*; **IV**, 283, *295*

Barnett, W. S., **IV**, 5, *23*
Barnouw, E., **IV**, *346*
Barocas, R., **III**, 420, *436*
Baron, R. M., **IV**, 378, *403*
Barr, H. M., **IV**, 106, 107, *125*
Barrera, M., **IV**, 386, *403*
Barret, J., **I**, 271, *280*
Barret, R. L., **III**, 259, 261, *271*
Barrett, J., **III**, 53, *56*
Barrett, K., **II**, 252, *257*; **IV**, 9, 19, *24*
Barrett, M. E., **IV**, 117, *121*
Barron, A. P., **IV**, 303, *317*
Barron, F., **III**, 283, *301*
Barry, H., **III**, **II**, 221, *232*
Barry, M., **II**, 69, 71, 72, *80, 82*
Barry, W. A., **IV**, 38, *54*
Barsch, R., **III**, 313, *329*
Barsch, R. H., **IV**, 61, 62, *79*
Bartenstein, E., **III**, 372, *391*
Barth, J. M., **I**, 79, *83*; **IV**, 381, *406*
Barth, R. P., **III**, 68, *84*, 221, 222, 223, 224, 225, 228, *229*
Barth, R. T., **IV**, 173, *182*
Bartko, W. T., **II**, 154, *156*; **III**, 44, *60*
Bartlett, E. E., **IV**, 176, *181*
Bartlett, K. T., **III**, 440, *455*
Bartob, M., **III**, 201, *205*
Barton, E. J., **IV**, 245, 246, *251*
Barton, M. E., **III**, 201, *203*
Baruch, G., **III**, *139*
Baruch, G. K., **II**, 144, 145, *156*; **III**, 29, 34, 35, *56*; **IV**, 283, *295*
Basham, R., **III**, 282, *301*, 371, *387*, 396, *417*; **IV**, 137, *155*
Basham, R. B., **I**, 26, *33*, 219, 220, *228*, 273, *279*; **III**, 40, 62, 124, *142*, 281, *303*; **IV**, 289, 293, *295*
Baskett, L. M., **I**, 146, 147, 150, *159*
Baskiewicz, A., **I**, 235, *251*
Baskin, B. H., **IV**, 60, 75, *79*
Baskin, G. S., **IV**, 107, *124*
Bass, D., **I**, 132, *139*
Bass, D. M., **I**, 131, *137*
Batavia, A. I., **IV**, 61, *80*
Bates, E., **I**, 21, *31*
Bates, J., **I**, 11, *37*; **II**, 290, *307*; **IV**, 138, *153*
Bates, J. E., **I**, 13, 14, 19, 22, 25, *31, 36, 37*, 74, *84, 89*, 258, 269, 272, 276, *278, 284*; **III**, 13, *25*, 162, 169, *171*, 376, *386*; **IV**, 16, 21, *23, 26*, 147, *159*, 207, 208, 216, *221, 223*, 224, 248, *252, 256*, 287, *295*, 301, 303, 304, 305, 307, 308, 311, *317, 319*, 382, 383, *406, 407*
Bates, R. W., **II**, 13, *24*, 62, *84*
Bateson, G., **IV**, 39, *52*, 354, 355, 359, *372*
Bateson, P., **IV**, 12, 17, *23*
Bateson, P. P. G., **IV**, 15, *26*
Bathurst, K., **II**, 139, 140, 141, 142, 143, 144, 145, 147, 148, 149, 150, 151, 152, 154, *156, 157*
Batra, S., **II**, 93, 94, *110*
Batshaw, M. L., **IV**, 71, *79*
Battison, S., **I**, 290, *303*
Battistelli, P., **III**, 93, 97, 99, *108*
Bauchner, H., **IV**, 90, *99*, 116, *126*
Bauer, J. K., **II**, 64, *79*
Bauer, W. D., **IV**, 142, 143, *153*
Baum, C., **IV**, 192, 194, *203*

Subject Index

About the Authors

MARC H. BORNSTEIN is senior research scientist and head of Child and Family Research at the National Institute of Child Health and Human Development. He holds a BA from Columbia College and MS and PhD degrees from Yale University. Bornstein was a J. S. Guggenheim Foundation Fellow, and he received a Research Career Development Award from the National Institute of Child Health and Human Development. He received the C. S. Ford Cross-Cultural Research Award from the Human Relations Area Files and the B. R. McCandless Young Scientist Award from the American Psychological Association. Bornstein has held visiting academic appointments in Munich, London, Paris, New York, and Tokyo. He is co-author of *Development in Infancy* and *Perceiving Similarity and Comprehending Metaphor,* and general editor of *The Crosscurrents in Contemporary Psychology Series,* including *Psychological Development from Infancy, Comparative Methods in Psychology, Psychology and Its Allied Disciplines* (Vols. I-III), *Sensitive Periods in Development, Interaction in Human Development,* and *Cultural Approaches to Parenting.* He also edited *Maternal Responsiveness: Characteristics and Consequences* and the *Handbook of Parenting* (Vols. I-IV), and he co-edited *Developmental Psychology: An Advanced Textbook, Stability and Continuity in Mental Development, Contemporary Constructions of the Child, Early Child Development in the French Tradition,* and *The Role of Play in the Development of Thought.* He is author of children's books and puzzles in *The Child's World* series. Bornstein studies human experimental, methodological, comparative, developmental, cross-cultural, and aesthetic psychology. He is editor of *Child Development.*

* * *

JEANNE BROOKS-GUNN is Virginia and Leonard Marx Professor of Child Development and Education, Teachers College, Columbia University. She is also director of the Center for Children and Families and the Adolescent Study Program at Columbia University. She received her PhD from the University of Pennsylvania, an EdM from Harvard University, and a BA from Connecticut College. Brooks-Gunn is president of the Society for Research in Adolescence and is a member of the National Academy of Sciences Panel on Child Abuse and Neglect as well as the Panel of Defining Poverty. Her research focuses on transitions during childhood and adolescence, intergenerational transmission of parenting behavior and beliefs, policy research on poverty, and interventions including parents as well as children and/or adolescents. She co-edited *Depression in Adolescence, Transitions Through Adolescence: Interpersonal and Contextual Issues,* and *Escape From Poverty: What Makes a Difference for Children?*

* * *

XINYIN CHEN is assistant professor of psychology at the University of Western Ontario. He obtained his BA at East China Normal University and his PhD at the University of Waterloo. He is a member of the Society for Research in Child Development and the International Society for the Study of Behavioral Development. His research interests include the cross-cultural study of parent–child and peer relationships.

* * *

W. ANDREW COLLINS is professor of child psychology at the Institute of Child Development, University of Minnesota. He received his PhD from Stanford University. Collins has served as director of the Institute of Child Development. A specialist in the study of social and cognitive processes in middle childhood and adolescence, he has investigated developmental aspects of children's and adolescents' responses to television and parent–child relationships during the transition to adolescence. He served as chair of the National Research Council's Panel on the Status of Basic Research on Middle Childhood (age 6–12) and was editor of *Development During Middle Childhood: The Years from Six to Twelve*. He is also co-author of *Adolescent Psychology: A Developmental View* and *Developmental Psychology*. Collins was editor of the *Minnesota Symposia on Child Psychology* and has served as associate editor of *Child Development*.

* * *

BARBARA A. DIVITTO is a psychologist for the Neurodevelopmental Center, North Shore Children's Hospital, Salem, Massachusetts. She received her BA from Mt. Holyoke College, MA from Tufts University, and PhD from Brandeis University. She has worked at the Pediatric Rehabilitation Program, Jewish Memorial Hospital, Boston, and the Developmental Disabilities Unit of Massachusetts General Hospital's School for Allied Health Professionals. She is co-author of *Born Too Soon: Preterm Birth and Early Development* and has been a board member and co-director of education for the Boston Institute for the Development of Infants and Parents.

* * *

CAROLYN POPE EDWARDS is professor of family studies at the University of Kentucky. She took her BA and EdD degrees from Harvard University. Edwards was formerly at the University of Massachusetts, Amherst, and Vassar College. She teaches infant and child development and early childhood education and has conducted cross-cultural research in Italy, Kenya, and Mexico. Her areas of interest are early childhood education, comparative childhood socialization, social and moral development, and sex differences in social behavior. Edwards co-edited *The Hundred Languages of Children: The Reggio Emilia Approach to Early Childhood Education,* co-authored *Children of Different Worlds: The Formation of Social Behavior,* and wrote *Promoting Social and Moral Development: Creative Ideas for the Classroom.*

* * *

DAVID J. EGGEBEEN is associate professor of human development in the Department of Human Development and Family Studies and senior research associate, Population Research Institute, both at the Pennsylvania State University. He received his PhD in sociology from the University of North Carolina–Chapel Hill. Eggebeen has served on the editorial board of *Demography*. He is also a member of the Program Effectiveness Panel of the U.S. Department of Education and is chair-elect of the American Sociological Association Section on Children. His current research interests are in patterns of intergenerational support in U.S. families, living arrangements among the elderly, and the linkage between changing family structure and children's socioeconomic circumstances.

* * *

BEVERLY I. FAGOT is professor of psychology at the University of Oregon and research scientist at Oregon Social Learning Center in Eugene, Oregon. Fagot received her BA from Occidental College and her PhD from the University of Oregon. She is on the editorial board of *Child Development* and *Developmental Review* and is a fellow in the American Psychological Association and the American Psychological Society. Fagot studies the development of gender understanding in children, and her current work examines social and cognitive competency in young children in relation to different types of parenting behaviors.

* * *

DAVID HENRY FELDMAN is professor in the Eliot-Pearson Department of Child Study at Tufts University and director of the Developmental Science Group at Tufts. He holds a BA from the University of Rochester, an EdM from Harvard University, and MAT and PhD degrees from Stanford University. He is the recipient of several grants and awards, including the National Association of Gifted Children's Distinguished Scholar for 1988; Fulbright Visiting Professor at Tel Aviv University; and fellow of the American Psychological Association. His media involvements have included appearances on the "Today" show, "Nova," "48 Hours," and CNN. Among his recent books are *Nature's Gambit: Child Prodigies and the Development of Human Potential, Changing the World: A Framework for the Study of Creativity,* and *Beyond Universals in Cognitive Development.*

* * *

WYNDOL FURMAN is professor of psychology at the University of Denver. He received his PhD from the University of Minnesota. Furman is interested in children's and adolescents' social networks. He has conducted research on sibling relationships, parent–child relationships, friendships, and peer relationships. Currently, Furman is examining adolescents' romantic relationships and their development.

* * *

SUSAN GOLDBERG is a research scientist in the Psychiatric Research Unit, The Hospital for Sick Children, and professor of psychology and psychiatry at the University of Toronto. She completed her PhD in experimental child psychology at the University of Massachusetts and has taught at Brandeis University. She is co-author of *Born Too Soon: Preterm Birth and Early Development,* and co-editor of *Infants Born at Risk* and *Interactions with High Risk Infants and Children.* Goldberg has served on the editorial boards of *Child Development, Developmental Psychology,* and *Infant Behavior and Development.* Her current research is based on a longitudinal study of social development and behavior problems of children diagnosed with cystic fibrosis or congenital heart disease in infancy.

* * *

MICHAEL L. HARRIS is a graduate student at the Institute of Child Development and the Psychology in the Schools Training Program at the University of Minnesota. He holds an MA degree from the University of Minnesota. Harris' major areas of research are preschoolers' development of emotion regulation and antecedents to chronic parent–child conflict during the transition from middle childhood to adolescence. His major areas of clinical training include mental health services for families delivered via children's schools and community-based mental health services for disadvantaged populations.

* * *

ROBERT M. HODAPP is associate professor in educational psychology at the Graduate School of Education at the University of California, Los Angeles. A graduate of Columbia University, Hodapp received his PhD from Boston University. He later worked at Yale University's Child Study Center. Hodapp's work is comprised of three related areas. First, he has expanded and updated developmental approaches to children with mental retardation. Second, he has examined the behavioral development of children with Down syndrome, fragile X syndrome, and Prader–Willi Syndrome. Third, he has explored caregiver–child interactions, families, and early intervention strategies concerning children with mental retardation. Hodapp is co-author of *Understanding Mental Retardation* and *Behavior and Development in Fragile X Syndrome.* He has also co-edited *Issues in the Developmental Approach to Mental Retardation* and the *Handbook of Mental Retardation and Development.*

* * *

GRAYSON N. HOLMBECK is associate professor of clinical psychology in the Department of Psychology at Loyola University Chicago. He is also the coordinator of the Child-Clinical and Family Subspecialty in the Clinical Psychology program at Loyola. He received his ScB in psychology from Brown University and his MS and PhD in clinical psychology from Virginia Commonwealth University. Holmbeck completed his clinical internship at Children's Memorial Hospital in Chicago. His research focuses on parent–adolescent relationships and child adjustment during the early and late adolescent periods. He is also interested in the interface between developmental and child-clinical psychology as it applies to adolescence. He is currently investigating the transition to early adolescence in families with children who have a physical disability (spina bifida).

* * *

HUGH LYTTON is professor emeritus of educational psychology at the University of Calgary, Canada. He received his training in school and clinical child psychology at the Tavistock Clinic, London, and his PhD in psychology at the University of London, England. His career has spanned school teaching and professional (child clinical and school) psychology in England and Scotland, and academic psychology through affiliations with the Universities of Exeter, England, and Calgary, Canada. He is a fellow of the British Psychological Society and of the Canadian Psychological Association. He has served on the boards of several psychological associations and psychological journals, as well as on committees of the Social Sciences and Humanities Research Council of Canada. His research interests—mainly in the areas of developmental and educational psychology—have focused on bidirectional effects in parent–child relations, and on issues surrounding the origins of moral and antisocial behavior in genetic-biological substrates and in interactions within the family and the social environment. He has published widely in psychological journals. His books include *Creativity and Education, Parent–Child Interaction: The Socialization Process Observed in Twin and Singleton Families,* and he has co-authored *Social Development: History, Theory and Research.*

* * *

ROBERTA L. PAIKOFF is assistant professor of psychology in the Department of Psychiatry at the Institute for Juvenile Research, University of Illinois, Chicago. She received her BS in human development and family studies at Cornell University and her PhD in child psychology from the University of Minnesota. Paikoff completed postdoctoral work in psychology at the Hebrew University of Jerusalem and in policy research at Educational Testing Service. Her work focuses on links between family factors and adjustment of mothers and daughters during middle adolescence, as well as on biological contributors to adolescent adaptation. She is currently involved in basic and intervention research examining family and individual factors contributing to HIV risk exposure in urban, African-American pre- and young adolescents. She is editor of *Shared Views in the Family During Adolescence* and co-editor of *Preventing Adolescent Pregnancy: Model Programs and Evaluations.*

* * *

JANE PIIRTO is professor in the Department of Graduate Teacher Education at Ashland University, Ashland, OH. She took her BA from Northern Michigan University, MA from Kent State University, MEd from South Dakota State University, and PhD from Bowling Green State University. Piirto has been a high school teacher and counselor, a college instructor of humanities, a coordinator of gifted and talented programs, and principal of Hunter College Elementary School. She has been a consultant and speaker throughout the United States, the Near East, Southern Asia. She has sat on the Arts in Education Advisory Panel, National Endowment for the Arts, and on the Arts in Education and Literature panels for the Ohio Arts Council. She is a poet and fiction writer. Her books include *mamamama, Postcards from the Upper Peninsula, The Three-Week Trance Diet, Understanding Those Who Create,* and *Talented Children and Adults: Their Development and Education.* Piirto has held Individual Artist Fellowships in poetry and in fiction from the Ohio Arts Council, and has won the Carpenter Press First Novel Contest and a Fulbright-Hays Fellowship.

* * *

KENNETH H. RUBIN is professor of psychology at the University of Waterloo. He obtained his BA at McGill University and his PhD at the Pennsylvania State University. He was treasurer and membership secretary of the International Society for the Study of Behavioral Development. Rubin was associate editor of *Child Development,* coordinator (president) of the Developmental Section, Canadian Psychological Association, and member-at-large, Developmental Section, American Psychological Association. His research interests focus on social, emotional, and personality development and developmental psychopathology. Rubin's books include *The Development and Treatment of Childhood Aggression* and *Social Withdrawal, Inhibition, and Shyness in Childhood.*

* * *

JAGJIT K. SINGH is assistant professor in the departments of Educational Psychology and Teacher Education and Supervision at the University of Calgary, Canada. She completed her PhD at the University of Calgary. Singh teaches courses in the use of computers in education, developmental psychology, cognitive psychology, and research methods. At present, her research areas include the use of computers in education, developmental psychology in health care, and concerns and practices of parents of twins. She has published journal articles on the use of computers in education, on developmental and cognitive psychology, and on developmental psychology for the health care professional.

* * *

SHANNON L. STEWART is a practicing clinical psychologist at CPRI, London, Ontario. She obtained her BA at the University of Waterloo, MA at the University of Guelph, and PhD at York University. She is a member of the Society for Research in Child Development and the International Society for the Study of Behavioral Development. Stewart's research interests include socioemotional development, social competence, and developmental psychopathology.

* * *

AMY SUSMAN is a graduate student at the Institute of Child Development and the Psychology in the Schools Training Program at the University of Minnesota. She completed her BA at Cornell University and MA at the University of Minnesota. Susman is engaged in research on parent–child relationships in early and middle childhood and in adolescence. She has been a public-policy intern with the Foundation for Child Development in New York City.

* * *

STEVEN H. ZARIT is professor of human development in the Department of Human Development and Family Studies and assistant director of the Gerontology Center, both at the Pennsylvania State University. He is also adjunct professor at the Gerontology Institute, University College of Health Science, Jönköping, Sweden. He received a PhD from the Committee on Human Development, University of Chicago, and previously held faculty positions at City College of New York and the University of Southern California. Zarit's professional activities include serving on the editorial boards of *The Gerontologist, Journal of Gerontology: Psychological Sciences,* and *Psychology and Aging,* and he was president of Division 20 (Adult Development and Aging) of the American Psychological Association. His current research interests focus on mental health of the elderly, especially the effects of caring for a dementia patient on family caregivers and how interventions such as day care may lower feelings of strain. He collaborates on a longitudinal study of functional competencies of the oldest old. He is author of *Aging and Mental Disorders,* co-author of *The Hidden Victims of Alzheimer's Disease: Families Under Stress,* and co-editor of *Caregiving Systems: Formal and Informal Helpers.*

* * *